Sustainable Security

T0334291

Sustainable Security

Rethinking American National Security Strategy

Edited by Jeremi Suri

and

Benjamin Valentino

OXFORD
UNIVERSITY PRESS

OXFORD
UNIVERSITY PRESS

Oxford University Press is a department of the University of Oxford. It furthers
the University's objective of excellence in research, scholarship, and education
by publishing worldwide. Oxford is a registered trade mark of Oxford University
Press in the UK and certain other countries.

Published in the United States of America by Oxford University Press
198 Madison Avenue, New York, NY 10016, United States of America.

CIP data is on file at the Library of Congress
ISBN 978–0–19–061147–7 (hbk)
ISBN 978–0–19–061148–4 (pbk)

1 3 5 7 9 8 6 4 2

Paperback printed by Webcom, Inc., Canada

Hardback printed by Bridgeport National Bindery, Inc., United States of America

CONTENTS

LIST OF FIGURES

LIST OF TABLES

ACKNOWLEDGMENTS

This volume is a product of sustained collaboration through the Tobin Project, a community of scholars and policymakers committed to cultivating rigorous academic understanding of the most significant problems facing the United States. The engagement of the Tobin community has strengthened this endeavor at every step along the way, and we have been fortunate to work with many great minds over the course of this initiative.

First among these is Stephen Van Evera, who chairs the Tobin Project's National Security initiative and has been integral to this project from its inception. It has been a privilege to work with Steve, and this book is much better for his suggestions, his critiques, and his encouragement to reach for transformative scholarship on the biggest threats to American security. We owe him a deep debt of gratitude, and we have done our very best to weave his vision and expertise into the scholarship represented in this volume.

This project was made possible by the generous support of the Carnegie Corporation of New York, whose long-term investment has been central to the development of the Tobin Project's work on security. We are grateful for their contributions to this effort, as well as their broader longstanding commitment to helping scholars make their work as valuable to society as possible. The statements made and views expressed herein are solely the responsibility of the authors.

We would like to thank all those who have participated in our meetings and workshops—scholars and policymakers alike—whose comments and guidance were invaluable as this volume took shape. We are grateful to Matthew Connelly and Paul Barford for contributing to early stage discussions of sustainable national security; Jeremy Shapiro, Jeremy Pressman, Colin Kahl, Elissa Slotkin, Robert Art, F. Gregory Gause III, and Carl Robichaud for their contributions to our meeting on US global security commitments; The Institute for the Study of Diplomacy for cohosting a seminar on grand strategy; Ambassador Thomas Pickering, Paula Newberg, Barry Posen, and William Hitchcock for their helpful comments at the seminar; and Ambassador James Dobbins, Stephen P. Cohen, Shuja Nawaz, Peter Mandaville, and Vikram Singh for contributing to our meeting on Afghanistan.

We would also like to thank Daniel Baer, Peter Harrell, Michael Phelan, Dafna Rand, and James Schear for their insights on the problems facing US foreign policy and the open questions they confronted; Risa Brooks, Mathew Burrows, David Ekbladh, M. Taylor Fravel, David Singh Grewal, and Joseph Nye for sharing their insights on long-term security issues at a workshop in Cambridge, MA; the Lyndon B. Johnson School of Public Affairs for hosting our May 3–4 workshop, and Terrence Chapman, Robert Chesney, Kyle Longley, Patrick McDonald, Larry O'Bryon, and Peter Trubowitz for their comments during the meeting; and Michael Beckley for participating in our May 28, 2013 workshop in Hanover, NH. We would also like to thank Omar Samad and New America for convening an illuminating discussion on Afghan neutrality.

We also gratefully acknowledge all those who participated in our December 2012 conference on sustainable national security strategy. We extend a special thanks to a few key figures who made the conference possible: Robert Art, who graciously moderated our forum on US regional security commitments; Jennifer Harris, Michael Phelan, and Kori Schake, whose comments as respondents helped strengthen chapter drafts; and David McKean, Esther McClure, Steven Feldstein, and Kaleb Redden, who were kind enough to provide formal remarks throughout the conference.

We are fortunate to have had the opportunity to collaborate with Scott Parris and Cathryn Vaulman, our editors at Oxford University Press; we thank them for all of their help in bringing this volume to print. We also wish to thank the four anonymous reviewers of the manuscript, whose thoughtful comments were invaluable to us during the revisions process.

Finally, we are grateful to the staff and leadership at the Tobin Project, whose hard work and commitment have been indispensable from the birth of this initiative to its close. Tobin's mission is to mobilize scholars to work on solving problems of great importance to our nation. As this project demonstrated, however, that work would not be possible without the tremendous effort and expertise of the dedicated people at Tobin. We are especially grateful to John Cisternino, the Tobin Project's Director of Research; Melanie Wachtell Stinnett, the Project's former director of Policy and Communications; and Sidharth Shah, who was vital to planning and shaping this inquiry. They made this project better in every way. We also thank Rebecca Chan, Miranda Priebe, and Sam Dunham, who all gave comments and suggestions that improved this volume and greatly facilitated the publication process; Medha Gargeya and Nathaniel Donahue, who helped prepare and edit the manuscript; and Robert Ward for his long-term work to make sure this volume reaches the audiences of scholars, policymakers, students, and citizens for whom we and the contributors meant it.

LIST OF EDITORS

Jeremi Suri is the Mack Brown Distinguished Chair for Leadership in Global Affairs and has a joint appointment in the Lyndon B. Johnson School of Public Affairs and the Department of History at the University of Texas at Austin. Professor Suri was previously with the University of Wisconsin, where he was the E. Gordon Fox Professor of History, the Director of the European Union Center of Excellence, and the Director of the Grand Strategy Program. He is interested in the formation and spread of nation-states, the emergence of modern international relations, the connections between foreign policy and domestic politics, and the rise of knowledge institutions as global actors. He is the author and editor of seven books, including a biography of one of America's most distinguished diplomats, *Henry Kissinger and the American Century* (Harvard University Press, 2007). His latest book, *Liberty's Surest Guardian: American Nation-Building from Washington to Obama,* was released in the fall of 2011. He also co-edited *Foreign Policy Breakthroughs: Cases in Successful Diplomacy* (Oxford University Press, 2016) with Robert Hutchings, and *The Power of the Past: History and Statecraft* (Brookings Institution Press, 2016) with Hal Brands.

Benjamin Valentino is an Associate Professor of Government at Dartmouth College. His research interests include the causes and consequences of violent conflict and American foreign and security policies. At Dartmouth he teaches courses on international relations, international security, American foreign policy, and the causes and prevention of genocide. He also serves as codirector of the Government Department Honors Program and the faculty coordinator for the War and Peace Studies Program at Dartmouth's Dickey Center for International Understanding. Professor Valentino's book, *Final Solutions: Mass Killing and Genocide in the 20th Century* (Cornell University Press, 2004), received the Edgar S. Furniss Book Award for making an exceptional contribution to the study of national and international security. His work has appeared in outlets such as *The New York Times, Foreign Affairs, The American Political Science Review, Security Studies, International Organization, Public Opinion Quarterly, World Politics,* and *The Journal of Politics.*

CONTRIBUTORS

Joshua William Busby is an Associate Professor of Public Affairs at the University of Texas-Austin, LBJ School of Public Affairs. Dr. Busby was a research fellow at Princeton's Woodrow Wilson School (2005–2006), Harvard's Kennedy School (2004–2005); and the Brookings Institution (2003–2004). He received his PhD in 2004 from Georgetown University. Busby is the author of two books on social movements published by Cambridge University Press. Busby is a Life Member in the Council on Foreign Relations. He has written extensively on climate change and national security in publications such as *International Security, Security Studies,* and *Political Geography,* as well as for several think tanks. Dr. Busby is one of the lead researchers on a project funded by the Department of Defense on Climate Change and African Political Stability (CCAPS). He is also the principal investigator of another DOD-funded project, Complex Emergencies and Political Stability in Asia (CEPSA).

Daniel Byman is a Professor in the Security Studies Program in the Edmund A. Walsh School of Foreign Service, with a concurrent appointment with the Georgetown Department of Government. He served as director of Georgetown's Security Studies Program and Center for Security Studies from 2005 to 2010. Professor Byman is a Senior Fellow and Director of Research at the Center for Middle East Policy at the Brookings Institution. He is the author or coauthor of seven books; his most recent book, *Al Qaeda, the Islamic State, and the Global Jihadist Movement: What Everyone Needs to Know,* was published by Oxford University Press in 2015. His articles have appeared in *Foreign Affairs* and *Foreign Policy,* as well as journals including *Political Science Quarterly, Studies in Conflict and Terrorism, International Security,* and *Journal of Strategic Studies.* From 2002 to 2004, he served as a Professional Staff Member with the 9/11 Commission and with the Joint 9/11 Inquiry Staff of the House and Senate Intelligence Committees. Before joining the Inquiry Staff, he was the Research Director of the Center for Middle East Public Policy at the RAND Corporation. He has also worked as an analyst on the Middle East for the US government.

Audrey Kurth Cronin is professor and the director of the International Security Program at George Mason University's School of Policy, Government, and International Affairs. Before joining George Mason in 2011, she directed the core course on war and statecraft at the US National War College. Prior to that, she was the Director of Studies for the Changing Character of War program at the University of Oxford, UK. She is a member of the Council on Foreign Relations and has served in the US Congressional Research Service, the Office of the Secretary of Defense/Policy, and the Office of the Secretary of the Navy. Academically,

Professor Cronin has a longstanding interest in the question of how conflicts end. While on the faculty at Oxford, she completed her fourth book, *How Terrorism Ends: Understanding the Decline and Demise of Terrorist Campaigns* (Princeton University Press, 2009). She has published widely in scholarly and policy journals. She received her AB (*summa cum laude*) from Princeton, and her MPhil and DPhil degrees from Oxford University.

Daniel W. Drezner is Professor of International Politics at the Fletcher School of Law and Diplomacy at Tufts University, a nonresident senior fellow at the Brookings Institution, and a contributing editor at the *Washington Post*. Prior to Fletcher, he taught at the University of Chicago and the University of Colorado at Boulder. He has also worked for the Civic Education Project, the RAND Corporation, and the US Department of the Treasury. Drezner is the author of five books, including *All Politics is Global: Explaining International Regulatory Regimes* (Princeton University Press, 2007) and *The System Worked: How the World Stopped Another Great Depression* (Oxford University Press, 2014), and has edited two others. He has published articles in numerous scholarly journals as well as in the *New York Times*, *Wall Street Journal*, and *Foreign Affairs*, and has been a contributing editor for *Foreign Policy* and *The National Interest*. He received his BA in political economy from Williams College and an MA in economics and PhD in political science from Stanford University.

Sumit Ganguly is a professor of political science, holds the Rabindranath Tagore Chair in Indian Cultures and Civilizations, and is the Director of the Center on American and Global Security at Indiana University, Bloomington. A specialist on the contemporary politics of South Asia, he has written extensively on questions of nuclear stability, ethnic conflict, and counterinsurgency in the region. He is an Associate Editor of *Security Studies* and serves on the editorial boards of *Asian Security*, *Current History*, *The India Review*, *International Security*, *Journal of Democracy*, and *Pacific Affairs*. His most recent book is *The Oxford Short Introduction to Indian Foreign Policy* (Oxford University Press, 2015). Next year, Cambridge University Press will publish his book, *Deadly Impasse: India and Pakistan at the Dawn of a New Century*.

John W. Hall is the Ambrose-Hesseltine Associate Professor of US Military History at the University of Wisconsin-Madison. His research focuses on early American warfare with a particular emphasis on intercultural conflict and cooperation between European and Native American societies during the eras of the American Revolution and the Early Republic and US defense policy more generally. A lieutenant colonel in the US Army Reserve, he previously served as a doctrinal concept developer in the Future Warfare Division of the US Army Training and Doctrine Command. He is the author of *Uncommon Defense: Indian Allies in the Black Hawk War* (Harvard University Press, 2009), has also published in the *Journal of Military History* and a number of edited volumes, and is currently working on a book entitled *Dishonorable Duty: The U.S. Army and the Removal of the Southeastern Indians*. He holds a BS in History from the US Military Academy at West Point and received his PhD in History in 2007 from the University of North Carolina-Chapel Hill.

Nancy F. Hite-Rubin is Assistant Professor of Political Economy at the Fletcher School of Law and Diplomacy at Tufts University. Her research and teaching interests lie at the intersection of comparative political economy and international relations, and she has done fieldwork on the West Bank, India, and the Philippines. She focuses mostly on comparative politics in developing and transitional countries and is keenly interested in the relationship between informal markets, access to state institutions, clientelism, and political psychology. Her book manuscript, *Economic Modernization and the Disruption of Patronage Politics: Experimental Evidence from the Philippines,* employs qualitative, field experimental, and quantitative research methodology to investigate how marginalized people respond to economic development. She received her PhD in Political Science from Yale University in 2012 and earned an LLM in Law and Economics from the University of Hamburg, Germany on a Fulbright Scholarship. She holds a BA in Economics (with distinction) from the University of Texas, Austin.

William Inboden is William Powers, Jr. Chair and Executive Director of the William P. Clements, Jr. Center for National Security at the University of Texas-Austin. He also serves as Associate Professor at the LBJ School of Public Affairs and is a Distinguished Scholar at the Robert S. Strauss Center for International Security and Law. Previously, he served as Senior Director for Strategic Planning on the National Security Council at the White House, where he worked on a range of foreign policy issues including the 2006 *National Security Strategy,* democracy and governance, contingency planning, counterradicalization, and multilateral institutions and initiatives. Inboden also worked at the Department of State as a Member of the Policy Planning Staff and a Special Advisor in the Office of International Religious Freedom, and has worked as a staff member in both the US Senate and the House of Representatives. He is the author of *Religion and American Foreign Policy, 1945–1960: The Soul of Containment* (Cambridge University Press, 2010). Inboden received his PhD and MA degrees in history from Yale University.

Jonathan Kirshner is the Stephen and Barbara Friedman Professor of International Political Economy in the Department of Government at Cornell University. His research and teaching interests focus on international relations, political economy (especially macroeconomics), and politics and film. He is the author of numerous books, including *American Power after the Financial Crisis* (Cornell University Press, 2014), *Currency and Coercion: The Political Economy of International Monetary Power* (Princeton University Press, 1995), and *Appeasing Bankers: Financial Caution on the Road to War* (Princeton University Press, 2007), which won the best book award from the International Security Studies Section of the International Studies Association. He is the editor of the volumes *Globalization and National Security* (Routledge, 2006) and *Monetary Orders: Ambiguous Economics, Ubiquitous Politics* (Cornell University Press, 2003), and, with Eric Helleiner, the coeditor of two volumes and the multidisciplinary book series Cornell Studies in Money. He previously chaired the Economics and National Security Program at the Olin Institute of Strategic Studies at Harvard. Kirshner is a recipient of the Provost's Award for Distinguished Scholarship and the Stephen and Margery Russell Distinguished Teaching Award from Cornell University. He is currently pursuing projects on classical realism, the international political implications of the financial crisis, and the politics of mid-century cinema.

Jennifer Lind is an Associate Professor of Government at Dartmouth College and Faculty Associate of the Reischauer Institute for Japanese Studies at Harvard University. She has previously been a Fellow at the Sasakawa Peace Foundation; a Visiting Scholar at the Waseda University for Advanced Study in Tokyo, Japan; and a consultant for RAND Corporation and for the Office of the Secretary at the US Department of Defense. Lind is the author of *Sorry States: Apologies in International Politics* (Cornell University Press, 2008). Her work has also been featured in *International Security, International Studies Quarterly, The Atlantic*, and *Foreign Affairs*. Lind's current research adresses the way countries rise to the status of great powers and the coming struggle for the Western Pacific between the United States and China. She holds an MA in Pacific International Affairs from University of California, San Diego and a PhD in Political Science from the Massachusetts Institute of Technology.

Sara Bjerg Moller is Assistant Professor at the School of Diplomacy and International Relations at Seton Hall University. Her research interests lie at the intersection of international cooperation and conflict processes. Her dissertation, "Fighting Friends: Institutional Cooperation and Military Effectiveness in Multinational Wars," analyzes the institutional design and effectiveness of multinational fighting arrangements in wartime. Her work has been published in the *Los Angeles Times, Boston Globe, National Interest, Middle East Times*, and *World Politics Review*. She received her PhD from Columbia University; prior to undertaking PhD studies, she worked as a Research Associate for Middle Eastern Studies at the Council on Foreign Relations.

Cindy Williams is a Research Affiliate of the Security Studies Program at the Massachusetts Institute of Technology, where she was a Principal Research Scientist until her retirement in 2013. She is also an elected fellow and a former member of the board of directors of the National Academy of Public Administration and a member of the Council on Foreign Relations, in addition to serving on the editorial board of *International Security*. Formerly, she was an Assistant Director of the Congressional Budget Office, where she led the National Security Division in studies of budgetary and policy choices related to defense and international security. Dr. Williams also served as a director and in other capacities at the MITRE Corporation in Bedford, Massachusetts; as a member of the Senior Executive Service in the Office of the Secretary of Defense; and as a mathematician at RAND. Dr. Williams holds a PhD in mathematics from the University of California, Irvine. She is coauthor, with Gordon Adams, of *Buying National Security: How America Plans and Pays for Its Global Role and Safety at Home* (Routledge, 2010). She is the editor of *Filling the Ranks: Transforming the U.S. Military Personnel System* (MIT Press, 2004) and *Holding the Line: U.S. Defense Alternatives for the Early 21st Century* (MIT Press, 2001), and co-editor, with Curtis Gilroy, of *Service to Country: Personnel Policy and the Transformation of Western Militaries* (MIT Press, 2006).

William C. Wohlforth is the Daniel Webster Professor in the Dartmouth College Department of Government. A widely recognized expert in international relations, he has published works on topics ranging from the Cold War to contemporary US grand strategy. He is the editor of five books and the author of three others, including *America Abroad: The United States' Global Role in the 21st Century* (Oxford University Press, 2016) with coauthor Stephen G. Brooks. He has published some sixty articles and book chapters, and his work has appeared in journals including *Foreign Affairs, International Security, American Political Science Review,* and *World Politics.* He is a member of the editorial boards of the *Cambridge Studies in International Relations, Security Studies,* and *International Security,* is a member of the Council on Foreign Relations, and has served as a consultant for the National Intelligence Council and the National Bureau of Asian Research. Before coming to Dartmouth in 2000, Wohlforth held faculty appointments at Princeton University and Georgetown University. He has taught undergraduate courses on a wide array of topics, including international politics, Russian foreign policy, leadership and grand strategy, violence and security, and decision making. He is currently writing a book on nationalism and war with Nicholas Sambanis and Stergios Skaperdas.

Sustainable Security

SUSTAINABLE SECURITY
RETHINKING AMERICAN NATIONAL SECURITY STRATEGY

Jeremi Suri and Benjamin Valentino

In recent years, observers of US defense and foreign policies have increasingly warned that America's national security strategy has become obsolete or unsustainable. Although it is widely recognized that the domestic and international conditions facing the United States have changed dramatically since the end of the Cold War, our defense and foreign policies—and the underlying ideas and institutions that support them—have changed surprisingly little. Is it simply good fortune that the same basic policies, allies, and budgets that protected us from the Soviet Union in 1988 have turned out to be the optimal ones for defending American interests against terrorist groups like Islamic State in Iraq and Syria (ISIS) or a rising China in 2013 and beyond? Or have we clung to familiar policies, friends, and institutions simply because change is difficult? Even supporters of America's current policies need to be more explicit in explaining why and how these inherited policies will remain effective and affordable in the long term.

A decade of foreign wars, a devastating global financial crisis, mounting public debt, and profound realignments in international political and economic power have inspired calls for fundamental change from the competing extremes of the American political landscape. A new generation of political actors in the United States does not share the assumptions of the Cold War generation that shaped current US foreign policy. To some, these developments call for a neo-isolationist strategy that would attempt to wall America off from international threats and unpredictable global economic forces. To others, new threats from terrorism, the proliferation of weapons of mass destruction, and a rising China justify an even more interventionist approach, in which the United States would expand its commitments to friendly nations and use its current military advantages to act forcefully, sometimes preventively, to protect American interests around the world.

If we wish to avoid either of these extremes, the United States needs a new set of ideas and principles to justify its worthwhile international commitments, and curtail ineffective obligations where necessary. Strategy is at least as much about choosing what *not* to do as it is about choosing what to do. Americans must be cautious about pursuing radical strategic changes, but they also must recognize that thoughtless adherence to the status quo is potentially self-defeating. America's national security strategy must be sustainable politically, as well as financially and militarily. Without a clear set of strategic ideas and principles to guide their decisions, American leaders will be unable to explain convincingly why some interests are worth fighting for and some are not.

In this volume we use the term "sustainable security" to describe a foreign policy that matches America's means to its ends, not just today, but in a way that can be maintained over the coming decades. Virtually all observers of the changing international environment acknowledge that the United States is in the midst of a transition from unquestioned hegemon in a unipolar post–Cold War regime to one player, still powerful, in a materially different world. The United States must craft its security strategy in a manner that does not assume American economic primacy as a foregone conclusion, but rather figures the long-term economic costs and benefits of different decisions into what will keep America strong. Policies that mortgage America's economic prosperity to maximize security will leave the United States neither prosperous nor secure in the future. Balancing our means and ends requires a deep reevaluation of US strategy, as the choices made today will shape the direction of US security policy for decades to come.

A new wave of rigorous, policy-relevant scholarship on how the United States can sustainably pursue its national security interests is necessary for the development of coherent strategic principles. Given the range of issues that might affect American security in the twenty-first century, developing such a strategy is beyond the abilities of any individual scholar, policymaker, or academic discipline. This volume, therefore, represents an effort to bring together leading historians and political scientists to rethink the foundations of American national security for a new era. The research presented in these chapters was conducted between 2011 and 2014 as part of the Tobin Project's national security initiative.

The research in this volume focuses on two related facets of national security. The first section of the book explores the material foundations of American national security and the opportunities for significant shifts in foreign policy strategy. The chapters in this part begin by focusing on the economic and financial foundations of policy, examining how US power is affected by recent trends in national and international political economy. The chapters address the relationships between topics such as defense budgets, public debt, the status of the US dollar as an international reserve currency, and the economics of America's global military posture, seeking to identify the factors that cultivate or undermine American power in the long term.

This first section of the book also includes a set of historical chapters that build on the analysis of political economy in earlier chapters to analyze similar moments in the past: How have other great powers attempted to shift their strategies under similar constraints? How has the United States managed strategic change in other periods? The chapters in this section pay particularly close attention to the domestic institutions, both military and civilian, that underpin national security policy. They probe the historical record for insights about how powerful countries have succeeded and failed in adjusting to broad shifts in political economy.

A chapter on climate change, and the geopolitics surrounding that topic, is also included in the first section of the book. This chapter examines a rapidly emerging challenge to stability, economy, and security among the most powerful international actors. Building on the political economic analysis of prior chapters, this one focuses on domestic effects that reverberate internationally, and the necessity for expanded cooperation among dominant states, especially China and the United States.

The second section of this book explores several of America's most important regional security commitments in Europe, the Middle East, South Asia, and East Asia. These are close case studies in the difficult strategic choices the United States must make about allocating limited military and economic resources. The authors ask whether and how these commitments continue to advance America's national interests and, if not, how they might be transformed. This part of the book also examines American public opinion regarding overseas commitments.

The two sections of the book are symbiotic. The chapters in Section I analyze the material pressures on policy and the historical impediments and opportunities for change. The chapters in Section II begin to reassess US security strategy, exploring the dilemmas that policymakers confront in managing contemporary commitments and resources. Together, the two sections point to possibilities for a more sustainable national security policy by applying the lessons of Section I to the difficult cases in Section II.

This volume is focused primarily on the material foundations of American national security. We chose to concentrate on international political economy, US national security institutions, and regional security commitments because each of these three topic areas has been understudied in relation to current US policy options. We also recognized that studying these three fields together would offer an opportunity to re-frame critical policy choices and generate new research insights. Taken together, the chapters in this volume can help to answer the following fundamental questions about US security strategy: How is US national security strategy shaped? How have the United States and other great powers shifted their security strategies to adapt to geopolitical and economic change in the past? How do current (inherited) US security commitments serve US interests in a changing world? As in the past, the intersection of international political economy, national security institutions, and regional security commitments will determine many elements of America's future power projection abroad.

Within this framework, the forthcoming chapters devote relatively little attention to the cultural and social foundations of American power. These are important topics, worthy of more extensive investigation. The scholars in this volume made a focused analytical choice: to understand the political, economic, and regional security dimensions of contemporary national security policy. We acknowledge the importance of many other factors, including the emerging challenges of climate change and cybersecurity, and we urge future researchers to explore, perhaps on the model of this volume, how other factors reshape US security in the twenty-first century.

AN ERA OF CONSTRAINED RESOURCES

Strategic crises are common and they rarely result in enduring shifts of power. The systemic elements of the international system—geography, the allocation of wealth, the mobilization of military capabilities, perceptions of political legitimacy, and routines of behavior—are generally more resilient than the pressures of a particular moment, even a major war. For this reason, American international predominance has continued with remarkable consistency across the last six decades, despite repeated policy miscalculations and misallocations of resources. American strategic leadership has been mediocre, at best, but American strategic predominance has remained largely invulnerable.

Many observers expect this trend to continue with the new energy resources emerging from North America, expansion of global markets for commerce, increased demands for political participation across the globe, and rising political-economic turmoil around East Asia and Europe, the only two regions capable of producing a strategic peer to the United States in the foreseeable future. According to this analysis, American predominance will continue even if America fails to adapt its national security strategy to a changing world. This is a comforting and humbling prediction, echoing German Chancellor Otto von Bismarck's contemptuous nineteenth century comment that "God has a special providence for fools, drunks, and the United States of America."

Perhaps America's luck is finally running out. There is reason to believe that the mediocrity of American strategic leadership is now imperiling the country's inherited strategic advantages. The crises facing the United States today are not new, but they appear to be reaching a historical tipping point because of the accumulated costs of past decisions, the density of current challenges, and, above all, the stagnation of American policymaking. Simply stated, the United States is operating in an incredibly difficult international environment with extensive commitments but limited reserves, and even more limited readiness at home to adjust to these circumstances. These pressures are not transitory, but the consequence of long-term trends that are unlikely to reverse themselves in the near future. The accumulated and current pressures on the United States do not make a strategic tip inevitable, but they make a serious consideration of new policy options and assumptions imperative. That is the motivation for this book.

The United States remains a wealthy and dynamic society that can spend more on its security than any of its peers. The United States also continues to support a more powerful military than most of its competitors combined. American military and communications technologies are, in many cases, at least one and often two generations ahead of others. The United States consistently deploys more advanced weapons in larger numbers and with better-trained operators than our adversaries. That will not change in coming years. American military expenditures are high in absolute terms, but remain at a historically sustainable level of about five percent of gross national product.

The trouble is not that the United States spends too little on the military, but that it may have too many commitments both at home and abroad. There are a dizzying number of latent demands on American force across the globe; and while political realities make it unlikely that American military spending will rise dramatically in the foreseeable future, no conceivably sustainable military budget could ensure that all American commitments are simultaneously protected. American ships patrol all the major waterways of the world, American bases constitute what one scholar calls a global "archipelago" of facilities, and American aircraft fly daily missions (manned and unmanned) above virtually all terrain. Basic American military operations are ubiquitous; they are labor intensive, and they are expensive. Within a political climate that demands an "all-volunteer" force, there is little available capacity in the incredibly large American military for multiplying regional conflicts that demand additional personnel and capacities. For all its extraordinary size and skill, the American military can easily become overstretched.

It might have reached that point already. In conflicts like those in Iraq and Afghanistan—and now a new war against the Islamic State of Iraq and Syria, as well as other terrorist groups—US armed forces quickly find themselves spread too thin to accomplish strategic aims. The civilians who direct American policy—including the president, the secretaries of state and defense, and the national security advisor—find themselves in perpetual crisis mode, reacting to new demands rather than thinking systematically about strategic priorities.

Another inherited burden on resources is demographic. As Cindy Williams argues, although the United States does not confront population decline (as in Europe and East Asia), the country faces ballooning health and retirement obligations that are crowding out other investments. After a half-century during which the United States has fielded the largest peacetime military force in its history, it is now obligated to finance higher economic transfer payments to veterans than ever before. An all-volunteer military compounds these problems because volunteers demand more long-term benefits for retention. These expenses are threatening to break the Pentagon's budget, just as they are producing exorbitant national debt obligations. The American military, like other major civilian institutions, is asked to address a growing number of current commitments and crises while it must devote a higher proportion of its resources than ever before to personnel who are no longer active. We may be at a tipping point where inherited costs undermine current investments.

Defense Secretaries Robert Gates and Leon Panetta both articulated these urgent points, as they called for more restraint in American military commitments and serious reform in health and retirement entitlements. Chairman of the Joint Chiefs of Staff Admiral Mike Mullen made the clearest public statement about these resource challenges. In September 2011, on the eve of another recurring budget battle in Congress, he told a group of business executives that the "biggest threat to our national security is our debt." Mullen focused on the higher costs for capital equipment and "increases in pay, and especially increases in the cost of health care."

Mullen closed his candid statement with a clear call for greater restraint in American military commitments and more attention to the prudent reallocation of resources: "We must consider the world as it is—the threats as we see them—not wishing away the danger nor blowing it out of proportion," Mullen said. "Pragmatism and practicality must be our watchwords moving forward," he added, "[and] strategy must become our acumen."

Despite the enormous influence of Gates, Panetta, and Mullen, these figures failed to make serious headway on reform. American policymakers in the Bush and Obama administrations were more cautious about intervening in foreign conflicts after long frustrating months of combat in Afghanistan and Iraq, but they have not shown any serious willingness to reduce costly inherited commitments around the world. If anything, the "Asian pivot" has created a new obligation to increase the American land, sea, and air presence in Asia, while maintaining military hegemony in the Persian Gulf, Western Europe, and all major waterways around the globe.

Civil wars and territorial disputes throughout East and South Asia, North Africa, and the Middle East threaten to suck in further American military forces, based on security guarantees that the United States has inherited, in some cases, from the early years of the Cold War. Resource pressures demand some degree of American retrenchment, but political calculations push policymakers to avoid all the difficult trade-offs. Without attention to trade-offs, there can be no coherent strategy.

Perversely, the across-the-board sequester budget cuts of 2013 reinforced the resource problem because they exclude reductions to entitlements, they leave inherited obligations in place, and they are accompanied by the increasing demands on American security forces around Syria, North Korea, Libya, Somalia, and other international trouble spots. The sequester simply asks the American military, and all other government agencies, to do more with less. This is a recipe for even greater overstretch and underachievement in American foreign policy. This is also a recipe for more strategic blunders like the Iraq War of 2003, where ambitious policy aims were accompanied by clearly insufficient resource commitments.

Observing the widening mismatch between ambitions and resources, numerous commentators have focused on the dysfunctional elements of American domestic politics. Neither partisanship nor politicization of foreign policy are new, but the heightened elements of both phenomena press dangerously on current resource vulnerabilities. It looks at times (especially during the government shutdown and threatened default of October 2013) like a perfect storm. The political posturing of American international dominance is blowing hard against the weakened walls of available American capabilities and domestic support.

American military personnel, diplomats, and other officials are now spread so thin that one must question whether they can continue to perform basic functions with the competence citizens expect. High standards of quality usually decline when personnel are asked to do more with less. The natural tendency is to cover up seemingly small holes in capabilities until they are exposed in disastrous fashion. There is an accompanying urge to silence warnings about potential shortfalls in fulfilling required missions. This has been the experience for other government agencies under similar conditions in the past.

Why should we expect US military, security, and diplomatic agencies to be immune to this dynamic? How can we hope to maintain the high standards we demand for international and domestic security when ambitions and resources are misaligned? The rising levels of suicide, depression, and violence within the military services are already a sign of serious internal troubles. The on-the-ground difficulties in Iraq and Afghanistan were another powerful warning. We have entered an era when rigid domestic political demands, coupled with multiplying foreign challenges, constrain the strongest military in the world.

These changes render the current crisis in American foreign policy more serious and difficult to ignore than those America has faced since the end of the Cold War. If the United States benefited from enormous strategic fortune in the past, as Bismarck observed, it appears to confront an unfortunate dynamic in the early twenty-first century: expanding international activities with an evermore constrained and polarized domestic base. This situation cannot continue for very long in a democratic system without a major strategic reevaluation. American political leaders need to be able to maintain a security strategy that both serves American interests and values, and is acceptable to the democracy. Our book hopes to contribute to this process in a reasoned and measured way. We can expect less reason and measure if change is required after a public catastrophe, perhaps something larger than the September 11, 2001 attacks, Hurricane Katrina, or the frustrating war in Iraq. Strategic change is most effective when it begins *before* a catastrophe, giving policymakers the chance to anticipate and mitigate future threats. Otherwise, rapid catastrophe-driven reform is likely to prove counterproductive, and maybe too little, too late.

SUSTAINABLE SECURITY

A sustainable national security strategy must effectively unite America's means with its ends, its limited resources with its global interests. The constraints on American political and economic resources must be matched with the threats the United States faces from beyond its shores. American policymakers cannot stretch resources continuously without diminishing returns abroad and at home. Sustainability in foreign policy implies focus, cost-effectiveness, and a careful management of resources. It discourages the tendencies toward full spectrum dominance, endless warfare, and multiplying foreign commitments in recent American policy. The chapters in this volume use the concept of sustainability to analyze a few important dimensions for American strategic reevaluation.

Unfortunately for American strategists, the international security environment has changed at least as radically in the last twenty years as have the constraints on national resources. Some of these changes, like the collapse of the Soviet Union and the end of the Cold War, have undoubtedly made America safer. Many others have presented new threats and challenges to the United States. There is a natural tendency toward threat inflation, and domestic politics often make it difficult to control popular calls for shows of military strength against terrorist groups and other violent but distant troublemakers. A sustainable security strategy requires the hard work of educating citizens about the limits of various threats, and the high costs incurred by reacting to every challenge. Difficult American experiences in Vietnam, Afghanistan, and Iraq show that overreaction to limited threats can be more damaging than the threats themselves.

The United States exists in a world almost without precedent for a leading international power. American military capabilities dwarf those of any other country. Yet the United States remains an explicit ally or close friend of almost every country on the World Bank's list of the twenty largest economies. The only exceptions are China and Russia, and few see a realistic threat of full-scale war with them any time soon, despite continued tensions around various East Asian islands and Ukraine. Never before has the leading international state had so many powerful friends and so few state adversaries aligned against it. The most pressing threats to the United States come from terrorists, rogue states, and other small actors who can harm large numbers of citizens (usually abroad). Their capacity for undermining overall American security, however, is quite limited. Terrorism is a danger to civilians; it is not a strategic challenge to US international supremacy.

Traditional security is not the problem for the United States. The most significant challenge for American policymakers, and a missing piece for a sustainable security strategy, is adjustment to international economic change. Long-term trends in economic growth are narrowing America's relative position, and limiting the resources that the United States can effectively allocate for traditional security commitments, especially if Americans want to continue investing in innovation and productivity at home. In 1994, when the last Russian troops left Germany, China's Gross Domestic Product (GDP) stood at $560 billion (using market exchange rates), compared to America's $8.4 trillion. Today, China's GDP has reached $8.4 trillion, an increase of almost fifteen-fold, while the US economy has more than doubled to $15.7 trillion. At this rate, China's economy is likely to surpass the United States' before the end of the decade.

Even if the Chinese economy does not grow larger than the American economy, however, the emerging parity of the two markets and the financial interdependence between them means that the United States will have less freedom to act unilaterally to protect its interests around the globe. The Chinese, and coalitions of other states, will have the power to inflict high costs on undesirable American actions by redirecting their financial resources, including their purchases of US government debt. Leaders in Washington will find it necessary to elicit significant military and financial assistance, not just acquiescence, from regional allies in order to share costs.

In contrast to the militaristic unilateralism that has dominated American foreign policy from the Global War on Terror to recent attacks on ISIS, a sustainable security policy for the United States will require extensive multilateralism— compromise on interests, consultation on actions, and serious burden-sharing. In a more competitive international economic environment, current American foreign policies will only be sustainable if the United States is not acting largely alone, and not paying most of the costs. Otherwise, American unilateral actions will inspire more local resistance and incur painful burdens on the national economy. A sustainable security policy must be attentive to the opportunity costs of military and other foreign policy expenditures. This is a central theme for each chapter in this book.

In addition to increased economic competition and the spread of terrorism, the United States faces a host of unconventional developments with the potential to affect America's security. As American business and military organizations have become more dependent on the Internet, they are now vulnerable to cyberattacks. Major climactic shifts are creating new geopolitical realities. These include the opening of Arctic sea lanes and increased competition between nations over newly accessible mineral, oil, and gas deposits in the Arctic and Antarctic. Climate change also threatens to alter patterns of human habitation and economic activity on a global scale, with unknowable consequences. Although the United States may be more secure than ever before, current policy confronts new and emerging threats that require strategic responses. This is an additional reason to manage security commitments wisely, allocating precious resources and attention for nascent challenges beyond those of the present moment.

Unfortunately, recent American foreign policy has focused almost exclusively on current threats and past commitments, not future needs. This is most evident in the startling observation that the broad contours of America's national security strategy have changed very little since the end of the Cold War. The number of active duty military personnel has declined by less than ten percent. America's defense budget has remained relatively constant at about 4.5 percent of GDP. In 1994, the United States operated twelve aircraft carriers. Today we have ten with another one under construction.

Perhaps the easiest way to appreciate the stagnation in America's national security strategy over the last two decades is to review America's network of alliances. America's main formal or informal defense commitments with Western Europe, Japan, South Korea, Taiwan, Israel, Egypt, and Saudi Arabia all predate the end of the Cold War. The only significant change to our alliance structure since then has been the expansion of NATO, which, despite the collapse of NATO's primary adversary, has committed the United States to the defense of twelve additional nations in Eastern Europe—a decision many have begun to question in light of Russia's increasing willingness to test the strength of those commitments. The United States has reduced the number of troops deployed in South Korea and Japan, but nowhere has Washington chosen to terminate its commitments to defend other nations. (The Philippines did ask the United States to close its major bases there in 1991, but the US retains an almost sixty-year-old mutual defense treaty with the Philippines.) It is difficult to believe that the same alliance portfolio the United States needed in 1950 just happens to be the one we need today. Adherence to inherited commitments and routines, rather than adjustment to emerging needs, threatens to make current policy unsustainable.

A key premise of this book is that the time has come for a comprehensive reassessment of America's overseas commitments in light of America's changed strategic and economic environment. Significant cuts to our defense budget are likely whether we reexamine our commitments or not. It would be wise to use this opportunity to ask whether we can bring our commitments back in line with our national interests and sustainable costs, rather than struggle to overstretch our budget to meet ever-growing commitments. It makes little sense, for example, to continue to debate the utility of the F-22 aircraft or how many carrier battle groups we need without examining the value to the United States of the overseas commitments these weapons were designed to defend.

The costs of America's commitments, of course, are not merely economic. Although our alliances were initially formed to deter conflict, many of America's overseas commitments also have the potential to draw the United States into wars it would prefer to avoid. The recent crisis in Ukraine reinforces this point. If Ukraine were indeed part of NATO, as some have advocated, the United States would have an obligation to join a potential war between Ukraine and Russia, even if leaders in Washington questioned American interests in that conflict. A similar dynamic exists in Asia, where Japan's actions in the Senkaku/Diaoyu islands threaten to draw the United States into a war against China. Extended security commitments quickly become unsustainable when regional conflicts call in American guarantees.

Although alliances are essential for effective multilateralism, they can be dangerous and even self-defeating if they become permanent and axiomatic. When the United States promises to ensure the security and welfare of countries, it also encourages free riding, and sometimes even reckless behavior. This has been evident throughout the Middle East, East Asia, and South Asia during the last decade. Permanent alliances also complicate relations with major powers like Russia and

China, who perceive themselves as permanent adversaries for these alliances. That perception makes cooperation with the United States on critical issues like trade, arms control, humanitarian intervention, and regional conflict more difficult. These costs are perhaps worth paying, but only if they are outweighed by benefits afforded by existing alliances. Weighing costs and benefits, and contemplating shifts in alliance commitments, is an exercise we have ignored for much too long.

Substantial costs might be justified if they are clearly outweighed by the benefits of existing alliances. The character of alliance benefits, however, is seldom made clear by those who advocate maintaining US commitments; they simply assert vague benefits that some of the chapters in this volume question. Indeed, in the post–Cold War world, it is hard to make the case that most of our allies do much to defend directly the security of the United States. To take two examples: Romania does little to protect the United States from Russia, and Taiwan does not protect the United States from China. American allies may assist in projecting power around the world, but in many cases the main reason the United States needs to project power is to protect these same allies. A cycle of alliance dependencies raises American costs with perhaps negative security returns.

Many of the arguments in favor of maintaining American alliances boil down to fears about regional instability that could occur should the United States pull back. Would a US withdrawal from Asia spark a conventional build-up or even nuclear weapons programs in Japan, South Korea, and Taiwan? Would it embolden China to threaten US freedom of navigation in the Pacific? Would a reduction of US support to Israel encourage Iran to develop nuclear weapons or set off a nuclear arms race in the Persian Gulf? Proponents of these commitments must make the case that the predicted threats are reasonably likely, that a military alliance with the United States is the most effective way of averting them, and that averting them is worth the costs and risks to the United States. Proponents must also address an alternative proposition: that extended American commitments in regions like the Middle East make conflict and instability more likely. Would some regions be better off with a smaller US presence? Would a more limited US posture prove more sustainable for the region and American interests?

This book poses four fundamental questions of America's security commitments, aimed at assessing core interests and long-term sustainability. First, what benefits does the United States obtain from a given alliance? Put differently, what negative consequences might the United States suffer if it ended a particular commitment, and how likely are those consequences to occur? Second, is a US military commitment necessary to defend our interests in the region, or are our allies capable of defending themselves? Third, is it possible that our commitments could be counterproductive—diminishing our allies' incentives to invest in their own defense or encouraging them to behave recklessly? Finally, what are the full costs of a given commitment to the United States, including the economic and political liabilities, and the risks of war?

The chapters in this book explore strategies for American foreign policy that focus on core national interests and recognize the limits on resources. The authors take the criticisms of current strategic overstretch and ineffectiveness seriously. They also affirm that the power of the United States requires some active measures of foreign defense, open trade, and continued international exchange of labor, capital, and ideas. The authors argue that a fundamental strategic reevaluation for the United States is necessary to reaffirm internationalist principles. In the past, strategic reevaluations—by William McKinley and John Hay after 1896, and Franklin Roosevelt after 1933—played a vital role in repositioning the United States to improve its security abroad, as it forged a new policy consensus at home. We are in similar historical terrain today. Assessing how we have come to our current predicament and examining realistic alternatives, in the light of past experience, is the only way to develop a sustainable strategy for American security into the middle of the present century.

OUR CONTRIBUTIONS

Each of the chapters in this volume addresses three questions: Why does the United States need a more sustainable security strategy? What are the key elements of a more sustainable security strategy? How might the United States construct such a strategy? Although our contributors offer different ideas and recommendations, they all agree that the time has come for a critical reexamination of the foundations of American security.

The first set of chapters focus on the links between money and power. Jonathan Kirshner examines the great recession of 2008 and its lingering effects on America's international economic position. He argues that the interrelated trends of domestic financial deregulation and financialization contributed directly to the crisis, to the rise in foreign-held US debt, and to the new fundamental weakness of the dollar as a global currency. Kirshner describes Chinese and other efforts to challenge the standing of the dollar, and he predicts more of the same. Kirshner's analysis argues for rethinking of assumptions about financial deregulation at home to give the United States a sounder basis for the support of its extended international economic, political, and military positions.

Daniel Drezner and Nancy Hite-Rubin examine the relationship between military spending and foreign direct investment. In a close analysis of the data, they find that high military spending by developed countries, particularly the United States, does not attract more capital investment to the country. Drezner and Hite-Rubin point to some correlation for developing countries, establishing basic security for investors, but they show that the high levels of American spending do not pay off. Instead, current American military spending at home and abroad contributes to capital depletion and indebtedness. Drezner and Hite-Rubin's analysis suggests that a sustainable security strategy must involve less military spending.

Cindy Williams digs into the effects of smaller budgets for the US military services. In a very fine-grained analysis, she argues that cuts can, in fact, strengthen American capabilities. To address the demographic challenges the military faces, Williams proposes reforms to pay structures, benefits, and overall numbers that will eliminate waste and discourage mission creep. Williams lays out what a smaller, more efficient, and more focused US military might look like. She anticipates a more sustainable defense establishment in future years.

The next three chapters add a historical dimension to the analysis of economy, strategy, and power. Jeremi Suri interrogates the sources of power growth and decline in eighteenth-century Great Britain, nineteenth-century China, and the twentieth-century United States. He analyzes the crucial roles played by domestic taxation and foreign borrowing for necessary economic and military investments. Suri argues that these financial instruments are crucial for a sustainable security strategy. Successful governments nurture institutional capabilities for effective taxation and inexpensive borrowing. He argues that the United States must strengthen these capabilities if it wishes to sustain its international power.

William Inboden focuses his attention on American security institutions, the National Security Council (NSC) in particular. He describes how important the coordination of different policymakers through the NSC is for the formulation and implementation of strategy, especially during periods of domestic retrenchment and foreign threat. Comparing the experiences of President Harry Truman with those of Presidents Bill Clinton and George W. Bush, Inboden distills a series of valuable guidelines for reforming American national security in a new era. Inboden's analysis shows that a sustainable foreign policy begins, in many ways, with effective national security institutions remade for the challenges of their time.

John Hall's chapter, which compares the experiences of European and American armies between the two World Wars, offers a number of lessons for contemporary policy that build on the economic and institutional insights of the prior chapters. He shows that higher budgets do not necessarily improve military preparation, and he also observes that strategic rigidity hinders necessary learning. For Hall, the key elements of military success include adaptability, innovation, and tolerance of dissent. He observes that these qualities are limited in the current US military by the pressures derived from "global constabulary obligations and the constraint of being perpetually ready for a major war." Hall's chapter argues that stricter scrutiny of budgets and security commitments might, in fact, help the US Army to develop a more sustainable strategy.

Joshua Busby's chapter neatly closes out this section with a concise description of the emerging political and economic implications of climate change. Busby addresses some of the clearest connections to security, and the likely consequences. He points to necessary areas for cooperation, and outlines some possible paths for US policy that link security and climate in sustainable ways.

The second section of the book applies the insights from the chapters in the first section to current geopolitical realities, focusing on America's extensive system of alliances and security commitments. This section begins with a chapter by Benjamin Valentino which explores the nature of American public opinion regarding our existing overseas alliances. Since the public ultimately bears the costs of these alliances, continued public support is necessary for sustaining them. Recently, however, many scholars and policymakers have expressed concern that widespread disillusionment among the public could lead to increased support for isolationism. Drawing on an original poll conducted especially for this volume, however, Valentino shows that fears of a new wave of isolationism have been greatly exaggerated and public support for American alliances remains strong. Thus the greater challenge in the coming years may be for those political elites and scholars who favor retrenchment to convince the public that ending or significantly reconfiguring our overseas commitments is a necessary part of a sustainable security strategy.

The remaining chapters in this section explore America's commitments to specific regions. William Wohlforth begins with a hard look at America's oldest and largest alliance, NATO. Although Wohlforth acknowledges that the "case for an agonizing reappraisal of the US security commitment to Europe has never seemed stronger," he ultimately concludes that the European alliance structure we have inherited through more than a half century of political, military, financial, and bureaucratic wrangling is about the best we can do. Wohlforth argues that because both the costs and the risks of the alliance are relatively low, "muddling through" is better than the alternatives of dramatically reducing or further expanding our commitments.

Daniel Byman and Sara Bjerg Moller provide a detailed inventory and appraisal of America's commitments to the Middle East, the region that has occupied more of the resources and attention of United States than any other since the end of the Cold War. Byman and Moller argue that permanent US military deployments in the region are not only unnecessary, but often counterproductive. They recommend a lower profile strategy that focuses on maintaining bases and prepositioned equipment, and negotiating access agreements should the United States need to intervene more directly. Ultimately, Byman and Moller acknowledge that the power of the United States to shape events in this critical region remains limited. Sometimes the best we can do is "prepare for the aftermath."

Jennifer Lind's chapter explores America's alliances in East Asia. Lind argues that although our alliances with Korea, Japan, the Philippines, and Taiwan do support some key American interests in the region, they also come with substantial risks. Our commitments risk entangling the United States in a costly and dangerous security spiral with China, or entrapping the United States in wars that are not in American interests to fight. Our alliances have also encouraged buck-passing and expense-passing by our allies who are capable of contributing much more to their own defense. Lind argues that the United States is unlikely to withdraw from these alliances, but that it could reform them by transforming them from "terminals" that serve only to help defend single allies into "hubs" that allow the United States project power in the region.

Sumit Ganguly focuses on one of America's most important, but also most troubled, overseas commitments: the relationship with Pakistan. As Ganguly shows, an array of critical US interests overlap in Pakistan, including the future of Afghanistan, the fight against Islamic extremism, and efforts to limit nuclear proliferation. Ganguly makes the strong case that if the United States wishes to do more than react to increasingly grave crises emanating from Pakistan, Washington has a long-term interest in helping to resolve the rivalry between India and Pakistan. He argues that the United States may have a key role to play in deescalating the rivalry, if it is willing to use the leverage available to it.

Finally, Audrey Kurth Cronin focuses on the future of America's relationship with Afghanistan, the location of America's longest war. Cronin argues that if the United States does not wish to be drawn back into Afghanistan, as it has been in Iraq, it must help Afghanistan establish and maintain a strict policy of neutrality and nonalignment. As Cronin writes: "Afghanistan has been most dangerous to itself and others when it has drawn too close to any one power or group, and most stable when it has acted as a political buffer and economic crossroads between two or more." A sustainable security strategy involves a disciplined acknowledgement of limits, as well as continued ambitions, by American policymakers in Afghanistan and other regions.

CONCLUSION: A SUSTAINABLE FOREIGN POLICY

American national interests are best served when short-term foreign policy decisions are woven into a strategic fabric that endures. Effective national strategies assign priorities to guide behavior in crises, they allocate resources for worthwhile investments, they affirm valuable relationships, and they caution against temptations and traps. Effective national strategies also educate the public, create clear expectations, and provide criteria for assessing success and failure. Strategies tell us clearly what is worth fighting for and what is not.

Together these qualities contribute to what we call a sustainable national strategy. We are concerned with the formulation and implementation of a new American national strategy that can serve the nation's interests at reasonable cost, with consistent support, and continuing benefits to Americans and non-Americans alike. A more sustainable strategy, like the Open Door in the late nineteenth century and containment in the Cold War, must be simple, resilient, and compatible with American institutions and values.

In the chapters that follow, the authors assess sustainability by focusing on political economy, institutions, policy routines, and threat assessments. The chapters are attentive to the *material* sources and measures of power. The chapters also analyze the *choices* that leaders and publics have made about strategy, and the ways those choices influence ongoing behavior. Of course, multiple sets of actors—domestic and international—express preferences at the same time. The chapters assess the intersections of different preferences, and their consequences for policy choices. A sustainable strategy must frame, organize, and prioritize diverse policy preferences, converting them into a coherent system of choices that serve national interests over time.

Strategies are ultimately composed of compromises among different preferences. They are necessarily imperfect and dependent on their time and context. They must reflect domestic political realities as well as material ones. The fairest way to assess the sustainability of a national strategy is to ask how it compares to viable alternatives. Is there a better way to protect national interests at reasonable cost? Is there a national strategy that can offer more benefits with fewer risks? These are the historical, economic, and political questions that ground rigorous analysis of what composes a sustainable national strategy for a large and powerful country in a world with seemingly endless policy demands. A sustainable strategy helps to provide necessary resources and limit excessive commitments.

America's national security strategy has seen more continuity than change over the last sixty years. Making major changes to any policy as enduring and complex as this brings significant challenges. Our current policy is the devil we know. Anything else is the devil we don't know. Countless political, economic, and even emotional interests have accreted over the decades to sustain the national security strategy we have today. Many of those who stand to lose from changes to the present policy, including current allies who will have to spend more on their own defense, know who they are and are therefore motivated to defend the status quo. Many of those who might gain from a new strategy, such as America's men and women who will not be asked to fight in future foreign wars, do not yet know it, and so cannot be counted upon to advocate for change. Nevertheless, the first steps to making such changes are carefully assessing why things are as they are, and imagining how things could be different. These are the goals of the scholars who have contributed to this volume. A sustainable national security strategy must ask tough questions and it must imagine better alternatives.

SECTION I

Recalibrating National Security Strategy

Jeremi Suri

Since the end of the Cold War the United States has spent more money on forward military activities than any other country. For many years after 1991 the United States spent more than the rest of the countries in the world added together. It is hard to overstate the breadth of American hegemony at the dawn of the twenty-first century.

The paradox is that these unparalleled expenditures were never enough. As crises unfolded in the former Yugoslavia, Rwanda, Somalia, Afghanistan, Iraq, Libya, and Syria, the United States seemed to have too few resources available for the challenges at hand. Establishing a presence everywhere often meant that the United States was not enough of a presence anywhere.

That was not the only problem. Although American military expenditures remained around the recent historical norm, five percent of annual gross national product, the domestic burden on the United States grew. This was particularly true during the severe economic downturn of 2008–2009, when the country faced a precipitous capital liquidity crisis, despite billions of dollars of federal stimulus money. Years before the "Great Recession," American military expenditures had contributed to a much larger annual budget deficit. The United States borrowed more money each year to finance various programs, including its vast military and security establishment. Policies to diminish taxation and deregulate industries contributed to the deficits as they reduced government revenue and regulation, while Washington was trying to do more for citizens at home and allies abroad. For all the public focus on terrorism after the September 11 2001 attacks on the United States, resource constraints emerged as one of the most important strategic challenges for a hyperexpansive American security posture.

Political economy has long been a foundational element of strategic studies, but recent observers of American policy have, curiously, given this topic insufficient attention. The technological revolution in military affairs, the spread of democracy, and counterinsurgency have instead dominated public debates about strategy in the early twenty-first century. Basic questions about how much the United States should spend on national security and where it should spend have been largely neglected, especially by international relations specialists. Rigorous assessments of costs and benefits, as well as alternative strategic postures, are almost nonexistent in the public domain. For all the creative and valuable writing on foreign policy, it is fair to say that the literature is dominated by a liberal Keynesian consensus that assumes the US government can always spend more and get more security value for its expenditures.

The forthcoming chapters interrogate this consensus, although they do not necessarily reject it. The authors examine the consequences of American "financialization" and indebtedness, the costs of American foreign commitments, and the importance of taxation and capital markets for security. The chapters analyze the possibilities for reforming a smaller military, redesigning national security institutions, and nurturing more flexible decision-making bodies. The authors combine a deep reading of history with a close analysis of current conditions to provide a clearer view of how resource constraints, and political economy in general, define the possibilities for American security policy. Climate change also matters because it constrains resources and undermines what were seen as permanent security anchors.

The overarching theme for this section is that American policymakers must think in more systematic ways about the costs of their foreign policy choices. They should not necessarily spend less, but they should weigh costs and benefits more rigorously, to insure that they are getting good value. This involves making careful choices about commitments and improving the management of those commitments within the national security bureaucracy. Weighing costs and benefits also requires focused analysis on where the resources will come from: who will pay the taxes, who will finance the loans, and who, most importantly, will enforce trade-offs.

The authors in this section have many different ideas, but they agree that the hegemonic aspirations of American security policy in the early twenty-first century are too costly. The chapters explain why and they point to ways in which the United States, drawing on its own history and other societies, can sustain its global leadership while better managing its resources. A sustainable US foreign policy is not isolationist, nor is it hyperexpansionist. A sustainable US foreign policy must find an effective posture in between.

Each chapter in this section offers unique insights into what will constitute a more balanced American strategic posture. It will surely involve a mix of domestic retrenchment and selective foreign intervention; smaller armies but larger roles for diplomats and other government representatives. A sustainable security policy will use resources in ways that depart from the unlimited (and sometimes reckless) presumptions of previous years.

1

DOLLAR DIMINUTION AND NEW MACROECONOMIC CONSTRAINTS ON AMERICAN POWER

Jonathan Kirshner

In the introduction to this volume, Jeremi Suri and Benjamin Valentino proffer the eminently sensible (if all-too-commonly overlooked) admonition "America's national security strategy must be sustainable politically, as well as financially and militarily." Since the end of the Cold War at least, in an era of US hegemony and the unquestioned role of the dollar as the world's currency, the need for national security strategy to be "financially sustainable" was not much worried about by American planners. But this luxury, one virtually unprecedented in history, can no longer be taken for granted.

This chapter considers new macroeconomic constraints on American power. Those new constraints will derive from a basic and generally underappreciated shift in the US engagement with the global macroeconomic order. Since before the Second World War—that is, for the entirety of practical and institutional living memory—the international monetary and financial system had served to enhance US power and capabilities in its relations with other states. From the turn of the twenty-first century, however, underlying problems left unattended threatened the possibility that what had been a traditional (if implicit) source of strength might become instead a source of chronic weakness. The global financial crisis of 2007–2008 was an inflection point that has increased this risk. That crisis, the worst since 1931, is distinguished by the fact that the United States was at its epicenter. Since World War II financial crises were widely understood to be things that happened to *others*—that is, to countries other than the United States. As a result of the crisis, the United States will likely be confronted with new constraints on its power and new complications regarding the management of the dollar as a global currency, problems compounded by the stripping away of its aura of financial invulnerability. Moreover, both these new constraints and the unfamiliarity of American elites and citizens in facing such constraints will matter. That is to say, new and real constraints will present themselves, but the domestic political process and domestic political choices will play a crucial role in determining the severity of those new constraints in practice.

I begin with a review of the setting on the eve of the global financial crisis, which is crucial to understanding its implications. Even before the crisis, many observers were anticipating a relative reduction in the dollar's role as an international currency, and for a number of reasons, the crisis has served as an accelerant of that process, increasing pressure on the dollar and heightening its vulnerability. In particular, a turning away from the American economic model, especially in Asia, and the encroachment on the international role of the dollar by the RMB (despite its relative immaturity) and Euro (despite its own considerable distress), will present new challenges to the greenback and to US macroeconomic management. This chapter elucidates the likely international political consequences of these developments for American power in particular but also for international politics more generally. In the abstract and with reference to historical parallels, I will explain two distinct types of challenges faced by states managing international currencies in relative decline: (1) the loss of the benefits associated with issuing international money, and (2) the difficulties associated with supervising a currency experiencing a contraction in its global use. As a practical matter, the principal consequences of international currency diminution include pressure on defense spending, reduced macroeconomic autonomy (and thus the ability to finance ambitious foreign policies), vulnerability to currency manipulation, and greater exposure to debilitating financial distress, especially during times of international political crisis. In contemporary politics, these difficulties are likely to be exacerbated by increased disagreement and contestation between states over the politics of international monetary relations and global financial governance.

Even without the financial crisis, the most likely scenario was for the dollar's international role to modestly diminish over time.[1] It was expected (and is still most likely) that for the foreseeable future, the dollar will remain the world's most widely used international currency. But it also should be clear that the greenback need not be supplanted for there to be a politically consequential contraction in its global role. Even as it remains the world's most widely used money, the dollar's use and influence will likely be encroached upon by the RMB in Asia; by the Euro (despite the daunting, politically vexing problems which have hobbled that currency) at the frontiers of the Eurozone and possibly the Middle East; and, perhaps most importantly (and least appreciated), by a greater *motivation* for diversity on the part of numerous and varied actors in the wake of the global financial crisis. As Suri and Valentino argue, to understand world politics, material power remains of course enormously important, but it is also very much the case that states make strategic *choices* that reflect the policy preferences of various actors. Disenchantment with the American financial model will matter when it comes to choices about money (an area where ideas are especially consequential), affecting both state choices and international politics.

ON THE EVE OF THE FINANCIAL CRISIS

Before the financial crisis, some scholars were raising alarms about the future of the dollar and the stability of the international financial system—concerns rooted in the dismantling of international capital controls and the unsustainability of enormous, historically unprecedented deficits on US external accounts. Given the large number of dollars held abroad and anxiety about large US budget deficits, a small crisis threatened to mushroom into a large one, implicating the dollar and its

[1] See for example Benjamin Cohen, "Towards a Leaderless Currency System," in *The Future of the Dollar*, Eric Helleiner and Jonathan Kirshner eds., (Ithaca, NY: Cornell University Press, 2009).

role as an international currency. In 2004, I wrote that "America is ... at greater risk for a major financial crisis than at any other time since the Second World War," which I thought would be sparked by a "medium-sized financial disturbance that emerges in the United States [and] work[s] its way through the system via the recently deregulated US financial economy and high-flying international capital markets." I argued further that as "a few firms were pulled down by the under-tow, a full-blown panic would emerge. In the United States, the paper losses would be enormous; the contraction of wealth and instinct for caution would throw the economy into recession. The elements that make this scenario more rather than less likely are in place."[2]

Although alarmists were correct about the risk of financial crisis and the factors that contributed to it, the 2007–2008 meltdown—rooted in the house-of-cards collapse of the American banking system and then transmitted abroad—actually bolstered the dollar in the short run as investors fled in panic for the (comparatively) safest haven. But the long-run implications of the crisis leave the US economy (and the greenback) weaker than before, and magnify real concerns about a debt-addled America and a dollar in (relative) decline.

To understand the implications of the crisis, it is necessary to consider its origins. The Global Financial Crisis of 2007–2008, the worst economic catastrophe since the Great Depression, whose aftershocks still ripple, was a fundamental disturbance of what I call the "Second US Postwar International Economic Order." This order, the "globalization project" of 1994–2007, is distinct from the first order forged by the United States—the Bretton Woods system of 1948–1973—in its political, ideational, domestic, and international manifestations. In contrast with the "embedded liberalism" of the first project, which was market-oriented but, chastened by the failures of the Depression, skeptical of unmediated market forces, the second order had as its touchstone the liberation of finance, at home and abroad.

Brimming with post–Cold War confidence, America embarked on a dramatic acceleration of the domestic financial deregulation that had been initiated in the 1980s. At home, the Clinton administration led a bipartisan charge to dismantle the Depression-era firewalls that had been designed to contain instability in the domestic financial sector. These trends were, if anything, accelerated by the transition to the Bush administration (coupled with continuity at Greenspan's Federal Reserve). Two signature pieces of legislation codified these changes. First was the repeal of Glass-Steagall, the Banking Act of 1933 that regulated and compartmentalized the reckless financial order that contributed so fundamentally to the Depression. This effort, in particular to dismantle the firewalls between commercial and investment banking (and insurance), was led from the Clinton White House by Treasury Secretary (and former Goldman Sachs co-chair) Robert Rubin, in close partnership with Senate Banking Committee Chair Phil Gramm, and with the blessing of Federal Reserve Board Chair Alan Greenspan. Writing on the eve of the financial

---

[2] Jonathan Kirshner, "Globalization and American Power," workshop memo, April 16, 2004. See also Kirshner, "Globalization, Power, and Prospect," in *Globalization and National Security*, Kirshner ed. (New York: Routledge, 2006), pp. 321–340. I was in good company: Paul Volcker estimated there was a seventy-five percent chance of a dollar crisis within five years, "Checking the Depth Gauge: How Low Might the Dollar Sink?" *The Economist*, November 11, 2004.

crisis, Greenspan called the repeal (The Gramm-Leach Bliley Act) "a milestone of business legislation" from which "we dare not go back."[3]

Dismantling existing regulations was only half of the story of the great 1990s financial liberalization project. The other half was the fight *not* to supervise and regulate new and fantastically expanding sectors of the financial economy, which produced massive wealth, fueled the rapid growth of industry—and were inherent carriers of systemic risk. The interrelated phenomena of securitization (the repackaging, blending, and resale of bundles of financial assets such as mortgages) and the astonishing growth of trading in derivatives (any asset whose value "derived" from another asset, from simple futures and options to extremely complex and enmeshed risk and insurance dispersal exotica) forged the financialization of the American economy. These activities were largely unsupervised by an oversight and regulatory apparatus that was designed long before such products came on the scene.

A few voices were raised in concern, such as that of the US Government Accountability Office, which warned that "the size and concentration of derivatives activity, combined with derivatives-related linkages, could cause any financial disruption to spread faster and be harder to contain." The GAO was worried this could lead to "systemic crisis" and urged modernization of the regulatory structure. But the report elicited a fierce industry push back and massive lobbying effort; its allies in government were also mobilized. Key players included Larry Summers (who would become Treasury Secretary in 1999) and Alan Greenspan, who insisted that "regulation of derivatives transactions that are privately negotiated are unnecessary." Expressing confidence in the self-interest of private actors, Greenspan saw "no reason to question the underlying stability" of derivatives markets. (Greenspan, technically in charge of the oversight of the US financial system, saw little attractive in that responsibility. But as it turned out, he was "delighted that being a regulator was not the burden I had feared.") With this wind at his back, Gramm took the ball and ran with it, championing the Commodity Futures Modernization Act, which prohibited the regulation of derivatives, including the credit-default swaps that would play a central role in the 2007–2008 financial crisis.[4]

Not surprisingly, the US financial sector became larger, more concentrated, and riskier in this environment. From 1980 to 2002, as manufacturing in the United States fell from twenty-one percent of GDP to fourteen percent, finance, the biggest and fastest growing sector in the American economy, grew from fourteen percent to twenty-one percent. In 2007, finance accounted for forty-seven percent of US corporate profits; from 1981 to 2008, financial sector debt increased from twenty-two to 117 percent of GDP, the tip of an iceberg of risk that metastasized in the wake of deregulation.[5]

[3] Alan Greenspan, *The Age of Turbulence* (New York: Penguin, 2007), pp. 198–199, 257, 375–376.

[4] US Government Accountability Office, *Financial Derivatives: Actions Needed to Protect the Financial System* (Washington, DC: GAO, 1994), pp. 11, 14–15, 39, 124, 126–127; Alan Greenspan, "The Regulation of OTC Derivatives," Testimony before the House Committee on Banking and Financial Services, July 24, 1998; Greenspan, *Age of Turbulence*, pp. 373–374.

[5] Greta R. Krippner, *Capitalizing on Crisis: The Political Origins of the Rise of Finance* (Cambridge, MA: Harvard University Press, 2011), pp. 28, 29, 39, 51; Simon Johnson and James Kwak, *13 Bankers: The Wall Street Takeover and the Next Financial Meltdown* (New York: Pantheon, 2010).

The continuing financialization of the American economy was buttressed by a fundamentalist ideology that "markets always know best," which created the permissive environment of unsupervised securitization and the housing bubble. Reinforcing this was the rise of a Washington-Wall Street culture, whereby bankers, politicians, and regulators became so enmeshed that the metaphor of the revolving door is inadequate. This was also an era, as Simon Johnson argued, when Wall Street "translated its growing economic power into political power" and "the ideology of financial innovation became conventional wisdom in Washington." The financial sector invested $5 billion in the political process from 1998 to 2008.[6] Wall Street kingpins like Robert Rubin and Henry Paulson took on senior positions in government and—especially eyebrow-raising for a country that commonly castigated other cultures for something called "crony capitalism"—government officials and regulators could anticipate lucrative industry positions. Summers was paid over $5 million for a part-time job at the hedge fund D. E. Shaw and received $135,000 from Goldman Sachs in exchange for a personal appearance a few months before joining the Obama administration. Friend-of-finance Phil Gramm left the Senate in 2002 and immediately took a lucrative perch at the financial giant UBS.

FALLOUT FROM THE CRISIS: MATERIAL, IDEATIONAL, AND STRATEGIC

The purpose of this narrative is not to assign blame, but to emphasize that the crisis will have both material *and* ideational consequences and to argue that both will matter. As a material phenomenon, the crisis will create new American vulnerabilities and accelerate two preexisting trends: reduced US international political capacity and the continuing emergence of China.

Although the United States has emerged from this crisis still as the world's preeminent economic and military power, what is particularly novel about the great financial crisis of 2007–2008 is not so much its "novelty"—international financial crises are very common phenomenon—but the fact that it "hit home." During the age of regulation—the 1940s, 1950s, 1960s, and 1970s—the United States experienced no major financial crisis. These only occurred (with regularity) in the unregulated 19th and early 20th centuries, and reemerged in the 1980s in the age of deregulation. This crisis, then, is distinguished mostly by the fact that the United States was at its epicenter, and that it bore many of its costs.[7] This is suggestive more generally of a new, and, importantly, unfamiliar level of exposure of the US economy to external financial pressures. (Unfamiliar to be sure, but in fact not so much "new" as a "return to normal.")

One challenge to American power concerns the long-run trajectory of the dollar as an international currency. Despite the fact that the dollar has served as a safe haven during this crisis, the longer-run prospects are more alarming. As before the crisis, the dollar remains, by any objective account, vulnerable to a crisis of its

---

[6] Johnson and Kwak, *13 Bankers*, pp. 87, 91.
[7] See Carmen Reinhart and Kenneth Rogoff, *This Time is Different: Eight Centuries of Financial Folly* (Princeton, NJ: Princeton University Press, 2009).

own. Paradoxically, one legacy of the dollar's historical attractiveness is that it has increased its vulnerability. Because the dollar has served as the world's "key currency," there are an enormous amount of dollars held abroad. Thus if there was a spark, somewhere, that touched off a financial crisis that implicated the dollar, given the state of underlying expectations about its future value, a sudden reversal of the dollar's fortunes is not inconceivable. In sum, the United States emerges from the crisis with sluggish economic growth, exposed economic weaknesses, and a more suspect dollar (an area where perceptions matter).

All this contrasts with China's relatively rapid recovery in the years following the crisis. Despite facing formidable economic challenges of its own, and even with its rate of growth slowing, differential rates of recovery from the global financial crisis still markedly accelerated preexisting trends of China's relative economic rise. To a large extent, China is not "rising" so much as it *has risen*. As Suri and Valentino observe, handicapping if and when China's economy might (or might not) overtake the US economy is irrelevant to the more important implications of general trends in the global economy for international politics. With the emergence of China and others, "the United States will have less freedom to act unilaterally to protect its interests around the globe."

Continued stability of the Chinese economy, of course, is by no means a sure thing.[8] Nevertheless, whatever the future holds, a larger Chinese economy will surely support a more formidable military; of even greater significance are the profound international *political* consequences of China's economic importance. The People's Republic is now the world's second largest importer, taking on over $1 trillion worth of other countries' goods each year. As a result China's status and influence have been enhanced. This does not much affect China's military prowess; but it does mean that China's international political influence will increase, and this will matter, as states that trade with China come to identify their own their interests with a sensitive eye to how foreign policy choices they consider might affect their relations with China.

Beyond these adjustments to the balance of power and influence, world politics will also be affected by the ideational consequences of the crisis—and in particular, the implications of a new divergence of opinion regarding global finance. Venerable old banks were not the only things that came crashing down in 2007–2008—the legitimacy of the Second US Postwar International Economic Order also collapsed. Even if one is inclined to reject the view that the American model of uninhibited finance was flawed, the following three propositions are uncontroversial and consequential: (1) for much of the world, the global financial crisis was the second major financial crisis of the past ten years; (2) the United States was the epicenter of the

---

[8] China's continued economic growth is by no means guaranteed. The People's Republic faces some formidable economic challenges in the coming years, and its rate of economic growth has decelerated and will most likely not return to the unprecedented, galloping rate of the thirty-plus years from the 1980s. Nevertheless, most projections of economic growth—even those that are cautious about China and optimistic about America—suggest that even if US growth tracks toward the high end of its potential, and even if China's growth rate checks in closer to the lower end of its commonly anticipated trajectory, each year (and over the years) China will grow faster than the United States, with long-run consequences for the balance of power.

crisis; (3) the interpretation of the crisis implied by US policy is not shared by some important international actors. In particular, the American response to the crisis suggests that a "market fundamentalist" approach—one that continues to embrace rational expectations theory and the efficient markets hypothesis—still holds sway. From this perspective, the global financial crisis was a "black swan," akin to a plane crash: a regrettable, but nevertheless rare and unpredictable event, and as such, about which little can be productively done—air travel, and the financial system, are as safe as we can practically expect them to be. Modest tweaks or reforms might possibly make the system even safer, but finance is essentially efficient and self-regulating.

This interpretation contrasts with what I would dub a "KKM" perspective, named after John Maynard Keynes, Charles Kindleberger, and Hyman Minsky: financial markets, especially ones left to themselves, are prone to crisis. This view holds that financial crises are common throughout history and invited by unregulated, unsupervised financial systems. It implies that the US financial-economic model 1990s is flawed and in need of fundamental reform. I would note that KKM clearly has history on its side[9]—but it matters not for this discussion who is right—it matters that a disagreement exists, and different actors now hold pointedly different ideas about organizing the financial economy.

THE AMERICAN FINANCIAL GLOBALIZATION PROJECT ABROAD

The American push for liberated finance—both at home and abroad—was a purposeful, political project: as Summers explained at the time, "[f]inancial liberalization, both domestically and internationally, is a critical part of the US agenda." The style of that push, I argue, primed actors throughout the world (not just in Asia, but in Latin America, Russia, and elsewhere), to push back when given the chance. The United States, and its ally, the International Monetary Fund (IMF), were not of a mood to encourage financial liberalization—they were inclined to insist. In the mid-1990s, the IMF moved to force member states to completely eliminate their capital controls (despite a lack of evidence to support the contention that this was appropriate economic policy). This ambitious project was in accord with America's perception of its national interest. But greasing the political wheels was an economic ideology—actually, a leap of faith—as the IMF declared on the eve of the Asian financial crisis that "international capital markets appear to have become more resilient and are less likely to be a source of disturbances." Some faiths are hard to shake; in April 2006, the IMF announced that "the rapid growth of derivative and structured credit markets in recent years, particularly among more complex products, has facilitated the dispersion of credit risk by banks to a broader and more diverse group of investors ... [which] has helped to make the banking and overall financial system more resilient and stable."[10]

---

[9] See for example, Rogoff and Reinhart, *This Time is Different*, p. 155.

[10] International Monetary Fund, "IMF Survey" 26, no. 9, May 12, 1997; International Monetary Fund, "Global Financial Stability Report" (April 2006), p. 133.

Bilaterally, the United States was, if anything, even more aggressive. In 1995, during negotiations for a free trade agreement with Chile, Treasury representatives insisted that elimination of Chile's modest, innovative, market-friendly controls on short-term capital inflows must be included as a condition of the deal. In 1996, as Korea sought membership in the Organization for Economic Cooperation and Development (OECD), the United States insisted that Korea speed the pace of financial deregulation and provide increased access for American firms. From the mid-1990s, as one account described, "[w]orking through the IMF or directly with other countries," Summers and Rubin, with the encouragement and support of Greenspan, "pushed tirelessly for ... free capital flows."[11]

The confluence of forces—ideas, interests, and power—that led the United States and the IMF to push, hard, for universal, uninhibited capital deregulation, are, like so many questions about monetary affairs, not easily disentangled.[12] The architects of the Second US Postwar International Economic Order were certain that markets, even financial markets, are always right and always know best. But interests and power are not to be underestimated. In the post–Cold War world of American unipolarity, the promotion of financial globalization was also was recognized as maximizing US comparative advantage and further enhancing American geopolitical primacy.

But the US/IMF push coincided, and not coincidentally, with an increase in global financial instability—most notably, but not at all exceptionally, with the Asian financial crisis of 1997–1998. Sparked by a currency crisis in Thailand in July 1997, an international financial crisis quickly and unexpectedly spread throughout region, engulfing the Philippines, Malaysia, Indonesia, Hong Kong, and, astonishingly, South Korea, which announced in November that it had no choice but to turn to the IMF for a rescue package or it would face national bankruptcy.

This crisis, and the US/IMF reaction to it, exposed an ideational and political fault line at the foundations of the American system. In Asia (and elsewhere), the crisis was easily recognized as a classic international financial crisis. But a different narrative held sway at the IMF, in Washington, and on Wall Street. In those quarters, blame was placed, squarely and entirely, on the Asian economies. IMF accounts were typically myopic, not to mention amnesiac, placing blame exclusively on the domestic economic policies of states whose economies and macroeconomic management the Fund had only recently been touting. The IMF's Stanley Fischer focused exclusively on domestic causes of the crisis: "weak financial institutions, inadequate bank regulation and supervision, and the complicated and nontransparent relations among governments, banks and corporations were central to the economic crisis." There is, of course, an unintended irony here—ten years later, this would have served as a particularly potent indictment of the *American*

---

[11] Nicholas Kristof and David E. Sanger, "How U.S. Wooed Asia To Let Cash Flow In," *The New York Times*, February 16, 1999 (regarding Chile and Korea); Kenneth Klee and Rich Thomas with Stefan Theil, "Defending the One True Faith," *Newsweek*, September 14, 1998, p. 22 (last quotes).

[12] On these themes see Jonathan Kirshner, ed., *Monetary Orders: Ambiguous Economics, Ubiquitous Politics* (Ithaca, NY: Cornell University Press, 2003).

financial model. But in any event, the point was clear: "I emphatically reject the view," Fischer argued, "that turbulence on international financial markets suggest caution with capital account liberalization." Greenspan, Rubin, and Summers were similarly unequivocal and (over)confident in their assessments; Greenspan placing the blame entirely on "poor public policy" within the affected states, Summers arguing that if anything, the IMF should "accelerate" rather than "slow the pace of capital account liberalization."[13]

Much of the world disagreed with that assessment (including Japanese and Brazilian representatives at the IMF), but although the drive to amend the IMF's charter stalled in the wake of the Asian crisis (and subsequent crises that quickly followed), the underlying philosophy continued to hold sway at the Fund, and, especially, in the United States. In 2003, while completing free trade agreements with Chile and Singapore, the United States demanded, over the vociferous objections of its counterparties, clauses in these trade treaties that demanded each country renounce the right to introduce any form of capital controls. What this had to do with free trade, whether it is remotely wise policy, and whether these were instruments the states in question did *not* want to give up were of little concern to Bush administration negotiators.[14]

In sum, in Asia and elsewhere, a defining attribute of the global financial crisis of 2007–2008 is that it came at the heels of the 1997–1998 crisis. Whereas recent US behavior suggests a belief that the crisis is epiphenomenal (as it emerges from the crisis with an even more concentrated financial sector playing by modified versions of most of the old rules and all of the old norms), in much of the rest of the world, the crisis is a "learning moment"—the valedictory lecture in a long and difficult course of study demonstrating that unbound finance does not work.

The current crisis, then, has delegitimized the culture of American capitalism, especially as it applies to finance, and, as noted above, this will affect both state choices and international politics. John Ikenberry and Charles Kupchan have argued that "socialization"—the embrace by elites in secondary states of the substantive beliefs of a great power—is an important source of influence for a hegemon. Their work focused on the establishment of hegemonic socialization, and how such legitimacy crucially buttresses its political influence.[15] What we will witness in the coming years is the flip side of that phenomenon, the likely *erosion* of that influence, as others come to reject the ideas that they once embraced or at least tolerated. With this legitimacy reversal, continuity in the United States and change elsewhere will

---

[13] Alan Greenspan, "The Current Asian Crisis," testimony before the Senate Appropriations Committee, The Federal Reserve Board, March 3, 1998. See also Stanley Fischer, "The IMF and the Asian Crisis," testimony before the International Monetary Fund, March 20, 1998 and Lawrence Summers, "Repairing and Rebuilding Emerging Market Financial Systems," testimony before the International Monetary Fund, March 9, 1998.

[14] Sidney Weintraub, "Lessons from the Chile and Singapore Free Trade Agreements," in *Free Trade Agreements: U.S. Strategies and Priorities*, Jeffrey Schott ed. (Washington, DC: Institute for International Economics, 2004), p. 87.

[15] G. John Ikenberry and Charles Kupchan, "Socialization and Hegemonic Power," *International Organization* 44, no. 3 (June 1990): 283–315.

contribute to a "new heterogeneity" of ideas about finance. States will commonly have divergent preferences about the global financial order, reducing US influence and making cooperation about the governance of money and finance more problematic. In particular, many states will search for ways to insulate themselves from the dangers of unmediated global finance.

The United States has emerged from the crisis with its financial model largely intact. The modest Dodd-Frank financial reforms are vaguely specified, and, in the words of Robert Shiller, represent "only a beginning of dialogue on how move our financial system into the twenty-first century." But this dialogue is not taking place. In the United States, the "regulatory landscape has been little changed," Paul Volcker observed in August 2013. "Here we are, almost three years after the passage of Dodd-Frank, with important regulatory and supervisory issues arising from the act unresolved." This matters, especially if the United States is "returning to normal" and becoming "more like others" with regard to the basic level of its exposure to potential financial crises. Even Robert Lucas recently observed "the fact that during the sixty-six years that [Glass-Steagall] remained in force the United States did not experience any widespread financial crises commands respect, or at least curiosity."[16]

Throughout the rest of the world, however, considerably more rethinking about the governance of money and finance is taking place. This need not cohere in a single, competing model that will vie for influence with the American way. Rather, the New Heterogeneity is just that—the flowering of a multitude of ideas about the viability of capital controls, the optimal level of inflation, and macroeconomic management more generally. Even at the IMF, a tolerance for new policy experiments characterizes what Ilene Grabel has dubbed "productive incoherence" with regard to strategies of economic governance.[17] Contrasting ideas about money and finance combined with a new wariness of American financial stability do not bode well for the trajectory of US international power and influence.

[16] Robert Shiller, "Democratizing and Humanizing Finance," in *Reforming U.S. Financial Markets: Reflections Before and Beyond Dodd Frank*, Randall Kroszner and Robert Shiller eds. (Cambridge: MIT Press, 2011), pp. 2, 5, 9. Paul Volcker, "The Fed & Big Banking at the Crossroads," *New York Review of Books*, August 15, 2013, p. 33. As one scholar observes, "post-crisis developments seem to indicate that the privileged position of banks has been entrenched rather than diminished." See Andrew Baker, "Restraining Regulatory Capture? Anglo-America, Crisis Politics and Trajectories of Change in Global Financial Governance," *International Affairs* 86, no. 3 (2010): 655. Robert Lucas, "Glass-Steagall: A Requiem," *American Economic Review* 103, no. 3 (2013): 43.

[17] Ilene Grabel, "Not Your Grandfather's IMF: Global Crisis, 'Productive Incoherence' and Developmental Policy Space," *Cambridge Journal of Economics* 35, no. 5 (2011): 812, 814, 816, 817, 825; see also Jonathan D. Ostry, et al., "Capital Inflows: The Role of Controls," IMF Staff Position Note, Washington, DC: IMF, February 19, 2010; Olivier Blanchard, Giovanni Dell'Aricca, and Paolo Mauro, "Rethinking Macroeconomic Policy" IMF Staff Position Note, February 12, 2010 ("the crisis clearly forces us to question our earlier assessment"), pp. 3, 11; IMF External Relations Department Morning Press, "Capital Controls: IMF Shifts its Stance With Plan for Capital Controls," April 6, 2011.

CHINA AND ACCELERATED RMB
INTERNATIONALIZATION

This changing orientation will be especially visible—and is already observable—in China. Prior to the global financial crisis, elites in China anticipated future RMB internationalization. But the dominant position of the dollar, the emergence of the Euro, and the fragility of China's sheltered, murky domestic financial sector tempered expectations about how quickly the RMB might take its place as an important international currency. Nevertheless, such ambitions, however distant, were clearly harbored, and as China continued its rise to great power status it was natural to assume that a greater international role for a maturing RMB would be part of that process. As a long-term project, Beijing could envision the day when the yuan would be the currency of choice in East Asia, a prospect that would further enhance its political leadership and influence there. In the wake of the crisis, that timetable has been accelerated *and* a new and important motivation has emerged—to establish some distance from the dollar, and to explore models of economic governance that offers some alternative to radically unmediated global finance. Whatever forms they take, such new approaches and initiatives will reflect the fact that, as Benjamin Cohen observes, "in both words and deeds, the Chinese have appeared to underscore a dissatisfaction with the status quo," and "Beijing appears to be working hard to tilt the global balance of monetary power as much as possible in its favor."[18]

The Japanese experience from the late 1980s holds a number of lessons that provide insight into the case of contemporary China. As Japan emerged as the second largest economy in the world, many Japanese officials imagined an internationalized yen as a major currency as a means of further enhancing Japan's growing influence. But with the stagnation of the Japanese economy in the 1990s, such attitudes fell into remission, only to resurface, in a very different guise, in the wake of the Asian financial crisis. After that crisis, a revived interest in larger role for the yen was rooted in defensive motivations—the search for greater insulation, autonomy, and greater space from the American vision of global financial order. As William Grimes explained, the revived debate was "fundamentally about *insulation*," rooted in disenchantments: with the instability associated with (American-championed) uninhibited financial globalization and deregulation; with the United States' ability to shift macroeconomic burdens of adjustment abroad (and chronic American pressure over ex-rate issues); and with the more general implications of the ideological divergence between the United States and Japan over their respective reactions to the Asian financial crisis.[19]

These themes all resonate with contemporary politics. On the one hand, China had always been wary of exposing itself to international capital markets, and understood that its controls had spared it from the Asian financial crisis and other tumult

---

[18] Benjamin Cohen, "The China Question: Can the Rise of the Middle Kingdom Be Accommodated?" in *The Great Wall of Money: Politics and Power in China's International Monetary Relations*, Eric Helleiner and Jonathan Kirshner eds. (Ithaca, NY: Cornell University Press, 2014), p. 41; see also Gregory Chin, "China's Rising Monetary Power," *Great Wall of Money*.

[19] William Grimes, "Internationalization of the Yen and the New Politics of Monetary Insulation," in *Monetary Orders*, Kirshner, pp. 177, 180, 181 (quote), 183–184, 193–194.

that had characterized global finance in a succession of crises since the mid-1990s. From the early 2000s, China embarked on a cautious path that accommodated controlled RMB appreciation and modest movements toward financial liberalization. And China's continued economic growth and its massive and increasing holdings of dollar assets assured that, at the very least, discussions of the country's role as a potential monetary powerhouse would take place. On the eve of the crisis, however, most observers would agree with the assessment that "China's power in the international financial system, certainly growing, should not be overestimated."[20]

But the global financial crisis changed this. It provided a new impetus to the promotion of the yuan, and it also, crucially, altered visions of the trajectory of its path. By exposing profound flaws in the American model, the crisis elicited what I call "buyer's remorse" in China, with regard to its development model that had bound it so tightly to the (weaker than previously assumed) US economy and made it such a stakeholder in the (even more vulnerable that once thought) US dollar. The crisis also redoubled the (already robust) wariness of Chinese elites about the risk of exposure to the global financial economy and reinforced demands for insulation. And the relative rates of recovery from the crisis—swift in China, sluggish in the United States (and Europe)—magnified the preexisting trends that were already suggestive of a rising China. Finally, and crucially, the crisis delegitimized the American model that China had been cautiously tacking toward, right up until the crisis, if invariably at a rate deemed inadequate by its Western tutors. The Americans had never stopped lecturing Beijing on the need to move faster—ever faster—on their path of convergence toward the US model. Just months before the crisis, Treasury Secretary Paulson was (again) lecturing that "the risks for China are greater in moving too slowly than in moving too quickly" with financial liberalization.[21] Chinese elites are now patting themselves on the back for resisting this bad advice.

Buyer's remorse also reflects a greater disenchantment with the US management of the dollar and its role in the international financial system more generally, two things about which Chinese observers are increasingly critical. These reassessments have contributed to a desire for insulation from anticipated future instability caused by American mismanagement and demands for reform of the global macroeconomic order for similar reasons. Nor are politics far behind: American policies force others to adjust "in accordance with the needs of the US dollar," argues Li Ruogu, Chairman and President of the China Export-Import Bank; "the United States used this method to topple Japan's economy, and it wants to use this method

---

[20] Carl E. Walter and Fraser J. T. Howie, *Red Capitalism: The Fragile Foundation of China's Extraordinary Rise* (Singapore: Wiley, 2011), pp. ix–x, 3; Rosemary Foot and Andrew Walter, *China, The United States, and Global Order* (Cambridge, UK: Cambridge University Press, 2011), pp. 117, 120, 123, 265–270; Gregory Chin and Eric Helleiner, "China as a Creditor: A Rising Financial Power?" *Journal of International Affairs*, 62, no. 1 (Fall/Winter 2008): 87 (quote), 92, 97–98, 99.

[21] Geoff Dyer, "Paulson Urges Beijing to Speed Up Reform," *Financial Times* March 8, 2007. Pieter Bottelier, "China and the International Financial Crisis," in *Strategic Asia 2009– 10: Economic Meltdown and Geopolitical Stability*, Ashley Tellis, Andrew Marble, and Travis Tanner eds. (Seattle, WA: National Bureau of Asian Research, 2009), p. 100 ("The crisis has confirmed Chinese leaders in their belief that they were correct in resisting US pressure.").

to curb China's development." Increasingly, there is the view that RMB internationalization is necessary to reform, and to pluralize, the international monetary system. "Only by eliminating the US dollar's monopolistic position" can the system be reformed. RMB internationalization is a necessary step toward a multiple currency system that would reduce the influence of the dollar, contribute to systemic stability, increase China's voice, and provide some insurance against a dollar crisis.[22]

In March 2009, Zhou Ziaochuan, Governor of the People's Bank of China, delivered a speech on "Reform of the International Monetary System." Nominally a call for a greater role for the SDR, the Governor's statement was properly understood as a challenge to the dollar.

As Chin and Wang argued, the speech reflects "the consensus Chinese view ... that a multi-reserve currency era is coming, even if only gradually, and that it would be in China's strategic interests to promote such a scenario." Publications by Chinese elites and academics increasingly illustrate this perspective.[23]

There remain barriers to the emergence of the RMB—in particular, the extent of the weakness in and discomforting opacity of Chinese banks and its domestic financial sector more generally, which many see as the rate limiting factor of the yuan's rise.[24] Nevertheless, after the crisis, Chinese leaders decided to step up the pace of RMB internationalization, promote regional monetary cooperation, and encourage reform of global monetary management.[25] Notably, there is both an increase on

---

[22] Li Ruogu, "The Financial Crisis and International Monetary System Reform," *China Finance* 5 (2010); Li Yang, "Reform of the Global Financial System and Asia's Choices: We Need Deeper Thinking," *Studies in International Finance* 10 (2010); Li Daokui and Yin Xingzhong, "New Structure of the International Monetary System: Research on the Post-Financial Crisis Era," *Journal of Financial Research* 2 (2010).

[23] Zhou Xiaochuan, "Reform of the International Monetary System," People's Bank of China, March 23, 2009; David Barboza, "China Urges New Money Reserve to Replace Dollar," *New York Times*, March 24, 2009; Gregory Chin and Wang Yong "Debating the International Currency System: What's in a Speech?" *China Security* 6, no. 1 (2010): 4, 5, 11, 12, p. 14 (quote); Zhang Yuyan, "Internationalization of the RMB: Endorse or Oppose," *International Economic Review* 1 (2010); Zhang Ming and Miguel Otero-Iglesias, "EU-China Collaboration in the Reform of the International Monetary System: Much Ado About Nothing?" *The World Economy* 37, no. 1 (2014): 151–168; Zhang Yuyan and Zhang Jingchun, "International Currency's Costs and Benefits," *World Affairs* 21 (2008).

[24] Walter and Fraser *Red Capitalism*, pp. 25, 27, 38, 77–78, 80, 138–39; Michael F. Martin, "China's Banking System: Issues for Congress," *CRS Report for Congress*, 7-5700, February 20, 2012; Sebastian Mallaby and Olin Wethington, "The Future of the Yuan: China's Struggle to Internationalize Its Currency," *Foreign Affairs* 91, no. 1 (January/February 2012): 136, 137; Jeffrey Frankel, "Historical Precedents for Internationalization of the RMB" (Council on Foreign Relations, Maurice Greenberg Center, November 2011), p. 13.

[25] Ming Zhang, "China's New International Financial Strategy amid the Global Financial Crisis," *China & World Economy* 17, no. 5 (2009): 23, 24, 27, 29, 31; Pieter Bottelier, "Future of the Renminbi as an International Currency," *ChinaUsfocus.com* April 29, 2011; Keith Bradsher, "In Step to Enhance Currency, China Allows Its Use in Some Foreign Payments," *New York Times*, July 6, 2009; George Koo and Henry Tang, "How Shall America Respond to Chinese Yuan as a Global Currency," *ChinaUsFocus.com* February 29, 2012.

the *supply side*—China's willingness to have the RMB deployed in a greater role internationally—and at the same time a clearly increased *demand*: a greater desire by states to find ways to transact business in ways that does not bind them tightly to, or at least provides some diversification away from, the dollar, the American financial model, and the US economy.[26]

This also means that a greater international role for the RMB might look somewhat different than would be drawn up on a chalkboard by those envisioning inevitable convergence toward the American model. Most Western analysis, for example, considers full currency convertibility and completely open capital markets as virtual prerequisites to establish the international financial centers that would be the platforms for and hubs of international money.[27] But as a matter of practice, this may or may not be the case. China seems poised to act as if, in fact, it is not, and seems set to embark on considerable internationalization of the RMB without first, or perhaps ever, fully liberalizing its capital account.[28] (This is, of course, an illustration of "new heterogeneity" of thinking.) According to Governor Zhou, the "definition of capital account convertibility is something that can be discussed, and how standards should be set should have a certain degree of flexibility." In addition, he insisted, "China has to have its own voice in the establishment of international standards." All this may be part of what rejecting the American model of financial governance looks like: putting the infrastructure in place for the yuan to become more internationalized, promoting its use as a vehicle currency, and encouraging other central banks to hold RMBs as reserves—while retaining some capital controls and other market- inhibiting devices.[29] But in whatever form, the bottom line remains

[26] Chen Siqing, "Deeper-Level Analysis of the Reasons for the U.S. Financial Crisis and Its Lessons for China's Banking Industry," *Studies of International Finance* 12 (2008); John Williamson, "Is the 'Beijing Consensus' Now Dominant?" *Asia Policy* 13 (January 2012), p. 3; Nancy Birdsall and Francis Fukuyama, "The Post-Washington Consensus: Development After the Crisis," *Foreign Affairs* 90, no. 2 (March–April 2011): 3; Foot and Walter, *China, The United States, and Global Order*, p. 271.

[27] See for example Mallaby and Wethington, "The Future of the Yuan: China's Struggle to Internationalize Its Currency," (January/February 2012), pp. 136, 137; Jeffrey Frankel, "Historical Precedents" (November 2011), p. 13; Takatoshi Ito, "The Internationalization of the RMB: Opportunities and Pitfalls," Working Paper, Council on Foreign Relations, November 2011, p. 11.

[28] And this position would appear to be gaining toeholds of legitimacy. See for example Olivier Jeanne, Arvind Subramanian, and John Williamson, *Who Needs to Open the Capital Account?* (Washington, DC: Peterson Institute for International Economics, 2012). On the relationship between internationalization and liberalization, see also Dong He, "Renminbi Internationa lization: A Primer," *Hong Kong Institute for Monetary Research*, July 31 2012, and Christopher A. McNally, "Abstract Sino-Capitalism: China's Reemergence and the International Political Economy," *World Politics* 64, no. 4 (October 2012): 760–762.

[29] Zhou Xiaochuan, "Several Issues in the Establishment and Implementation of Financial Industry Standards" *ChinaFinance* (January 5 2012). On internationalization ahead of liberalization, see Robert N. McCauley, "Internationalizing the Renminbi and China's Financial Development Model" (Council on Foreign Relations, Maurice Greenberg Center, November 2011), pp. 1, 3 ("In internationalizing the Renminbi within a system of capital controls, the Chinese authorities set out on a path with no signposts"), 13, 21.

that China is moving ahead with a panoply of measures that reflect "a desire to carve out China's own space within a US-dominated global financial system," a process that "accelerated with the outbreak of the global financial crisis"[30]

Some scholars have expressed skepticism regarding the import of the measures undertaken by Beijing, suggesting that they are largely nascent, symbolic, and limited.[31] And it is the case that we are early in this game, and that the RMB is currently a marginal presence as a global reserve currency. But these steps are consistent with the pre-positioning of an apparatus that would support the emergence of the yuan as an important international currency. And, crucially, as noted above, China's willingness to increase the "supply" of international monetary options has coincided, for similar reasons, with greater demand for alternatives to the dollar and to the ideology of unbridled financial globalization as well. The emergence of the RMB is not simply a "supply side" story—there is a robust "demand side" as well.[32]

Interest in different international monetary possibilities is also on the rise. One manifestation of this—of both disenchantment with the American way and a desire for greater voice—is China's sponsorship of the Asian Infrastructure Investment Bank (AIIB), and of the eagerness of others to sign on. Once again, it is important not to let underlying trends run ahead of the facts of the ground, and there is no need to share Summers's hyperbolic reaction to the AIIB ("This past month may be remembered as the moment the United States lost its role as the underwriter of the global economic system.") but on balance the AIIB will enhance China's influence at the expense of the United States, Japan, and the international institutions that those two countries dominate.[33] And whatever the stakes, it is notable that the United States tried, and miserably failed, to undercut the AIIB's emergence. Summers, likely, was fondly recalling his late-1990s role in crushing Japan's proposed Asian Monetary Fund, which was also perceived as a challenge to the leadership of the United States and intuitions it dominated. But China will more assertively, and more successfully, seek to establish opportunities to promote its voice and its interests—and likely find willing partners.

In sum, even while keeping new developments in context and recognizing that China faces its own real problems and challenges, the RMB will likely emerge as an important international money, and will be associated with and help reinforce a

---

[30] James Kynge and Josh Noble, "China: Turning Away from the Dollar," *Financial Times*, December 9, 2014.

[31] Yang Jiang, "China's Monetary Diplomacy: Venturing Beyond Bilateralism?" in *The Great Wall of Money: Politics and Power in China's International Monetary Relations*, Eric Helleiner and Jonathan Kirshner eds. (Ithaca, NY: Cornell University Press, 2014).

[32] Steven Liao and Daniel McDowell, "Redback Rising: China's Bilateral Swap Agreements and Renminbi Internationalization," *International Studies Quarterly* 59, no. 3 (2015): 401–422; Simon Rabinovitch, "China and Japan Agree on Currency Push," *Financial Times* December 27, 2011; Wang Xiaotian and Gao Changxin, "China-Japan Currency Deal Ushers in a New Era," *ChinaDaily.com.cn*, May 30, 2012; Kosuke Takahashi, "Japan and China Bypass US in Direct Currency Trade," *The Asia-Pacific Journal* 10, 24, no. 3 (June 11, 2012); "China and Australia in $31bn Currency Swap," *Financial Times*, May 22, 2012; "China and Brazil in $30bn Currency Swap Agreement," *BBC News*, June 22, 2012.

[33] Lawrence Summers, "A Global Wake-Up Call for the U.S.?" *Washington Post* April 5, 2015.

continued rise in China's international political power and influence. It should be remembered, in addition, that it is not just China who will be encroaching on the dollar (nor is it solely actors in Asia that will seek greater insulation from potential American financial instability). The World Bank, for example, in its 2011 *Global Development Horizons* report, anticipates an increasingly multipolar world economy, and, notably, a multipolar currency order, with the RMB, and especially the Euro, increasing in importance as international currencies.[34]

Currently flat on its back, Europe is down but not out, and in the longer run, the Euro will resume its encroachment on the dollar's international role. Certainly, Europe's own troubles have exposed the weaknesses of the Euro as a potential peer competitor to the dollar, a status that the European currency seemed close to achieving before the global financial crisis exposed its own the problems and, not to be underestimated, contradictions.[35]

To a considerable extent Europe's crisis has handed (yet another) get-out-of-jail-free card to the profligate dollar, left again as the only game in town. And the Euro's dysfunction, and the political paralysis of the countries that oversee it, is not to be underestimated. As Randall Germain and Herman Schwartz elucidate in their trenchant inquest into the Euro disaster, the global financial crisis did not cause the Euro's fundamental weakness so much as expose it. Monetary integration ran far ahead of political integration in Europe, and "the EU lacks the will, ideas, and the capacity to promote the Euro into the status of a top international currency." Germain and Schwartz identify another Euro-pathology: Triffin's dilemma, which holds that reserve currencies walk a tightrope between too much liquidity, undermining confidence in a system's key currency, or too little, resulting in strangling deflation. In the 1960s, the United States made its choice, and the Bretton Woods system was indeed unsustainable. But the guardians of the Euro, especially Germany, are choosing death by ice rather than by (even the slightest risk of) fire. Essentially, "the current Euro-crisis replicates the deflationary problems" of the gold standard. The Euro is committing suicide by asphyxiation—thus the dollar endures, unchallenged.[36]

But the failure of others offers only a thin reed of support for the dollar. Against all evidence, Europe will eventually come to solve its problems. Especially with regard to the prospects for international money, the crisis will almost certainly force the EU into a "corner solution": forward or back. The global financial crisis was the

[34] World Bank, "Global Development Horizons 2011—Multipolarity: The New Global Economy," Washington, DC: World Bank, 2011, pp. 7, 13, 126, 131, 140, 144, 152.

[35] The Euro was always a *political* project; part of an effort to forge a common European entity and identity. Considered solely from an economic perspective, the Euro project was incoherent. The monetary union had invited problems and allowed pressures to develop, and when faced with real difficulties, states found themselves disarmed of essential policy defenses. Joining the Euro meant the abdication of monetary policy and exchange rate policy, without gaining any new policy levers. On the problems of the Euro, see Martin Feldstein, "The Failure of the Euro: The Little Currency that Couldn't," *Foreign Affairs* 91, no. 1 (January/February 2012): 105–116.

[36] Randall Germain and Herman Schwartz, "The Political Economy of Failure: The Euro as an International Currency," *Review of International Political Economy* 21, no. 5 (2014): 1095–1122; see also K. O'Rourke and A. Taylor (2013) "Cross of Euros." *Journal of Economic Perspectives*, 27, no. 3: 167–192.

stress test that has exposed the fault line of the entire project: the economics of the European Union had run ahead of the politics.[37] Either it will have to move forward with greater political integration, or, with regard to the common currency at least, devolve toward a smaller core of participants. But in either scenario, over time the Euro is likely to emerge as an even stronger player on world markets. And, again, in a relative sense, this can only come about at the expense of the dollar's reach.

PRESSURE ON THE DOLLAR'S ROLE AS AN INTERNATIONAL CURRENCY: SORTING OUT THE RISKS TO THE DOLLAR

What does it matter if the international role of the dollar comes under pressure? Three types of consequences follow: the loss of benefits, the management of new burdens, and challenges specific to the American case. I consider these in the abstract, with illustrative historical analogies, and as applied to contemporary politics.

The main perks of issuing "key" currency are (1) autonomy and balance of payments flexibility, and (2) structural power. With regard to the former, in the United States it is underappreciated to what extent the special place of the dollar has allowed America to shake off the (often costly) burdens of macroeconomic adjustment and essentially dump them on others.[38] In addition, the United States has been able to sustain deficits on its international accounts that other states could not have, and to adopt economic policies that, attempted elsewhere, would have been overwhelmed by a withering "disciplinary" response from international financial markets. The erosion of these perks will circumscribe US power and autonomy, and fights over the burdens of adjustment—the normal stuffing of international monetary politics—will become more a more common and a more salient feature of foreign policy, at least from an American perspective.

The dollar-centric international system has also rewarded the United States with structural power. Structural power is not easily measured, nor obviously "coercive," but reflects "the power to decide how things shall be done, the power to shape frameworks within which states relate to each other."[39] Structural power also affects the pattern of economic relations between states and their calculations of political interest. States that use the dollar (and especially those that hold their reserves in dollars) develop a vested interest in the value and stability of the dollar. Once in widespread use, the fate of the dollar becomes more than just America's problem— it becomes the problem of all dollar holders.

---

[37] Rawi Abdelal argues that the framers of the Eurozone understood that eventually and inevitably some sort of reckoning would force a reassessment of monetary arrangements in Europe. But they also understood that it would take some sort of crisis (if not quite this big) to propel the union forward. Rawi Abdelal, *Capital Rules: The Construction of Global Finance* (Cambridge, MA: Harvard University Press, 2007), chapter 4.

[38] See Benjamin Cohen, "The Macrofoundations of Monetary Power," in *International Monetary Power*, David M. Andrews ed. (Ithaca, NY: Cornell University Press).

[39] Susan Strange, "Finance, Information and Power," *Review of International Studies* 16, no. 3 (July 1990): 259–274.

A relative contraction of the dollar's international role, then, would reduce both the "hard" and "soft" power the United States previously enjoyed—its coercive power enhanced by greater autonomy and its structural power implicitly shaping the preferences of others. Further, the United States would face additional burdens—not from the loss of perks, but from the costs associated with managing a currency in relative decline. For issuers of once dominant international money, those new difficulties arise from what can be called the overhang problem, and from a loss of prestige.

The overhang problem arises as a function of a currency's one-time greatness. At the height of its attraction, numerous actors are eager to hold international money—governments for reserves, and private actors as a store of value (and often as a medium of exchange). But once the key currency is perceived to be in decline, it becomes suspect, and these actors will, over time, look to get out—to exchange it for some other asset. The need to "mop up" all this excess currency creates chronic monetary pressure on the once great currency; and macroeconomic policy will take place under the shadow of the overhang.[40]

The loss of prestige is also a crucial consequence of managing a currency in decline. Prestige is a very slippery concept, but it finds a home in monetary analysis under the rubric of credibility, which is generally acknowledged to play a crucial role in monetary affairs (even if it, too, is not easily measured). The unparalleled reputation and bedrock credibility of the key currency during its glory days is a key source of the power it provides. The willingness of markets to implicitly tolerate imbalances in accounts and impertinent macroeconomic politics that would not be tolerated in other states rests on these foundations.

The loss of prestige and reduced credibility (which the challenge of the overhang exacerbates) imposes new costs on the issuer of a currency in relative decline. Whereas in the past the key currency country was exempted from the rules of the game—that is, placed on a much longer leash by international financial markets than other states—the opposite becomes true. With eroding prestige and shared expectations of monetary distress, market vigilance is heightened and discipline imposed more swiftly by the collective expectations of more skeptical market actors. A presumption of confidence is replaced with a more jaundiced reading of the same indicators, and the long leash is replaced by an exceptionally tight choker.

Some of these problems can be illustrated by historical analogies. The experience of the British pound in the decades following World War II offers one such example of the challenges faced by an international currency under pressure. In the 19th and early 20th centuries, sterling served as the international currency of choice, and the pound's key currency status enhanced British power. But eventually the management of sterling-in-decline became a vexing problem for British authorities, complicating economic management and exacerbating its chronic financial crises in the 1960s. With sterling invariably on the ropes on international financial markets, the demand for a clean bill of macroeconomic health placed British budgets—and British military spending and overseas commitments—under constant pressure.

---

[40] In theory, with floating rates, the "overhang" can be ignored and excess currency "mopped up" by depreciation. In practice, states are very sensitive to the management of this type of problem even in the absence of fixed rates.

The limits of British power and the constraints of financial fragility were brought into stark relief with the Suez Crisis in 1956. On October 31 of that year, British and French forces attacked Egypt with the stated goal of seizing the Suez Canal, but with the additional goal of causing the overthrow of Egypt's President Nasser. But on November 6, just days short of victory, and to the great dismay of the French, Britain called a halt to the operation. Harold Macmillan, Chancellor of the Exchequer (and to that point one of the most forceful proponents of the Suez adventure), informed his cabinet colleagues that a run on the pound, which he claimed had been "viciously orchestrated" in Washington, had become overwhelming, and the country did not have adequate reserves to save the currency on its own. Moreover, the Americans made clear that they would block Britain's ability to seek help from the IMF. On the other hand, if (and only if) the British agreed to an immediate cease-fire and prompt withdrawal from the Suez Canal zone, the United States would facilitate IMF support and provide additional emergency financial relief of its own.[41]

Britain caved in, and the entire affair was a formative experience for a generation of British politicians, who came away with an instinctive sensitivity to the economic limits of British power. That sensitivity would be reinforced by decades of less spectacular but nevertheless chronic hard knocks. Currency weakness and resulting pressure on government spending—austerity to balance the budget, austerity to shore up confidence in the pound, always and everywhere, austerity— would become a defining problem for British governments in the mid-1960s (and beyond), ultimately forcing the country to reluctantly abandon its military role "East of Suez." President Johnson considered sterling's weakness a "major foreign policy concern" and was eager to take steps that would take the pressure off the British currency and thus "sharply reduce the danger of sterling devaluation or . . . British military disengagement east of Suez." But economic pressure on sterling, which staggered from crisis to crisis throughout the period, was unrelenting and ultimately decisive.[42]

Sterling crises in autumn 1964 and again in summer 1965 rocked the British economy. Prime Minister Wilson's response was to cut defense spending without

[41] Jonathan Kirshner, *Currency and Coercion: The Political Economy of International Monetary Power* (Princeton, NJ: Princeton University Press, 1995), pp. 64–70; Harold Macmillan, *Riding the Storm* (New York: Harper and Row, 1971), p. 164. See also Diane B. Kunz, *The Economic Diplomacy of the Suez Crisis* (Chapel Hill: University of North Carolina Press, 1991); Lewis Johnman, "Defending the Pound: The Economics of the Suez Crisis, 1956," in *Postwar Britain, 1945–64: Themes and Perspectives*, Anthony Gorst, Lewis Johnman and W. Scott Lucas eds. (London: Pinter, 1989); Howard J. Dooley, "Great Britain's 'Last Battle' in the Middle East: Notes on Cabinet Planning during the Suez Crisis of 1956," *International History Review* 11, no. 3 (August 1989).

[42] Phillip Darby, *British Defense Policy East of Suez 1947–68* (London: Oxford University Press, 1973), p. 293; Michael Chichester and John Wilkinson, *The Uncertain Ally: British Defense Policy 1960–1990* (Aldershot, UK: Gower, 1982), pp. 9–10; Jeremy Fielding, "Coping with Decline: US Policy Toward the British Defense Reviews of 1966" *Diplomatic History* 23, no. 4 (Fall 1999): 633–637, 645; "Memorandum From President Johnson to Secretary of the Treasury Fowler," in *Foreign Relations of the United States: 1964–1968*, Volume 7, Kent Sieg ed. (Washington, DC: Government Printing Office, 2003), p. 173.

addressing overall military posture, a tightrope which could only be negotiated for so long. With the February 1966 defense review the rope frayed further, with defense cuts eroding British overseas capacities. But sterling crisis and relentless pressure on budgets continued, and 1967 would feature the blows that finally burst the sterling piñata. Yet another defense white paper bowed to the inevitable and finally outlined a phased withdrawal from Singapore, Malaysia, and Aden—British forces would be cut in half by 1971 and gone completely by 1977. Some pretense was maintained regarding Britain's positions in Persian Gulf, but these fig leaves were swept aside by the financial crisis that led to sterling's devaluation in November. Chancellor of the Exchequer Roy Jenkins insisted on a fundamental reassessment of defense policy. Not only was military spending cut further, but the timetable for withdrawal from East of Suez was accelerated and would be complete by the end of 1971. This met with vigorous opposition from the Tories, but pressure on sterling presented stubborn truths. Returning to power in 1970, faced with sluggish growth and the need to fight inflation, the Conservatives could not escape the same financial constraints that had plagued Labour, and the new posture was retained.[43]

Notably, even with the East of Suez question settled, with the devaluation of sterling, and the shift to a floating exchange rate, the relationship between Britain's fragile finances and its military capabilities remained. The 1976 financial crisis forced Britain to seek help from the IMF, which insisted on still further cuts to domestic spending. An additional £300 million was squeezed from the military, despite vociferous protests from the Chiefs of Staff.[44]

There are, of course, fundamental differences between postwar sterling and the contemporary dollar. But as a more extreme case, it helps to expose and magnify the mechanisms by which currency diminution can affect national security. The politics of austerity—everywhere—will not spare military budgets, especially in peacetime and especially if such budgets appear large. And it will be generally so that a currency in decline faces increased (and more skeptical) market scrutiny—especially during moments of international crisis and wartime. Markets tend to react negatively to the prospects for a country's currency as it enters crisis and war, anticipating increased prospects for government spending, borrowing, inflation, and hedging against general uncertainty.[45] In that sense, the Suez analogy is not inappropriate. Nor was this an isolated incident—weak currencies make for timid states.

[43] Clive Ponting, *Breach of Promise: Labour in Power 1964–1970* (London: Hamish Hamilton, 1989), p. 55; Darby, *British Defense Policy*, pp. 283, 304; Fielding, "Coping with Decline," pp. 634–636, 651; Michael Dockrill, *British Defence Since 1945* (Oxford: Basil Blackwell, 1988), pp. 94–95, 97, 101, 103; J. C. Hurewitz, "The Persian Gulf: British Withdrawal and Western Security," *Annals of the American Academy of Political and Social Science* 401 (May 1972): 107, 114; Chichester and Wilkinson, *The Uncertain Ally*, pp. 20, 23, 31–32.

[44] Kathleen Burk and Alec Cairncross, *Goodbye Great Britain: The 1976 IMF Crisis* (New Haven, CT: Yale University Press, 1992), pp. 20, 78, 105; Dockrill, *British Defence*, pp. 104, 106, 107; Chichester and Wilkinson, *The Uncertain Ally*, pp. 47–48; 53; "Britain's Defensive World Role," *The Economist*, November 24, 1979, p. 27.

[45] Jonathan Kirshner, *Appeasing Bankers: Financial Caution on the Road to War* (Princeton, NJ: Princeton University Press, 2007).

This axiom is well illustrated by the experiences of interwar France, a case that offers something of a laboratory for the national security consequences of currency weakness. In this instance, the franc came under withering pressure somewhat "voluntarily"—that is, domestic politics in France enforced an almost obsessive fixation on "defending the franc," which need not have been the only policy choice (indeed, the socialists finally, if very reluctantly, abandoned the cause in 1936).[46] But the pressure, even if to some extent self-imposed, illustrates again two mechanisms via which monetary distress fuels national (in)security—through the relentless march of austerity and existential anxiety about the power of financial markets.

Monetary orthodoxy and thus constant pressure to balance the budget meant that finance was the "soft underbelly" of France's defense posture. These interconnections cannot be overestimated—it was accepted as an article of faith that the franc rested on the foundation of the balanced budget—and defense spending was gutted in an effort to achieve that end. From 1930–1933, defense spending was cut by twenty-five percent—in fact military spending at the 1930 level would not be reached until 1937. Between 1933 and 1938, German defense spending would practically triple France's, and during roughly the same period, real military spending in Germany would increase by 470 percent, in France, forty-one percent. Pressure on the franc routinely provided the major impetus for new rounds of deflation and budget cuts, and repeatedly new weapons programs and efforts at modernization were the first, easiest place to find savings from the defense budget.[47]

A commitment to maintaining the convertibility of the franc into gold at the level established in 1928, even more than the budget cuts, circumscribed French foreign policy. In 1933, the Bank of France explained that it was "resolved to consent to no measure whatsoever that could again endanger the stability of the franc." This contributed to France's sluggish response to Germany's rearmament, which was clearly understood in France by the end of 1932.

The constant threat that a financial crisis would force the franc off gold paralyzed French leaders and contributed to a conciliatory bias in French foreign policy. Adherence to orthodoxy in France required, if not appeasement, something very close to it. In 1934, financial journalist Paul Einzig expressed his grave concern

---

[46] H. Clark Johnson, *Gold, France and the Great Depression, 1919–1932* (New Haven, CT: Yale University Press, 1997); Kenneth Moure, *The Gold Standard Illusion: France, The Bank of France, and the International Gold Standard, 1914–1939* (Oxford: Oxford University Press, 2002); Martin Wolfe, *The French Franc Between the Wars 1919–1939* (New York: Columbia University Press, 1951), esp. pp. 35, 83.

[47] Kenneth Mouré, *Managing the Franc Poincaré: Economic Understanding and Political Constraint in French Monetary Policy, 1928–1936* (Cambridge, UK: Cambridge University Press, 1991), pp. 17–18; 22, 27, 121; Barry Posen, *The Sources of Military Doctrine: France, Britain and Germany Between the World Wars* (Ithaca, NY: Cornell University Press, 1984), p. 20. Robert Murray Haig, "The National Budgets of France, 1928–1937," *Proceedings of the Academy of Political Science* 17, no. 4 (1938): 26, 29; Talbot Imlay, *Facing the Second World War: Strategy, Politics and Economics in Britain and France 1938–1940* (Oxford: Oxford University Press, 2003), p. 25; Bradford Lee, "Strategy, Arms, and the Collapse of France 1930–40," in *Diplomacy and Intelligence during the Second World War*, F. H. Hinsley and Richard Langhorne eds. (Cambridge, UK: Cambridge University Press, 1985), pp. 59, 63, 64, 65.

that "monetary orthodoxy will be sufficiently influential to delay urgent armament expenditure in order to avoid jeopardizing the stability of the franc."[48]

But this was the course followed by France until September 1936. Each year leading up to that point France recognized new German challenges and remained passive. A dramatic increase in German military spending in March 1934 had no effect on French policy. In March 1935, Germany announced that its army would expand to thirty-six divisions, more than five times the ceiling mandated by the Versailles treaty. Yet France again stood passively, aside from raising protests and seeking to stitch together a multilateral response, which came to nothing. The threat of capital flight reinforced the policy of appeasement. In the words of one critic, due to such fears, the "government was condemned to a certain impotence."[49]

This would have more severe consequences one year later. On March 7, 1936, Germany remilitarized the Rhineland. Not only was this in direct violation of the Versailles treaty, it also closed the corridor through which France would have, in theory, come to the defense of its eastern allies. Yet again, France took no action, a policy that has been called "the first capitulation." Certainly a number of factors involving both domestic and international politics contributed to this outcome. But financial questions were decisive, and essentially ruled out the use of force, or even the threat of force.[50] Worse, mobilization was incompatible with the protection of the franc. It would have required devaluation.

This stark fact guaranteed French inaction. As one student of the crisis observed, "Hitler and the rest of the world knew" that the French government would "above all . . . do nothing that would endanger the franc." Even *couverture*, the state of armed readiness that would precede a general mobilization, would have cost thirty million francs a day, an expense that would "undoubtedly provoke a run on the franc." Because of the fragility of France's financial position, full mobilization would have led to an immediate "full-scale monetary crisis," and would have

[48] Mouré, *Managing the Franc*, p. 151. Emile Moreau, *The Golden Franc: Memoirs of a Governor of the Bank of France* (Boulder: Westview, 1991), pp. 128, 513–515, 517–518; J. Nere, *The Foreign Policy of France from 1914–1945* (London: Routledge & Kegan Paul, 1975), pp. 127, 129–130; Anthony Adamthwaite, *France and the Coming of the Second World War* (London: Frank Cass, 1977), p. 27 ("the franc was the Achilles heel of French Policy"); Haim Shamir, *Economic Crisis and French Foreign Policy, 1930–1936* (Leiden: E. J. Brill, 1989), pp. 16–17, 26, 44; Paul Einzig, *France's Crisis* (London: Macmillan, 1934), pp. viii, ix, 12, 102 (quote), 119.

[49] Nere, *French Foreign Policy*, p. 152; Rene Girualt, "The Impact of the Economic Situation on the Foreign Policy of France, 1936–1939," in *The Fascist Challenge and the Policy of Appeasement*, Wolfgang Mommsen and Lothar Kettenacker eds. (London: Allen and Unwin, 1983), p. 223 (quote), see also pp. 214, 216; Shamir, *Economic Crisis*, pp. 133, 211, 215. Robert Frankenstein, "The Decline of France and French Appeasement Policies, 1936–9," in *The Fascist Challenge*, Mommsen and Kettenacker, p. 237.

[50] R.A.C. Parker, "The First Capitulation: France and the Rhineland Crisis of 1936," *World Politics* 8, no. 3 (April 1956): 367, 371; Nere, *French Foreign Policy*, pp. 186–89; Raphaelle Ulrich, "Rene Massigli and Germany, 1919–1938," in *French Foreign and Defense Policy*, Robert Boyce ed., (London: Routledge, 1998), p. 143; James Thomas Emmerson, *The Rhineland Crisis 7 March 1936: A Study in Multilateral Diplomacy* (Ames: Iowa State University Press, 1977), pp. 39, 41, 47; Shamir, *Economic Crisis*, p. 218.

"exposed the virtual bankruptcy of the French treasury and toppled the franc." Any doubts about this relationship were erased as capital flight and pressure on the franc increased in the few days before it was known that France would not take any strong measures of resistance. On Sunday March 8 there were rumors that France might use force against Germany, and on Monday the franc came under renewed pressure in international markets. This pressure did not abate until Wednesday, after the announcement that France would act only with multilateral support and within the framework of the League of Nations, which made it clear that there would be no military response to the German provocation.[51]

Twenty-first century America is not postwar Britain, nor is it interwar France. But the experiences of those countries provide important insights into the types of challenges faced by a country attempting to navigate its grand strategy while nursing a suspect currency. And greater skepticism about the dollar is a new fact of life. Actors may continue to hold their dollars, and even accumulate more of them. But they now do so through gritted teeth. Wariness of the American model adds another stone to the burdens borne by the dollar, the future of which will influence US power in the coming decades. As noted above, the "three Ds"—dollars, deregulations, and deficits—have left the greenback still exposed; the necessary policy responses to the crisis only increase suspicions about the dollar's long run health; potential alternatives loom in the distance. Moreover, and crucially, the dollar no longer enjoys the political "safety net" it once enjoyed. Politics always has and will continue to shape the international monetary order. During the Cold War, monetary squabbles took place between the United States and its strategic allies and military dependencies. No longer.

In sum, the dollar is vulnerable in ways that are unprecedented since before World War I. Even in the absence of a major dollar crisis, and even though the greenback will remain the world's most prominent currency, the relative diminution of the dollar's international role will present new constraints on US power. This is because American power has been supplemented and at times facilitated by dollar primacy, which has made it easier to project its power abroad and afforded an assortment of other political perks. Were some dollar diminution to take place, the United States would not only lose that capacity and those perks, it would also face new limitations associated with the macroeconomic management of an international currency in relative decline.

In a scenario where the dollar's role has receded, and especially as complicated by an increasingly visible overhang problem, American policies would no longer be given the benefit of the doubt. Its macroeconomic management would be subject to intense scrutiny in international financial markets and its deviations from financial rectitude would start to come at a price. In the past, periods of notable dollar weakness led to US borrowing via mechanisms that involved foreign currency payments, designed to insure creditors against the possibility of a decline in the value of the dollar. These experimental mechanisms of the late 1960s and 1970s were only used

---

[51] Emerson, *The Rhineland Crisis*, p. 78 (quotes); see also pp. 105, 111, 247. Stephen Schuker, "France and the Remilitarization of the Rhineland, 1936," *French Historical Studies* 14, no. 3 (Spring 1936): 304, 330, 334, 335 (quotes); "French Financial Weakness," *The Economist*, March 28, 1936, p. 711.

on a modest scale, but they suggest the antecedents of future demands that might be imposed by creditors.[52] It would also become more difficult to reduce the value of US debts via devaluation and inflation, devices which have served the United States well in the past, but which in the future would both work less well and further undermine the dollar's credibility.

Reduced autonomy, eroding structural power, vanishing prestige, and a growing overhang problem all suggest a challenging general macroeconomic context for American power in the coming years. More specific problems also loom large, in the form of the risk of debilitating crisis and vulnerability to economic coercion. The danger of financial crisis remains—the underlying vulnerabilities of the US financial system have not been addressed. Another crisis could come. And it could arrive during a national security crisis.

The overextended dollar might also leave the United States vulnerable to economic coercion by other states. There is a real threat here, though one less apocalyptic than often suggested by those expressing concerns that China might threaten to dump its enormous dollar holdings as an act of political coercion against the United States. This possibility is severely circumscribed by the fact that it is not in China's interest to do so, leaving this as a mostly empty threat.[53] China now has, as I have argued above, "buyer's remorse" with regard to its vast dollar holdings. But it did not accumulate those dollar assets as an act of philanthropy, and it currently finds itself as a major stakeholder in the future of the dollar and the health of the US economy. China would be a big loser in a confrontation that undermined either the greenback or American consumer demand. Despite its remarkable record of economic growth, China's economy has visible fragilities. Significant dollar depreciation would be a blow to China's economy; a collapse in the dollar that reduced American demand for imported goods would be a disaster. Thus China could conceivably dump its dollars, but this would be the economic equivalent of the nuclear option. It is possible to imagine scenarios, especially regarding confrontations over Taiwan, where China might try and engage in dollar brinksmanship or even pull the currency trigger—but short of that, China's vested interest in the dollar undercuts the potential political advantages of such a gambit.

But this does not leave the dollar in the clear. China has a subtler lever of monetary power at its disposal. It has the capacity to modulate the rate at which it acquires dollar assets, as well as the ability to manipulate the timing and publicity associated with the rebalancing of its reserve portfolio (an effort already underway). And this channel of influence is more of a one-way street. A more confident—or more aggrieved—China might use this more subtle technique of monetary power to get the attention of the United States during moments of political conflict.

---

[52] John Makin, "Swaps and Roosa Bonds as an Index of the Cost of Cooperation in the 'Crisis Zone,'" *Quarterly Journal of Economics* 85, no. 2 (May 1971); Anna Schwartz, "From Obscurity to Notoriety: A Biography of the Exchange Stabilization Fund," *Journal of Money, Credit, and Banking* 29, no. 2 (May 1997).

[53] Daniel Drezner, "Bad Debts: Assessing China's Financial Influence in Great Power Politics," *International Security* 34, no. 2 (2009); also Gregory Chin and Eric Helleiner, "China as a Creditor," *Journal of International Affairs* 61, no. 2 (Fall/Winter 2008).

Although the circumstances are (again) notably different, this capacity is parallel to the Franco-British monetary relationship in the late 1920s and early 1930s. In that period, the functioning of the international monetary system gave France the ability to draw gold from Britain essentially at will. France rather self-consciously used this power to try and push Britain around whenever the two states came into disagreement on important international political issues. If Sino-American relations deteriorate over economic or international political issues, it is likely that US macroeconomic stability will be ruffled by China shuffling its dollar cards, even if it never folds them. Once again, even though the circumstances are quite distinct, the lessons are relevant—and alarming. France did not hesitate to resort to the exercise of monetary power (and it would be naïve to assume that China would abstain from the practice). France's efforts at monetary diplomacy ultimately backfired, and contributed to the collapse of the international financial system and the Great Depression (a reminder that even though China has every incentive to avoid undermining the world economy, intentions are not always adequate to prevent costly blunders).

In the late 1920s, France was determined to take full advantage of one of the few high cards it held. Toward Germany (and Eastern Europe more generally) France sought to use the financial system, an area of relative strength, as a lever of influence. Toward Britain, as noted, France resorted to boat-rocking—expressing its preferences, as necessary, by exposing the precarious nature of British finances. Whenever Britain and France came into conflict, gold flowed from Britain to France. Those conflicts were invariably over some aspect of the German question, such as negotiations over adjusting reparations.[54]

Push came to shove, unfortunately, in 1931, during the Creditanstalt crisis, an event with eerie parallels to more recent events. On May 8, the bank informed the Austrian government that it was on the brink of failure. Understanding immediately that the Creditanstalt was a "too big to fail" institution—it was the largest bank in Austria, indeed, the largest European bank east of Germany—the normally conservative, noninterventionist government immediately went to work on a rescue package. Despite the efforts of the government, runs on banks throughout Austria occurred. Things got out of hand, the Creditanstalt failed, and the crisis spread to Germany, whose financial sector was left in ruins.[55] The crisis then spread to London, where, in September, a hemorrhaging of reserves forced the pound off the gold standard for the first time (outside of wartime suspensions) in two hundred years. Major aftershocks from the British break with gold were felt in the United States and as far away as Japan—where they were a decisive factor in the radicalization of politics there.

[54] Paul Einzig, *International Gold Movements* (London: Macmillan, 1931), p. 33; Kirshner, *Currency and Coercion*, chapter 6; see also Sir Frederick Leith-Ross, *Money Talks: Fifty Years of International Finance* (London: Hutchinson and Co., 1968); and Moreau, *The Golden Franc.*

[55] Aurel Schubert, *The Credit-Anstalt Crisis of 1931* (Cambridge, UK: Cambridge University Press, 1991), pp. 3–4. 7, 11–12; Michael Bordo and Harold James, "The Great Depression Analogy," *Financial History Review* 17, no. 2 (2011): 128; Iago Gol Aguado, "The Creditanstalt Crisis of 1931 and the Failure of the Austro-German Customs Union Project," *The Historical Journal* 44, no. 1 (2001): 200.

Why was the crisis uncontained? In a word, politics.[56] Once the troubles of the Creditanstalt were made public, it was understood that Germany would be "at once exposed to the danger of panic withdrawal of capital." Britain, hoping to prevent a generalized European banking crisis, favored finding a way to support the rescue efforts of the Austrian government. France, in contrast, saw a political opportunity. Austria and Germany had been moving toward a Customs Union, but France had argued, reasonably, that such an agreement was forbidden by the Versailles Treaty. Now France could do more than argue—it made any assistance to Austria contingent on the abandonment of the Customs Union scheme—which it presented as an ultimatum on June 16.[57]

The Americans and the British, who had, in May, backed an initial loan to Austria through the Bank for International Settlements (more help was now needed), were displeased by what internal US documents described as "blackmail." Secretary of State Henry Stimson personally told the French Ambassador in Washington that such behavior was not "the proper way to meet a financial crisis." (Actually, France's efforts went beyond blackmail; with the banking crisis there was a flight from the Austrian shilling, and France withdrew funds from Austria in an effort to pour gasoline on that fire.) Faced with France's demand, the Austrian government announced its resignation, which threatened such chaos that the next day the Bank of England stepped in with a large emergency short-term loan of its own. This temporarily saved the Austrian government, but weakened the position of sterling.[58]

The British credit provided a respite from the storm but could not restore the continent's fragile finances, and soon enough Germany found itself tested—and wanting—by the financial pressures unleashed by the Austrian crisis. On June 25th the situation was dire enough that even France joined in with the Bank of England, the Bank for International Settlements, and the US Federal Reserve Banks to collectively provide a $100 million loan to Germany. But when that proved insufficient, and it was clear that Germany would need more help from abroad, France introduced a range of political conditions on any new loans, including demands for concessions on naval disarmament, reparations, the Customs Union issue (once again), and recognition of French interests in Central Europe and the Balkans. Instead, Germany retreated behind a wall of exchange controls (which would be adapted and integrated into Nazi grand strategy a few years later), essentially divorcing itself from global financial markets. With the German avenue dammed, the crisis

[56] See for example Theo Balderston, "The Banks and the Gold Standard Crisis of 1931," *Financial History Review* 1, no. 1 (April 1994): 65; George Glasgow, "The Financial and Economic Crisis," *Contemporary Review* 140 (July/December 1931), pp. 140–141.

[57] League of Nations, *World Economic Survey 1931–1932* (Geneva: 1932), p. 72; Aguado, "The Creditanstalt Crisis," pp. 203, 204, 216; Edward W. Bennett, *Germany and the Diplomacy of the Financial Crisis, 1931* (Cambridge, MA: Harvard University Press, 1962), pp. 41, 71, 73, 117, 149–150.

[58] *Foreign Relations of the United States, 1931*, Vol. 1 (Washington, DC: 1946), pp. 23, 24 ("blackmail"), 26, (Stimson); Schubert, *The Credit-Anstalt Crisis*, pp. 14–15, 160–161; Bennett, *Diplomacy of the Financial Crisis*, pp. 151–152. Aguado, "The Creditanstalt Crisis," pp. 211, 214, 216.

floodwaters were diverted to Britain, and the stage was set for the crisis that would be visited upon sterling in September.[59]

An important difference between the global financial crises of 1931 and 2007 was that in the former case, the perception of intense security dilemmas across Europe inhibited cooperative efforts that might have contained the crisis, and encouraged short-sighted unilateralism that was collectively disastrous. A reminder that politics always has a formative influence on the pattern of international monetary and financial relations; that the relatively benign security environment in 2007 contributed to the containment of that crisis (it could have been much worse); and that there are no guarantees that the international political environment will be as forgiving next time.

CONCLUSIONS: NEW HETEROGENEITY ABROAD—PARALYSIS AT HOME?

Before the financial crisis, trends at home and abroad suggested new macroeconomic constraints on American power. Assuming continuity in these underlying factors—although this certainly need not be the case, and international relations theorists have repeatedly erred in implicitly assuming continuity over change with regard to trends in world politics[60]—I have argued that the crisis has accelerated those underlying trends, and left the United States more vulnerable to the possibility that macroeconomic factors that will inhibit, rather than enhance, its capabilities on the world stage, a reversal of the experiences of the past seventy years.

My principal argument in this chapter is that the global financial crisis will present (like the Great Depression and the inflation of the 1970s) a "learning moment" in world politics, but that much of that learning will take place *outside* of the United States. And that lesson will be–to varying extent, import, and consequence—that unbridled capitalism (and, especially, unbound finance), does not work, and that the American model is disreputable. The emergence of a new heterogeneity of thinking about money and finance will mark the end of the Second Post-War American

---

[59] Bennett, *Germany and the Diplomacy of the Financial Crisis* pp. 177–78, 190, 219, 231, 237, 248; *Federal Reserve Bulletin*, Washington, DC: US Government Printing Office, November 1930, p. 383; *Foreign Relations of the United States, 1931*, p. 96.

[60] Major game changing discontinuities are plausible, and easily imagined, and would require a reassessment of my conclusions. A major financial crisis with the United States at its epicenter— either a dollar panic, or what would become known as "too big to fail two"—would radically accelerate the decline of the dollar as an international currency. The complete implosion of the Euro would bolster the dollar as the only safe harbor in sight, although that assumes that such a crisis would not pull down a major US financial institution along with it, which might be wishful thinking—and not to be underestimated are the effects on the economies of the United States and China that would result from a deepening of Europe's economic distress. Finally, it is easy to imagine an interruption in China's economic growth, which, again, would bolster the dollar and decelerate the shift in the balance of power away from the United States. However, given the likely consequences of economic distress in China, spillover harm to its trading partners, and a legitimacy crisis for the CCP, the "costs" of a slowly growing China will outweigh the "benefits."

Order. States will increase their demand for autonomy and insulation from global financial instability, and, due to ideological shifts and the acceleration of underlying material trends, US power and influence will be relatively diminished on this new environment.

In addition to changes to the balance of power and political influence, these developments will also contribute to more acrimonious and chronic macroeconomic squabbling between states, which will place additional pressure on the management of the dollar. The underlying problem is that, in general, monetary cooperation is inherently difficult. States invariably seek to shift the burdens of adjustment abroad—costs that can be quite high and politically unwelcome. (Much of Europe's current crisis is a fight over how to distribute the burdens of macroeconomic adjustment.) Typically, it takes a confluence of exceptional factors for monetary cooperation to be sustained, each of which mitigates the costs of those burdens. A concentration of monetary power can help foster cooperation, because a hegemon can take on a disproportionate share of the costs of adjustment, or it can supervise, police, and enforce arrangements about the nature of adjustment. Ideological homogeneity can foster cooperation by giving a cloak of economic legitimacy to the economic distress associated with adjustment. And shared, salient security concerns can increase the willingness of partners to bear the costs of adjustment, because they care more about the security situation.

Note that in contemporary international politics all of these variables are moving in the "wrong" direction. US relative power (and monetary power) is in relative decline. I have argued that there is a new heterogeneity of ideas about money and finance. And the security interests of key players at the monetary table have not been this divergent (if not necessarily oppositional) in over a century.[61] In particular, it is notable that every major effort to reconstitute the international monetary order in the second half of the twentieth century was undertaken by the United States and its political allies and military dependencies. That is no longer the case.

The implication of these problems can be overstated, and it is important to understand them in context. Dollar "optimists" correctly point to the extraordinary and unique strengths of the US economy, and the additional advantages of incumbency for the dollar as international money.[62] These are good reminders that dollar is extremely unlikely to simply go away, and discussions of its "eclipse" are premature, to say the least. My argument is simply that its international role *is* very likely to *relatively* diminish over time, and that this change in status—even as modest as remaining "first among equals"— will have significant consequences for American power. Optimists also note—again correctly—that for all of the dollar's observable problems, comparatively speaking, it remains the most attractive international money. That is, it remains champion due to the glass jaws of would-be competitors.

---

[61] Participants at every major monetary conference of the twentieth century were by and large political allies.

[62] See for example Doug Stokes, "Achilles' Deal: Dollar Decline and U.S. Grand Strategy After the Crisis," *Review of International Political Economy* 21, no. 5 (2014); Daniel Drezner, *The System Worked: How the World Stopped Another Great Depression* (Oxford: Oxford University Press, 2014); Eswar Prasad, *The Dollar Trap: How the U.S. Dollar Tightened Its Grip on Global Finance* (Princeton, NJ: Princeton University Press, 2014).

Nevertheless, however accurate, such a static observation overlooks the fact that this—the lack of alternatives—is the dollar's most important remaining foundation. All of the other pillars that served to provide the bedrock support for the dollar order—common economic ideology, the concentration of power, shared security concerns, and faith in the American economy and its unique invulnerability to financial crisis—have eroded away. The dollar dominates, but its exposure and others' motivations for greater diversity have never been higher.

In sum, the stage is set for chronic squabbling over international monetary and financial cooperation and governance in the coming decades, and the United States will find it harder to simply shrug off the burdens of macroeconomic adjustment (which will inevitably present themselves) onto others. This will compound the new US sensitivity to external constraints. And a key word here is *new*. It is not just that the United States will very likely face external constraints—pressures for adjustment, new macroeconomic vulnerabilities, the danger of financial crisis—it is that such pressures are unfamiliar to the US political system. And that system is already under considerable stress, dealing (or failing to deal) with formidable domestic economic problems, first among which is the need to put its fiscal house in order. Given the strands of unilateralism and isolation that weave their way throughout American history, it is possible that domestic politics will indeed magnify the "real" effect of these new pressures, and present an Achilles heel of American power.

Sustainable national security strategies rest on economic and political foundations. Both global economic trends and domestic political contestation suggest that a careful assessment of the underpinning logics and long-run wisdom and viability of America's global strategy—which should reflect its priorities, capabilities, and ambitions—is in order. In particular, US planners need to be alert to both the international economic and domestic political consequences of another American financial crisis—a possibility that, unfortunately, cannot be causally dismissed. As Barry Eichengreen has argued, the success of the emergency measures introduced in the heat of the moment prevented a second Great Depression, but "their very success encouraged second thoughts," and "weakened the incentive to think deeply about causes." This has left in place, according to Financial Times columnist Martin Wolf, a financial structure that is "irretrievably unstable," and it is "grotesquely dangerous."[63] Moreover, domestic politics are much more brittle now than they were then. During the 2007–2008 crisis, the correct policies were initially chosen; but, applied half-heartedly and incompletely, these measures are commonly considered to have been a failure by the general public. This perception, coupled with the (more accurate) resentment that the tycoons who caused the crisis were largely sheltered from its consequences, has likely exhausted the political will that would be necessary to introduce the emergency measures required to deal with the next big crisis. Thus the economic and political consequences of the next crisis on American national security strategy will almost certainly be even greater.

---

[63] Barry Eichengreen, *Hall of Mirrors: The Great Depression, The Great Recession, and the Uses—and Misuses—of History* (New York: Oxford University Press, 2015); Martin Wolf, *The Shifts and the Shocks: What We've Learned—and Still Have to Learn—from the Financial Crisis* (New York: Penguin, 2014).

ACKNOWLEDGMENTS

For helpful comments, I thank Jeremi Suri, Stephen Van Evera, and the participants in Tobin Project Conferences on Sustainable National Security Strategy. Thanks also to Wendy Leutert for research assistance and all translations. An earlier version of this chapter appeared as "Bringing Them All Back Home? Dollar Diminution and American Power," *The Washington Quarterly* 36:3 (Summer 2013), pp. 27–45. This chapter draws from my book, *American Power after the Financial Crisis* (Ithaca, NY: Cornell University Press, 2014).

2

DOES AMERICAN MILITARY POWER
ATTRACT FOREIGN INVESTMENT?

Daniel W. Drezner and Nancy F. Hite-Rubin

A future of limited US defense budgets has triggered anxiety from some quarters of the US national security community. Advocates for a large military argue that the world is safer and more prosperous today precisely because of the United States' outsized security capacities and deep engagement with the rest of the world. When budgetary constraints began to appear on the horizon in 2010, the presidents of American Enterprise Institute, Heritage Foundation, and Foreign Policy Initiative explicitly argued in the *Wall Street Journal* that "military spending is not a net drain on our economy (Brooks, Fuelner and Kristol 2010)." This argument is one of several that have been made about the positive economic benefits to the United States of possessing military predominance and deep engagement with the rest of the world (Brooks, Ikenberry, and Wohlforth 2012–13; Kagan 2012; Ikenberry 2011; Brooks and Wohlforth 2008).

Critics, however, have long questioned whether military preeminence yields the benefits claimed by proponents (Jervis 1993; Gholz, Press and Sapolsky 1997; Walt 2006). Those criticisms have only intensified since the 2008 financial crisis (Friedman, Gholz, Press, and Sapolsky 2009; Preble 2009; Pape 2009; Gholz and Press 2010; Mearsheimer 2011; MacDonald and Parent 2011; Betts 2012; Posen 2014). While arguments in favor of military predominance are frequently asserted in policy circles, there is less discussion about their theoretical and empirical foundation. What can international relations scholarship say about the relative economic benefits of military primacy?

There is a welter of different causal mechanisms through which military power is hypothesized to lead to positive economic benefits (Norrlof 2010; Drezner 2013; Maass, Norrlof, and Drezner 2014). The focus of this chapter will be whether military spending attracts private capital. A staple of international political economy research over the past few decades has been identifying the drivers behind cross-border investment. A number of empirical investigations have explored the ways in which a country's resource endowments, political institutions, and external relations affect its ability to attract private capital

We are grateful to the Tobin Project for their generous funding and support for this project. We are also grateful to attendees at the University of Texas at Austin, Brookings Institution, and American University for their thoughtful feedback on previous drafts of this chapter.

inflows. Curiously, however, the effects of military power have remained relatively unexplored in this literature. Do a country's military capabilities enhance or discourage foreign investment?

The absence of empirical inquiry on this issue is curious. Theoretically, there are numerous hypothesized ways in which military power could affect private sector investment decisions. Some argue that the greater a country's military capabilities, the more it can attract private capital seeking security, a form of geoeconomic favoritism. (Norrlof 2010). Others argue that defense spending "crowds out" foreign direct investment by revealing a less friendly business environment for investors (Acemoğlu and Robinson 2012). From a policy perspective, determining the precise relationship between American military power and investment flows is crucial for long-range calculations of US grand strategy and defense planning. If there are positive economic externalities from US defense spending, that kind of "dynamic scoring" should be factored into future budgetary plans. If, however, US military expenditures are negatively correlated with investment flows, that consideration needs to be factored into any determination of the sustainable level of defense spending. At this point, there are merely claims and counterclaims about the alleged economic benefits. Without more rigorous testing, such assertions, accurate or not, can gain traction in the US foreign policy community.

This chapter empirically tests the effect of defense spending on foreign direct investment (FDI) inflows for the post–Cold War era on a set of developed economies, with a special emphasis on North America. Using multiple measures of the dependent variable, the results suggest that high levels of investment in military capabilities do not lead to geoeconomic favoritism. In other words, military expenditures do not attract inward flows of foreign direct investment in affluent states. This result, combined with prior research (Drezner 2013), casts significant doubts on the argument that an advanced great power's military capabilities generate positive economic externalities. For the United States, the policy implications are clear: elevated levels of military spending crowd out foreign investments. This fact needs to be incorporated into any debate about sustainable levels of defense spending. The econometric results do call into question, however, whether this finding is generalizable to other states.

The rest of this paper is divided into five sections. The next section briefly reviews the literature on the political economy of FDI, and the relative poverty of analysis connecting military power with foreign direct investment. The second section considers the arguments put forward about the relationship between military power and foreign investment. The third section outlines the testing strategy and methodology. The fourth section presents the econometric results. The final section summarizes and concludes.

THE LITERATURE

The study of foreign direct investment is as old at the international political economy subfield itself (Gilpin 1975). Indeed, the wave of expropriations and nationalizations in the 1960s and 1970s was one of the triggers for the international political economy (IPE) research program. As it has evolved, however, the security questions that initially motivated the research program have faded somewhat. This is surprising. In their survey of the field, Frieden and Martin (2002, p. 131) note that the political and security dimensions of foreign investment have received "relatively sketchy theoretical and empirical work." Biglaiser and DeRouen (2007, p. 836) go further, observing, "few contemporary studies consider security concerns and FDI inflows, a well-researched topic by scholars historically."[1] Li and Vashchilko (2010, 765–766) state, "there is very little work on how the quality of interstate security relations influences bilateral investment flows."

In general, research into the patterns of foreign direct investment can be broken down into three categories. Economists have focused overwhelmingly on the economic and policy conditions of the host country. Beginning with John Dunning's eclectic "ownership, location and internationalization" (OLI) framework, this vein of research examines the fundamentals of the host economy, as well as the country's policies towards foreign investment as key drivers of private capital flows. Economic fundamentals include the country's economic size and growth rate, inflation, labor costs, and resource endowments (Kinda 2010). Policy variables include the imposition of capital controls, policies of taxation, technology transfer, local content, and the repatriation of profits.

The second category of research examines the institutional dimensions of the host country. As Raymond Vernon (1971) observed more that forty years ago, the "obsolescing bargain" of foreign direct investment means that companies must be concerned about the ability of host countries to credibly commit to not altering the foreign investment climate after the firm has committed to asset-specific investments. In recent years, the treatment of foreign investors in Argentina and Russia has certainly highlighted the ongoing nature of this policy concern. A fair amount of empirical research has been devoted to the effect that investment-specific institutions, such as bilateral investment treaties and preferential trade agreements, have on FDI (Neumayer and Spess 2005; Kerner 2009; Büthe and Milner 2008).

At a deeper level, there has been a surfeit of studies looking at whether the host country's regime type and political insitutions affect FDI inflows (Oneal 1994; Jensen 2003 and Jensen 2008; Li and Resnick 2003; Blanton and Blanton 2007; Schulz 2009; Asiedu and Lien 2011). Originally, it was thought that authoritarian institutions would attract FDI because of the host country's ability to suppress any political or labor discontent (Oneal 1994). Over time, however, the pendulum has shifted in favor of democratic institutions. Because democracies allow political leaders to credibly commit, states with democratic regimes are perceived to be more likely to honor their contracts (North and Weingast 1989; Schultz and Weingast 2003; Besley and Persson 2007; Acemoğlu and Robinson 2012). Foreign investors are thought to be more vulnerable to the development of "extractive" political

---

[1] See Krasner (1978) and Lipson (1985) for examples of this earlier IPE generation of FDI research, and Schneider and Frey (1985) for a fuller review of this generation of economic research.

institutions. Politically powerful actors can exploit the coercive apparatus of the state to develop political institutions that reward members of the selectorate with private goods—rather than the public goods necessary to attract inward capital flows (Bueno de Mesquita et al. 2003). As Daron Acemoğlu and James Robinson (2012) have observed, countries based on "extractive" political institutions are more likely to possess comparatively more sclerotic economies.

The final dimension of FDI research has looked at the role of security in affecting FDI flows. Although this dimension has faced comparative neglect in recent decades, there has been some work on this topic. One vein of research follows on from statistical tests showing that trade follows the flag—that is, trade flows are likely to be higher within a security alliance than not (Pollins 1989a and Pollins 1989b; Gowa and Mansfield 1993; Gowa 1994; Keshk, Pollins, and Reuvney 2004). Some scholars have investigated to see whether foreign direct investment flows also follow the flag (Gupta and Yu 2007). Biglaiser and DeRouen (2007) suggest that US foreign direct investment flows respond positively to the overseas deployment of US troops. The bulk of this literature does not address the question of military capabilities at all, but rather the connection between investment, alliances, and violent conflict.

A few studies have focused exclusively on the relationship between American military power and the reactions of private capital. Carla Norrlof's (2010, p. 171) work represents the most direct effort to test the relationship between US military prowess and financial strength. She argues, for example, that when the United States has won wars since 1979, "funds have more readily flowed to the United States." When the United States has gotten bogged down in military quagmires, on the other hand, the reverse has been true. Her evidence for testing this assertion, however, rests solely on an annual bivariate comparison of US military performance with financial flows into the United States. The failure to consider other causal factors in determining the flow of funds—such as economic growth, monetary policy, or fiscal policy measures—introduces significant omitted variable bias into her analysis. Beyond Norrlof, however, there has been no large-n econometric analysis of how a country's military capabilities affect foreign direct investment inflows.

HOW CAN MILITARY POWER AFFECT FOREIGN DIRECT INVESTMENT?

There are ways in which military power can be hypothesized to attract inward foreign direct investment. Private capital, for example, might interpret military power as a powerful market signal. At a minimum, the most obvious benefit from military and paramilitary forces is the security it provides to potential investors. All else equal, a country is far more likely to attract foreign capital if it is secure from foreign invasion. This security, in turn, can make the country an attractive place for foreign investment (Norrlof 2010, chapter 6; Beckley 2011–2012). A country with sufficient military capabilities also possesses a monopoly on the use of legitimate coercive violence within its borders. By bolstering property rights and reducing risk, military capabilities can act as a magnet for foreign capital inflows. We will label the possible positive effects of military power on foreign direct investment as the *geoeconomic favoritism hypothesis.*

At the same time, it is easy to hypothesize how military power would act as a deterrent on foreign direct investment. A large military creates a number of possible problems for foreign investors. From a macroeconomic perspective, a large military leads to large amounts of government spending, which can trigger higher interest rates or inflation. A state that spends more on military power might be underinvesting in civilian public goods such as infrastructure or health care. It is also possible that states with military power might be more likely to take actions that limit the rate of return on foreign investment. Governments that control larger militaries are more likely to be able to expropriate foreign investment by force. They are also more likely to trigger the security dilemma with other states, increasing the likelihood of violent conflict (Jervis 1978). We will label the possible negative effects of military power on foreign direct investment as the *crowding out hypothesis.*

The empirical literature on the effects of aggregate military power on inward foreign direct investment is thin. To be sure, some measure of military power is generally acknowledged to be a necessary prerequisite for developing an attractive climate for foreign investment (Bergsten 1975; Cohen 1977; Helleiner and Kirshner 2009). Since the beginning of the modern Westphalian state system, leaders have equated military power with economic plenty (Viner 1948). As a necessary condition, it certainly must be the case that a state's ability to defend its borders determines its ability to develop its economy, capital markets, and regional economic ties (Gerace 2000; Norrlof 2010). In this way, military capabilities can help to reduce political risk, which is a significant explanatory factor for cross-border capital flows (Papaioannou 2009).

That said, the historical literature does not lend significant support to geoeconomic favoritism. Most analyses of the effect of military power on investment have been on *outward* FDI—namely, the ability of the home country to protect its overseas investments (Lipson 1985; Tomz 2007). Comparatively less work has focused on whether military power or military statecraft affects foreign investment inflows. The direction of causality in this relationship is difficult to ascertain, however. Most historical research draws the opposite conclusion: the primary causal arrow moves from economic vitality towards a strong military. This was Paul Kennedy's (1987) conclusion in *The Rise and Fall of the Great Powers,* and matches the general consensus of most scholars who work on hegemonic stability, power transition, or long cycles (Organski 1969; Modelski 1978; Gilpin 1981). Jonathan Kirshner's work (2007, p. 206) demonstrates that financial interests are interested in the minimization of risk. Kirshner shows that, historically, the financial sector has staunchly opposed initiating the use of force in world politics. Even military hegemons must therefore be wary of alienating global capital.

The hypotheses to test the effect of military power on inwards flows of foreign direct investment are straightforward:

H1 (geoeconomic favoritism): *Ceteris paribus,* military power will be positively correlated with greater inflows of foreign direct investment.

H2 (crowding out): *Ceteris paribus*, military power will be negatively correlated with greater inflows of foreign direct investment.

EMPIRICAL METHODS AND DATA

We construct a unique data set to thoroughly test the hypothesized relationships between foreign direct investment and military power. The data are organized in a pooled time-series cross-sectional format (TSCS) covering the post–Cold War era. There is considerable variation in military spending and FDI inflows across time and space, enabling us to test our hypotheses. We use the Correlates of War project's data on annual military expenditures to proxy military power.

We utilize separate measures of foreign direct investment inflows to ensure panel balance and robustness of our findings. The model is tested using multiple controls for both economic and political determinants of FDI. We also incrementally stage the complexity and stringency of the model specification in order to control for heteroskedasticity, autocorrelation, and cross-sectional dependence in the data. Because we are principally interested in the role of American military power in attracting FDI, we focus our analysis in this chapter on the relationship across military expenditures and FDI flows into developed economies. Because, almost by definition, developed world governments have investor-friendly policies and institutions, we can focus more on the variation in military power across these economies. The empirical analysis covers ninety-two countries (see Appendix 1) from the end of the Cold War through 2007.

FDI Inflows

Our dependent variable is a measure of net FDI inflows into the host country in a given year, measured in current US dollars. We utilize two separate measures of foreign direct investment inflows—one relying on the PRS group and one relying on World Bank data. The PRS group is a subscription-based service that provides data on foreign investment and country-specific political and economic factors.[2] Both PRS and the World Bank utilize the same definition and measures for reporting FDI inflows, with the groups' measurements covarying at over ninety percent. The utilization of two independent measures of FDI helps to ensure the robustness of our results.

Military Spending

Our military expenditure data are from the National Material Capabilities (NMC), which is part of the Correlates of War Project at the University of Michigan. Its variable military expenditures measurement (*milex*) is a country-year measure in

---

[2] https://www.prsgroup.com.

current US dollars. Our project utilizes the most recent version (4.0) that covers 158 countries across our time series from 1990–2007.

Political and Economic Controls

There are many institutional, economic, and political factors that account for changes in FDI inflows from one year to the next. Our data set is constructed to comprehensively control for these competing explanations, ensuring that relationships we detect between military spending and FDI inflows are not spurious. We increase the number of controls used in our model specifications in a stepwise fashion.

Our control measure for population, *pop*, is also taken from the Composite Index of National Capability V4. These data are collected annually by individual country and are balanced very well with the military spending variable, *milex*, over the 1990–2007 time frame. In addition to population control, we utilize the CINC's measure for primary energy consumption: *pec*. This energy consumption variable is measured in thousand coal-tons by country-year.

We use the ICRG-PRS group's political risk measures for control variables. The International Country Risk Guide (ICRG) collects political and economic information, and converts these into annual "risk points" or indexed assessments of financial risk in a given country along several dimensions. Five of these dimensions are used in our data set. The first dimension is corruption (*corr*), which the ICRG measures annually on a 0-6 scale. This score is based on the "corruption within the political system that is a threat to foreign investment . . ."[3] Another dimension that we utilize is foreign debt (*f_debt_gdp*), an annual measure of gross foreign debt expressed as a percentage of GDP. The third dimension we include is an annual measure of government budget balance (*bb_gdp*), expressed as a percentage of GDP. Fourth, the ICRG provides a six-point index measure of "law and order"[4] (*law_o_*). The ICRG calculates this risk point based on a combined score that measures the strength and impartiality of the legal system, along with an assessment of the observance of law in practice. Finally, we utilize the ICRG's combined economic risk rating, (*riskr_*), which rates investor risk for each country yearly from 0 (highest risk) to 50 (least risk).[5]

---

[3] . . . which the group defines as "a measure of corruption within the political system that is a threat to foreign investment by distorting the economic and financial environment, reducing the efficiency of government and business by enabling people to assume positions of power through patronage rather than ability, and introducing inherent instability into the political process." (Refer to ICRG Methodology for maximum points for this variable, as well as for related formulas for calculating risk.)

[4] Two measures comprising one risk component. Each subcomponent equals half of the total. The "law" subcomponent assesses the strength and impartiality of the legal system, and the "order" subcomponent assesses popular observance of the law. (Refer to ICRG Methodology for maximum points for this variable, as well as for related formulas for calculating risk.)

[5] Economic risk rating—a means of assessing a country's current economic strengths and weaknesses. In general, where strengths outweigh weaknesses a country will show low risk, and where weaknesses outweigh strengths, the economic risk will be high. To ensure comparability between

One of the challenges in constructing the necessary data set for testing our hypotheses was finding available data that cover most of the world's countries over our time frame (1990–2007). This was particularly true for empirical data on institutions that regulate the movement of capital. We constructed our own data set for bilateral investment treaties (BIT). The variable *bit* is a country-year measure of the number of active bilateral investment treaties. The intuition behind our measure is that the greater the number of active BITs a country has in a given year, the more capital investment is likely to follow. We have 4199 country-year observations, with countries in our data set averaging fourteen treaties in any given year.

FINDINGS

Our analysis leads us to reject the hypothesis that increasing US military spending attracts inward foreign direct investment. However, there is striking evidence that this relationship holds for less powerful states. Our main finding is that military spending and foreign direct investment exhibit a significant nonlinear relationship. This nonlinearity hinges upon the states' level of economic development. In advanced economies (including the United States), the link between spending and FDI does not hold. Yet the relationship is positive and significant for many countries in our sample. In these emerging market countries the link is robust and worthy of further exploration.

The following analysis actually provides considerable support for both hypotheses, and hence a nonmonotonic correspondence of military spending to investment. Although the overriding relationship between military spending and FDI is positive and significant, there is a subset of countries where the opposite trend holds. In the more diversely represented World Bank data sample the relationship appears to be null, and in some cases, even significantly negative. This suggests that under certain factors, military spending deters foreign direct investment (crowding-out hypothesis). These competing relationships are demonstrated by comparative analyses utilizing PRS group and World Bank measures of FDI. The PRS data are focused on emerging market economies, for which the geopolitical favoritism hypothesis is robust. However, when the data analysis is shifted towards LDC and OECD countries using the World Bank data set, the relationship washes out. We contend that there is an underlying factor explaining why military spending functions to attract FDI in emerging market economies, and not among OECD member states.

The analysis presented in Table 2.1 indicates that the relationship between logged military spending and logged net foreign direct investment is significantly

countries, risk components are based on accepted ratios between the measured data within each country's national economic/financial structure, and then the ratios are compared, not the data. Risk points are assessed for each of the component factors of GDP per head of population, real annual GDP growth, annual inflation rate, budget balance as a percentage of GDP, and current account balance as a percentage of GDP. Risk ratings range from a high of 50 (least risk) to a low of 0 (highest risk), though lowest de facto ratings are generally near 15.

Table 2.1 Main Regression Results

Variables	PRS Group Measure of FDI			World Bank Measure of FDI		
	Model 1	Model 2	Model 3	Model 4	Model 5	Model 6
Log Military Spending	0.226**	0.241***	0.331***	0.0161	0.0913	0.254**
	(0.0854)	(0.0784)	(0.105)	(0.153)	(0.0943)	(0.101)
Log GDP per capita	2.012***	1.595***	1.758***	3.237***	1.803***	1.968***
	(0.265)	(0.176)	(0.312)	(0.197)	(0.305)	(0.313)
Log Population	1.303**	2.074***	−0.302	0.75	2.319**	−0.221
	(0.522)	(0.451)	(0.636)	(0.526)	(0.807)	(0.826)
Cumulative BITS	0.0208***	0.0269***	0.0278***	0.0238***		
	(0.00383)	(0.00603)	(0.0063)	(0.00546)		
Corruption	−0.000761	0.00996	0.0242	−0.0567	0.0473	0.0447
	(0.0487)	(0.0507)	(0.0634)	(0.0525)	(0.0412)	(0.0742)
Economic Risk	0.0273***	0.00990*	0.0106*	0.0471***	0.0139	0.0157**
	(0.00814)	(0.00513)	(0.00512)	(0.0137)	(0.00864)	(0.00542)
Foreign Debt (% of GDP)	−0.00182*	−0.00162*	−0.00135	−0.000163	−0.00129	−7.89E−05
	(0.000866)	(0.000877)	(0.00152)	(0.00107)	(0.000881)	(0.0015)
Budget Balance (% of GDP)	0.00865*	0.00770*	0.00736	0.00984	0.00763	0.00649
	(0.00482)	(0.00412)	(0.00429)	(0.00657)	(0.00461)	(0.00465)
Energy Consumption (coal tons)	−0.480**	−0.360**	−0.142*	−0.468	−0.374	−0.0203
	(0.171)	(0.16)	(0.0711)	(0.371)	(0.322)	(0.126)
Law and Order	0.0461	0.0603	0.120*	0.0827	0.0974	0.140**
	(0.0316)	(0.0397)	(0.0594)	(0.0638)	(0.0591)	(0.0632)
Total Trade (% of GDP)			0.00945***			0.00721***
			(0.00298)			(0.00238)
GDP Growth (%)			0.0132			0.0146
			(0.0106)			(0.0149)
Democracy Score (Polity 2)			0.0206			−0.0148
			(0.0226)			(0.0243)
Index of Globalization			0.0441***			0.0667***
			(0.00525)			(0.00709)
Trade Freedom			−0.000199			−0.000822
			(0.00335)			(0.00375)
International Liquidity		−0.00104			−0.00455	
		(0.00242)			(0.00364)	
Inflation		−0.000222**			−0.000259***	
		(9.18E−05)			(6.87E−05)	
Real GDP Growth (%)		0.0534***			0.0646***	
		(0.0161)			(0.0145)	
Foreign Currency Reserves		0.000926**			0.000816	
		(0.000379)			(0.000552)	

(Continued)

Table 2.1 Contiuned

Variables	PRS Group Measure of FDI			World Bank Measure of FDI		
	Model 1	Model 2	Model 3	Model 4	Model 5	Model 6
Constant	−49.66***	−50.57***	−37.56***	−44.02***	−34.51***	−23.07**
	(4.627)	(3.527)	(8.304)	(4.493)	(4.78)	(8.964)
Observations	1,384	1,359	1,065	1,432	1,385	1,072
Country Clusters	89	89	87	91	89	87

Notes: Estimation of pooled OLS/WLS and fixed effects (within) regression models with Driscoll and Kraay standard errors. *** $p<0.01$, ** $p<0.05$, * $p<0.1$

and positively correlated. The dependent variable in all six specifications is net foreign direct investment inflows by country-year. The first three columns show model specifications using PRS data for FDI, with the core controls (Model 1), additional economic controls (Model 2), and additional political controls (Model 3). The remaining columns contain specifications using the World Bank as the data source for FDI: core controls (Model 4), additional economic controls (Model 5), and additional political controls (Model 6). The relationship between military spending (*lmilex*) and FDI is strongly significant and positive in Models 1,2, 3, and 6. The additional variables in the expanded economic and political specification pick up some of the variation in the dependent variable. However, comparisons across these models show that the robustness of the military spending–FDI relationship is roughly equivalent across all specifications.

The above results hold with alternative regression models. We present the regression results utilizing the *xtscc,* as it is the most conservative estimator. The xtscc provides Driscoll and Kraay (1998) standard error estimates which are robust to disturbances that are heteroscedastic, autocorrelated, and cross-sectionally dependent. By controlling for cross-sectional dependence, xtscc regressions are more stringent than controlling for temporal lags and fixed effects alone. However, it does not appear that the additional stringency is divisive, since the relationships are roughly equivalent with varying estimators. We find that neither exclusion of control variables or relaxing the model assumptions alters our substantive conclusions.

It is worth noting that military spending is strongly associated with FDI inflows in all specifications using the PRS data set, but not necessarily using World Bank data. This contrast in significance holds regardless of which estimator is used. This was at first confusing, given that both sources of military spending utilize the exact same measurement and definition for FDI. The contrasting relationship is explained in part by the countries covered by the PRS versus the World Bank data source. The regression tests in Models 1–3 utilize similar numbers of observations and country clusters as the ones in 4–6, but these countries are not the same. The PRS group provides a subscription-based service to international investors. For this reason, their incentive is to focus on data collection in emerging and frontier markets rather than very poor or inaccessible markets. For example,

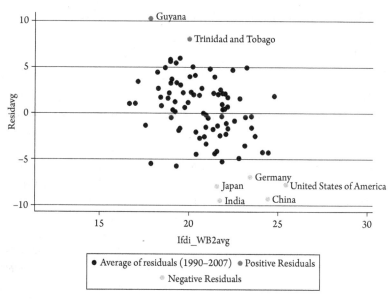

Figure 2.1 Residual Analysis
This is a scatterplot of residuals from our regression utilizing World Bank data for FDI.

while the World Bank data source covers Guyana, it is not complete in reporting Guyana's FDI during the period 1990–2007. In contrast, the PRS group does not cover Guyana but provides more complete measures of FDI for the smaller set of countries included in their database.

The residual analysis presented in Figure 2.1 highlights the varied relationship across military expenditures and FDI for large markets and emerging markets versus less developed states. The scatter plot displays the average residual for each country on the y-axis and the average logged FDI inflows on the x-axis. Since these are average values, taken over the 1990–2007 time frame, each country represents one data point. The residuals are relatively small for emerging market states, indicating that these data points fit the model specification well. The average residual for the United States is large and negative, indicating that the historical variation in US military expenditures does little to explain fluctuations in attracting foreign capital. Visual inspection makes it clear that Japan, Germany, India, China, and the United States have the most striking negative residuals. This means that the estimated model does not predict foreign direct investment inflows very closely for these countries. Negative residuals indicate that these countries have on average higher FDI inflows than the model predicts they would have.

To explore this divide in our ability to link FDI and military spending in some countries and not others, we conduct a split analysis. This positive and significant FDI-military spending relationship holds in emerging market countries that typically compete for capital. The analysis in Table 2.2 picks up on an interesting distinction between countries that seem to benefit from greater military spending, and those that do not. Here, we split the sample of countries represented in the data set between the global "North" vs. "South" typology. The first column on

Table 2.2 Military Spending and FDI Split Analysis: Global North and Global South

VARIABLES Sample =	ALL	"North"	"South"
Log Military Spending	0.258***	−0.394	0.296***
	(0.0834)	(0.368)	(0.0488)
Log GDP per capita	1.921***	3.493***	2.010***
	(0.265)	(0.503)	(0.305)
Log Population	1.628***	−1.735	2.095***
	(0.549)	(1.11)	(0.489)
Cumulative BITS	0.0191***	0.0206***	0.000509
	(0.00444)	(0.00403)	(0.0064)
Corruption	0.00728	−0.0637	0.0532
	(0.0523)	(0.0886)	(0.0501)
Economic Risk	0.0220***	−0.0226	0.0296***
	(0.00711)	(0.0158)	(0.00665)
Foreign Debt (% of GDP)	−0.00138	0.00807**	−0.00188**
	(0.000889)	(0.00355)	(0.000656)
Budget Balance (% of GDP)	0.00890*	0.0270*	0.00714
	(0.00507)	(0.0149)	(0.00414)
Energy Consumption (coal tons)	−0.386**	−0.652**	−0.22
	(0.167)	(0.298)	(0.184)
Law and Order	0.0513	0.0513	0.0725*
	(0.0345)	(0.0631)	(0.0394)
International Liquidity	−0.0003	0.0411*	−0.0016
	(0.00327)	(0.0212)	(0.00189)
Constant	−52.43***	−36.67***	−60.47***
	(4.439)	(6.068)	(4.614)
Observations	1,360	506	854
Number	89	31	58

Notes: Estimation of pooled OLS/WLS and fixed effects (within) regression models with Driscoll and Kraay standard errors. *** $p<0.01$, ** $p<0.05$, * $p<0.1$

the left displays results for the full data set. Again, our main finding is that there is a significant positive relationship between military expenditure and investment inflows. In contrast with our main finding, however, the results in column 2 show that the relationship is no longer valid if one limits the sample to countries in the Global North. The findings for the subset of countries belonging to the Global South are, however, significant. This indicates that the geoeconomic favoritism hypothesis is valid in countries belonging to the Global South. The crowding out hypothesis, however, applies to the advanced industrialized economies—including the United States. Increasing US military spending is unlikely to generate higher FDI inflows.

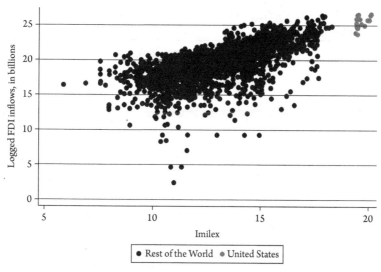

Figure 2.2 FDI Inflows and Military Spending (1990–2007)

In concluding the analysis section, some modesty is in order. It is worthwhile to delimit what can and cannot be established with the regression methodology at hand. We extensively control for a multitude of factors that predict FDI. Given the extended model specifications and robustness checks, we are confident that a marginal increase in military spending corresponds to marginal increase in inward FDI flows in the developing world. These data provide us insight on the role of military spending in attracting foreign investment during a period of US hegemony.

The scatter plot presented in Figure 2.2 above illustrates that the US was the clear frontrunner in both military expenditures and attracting foreign capital. Logged military expenditures are demonstrated on the x-axis whereas logged FDI is on the y-axis. What this shows is that the United States (denoted in gray) is an outlier. However, we cannot presume that the United States is an influential outlier from this illustration alone. One may be inclined to draw an imaginary line through the scatter plot, estimating a positive slope that cuts straight through the US data. This would be foolhardy since the illustrated correlation does not take into account several important controls, or make adjustments for country-fixed effects and time trends. This important work is done by the regression analysis. Table 2.3 shows us why an imagined line connecting the black dots to the gray dots in Figure 2.2 is misguided. The first two columns present the relationship between spending and investment for just North America. Despite having only thirty-five observations, the relationship between military spending and investment is flipped completely. Here we see that there is a negative historical correlation across increases in military spending and inward investment flows. Thus, we conclude that it doesn't pay to be the leader of the pack. Furthermore, removing the United States and Canada from the data set (columns three and four) does not alter the significance of our finding that military spending attracts investment into less dominant markets.

Table 2.3 Military Spending and FDI Split Analysis: North America and Excluding North America

FDI Source Sample Used	(PRS Group) North America	(World Bank) North America	(PRS Group) Excluding N. America	(World Bank) Excluding N. America
Log Military	–1.061**	–1.246**	0.265***	0.0842
Spending	(0.458)	(0.459)	(0.0787)	(0.107)
Log GDP per capita	5.434	5.64	1.899***	2.171***
	(3.584)	(3.73)	(0.267)	(0.353)
Log Population	–11.65	–11.24	1.643***	1.848**
	(10.17)	(10.84)	(0.547)	(0.829)
Cumulative BITS	0.0265	0.0242	0.0190***	0.0238***
	(0.0192)	(0.0185)	(0.00441)	(0.00546)
Corruption	–0.325	–0.333	0.00614	0.0392
	(0.284)	(0.297)	(0.05)	(0.0391)
Economic Risk	0.0573	0.0541	0.0217***	0.0296***
	(0.102)	(0.0958)	(0.0071)	(0.00906)
Foreign Debt	0.0288**	0.0343**	–0.00143	–0.00137
(% of GDP)	(0.0127)	(0.0125)	(0.000878)	(0.000801)
Budget Balance	0.158***	0.168***	0.00869*	0.00915
(% of GDP)	(0.0456)	(0.0455)	(0.00498)	(0.00591)
Energy Consumption	–1.18	–1.714	–0.385**	–0.44
(coal tons)	(1.887)	(1.777)	(0.166)	(0.355)
Law and Order	0.121	0.0163	0.049	0.0879
	(0.454)	(0.414)	(0.0355)	(0.053)
International Liquidity	0.125***	0.124***	–0.000481	–0.00391
	(0.029)	(0.029)	(0.00313)	(0.00356)
Constant	51.95	75.28	–52.11***	–36.06***
	(83.29)	(79.46)	(4.503)	(5.468)
Observations	35	35	1,325	1,351
Number of Groups	2	2	87	87

Notes: Estimation of pooled OLS/WLS and fixed effects (within) regression models with Driscoll and Kraay standard errors. *** $p<0.01$, ** $p<0.05$, * $p<0.1$

Our data set enables us to observe the post-Cold War correlation across military spending and inward FDI flow. Our finding that military spending only functions to attract investment in less developed nations is born from testing observational data. What we cannot infer from the regression analysis is how geoeconomic favoritism may or may not hold outside of the period of US hegemony.

CONCLUSION

A bevy of domestic and international factors have been used to explain the pattern of private capital flows—and yet the role of military spending has not been closely examined. Some argue that the greater a country's military capabilities, the more it acts as an attractor for private capital seeking security. Others argue that defense spending "crowds out" foreign direct investment by revealing a less friendly business environment for investors.

This paper empirically tests the effects of military spending on FDI inflows for the post-Cold War era on a broad-based set of economies. The relationship between military expenditures and inward FDI flows is nonlinear. While the geoeconomic favoritism hypothesis does seem to matter for some countries, it does not hold at all for the United States. Indeed, the United States is an empirical outlier that bolsters the crowding-out hypothesis.

Our explanation for this finding is that for the United States, its military hegemony means that the law of diminishing marginal returns on geoeconomic favoritism has kicked in with a vengeance. Simply put, if a country is viewed as secure from external attack and has a strong domestic rule of law, then investors will not view any increase in military capabilities as affecting political risk. Host economies that possess secure external and internal environments present little political risk to foreign investors. For these countries, greater military spending generates minimal new information. Rather investors will discount the utility of any increase in military capabilities from secure great powers. Since the United States possesses a strong domestic rule of law and is the only great power to possess regional hegemony, it gains little economic favor from boosting its defense capabilities any further.

Obviously, further research is needed. Nevertheless, if these preliminary findings hold, the policy implications of these results are clear. The arguments that defense hawks have made about the unexplored economic benefits of military hegemony have been vastly exaggerated. Indeed, it would seem that, if anything, greater levels of military spending generate deleterious economic effects. This is not to say that greater defense military capabilities might not be justified because of shifts in the global distribution of power or the external security environment. The idea that there are hidden economic benefits from military hegemony, however, is a chimera.

More significantly, as Kennedy (1987) and others have noted, military power flows from economic power at the hegemonic level. Military overstretch can, however, act as a drag on a great power's economy. The hawkish argument that American military spending should be "dynamically scored" to account for positive economic externalities is incorrect. Indeed the opposite would appear to be true. When applying the lessons from this analysis to debates about American grand strategy, the prescription seems clear. There is an overreliance on military preponderance that is badly misguided. The United States would profit more from investing in nonmilitary power resources than in more military assets.[6] An excessive reliance on military might, to the exclusion of other dimensions of power, will yield negative returns.

---

[6] One could argue that the recent increase in the US use of economic statecraft is evidence that the Obama administration is aware of this tradeoff (Drezner 2015).

APPENDIX 1: COUNTRY BALANCE COMPARISON OF WORLD BANK VERSUS PRS GROUP FDI DATA

Table 2.4 Balance Comparisons with Military Expenditure and FDI Measures (1985–2010)

PRS Countries	# Obs	World Bank	# Obs
Algeria	25	Algeria	16
Argentina	25	Angola	14
Australia	25	Argentina	18
Austria	25	Australia	16
Bangladesh	25	Austria	18
Bolivia	25	Azerbaijan	14
Bulgaria	25	Bangladesh	14
Canada	25	Belgium	18
Chile	25	Bolivia	17
China	25	Botswana	17
Colombia	25	Bulgaria	17
Congo	25	Cameroon	14
Costa Rica	25	Canada	17
Denmark	25	Chile	18
Dominican Republic	25	China	18
Ecuador	25	Colombia	18
Egypt	25	Congo	12
El Salvador	25	Costa Rica	18
Finland	25	Cuba	15
France	25	Czech Republic	15
Germany	25	Republic of the Congo	14
Ghana	25	Denmark	17
Greece	25	Dominican Republic	18
Guatemala	25	Ecuador	16
Guinea	25	Egypt	18
Honduras	25	El Salvador	15
Hungary	25	Finland	17
India	25	France	18
Iran	25	Gabon	8
Ireland	25	Germany	16
Israel	25	Ghana	18
Italy	25	Greece	18
Jamaica	25	Guatemala	18
Japan	25	Guinea	12
Kazakhstan	25	Guyana	13
Kenya	25	Haiti	6

(Continued)

Table 2.4 Continued

PRS Countries	# Obs	World Bank	# Obs
Kuwait	25	Honduras	18
Malaysia	25	Hungary	18
Mexico	25	India	17
Morocco	25	Indonesia	13
Myanmar	25	Iran	13
Netherlands	25	Ireland	15
New Zealand	25	Israel	18
Nicaragua	25	Italy	18
Nigeria	25	Jamaica	18
Norway	25	Japan	17
Oman	25	Kazakhstan	16
Pakistan	25	Kenya	16
Panama	25	Kuwait	11
Papua New Guinea	25	Libya	10
Paraguay	25	Malaysia	18
Peru	25	Mexico	18
Philippines	25	Morocco	18
Poland	25	Myanmar	18
Portugal	25	Netherlands	18
Romania	25	New Zealand	17
Singapore	25	Nicaragua	16
South Africa	25	Nigeria	18
South Korea	25	Norway	16
Spain	25	Oman	18
Sri Lanka	25	Pakistan	18
Sudan	25	Panama	18
Sweden	25	Papua New Guinea	17
Switzerland	25	Paraguay	18
Syria	25	Peru	17
Thailand	25	Philippines	18
Trinidad and Tobago	25	Poland	18
Tunisia	25	Portugal	18
Turkey	25	Romania	17
Ukraine	25	Saudi Arabia	10
United Arab Emirates	25	Singapore	18
United Kingdom	25	Slovakia	15
United States	25	South Africa	15
Uruguay	25	South Korea	18
Venezuela	25	Spain	18
Zambia	25	Sri Lanka	18

(Continued)

Table 2.4 Continued

PRS Countries	# Obs	World Bank	# Obs
Zimbabwe	25	Sudan	10
Total	1925	Sweden	17
		Switzerland	17
		Syria	15
		Thailand	18
		Trinidad and Tobago	16
		Tunisia	18
		Turkey	17
		Ukraine	16
		United Arab Emirates	12
		United Kingdom	18
		United States	18
		Uruguay	15
		Venezuela	17
		Zambia	17
		Zimbabwe	11
		Total	1,482

APPENDIX 2: MARGINS PLOT

Here we regressed our main model:

xtreg lfdi_WB lmilex lgdp ltpop bit_ corr_ riskr_ f_debt_gdp_ bb_gdp_ lpec law_o_int_liq_ i.year , fe

The margins plot shows the size of the ninety-five percent confidence interval around the linear prediction for logged foreign direct investment inflows at varying levels of logged military spending (lmilex). Note that the predictive band is wider at both relatively high and low levels of military spending. This indicates to us that the model fits more closely for military spending values that are closer to the mean.

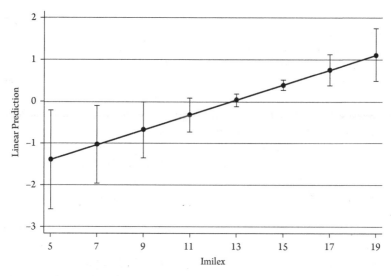

Figure 2.3 Predictive Margins with 95% CIs

APPENDIX 3: MILITARY SPENDING AND FDI INFLOWS

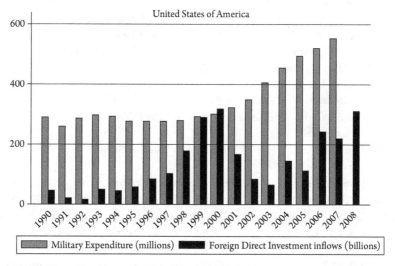

Figure 2.4 Military Spending and FDI Inflows (1990–2007)

REFERENCES

Acemoğlu, Daron, and James A. Robinson. 2012. *Why Nations Fail: The Origins of Power, Prosperity, and Poverty.* New York: Crown.

Asiedu, Elizabeth, and Donald Lien. 2011. "Democracy, Foreign Direct Investment and Natural Resources." *Journal of International Economics* 84 (1): 99–111.

Beckley, Michael. 2011–2012. "China's Century? Why America's Edge Will Endure," *International Security* 36 (3): 41–78.

Bergsten, C. Fred. 1975. *The Dilemmas of the Dollar: The Economics and Politics of United States International Monetary Policy.* New York: New York University Press.

Besley, Timothy, and Torsten Persson. 2007. "The Origins of State Capacity: Property Rights, Taxation, and Politics." NBER Working Paper, No. 13028, April.

Betts, Richard K. 2012. *American Force: Dangers, Delusions, and Dilemmas in National Security.* New York: Columbia University Press.

Biglaiser, Glen, and Karl DeRouen. 2007. "Following the Flag: Troop Deployment and US Foreign Direct Investment." *International Studies Quarterly* 51 (4): 835–854.

Blanton, Shannon Lindsey, and Robert G. Blanton. 2007. "What Attracts Foreign Investors? An Examination Of Human Rights and Foreign Direct Investment." *Journal of Politics* 69 (1): 143–155.

Brooks, Arthur, Edwin Fuelner, and William Kristol. 2010. "Peace Doesn't Keep Itself." *Wall Street Journal*, October 4.

Brooks, Stephen, G. John Ikenberry, and William C. Wohlforth. 2012–2013. "Don't Come Home, America: The Case against Retrenchment." *International Security* 37 (3): 7–51.

Brooks, Stephen G., and William C. Wohlforth. 2008. *World Out of Balance: International Relations and the Challenge of American Primacy.* Princeton, NJ: Princeton University Press.

Bueno de Mesquita, Bruce, Alistair Smith, Randolph M. Siverson, and James D. Morrow. 2003. *The Logic of Political Survival.* Cambridge: MIT Press, 2003.

Büthe, Tim, and Helen V. Milner. 2008. "The Politics of Foreign Direct Investment into Developing Countries: Increasing FDI Through International Trade Agreements?" *American Journal of Political Science* 52 (4): 741–762.

Cohen, Benjamin J. 1977. *Organizing the World's Money: The Political Economy of International Monetary Relations.* New York: Basic Books.

Drezner, Daniel W. 2013. "Military Primacy Doesn't Pay (Nearly As Much As You Think)." *International Security* 38 (1): 52–79.

Drezner, Daniel W. 2015. "Targeted Sanctions in a World of Global Finance." *International Interactions* 41 (4): 755–764.

Driscoll, John C., and Aart C. Kraay. 1998. "Consistent Covariance Matrix Estimation with Spatially Dependent Panel Data." *Review of Economics and Statistics* 80 (4): 549–560.

Frieden, Jeffry, and Lisa L. Martin. 2002. "International Political Economy: Global and Domestic Interactions." In *Political Science: The State of the Discipline*, edited by Ira Katznelson and Helen Milner, 118–146. New York: W.W. Norton.

Gerace, Michael. 2000. "State Interests, Military Power, and International Commerce: Some Cross-National Evidence." *Geopolitics* 5 (1): 101–124.

Gholz, Eugene, and Daryl Press. 2010. "Footprints in the Sand." *American Interest* 5 (4): 59–67.

Gholz, Eugene, Daryl G. Press, and Harvey M. Sapolsky. 1997. "Come Home, America: The Strategy of Restraint in the Face of Temptation." *International Security* 21 (4): 5–48.

Gilpin, Robert. 1975. *U.S. Power and the Multinational Corporation: The Political Economy of Foreign Direct Investment.* New York: Basic Books.

Gilpin, Robert. 1981. *War and Change in World Politics.* New York: Cambridge University Press.

Gowa, Joanne. 1994. *Allies, Adversaries, and International Trade.* Princeton, NJ: Princeton University Press.

Gowa, Joanne, and Edward Mansfield. 1993. "Power Politics and International Trade." *American Political Science Review* 87 (2): 408–420.

Gupta, Nandini and Xiaoyun Yu. 2007. "Does Money Follow the Flag?" Working Paper, available at the Social Science Research Network, http://ssrn.com/abstract=1316364.

Helleiner, Eric, and Jonathan Kirshner, eds. 2009. *The Future of the Dollar.* Ithaca, NY: Cornell University Press.

Ikenberry, G. John. 2011. *Liberal Leviathan: The Origins, Crisis, and Transformation of the American World Order.* Princeton, NJ: Princeton University Press.

Jensen, Nathan M. 2003. "Democratic Governance and Multinational Corporations: Political Regimes and Inflows of Foreign Direct Investment." *International Organization* 57 (3): 587–616.

Jensen, Nathan M. 2008. "Political Risk, Democratic Institutions, and Foreign Direct Investment." *Journal of Politics* 70 (4): 1040–1052.

Jervis, Robert. 1978. "Cooperation Under the Security Dilemma." *World Politics* 30 (2): 167–214.

Jervis, Robert. 1993. "International Primacy: Is the Game Worth the Candle?" *International Security* 17 (4): 52–67.

Kagan, Robert. 2012. *The World America Made.* New York: Knopf.

Kennedy, Paul. 1987. *The Rise and Fall of the Great Powers.* New York: Random House, 1987.

Kerner, Andrew. 2009. "Why Should I Believe You? The Costs and Consequences of Bilateral Investment Treaties." *International Studies Quarterly* 53 (1): 73–102.

Keshk, Omar, Brian Pollins, and Rafael Reuvney. 2004. "Trade Still Follows the Flag: The Primacy of Politics in a Simultaneous Model of Interdependence and Armed Conflict." *Journal of Politics* 66 (4): 1155–1179.

Kinda, Tidiane. 2010. "Investment Climate and FDI in Developing Countries: Firm-Level Evidence." *World Development* 38 (4): 498–513.

Kirshner, Jonathan. 2007. *Appeasing Bankers: Financial Caution on the Road to War.* Princeton, NJ: Princeton University Press.

Krasner, Stephen D. 1978. *Defending the National Interest.* Princeton, NJ: Princeton University Press.

Li, Quan, and Adam Resnick. 2003. "Reversal of Fortunes: Democratic Institutions and Foreign Direct Investment Inflows to Developing Countries." *International Organization* 57 (1): 175–212.

Li, Quan, and Tatiana Vashchilko. 2010. "Dyadic Military Conflict, Security Alliances, and Bilateral FDI Flows." *Journal of International Business Studies* 41 (5): 765–782.

Lipson, Charles. 1985. *Standing Guard: Protecting Foreign Capital in the Nineteenth and Twentieth Centuries.* Berkeley: University of California Press.

Maass, Richard W., Carla Norrlof, and Daniel W. Drezner. 2014. "The Profitability of Primacy." *International Security* 38 (4): 188–207.

MacDonald, Paul K., and Joseph M. Parent. 2011. "Graceful Decline? The Surprising Success of Great Power Retrenchment." *International Security* 35 (4): 7–44.

Mearsheimer, John J. 2011. "Imperial by Design." *National Interest* 111 (January/February): 16–34.

Modelski, George. 1978. "The Long Cycle of Global Politics and the Nation-State." *Comparative Studies in Society and History* 20 (2): 214–235.

Neumayer, Eric, and Laura Spess. 2005. "Do Bilateral Investment Treaties Increase Foreign Direct Investment to Developing Countries?" *World Development* 33 (10): 1567–1585.

Norrlof, Carla. 2010. *America's Global Advantage: US Hegemony and International Cooperation.* Cambridge, UK: Cambridge University Press.

North, Douglass, and Barry Weingast. 1989. "Constitutions and Commitment: The Evolution of Institutions Governing Public Choice in Seventeenth Century England." *Journal of Economic History* 49 (4): 803–832.

Oneal, John R. 1994. "The Affinity of Foreign Investors for Authoritarian Regimes." *Political Research Quarterly* 47 (3): 565–588.

Organski, A.F.K. 1969. *World Politics,* 2nd edition. New York: Knopf.

Papaioannou, Elias. 2009. "What Drives International Financial Flows? Politics, Institutions, and Other Determinants." *Journal of Development Economics* 88 (2): 269–281.

Pape, Robert A. 2009. "Empire Falls." *National Interest* 99 (January/February): 21–34.

Pollins, Brian. 1989a. "Does Trade Still Follow the Flag?" *American Political Science Review* 83 (2): 465–480.

Pollins, Brian. 1989b. "Conflict, Cooperation, and Commerce: The Effect of International Political Interactions on Bilateral Trade Flows." *American Journal of Political Science* 33 (3): 737–761.

Posen, Barry. 2014. *Restraint: A New Foundation for U.S. Grand Strategy.* Ithaca, NY: Cornell University Press.

Preble, Christopher A. 2009. *The Power Problem: How American Military Dominance Makes Us Less Safe, Less Prosperous, and Less Free.* Ithaca, NY: Cornell University Press.

Schneider, Friedrich, and Bruno S. Frey. 1985. "Economic and Political Determinants of Foreign Direct Investment." *World Development* 13 (2): 161–175.

Schulz, Heiner. 2009. "Political Institutions and Foreign Direct Investment in Developing Countries: Does the Sector Matter?" *Available at SSRN 1403983.* http://papers.ssrn.com/sol3/papers.cfm?abstract_id=1403983.

Schultz, Kenneth, and Barry Weingast. 2003. "The Democratic Advantage: Institutional Foundations of Financial Power in International Competition." *International Organization* 57 (1): 3–42.

Tomz, Michael. 2007. *Reputation and International Cooperation: Sovereign Debt across Three Centuries.* Princeton, NJ: Princeton University Press.

Vernon, Raymond. 1971. *Sovereignty at Bay.* New York: Basic Books.

Viner, Jacob. 1948. "Power versus Plenty as Objectives of Foreign Policy in the Seventeenth and Eighteenth Centuries." *World Politics* 1 (1): 1–29.

Walt, Stephen M. 2006. *Taming American Power: The Global Response to U.S. Primacy.* New York: W.W. Norton.

3

PRESERVING NATIONAL STRENGTH IN A PERIOD OF FISCAL RESTRAINT

Cindy Williams

INTRODUCTION

The US government faces a challenging fiscal outlook. Debt held by the public in 2014 was larger as a share of the economy than at any time in US history, with the exception of seven years during and after World War II. Between 2011 and 2013, national leaders took steps to rein in future debt through budget cutbacks and tax increases. Absent further policy changes, however, that debt will mount within a few decades to levels never before experienced by this country.[1] The consequences for the American economy and for the nation's place in the world could be severe.

If the President and Congress cannot agree within a few years to additional debt control measures, then the choices available to future policymakers as national security challenges emerge will be increasingly constrained. As a result, the growing debt will have serious implications for the military and political strategies discussed in other chapters of this book. On the other hand, if policymakers do take the fiscal measures that are needed during the next few years to hold the debt in check, those actions will in themselves put limits on national strategic choices.

National defense constitutes one of the largest elements of US federal expenditure, in 2013 second only to Social Security.[2] Among the programs that leaders can control through annual budget requests and Congressional appropriations, defense represents the single largest expenditure, comprising more than one-half of appropriated federal funding in 2013.[3]

---

[1] Congressional Budget Office, *The 2013 Long-Term Budget Outlook* (CBO: Washington, DC: September 2013), p. 115.

[2] In the federal budget, the national defense category includes spending for the Department of Defense, programs related to nuclear weapons in the Department of Energy, and national defense programs in other federal agencies, particularly the FBI. Unless otherwise stated, all years discussed in this chapter are fiscal years.

[3] US Office of Management and Budget, "Fiscal Year 2014 Mid-Session Review," July 8, 2013, Table S-4. Expenditures controlled through annual appropriations are termed "discretionary." Other programs, termed "mandatory," receive funding in accordance with extant law; examples include Social Security, Medicare, and pension programs for federal workers. In 2013, discretionary programs comprised about thirty-five percent of total federal spending. Mandatory spending, including interest payments on the federal debt, accounted for the other sixty-five percent. National defense made up some fifty-two percent of discretionary expenditures.

As such, defense is deeply intertwined with the nation's fiscal and economic future. Because defense is such a big player in the federal budget, it is an important contributor to the growing federal debt. In fact, at least one-quarter of the $12 trillion federal debt held by the public in 2013 can be attributed to the rise in defense spending between 2001 and 2013.[4]

On the other hand, the military is an important player in the overall economy. The Department of Defense is the largest employer in the United States, with about 1.3 million active-duty service members, 800,000 uniformed members of the National Guard and Reserves, and nearly 800,000 civilian employees. It also supports contracts worth hundreds of billions of dollars annually. Moreover, the linkage between defense spending and the economy is not just one-way. In the future, the federal fiscal situation and the state of the economy will be important factors in decisions about what the nation can afford to spend on defense, and thus on the size and capabilities of the armed forces and the strategy they can support.

This chapter examines the nation's fiscal challenges and considers what part the defense establishment might be asked to play in addressing them. It explores the potential cutbacks to defense budgets and what they might mean for future national security strategy and for the military's forces and capabilities. The chapter finds that keeping the economy strong for the future will require improving the government's fiscal outlook, which in turn is likely to necessitate significant cutbacks in defense spending. To deal with the likely budget reductions, national leaders will face important, strategic choices about the future size and shape of the armed forces, their equipment, and the way they train and operate.

The nonwar portion of the national defense budget peaked in 2010 at about $580 billion (in fiscal year 2013 dollars).[5] The Budget Control Act (BCA) of 2011 mandates a reduction of that budget to roughly $500 billion—about fourteen percent below its peak level—for the years between 2014 and 2021. The cuts dictated by the BCA fall short of bringing anticipated future deficits down to sustainable levels, however. As a result, nonwar defense budgets may ultimately shrink even further than the levels set under that law—even if the law is ultimately overturned.[6] Lowering the defense budget to about $470 billion a year—a real decline of about twenty percent relative to the 2010 peak—would be consistent both with the magnitude of the nation's structural fiscal problems and with historical reductions to US defense spending as wars end.[7]

---

[4] The $1.4 trillion cost of the wars in Iraq and Afghanistan is widely reported. Nonwar spending above the 2001 level added about another $1.4 trillion. Since taxes did not rise to pay for the wars or the added nonwar military spending, defense contributed $2.8 trillion plus accumulated interest to the debt.

[5] Unless otherwise stated, all spending and revenue figures discussed in this chapter are adjusted for inflation to fiscal year (FY) 2013 dollars.

[6] Since the Act took effect, Congress has granted partial reprieves from its limits through a series of appropriations, but it has not overturned the requirement to reduce budgets in accordance with the BCA in later years.

[7] Including the costs of the wars in Iraq and Afghanistan brings the 2010 figure to about $749 billion. Assuming no war costs for the future, the $470 billion figure represents a thirty-seven

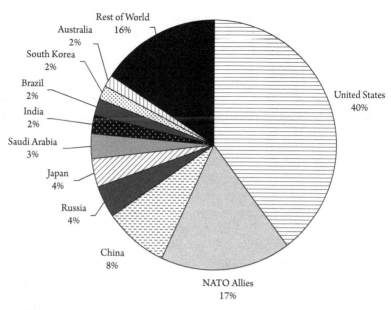

Figure 3.1 World Defense Expenditures in 2012

The United States lays out about forty percent of all the world's military expenditures (see Figure 3.1). At \$470 billion, the US military would still outspend every other military in the world. The armed forces would be smaller than today's, but if the reductions are handled sensibly, the US military will remain by far the strongest, best equipped, best trained, and best maintained in the world.

US nonwar defense spending rose by about fifty percent in real terms from its post–Cold War low in FY 1998 to its peak in FY 2010. Part of the reason for that rise was the rapid growth in spending for pay and benefits for military and civilian personnel and military retirees. Absent policy reform, this internal cost growth will crowd out the funds available for force structure, equipment modernization, and training. This chapter considers two policy changes that would reduce the anticipated rise in the costs of pay and benefits.

Even if the department's internal costs can be brought under control, likely budget cuts will require defense leaders to downsize the force and reexamine plans for new equipment. The changes will restrict the missions that the armed forces are able to undertake at low or moderate levels of risk.

A more restrained mission set is arguably in order in any case. After the Cold War ended, policymakers on both sides of the political aisle embraced an increasingly expansive collection of aims for US foreign and security policy. Beginning in the late 1990s, they gave virtually no thought to cost. In addition to preparing for high-intensity warfare in major military operations, the aims included stopping the

percent drop in spending. In the aftermath of World War II, the military budget plummeted to a fraction of its wartime high. It dropped nearly forty percent following the Korean War, thirty percent after Vietnam, and thirty-three percent as the Cold War ended.

spread of nuclear weapons, ending civil wars in distant lands, deposing dictators, conducting stability and counterinsurgency operations, and building market economies and democratic institutions.

Events of the past fifteen years provide a glimpse of the high costs of those expansive aims. The budgetary costs attributed to the wars in Afghanistan and Iraq exceed $1.4 trillion. More than 6,700 US troops have died, and tens of thousands have suffered combat injuries. By some estimates, hundreds of thousands have come home with brain injuries or posttraumatic stress disorder. Many service members have deployed multiple times and spent years away from their families.

Expansive aims have also created problems for the military as an institution. The wars in Iraq and Afghanistan took a toll on the numbers and quality of recruits for the army's active and reserve components.[8] Multiple long deployments also eroded retention.[9] Most fundamentally, a dozen years of training for stabilization, reconstruction, and counterinsurgency operations have left in doubt the army's readiness for high-end maneuver warfare.[10]

The White House and Department of Defense outlined their most recent national security strategy in January 2012.[11] The strategy calls for reduced emphasis on prolonged stability and counterinsurgency operations and increased attention to Asia and the Pacific. The 2012 update was somewhat more selective in its aims than previous post–Cold War strategy documents. Nevertheless, the update still called on US armed forces to underwrite a "rules-based" international order, to "confront and defeat aggression anywhere in the world," and to broaden already extensive military-to-military partnerships with other nations.[12]

In July 2013, Secretary of Defense Chuck Hagel indicated that the January 2012 strategy was unaffordable under the spending limits of the Budget Control Act, even if Congress helps the department to bring its personnel costs under control.[13] A more restrained strategy is in order.

---

[8] Beth Asch, Paul Heaton, James Hosek, et al., *Cash Incentives and Military Enlistment, Attrition, and Reenlistment* (Santa Monica, CA: RAND, 2010), pp. 24–26.

[9] James Hosek and Francisco Martorell, "How Have Deployments during the War on Terrorism Affected Reenlistment?" (Santa Monica, CA: RAND, 2009).

[10] "To again become masters of combined arms maneuvers will require revitalizing home-station training, modernizing the Army's training centers, and preparing our soldiers to confront enemies equipped with the most advanced weaponry" (Secretary of Defense Leon Panetta as quoted in Chris Carroll, "Army Must Maintain Conventional Warfare Skills, Panetta Says," *Stars and Stripes*, October 12, 2011; see also Gian P. Gentile, "The Death of the Armor Corps," *Small Wars Journal*, April 17, 2010.

[11] The White House and Department of Defense, "Sustaining Global Leadership: Priorities for the 21st Century" (January 2012).

[12] Ibid.

[13] "Sequester-level cuts would break some parts of the strategy, no matter how the cuts were made," Secretary of Defense Chuck Hagel and Vice Chairman of the Joint Chiefs of Staff Admiral James A. Winnefeld, "Department of Defense Briefing by Secretary Hagel and Adm. Winnefeld From the Pentagon," July 31, 2013.

A strategy of restraint seems ideally suited to the nation's fiscal picture. Such a strategy would bring an end to efforts to reform the rest of the world's governments in favor of protecting a narrower range of US national security interests—including American safety, sovereignty, territorial integrity, and relative power position. Restraint means that the United States stays its hand from intervening in the internal affairs of other countries; that it goes to war only when necessary to serve its own security interests; and that allies provide more for their own security.[14] Such a strategy is well aligned with the smaller US forces this chapter considers.

A strategy of restraint is not a strategy of military weakness. In fact, restraint today can allow the United States to marshal its economic resources for the future. It can give the armed forces the time they need to regroup and rebuild strength for likely future missions while focusing today's training on a leaner menu of crucial tasks. With smart choices, the United States can retain a very strong military, fully ready, equipped, and capable of succeeding in the most important missions, with budgets significantly smaller than today's.

As they make those choices, leaders face crucial decisions in how the defense budget is allocated among the military services; between the size of the military and the way it is equipped; and between the size of the force that can be brought to bear for immediate operations and the staying power the force might have in the event of longer wars or wars where the nation has more time to prepare. To gain insight into those choices, this chapter explores three options:

- Proportional cuts: Reduce the budget of each military department by the same fraction;
- A rebalanced force: Emphasize forces for rebalancing toward Asia and the Pacific;
- Reversible cuts: Preserve expandability and rotational capacity by adjusting the peacetime staffing levels of some units and retuning the mix between active-duty and reserve forces.

Each of these alternatives has its own merits.

The chapter is organized as follows: The next section briefly reviews the part defense might play in coming to grips with the nation's fiscal challenges. The chapter continues with a look at rising pay and benefits and two remedies for reining them in. Then three sections look at the three options for downsizing the military. The chapter ends with a brief concluding section.

COMING TO GRIPS WITH THE NATION'S FISCAL CHALLENGES

In September 2011, Chairman of the Joint Chiefs of Staff Admiral Mike Mullen cited the growing federal debt as "the biggest threat" to US national security.[15]

---

[14] See, for example, Barry R. Posen, "Pull Back: The Case for a Less Activist Foreign Policy," *Foreign Affairs* 92, no. 1 (January/February 2013): 116–129.

[15] Army Sgt. 1st Class Tyrone C. Marshall Jr., "Debt is Biggest Threat to National Security, Chairman Says," *American Forces Press Service*, September 22, 2011.

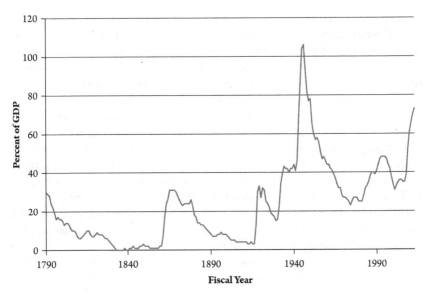

Figure 3.2 US Federal Debt Held by the Public, 1790 to 2013

Indeed, the expanding debt has important implications for the nation's economy, and the economy is the engine of American power.

In 2013, US debt held by the public was about seventy-three percent of gross domestic product (GDP), larger as a share of the economy than at any point in US history with the exception of a few years during and after World War II (see Figure 3.2).[16] Debt grew rapidly between 2008 and 2013, in part because of the economic downturn that began in 2008. Economic slowdowns typically make it harder to balance the budget; tax revenues shrink as unemployment rises, at the same time that demands for federal benefits increase.

Not all of the federal debt can be blamed on the weak economy, however. Instead, much of the debt in 2013 is related to a structural imbalance between federal spending and revenues. Since the late 1960s, federal revenues have failed to keep up with spending in most years (see Figure 3.3). On average between 1973 and 2012, tax

[16] Congressional Budget Office, *The 2013 Long-Term Budget Outlook* (Washington, DC: CBO, September 2013), Fig. 1-1. Debt was higher than the 2013 level between 1944 and 1950. The federal government draws a distinction between debt held by the public—virtually any entity other than the government itself—and debt held by government accounts, largely what the US government owes itself as a result of borrowing from trust funds like the ones for Social Security. Debt held by the public is typically of more interest to economists, but total debt (which includes both debt held by the public and debt held by government accounts) is the measure subject to the congressionally mandated debt ceiling. In 2013, debt subject to the ceiling is expected to reach about $17 trillion, about the same size as the GDP. Unless otherwise stated, GDP figures in this chapter reflect the technical changes announced by the Bureau of Economic Analysis of the US Department of Commerce on July 31, 2013. Those changes in the way GDP is calculated make historical and current GDPs appear somewhat higher than previous calculations. As a result, measures expressed as shares of GDP look a bit lower.

receipts lagged outlays by about three percent of GDP.[17] Absent fundamental policy changes, those structural fiscal imbalances will persist even as the economy and the employment picture improve.

The future size of the debt will depend on the state of the economy; demands on social programs like Social Security, Medicare, and Medicaid; and the laws, including annual appropriations, that govern spending and taxes.[18] It will also depend on the extent to which the debt itself poses problems for the economy.

A large debt that grows year after year poses important fiscal and economic risks. For example, creditors concerned about the ability of the federal government to make good on the growing debt will likely charge higher interest rates on the money they lend; just keeping up with interest payments would become increasingly difficult for the Treasury. There is also a risk that burgeoning debt will crowd out productive investment and thus reduce productivity. High interest rates and low productivity create a drag on the economy, generating a feedback cycle in which the debt worsens the economy and the less productive economy worsens the debt. Moreover, policymakers faced with a future economic or financial crisis will likely find it increasingly difficult to adopt measures like fiscal stimulus or bailouts to help the nation weather the storm.[19]

The BCA's spending cutbacks and the increased taxes that Congress enacted in January 2013 are far from sufficient to restrain the federal debt at its current level as a share of GDP or return it to historical levels. The Congressional Budget Office (CBO) runs simulations to explore how spending, revenues, and debt might unfold over multiple generations under a variety of assumptions.[20] One such simulation assumes that tax and spending laws remain essentially as they are in 2013 for decades.[21] For example, the scenario supposes that the budget cuts mandated by the BCA remain in effect for about a decade; Medicare payment rates to physicians decline significantly as currently scheduled, beginning in January 2014; and some seventy-five tax breaks that are set to expire will indeed expire on schedule.[22]

Under that scenario, expenditures will decline for a few years from the 20.8 percent share of GDP they hold in 2013.[23] Beginning around 2019, however, federal spending will outstrip economic growth for decades, fueled by the rising costs of federal health programs and, to a lesser extent, Social Security, as increasing numbers of baby boomers retire and the underlying costs of healthcare grow faster than

[17] Congressional Budget Office, *The 2013 Long-Term Budget Outlook* (Washington, DC: CBO, September 2013), p. 22.

[18] While the size of the debt depends on the state of the economy, it also affects the economy, as discussed later in this chapter.

[19] Congressional Budget Office, *The 2012 Long-Term Budget Outlook* (June 2012), p. 30; Cindy Williams, "The Future Affordability of US National Security," The Tobin Project, November 2011.

[20] The most recent of these is Congressional Budget Office, *The 2013 Long-Term Budget Outlook* (Washington, DC: CBO, September 2013).

[21] Ibid.

[22] Ibid., p. 85.

[23] Ibid., p. 22.

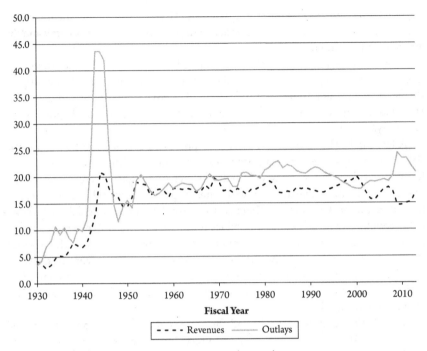

Figure 3.3 Revenues and Outlays as a Share of GDP (Percent)

the economy.[24] By 2038 spending will climb above twenty-six percent of GDP—a level previously reached only for three years during World War II.[25] Revenues will not keep up with the rise in spending, as shown in Figure 3.3. As a result, the interest payments the government owes its creditors will rise every year, thus further increasing the outlay total.

As a result, even if there is no negative feedback between the rising debt and economic performance, new deficits will accumulate every year, pushing the debt from seventy-three percent of GDP in 2013 to one hundred percent of GDP by 2038.[26] If likely negative feedback is considered in the simulation, debt will grow to 109 percent of GDP by 2038—about the same level as its World War II peak. Unless things change, the debt will continue to climb unsustainably for decades after that, reaching two hundred percent of GDP by 2075 if negative economic feedback is not a factor and a larger multiple of GDP if feedback is included.[27]

[24] Ibid., p. 3.

[25] Ibid., p. 22.

[26] Ibid., p. 27

[27] The debt picture could be much worse. In an alternative scenario, CBO assumes that Congress overturns the BCA's remaining budget cuts; that consistent with past practice, Medicare's payment rates are spared from planned reductions; and that lawmakers ultimately extend the seventy-five tax breaks now scheduled to expire. Under those circumstances, and including economic feedback, debt held by the public will grow to 190 percent of GDP by 2038, far higher than ever before experienced by the United States. Congressional Budget Office, *The 2013 Long-Term Budget Outlook* (Washington, DC: CBO, September 2013), p. 114.

Putting the federal government on a sustainable fiscal path will require an increase in taxation, a reduction in anticipated spending, or some combination of the two. The sooner those changes occur, the less money will have to move from one side of the fiscal ledger to another. CBO calculates that if current laws remain in place and economic feedback is not a factor, then policymakers must shift 0.8 percent of GDP out of spending or into taxes by 2015 to hold debt at its 2013 level (seventy-three percent of GDP) for 25 years.[28] If leaders wait until 2017 to make the fiscal adjustments, then one percent of GDP must be shifted from one side of the books to the other.[29] Restoring debt to the thirty-eight percent share of the economy it held before the financial crisis of 2008 would require a shift of at least two percent of GDP, depending on how soon the changes take place.[30]

It is hard to say what share of any new budget cuts might be taken from defense. In the past, defense has been a major bill payer for deficit reduction efforts, particularly when those efforts coincide with the ending of wars. Moreover, even the non-war portion of the defense budget grew rapidly between 1998 and 2010, making defense a prime target for cuts. The BCA cutbacks, while significant, only return nonwar defense budgets in real terms to their 2007 level (see Figure 3.4).

Two plausible formulas for keeping the debt near its 2013 level as a share of GDP lead to about the same result: The defense budget probably faces additional reductions beyond those of the BCA.

One formula for holding the debt in check for twenty-five years would be to increase taxes enough to take care of one-quarter of the fiscal problem, rein in entitlement spending to deal with another quarter, and deal with the remaining one-half of the problem through cutbacks to appropriated programs. Such a formula echoes the promises of some leaders to cut spending by three dollars for every dollar in raised taxes. A second plausible formula reflects the "no-new-taxes" promise to which some other political leaders adhere. Under this principle, the full burden of fiscal improvement would fall on spending cuts, which would be spread proportionately among the government's major budget functions. Under the assumption that policymakers wait to act until 2017, either formula would reduce the nonwar defense budget to about $470 billion (in 2013 dollars), about $20 billion below the BCA's limit for 2014, and about $30 billion below the Act's average limit on that budget over the decade.[31]

Because the debt in 2013 is near an all-time high, however, policymakers may ultimately want to reduce it below the current level. Returning debt held by the public to the thirty-eight percent of GDP it held before the financial

---

[28] Ibid., p. 10.

[29] Author's estimate based on Congressional Budget Office, *The 2013 Long-Term Budget Outlook* (Washington, DC: CBO, September 2013), p. 12.

[30] Ibid., p. 11.

[31] Author's calculation based on Congressional Budget Office, *The 2013 Long-Term Budget Outlook* (Washington, DC: CBO, September 2013), pp. 11–12. CBO assumes that war spending continues at about its 2013 level for decades. The calculation here assumes that war spending can be reduced to zero and held there, and that the eighty billion dollars CBO counts toward the wars is treated as savings across the entire non-interest-related budget.

crisis of 2008 would require significantly more aggressive action. Using either of the two formulas described here to allocate the needed fiscal shift among the various contributors to the debt, budgets for national defense might fall to about $430 billion, some $60 billion lower than the 2014 cap set on defense by the BCA.

Given the nation's fiscal challenges, either of these paths for defense spending seems plausible. The remainder of this chapter considers how national leaders could shape and manage a national defense budget of $470 billion, consistent with holding debt at today's level as a share of GDP. At that level, defense spending would be about thirty-eight percent lower than at its 2010 peak (including war funds) and nearly twenty percent lower than the 2010 nonwar budget. In real terms, the budget would be about the same as it was in 2003 (see Figure 3.4).

Unfortunately, the 2003 defense budget will no longer buy the military forces and capabilities of 2003. This is because in certain categories of the budget, costs grew significantly faster than inflation between 2003 and 2013. This internal cost growth is particularly severe in two areas: military healthcare and the pay and benefits of military and civilian personnel. Moreover, the costs in those areas continue to grow. Looking to the future, even if the budget remained constant in real terms over the coming decade, forces would still have to be cut significantly just to make room for the cost growth above inflation. Experts have offered numerous ways of achieving control over costs in those areas.

The next section of this chapter looks at two examples.

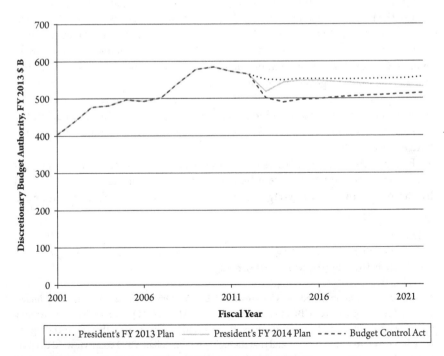

Figure 3.4 Nonwar Budgets for National Defense under Three Plans

DEFENSE SPENDING FOR HEALTHCARE AND PAY

Department of Defense spending for pay and benefits grew dramatically between 1998 and 2013. Absent policy changes, continued cost growth in those areas will crowd out spending for force structure, equipment modernization, and readiness in the coming years. This section recommends two illustrative policy changes that would slow that anticipated growth. The first would adjust the cost-sharing arrangements for military healthcare, particularly for retirees. The second would hold the pay raises for service members and federal civilians to the level of inflation across the economy for four years.

Taken together, the recommended changes would avert an average of $20 billion in anticipated cost growth annually over the coming decade. Those savings are enough to keep at least two active-duty army brigades, twelve navy ships, and three air force fighter squadrons from the chopping block. Absent these and other personnel reforms, the Department of Defense will find itself having to reduce the armed forces much more than the amounts discussed in the next section of this chapter.

The following subsections look at healthcare costs and pay in turn.

Adjust the Cost-Sharing Arrangements for Military Healthcare

Healthcare for service members, their families, and military retirees is the fastest-growing element of the defense budget. Spending in this category more than doubled in real terms between 1998 and 2013. Absent significant policy changes, it will expand another forty-three percent beyond inflation by 2021, the last year covered by the BCA.[32] Assuming the BCA remains in place, military healthcare costs alone will at that point comprise about sixteen percent of the total budget for the Department of Defense. If defense budgets were then held constant for a decade after 2021, military healthcare would consume about one-fifth of the department's budget by the end of the period.[33] At some point there will be no money left for the pointy end of the spear.

That military healthcare costs have grown should come as no surprise; after all, healthcare costs have grown rapidly across the United States. But the Defense Department's healthcare bills have grown significantly faster than those in the civilian world, for two reasons. The first is a broad expansion of the healthcare entitlement for military retirees and their spouses who are old enough to qualify for Medicare (typically sixty-five years old). In 2000, Congress authorized the Tricare-for-Life program, which provides wraparound coverage for those retirees and their Medicare-eligible dependent family members and survivors. The Department of Defense established an accrual account to recognize the future costs of those benefits for service members currently in the force. In 2013, that account cost more than $8 billion.

---

[32] Congressional Budget Office, *Long-Term Implications of the 2013 Future Years Defense Program* (July 2012), p. 21.
[33] Ibid.

The second reason for growing costs is that the cost-sharing arrangements for Department of Defense healthcare plans are much more favorable to retirees' pocketbooks than those of other plans available to them. For military retirees over sixty-five, Tricare-for-Life charges no premium; for most medical services, it also charges no deductibles or copayments. As a result, almost all Medicare-eligible retirees use the military coverage.

Military retirees under age sixty-five qualify for a different program, called Tricare. When the Department of Defense established Tricare in the mid-1990s, a working-age retiree typically paid about twenty-seven percent of the total cost of the plan through premiums, deductibles, and copays.[34] Between then and 2012, Tricare's costs to beneficiaries were generally not adjusted for inflation. Recently, Congress has allowed adjustments that reflect the annual change in the overall cost of living. But premiums, deductibles, and copays were never adjusted to reflect the much faster inflation in the medical sector or even to recognize the cumulative rise in the cost of living over nearly two decades. By 2012, working-age retirees bore only eleven percent of the costs of their Tricare plans.[35]

Over the same period, the costs borne by civilians under nonmilitary employer-based policies grew rapidly. The result is that by 2012, Tricare costs paid by a typical working-age military retiree were less than twenty percent of what he or she would pay under a civilian employer's plan.[36]

More than seventy percent of working-age military retirees can get medical insurance through an employer or professional organization.[37] As the gap between Tricare and private-sector user fees widened, however, the government plan attracted increasing numbers of retirees who formerly chose that other coverage. Healthcare costs previously borne by retirees' postmilitary employers or their spouses' employers were transferred wholesale to the Department of Defense.

Since 2006, the Department of Defense has repeatedly asked Congress to adjust the increasingly skewed cost-sharing arrangements for military retirees. With the exception of small adjustments to reflect recent changes in the cost of living, Congress rejected the proposals. In 2014, the department reiterated its request for more sensible cost-sharing, including: impose premiums on new beneficiaries of Tricare-for-Life; add premiums for parts of Tricare that previously did not require them; gradually adjust Tricare premiums to reflect nearly two decades of medical-sector inflation; increase deductibles; and raise copays for prescription drugs and some medical services.[38] The request specifically exempts from higher payments the

[34] Carla Tighe Murray, "Approaches to Reduce Federal Spending on the Defense Health System," Presentation at the Western Economic Association Conference, July 1, 2013 (Washington, DC: CBO).

[35] Ibid.

[36] Ibid.

[37] Louis T. Mariano, Sheila Nataraj Kirby, Christine Eibner, and Scott Naftel, *Civilian Health Insurance Options of Military Retirees* (Santa Monica, CA: RAND, 2007), p. xv.

[38] United States Department of Defense, Office of the Under Secretary of Defense (Comptroller)/ Chief Financial Officer, *Overview, Fiscal Year 2014 Budget Request* (April 2013), pp. 5–4 to 5–6.

survivors of service members who died on active duty, as well as service members who retired for medical reasons.[39]

Making those changes would reduce retirees' incentives to rely on the military plan when other plans are available and would save an average of about $10 billion annually over the coming decade.[40] Unfortunately, as in previous years, Congress is poised to reject most of the department's suggestions.

Another alternative is to require retirees who have other employer-based options to take them instead of turning to Tricare. The department signaled in its 2013 Strategic Choices and Management Review that it is considering that.[41] Indeed, the department would save money even by paying retirees to shift to other plans.

The politics behind lawmakers' reluctance to change the healthcare cost-sharing arrangements for military retirees are complicated. Part of the reluctance stems from concerns about failing to provide for those who served and sacrificed for their country—particularly in a time of war. But the reluctance also reflects in no small measure the persistent and coordinated prodding by associations that represent military retirees, families, and veterans. Those associations work together through The Military Coalition to orchestrate a unified legislative agenda, coordinate testimony before Congress, suppress public dissent, shame policymakers who promote changes to the cost-sharing equation, and persuade every member of Congress to adhere to the status quo.[42]

Limit Pay Raises for Service Members and Federal Civilians for Four Years

Between 1998 and 2013, military basic pay grew more than sixty percent faster than the consumer price index and significantly faster than pay in the private sector.[43] When the cash allowances provided to military personnel to offset the costs of food and housing are included in the calculation, the rise in military cash pay was even more dramatic. Pay for federal civilian workers—including nearly 800,000 civilians

---

[39] Office of the Under Secretary of Defense (Comptroller)/Chief Financial Officer, *Overview, Fiscal Year 2014 Budget Request* (April 2013), pp. 5–4 to 520136.

[40] Congressional Budget Office, *Long-Term Implications of the 2013 Future Years Defense Program* (July 2012), p. 21.

[41] Deputy Secretary of Defense Ashton B. Carter and Vice Chairman of the Joint Chiefs of Staff James A. Winnefeld, Jr., Prepared Testimony, House Armed Services Committee, August 1, 2013.

[42] For a list of organizations the coalition includes and an example of coordinated testimony, see "Statement of the Military Coalition (TMC) before the Senate Armed Services Subcommittee on Personnel concerning Military Personnel, Compensation, and Healthcare Matters," March 26, 2014, p. 1. Accessed on April 13, 2016, at http://www.armed-services.senate.gov/imo/media/doc/TMC_Testimony_03-26-14.pdf. See also Arnold L. Punaro, "Leadership and Perseverance: Overcoming the Barriers to Change," in Cindy Williams ed., *Filling the Ranks: Transforming the U.S. Military Personnel System* (Cambridge, MA: The MIT Press, 2004), pp. 265–288.

[43] Author's calculation based on Bureau of Labor Statistics data and Department of Defense, "National Defense Budget Estimates for FY 2013" (March 2012), chapter 5.

who work in the Department of Defense—grew almost as rapidly through 2009.[44] As a result, both uniformed service members and defense civilian workers today are substantially better off relative to their counterparts in the private sector than they were in 1998.

Men and women in uniform face risks, hardships, and sacrifices unlike those faced by civilians, and they deserve to be paid well. In fact, US service members are extremely well paid in comparison to their civilian counterparts.

The British government uses a concept called the X-factor, which is meant to recognize explicitly the net differences between military and civilian life. An Armed Forces' Pay Review Body estimates the X-factor each year. Military pay is generally set to equal the average pay of comparable civilians, plus the X-factor. During the past two decades, British estimates of the X-factor ranged between eleven and fifteen percent.[45]

In the United States, the pay differential between service members and civilians is much greater than that. Although the United States does not calculate an X-factor, it is possible to impute one by comparing service members' cash pay to that of comparable civilians. That comparison reveals an implicit US X-factor of ninety to one hundred percent for enlisted personnel and seventy to ninety percent for officers.[46] In other words, military pay is on average between seventy percent higher and twice as high as that of civilians with similar levels of education and experience.

That comparison looks at average salaries. A different comparison, used by defense planners for several decades, looks instead at wage percentiles. In the past, the Department of Defense aimed to keep military pay near the seventy-fifth percentile for civilians with comparable levels of education and experience. For the enlisted force, the civilian comparison group was high school diploma graduates. For officers, it was holders of college degrees. Today, the military pay advantage far exceeds that aspiration. Indeed, the average pay of enlisted members—most of whom have high school educations but little college—now falls at the ninetieth percentile of wages for civilians who hold a high school diploma or have an associate's degree.[47] Average officer pay stands at the eighty-third percentile of wages for civilians with bachelors or advanced degrees.[48] US men and women are very well paid in comparison with their civilian counterparts.

---

[44] In 2010, the civilian pay raise was smaller than that of the military. Civilian pay was frozen at the 2010 level between 2011 and 2013.

[45] See for example Armed Forces' Pay Review Body, "Forty-Second Report 2013" (London: Crown Copyright, March 2013).

[46] Author's calculations, based on Department of Defense, "Report of the Eleventh Quadrennial Review of Military Compensation," June 2012, pp. 27–29. Pay here is so-called regular military compensation, which includes basic pay, allowances for housing and food, and the tax advantage that accrues because the housing and food allowances are not taxable. The comparison is between enlisted personnel and civilian high-school diploma graduates, and between officers and civilian holders of bachelors' degrees.

[47] Pay here means regular military compensation. Department of Defense, "Report of the Eleventh Quadrennial Review of Military Compensation," June 2012, p. xvii.

[48] Ibid.

Good pay is important to the recruitment and retention of high-quality person-nel—both military and civilian. At the peak of the wars in Iraq and Afghanistan, military recruitment was difficult. As of this writing, however, military recruiters are in the position of turning away good candidates for service. On the civilian side, hiring for the Department of Defense is nearly frozen; even employees brought in under the prestigious Presidential Management Fellowship program are not being offered employment beyond the two years of their fellowships. Retention is also strong for both military personnel and civilians.

In the current environment, slowing down military pay growth and limiting civilian raises for a period of several years makes sense. By limiting the annual pay raise for service members and civilians to the rate of inflation across the GDP for four years, the Department of Defense could save an average of ten billion dollars a year between FY 2014 and FY 2023.[49]

The Department of Defense proposed such limits on military and civilian pay raises in its 2014 budget request. Opposition from the military associations was swift and fierce, however. As of this writing, both chambers of Congress have rejected the proposal. If Congress continues to block these and similar reforms, the nation's military capability will erode from the inside even if budgets are not cut back.

Slowing the internal cost growth anticipated for the Department of Defense can make room for other areas of spending within a budget that is constant in real terms. Such measures are unlikely to pull defense spending much below today's level, however. The remainder of this chapter explores three options for reshaping military forces to bring spending down to a more affordable level.

OPTIONS TO REDUCE MILITARY FORCES

This chapter looks at three options to reshape the armed forces in keeping with a nonwar budget of $470 billion (about a twenty percent real cutback in funding relative to the Defense Department's peak nonwar budget in FY 2010):

- Proportional cuts: Reduce the budget of each military department by the same fraction;
- A rebalanced force: Emphasize forces for fights in the Asia-Pacific region;
- Reversible cuts: Preserve expandability and rotational capacity through reserves and leadership cadres.

All three options fit comfortably with a grand strategy of restraint that empha-sizes core US security interests. Under such a strategy, the United States would eschew military intervention to topple dictators or stop civil wars in other countries,

---

[49] Author's calculation, based on data from Office of the Under Secretary of Defense (Comptroller), "National Defense Budget Estimates for FY 2013" (March 2012), Table 6-2; and Congressional Budget Office, "Long-Term Implications of the 2013 Future Years Defense Program" (July 2012), p. 19.

stop trying to promote democracy around the globe through military means, and encourage allies to provide more for their own defense.[50]

The options differ in the degree to which the armed forces would be shaped to address future challenges in the Asia-Pacific region and in their capacity to participate in a large war that unfolds rapidly or one that lasts more than a year or two. Of the three options, the proportional-cuts alternative could put the most active-duty boots on the ground in the event of an immediately unfolding land war, but it is less well suited to fights in Asia than the other two. The second choice would rebalance the armed forces in the direction of the naval and air forces and thus be better tailored to future challenges in Asia. However, its smaller army would have less capacity than that of the proportional-cuts option to conduct extended wars of the sort the United States fought in Iraq and Afghanistan. The third alternative trades some forces from the active side to provide a deeper bench of reserves and other units that would improve its capacity for a major war and its staying power for longer wars.

For decades, national leaders have allocated funds among the three military departments—the army, the Department of the Navy (which includes the navy and the Marine Corps), and the air force—using nearly the same formula every year. When the overall defense budget dropped, the budget of each military department was cut by the same percentage. If defense budgets rose by five percent, so did the budgets of the army, navy, and air force. The result is that from one year to the next, the share of the budget going to each service remained nearly constant (see Figure 3.5).[51]

In January 2012, the White House and the Department of Defense together unveiled the most recent national security strategy.[52] With the war in Iraq ended and combat operations in Afghanistan winding down, the document prescribes rebalancing the national security effort toward the Asia-Pacific region. It suggests that in the future, rising powers like China will pursue a wide range of means to thwart the ability of the US military to operate effectively in distant theaters—what the Department of Defense calls the "anti-access/area denial challenge." The document sees building the capacity to operate around the globe despite the anti-access challenge as a top priority for the armed forces.[53] It puts the types of military operations of the past decade—stability operations, counterinsurgency, and humanitarian operations—at the bottom of the list of future military concerns.[54]

[50] Barry R. Posen, "Pull Back: The Case for a Less Activist Foreign Policy," *Foreign Affairs* 92, no. 1 (January/February 2013): 116–129.

[51] Not all of the defense budget goes to the services. In 2013, nearly one fifth of the nonwar budget for the Department of Defense went to so-called defense-wide activities that are managed outside of the services. Defense-wide programs include those of defense agencies like the Defense Intelligence Agency, the Missile Defense Agency, and the Defense Commissary Agency. They also include most of the Defense Health Program.

[52] The White House and Department of Defense, "Sustaining US Global Leadership: Priorities for 21st Century Defense" (January 2012).

[53] The White House and Department of Defense, "Sustaining Global Leadership" (January 2012), pp. 4–6.

[54] While the document is not explicit about whether the list of missions it offers is meant to be in priority order, much of the official discussion upon its release indicated that the order in which missions occur on the list is meant to reflect their priority.

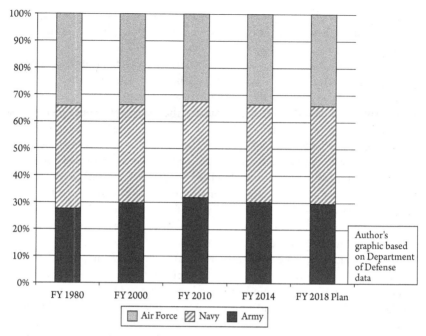

Figure 3.5 Military Departments' Shares of Total Budget for the Services, Selected Years

Many observers believe that a war in the Asia-Pacific region would be fought largely at sea and in the air. Thus the rebalancing that the department embraced in January 2012 would seem to require relatively more of the navy and to some extent the air force, and comparatively less of the army than the boots-on-the-ground wars of the past decade.

Rather than shifting more money toward the navy, however, the budget plans the Department of Defense submitted after it announced the rebalancing strategy extend the past trend of allocating money to the services in nearly constant shares. Even by FY 2018—well after combat operations in Afghanistan are meant to end— the plan submitted in April 2013 would leave the Department of the Navy with the same budget share as it enjoyed in 2010.[55]

---

[55] The air force argues that its actual spending power is significantly less than the share reflected here. Indeed, in FY 2012, nearly $34 billion—about twenty-one percent of the total air force budget—falls into a category that the service calls "non-blue" or "pass-through funding." This category includes spending for intelligence agencies like the CIA, whose funding resides largely inside the Department of Defense budget but is not controlled or managed by the department. It also includes funding for healthcare accounts that the air force does not control. For a discussion of the non-blue budget, see Adam J. Hebert, "Beyond the Blue Budget," *Air Force Magazine* 93, no. 4 (April 2010). For the purposes of this chapter, the actual share of defense spending devoted to each military department does not matter; the question is whether that share rises or falls in successive budgets. In fact, air force non-blue funds rose between FY 1990 and FY 2012 from seventeen percent to twenty-one percent of the budget, indicating a shift out of service-controlled accounts in the air force budget of about one percent of the total defense budget. This

The proportional-cuts option examined in this section assumes that the Department of Defense will continue the same practice through the coming decade. Each military department's budget will be reduced by the same percentage.

In keeping with its altered strategy, the Department of Defense Strategic Choices and Management Review (SCMR) of 2013 recommended an end to that constant-shares practice.[56] The rebalanced force alternative examined in this chapter assumes that leaders can follow that recommendation. The alternative would increase the Department of Navy's share of the budget and reduce the share held by the army.

The rebalanced force outlined here would eliminate forty percent of the army's active-duty combat brigades. Its navy and air force would be more generously funded than those of the proportional-cuts option, and significantly better tailored to operations in an access-challenged environment like the one expected in the Pacific. If the nation's leaders can hew to the strategic guidance of January 2012 and avoid involvement in stability operations, counterinsurgencies, and nation-building efforts for a decade or two, then the option makes good sense.

On the other hand, some experts worry that the nation's future leaders will not hold back from such involvement, regardless of articulated strategy and despite the smaller ground force. Moreover, as world events unfold in the future, they fear that the United States could find it necessary to mobilize for major war. The reversible-cuts option described here offers ways to hedge against those possibilities by building more expandability into the force through a larger reserve and through a new type of leadership unit in the army. The next three sections explore the three options in turn.

Proportional Cuts

The first option would reduce the budget of each military department—the army, navy, and air force—by the same percentage. The option would also adjust Department of Defense spending that falls outside of the military departments—so-called defense-wide spending—by the same fraction. It would hold expectations for force readiness at today's levels, and generally modernize the remaining units as currently planned. It would reduce the services' reserve components by about the same fraction as their active components.[57]

---

rise in non-blue funding may thus have caused the air force to suffer a small decrease in the share of the defense budget that it actually controls, relative to the other services. On the other hand, the other military departments also hold pass-through accounts, and it is possible that those accounts also grew disproportionately during the past two decades. What we can say is that if the air force-controlled budget has suffered disproportionately in comparison with the budgets of the army or navy, the damage since 1990 is no more than one percent of the total defense budget. Data on air force blue and non-blue spending since FY 1990 were provided to the author by Air Force Public Affairs and the Office of the Air Force Comptroller.

[56] Secretary of Defense Chuck Hagel and Vice Chairman of the Joint Chiefs of Staff Admiral James A. Winnefeld, "Department of Defense Briefing By Secretary Hagel and Adm. Winnefeld From the Pentagon," July 31, 2013.

[57] The army's reserve component consists of the Army Reserve and the Army National Guard. The navy's consists of the Navy Reserve. The Marine Corps' is the Marine Reserve. The air force

The result would be a military shaped about like the one the Department of Defense plans to keep (as of 2013), but with about sixteen percent fewer active-duty personnel and about twenty-two percent smaller forces. Such a military would be consistent with a grand strategy that is significantly more restrained than that of the past two decades. Like the force of the past two decades, however, this one would support a grand strategy that sees the major risks and threats posed to US interests from various regions of the world as being of about equal likelihood and importance.

This force retains a sizeable nuclear deterrent consisting of a triad of systems: land-based intercontinental ballistic missiles, submarine-launched ballistic missiles carried on nuclear submarines, and nuclear-armed bombers. It also keeps a significant ballistic missile defense program, a healthy military space program, and an intelligence effort that retains most of the post-9/11 expansion of intelligence capabilities and activities.

The force created under this alternative would be extremely capable in a wide range of operations, including those involving intense combat as well as humanitarian, peacekeeping, or counterinsurgency operations. Of the three options considered in this chapter, this force would keep the largest number of soldiers and the most brigades in the active-duty army. It could thus provide the most land-based international presence in peacetime. It also offers the greatest capacity to put boots on the ground quickly if the United States again becomes involved in wars like those in Afghanistan and Iraq. The force would be well suited to a single long war similar to the one in Iraq between 2003 and 2011. Without a buildup of units, personnel, and equipment, however, it would be too small to conduct multiple simultaneous wars of that size and duration.

With the navy reduced in lockstep with the other services, this force is not as well suited as the other two options to operations in the Pacific. As such, it is not well suited to the strategy of rebalancing toward the Asia-Pacific that the White House and the Department of Defense embraced in the strategic update of January 2012. Moreover, it lacks the deeper bench of reserves and leaders that the reversibility option offers. Thus it could take multiple years to bring this force up to a suitable level of readiness for a large ground war of long duration.

The following subsections explore in greater detail what each service might look like under a proportional-cuts plan, and considers the future capability of the resulting military. The section ends with a brief summary of the merits and drawbacks of the option.

The Army under Proportional Cuts

The plan put forward by the Department of Defense with its budget request for FY 2013 would reduce the size of the active-duty combat army from forty-five to thirty-seven maneuver brigades. It would retain all twenty-eight of the combat brigades

reserve component includes the Air Force Reserve and the Air National Guard. In this article, the number of troops in the Guard and Reserve represents the number in the so-called "selected reserve"—those who are paid and who train regularly; it excludes the 220,000 members of the Individual Ready Reserve.

currently in the army's reserve component.[58] The proportional-cuts option would cut eight more brigades from the active force, leaving twenty-nine combat brigades in the service's active component. The active-duty army would shrink from 562,000 soldiers in FY 2012 to 410,000 troops under this plan.

On the reserve side, this option would eliminate six of the twenty-eight current brigades, leaving twenty-two brigade combat teams in the Guard and Reserve and fifty-one brigade combat teams across the total force. The number of army reserve component personnel would decline from about 563,000 in 2012 to roughly 470,000. Thus the total army—that is, the active plus reserve components—would retain 880,000 soldiers.

The army canceled its most expensive equipment investment programs in recent years, leaving the service with a relatively lean nonwar budget for research and development and for procurement of new equipment. Under this plan, equipment purchases would be slowed to match the new anticipated size of the army, but no procurement programs would be canceled. The army will likely find, however, that it cannot afford an expensive replacement for its Bradley Fighting Vehicle, and that a program that upgrades and refurbishes existing Bradleys makes more sense. Research and development programs would be trimmed consistent with the overall budget reduction.

With 410,000 active-duty soldiers, the army would be about fifteen percent smaller than it was in 2001. At that size, it would still be able to provide a presence on the Korean peninsula. Policymakers would want to reconsider current plans for keeping a two-brigade force permanently in Europe, however; a bare-bones operation to support the occasional rotation of a brigade onto the continent might make more sense. In addition, the army would want to reconsider its plans for exercising with and training foreign troops, cutting back on some of those activities to ensure sufficient time for US units to conduct training in their own critical skills.

The service would still be highly capable of and ready for missions at the lower end of the conflict spectrum, including humanitarian operations, peacekeeping operations, and disaster relief—but using it persistently in those roles would eat into its capacity to fight in a big war. With participation of the Guard and Reserve, the army would be fully capable of conducting an operation of the combined size of Iraq and Afghanistan that lasted for a year or so. Alternatively, it could conduct two operations, aimed at defending against an enemy invasion, each on the level of the Persian Gulf War of 1991. With participation from the Marine Corps and the Guard and Reserve, US armed forces would still have the capacity to win decisively in one

---

[58] In addition to eliminating eight brigades altogether, the army has announced plans to disband another five of the remaining thirty-seven brigades and shift their units and people to expand each of the thirty-two brigades that will then remain. The thirty-two restructured brigades would return from the current configuration that includes just two maneuver battalions to a model more like what the army had before the so-called modularity reform of the 2000s, in which each combat brigade held three maneuver battalions. The plans for how to make the change are not complete, however, and the army may decide not to restructure its brigades because of the budget cuts imposed by the Budget Control Act of 2011 (BCA). For those reasons, the numbers of combat brigades discussed in this chapter are not adjusted for those structural changes.

of those wars. Like the force currently planned by the Department of Defense, however, the US military would no longer be large enough to carry out "win and hold" operations—that is, operations in which ground forces must push enemy forces back, make their way to the enemy's capital, and remain as an occupying presence—in two places at the same time.

This army would not be able to sustain the needed rotations for a long war similar to the combined effort in Iraq and Afghanistan. If policymakers again commit to a war or combination of wars requiring as many as 200,000 ground troops for years at a time, they would need to expand the size of the service.

The Navy and Marine Corps under Proportional Cuts

The US Navy has a fleet of 284 warships in 2013. It hopes over the coming decades to expand the fleet to more than three hundred ships.[59] The Marine Corps has three Marine Expeditionary Forces (MEFs), with three active-duty divisions and one reserve division.

For decades, the navy has persistently built fewer ships than its plans called for. Part of the reason for this is continual, unanticipated growth in the costs of its ships. Another factor is that the navy makes long-term shipbuilding plans under the assumption that future budgets will be significantly larger than past ones—or that the service itself will be able to devote a larger share of its budget to shipbuilding than it has in the past. For example, the navy's fiscal year 2013 shipbuilding plan assumes that it will be able to spend about ten percent more on ship construction and conversion during the coming decade than on average over the past three decades—despite the budget constraints already in place in the Defense Department's fiscal year 2013 plan. The reality is that the budget will likely be ten percent lower than anticipated in that plan. Between 2023 and 2032, the service assumes its shipbuilding funds will exceed those of past decades by thirty-five percent.[60]

Under the proportional-cuts alternative, the navy could afford to build and operate a fleet of about 235 ships. Sized at this level, the navy could fit its shipbuilding program more realistically to its future budget. The number of active-duty sailors and marines would decline from 528,000 in FY 2012 to 440,000 (about 280,000 sailors and 160,000 marines).

This option assumes that the navy would retain ships of various types in the new plan in proportion to their numbers in the navy's current plan for two decades from now. Table 3.1 illustrates the number of ships of each type the navy would have under each of the options outlined in this paper, compared with the number in the navy's plan for fiscal year 2032.

The proportional-cuts fleet would eliminate two of the navy's eleven aircraft carriers and their associated air wings, keeping a total of nine carriers (see Table 3.1). The

---

[59] Ron O'Rourke, "Navy Force Structure and Shipbuilding Plans: Background and Issues for Congress" (Congressional Research Service, August 9, 2012), p. 9.
[60] Congressional Budget Office, *An Analysis of the Navy's Fiscal Year 2013 Shipbuilding Plan* (July 2012), p. 11.

Table 3.1 Navy Ships under the Navy's Plan and under Three Options

	Number of Ships		
Ship Type	Navy plan for 2032	Proportional Cuts	Rebalanced Force and Reversible Cuts[a]
Aircraft Carrier	11	9	8
Surface Combatants and Mine Countermeasures	135	108	90
Attack Submarines and SSGNs	45	36	44
Ballistic Missile Submarines	10	8	10
Amphibious Warfare Ships	32	25	30
Combat Logistics and Support Ships	62	49	53
Total Ships	295	235	235

[a] Under the reversible cuts option, the navy would also retain nine additional ships in storage.

navy already plans to operate a ten-carrier fleet during FY 2013 and FY 2014, and the Department of Defense has indicated that the risk of that carrier fleet is acceptable in the context of its presence missions, the war in Afghanistan (which at the time of the DoD assessment was still ongoing), and other potential near-term operations.[61] With nine carriers and the surface fleet proposed in this option, the navy would likely abandon the goal of keeping a carrier in the Mediterranean or the Atlantic for much of every year. It could still keep the surface elements of one carrier battle group based in Japan and one operating full-time in the Indian Ocean. In addition, the fleet would retain the capacity to surge at least three more carrier groups within about one month.

The proportional-cuts option falls short of the number of attack submarines the navy might need to support nine carrier battle groups and conduct the other operations expected of them. It also deepens a shortfall that already exists in the number of amphibious warfare ships the Marine Corps would like to support its expeditionary operations.[62] This makes the option unsuitable for a strategy that emphasizes challenges in the Asia-Pacific region.

The alternative cuts back the number of nuclear ballistic missile-carrying submarines—the most secure and survivable leg of the nation's nuclear triad of submarines, long-range bombers, and intercontinental ballistic missiles (ICBMs).

The Defense Department's FY 2013 plan would remove about 20,000 marines from the active side of the Marine Corps between FY 2012 and FY 2017. It would also thin out the marines' divisions by eliminating four active-duty and one reserve marine infantry battalion as well as several tactical air and artillery units. The Marine Corps is required by law to retain three divisions, but the department has significant leeway regarding how the divisions are configured.

The proportional-cuts option outlined here would reduce the Marine Corps by another 22,000 marines by removing additional units at the lower echelons. At that

---

[61] Department of Defense, *Quadrennial Defense Review Report* (February 2010), pp. 45–47.
[62] Congressional Budget Office, *An Analysis of the Navy's Amphibious Warfare Ships for Deploying Marines Overseas* (November 2011), p. 9.

point, the Corps would likely find its three nominal divisions so thin that it would prefer to work with Congress to end the legislative mandate requiring the service to retain three divisions.

The Air Force under Proportional Cuts

The air force in 2012 had sixty combat-coded tactical air squadrons between its active and reserve components.[63] Under the plan put forward with the FY 2013 budget, the service plans to shed six of them, reducing the total number to fifty-four.[64] The proportional-cuts option would quickly eliminate another eleven squadrons, leaving the service with forty-three squadrons and about 880 fighter and attack planes. The option assumes proportional reductions to other elements of the service's force structure, including airlift and air refueling, surveillance aircraft, long-range bombers, intercontinental ballistic missiles, and space operations units. Active-duty end strength would drop to 274,000 airmen in the active force and 142,000 in the Guard and Reserve, compared with about 333,000 active-duty airmen and 178,000 guardsmen and reservists in 2012. Some 416,000 airmen would remain across the total air force.

During the past two decades, the capability of the air force to deliver weapons precisely on targets has grown markedly, despite cutbacks in the size of the tactical force. The same period witnessed the growth of a fleet of unmanned aerial vehicles that increasingly took on combat as well as surveillance and communications roles. The Defense Department's 2010 Quadrennial Defense Review and the January 2012 strategy update published by the White House and the Department of Defense both note that the advanced technologies incorporated in present and future systems mean the service can do more than before with fewer aircraft.[65]

Moreover, the tactical air force today is greatly oversized for the wars it was called upon to fight in recent years, including the onset of operations in Afghanistan in 2001, support for the initial invasion of Iraq in 2003, and the air war over Libya in 2011. With their short ranges and land basing, air force tactical aircraft are arguably not well suited for wars that pose significant anti-access challenges—as even a near-term operation in the Pacific might. On the other hand, air force fighters and attack aircraft would be of great use in wars against an enemy like Iran or Syria. Those countries' air defenses are significant, but defeating them and establishing control of the air would by no means require the air force to be sized at the level envisioned in the FY 2013 budget.

The land-based tactical fleet of the proportional-cuts option would still be able to provide close air support to the smaller army envisioned under the option. It would also retain more than 150 F-22s capable of air-to-air operations against

---

[63] Combat-coded squadrons are those not held solely for training.

[64] US Air Force White Paper, "USAF Force Structure Changes: Sustaining Readiness and Modernizing the Total Force," February 2012, p. 3.

[65] Department of Defense, *Quadrennial Defense Review Report* (February 2010); The White House and Department of Defense, "Sustaining Global Leadership: Priorities for the 21st Century" (January 2012).

highly capable enemy fighters in a challenging air defense environment. Programs aimed at developing that aircraft's ability to bomb targets on the ground would be ended.

This option would preserve air force plans to develop a new long-range bomber, but would reduce the total number of bombers in the force proportionally with the cutbacks to fighter and attack aircraft. Given the Defense Department's concerns over challenged access and area denial, such proportional cutbacks to the bomber force could leave the air force short of assets important to future fights.

The drawdown of air force mobility and tanker assets discussed here could pose a problem for the other services. The air force plan for FY 2013 already calls for the elimination of 150 such aircraft—about fifteen percent of the fleet—during the coming five years. The proportional-cuts option would take another twenty percent. The army is already concerned that air force airlift resources will not meet its needs in a rapidly unfolding ground war. Even at its smaller size, the army may find itself short of the airlift it relies on to flow forces rapidly into theater. Assuming the air force is constrained to a proportional share of budget cuts at the level envisioned here, a better choice for the Department of Defense overall might be for the service to shed more tactical units and retain a larger share of its other fleets.

Reductions under this option would trim the ICBM force consistent with the other cuts to the service. The air force argues that such a reduction is inefficient; eliminating a few dozen missiles does nothing to reduce the costs of command and control, infrastructure, and upkeep that drive spending for the fleet. Achieving sizeable savings would require the elimination of the entire force, as suggested under the second option.

Intelligence, the Defense Agencies, and Cyberoperations under Proportional Cuts

Intelligence spending reportedly makes up a significant fraction of the Department of Defense budget. By some estimates, as much as ninety percent of the $80 billion total intelligence budget for FY 2012 fell somewhere in the defense budget. Much of it is believed to reside in the budgets of the military departments. The proportional-cuts option would reduce intelligence spending in the Department of Defense by sixteen percent relative to the department's FY 2013 plan, consistent with cutbacks to the military departments. The resulting intelligence budget would come to about $60 billion (FY 2013 dollars).

Beginning in 1998, the nation's intelligence spending rose more sharply than the overall military budget, more than doubling in real terms between 1998 and 2010.[66] Intelligence budgets have since declined modestly. The President's FY 2013 budget called for another twelve percent reduction in real terms, to about $72 billion.

---

[66] In 1998, the Director of Central Intelligence disclosed a total intelligence budget of $26.7 billion current dollars, about $37 billion in FY 2013 dollars. In recent years, the Director of National Intelligence has routinely released total figures for intelligence spending. In 2013 dollars, the FY 2010 intelligence budget came to nearly $85 billion. The figures discussed here include spending attributed to the wars in Iraq and Afghanistan.

Under this option, intelligence spending would still be more than sixty percent higher in real terms than in 1998.

The Department of Defense spends about $4.5 billion annually on cybersecurity.[67] That money is distributed among the services and defense agencies. In the spirit of proportional cuts, this option would trim cyberbudgets along with spending for other activities by sixteen percent relative to their 2013 levels.

The option would also trim the budgets of the independent defense agencies by a total of sixteen percent relative to the President's FY 2013 plan. (Some of those agencies, such as the Defense Intelligence Agency, the National Geospatial-Intelligence Agency, the National Security Agency, and the National Reconnaissance Office, are part of the intelligence community and included in the discussion of intelligence spending in the paragraphs above; their budgets would not be cut twice.) Non-intelligence agencies in this group include support agencies like the Defense Logistics Agency and acquisition organizations, such as the Missile Defense Agency and the Defense Advanced Research Projects Agency. In this option's spirit of proportional budget reductions, each agency's budget would be reduced by sixteen percent—though in reality, the Department of Defense could choose to offset smaller cuts to some agencies with larger cuts to others.

In addition, some of the agencies that exist today can be eliminated in the coming years. These include the Office of the Special Inspector General for Iraq Reconstruction and the Office of the Special Inspector General for Afghanistan Reconstruction.

Smaller but Shaped as Before

The proportional-cuts force is smaller across the board than today's, but shaped about the same as the force inherited from the Cold War. Like any of the forces described in this chapter, this one would be highly capable and still the strongest military in the world. The option could deliver very effective forces to a wide range of military operations, but it is not especially well tailored to any particular mission.

Because the force in 2013 reflects to a large extent its Cold War roots, this force—a smaller version of today's—in many ways resembles the one designed for the Cold War—ready to fight if needed in a land war in Europe or the Middle East, while retaining presence through maritime forces and some land-based forces in Asia. At only about one-half the size of the Cold War force, however, it is far from capable of sustaining itself through a major ground operation of the sort envisioned in the 1970s and 1980s.

A Rebalanced Force

The second alternative would cut the total defense budget to the same size as under the proportional-cuts option. In contrast with that option, however, it would

---

[67] The President's budget for fiscal year 2014 requests $4.7 billion for investment in cyberoperations.

distribute funds among and within the services to emphasize forces for potential future fights in the Asia-Pacific region. The option rebalances force structure to emphasize the maritime operations that seem more likely in the Asia-Pacific region. It reduces the army more sharply than the other services. In the air force, it reduces land-based tactical air forces that would be most vulnerable to anti-access challenges in the region, and sizes them to provide battlefield support to a smaller army. The option favors naval forces, particularly those that could be most useful in a maritime war against a rising power in Asia.

This option is well suited to a strategy that is significantly more restrained in its global ambitions than the grand strategy of the past two decades, and that sees future challenges to US core interests as most likely to unfold in Asia. It retains a sizeable nuclear deterrent force. In contrast with the first alternative, however, it eliminates the land-based intercontinental ballistic missile force and relies exclusively on a dyad consisting of submarine-launched ballistic missiles and long-range, nuclear-armed bombers.

The rebalanced force described here would be effective in a wide range of missions and every point on the spectrum of conflict. Though smaller, its land forces would still be the best in the world at high-intensity operations, and also adaptable to smaller-scale missions at the lower end of the conflict spectrum, including humanitarian and stability operations. Its maritime and air forces would be well positioned for future challenges that might arise in the Asia-Pacific region and particularly well suited to fights in access-challenged environments.

Of the three forces described in this chapter, this one would provide the most maritime presence around the globe for today's missions and would be the best prepared for a rapidly unfolding war fought on sea and in the air. It is significantly better suited to maritime operations than the previous proportional-cuts force. It could provide more day-to-day presence and greater readiness for immediate action of any kind than the third option, described in the next subsection. But it also lacks the potential staying power of the third option, which would make more extensive use of reserves and prepare some units to expand quickly.

The following subsections explore what each service might look like in this smaller, rebalanced force. They also consider the future capability of the rebalanced force.

The Army in a Rebalanced Force

In the rebalanced force, the army's nonwar budget would fall by twenty percent compared with the President's request for FY 2013 (about twenty-five percent from its peak in FY 2010). The result would be an active-duty army of twenty-seven maneuver brigades and about 390,000 soldiers. The service would also eliminate eight of its current twenty-eight combat brigades in the Guard and Reserve, leaving its reserve component with twenty Brigade Combat Teams and 445,000 guardsmen and reservists. The total army would thus retain forty-seven combat brigades and 835,000 soldiers. At that size, it would still be one of the largest armies in the world and by any useful measure the strongest.

This option would reduce the army's procurement programs consistent with the new force structure, but does not require the army to cancel key development or procurement programs. As in the proportional-cuts option, however, the service might find its new combat vehicle program to be overly expensive, and choose instead to refurbish and upgrade existing Bradley Fighting Vehicles, or alternatively to enter production of an upgraded version.

With the 390,000 active-duty troops of this option, the army would be nearly twenty percent smaller than it was in 2001. Consistent with the rebalancing toward Asia, the service would remove virtually all permanent presence from Europe. It would still be able to provide a small presence on the Korean Peninsula. In keeping with the rebalancing strategy, the army would no longer be the tool of first resort for solving problems around the globe. Rather the service would focus on preparing to fight a major war in situations where core US interests come under serious challenge. The service would still be highly capable of and ready for missions at the lower end of the conflict spectrum, including humanitarian operations, smaller peace-keeping operations, and disaster relief—but using it in those roles would reduce its immediate capacity to fight in a big war.

With participation of the Guard and Reserve, the army would be capable of conducting an operation of the combined size of Iraq and Afghanistan that lasted for a year or so. Alternatively, it could conduct two operations, aimed at defending against an enemy invasion, on the level of the Persian Gulf War of 1991. With participation from the Marine Corps and the Guard and Reserve, US armed forces would still have the capacity win decisively in one of those wars. Like the force currently planned by the Department of Defense, however, the US military would no longer be large enough to carry out "win and hold" operations in two places at the same time.

This army would not be able to sustain the needed rotations for a long war similar to the combined effort in Iraq and Afghanistan. Moreover, the Guard and Reserve would be able to provide at most three brigades at a time to support those rotations. If policymakers again commit to a war or combination of wars requiring nearly 200,000 ground troops for years at a time, they would need to grow a significantly larger army.

The Navy and Marine Corps in a Rebalanced Force

The rebalanced force option would reduce the Department of Navy budget by just ten percent relative to the FY 2013 plan, or about fourteen percent compared with FY 2010. Consistent with a strategy of rebalancing the military for future fights in the Asia-Pacific region, the option makes adjustments within the sea service to prepare it better for a blue-water fight in an access-challenged environment.

This option keeps about 294,000 active-duty sailors in the navy and 168,000 active-duty marines. It cuts the Navy Reserve to 52,000 sailors and the Marine Reserve to 37,000 marines.

If the navy cut the number of ships in each class by the same fraction, it could afford about 250 ships under this option. In keeping with the goal of rebalancing, however, the option trims some ship categories less severely, while making deeper cuts to other categories. The result is a fleet that is better matched to anticipated missions and also better organized to make full use of the capabilities of each element.

The rebalanced force option reduces the carrier fleet from the nine ships of the proportional-cuts option to eight ships here. It reduces the number of Littoral Combat Ships from fifty-five ships in the current plan to thirty, but retains enough large surface combat ships to support fully the remaining carriers. It builds relatively more nuclear-powered attack submarines than the proportional-cuts alternative, retaining a fleet of forty-four SSNs for the longer term. It also restores three of the amphibious warfare ships eliminated under the first option, bringing the number of ships supporting the Marine Corps to thirty.

This eight-carrier navy would abandon the goal of keeping a carrier in the Mediterranean or the Atlantic for much of every year. It could still keep one carrier battle group based in Japan and one operating full-time in the Indian Ocean. In addition, the fleet would retain the capacity to surge at least two more carrier groups within about one month, with the potential for a third within two or three months.

The larger attack submarine fleet of this option is better suited to support in full the remaining eight carrier battle groups and conduct other operations that will be crucial in an accessed-challenged environment. The option also sizes the amphibious fleet to match the expeditionary needs of the Marine Corps more closely.[68]

The rebalanced force option retains a fleet of ten nuclear ballistic missile-carrying submarines—two more than the previous option. The larger fleet recognizes the crucial role of this leg of the triad in nuclear deterrence and offsets the elimination of the ICBM force proposed in the discussion of the air force below. This option retains a Marine Corps modestly larger than that of the previous alternative.

The Air Force in a Rebalanced Force

The rebalanced force option reduces air force spending by eighteen percent in real terms relative to the President's budget request for FY 2013, or about twenty-two percent compared with FY 2010. It retains about 267,000 airmen in the active component and 138,000 in the Guard and Reserve.

Compared with the President's FY 2013 plan, this alternative would eliminate twelve fighter and attack squadrons, leaving the service with forty-two squadrons, with about 850 fighter and attack planes. The option would make smaller cuts to the airlift, air refueling, and surveillance fleets that would provide important support during a major war in an access-challenged environment. Under this plan, air force mobility and tanker assets would be better matched to meet the needs of the army in a rapidly unfolding ground war.

---

[68] Congressional Budget Office, "An Analysis of the Navy's Amphibious Warfare Ships for Deploying Marines Overseas" (November 2011), p. 9.

The resulting land-based tactical fleet would be well matched to provide close air support to the smaller army of this option. It would also retain 150 F-22s capable of air-to-air operations against highly capable enemy fighters in a challenging air defense environment. Programs aimed at developing that aircraft's ability to bomb targets on the ground would be ended.

This option would outfit the air force with relatively more long-range bombers than under the proportional-cuts alternative. It would preserve air force plans to build its new bomber, but drop any expectations for all-aspect stealth and focus the research and development program on producing an affordable plane that can be equipped with nuclear as well as conventional payloads. The new bomber would be designed to carry significant numbers of cruise missiles in addition to precision-guided bombs, and thus better suited to operations in a severely access-challenged environment.

The reductions and reshaping suggested in this option will result in an air force that is still the best in the world. It will be fully capable of supporting ground operations in a major war where land basing is not under serious challenge. Together with the air assets of the navy and Marine Corps, the service will be better positioned to suppress enemy air defenses, establish and sustain control of the airspace, and conduct important air-to-ground missions even when access is challenged.

This option would retain vital space operations elements. It would wholly eliminate the ICBM force. The elimination of more vulnerable ICBMs would be offset by the navy's retention of a relatively larger fleet of secure and survivable SSBNs, and by the new air force bomber.

Intelligence, the Defense Agencies, and Cyberoperations under Rebalanced Forces

Like the proportional-cuts option, the rebalanced force option reduces intelligence spending in the Department of Defense by sixteen percent relative to the FY 2013 plan, or about twenty percent compared with FY 2010 budgets. This would bring intelligence spending to a level about sixty-two percent higher in real terms than in 1998. The option would also trim the budgets of the independent defense agencies by a total of sixteen percent relative to the President's FY 2013 plan (with care not to assess the intelligence agencies twice). Reflecting the option's focus on Asia and emerging concerns about China's offensive cyber capabilities, the option would increase the share of total defense spending devoted to cyberoperations.

A Smaller Force, Better Suited to the Future

The rebalanced force outlined here reflects more clearly the Defense Department's shift in emphasis toward Asia and the Pacific. Compared with the FY 2012 budget, it shifts two percent of the total defense budget away from the army and into the air force and navy. It expands the Department of Navy's share of total defense spending from about twenty-nine percent under the President's plan to thirty-one percent.

The option results in a military significantly smaller than today's, but one that is shaped more in keeping with the missions currently envisioned by the Department of Defense. It is suited to a grand strategy much less ambitious and interventionist than that of the past two decades; in particular, it is decidedly less ready to undertake a long counterinsurgency war than the military of 2012. This force should not be called upon routinely to settle problems around the globe that are not directly tied to US vital interests. If it is, there is a risk that it will not be ready to fight and win the major wars for which it is shaped.

Nevertheless, the force retains the capability to win decisively in a major theater war, while conducting a smaller operation elsewhere. Even under this option, the United States will retain by far the most powerful military in the world.

Reversible Cuts

The rebalanced force outlined in the previous section would eliminate about forty percent of the army's active-duty and reserve component combat brigades. If the nation's leaders adhere to the strategic guidance articulated by the White House and the Department of Defense in January 2012 and avoid future involvement in stability operations, counterinsurgencies, and nation-building efforts for a decade or two, then the option makes good sense.

On the other hand, future leaders may ultimately press forward with such operations despite the published strategy and even though the ground forces are not sized to support multiple rotations for long expeditionary wars. Moreover, as world events unfold in the future, the United States could find it necessary to mobilize for major war. The reversible-cuts option offers several ways to hedge against those possibilities. The option is well suited to a grand strategy that is significantly more restrained in its ambitions for foreign military intervention and global shaping than that of the past two decades and emphasizes challenges in the Asia-Pacific region, but wants to hedge against other possibilities.

Compared with the rebalanced force discussed in the previous section, this option beefs up the army and Marine Corps reserve components. Since the end of the Cold War, the reserve component has functioned increasingly as an operational reserve, routinely making important contributions to wars, stability operations, humanitarian operations, and disaster relief efforts. This stands in stark contrast to the Cold War concept of a strategic reserve designed largely to supplement and backfill the active forces in the event of a global war.

The army and Marine Corps reserve components were an important part of the rotation base for operations in Iraq and Afghanistan. In the wake of those wars, the Guard and Reserve are arguably better equipped and better trained than they have been for decades. Moreover, the Guard and Reserve are significantly less expensive in peacetime than their active-duty counterparts.

Both the proportional-cuts option and the rebalanced force would reduce each service's reserve component by about the same fraction as its active component. In contrast, the reversible-cuts option trims the army's reserve component by a smaller fraction than its active component and improves Guard and Reserve training relative to current practice. More plentiful and better trained reserves can serve as a hedge in the event that more ground forces are needed during the coming decades—either to fill in a rotation base in the event of a war that lasts for multiple years or to expand the size of the force that can be brought to bear in a major mobilization.

Second, the reversible cuts option develops active-duty units of a new type within the army: leadership cadres consisting of officers and senior noncommissioned officers, with very limited staffing at the junior level. In peacetime, those units would allow the service to keep relatively more officers and senior enlisted soldiers than in today's hierarchy. Mid-grade officers and noncommissioned officers would rotate through the units, where they would do the planning needed to bring the units up to full speed in the event of a war; they would also continue to develop the skills honed during their regular rotations with fully staffed units. In the event of a long war or mobilization for major war, they would form the leadership and training backbone for units that could be staffed up to full strength by bringing in new recruits or recently discharged soldiers. Third, the option takes steps to place into storage nine ships that the navy currently plans to retire before the end of their useful lives. Finally, it readjusts the active-reserve mix for fighter and airlift squadrons in the air force.

The following subsections consider what the services would look like and what their capabilities would be under this option.

The Army under Reversible Cuts

The reversible cuts option provides the army with the same total budget as the rebalanced force option, but devotes more of that budget to the Guard and Reserve than the previous alternative. It also creates new leadership units in the active force as a way of developing officers and senior enlisted troops who could lead and train additional units should they be needed for a larger or longer land war than the force could otherwise support.

The result is an active-duty army consisting of twenty-four brigade combat teams and six thinly-staffed brigades that consist principally of officers and senior noncommissioned officers. In contrast to the proportional-cuts or rebalanced force alternatives, this option would preserve all twenty-eight of the brigade combat teams currently in the army's reserve component. Under this option, the active-duty army would shrink to 370,000 soldiers; the Army National Guard and the Army Reserve would have about 550,000 soldiers. The option also expands the training schedule for the reserve component to provide one extra month of training every five years for every Guard and Reserve combat brigade.

While the active-duty army would be smaller than in the other options, the total army would be larger, with 920,000 troops instead of the 835,000 of the previous option. In the event of a large or long war, it could expand relatively quickly to provide significantly more combat capability, with the potential for fifty-eight combat brigades as compared with forty-seven brigades under the rebalanced force.

The Army National Guard and the Army Reserve made substantial contributions to the wars in Iraq and Afghanistan. One result is that today the service's reserve component is arguably better trained and more ready than it has been for generations. Another result is that it is better equipped than it was for most of the Cold War.[69]

Unless steps are taken to preserve those gains, the peacetime readiness of the Guard and Reserve is likely to erode rapidly as units revert to their former training schedule of one weekend every month and two weeks in the summer. The army hopes to avoid some of that erosion, and capitalize on the gains in readiness made during the wars, by expanding the training schedule for some units.[70] The reversible cuts option would extend the army plan to all reserve-component combat units, allowing for one extra month of training every five years for each brigade.[71] Under the option, every brigade would get six weeks of summer training, instead of the two weeks formerly provided, in the year before it is meant to be available to deploy. The change should greatly improve the readiness of the reserve component to provide rotational forces in the event of a long war. It will also mean that as many as one-half of the reserve component's brigades can quickly be readied to contribute to the fight in the event of a rapidly unfolding war with heavy troop requirements.

In addition, this option would keep all twenty-eight combat brigades presently in the army's reserve component. The equipment for twenty-eight brigades already exists, and it could be supplemented as needed with equipment from disbanded active brigades.

A reserve force is one way to retain capacity that is not as ready for immediate action in peacetime as its active-duty counterpart. Under the US Guard and Reserve model, forces are close to fully staffed in peacetime, but most of the members serve part time. A different model for storing useful capacity for wartime is to create forces that are partially staffed in peacetime with members who serve full

---

[69] For example, Army National Guard equipment on hand is now ninety-two percent, compared with just sixty-five percent in 2005. The National Guard is scheduled to receive even more new equipment during the coming year as a result of the reset program. See Statement by Lieutenant General William Ingram, Jr., Director, Army National Guard, before the Subcommittee on Defense of the Senate Appropriations Committee, "The Fiscal Year 2013 Guard and Reserve Budget," May 23, 2012, p. 5.

[70] In recent years, the army shifted its concept for preparing its active and reserve forces for war to a rotational model called Army Force Generation, or ARFORGEN. For the reserve component, ARFORGEN puts each combat brigade on a five-year cycle of reset, readiness, and availability, with the expectation that units in the final year of the cycle would be called up first should the need arise. The army currently plans to expand training, from the usual one weekend per month and two weeks in the summer, for some units during their fifth year of the cycle. The specific amount of added training and what it will cost are not yet clear to the author. See Statement by Lieutenant General William Ingram, Jr., "The Fiscal Year 2013 Guard and Reserve Budget," May 23, 2012, pp. 2–3.

[71] I estimate that the costs of the added training could be offset by eliminating one-half of one of the active-duty brigades.

time.[72] The reversible-cuts option would create several partially staffed brigades in the active-duty army.

The army can train a newly recruited private to be ready for action in less than a year. In contrast, it takes many years to develop its officers and senior enlisted leaders. In past years, the army stockpiled more captains and lieutenant colonels than it needed to command its companies and battalions, to provide a base for expansion and mobilization in the event of major war. That practice caused significant career dissatisfaction and turbulence, however, as large numbers of officers had to rotate through a small number of open positions to get the leadership experience they needed. The practice was arguably detrimental to force quality as well, because command tours had to be shortened to make room for the next round of officers.[73]

To expand the pool of leaders in a shrinking army and avoid problems associated with the former pattern of stockpiling officers, this option creates six new leadership brigades in the active army.[74] Those leadership cadres would be manned at about the twenty-five percent level with officers and senior enlisted members, but would lack the junior-ranked soldiers who constitute the bulk of an ordinary brigade. They would be outfitted with equipment drawn from the active brigades that will be eliminated under any of the options considered in this paper. Most of their equipment could be placed into storage, although it might make sense to keep some of it to be maintained by the cadre or by Guard and Reserve units with which the cadre trains.

These understaffed brigades would lack the junior soldiers they would need to deploy in peacetime, and would not be expected to fight in their understaffed configurations. Instead, the leadership cadres would concentrate in peacetime on planning and preparations for expanding their brigades and readying them for action in the event of war. A leadership brigade could also be attached in peacetime to a Guard and Reserve brigade, where it would provide core full-time leadership and expertise to the part-time force.[75]

---

[72] For this insight, see Christopher Ordowich, "Considering a Cadre-Augmented Army," Dissertation for the Pardee Rand Graduate School (Santa Monica, CA: RAND Corporation, 2008).

[73] Cindy Williams ed., *Filling the Ranks: Transforming the U.S. Military Personnel System* (Cambridge, MA: The MIT Press, 2004).

[74] I estimate that the costs of eight reserve component brigades could be offset by eliminating two active-duty brigades. This is consistent with an examination of the relative operation and support costs of the active and reserve components of the army in recent budgets. It is a bit more conservative than estimates prepared by the Congressional Budget Office during the early 1990s. See "CBO Testimony," Robert D. Reischauer, Statement before the Committee on Armed Services, United States Senate, May 10, 1990, p. 31. The cost of the new cadre units could essentially be offset by eliminating one active-duty brigade. This calculation is consistent with the estimate of costs for such cadre units presented in Ordowich, "Cadre," 2008.

[75] For a discussion of how such brigades might function, see Ordowich, "Cadre," 2008.

No individual would be assigned permanently to a leadership cadre. Rather, in peacetime, the cadres would draw on officers and senior noncommissioned officers from across the active-duty force. An individual might expect to rotate into a leadership cadre about twice during his or her career.[76]

In wartime, each leadership cadre would become the core around which a full brigade could be formed. The junior soldiers needed to fill out each brigade could come from those members of the Individual Ready Reserve who separated recently from active service, or by expanded recruiting, or using a combination of the two.[77] (In the event of a major war, the nation's leaders could also opt to restore the draft or to use the Selective Service System for a more limited call-up.)

In wartime, it would take more than a year to fill the cadres and train them up. If world events signal that the nation needs to prepare for a major war, national decision makers could take the personnel actions needed to bring cadres up to full strength. In that event, the cadres could be ready for action even on day one of the war. If major war unfolded with little warning, on the other hand, the cadres could be made available by the second or third year of the war. In the event of a war like the ones in Iraq and Afghanistan—for which rotational forces are needed over a period of several years—the filled-in cadres would provide added units to rotate into the fight, perhaps beginning in the third year of combat.[78]

Leadership cadres would be significantly cheaper than fully manned units in peacetime. The full-time but underfilled cadre model complements and offers some advantages over the part-time but fully staffed reserve model, in that it retains more of the army's most precious resource—experienced officers and noncommissioned officers. It offers a more organized and useful way of retaining the leadership capacity that might be needed in the future than the former turbulent practice of rotating excess captains and lieutenant colonels quickly through leadership positions in fully staffed units.

Like the army of the other two options, this army would be one of the largest in the world and by an appropriate measure still the most capable. Like that of the balanced-cuts option, it would be well suited to a strategy more restrained than today's, particularly one that emphasizes operations in the Asia-Pacific region. It would be extremely capable of high-intensity combat but still useful and ready for humanitarian or stability operations at the lower end of the conflict spectrum. The choice to use it persistently in those lower-end operations would limit its capacity to swing quickly to combat operations in the event of a larger regional war, however.

This army's active-duty force would be smaller than that of the previous balanced-cuts option and thus ready to put fewer boots on the ground into an immediately unfolding war. The total army would be significantly larger, however, and reserves would be well prepared to enter the fight relatively quickly if needed. While

---

[76] For an excellent and comprehensive discussion of what cadres might cost and how the cadre concept could operate in peacetime and in war, see Ordowich, "Cadre," 2008.

[77] The Individual Ready Reserve consists of former active-duty service members who are not assigned for training to reserve units and are not paid unless called to active service.

[78] The schedule for bringing a leadership cadre into the fight depends heavily on the timing of the decision to do so. See Ordowich, "Cadre," 2008.

smaller in peacetime than the armies of the other two options, this one could expand relatively quickly to a significantly larger force if needed for a large war and for wars of long duration. Thus while it is well suited to a restrained strategy that emphasizes the Asia-Pacific, it offers leaders a more rapid path to expansion for larger ground wars should the international environment change.

The Navy and Marine Corps under Reversible Cuts

As part of its cost cutting effort, the navy currently plans to retire seven cruisers and two of the older dock landing ships that support the Marine Corps. All nine ships still have several years of useful service life remaining. The reversible cuts option would require the navy to retain those ships in storage, to be brought back into service in the event of war.[79] To offset the costs of ship storage and maintenance, the option trims the number of sailors in the active-duty navy by 4,000.

The result is a 235-ship peacetime navy that can be expanded, perhaps within a year, to a 244-ship navy. Bringing the stored ships to readiness might take from six months to a year.[80] Personnel for the expanded force could be drawn from the Individual Ready Reserve, with leaders coming from cohorts that separated most recently from service. In the event of a major war, national leaders would need to call such personnel up expeditiously to give them an opportunity to retrain while the ships are restored to readiness.

Like the navy of the previous balanced-cuts option, this navy would be the strongest in the world. It is very well suited to deal with future challenges in the Asia-Pacific region. It sacrifices a small amount of near-term presence to ensure a larger fleet should the navy find itself in need of the ships it plans to retire.

The Air Force under Reversible Cuts

Today, about seventy percent of air force tactical squadrons reside in the active component. Yet reserve component squadrons are cheaper and in most regards just as ready as those of the active force.[81] Retaining a relatively larger reserve and a smaller active force would increase the number of squadrons in the total air force, potentially expanding the service's capability in both peacetime and war.

Compared with the rebalanced force alternative, this option retains twelve additional tactical squadrons in the reserve component while eliminating eight

---

[79] I estimate that each ship can be stored and kept at a modest level of readiness for an annual cost of less than $10 million. This is consistent with estimates (adjusted for inflation) from Lane Pierrot, *Structuring U.S. Forces After the Cold War: Costs and Effects of Increased Reliance on the Reserves* (Washington, DC: Congressional Budget Office, 1992), pp. 32–33.

[80] Lane Pierrot, *Structuring*, p. 35.

[81] I estimate the cost of a reserve squadron to be about seventy percent of the cost of an active squadron. This is consistent with "CBO Testimony," Robert D. Reischauer, Statement before the Committee on Armed Services, United States Senate, May 10, 1990, p. 31. For an excellent discussion of the readiness of Air National Guard units, see Luke Ahmann and Liesl Carter, "Total Force Optimization," Paper for the National Security Fellows Program, John F. Kennedy School of Government, 2012.

squadrons from the active force of the previous alternative. It thus reverses the mix from an active-duty-heavy tactical force to one weighted toward the reserves. The result is a total air force with forty-six tactical squadrons—four more than under the previous option. The reversible cuts option also adjusts the personnel mix, with 255,000 airmen in the active force and 156,000 in the reserve component.

Air force mobility forces could also be redesigned to place more emphasis on the reserve component, which is arguably more cost-effective in peacetime than the active component.[82] That change would expand the number of airlift squadrons in the total air force, while adding several thousand airmen to the reserve component and modestly reducing the number active-duty airmen, in comparison with the rebalanced-force option.

Like the air force of the rebalanced-force option, this one will still be the most powerful air force in the world. Compared with the proportional-cuts option, it is better suited to fights in an access-challenged environment and significantly better tailored to support the other services with close-air support, airlift, and space operations. Compared with the rebalanced-force option, it provides more rapid generation of additional force should it be needed.

Intelligence, the Defense Agencies, and Cyberoperations under Reversible Cuts

The reversible cuts option treats the intelligence budget, the defense agencies, and cyberoperations in the same way as the rebalanced force option outlined in the previous section.

Smaller Active Forces with More Room to Grow

The reversible-cuts force is ideally suited to a strategy that emphasizes challenges in the Asia-Pacific region and eschews wars to topple dictators, bring democracy to countries around the world, and intervene in civil wars in distant lands—but that views future events as uncertain and wants to preserve a wide range of options for future leaders. The active-duty force of this option is smaller than that of the first two options, but its total force is larger, making it better suited to larger wars for which the nation has a year or so to prepare, or for longer wars in which frequent rotations become burdensome for active-duty units to sustain.

Three Strong, Highly Capable Forces

Table 3.2 summarizes the force structure and end strength for each service in the force of 2012, the force as envisioned by the Department of Defense, and the force under each of the three options considered in this paper. All three armed forces are quite large by international standards and significantly stronger than any other

[82] Ahmann and Carter, "Total Force Optimization," 2012.

Table 3.2 Comparison of Options

	2012 Force	Planned Force	Proportional Cuts	Rebalanced Force	Reversible Cuts
Army Brigades					
Active Component	45	37	29	27	24 (+6 cadres)
Reserve Component	28	28	22	20	28
Army End Strength					
Active Component	562,000	490,000	410,000	390,000	370,000
Reserve Component	563,200	558,200	470,000	445,000	550,000
Navy Ships	284	300+	235	235	235 (+9 in storage)
Navy End Strength					
Active Component	325,700	319,500	280,000	294,000	290,000
Navy Reserve	66,200	57,100	50,000	52,000	52,000
Marine Corps Divisions					
Active Component	3	3	2+	2+	2+
Reserve Component	1	1	1	1	1
Marine Corps End Strength					
Active Component	202,100	182,100	160,000	168,000	168,000
Marine Reserve	39,600	39,600	35,000	37,000	37,000
Air Force Tactical Squadrons					
Active and Reserve	60	54	43	42	46
Air Force End Strength					
Active Component	332,800	328,600	274,000	267,000	255,000
Reserve Component	178,100	170,700	142,000	138,000	156,000
Total End Strength					
Active Component	1,422,600	1,320,200	1,124,000	1,119,000	1,083,000
Reserve Component	847,100	825,600	697,000	672,000	795,000
Total Force	2,269,700	2,145,800	1,821,000	1,746,000	1,878,000

military in the world. The proportional-cuts option results in the largest active-duty force and the greatest potential for putting boots on the ground quickly in the event of war. The rebalanced force is better suited to the maritime fights that seem more likely in Asia and the Pacific.

The reversible-cuts option retains the largest total force, with nearly as many troops in the Guard and Reserve as anticipated under the Defense Department's current plans. While that option could not provide as many units into theater as quickly as the rebalanced force, it would have more staying power and greater rotational capability for a long war, and be more readily expandable in the event of a war for which the nation had warning time of a year or more.

None of the three options cuts the number of active-duty troops by more than eighteen percent relative to the department's planned force. The total force in each case is at least eighty percent as large as the one the department currently plans to keep.

Under any of the three options, the United States will retain the strongest, best-funded, best-equipped, and best-trained armed forces in the world, with significant operational and strategic depth provided by a sizable and well-equipped reserve component. In all of the cases, the forces will be fully capable of winning decisively in at least one major theater war. Units will be highly ready to deploy to a distant theater. In addition, leaders will be able to send multiple ground-force brigades to conduct humanitarian or peacekeeping missions far from home. The navy will sustain significant presence in areas of high interest. But none of the active-duty forces outlined here will be able to sustain a long, large occupation or counterinsurgency operation without drawing heavily on the Guard and Reserve and without additional military buildup.

STRENGTH IN A TIME OF AUSTERITY

The Budget Control Act of 2011 significantly reduces federal budgets for defense and domestic programs relative to earlier expectations. Despite the Act's cutbacks from previously anticipated budgets, however, the nation still faces a debt that will grow within three decades to the largest share of the economy it has ever held.

Policymakers have a range of choices to bring future debt under control. Unfortunately, one of those choices—raising taxes—is anathema to Republicans. The second—reining in the growing costs of entitlements like Social Security and Medicare—is very hard for Democrats to accept. If the two parties cannot come to some bargain in those areas, then they will continue to look to nonentitlement expenditures as a preferred area of savings. Defense will likely continue to be a prime target for deficit reduction efforts.

How much defense will ultimately be cut depends on the future state of the economy, the international situation, the seriousness with which political leaders choose to confront the growing debt, and whatever compromises they can make on taxes and entitlements. This chapter explores how the Department of Defense could deal with a ten-year budget that cuts a bit deeper than that of the BCA, returning nonwar defense spending to its 2003 level in real terms.

Such a cut will not be easy for the department, in part because the costs of pay and healthcare benefits grew much faster than inflation between 2003 and 2013. If no action is taken to slow the future growth of those costs, then as the defense budget pie shrinks they will consume an increasing slice of it.

Since 2006, defense leaders have asked Congress repeatedly to trim the pay raises offered to military personnel and to ask military retirees to pay a larger share of the costs for their health insurance. Until now, Congress has refused. With the war in Afghanistan coming to a close and the defense budget shrinking, however, the time is right for Congress to reconsider.

By accepting the modest changes to pay and benefits that this chapter describes, lawmakers can save at least two active-duty army brigades, twelve navy ships, and three air force fighter squadrons from being cut. If lawmakers decide not to act, then the Department of Defense will have to cut more from the forces than discussed here.

Defense leaders face important strategic choices as they shape the force for a more austere future. Whatever path they decide on, the strategy will have to be much more restrained than that of the past two decades.

If leaders follow past practice and spread the pain of budget cuts evenly among the services, then armed forces a decade from now will look like a smaller version of today's. The United States will still have the most capable military in the world, effective at a wide range of missions and capable of putting hundreds of thousands of boots on the ground into the Middle East or other regions at a moment's notice. That force would not be as ready as it could be to respond to challenges in the Asia-Pacific region, however.

Alternatively, leaders could take the opportunity of downsizing to reshape the armed forces in line with the emerging international environment. By spending relatively more of the reduced budget on the navy and air force and less on the army, policymakers can tailor the armed forces to deal more effectively with the anti-access environments expected in Asia and the Pacific.

Finally, leaders need to think about how much of the force must be ready to go to war at a moment's notice. The reserves are significantly cheaper in peacetime than active-duty forces. As a result, if they are not called up persistently, the nation can afford more Guard and Reserve units than active-duty units for the same dollar. The same can be said of suggested new leadership units that allow the army to retain extra officers and senior noncommissioned officers in case they are needed to train and lead new units. A larger but less ready force could be particularly useful if, after adopting a more restrained strategy, the nation nevertheless finds itself in a major war or a sizeable military operation that goes on for years at a time.

The Department of Defense has already started down the path toward a more sustainable future. Budgets are significantly lower in 2013 than they were in 2010. The strategy update of 2012 and the 2013 discussion of the strategic choices and management review make clear that the tighter budgets of the future demand a more focused and restrained strategy.

The Department of Defense is also ready to get better control over rising personnel costs, if it can persuade Congress to agree to changes in that area. With the war in Afghanistan still ongoing, however, shifting the defense budget into lower gear has been hard both for the department and for Congress. The end of the war offers an important opportunity for leaders in the department, the White House, and the Congress to bring national security budgets and strategy fully into line with a sustainable fiscal future.

4

STATE FINANCE AND NATIONAL POWER
GREAT BRITAIN, CHINA, AND THE UNITED STATES
IN HISTORICAL PERSPECTIVE

Jeremi Suri

POWER FALLACIES

Foreign policy analysis is only as good as the empirical foundation on which it stands. Policymakers need sophisticated theories to make sense of the deluge of information they confront on a daily basis, but theories that misread basic global dynamics are like business plans that misinterpret the market. Impressive ideas and shiny products elicit bankruptcy, rather than profit, when they are out of touch with their surroundings. Understanding the trends in the external world—what Hegel called the "spirit of history"—is more important than building the best model.

For about a generation, scholars of foreign policy (including both political scientists and historians) have written about national power with little attention to the most important recent empirical insights concerning the actual content of national power. In particular, scholars of foreign policy have treated national power as an end rather than a process, as a largely fixed and quantifiable measure rather than a set of evolving and ever-changing relationships. The noun "power" sounds fixed and firm, but the concept is, in historical terms, much more fluid and changeable on short notice.

Ubiquitous discussions of "hard" and "soft" power reinforce the false assumption that power is something discrete, measureable, and modular. The categories themselves seem fixed and ahistorical. According to many writings, power is a direct object of state policy: it is "built," it is "deployed," and it "declines." Power often sounds like savings in the bank: you can have more or less; you can save it or spend it; and you can gain or lose interest on it, depending on how you invest.[1]

This logical but empirically questionable way of talking about power contributes to three guiding assumptions that are, on closer inspection, largely unfounded. First, common discussions of power assume that having more stuff is good. We

---

[1] For one of the most thoughtful and influential books on the subject, see Joseph S. Nye, Jr., *The Future of Power* (New York: Public Affairs, 2011), especially chapter 1. For one of the most insightful analyses of international politics that remains anchored in the concept of power as a fixed and ahistorical quantity, see John J. Mearsheimer, *The Tragedy of Great Power Politics* (New York: W.W. Norton, 2001).

might call this the *materialist fallacy*. The general argument is that if you have more weapons, more resources, and perhaps more people (large populations appear good, crowded populations appear bad), you are likely to be more powerful. The intuition is that someone with plentiful capabilities can mobilize lots of stuff to make more of what he or she needs, and conquer others at little cost. Material definitions of power call for an accounting of who has more or less than another.

For Americans—who are blessed with material abundance—assessments of this kind make sense. Historical evidence, however, points the other way. As often as not, those societies with the most stuff have found themselves facing defeat at the hands of adversaries with so much less. Think of the Athenian defeat by Sparta and the Roman collapse to a collection of roaming paramilitary groups. The early modern world replayed this pattern with repeated victories by the cold, wet island of Britain over richer, better-endowed empires centered on Spain and France. The rise of the island nation of Japan in nineteenth century East Asia is a similar story, contrasted with the latent power of the huge mainland empire of China. Other things being equal, having more stuff is preferable, but it is not a clear path to lasting power.[2]

The second flawed assumption concerns technology. Observers of foreign policy generally assume that more advanced technology contributes to international reach and effectiveness. According to this argument (which I will call the *innovation fallacy*), scientific and engineering innovations offer the societies that excel in these areas a big advantage. This is a powerful argument for explaining why Britain dominated ocean trade and warfare in the eighteenth and nineteenth centuries. The British had the most advanced ships, navigational instruments, and seaborne weapons. The British invested consistently in maintaining this technological edge, at least until the rise of a German naval challenger in the 1890s.[3]

Americans idealize inventors. We like to think that the innovators always win. That is simply not true. As often as not, innovators suffer from indiscipline, overcommitment, and hubris. Innovators often believe that they can find a "solution" to any problem. In foreign policy, innovators have frequently failed to achieve their aims, and they have hurt their societies in the stubborn quest for a game-changing breakthrough against great odds. Historians Geoffrey Parker and John Elliott have described this phenomenon in Imperial Spain and its efforts to bring innovation to the management of a vast and unwieldy empire that included Northern Europe and South America.[4] T.E. Lawrence famously exposed how British efforts in the Middle East were indeed clever, but still inappropriate for such a diverse and complex region.[5] Closer to our present time, David Halberstam was the first in a long

[2] William H. McNeill's writings remain the best on this topic. See: *The Pursuit of Power: Technology, Armed Force, and Society since A.D. 1000* (Chicago: University of Chicago Press, 1982).

[3] See Paul M. Kennedy, *The Rise and Fall of British Naval Mastery*, 2nd Edition (Amherst, NY: Humanity Books, 1998).

[4] See Geoffrey Parker, *The Grand Strategy of Philip II* (New Haven, CT: Yale University Press, 1998); John H. Elliott, *The Count-Duke of Olivares: The Statesman in an Age of Decline* (New Haven, CT: Yale University Press, 1986).

[5] See T.E. Lawrence, *Seven Pillars of Wisdom: The Complete 1922 Text* (Blacksburg, VA: Wilder, 2011).

line of distinguished authors to show how "the best and the brightest" Americans endeavored, unsuccessfully, to substitute innovation for good sense in Southeast Asia during the Cold War.[6] Some observers have made similar observations about the less-than-successful efforts of America's talented counterinsurgency innovators (John Nagl, Raymond Odierno, David Petraeus, and others) in twenty-first century Iraq and Afghanistan.[7] Innovation does not always increase national power. It often has the opposite effect.

Culture, for some observers, is the key to making innovation produce positive results. This is the third flawed assumption about power, what I will call the *cultural fallacy*. According to this argument, labeled "soft power" by Joseph Nye and others, countries gain international leverage from the consent, or at least acquiescence, that emerges from the spread of ideas, images, and practices.[8] Widely circulating ideas and images also empower new groups who evoke sympathy while the same ideas and images challenge assumptions about the legitimacy of traditional rulers, practices, and laws. Foreign citizens and leaders, by this logic, are less likely to resist and more likely to cooperate when they are convinced that they are on the popular side of a conflict. Entertainment and persuasion are more effective than guns and threats for those that treat power as culture.

More often than not, according to this argument, the popular side is the American or at least the "Western" side. Think of youth culture, rock 'n'roll music, and fast food as primary examples of Westernization through cultural diffusion. Behavior patterns often follow images and sounds that are widely circulated in traditional and especially social media. In the words of one scholar, popular culture frequently makes American interests "irresistible" abroad.[9] Some writers refer to an "Americanization" of the world by largely nonmilitary means.[10]

[6] See David Halberstam, *The Best and the Brightest* (New York: Random House, 1969). For a sophisticated and provocative elaboration on Halberstam's thesis, see Robert D. Dean, *Imperial Brotherhood: Gender and The Making of Cold War Foreign Policy* (Amherst: University of Massachusetts Press, 2001). For a close study of how "the best and the brightest" viewed Indochina before the escalation of American intervention, see Fredrik Logevall, *Embers of War: The Fall of an Empire and the Making of America's Vietnam* (New York: Random House, 2012).

[7] See Rajiv Chandrasekaran, *Little America: The War Within the War for Afghanistan* (New York: Knopf, 2012); Seth G. Jones, *In the Graveyard of Empires: America's War in Afghanistan* (New York: W.W. Norton, 2009).

[8] See Joseph S. Nye, Jr., *Soft Power: The Means to Success in World Politics* (New York: Public Affairs, 2005). For a thoughtful set of essays that engage "soft power" as a theoretical concept and an empirical phenomenon, see Inderjeet Parmar and Michael Cox, eds., *Soft Power and U.S. Foreign Policy: Theoretical, Historical, and Contemporary Perspectives* (London: Routledge, 2010).

[9] See Victoria de Grazia, *Irresistible Empire: America's Advance through Twentieth Century Europe* (Cambridge, MA: Belknap Press of Harvard University Press, 2005).

[10] Books on this topic have clever and seductive titles that, in some cases, substitute for serious analysis of policy and social change. See Robert W. Rydell and Rob Kroes, *Buffalo Bill in Bologna: The Americanization of the World, 1869–1922* (Chicago: University of Chicago Press, 2005); Reinhold Wagnleitner, *Coca-Colonization and the Cold War: The Cultural Mission of the United States in Austria After the Second World War* (Chapel Hill: University of North Carolina Press, 1994).

The spread of American-influenced popular culture is undeniable, but so is the evidence that popular culture does not necessarily increase national power. Popular culture often empowers resistance against its initial source. This is the old pattern of rising expectations that Alexis de Tocqueville first articulated in his analysis of the French Revolution. Masses of citizens revolt when they see that they can have more, and they feel that someone, or some state, is standing in the way.[11] For African slaves in Haiti, the promise of French *liberté* and *egalité* inspired a bloody revolt against Paris.[12] For British settlers in North America, the expectation of property ownership free of onerous taxes, as advocated by British "country radicals," also encouraged rebellion.[13]

Surveying the spread of American ideas and images of freedom in the twentieth century, one observes similar phenomena. The deeper the penetration of American culture, the more likely one finds active, sincere, and popular figures commanding local influence by their open challenge to American power. The Arab uprisings of 2009–2012 are a recent example of this dynamic: courageous citizens in Iran, Tunisia, Egypt, and other societies performed protests that appealed to the "democratic" aspirations of foreign viewers, but they also condemned the local leaders and interests most closely tied to foreign interests. Cultural diffusion encourages simultaneous imitation and resistance, focused on the same sources. As de Tocqueville recognized, those who inspire protest soon find themselves the target of the men and women making revolution.[14]

The common but questionable assumptions about the nature of national power—the materialist, innovation, and cultural fallacies, as I have called them—are sometimes true and sometimes false. They are fallacies because they assert a universal validity when they are, more accurately, contingent and context-specific. They are neither "independent variables" in the parlance of political science, nor laws of change in the conversation of some historians. The fallacies have little inherent predictive value for assessing the growth or decline of national power. They work as *post hoc* explanations for the rise and fall of states only because we already know the results. On close inspection, the winners of international politics only become more wealthy, innovative, and culturally attractive *after they have won*. To the winner go the spoils of historical inevitability.

---

[11] See the classic work by Alexis de Tocqueville: *The Old Regime and the French Revolution*, trans. Stuart Gilbert (New York: Random House, 1983). For an application of de Tocqueville's ideas to the Cold War, see Jeremi Suri, *Power and Protest: Global Revolution and the Rise of Détente* (Cambridge, MA: Harvard University Press, 2003).

[12] See Laurent Dubois, *Avengers of the New World: The Story of the Haitian Revolution* (Cambridge, MA: Harvard University Press, 2004).

[13] The classic work on this topic is: Bernard Bailyn, *The Ideological Origins of the American Revolution* (Cambridge, MA: Belknap Press of Harvard University Press, 1967). See also Gordon S. Wood, *The Radicalism of the American Revolution* (New York: Random House, 1991).

[14] For an early and useful survey of scholarly interpretations of the Arab Spring, see Kenneth M. Pollack, Daniel L. Byman, et. al., *The Arab Awakening: America and the Transformation of the Middle East* (Washington DC: Brooking Institution Press, 2011).

POWER CAPACITIES

States do not "innovate" their way out of difficult circumstances, despite claims to the contrary. States also cannot reverse geopolitical shifts, especially when they have contributed to these shifts through their own behavior. What states can do is adapt and adjust to challenges, mobilizing new domestic capacities for cooperation, competition, and sometimes fighting wars. A successful international state is, there-fore, a regime with effective internal political capacity. A failed international state is one that cannot draw on organized and consistent capacity at home.

Although poets, novelists, journalists, and moviemakers often dramatize the popular convulsions that make for social and political upheaval in long stagnant societies, historians have argued that silent transformations in the management of finance have a much greater effect on national power and its global expressions. Similarly, ambitious ideological projects and impressive territorial conquests have less enduring influence on the leverage of states than the mobilization and manage-ment of capital. Power turns out to depend less on common displays of charisma and strength, and more on unseen manipulations of markets and money.

According to what is now a large and impressive literature, banking, taxation, and government spending have had greater influence on the international reach of states than regime type, aggregate production, or even military aggrandizement. The institutions for acquiring, deploying, and managing revenue have been more important than the obvious and often commented-upon attributes of political, industrial, and military force. From early modern Britain to the modern United States, the bankers and accountants frequently trumped the politicians, the indus-trialists, and the generals in determining the contours of national power. Analysis of foreign policy has, to date, failed to focus appropriately. Too many pundits are enthralled with those who speak loudly, rather than those who allocate the real cur-rencies of international influence.[15]

Finance is not determinative of state power. It is, of course, deeply connected to the material endowments, innovative capacities, and cultural resources of a soci-ety. The availability of inexpensive capital for investment and spending, however, is the necessary foundation for all manifestations of state power. Without sufficient capital, even the most advanced, cohesive, and legitimate government cannot sus-tain continued expansion of its capabilities. Available capital will not substitute for the other attributes, but it will allow the *possibility* for more state activity in pursuit of security and prosperity. A functioning system of finance is fundamental to sus-tained state power. The historical record is quite clear on this point.[16]

---

[15] On this point, see the classic works by Robert Gilpin: *The Political Economy of International Relations* (Princeton, NJ: Princeton University Press, 1987); and *Global Political Economy: Understanding the International Economic Order* (Princeton, NJ: Princeton University Press, 2001). See also Niall Ferguson, *The Cash Nexus: Money and Power in the Modern World, 1700–2000* (New York: Basic Books, 2001).

[16] Paul Kennedy's foundational work examines this history in depth, affirming the fundamental importance of sound finance for the sustenance of great powers. Kennedy shows that nations can grow and expand without sound finance, but they cannot sustain that growth and expansion if they confront domestic capital shortages due to burdensome foreign military and occupation

Effective state finance involves credible and competent institutions and practices of governance and commerce that affirm the role of those institutions. Simply explained, the government must tax consistently, investors must believe that their loans will be honored, and consumers must trust that their property will be protected. Institutions, however, are only one part of finance. State leaders must attract and manage available capital to support productive uses, especially for economic growth and military security. This is the key historical variable: are effective institutions managed to encourage the allocation of capital for growth and security? Do citizens and investors have confidence that state institutions will continue to encourage effective capital accumulations and allocations for the public good?[17]

State power is, in the long run, a reflection of financial capacity (embedded in institutions of banking and taxation) and forward-looking leadership (exercised by figures who use their authority to incentivize productive capital investments). Effective leaders must do more than rule; they must attract wealth and encourage its uses for the improvement of the population and the state. Effective leaders are builders and protectors of national (and international) financial institutions that increase the capacity of the state and its people to push their self-interested agendas. Power is, ultimately, found in the acquisition, management, and deployment of capital for strategic purposes. Finance is the lubricant for all parts of state power.

There are many different theories for state power in the modern international system: realist, constructivist, and liberal, among others.[18] This focus on finance does not necessarily privilege one of these theories over another. What close attention to finance argues is that all descriptive and normative accounts of state power presume capital for mobilization of military, political, and cultural resources. To paraphrase Machiavelli, a prince can neither be feared nor loved if his treasury is barren. The successful prince must find ways to generate new wealth. Taxation and expropriation are two common mechanisms employed by many leaders for this purpose, but they are not sufficient in a competitive international system, and they are frequently counterproductive. The historical record since the eighteenth century

expenses. See Paul Kennedy, *The Rise and Fall of the Great Powers: Economic Change and Military Conflict from 1500 to 2000* (New York: Random House, 1987), especially xv–xxv, and pp. 73–139. See also Paul Kennedy, ed., *Grand Strategies in War and Peace* (New Haven: Yale University Press, 1992).

[17] This paragraph draws upon a number of notable studies, including: Daron Acemoğlu and James Robinson, *Why Nations Fail: The Origins of Power, Prosperity, and Poverty* (New York: Crown, 2012); Ian Morris, *Why the West Rules—For Now: The Patterns of History and What They Reveal About the Future* (New York: Farrar, Straus, and Giroux, 2010); David S. Landes, *The Wealth and Poverty of Nations: Why Some Are So Rich and Some So Poor* (New York: W.W. Norton, 1998); Jared M. Diamond, *Guns, Germs, and Steel: The Fates of Human Societies* (New York: W.W. Norton, 1997).

[18] For recent representative works, see Kenneth N. Waltz, *Theory of International Politics* (New York: McGraw-Hill, 1979); Alexander Wendt, *Social Theory of International Politics* (New York: Cambridge University Press, 1999); G. John Ikenberry, *Liberal Leviathan: The Origins, Crisis, and Transformation of the American World Order* (Princeton, NJ: Princeton University Press, 2011).

points to an alternative path, beginning with what some have identified as the first modern "financial revolution."

THE "FINANCIAL REVOLUTION" OF THE EIGHTEENTH CENTURY

Writing almost fifty years ago, British historian P.G.M. Dickson described what he called the "financial revolution" in England during the early eighteenth century—the period when the small island nation began its rise as an international power. Dickson observed the continued inferiority of English manufacturing and military activities in comparison to Spain and France. Both of the continental states had larger, richer populations and larger, richer empires. The English defended themselves against difficult odds and they leaped ahead of their competitors because of one major development in the late seventeenth century: the creation of a new system for the management of revenue and credit, centered on London. This new system did not arise overnight, and did not reflect the "genius" of any particular figure. The new system of credit emerged from conditions encouraged by the new English monarchy, after the Glorious Revolution, and the collection of North European bankers and businesspeople who sought better investment opportunities for their capital, as well as more long-term profit.[19]

Before these changes in the late seventeenth century, English investment deficiencies contrasted with the surplus capital that flowed into Spain from its Latin American silver mines. While the English were resource poor, living on a cold wet island, the Spanish benefited from an abundance of resources, extracted from a large mineral-rich empire. The French had similar advantages over England, especially based on the Bourbon monarchy's large territorial holdings within continental Europe. The English also were not "natural" bankers; they did not have a historical advantage in this area and their monarchy, like others, had relied on foreign financiers.

The "financial revolution" was born of a specific time period, and the pressing necessity for English economic reform in the aftermath of the Glorious Revolution. English leaders recognized that their new monarchy needed new tools of power if it was going to compete with neighbors who were growing stronger and more aggressive. English citizens, through Parliament, demanded levers to control the new monarchy and insure that it used its powers for the common good. The "financial revolution" was the most enduring outcome of the political upheavals that, in the end, transformed England's position in the world. It was neither planned nor anticipated, but it quickly became an emerging competitive advantage for England. The "financial revolution" had wider immediate effects in boosting state capacities than the new claims of political rights in England, and it provided a secure context for new political rights to gain permanence in domestic and imperial practice.

---

[19] See P.G.M. Dickson, *The Financial Revolution in England: A Study in the Development of Public Credit, 1688–1756* (London: St. Martin's, 1967).

Daron Acemoğlu and James Robinson appropriately call this transformation "the turning point" for the remarkable centuries-long rise in British prosperity and security. Through an empowered Parliament, a consensual monarchy, an expanded banking system, and a well-regulated market for economic exchanges, the "capability and capacity of the state increased in all directions."[20] In the eighteenth century the English government was simultaneously able to tax and spend more than ever before. The oversight of Parliament after the Glorious Revolution meant that the capital acquired by the central government was allocated for productive public investments, and the organized merchant and labor groups throughout the country insured that taxes were not too destructive to commerce. The rough balance struck in England between the need to tax capital and encourage its investment, with government support, contributed to the development of powerful new resources for expanding wealth and security throughout the country. The "financial revolution" constituted a new set of fiscal practices that strengthened state and society in enduring ways. The "financial revolution" had two key components: credit and taxes.

CREDIT

England, according to Dickson, converted its penury into prosperity by developing the first modern system of credit. The new king, William III, and his successor Queen Anne, encouraged the formation of a vast banking sector centered in London, where men (some Jewish exiles from the continent) exchanged loans of cash for contracts on agricultural and manufactured goods that would be produced in the future. Savvy investors also traded on risk, insuring one another's shipping and production against uncertainty, in exchange for up-front fees. England provided a stable political environment for finance capital, and government figures welcomed bankers and brokers ("jobbers") in London. The Bank of England (founded in 1694) and the infamous South Seas Company (founded in 1711) provided government sanction for finance capital, and direct avenues for investment by international traders assembling in London.[21]

Amsterdam had been the previous European center for these activities, but late-seventeenth-century London quickly became a more attractive locale because of its friendly business climate, combined with greater separation from French and Spanish threats. England also had the advantage of a sizeable hinterland and extensive ocean access, with a growing navy, financed in part by new credits. The political disunity of the United Provinces and their strategic vulnerability made them a less attractive investment hub when London opened, after the Glorious Revolution, as a welcoming alternative.[22]

---

[20] Acemoğlu and Robinson, *Why Nations Fail*, 196.

[21] Dickson, *The Financial Revolution in England*. For a more recent elaboration of Dickson's argument, see Carl Wennerlind, *Casualties of Credit: The English Financial Revolution, 1620–1720* (Cambridge, MA: Harvard University Press, 2011). Wennerlind gives more emphasis than Dickson to the role of state-sanctioned violence in the enforcement of credit in seventeenth century England.

[22] See Kennedy, *The Rise and Fall of the Great Powers*, 76–86.

The capital market in what became known as the "City" created numerous opportunities for the English government to borrow more money at lower cost than ever before. This is what made the "financial revolution" a significant geopolitical phenomenon. The Crown had procured loans in prior wars at an average rate of eight percent on short-term obligations. These loans came due as soon as a war concluded, and they placed an enormous immediate burden on the monarchy, especially when wars did not produce promised profits—as was almost always the case. The cycle of war, bankruptcy, and more war that characterized seventeenth-century Europe was a result of recurring debt burdens. After fighting one war on credit, monarchs had to find new wars that promised to pay off their debts. The cycle thus continued.

With new capital instruments around early eighteenth-century London, the English Crown gained access to loans on much better terms. The state began to borrow at about three percent (rather than eight percent) on long-term (rather than short-term) obligations. These debts were denominated in bonds and other paper instruments that allowed for a pooling of capital from diverse investors, and a flexible negotiation of terms. Government obligations could be traded and renegotiated in what became an active secondary credit market.[23]

Although London bankers were mostly independent profit-seekers, they attracted more money to London than ever before, and they managed an organized and predictable system of exchange. This system made borrowing easier for families and businesses—the most important of which was the monarchy. The system also encouraged a rational allocation of resources to public and private endeavors that promised real returns, not simply glory or other illusory gains. In return for favorable terms as a respected and credible borrower, the governments of William III and his successors provided legal sanction for London credit markets and judicial enforcement of contract obligations, even those that bound the Crown. Increased access to credit was accompanied by more creditable behavior, and one attribute reinforced the other.[24]

In this credit-rich context, during the eighteenth century the Crown accumulated an unprecedentedly high national debt. The large national debt was, however, easier and less costly to service than in the past. At a lower interest rate, servicing the debt required a smaller proportion of the Crown's annual budget. In a fluid market of financial instruments, the crown could also borrow readily to pay off unexpected obligations, re-finance existing debt, and renegotiate more favorable loan terms. The credit market in London gave the Crown flexibilities that greatly strengthened its options in war and other forms of international competition.[25]

William III and his successors allocated their borrowed capital to a series of wars in what was a period of intensive conflict and empire-building on four continents. They also invested in new institutions to manage the combination of capital and warfare that defined emerging English state power. In 1757 the Crown successfully extended its rule over parts of the Indian subcontinent through the East India Company with extensive military deployments paid for on credit. In 1783, in

[23] Ibid.

[24] See Wennerlind, *Casualties of Credit*, chapters 3 and 4.

[25] See Kennedy, *The Rise and Fall of the Great Powers*, 76–86.

contrast, the Crown withdrew from what became the independent United States after a costly war, also paid on credit. The Indian and American wars had different outcomes, but a small island nation could fight both of them (and other costly conflicts) because of extensive credit availability.[26]

The key point is that the English government could borrow enough money to fight these wars, despite a poor resource base, and continue to invest in basic needs at home. The wars produced mixed outcomes for English national interests, but the Crown remained solvent and continued to borrow at low rates. Credit allowed England to grow at home and punch above its weight abroad. It allowed England to address major challenges, and weather the mixed results of war.

The French monarchy, in contrast, had a much larger resource base, but went bankrupt because it could not service its existing debts or borrow new money at reasonable rates. The Spanish monarchy faced a similar credit crunch. Access to credit, more than domestic resources or traditional military capabilities, determined national power in the eighteenth century. Finance forged enduring state capacity.

TAXES

Historians following Dickson have expanded our understanding of national power and state capacity beyond credit to focus on taxation. John Brewer has written about what he calls the "sinews of power" that extend into the ability of the state to mobilize capital directly from the citizen body. The true revolution in eighteenth-century England, according to Brewer, was that the Crown could draw in more capital from its citizens on an annual basis, while simultaneously gaining increased allegiance from the taxed population. This was particularly striking because increased Crown taxes followed the Glorious Revolution, when English parliamentarians and subjects had, in fact, overthrown a monarchy that tried to increase taxes.[27]

Brewer argued that the genius of English power in the eighteenth century was the increased role of Parliament as a taxing institution, raising revenue for the Crown through mechanisms that promised more public accountability and service of the national interest. Parliament relied on increased trade tariffs, according to Brewer, but it used this taxing mechanism sparingly. Members of Parliament recognized that they wanted to encourage trade, not excessively tax it. They also wanted to maintain their control over the Crown through taxes that were less automatic, and required the monarch to make a direct case to the legislature, on an annual basis, about the needs and uses of tax revenue. Parliament relied heavily on excise taxes—surcharges on purchases, landholdings, and transactions—that were renewed annually to provide the crown needed revenue, but also affirmed parliamentary consent. Increased excise taxes raised capital from the population, and they gave the population more say in policy through the annual debates in Parliament.[28]

---

[26] Ibid., 86–139.

[27] See John Brewer, *The Sinews of Power: War, Money, and the English State, 1688–1783* (Cambridge, MA: Harvard University Press, 1990).

[28] Brewer has a brilliant chapter on the debates about excise taxes and Parliament's role. See *The Sinews of Power*, 137–161.

Propertied male citizens paid more to the state, but they felt empowered to believe that the state would be more responsive to their needs. Taxation was not a tribute to the monarch; it was now a contract between the governors and the governed. In this contractual arrangement, the English state could tax more in the common defense than most of its peer competitors. And, in fact, it did that throughout the eighteenth and nineteenth centuries. Brewer described this phenomenon as both the triumph of democracy and the rise of the "fiscal-military state." These were mutually reinforcing developments.[29]

From the perspective of creditors, the new tax regime in England made the state a more attractive borrower. Bankers believed that the state had the capacity to raise internal revenue, when necessary, to service loans. Bankers also recognized that parliamentary consent limited the adventurism of the Crown, encouraging wise investments of borrowed capital and less waste. Most of all, the tax regime gave everyone an interest in the growth of English national power. If the Crown fought and won its wars at low cost, creditors would profit and citizens would pay less tax. If the Crown squandered its resources, the pain would be distributed among citizens and creditors alike. Taxation gave credit a firm foundation in national consent, rather than elite whims.

National power for Dickson, Brewer, and the many historians who have followed their lead was constituted by the deep connection between credit and taxation. National power was the state's capacity to raise money for weapons, investments, and trade. National power was about processes of *resource procurement and management by government*, not aggregate resource production. Money required territory and goods for trade, but it also mattered more than either or both together.

France had a much larger gross domestic product than England in the eighteenth century. France had a much larger army. France also had a greater basic resource endowment. Those attributes did not give the Parisian government the upper hand against a small, weaker, and poorer England. The government in London outstripped Paris because it had easier access to money raised on credit markets and taxed from its population. The capacity to raise money through a centralized government meant more than anything else.

During the Napoleonic Wars of the late eighteenth and early nineteenth centuries, when Britain's security was most imperiled by a massive French army rolling over the European continent and an attempted French naval blockade of the British Isles, the London government was able to tax its population more than any of its peers. A succession of prime ministers used that domestic capital to finance, often through direct foreign subsidies, a coalition that ultimately defeated Napoleon's dominant military juggernaut. Britain financed the victory in a way that none of the other richer European states could at the time. London was remarkably effective at converting taxes and credits into guns and subsidies over more than two decades of prolonged warfare.[30]

---

[29] Brewer, *Sinews*, esp. 167–217.

[30] The seminal work on British finance and the Napoleonic Wars is John M. Sherwig, *Guineas and Gunpowder: British Foreign Aid in the Wars with France, 1793–1815* (Cambridge, MA: Harvard University Press, 1969), esp. 345–356.

The state's capacity to raise money was the foundational source of national power. In these terms, no one had a better system for producing power capacities than England in the eighteenth and nineteenth centuries. The English borrowed more than their peers, and they paid more taxes than most of their peers. They raised the capital to exert international power with a consistency and a geographical breadth that no one with lesser financial capabilities could match. This was quite an achievement for a small, wet island near so many bigger states.[31]

GENTLEMANLY CAPITALISM, EMPIRE, AND THE GREAT WAR

Until the First World War the English processes of credit and taxation fueled the growth of empire. Historians P.J. Cain and A. G. Hopkins, in what is now the authoritative history of British imperialism, document how finance centered in London gave the crown and its leading representatives the ability to maintain a dominant Navy, a profitable global trading system, a far-flung land empire, and a universally respected currency. Even as late as 1914, the British could borrow more money at less cost than any other society. Great Britain also had a citizen body that paid high taxes, and accepted limits on domestic consumption for the sake of managing a worldwide empire. Over two centuries, the British financed growing state capacities more efficiently than any of their peers.[32]

Cain and Hopkins remind us that British power did not turn on the Industrial Revolution or the experience of military prowess at sea, as some have claimed. The British could lead in these two areas because they had the best finances for technology, training, and production. Britain's comparative advantage was fundamentally financial, and it was self-reinforcing in a way that industrial and military advantages were not. Other states—France, Germany, Russia, Japan, and the United States—caught up to British production and military capability at times. They could *not* supersede the accumulated credibility that London had established as the safest, most creative, and most attractive financial center in the world. The money flowed most freely to London from home and abroad, and the crown deployed that capital as no one else could. Cain and Hopkins aptly call this the triumph of "gentlemanly capitalism"—the fusion of sophisticated finance with a landed elite that was willing to work with the market to maximize state capacity.[33]

---

[31] On the extraordinary achievements of British power, despite its limited domestic resource base, see John Darwin, *The Empire Project, The Rise and Fall of the British World-System, 1830–1970* (Cambridge, UK: Cambridge University Press, 2009).

[32] See P.J. Cain and A.G. Hopkins, *British Imperialism, 1688–2000*, 2nd Edition (London: Longman, 2001).

[33] See the seminal articles by P.J. Cain and A.G. Hopkins: "The Political Economy of British Expansion Overseas, 1750–1914," *The Economic History Review* 33, no. 4 (November 1980): 463–490; "Gentlemanly Capitalism and British Expansion Overseas I: The Old Colonial System, 1688–1850," *The Economic History Review* 39, no. 4 (November 1986): 501–525; "Gentlemanly

The Glorious Revolution empowered the gentlemanly capitalists around Parliament and the court of the new king. The First World War, however, destroyed the gentlemanly capitalists and their effective processes of credit and taxation. Fighting for four years at unprecedented cost, Britain ran out of credit. By 1918 London could no longer borrow at affordable rates from the United States and other capital markets. The center of global finance shifted from London to New York. The bloody nature of the war also smothered the British tax base. The most able-bodied citizens—including the gentlemanly capitalists—gave their lives on the battlefields of Northern Europe. Britain lost the citizens in war who had paid the high taxes that had financed the empire.[34]

England's rise and fall as a global power was about the rise and fall of English finance, more than anything else. Credit and taxation were the essential instruments of power, as Brewer has argued. Efficient and attractive processes for credit and taxation developed around late-seventeenth-century London fueled the state capacities that the crown deployed for naval strength, imperial conquest, extended warfare, and economic gain. Efficient and attractive processes for credit and taxation turned a small island into a world power. When these processes crashed in a long and destructive total war, they reduced British world power to second-rate status. After 1914 Britain lacked the capacity to finance its global role. For the next century, it needed the financial (and military) assistance of the United States, as never before.

QING CHINA'S FAILED MODERNIZATION

In the late nineteenth century China faced a series of strategic challenges on an even larger scale than Great Britain. The empire that had dominated the Asian mainland for at least five hundred years suffered from military and political vulnerabilities that imperiled its basic security. Great Britain, France, Germany, Japan, and to a smaller extent the United States, were carving up pieces of Chinese territory. The external powers formed an archipelago of "concession areas" that they controlled in and around the Chinese Pacific coastline. The foreign powers grabbed these territories through the use of superior military technology, organized economic incursions, and forceful political intervention.[35]

British seizure of Hong Kong after the "First Opium War" of 1839–1842 was an extreme example of how other countries demanded access to the Chinese market for their exports, with special "extraterritorial" protection for foreign workers, control over local policing, and the imposition of foreign law.[36] The United States even

---

Capitalism and British Expansion Overseas II: New Imperialism, 1850–1945," *The Economic History Review* 40, no. 1 (February 1987): 1–26. For a detailed critique of the "gentlemanly capitalism" concept, see Andrew Porter, "'Gentlemanly Capitalism' and Empire: The British Experience since 1750?" *The Journal of Imperial and Commonwealth History* 18, no. 3 (June 1990): 265–295.

[34] See Kennedy, *The Rise and Fall of the Great Powers*, 194–274; Niall Ferguson, *The Pity of War: Explaining World War I* (New York: Basic Books, 1998), chapters 5, 9, and 14.

[35] See John King Fairbank, *The Great Chinese Revolution, 1800–1985* (New York: Harper and Row, 1986).

[36] The classic study of this history remains John King Fairbank, *Trade and Diplomacy on the China Coast: The Opening of the Treaty Ports, 1842–1854* (Cambridge, MA: Harvard University Press, 1964).

created a federal district court in the early twentieth century to adjudicate legal disputes in American-controlled parts of China.[37] In the case of Japanese-controlled areas, Tokyo pursued brutal settlement policies designed to eliminate local Chinese populations and replace them with Japanese colonists. This was a "century of humiliation" as remembered in Chinese historical accounts today.[38]

From the early twentieth century to the present, Chinese and foreign observers have blamed the weakness of the Middle Kingdom on the obvious failings of the Qing regime. First, writers have pointed to the tradition-bound nature of Chinese society, with a bureaucracy still built around mastery of Confucian texts and an economy dominated by conservative landed elites. Second, observers have emphasized the isolationist and ethnocentric qualities of Qing China. According to William H. McNeill and others, these qualities discouraged innovation and growth at a time when Japan and the West were, in contrast, mobilizing innovation and growth for the purposes of state power.[39] Third, and perhaps most obvious, commentators have argued that the Qing dynasty entered a period of rapid decline as the imperial family became progressively isolated and ill-equipped for managing the complex pressures that accompanied a more competitive international system.[40]

Bernardo Bertolucci's stunning film, *The Last Emperor*, captures this last point with memorable scenes of the final child monarch, Pu Yi, struggling to understand modern society as his state crumbles around him. Pu Yi spent some of the last years of his life in a communist prison camp. He symbolized the end of an old, tradition-bound China. Mao Zedong's government released Pu Yi from prison in 1959 after he renounced his own family and embraced the new world order of the Chinese Communist Party. Mao Zedong's government was catastrophic in the death and destruction that it spread, but it was modern, internationalist, and vigorous in all the ways that the late imperial regime was not. The failure of a backward-looking, isolated, and leaderless China inspired a nightmare of the opposite qualities, according to the conventional wisdom articulated by Bertolucci and so many other observers.[41]

---

[37] See Eileen P. Scully, *Bargaining with the State from Afar: American Citizenship in Treaty Port China, 1844–1942* (New York: Columbia University Press, 2001).

[38] See Louis Young, *Japan's Total Empire: Manchuria and the Culture of Wartime Imperialism* (Berkeley: University of California Press, 1998).

[39] See William H. McNeill, *The Rise of the West: A History of the Human Community* (Chicago: University of Chicago, 1991).

[40] See Frederic Wakeman, Jr., *The Fall of Imperial China* (New York: Free Press, 1977).

[41] See Bernardo Bertolucci, Director, *The Last Emperor*, DVD, Columbia Pictures, October 1987. For background on the film and various interpretations, see Bruce H. Sklarew et al., eds., *Bertolucci's The Last Emperor: Multiple Takes* (Detroit: Wayne State University Press, 1998). Many scholars of China have pointed to the "Republican" period—between the fall of the Qing Empire in 1912 and the victory of the Communist Party in 1949—as a lost opportunity for more open, stable, and sustainable Chinese economic and political development. See Frank Dikötter, *The Age of Openness: China before Mao* (Berkeley: University of California Press, 2008); Brett Sheehan, *Trust in Troubled Times: Money, Banks, and State-Society Relations in Republican Tianjin* (Cambridge, MA: Harvard University Press, 2003); Frederic Wakeman, Jr., and Richard Louis Edmonds, eds., *Reappraising Republican China* (New York: Oxford University Press, 2000).

There is, of course, some truth to this depiction. There is also a lot that is misleading in this standard account. Odd Arne Westad's recent study of Chinese society persuasively argues that Qing China was filled with many modernizing, cosmopolitan, and capable figures who worked to reform the Chinese state and economy in parallel with their counterparts in Europe and Japan. Westad shows how diverse and international figures brought a creative mix of ideas and policy proposals to a frequently receptive regime. Westad claims that Qing China was a dynamic "hybrid" society, not the isolated, tradition-bound, self-enclosed kingdom of retrospective depictions. China's "backwardness" is largely a *post hoc* explanation for the chaos and collapse of the twentieth century, and the rise of the Mao's Chinese Communist Party.[42]

The evidence for this historical revisionism about China is overwhelming. Historians have analyzed the dynamic and promising efforts at "self-strengthening" in China during the second half of the nineteenth century, led by impressive figures like Li Hongzhang, Liang Qichao, Li Dazhao, and many others. These men had traditional credentials as Confucian scholars, but they also studied foreign ideas (especially through education in Japan) and brought them into Chinese policy discussions. Li Hongzhang, in particular, led Qing efforts to reduce opium abuse, improve general literacy, modernize military training, and negotiate effective alliances with foreign powers—especially Russia and the United States. Li was the first Chinese official to visit St. Petersburg and Washington DC in 1896. He met with US President Grover Cleveland to discuss enhanced Sino-American economic and political cooperation, and he allegedly introduced chop suey to New York City audiences.[43] Li Hongzhang, Liang Qichao, and Li Dazhao were part of a growing group of self-conscious international modernizers with a wide following in late Qing China.[44]

Jung Chang has recently published an impressive biography of Empress Dowager Cixi, who largely controlled the Chinese imperial regime through a

---

[42] See Odd Arne Westad, *Restless Empire: China and the World Since 1750* (New York: Basic Books, 2012). Jonathan Spence makes a similar argument in his magisterial account: *The Search for Modern China*, 3rd Edition (New York: W.W. Norton, 2012). See also Mary C. Wright, *The Last Stand of Chinese Conservatism: The T'ung-chih Restoration, 1862–1874* (Stanford: Stanford University Press, 1957).

[43] Daniel B. Schneider, "The Origins of Suey," *New York Times* (May 6 2001). Available at: http://www.nytimes.com/2001/05/06/nyregion/fyi-150452.html.

[44] Although it is frequently ignored in discussions of nineteenth-century China's alleged "backwardness," the literature on the influence of the Chinese modernizers is enormous. For some of the seminal works see: Wright, *The Last Stand of Chinese Conservatism*; Michael H. Hunt, *The Making of a Special Relationship: The United States and China to 1914* (New York: Columbia University Press, 1983); Vera Schwarcz, *The Chinese Enlightenment: Intellectuals and the Legacy of the May Fourth Movement of 1919* (Berkeley: University of California Press, 1986); Xiaobing Tang, *Global Space and the Nationalist Discourse of Modernity: The Historical Thinking of Liang Qichao* (Stanford: Stanford University Press, 1996); Pankaj Mishra, *From the Ruins of Empire: The Intellectuals Who Remade Asia* (New York: Farrar, Straus, and Giroux, 2012), chapter 3.

Figure 4.1 Li Hongzhang, during his Visit to the United States in 1896.

series of young and ill Emperors during the four decades after 1861. Drawing on a wealth of newly accessible Chinese documents, Chang depicts Cixi as an astute and cagey modernizer, encouraging men like Li Hongzhang to learn from the West and reform antiquated Chinese educational, military, and business institutions. During Cixi's reign, Chinese international trade grew and the Empress imported foreign experts, most famously Robert Hart, to manage this process. Chang shows how the duties on foreign trade, collected by Cixi, allowed her to finance other modernizing activities that ran against the interests of the established mainland families and bureaucracies.[45]

Empress Cixi's nearly fifty years of power—roughly parallel to Queen Victoria in Great Britain—clearly affirm that Chinese leaders were not necessarily tradition-bound or "behind" their counterparts in other countries. They were, in some ways, more advanced in their intellectual sophistication and their efforts to bridge the old with the new. Li Dazhao, for instance, helped to found the Chinese Communist Party through a small study group that articulated a vision of peasant transformation and nationalist assertion. Li Dazhao and his fellow communists, including

---

[45] See Jung Chang, *Empress Dowager Cixi: The Concubine Who Launched Modern China* (New York: Knopf, 2013). For more on Robert Hart's role in Chinese trade and modernization, see Richard J. Smith, John K. Fairbank, and Katherine F. Bruner, eds., *Robert Hart and China's Early Modernization: His Journals, 1863–1866* (Cambridge, MA: Harvard East Asian Studies Center, 1991).

young Mao Zedong, were easily as sophisticated and forward-looking as Woodrow Wilson, Vladimir Lenin, and Benito Mussolini.[46]

The chief hindrance confronting the Chinese modernizers was the absence of state capacity. Their ideas floated through Chinese society without a strong set of institutions on which they could rely for practical implementation. Compared to the states of Western Europe, Russia, Japan, and the United States, Qing China had the weakest institutions of governance. For all the pomp and circumstance surrounding the Emperor as the "Son of Heaven," he reigned but he hardly ruled.

During the late nineteenth and early twentieth centuries, China suffered from ineffectual state institutions. Many parts of mainland China, along the coast and within the interior, were largely ungoverned by a central administration between 1912 and 1949. This fact explains the survival of Mao's Communist Party as an insurgent force, despite decades of effort by the Guomindang regime and Japanese invaders to crush it.[47]

The weaknesses of the Chinese state were structural and historical. The Qing imperial court had very limited revenue-generating authority. It had massive accrued wealth in land and jewels, but few mechanisms for annual taxation. The Emperor could collect trade tariffs, but even these were difficult to enforce when many coastal trade ports cut their own deals with foreign shippers and businesspeople. In fact, precisely when Empress Cixi turned to trade tariffs as a new revenue generator, political turmoil gave local figures more leverage to assert their own decentralized control over exchanges with foreigners. During the second half of the nineteenth century, the Emperor lacked the policing power, institutional reach, or public legitimacy to demand that merchants and officials pay the central government for the right to trade.

These were governing powers the Emperor had never possessed in the recent past; they were nearly impossible to create in a time of increasing state fragmentation. Although the Emperor continued to receive tribute as the titular leader of China, his receipts paled in comparison to the revenue generation of trade for other central governments at the time, especially Japan and the United States.[48]

[46] See Maurice J. Meisner, *Li Ta-chao and the Origins of Chinese Marxism* (Cambridge, MA: Harvard University Press, 1967); Arif Dirlik, *The Origins of Chinese Communism* (New York: Oxford University Press, 1989).

[47] On this point, see the classic account by Edgar Snow: *Red Star Over China* (New York: Random House, 1944). See also William Hinton, *Fanshen: A Documentary of Revolution in a Chinese Village* (Berkeley: University of California Press, 1966).

[48] The United States, in particular, benefited from a large federal budget surplus in the 1880s due to federally enforced tariffs on expanding international trade. See Douglas A. Irwin, "Higher Tariffs, Lower Revenues? Analyzing the Fiscal Aspects of the 'Great Tariff Debate of 1888,'" National Bureau of Economic Research, Working Paper 6239 (October 1997), available at: http://www.nber.org/papers/w6239.

QING TAXES

The Chinese central government had relied for at least a century on a very low and unchanging land tax. That was the main source of annual revenue for the imperial regime. The Emperor also maintained a small tax on salt, and he received tribute from wealthy families, traders, and foreign representatives who approached the Middle Kingdom with decreasing deference. Tax extraction, as a whole, was very low. State institutions for regulating wealth and procuring resources from the public were weak and ineffectual. By the second half of the nineteenth century, the Emperor's reach was highly constrained, and his authority over the country's economy was more symbolic than real.

In some interior regions, local families and officials controlled fiscal resources. In many coastal areas, foreign groups increasingly dominated economic decisions and revenue allocations. In marked comparison to the "fiscal-military state" that evolved in eighteenth century Great Britain, Qing China devolved into a hollow and bankrupt state in the nineteenth century as it sought to modernize from the center without sufficient mechanisms for extracting resources from the coasts and hinterlands. As Daron Acemoğlu and James Robinson explain, nations with traditionally strong leaders who lack effective institutions for investing resources are bound to fail, often precipitously.[49]

Although the taxes and tribute added to the Emperor's riches, they offered little capital for building a modern military or investing in domestic economic development. Even in earlier centuries of Qing power, the central government had operated with little capital. In war and in peace, the Emperor's presence in China was powerful, but his direct control over resources was very limited. Qing China had impressive rulers but emasculated institutions for doing anything more than maintaining the status quo. The primary limitations did not come from Chinese traditions, which were largely adaptable, but from Chinese governing institutions which were capital poor.[50]

The "self-strengtheners" of the late nineteenth century, like Li Hongzhang, learned this hard lesson when they tried to create an advanced military, along with modern schools and factories. Li had political authority and support from the central government, but he did not have the money to pay the army, hire the teachers, and build the factories that he sought for China. He faced resistance from the established bureaucrats who had access to the few available government resources. Li could not buy them off, and he could not hire a new governing corps to supplant the established officials. In contrast to the more intrusive Meiji regime in Japan, the Qing state did not have the internal reach it needed to mobilize the country's vast resources for centralized development. The failure of Qing China was the failure to become sufficiently extractive.[51]

---

[49] Acemoğlu and Robinson, *Why Nations Fail*, esp. 368–403.

[50] This is one of the central points of Arthur Waldron's brilliant efforts to uncover the myths of the Great Wall of China and the state that allegedly built it. See *The Great Wall of China: From History to Myth* (Cambridge, UK: Cambridge University Press, 1992).

[51] For the best account of Qing China's financial and institutional weaknesses for pursuing a modern agenda, especially in contrast to Meiji Japan, see Wright, *The Last Stand of Chinese*

Historian Huaiyin Li has shown that in the seventeenth and eighteenth centuries the low taxes of the Qing regime produced enough revenue to cover the
small costs of maintaining the state and fighting border wars in the East. The central government, in fact, had a surplus of reserves until the end of the eighteenth
century. Tribute from citizens and neighbors provided additional resources and
assured stability in a Sinocentric regional order. The Emperor asserted his authority as a symbol and a broker, rather than a dynamic state ruler. Foreign threats to
Chinese territorial integrity were not significant in the seventeenth and eighteenth
centuries.[52]

The nineteenth century brought a crisis of governance as Chinese citizens and
neighbors began to demand more from the Emperor and the state. The Chinese
population grew rapidly, especially in poor rural areas. With more pressure on
the land, landholders had trouble paying their taxes to the state. Local authorities
looked to the central government, as they had not before, to maintain basic order.
This was especially true as a series of popular revolts spread across the mainland.
The longest and most devastating of these revolts was the Taiping Rebellion, which
over the course of fifteen years (1850–1864) resulted in more than 20 million
deaths![53]

The Emperor had to pay for costly military forces to put down these rebellions
as he also built new defenses against the foreign incursions on the Pacific coast.
Modernizers like Li Hongzhang simultaneously demanded government capital
for new military academies, basic infrastructure, law enforcement, and diplomatic activity. By the middle of the nineteenth century, the revenue-constrained
Chinese Emperor could not possibly cover the multiplying demands on his treasury. The central government lacked money, and it did not have an institutional
mechanism for raising new capital. If anything, the old processes for land taxation
and imperial tribute were producing less revenue just when the Emperor needed
so much more. The Chinese state was in crisis because it lacked sufficient taxing
power.[54]

Conservatism. Michael Hunt describes how some Chinese "self-strengtheners," especially
Li Hongzhang, looked to the United States for assistance. See Hunt, *The Making of a Special
Relationship.* Li sought to build partnerships with the United States, but he had no mechanism for receiving foreign aid. The United States never considered financial assistance to Qing
China. American investments in China were private, although they benefited from US gov-
ernment efforts to open opportunities and enforce contracts, especially in the years between
1909 and 1929. On this point, see Thomas J. McCormick, *The China Market: America's Quest
for Informal Empire, 1893–1901* (Chicago: Ivan Dee, 1967); Emily S. Rosenberg, *Spreading the
American Dream: American Economic and Cultural Expansion, 1890–1945* (New York: Hill and
Wang, 1982).

[52] Huaiyin Li, "Geopolitics, Fiscal Constitution, and Statecraft: The Qing Empire Revisited."
Paper presented at the Institute for Historical Studies, University of Texas at Austin, November
12, 2012.

[53] On the Taiping Rebellion and its connection to broader challenges to Qing rule, see Jonathan
D. Spence, *God's Chinese Son: The Taiping Heavenly Kingdom of Hong Xiuquan* (New York: W.W.
Norton, 1996).

[54] See Li, "Geopolitics, Fiscal Constitution, and Statecraft: The Qing Empire Revisited."

QING CREDIT

Unlike Great Britain (which also faced tax deficiencies in the late nineteenth century), the Chinese Emperor could not borrow money. The Qing court refused to participate in the standard practices of international banking: transparent accounting, commitment of collateral, and promise of contract. The Emperor's legitimacy as the "son of heaven" meant that he was above these worldly agreements. Holding the Emperor to contract—through bonds or other loans—was not possible because he did not acknowledge accountability to any secular institutions or groups. Chinese Emperors did not engage in market commerce; they lived in a world of tribute and gift-giving. In the terms of anthropologists, the financial economy of credit contradicted the moral economy of imperial beneficence.

Despite their efforts to imitate foreign economies, the Chinese modernizers failed to create a banking system that would attract capital. They made very little progress in building new financial institutions or practices. Foreign capital came into China for railroads, shipping, and some manufacturing, but investors held tight control over their capital because they did not trust local institutions to manage finances in a credible and competent way. In many cases, established Chinese financial institutions could not even process the new quantities of currency and other investment coming into the mainland in highly decentralized ways after the Opium Wars.[55]

Foreign investors had no reason to invest in government bonds or other instruments for public finance used so frequently by Great Britain and other European states at the time. China benefited from enormous cash remittances flowing back to the mainland from workers overseas, but this money also stayed within tightly controlled family networks. Foreign remittances were private. They lacked a public market for credit, or even public savings.[56]

The only available source of cash for the Emperor was, ironically, the sale of the Chinese territory that he sought to protect. From the time of the First Opium War in the 1840s he began ceding land to wealthy families and foreign powers in return for payments and promises of security. The Emperor used land as his only reliable source of credit. There was a severe limit, of course, to the amount of land the Emperor could convert to capital when his highest goal was to control, not cede, Chinese territory. The dense Chinese population also made land transfers of any kind incredibly difficult.

The modernizers tried to use land capital to strengthen the state, but the method of acquisition discouraged productive investments. If territorial concessions were the most lucrative source of money, then it made sense to refrain from territorial investments and export capital instead. Short of money at home,

[55] Brett Sheehan describes efforts by Li Hongzhang and others to create modern banks in China, but these had limited effect due to the weakness of the state and the political pressures of local and foreign groups who wished more direct control over resources. Qing China lacked a centralized system of law and enforcement for modern banking. See Sheehan, *Trust in Troubled Times*, 19–44.

[56] On the history of Chinese emigrants and their relationship to the mainland, see Lynn Pan, *Sons of the Yellow Emperor: A History of the Chinese Diaspora* (New York: Little Brown, 1990).

the Chinese quickly found that their territorial deals encouraged an increase in capital flight. Appeasement of foreign powers was not a viable financial strategy in this context.

QING COLLAPSE

The complete financial collapse of the Chinese state in 1911 marked the end of the Qing dynasty. Pu Yi and the imperial family had gone bankrupt, they could not raise new money, and they could not command basic loyalty from the population. None of the foreign powers were willing to loan the last Emperor enough money for the survival of his government. He was a ruler who still commanded the awe of many citizens, but he had lost all of the financial tools that were necessary to convert status into governing power. Pu Yi's financial fall left a political vacuum throughout society.

During the next four decades, different groups of domestic strongmen and foreign actors struggled for control of the Chinese mainland. They established small "warlord" areas of authority where they could finance institutions of local governance. The Guomindang, under the leadership of Sun Yatsen and then Chiang Kai-Shek, relied largely on the seizure of local resources and aid from both the United States and the Soviet Union, especially during the Second World War. The Chinese Communists, under Mao Zedong, implemented their strategy of peasant mobilization, encouraging local citizens to join a popular effort to nationalize all wealth in a people's party. Mao's strategy succeeded in the years after 1945 because it provided a firm basis in local peasant revenue to finance a revolution. Mao and the Chinese Communist Party had more consistent access to domestic capital than the better armed, but bankrupt, Guomindang.[57]

Looking back two hundred years from the day the Chinese Communists seized Beijing on October 1, 1949, there was little reason to believe that the government in Great Britain would survive while the one in China would come to such dismay. Both states faced growing external threats, and both states had difficult domestic challenges. Both states were in decline by the last decades of the nineteenth century. Great Britain survived because it could continue to rely on effective inherited systems of taxation and credit. Qing China disintegrated because it could not tax sufficiently and it could not raise credit. Financial capabilities were the margin of difference between survival and defeat. Financial capabilities were the crucial hinges of state power in the cutthroat competition of early twentieth century international politics.

THE UNITED STATES SINCE 1941

Mobilizing for war on two fronts amid the aftereffects of the worst economic downturn in American history, the United States benefited from the exact state capacities

---

[57] For a good introduction to these topics, see Dikötter, *The Age of Openness*; Philip Short, *Mao: A Life* (New York: Hodder and Stoughton, 2000).

that Qing China lacked a half-century earlier. The United States had strong and active state institutions, furthered beyond precedent by the expansion of the federal government through various New Deal programs. The United States also had a chief executive who was willing and able to manipulate the capacities of the strong American state for clear purpose.[58]

President Franklin Roosevelt did not command a large experienced military in 1941. He did not have a rapidly growing domestic economy from which to draw needed resources. Above all, he did not have a firmly united population, committed to a common vision of international change. President Roosevelt had one primary source of power: the ability to raise credit and to tax. He did not have surplus cash in the treasury in December 1941, but he could rapidly borrow money and increase domestic revenues for the purpose of preparing for war. Roosevelt could also borrow and tax to reallocate capital from peacetime consumption to war production.

Within a few short years, the laggard post-Depression American economy became a dynamic engine of growth because of the wartime capital borrowed, taxed, and redeployed by the US government. The fascist regimes in Germany, Japan, and Italy also mobilized capital to finance their wars, but they could not borrow as cheaply as the United States, and they had much smaller tax bases at home. By the early 1940s, they had already drawn out much of the domestic wealth in their societies for foreign military purposes. As a consequence, Germany, Japan, and Italy had to look to conquered territories for resources, while the United States could build efficiently from within.,[59]

Between 1942 and 1945 the American position strengthened as Washington drew more aggressively on its financial capacities. In contrast, the economies of the fascist states precipitously declined as they ran out of financial capacities. Effective American borrowing and taxation allowed for the gargantuan spending that underpinned the successful democratic war effort. There could be no "Four Freedoms" without strong state-run finance. The American ability to attract and mobilize money won the war.[60]

[58] On the growth of federal government capacities during the New Deal, the best book remains: William Leuchtenburg, *Franklin D. Roosevelt and the New Deal: 1932–1940* (New York: Harper and Row, 1963). See also Arthur M. Schlesinger, Jr., *The Coming of the New Deal* (Boston: Houghton Mifflin, 1958), esp. 511–588; David M. Kennedy, *Freedom From Fear: The American People in Depression and War, 1929–1945* (New York: Oxford University Press, 1999), esp. 323–380.

[59] Adam Tooze argues that Nazi leaders recognized their financial disadvantages in competition with the United States. The Nazis and other fascist regimes pursued policies of conquest, in part, as failed efforts to overcome financial disadvantages. Genocidal aggression, poor diplomacy, and excessive militarism meant that fascist conquests, in fact, worsened their financial disadvantages, creating unprecedented disasters for domestic economies in Germany, Italy, and Japan—as well as the occupied territories, of course. See Adam Tooze, *The Wages of Destruction: The Making and Breaking of the Nazi Economy* (New York: Penguin, 2006).

[60] On the remarkable productivity of the American economy during the Second World War, and the key role of taxation, see Kennedy, *Freedom From Fear*, 615–668. See also Harold G. Vatter, *The U.S. Economy in World War II* (New York: Columbia University Press, 1985); Richard Overy,

The same was true for much of the Cold War. Historians have noted that despite the anti-statist ideology of American rhetoric after 1945, citizens paid higher personal taxes than ever before and they authorized the federal government to borrow more than ever before as well. Presidents from Dwight Eisenhower to Ronald Reagan lamented the growth of government, but they consistently added to the revenue-generating capacities of the American state for the purpose of building weapons, assisting allies, investing in infrastructure, and supporting poor and aging American citizens. The ingenuity and expansion that allowed the United States to defeat the Soviet Union took trillions of dollars, raised and spent by Washington DC. The wealth creation that greatly improved standards of living from the era of the Depression took trillions of dollars, also raised and spent by Washington DC.[61]

No other government raised as much capital as the US government during the Cold War. Washington could do this because it had institutional capacities that allowed for effective taxation on personal incomes and business profits. Washington could also borrow easily and cheaply because the United States attracted so many investors, and because the American banking system inspired more trust than any other. After the United States abandoned the Bretton Woods system of fixed currency exchanges in 1971, people around the world continued to hold dollars and treasury bills, considering them "as good as gold" because the American financial system stood behind them. As in the Second World War, financial resources and management constituted the core of American strength in the Cold War. The Soviet Union could never compete in this area.[62]

Since 1991 the United States has remained a beneficiary of seemingly endless capital investment at very low interest rates. Under Presidents George H.W. Bush and Bill Clinton the United States increased its tax collections to allow additional domestic and international spending, as well as balanced budgets. When the terrorist attacks of September 11 2001 occurred, the United States was in a very strong position to take on vast new spending obligations for security, assistance (domestic and foreign), and warfare. Americans were able to affirm all of these new obligations without any diminishment in their consumption. The strength of American finance underpinned expansive "guns and butter" policies in the early twenty-first century.

Why the Allies Won (New York: W.W. Norton, 1995); Alan Milward, *War, Economy, and Society, 1939–1945* (Berkeley: University of California Press, 1979).

[61] See James T. Sparrow, *Warfare State: World War II Americans and the Age of Big Government* (New York: Oxford University Press, 2011); Michael J. Hogan, *A Cross of Iron: Harry S. Truman and the Origins of the National Security State, 1945–1954* (Cambridge, UK: Cambridge University Press, 1998); Robert M. Collins, *More: The Politics of Economic Growth in Postwar America* (New York: Oxford University Press, 2000).

[62] See Barry J. Eichengreen, *Exorbitant Privilege: The Rise and Fall of the Dollar and the Future of the International Monetary System* (New York: Oxford University Press, 2011); Francis J. Gavin, *Gold, Dollars, and Power: The Politics of International Monetary Relations, 1958–1971* (Chapel Hill: University of North Carolina Press, 2004); Eric Helleiner and Jonathan Kirshner, eds., *The Future of the Dollar* (Ithaca, NY: Cornell University Press, 2009); Stephen Kotkin, *Armageddon Averted: The Soviet Collapse, 1970–2000* (New York: Oxford University Press, 2001).

The challenge after the Great Recession of 2008 is continuing to finance all of these obligations. Even with necessary fiscal austerity and strategic retrenchment, the United States will still maintain costly domestic and international obligations for the foreseeable future. The security threats (traditional and nontraditional), the domestic demographics, and various popular political commitments point toward more spending, not less. American power will continue to rely deeply on finance—on the capacity of the United States government to borrow and spend efficiently.

The key question for current policymakers, therefore, is whether we are nurturing the correct financial capacities. This is *the* vital national security question. Does our current system of taxation allow for the appropriate revenue streams to finance our national power? Does our system of budgeting protect our access to capital at low borrowing costs?

CONTEMPORARY IMPLICATIONS

Too much of our current debate in the United States focuses on questions of austerity: what should we cut? Frugality is a definite virtue, but the historical record does *not* tell us that penny-pinching and power are one and the same. They often are not. The secret to sustaining national power since the eighteenth century has revolved around finding low-cost capital to spend on more things. That was the English strategy after the Glorious Revolution and the American strategy after the Great Depression. Qing China and the Soviet Union failed because they could not do the same.

Powerful states grow, innovate, and expand because they raise the money to do more. Declining states are the ones that run out of money and start doing less. Low taxes and small deficits are not the historical formulas for continued national power. Taxing more to buy more security and growth, and borrowing more to increase productive investment—those are processes that have seeded national power in the past.

The historical record does not offer license to legislate smothering taxes or carry crippling debts. Just the opposite: profligate taxing, borrowing, and spending can rapidly ruin a country's credit and corrupt its values. The historical record does, however, warn against the seductive assumption that taxing less and borrowing less are necessarily good things. The alternative to too much tax is not tax-free living. The alternative to too much borrowing is not an avoidance of credit. The correct balance involves adequate taxation and borrowing to increase the capacities of a society. Doing less undermines national power in the long-run.

National power is fundamentally financial. National power requires more money, not less. The strongest states are the ones that use their capacity to tax and borrow for dynamic purposes—not empty clichés about frugality, freedom, or social justice.

5

REFORMING AMERICAN POWER
CIVILIAN NATIONAL SECURITY INSTITUTIONS
IN THE EARLY COLD WAR AND BEYOND

William Inboden

An article in *Foreign Affairs* on the need for a major reform of the American national security system argued that:

> Recommendations for fundamental reforms in the organization and administration of foreign affairs have been made by high-level committees and task forces on the average of every two years since World War II. Despite the near unanimity of diagnosis, little has been done to deal with the serious problems uncovered; they are still with us, unsolved and debilitating. . . . The advent of a new administration, both popular and Congressional disenchantment with the results of America's involvement in the world over the last two decades, and the growing sentiment that we must put our domestic house in order as a matter of first priority, all suggest that the country can no longer afford the inefficiencies which too often have characterized its foreign programs in an era of rising budget curves.[1]

The article was published in January 1969. If nothing else, the fact that it could just as easily have appeared in the January 2016 issue of *Foreign Affairs* serves as a reminder that lamentations over the alleged inadequacies and dysfunctions of America's national security institutions are nothing new. Similar articles and studies could be cited from just about every decade from the 1940s up to the present day. The Protestant Reformers of the sixteenth century adopted the motto *ecclesia semper reformanda est* ("the church is always to be reformed"); perhaps its modern American national security counterpart is "the government is always to be reformed."

However, if dissatisfaction with government and demands for reform are virtual constants, substantial actions for reform are merely episodic. This chapter will examine the most consequential and paradigmatic period of institutional reform in modern American history, amid tremendous international flux: the end of World War II and beginning of the Cold War. To explore the questions of continuity and discontinuity in reform efforts, it will also look briefly at two other periods: the end

---

[1] Lannon Walker, "Our Foreign Affairs Machinery: Time for An Overhaul," *Foreign Affairs* 47, January 1969, 309–320. I am indebted to Celeste Ward Gventer for bringing this article to my attention.

of the Cold War and the era following the September 11, 2001 attacks. These eras are chosen not because they are exhaustive of reform efforts, but because they provide interesting case studies of disproportionately influential reform efforts that took place amid considerable geopolitical ferment.

There are few topics more soporific than bureaucratic process and organization, and if that is all this chapter explores then it has little basis, or even hope, to claim the reader's time and interest. But bureaucratic organization is merely the surface issue. The deeper questions animating this study are what is the nature of power and how does the American government wield it? The exercise of power for the purpose of national interests lies at the heart of how national security institutions are constituted and organized, and their effectiveness should be judged by this standard. How an American president imposes his will on his own government and directs the power of his nation in the international arena are some of the most persistent challenges and defining aspects of any presidency.

Yet even here the historian encounters a paradox. In national security terms, some of the most consequential and arguably effective American presidents of the modern era, such as Franklin D. Roosevelt, Richard Nixon, and Ronald Reagan, all presided over administrations whose national security organization and processes were at best less than ideal, and at worst downright chaotic and dysfunctional. Despite these organizational inadequacies and failures—or possibly because of them—these three presidents were still able to wield their power and implement their foreign policies effectively, and all left substantial legacies. Scholars continue to debate the reasons for the peculiar successes of these administrations, a question that is beyond the scope of this paper but likely involves some combination of presidential personality, ideology, force of will, the presence of a small number of highly capable lieutenants, and the elusive tides of history. Nor should one disregard the counterfactual that these presidencies might have been even more effective had they created a well-organized national security interagency system.

Nevertheless, two modest assumptions inform the purposes of this chapter. First, that the repeated, almost perpetual efforts to reform and improve American national security institutions reveal a general consensus among national security professionals that an organized and well-crafted system is a desirable goal. Second, that an organized and well-crafted set of national security institutions are a help to effective national security policy. With them, poor policies can be avoided or mitigated, and wise policies can be created and implemented. Without them, the consequences of poor policies have the potential for greater damage, and the benefits of wise policies have less opportunity to be realized. Perhaps Sen. Henry "Scoop" Jackson said it best in 1961 when he concluded his Subcommittee on National Policy Machinery's two-year review of the US government's national security system: "Good national security policy requires both good policymakers and good policy machinery. But organizational changes cannot solve problems which are not really due to organizational weaknesses. More often than not, poor decisions are traceable not to machinery but to people."[2]

---

[2] Senator Henry Jackson, "Organizing for National Security," November 15 1961, in Dorothy Fosdick ed., *Henry M. Jackson and World Affairs: Selected Speeches, 1953–1983* (Seattle: University of Washington Press, 1990), pp. 84–85.

This chapter will not attempt an exhaustive and comprehensive assessment of every aspect of national security institutional reform during the periods in question—a subject that alone merits an entire book or even series of books. Rather it will distill and highlight particular episodes or themes that are judged to be especially revelatory and potentially relevant for today's context. The National Security Council will receive a special measure of attention, as it is the institutional epicenter for the wielding of national power and often illustrative of broader reform efforts across government.

The following points summarize the main conclusions that emanate from this historical survey:

- Significant reforms most often result from a major shock, such as a surprise attack or a scandal. These shocks have a catalytic effect in revealing inadequacies in prevailing institutions, and generating sufficient political will to force major changes on entrenched bureaucratic interests.
- Major reforms usually have multiple authors and multiple constituencies. In the short term this makes for a messier process, but in the long term it makes reforms more sustainable because permitting multiple authors up front often creates multiple stakeholders at the end. The primary authors of reform can include Congress, expert commissions, eminent leaders, and the departments and agencies of the Executive branch itself.
- The inflection points considered in this paper all occurred during times of crisis yet also times of relative US power *ascendance*, rather than austerity and decline. This is not determinative, but at least suggestive that the times of crisis and ascendance may have a more catalytic effect on institutional reform efforts, whereas times of stagnation and decline may stifle institutional reform efforts and instead produce a cautious, status quo, even bunker mentality. Yet some of the insights drawn from successful reform efforts during times of power ascendance can also apply to reform efforts when a nation is not internationally ascendant. International change (whether during ascendance or decline) seems to be the most important geopolitical factor spurring reform. In turn, successful institutional reforms can take place during times of international ascendance, stagnation, or decline.
- Institutional reforms occur in real time, in the context of unfolding global events, and these events further shape the reform trajectory.
- The reform of US national security institutions is best considered as an ongoing, episodic process rather than a series of discrete outcomes.
- There can be unintended consequences. Reforms often evolve and function in ways different than their architects originally intended, and with sometimes ironic outcomes and consequences.
- Institutional structure is often secondary to individual will. Each president and his senior team ultimately seek to bend the institutions of government to their particular purposes, no matter how well- or how ill-suited those institutions might be.

1942–1950: EXPANDING "NATIONAL SECURITY" AT THE OUTSET OF THE COLD WAR

Japan's attack on the American fleet at Pearl Harbor on December 7, 1941 brought the United States into World War II, and brought in a new paradigm of national security institutions. The strategic shock of Pearl Harbor revealed not only an intelligence failure but also wholesale inadequacies in the ways that the American government was organized to wield power and protect its interests.[3] Even as the United States mobilized to fight the war, some American leaders began thinking about how their government should be reorganized not just for the war effort but especially for the postwar world. In hindsight, three challenges loomed especially large. These included resolving what might be called the "Roosevelt Problem" of a strong presidential personality and weak institutional system; devising an institutional mechanism to coordinate political and military affairs; and equipping the United States to exercise all elements of national power in its new role as guarantor of global security. Numerous other nettlesome organizational issues also preoccupied policymakers, such as the relationship between the army and the navy, and the creation and organization of a permanent intelligence agency. Undergirding all of these issues was an emerging geopolitical and existential reality: the United States was entering a new era, historically without precedent, as a global superpower with permanent international commitments. To be fit for its new role, the American government needed not merely to reform but to fundamentally reinvent itself.

At the center of this stood the beguiling figure of President Franklin Delano Roosevelt. The Roosevelt White House is pivotal in many ways; he stands simultaneously as the last president of the premodern era and the first president of the modern era. He strengthened the presidency in many enduring ways, including through pioneering mass communication techniques, overseeing a massive expansion in the size and scope of the federal government and federal power, and leading the United States to becoming the world's dominant military power. Yet he was also the last president to govern during a time when the United States had a relatively weak standing military and no alliances or permanent international commitments, with a small White House staff, and without a national security bureaucracy as an instrument through which he could wield presidential power. Despite these latter limitations—or perhaps even because of them, as scholars such as Matthew Dickinson have argued—Roosevelt masterfully oversaw the integration of political and military power during America's participation in the Allied victory in World War II.[4]

The "Roosevelt Problem" that resulted, of course, was the near impossibility of maintaining this system without a uniquely gifted and crafty president

---

[3] On Pearl Harbor as a shock to the American strategic posture, see John Lewis Gaddis, *Surprise, Security, and the American Experience* (Cambridge, MA: Harvard University Press, 2004). On Pearl Harbor's central role in catalyzing the eventual passage of the 1947 National Security Act, see Douglas T. Stuart, *Creating the National Security State: A History of the Law that Transformed America* (Princeton, NJ: Princeton University Press, 2008).

[4] Matthew Dickinson, *Bitter Harvest: FDR, Presidential Power and the Growth of the Presidential Branch* (New York: Cambridge University Press, 1996). I appreciate Philip Zelikow for bringing this book and its related arguments to my attention. For recent scholarship on Roosevelt's wartime leadership and strategy development, see David Kaiser, *No End Save Victory: How FDR Led the Nation Into War* (New York: Basic Books, 2014) and Nigel Hamilton, *The Mantle of Command: FDR at War, 1941–1942* (New York: Houghton Mifflin, 2014).

such as Roosevelt. Moreover, even some of Roosevelt's biggest supporters quietly shared the concerns of his most vociferous critics that under him the presidency risked being more about the man than the institution—it had become the "imperial presidency" in Arthur Schlesinger Jr's famous formulation.[5] In Dickinson's description, "despite the successful Allied military collaboration, many of those who worked most closely with FDR thought his administrative system poorly suited for the postwar era."[6] Wilson Miscamble's nuanced study of the transition from Roosevelt to Truman renders the verdict thus: "Roosevelt's personalization of his office and of American foreign policy made his juggler's act an especially difficult one to follow. Truman possessed none of his predecessor's nimbleness, nor did he desire to be such a solo or dominating performer. Roosevelt's death therefore immediately and inevitably prompted a major change in the *way* in which foreign policy was formulated."[7] Hence the problem: how to maintain the institutional strength of the presidency without leaving it susceptible to potential demagoguery from future aspirants, or hindering the effectiveness of subsequent presidents who lacked Roosevelt's singular wiles.

World War II also revealed a second challenge that was at once as old as warfare itself yet also novel to an American government accustomed to separating military and political matters: how to ensure coordination of political and military means and ends. In 1955 Ernest May observed that "long years of isolated safety smothered the idea of political-military collaboration" throughout American history. The ordeal of World War II and the dawn of the Cold War and the nuclear age changed this. "Not before the 1940s would the majority of Americans have endorsed the rationale that underlies the National Security Council." But now, "living in a world as sensitive as a can of nitroglycerin, Americans accept the need for exact weighing of political and military factors before each policy decision."[8] This change in strategic philosophy also needed a corresponding change in institutions, to ensure the integration of political and military considerations.

The third challenge perhaps loomed largest. It was not just a matter of coordinating political and military action, but of equipping the United States to play an unprecedented role on the global stage in an era when the nature of power itself became more multidimensional. This meant expanding the very meaning of "national security" and the concept of national power. No longer would "national security" mean only the military defense of the

[5] Arthur Schlesinger, Jr., *The Imperial Presidency* (Boston: Houghton-Mifflin, 1973).

[6] Dickinson, *Bitter Harvest*, 196. Note that Dickinson himself does not entirely share this assessment, and in fact argues that FDR's management style and system may be worth emulating by presidents today.

[7] Wilson D. Miscamble, *From Roosevelt to Truman: Potsdam, Hiroshima, and the Cold War* (New York: Cambridge University Press, 2007), p. 37. For a transatlantic perspective on Roosevelt's leadership, the international power transition and emergence of Cold War tensions, see David Reynolds, *From World War to Cold War: Churchill, Roosevelt, and the International History of the 1940s* (New York: Oxford University Press, 2006).

[8] Ernest R. May, "The Development of Political-Military Consultation in the United States," *Political Science Quarterly* 70, no. 2 (June 1955): 161–180.

nation's borders, and no longer would national power be regarded merely as the strength of arms.

While the needs described above may appear clear in hindsight, the actual motives and mechanisms for the creation of these new national security institutions varied greatly at the time. Each actor brought a set of parochial concerns and motives. The army and navy each sought jealously to guard their traditional prerogatives (and in the navy's case its independence); Congress sought to assert its authority; the White House sought to protect its executive role; numerous other strategists and statesmen injected their convictions and concerns. Expert commissions and study bodies such as the Eberstadt Report and the hearings of the Joint Committee on the Investigation of the Pearl Harbor Attack injected additional ideas into the process, as well as serving as proxies for other agendas. Looming over all of this were the acute existential concerns—held not just by average citizens and editorial boards, but also by some of the nation's most influential political leaders—that the United States not become a "garrison state" of stifling federal power, bureaucracy, and militarism.[9]

All of this occurred in the crucible of global crisis. The various efforts to research, debate, and draft legislation creating the new institutions of national security did not enjoy a sabbatical repose from history. Rather they took place as new threats loomed and demands for American leadership and intervention grew louder around the world. Just months after the final surrenders of World War II had been signed, and as most Americans hoped for nothing but demobilization and a return to peace and prosperity, the fragile world order appeared to crumble anew before it had even been rebuilt. Civil war resumed in China as the Communists renewed their campaign to defeat the Nationalists. Stalin appeared to press for more Soviet control in places like Iran and Eastern Europe. In late February 1946, George Kennan sent his "long telegram" from Moscow seeking to disabuse official Washington of any naïve hopes for a conciliatory relationship with the USSR. Two weeks later, Winston Churchill visited Fulton, Missouri and warned that "from Stettin in the Baltic to Trieste in the Adriatic an iron curtain has descended across the Continent." As the year went on, communist insurgencies grew in Greece and Turkey, and by the end of 1946 a severe winter had descended on western Europe that threatened millions with starvation in the still war-torn land.

Even as it engaged in negotiations on multiple fronts over the provisions of what would become the National Security Act, the Truman administration was designing and launching some remarkably ambitious initiatives that would define the Cold War and permanently transform American national security policy. These included President Truman's landmark address to Congress on March 12, 1947 inaugurating the Truman Doctrine and calling for American support against communist insurgencies in Greece and Turkey; and the June 5, 1947 Harvard

---

[9] Two of the most exhaustive treatments of this question, albeit from different perspectives, are Michael Hogan, *A Cross of Iron: Harry S. Truman and the Origins of the National Security State, 1945–1954* (New York: Cambridge University Press, 1998); and Aaron Friedberg, *In the Shadow of the Garrison State: America's Anti-Statism and its Cold War Grand Strategy* (Princeton, NJ: Princeton University Press, 2000).

commencement address by Secretary of State George Marshall announcing what would become the Marshall Plan of massive aid for reconstructing Europe. Both serve as reminders that the reform of national security institutions takes place not only amid the tumult of world events but also the ongoing conduct of statecraft. No analogy can fully capture the complexities of this situation in the years 1946 and 1947, but it is as if the Truman administration was hurtling down a highway in a bus that was still being assembled while its passengers squabbled, as the highway itself was being paved, during a simultaneous earthquake that shifted the ground underneath while a thunderstorm darkened the skies overhead. What may appear in the hindsight of history as a smooth process with a clear outcome was anything but at the time. Yet as important as these international challenges were in shaping the environment in which America's national security institutions were created, this context is curiously absent from most of the academic literature on the National Security Act.[10]

The acute sense of crisis that beset these years should not obscure an equally important fact: at the time the United States stood at the zenith of its international power and influence. Indeed these immediate postwar years may mark the relative high point of American geopolitical power at any point in history before or since. At the end of 1945, the United States alone produced about *half* of all global economic output, possessed the world's most dominant military with a global reach, and would enjoy a monopoly on atomic weapons until the end of the decade. This hard power leverage translated into substantial soft power as well (the concept existed at the time even if the term itself would not be popularized for another half century), which the United States mobilized in leading the construction of the postwar international economic and political order through new institutions such as the United Nations, World Bank, and International Monetary Fund.

Amid this peculiar combination of strength and vulnerability, America's leaders realized the need to reform, even create, new institutions designed to wield power effectively. The puzzle had one additional dimension: the relative weakness of the office of the presidency. Ironically, while governing the most powerful nation in the world, the president of the United States faced considerable constraints on his power, including the checks and balances provided by Congress and the judiciary, federalism's decentralization of power to the states, and the federal bureaucracy's resistance to presidential direction. How could the American president be better equipped to wield national power in this new world, while maintaining constitutional fidelity?

The specific provisions of institutional reform exemplified by the National Security Act did not arise *ex nihilo*, but reflected ideas and derived from predecessor

---

[10] For example, Stuart's otherwise strong book on the National Security Act neglects this historical context, as does Amy Zegart, *Flawed by Design: The Evolution of the CIA, JSC, and NSC* (Stanford, CA: Stanford University Press, 1999). Such context is also missing in Karl F. Inderfurth and Loch K. Johnson, eds., *Fateful Decisions: Inside the National Security Council* (New York: Oxford University Press, 2004).

institutions that had existed for years, even decades, before. Ernest May credits Assistant Secretary of the Navy Franklin D. Roosevelt with first suggesting the concept of a National Security Council in 1919 when he wrote to the secretary of state proposing a "Joint Plan Making Body" comprised of senior officials from the Departments of War, Navy, and State. In a historical episode replete with irony, Roosevelt's letter appears to have been misrouted to the Latin American Affairs division and was never read or even opened by the secretary of state. Thus a clerical error may have prevented the young Roosevelt's idea from coming to fruition, and in turn may have spared what became his institution-averse presidency two decades later from having to deal with a coordinating body that hindered the president's flexibility.[11] The eve and then advent of World War II did produce some efforts at coordination. In 1938, Roosevelt agreed to the proposal of his Secretary of State Cordell Hull for the creation of the Standing Liaison Committee comprised of the Undersecretary of State, the Army Chief of Staff, and the Chief of Naval Operations. Once the war began, the informal yet regular meetings of the leaders of the relevant departments eventually became institutionalized in 1945 in the creation of the State, War, Navy Coordinating Committee (SWNCC).[12] The SWNCC impressed new President Harry Truman with its smooth functioning at the Potsdam conference in 1945, and laid the foundation for his eventual support for the creation of the NSC.[13] Another important actor emerged toward the war's end in the person of Navy Secretary James Forrestal, whose diary entry of November 23, 1944 noted "I talked with Harry Hopkins tonight about the necessity for creating something similar to the Joint Chiefs of Staff on the civilian side of the American government. I said I felt that if we did not create something similar to the British system for coordinated and focused government action we should not be able to deal with the problems and relationships arising during the postwar period."[14]

Meanwhile, these efforts at executive branch policy coordination took place amidst growing calls in some quarters for more military unification. Representatives of the army often led these efforts, exemplified by General George C. Marshall's development of an ambitious plan toward the end of World War II for unification of the military services under one combined branch. In this Marshall found a supporter in Truman, especially once the latter assumed the presidency in 1945. Not that these sentiments were entirely new to Truman. A few months earlier as the vice presidential nominee, he had penned an article in *Collier's* magazine titled "Our Armed Forces Must Be Unified." Truman wrote that "proof that a divine Providence watches over the United States is furnished by the fact that we have managed to escape disaster even though our scrambled military setup has been an open invitation to catastrophe." He then called for "the integration of every

[11] May, "Political-Military Consultation," 168.

[12] Richard A. Best, Jr., "The National Security Council: An Organizational Assessment," Congressional Research Service, December 28, 2011.

[13] Inderfurth and Johnson, *Fateful Decisions*, 3.

[14] Walter Millis, ed., *The Forrestal Diaries* (New York: Viking, 1951), p. 19.

element of America's defense in one department under one authoritative, responsible head."[15]

Ironically, these two needs—for military unification and for greater executive branch policy coordination—may have *complemented* each other in Truman's mind, but they became *competing* demands in the hands of adversaries contending over how to reform American national security institutions. Even though the focus of this paper is on reform of civilian institutions, the eventual outcome of civilian institutions cannot be understood apart from contests over military institutions.[16] Thus in 1945 as Navy Secretary Forrestal observed with alarm what appeared to be a growing political consensus for unifying the army and navy (a prospect anathema to the navy, which feared that unification effectively meant subordination to the dominant army), he attempted the diversionary maneuver of commissioning an expert report. For this Forrestal chose his longtime friend and collaborator Ferdinand Eberstadt, a New York investment banker who had helped lead the military's industrial policy during World War II. In June, 1945, Forrestal requested that Eberstadt produce a study on the questions of military unification and executive organization for the postwar period. Three months later Eberstadt and his team delivered and widely disseminated their conclusions. Aside from its predictable recommendation against unification of the army and navy, the Eberstadt Report also urged the creation of a National Security Council "to afford a permanent vehicle for maintaining active, close, and continuous contact between the departments and agencies of our Government responsible, respectively, for our foreign and military policies and their implementation." Crucially, the report added the caveat that the NSC "would be a policy-forming and advisory, not an executive, body."[17] This last point anticipated a recurring tension over the role and responsibilities of the NSC.

The vast majority of political energy and contention on all sides was devoted to the titanic struggle over the structure and organization of the US military. Those few figures who did pay any attention to the proposed NSC were concerned to keep it institutionally weak and thus unable to challenge the prerogatives of the President or the responsibilities of the State Department for conducting diplomacy. Much of this centered on defining the NSC's responsibilities to be merely "advisory" and not "executive"; in other words, the NSC would not have any decision-making authority. For example, early in 1947 Secretary of State Marshall wrote to Truman of his concerns that the proposed NSC would undermine both the authority of the State Department and the presidency, complaining that it was a "critical departure from the traditional method of formulating and conducting foreign policy" and that it would "dissipate the constitutional responsibility of the president for the conduct of foreign affairs."[18] Mindful of such fears, during the Senate debate on the National Security Act, Senators Leverett Saltonstall (R-MA) and Raymond Baldwin (R-CT) engaged in a revealing colloquy. Saltonstall asked of Baldwin "Does the Senator

---

[15] Quoted in Stuart, *Creating the National Security State*, 86.

[16] This is central to Amy Zegart's argument that the NSC emerged almost as a byproduct of the fierce dispute between the army and navy over military unification.

[17] Eberstadt report excerpted in Inderfurth and Johnson, *Fateful Decisions*, 17–20.

[18] Quoted in Stuart, 129.

agree with me when I say that the purpose of creating the National Security Council is not to set up a new function of government with extraordinary powers, but solely to provide an organization to give advice to the President . . .?" To which Baldwin replied "I agree wholeheartedly . . . it is not essentially an administrative agency. It is an advisory council."[19]

The inordinate amount of attention devoted to the military unification provisions of the National Security Act and the comparative neglect of its provisions creating the National Security Council and the Central Intelligence Agency reveal one of the ironic themes of institutional reform: sometimes what become the most significant developments are little noticed or appreciated when they occur. If the NSC received little attention during the negotiations over the Act, what became the CIA received even less. The creation of the CIA came out of a rough consensus on the need for some manner of coordination of intelligence, but little appetite for the creation of a strong new intelligence organization, especially since each service branch and the State Department all sought jealously to preserve control over their own respective intelligence units (each one relatively weak already). In Amy Zegart's description, "the original CIA was never supposed to engage in spying. It was never supposed to sponsor coups, influence foreign elections, or conduct any other kind of subversive operations. It was never supposed to be more than an analysis unit . . . To put it plainly, the CIA was supposed to be weak." Moreover, "its provision in the National Security Act was among the least noticed and least debated of all."[20] In sum, according to the statute a weak NSC oversaw an even weaker CIA.

On July 26, 1947, Congress passed the National Security Act. In addition to establishing the Department of Defense, NSC, and CIA, it also created a "National Security Resources Board" to advise the president on the mobilization of domestic resources for national security needs. Truman signed the bill at the airport while preparing to fly home to Missouri to visit his ailing mother, who died that same day. In his diary entry that evening Truman described the Act merely as the "Unification bill," revealing his belief at the time that the law's main significance lay in its provisions bringing the service branches closer together under the newly created office of the Secretary of Defense.[21] Overall, Douglas Stuart's verdict on the Act is apt: "No one really understood what had been agreed upon on July 26, 1947. The legislation had established a new institution to assist the president in the coordination of foreign and defense policy, but it was up to the president to decide how to use it, or whether to use it at all."[22]

Two weeks after the law's passage, George Kennan took up these questions. In his new capacity as the inaugural Director of the State Department's Policy Planning Staff, Kennan wrote a memo to Truman titled "Suggestions Regarding the National Security Council and the National Security Resources Board." Reassuring Truman that the creation of these bodies "has in no way either increased the President's

---

[19] "Legislative Debate on the National Security Act of 1947," in Inderfurth and Loch, 21.

[20] Zegart, *Flawed by Design*, 163.

[21] July 26 entry, President Harry S. Truman's 1947 Diary Book, Harry S. Truman Library. Posted on the Truman Library website at http://www.trumanlibrary.org/diary/transcript.htm.

[22] Stuart, 143.

authority or decreased his responsibility," Kennan stressed the merely advisory nature of the NSC and said it "should in no sense restrict or circumscribe [Truman's] freedom to reach a 'Presidential position.'" Instead Kennan surmised that the NSC would be most effective "if the President refrained from attending the majority of Council meetings. This would assure the advisory nature of the Council's actions and guard against its becoming an operating body." Instead Kennan suggested, no doubt with Marshall's approval, that the secretary of state serve as chair of the NSC meetings. Accurately anticipating what lay ahead, Kennan noted the uncertain relationship between the NSC and the rest of the Cabinet, which "must be worked out on an evolutionary, trial-and-error basis."[23]

Kennan's memo also highlighted the expanding nature of national power and its ramifications for the concept of national security.

> In appraising the recommendations of the Council, however, the President will need to assess political capabilities, financial capabilities, and consider security objectives in the light of other objectives. The subject of the national security, broadly viewed, is a matter of concern to all the departments of the Government. But the inclusion on the Council of all Cabinet members who have an interest in national security would actually entail recreating the full Cabinet.[24]

American national power was no longer merely synonymous with its military and economic resources. And national security was no longer confined merely to the military's defense against aggressors. Rather, national power comprised *all* of the resources of the nation, material and ideational, natural and manufactured, coercive and seductive, that would be developed and employed on behalf of national security. National security, in turn, meant not just defending the nation's borders but protecting the values and identity of the United States, what came to be known as the "American way of life." The emerging global contest with the Soviet Union encompassed all of these dimensions of power and security: economic, diplomatic, ideological, and military. It only followed that every cabinet secretary would have an interest in it. The law itself sought, however imperfectly, to establish this concept, stating that the function of the NSC "shall be to advise the President with respect to the integration of domestic, foreign, and military policies relating to the national security."[25]

Truman appears initially to have agreed with Kennan's advice against attending many NSC meetings. The President chaired the inaugural NSC meeting two months later on September 26, 1947. At the meeting Truman reminded all present that "the Act establishes this Council purely as an advisory body, with no policymaking or

---

[23] August 8, 1947 Memorandum to the President from the Director of Policy Planning. From Department of State Record Group 59; Executive Secretariat, Subject Files, 1947–1965; Records of Actions, Entry A1 1586F; Box 3, Folder "NSC Admin 1947–1949." National Archives, College Park, MD.

[24] Ibid.

[25] The National Security Act of 1947, Title I, Section 101, in Inderfurth and Johnson, 24. For more on this evolving and expanding conception of "national security," see Stuart, 2–9.

supervisory functions except in its direction of the Central Intelligence Agency." Or as Secretary of Defense Forrestal put it more pungently in his diary, "the President indicated that he regarded it as *his* council, and that he expected everyone to work harmoniously without any manifestations of prima donna qualities." Truman also announced that he intended only "to sit with the Council on an average of once every month."[26] In asserting these terms, Truman should not be misunderstood as not valuing the NSC. While he was wary of its potential dilution of his executive authority, at the same time his deliberate absence from most NSC meetings by no means deprived him of the utility of the NSC. He would still benefit from the results of its deliberations as options and decisions developed at NSC meetings were presented to him—perhaps even more so than if he were present, since his valuable time was spared and his national security team would be able to deliberate freely without his presence potentially coloring their debates.

His stated intention to attend once a month notwithstanding, Truman attended no other NSC meetings thereafter for almost a year. In Truman's stead and at his direction, Secretary of State Marshall served as chairman, or if Marshall were absent then Secretary of Defense Forrestal filled the chair. This changed the next year with the first of what would become several Berlin crises during the Cold War: the Soviet Union's blockade of West Berlin. Following the June 27, 1948 termination by the Soviets of all rail and road traffic to West Berlin, the American commander General Lucius Clay immediately launched an airlift to resupply the isolated city. The NSC first took up the case of Berlin at its July 15 meeting, and began working on a strategy for the growing crisis beyond the immediate tactical necessity of air supply. Truman began a more active involvement with the NSC, chairing three of the next five NSC meetings from July to September. His participation in these meetings is all the more remarkable considering that he was also consumed by campaign travel in the closing months of one of the most fiercely contested presidential elections in American history, when November would bring his narrow victory in the famed "Dewey Defeats Truman" race.[27]

The Berlin Airlift became a pivotal episode in the evolution of the NSC, more so than has been appreciated by most scholarship.[28] It catalyzed Truman's reengagement in chairing meetings, required deft political and military coordination

---

[26] "Opening Statement at First Meeting of National Security Council," September 26, 1947 Agenda for the 1st Meeting of the National Security Council; Record Group 273 Records of the National Security Council; Official Meeting Minutes (OMM), Entry 5, Box 1, Folder: 1st Meeting. National Archives, College Park, MD. Forrestal quote from *The Forrestal Diaries*, 320. Emphasis original. Note also the unintended irony in Truman's opening statement that the NSC would have no policymaking or supervisory functions except over the CIA—within a few years the opposite would be true, as the NSC attained more authority while the CIA became more independent.

[27] Minutes of the 16th–20th—Meetings of the National Security Council; Record Group 273 Records of the National Security Council; Official Meeting Minutes (OMM), Entry 5, Box 1, Folders: 16th, 17th, 18th, 19th, 20th Meetings. National Archives, College Park, MD.

[28] A conventional view in much of the extant NSC scholarship is that Truman essentially ignored the NSC for its first three years and only reversed course to embrace it after the outbreak of the Korean War. This view emerges in, among others, Inderfurth and Loch; David Rothkopf,

such as the decision to deploy atomic-capable B-29 bombers to England as a show of political resolve, and represented the integration of several elements of national power: the military's airlift capability, economic resources in the provision of food, diplomacy in the delicate signaling of firmness without escalation, and an ideological offensive displaying the American commitment to defend free societies as well as the propaganda value of displaying Soviet malevolence to the world. This comprehensive view of national security and national power was also reflected in the range of tools being used in the emerging Cold War, such as the Truman Doctrine's provision of aid to anticommunist forces in Greece and Turkey, and the Marshall Plan's massive support for the reconstruction of Europe—an economic program with a substantial political impact.

Douglas Stuart has called the National Security Act "the second most important piece of legislation in modern American history—surpassed only by the 1964 Civil Rights Act."[29] But as much of a landmark as it was, what is striking in hindsight is how little of the National Security Act's original provisions survived intact within the first few years after its passage. This illustrates an important reality about institutional reform. It occurs more in periods than moments, in windows of years before and after the passage of new measures. In the case of the National Security Act, almost as soon as it became law it began to change. Several factors drove these changes, factors that would recur over time as the primary drivers of institutional reform. These included the external demands of geopolitics, the internal demands of Congress, the input of expert commissions, the continued bureaucratic maneuvering of military and civilian national security officials, and the executive branch's own ongoing assessments of what did and did not work. Undergirding all of these factors were the needs of the president for institutions he could wield effectively as instruments of comprehensive national power.

Truman made some of the changes unilaterally, such as when he expanded the membership of the NSC in late 1948 to include regular participation by the Treasury Department, as well as occasional participation by the Commerce Department and the attorney general.[30] This inclusion of officials responsible for the nation's economic and legal policies further institutionalized an expanding view of national power. Other changes were prompted in 1949 by outside reviews, principally the Commission on Organization of the Executive Branch of Government headed

---

Running the World: The Inside Story of the National Security Council and the Architects of American Power (New York: Public Affairs 2005), p. 57; Stanley Falk, "The National Security Council Under Truman, Eisenhower, and Kennedy," *Political Science Quarterly*, 79, no. 3 (September 1964): 403–434; and Anna Kasten Nelson, "President Truman and the Evolution of the National Security Council," *Journal of American History*, Vol. 72, no. 2 (September 1985): 360–378. In contrast and to his credit, Stuart appreciates the significance of the Berlin crisis as a transition point in Truman's posture toward the NSC.

[29] Stuart, 1.

[30] Minutes of the 26th—44th Meetings of the National Security Council; Record Group 273 Records of the National Security Council; Official Meeting Minutes (OMM), Entry 5, Box 1, Folders: 26th-40th Meetings; Box 2, Folders: 41st–44th Meetings. National Archives, College Park, MD.

by former president Herbert Hoover, with a subcommittee headed by Ferdinand Eberstadt. Taken together, the findings of the second Eberstadt Report, the Hoover Commission, input from the Truman administration, and strong opinions of leading members of Congress all led to the passage in 1949 of a substantial package of amendments to the National Security Act. The most meaningful effect shifted more power from the military services to other civilian national security leaders, exemplified by the statutory elimination of the three service secretaries (army, navy, air force) from NSC membership and the addition of the vice president. The previously limited authority of the secretary of defense was also expanded, as the erstwhile National Military Establishment became the Department of Defense.

The understanding of national power to include intelligence and ideological warfare led to further institutional changes. In January 1949, another expert commission on intelligence led by Allen Dulles, William Jackson, and Mathias Correa produced an exhaustive study recommending increasing the authority and activities of the CIA. The Truman administration implemented some of these changes under the existing ambiguous language of the 1947 Act, while Congress institutionalized other provisions with the passage of the 1949 Central Intelligence Act. Individual leadership made a difference as well, as the ambitious Walter Bedell Smith replaced the ineffective Roscoe Hillenkoetter at the helm of the CIA, increasing its influence and operations.[31] The escalating contest of ideas with communism led to an expansion of the NSC's role in ideological warfare. This had been a concern from the beginning. One of Secretary of Defense Forrestal's earliest memos to the NSC in 1948 urged "that our foreign information activities be effectively developed and that they be coordinated with the other phases of our foreign and military policies." The Truman administration's efforts in this regard led in 1951 to the creation of the Psychological Strategy Board under the NSC, with its own full-time staff overseen by interagency representatives of State, Defense, and the CIA.[32]

If the Berlin blockade of 1948 provided the first external catalyst that elevated the NSC's prominence, North Korea's invasion of South Korea on June 25, 1950 was the strategic shock that solidified America's Cold War institutional posture. In response, Truman began regularly chairing NSC meetings and increased their frequency to a weekly basis, and increased its permanent staff membership while decreasing the number of meeting participants (to keep discussions focused and at a suitably high level). The Korean War galvanized other dimensions of the Cold War as well, most famously resolving the internal debates over NSC-68 in favor of its recommended massive increases in defense spending. Consistent with its expansive views of national power and national security, the Truman administration worked

---

[31] Minutes of the 37th Meeting of the National Security Council (includes copy of Dulles-Jackson-Correa Report). Record Group 273 Records of the National Security Council; Official Meeting Minutes (OMM), Entry 5, Box 1, Folders: 37th Meeting. National Archives, College Park, MD. Also Stuart, 258–267 and Zegart, 163–195.

[32] Minutes of the 9th Meeting of the National Security Council (contains copy of Forrestal memo). Record Group 273 Records of the National Security Council; Official Meeting Minutes (OMM), Entry 5, Box 1, Folders: 9th Meeting. National Archives, College Park, MD. Also Falk, "National Security Council," 416.

with Congress in 1951 to pass the Mutual Security Act, creating a new foreign assistance organization whose director would sit on the NSC. This trend toward expansion and addition of agencies was not irresistible, however. The National Security Resource Board, initially envisioned by the 1947 Act's architects as almost equal in importance to the NSC, withered under the pressures of domestic political resistance and lack of support from the Truman administration, until it was eliminated altogether by the Eisenhower administration.[33]

The Truman administration's project of national security institutional reform is best understood as a discrete process that unexpectedly began at Pearl Harbor, accelerated with the advent of the Cold War, and was consolidated in the shadow of the Korean War. Within the US Government, multiple factions brought multiple agendas, but what united them were the beliefs that national power now encompassed diplomatic, intelligence, military, economic, and ideological resources; and that national security meant protecting and promoting democratic capitalism in a global conflict. As chief executive, Truman himself worked with and sometimes worked against the system until it became the instrument that he desired.

Although Truman did not appreciate it at the time, the success of his institutional reforms also depended on his detested successor in the Oval Office, the Republican Dwight D. Eisenhower. In one of presidential history's recurring ironies, Eisenhower campaigned in 1952 as a critic of Truman's national security system and policies, only to largely adopt that same structure once in office. It was this embrace of Truman's institutions by a successor of the opposing party that in turn helped institutionalize Truman's reforms and give them bipartisan legitimacy. Admittedly, Eisenhower made his share of modifications to the strategic framework of containment and to the actual functioning and structure of the NSC. But these were modifications, not rejections. As Joseph Nye observes, "the key decisions of American strategy—containing the Soviet Union and maintaining a permanent presence abroad—were made by Truman, but they were consolidated into a prudent and sustainable system by his successor, Dwight Eisenhower." Specifically, Eisenhower "consolidated and improved Truman's institutional changes, such as the National Security Council (NSC) process."[34] Eisenhower's adoption of this system thus ensured that it would be preserved intact, albeit with continual modification, by every subsequent president.

Nevertheless, in the ensuing decades few of the system's architects, including Truman, would have recognized it as it evolved to produce a National Security

---

[33] Falk, 416; Stuart, 279–280.

[34] Joseph Nye, *Presidential Leadership and the Creation of the American Era* (Princeton, NJ: Princeton University Press, 2013), pp. 46, 49. For more on the evolution of the containment doctrine from Truman to Eisenhower, see John Lewis Gaddis, *Strategies of Containment: A Critical Appraisal of American National Security Policy During the Cold War* (New York: Oxford University Press, 2005). For more on Eisenhower's National Security Council, see Robert Bowie and Richard Immerman, *Waging Peace: How Eisenhower Shaped An Enduring Cold War Strategy* (New York: Oxford University Press, 2000). On the Truman-Eisenhower rivalry and subsequent reconciliation, see Steve Neal, *Harry and Ike: The Partnership that Remade the Postwar World* (New York: Scribner, 2002).

Advisor of equal stature with cabinet secretaries, or an intelligence community dominated by the CIA, or an NSC staff involved in the creation and execution of national security policy. But they would likely have recognized some of its results, such as American victory in the Cold War, and some of its problems, such as perpetual bureaucratic turf wars, and periodic scandals.

THE END OF THE COLD WAR

The NSC as an institution evolved throughout the rest of the Cold War. The Eisenhower administration expanded the staff size and adopted more formal procedures; the Kennedy administration elevated the role of the National Security Advisor to be essentially coequal with cabinet secretaries; and the Nixon administration saw Henry Kissinger consolidate power in the NSC to an unprecedented degree. These various incarnations of the NSC at times produced policy successes and other times failures, yet all were adaptations of a fairly functional system—until the breakdown that took place during the Reagan administration.

The strategic shock that shook the American national security system in 1986 came not from a Soviet surprise attack but from a homegrown scandal. In an ironic twist of history it was a rogue operation, spanning multiple continents, of trading arms for hostages to fund a guerrilla war that led to the birth of the modern NSC system. The details of the Iran-Contra scandal have been related exhaustively elsewhere and need not concern us here. Rather its significance for the question of institutional reform is twofold—first, that an internal scandal emanating from the NSC, rather than an external threat, prompted a major reform effort; and second that this reform effort was completed just in time for a second strategic shock: the sudden collapse of the Soviet bloc and the end of the Cold War.

The geopolitical context is important. The Iran-Contra scandal was largely a self-inflicted wound during a time when the United States was reascendant as a global power. By 1985, a revived economy and military expansion had improved the nation's confidence and credibility abroad, just as its Soviet adversary was showing signs of brittleness. Conciliatory gestures from the new Soviet leader Mikhail Gorbachev provided further cause for optimism. As foolish and damaging as the Iran-Contra episode was, it also occurred at a time when America was otherwise well-positioned and on a positive trajectory. The domestic political conditions for reform of civilian national security institutions were especially ripe given the passage in 1986 of the Goldwater-Nichols Department of Defense Reorganization Act, which substantially revised the organization of the military to achieve greater operational jointness, unity of command, and ultimately combat effectiveness.

To investigate Iran-Contra and draw some constructive lessons from it, the White House created the President's Special Review Board, known informally as the "Tower Commission" after its chairman, former Senator John Tower of Texas. Political expediency certainly played a role in Reagan's decision to create the Commission, as his administration faced pressures on multiple other fronts including Congressional investigations and the appointment of an independent counsel. Taken together, these various investigations also produced the requisite political will and consensus for needful institutional reforms. Brent Scowcroft was the only one of the three members of the Tower Commission to have previously served on the NSC staff, including as National Security Advisor for President Ford. In writing the Tower Report, Scowcroft and his colleagues focused on the role of the National Security Council system, the breakdown of which lay at the core of the scandal. Importantly, in the words of the report, their conclusion "validates the current National Security Council system," and its recommendations were for reform of the system rather than a wholesale scrapping of it.[35] These reforms included a strengthened role for the National Security Advisor and NSC staff in serving as "honest brokers" of inter-agency positions, clarified lines of authority and responsibility, and recommending an end to any operational duties or covert actions overseen by NSC staff. The Reagan White House embraced the Tower Commission's recommendations, and a chastened Reagan ordered them implemented during his last two years in office.[36] In turn, by almost all accounts the Reagan administration NSC system—in both of its incarnations as the gathering of cabinet-level principals and as the NSC staff—functioned quite smoothly under the Tower Commission reforms. Under National Security Advisors Frank Carlucci and his successor Colin Powell, the staff refrained from operational mischief and returned to a more coherent structure. Meanwhile, when Carlucci replaced Casper Weinberger as Secretary of Defense, the once toxic feuds between State and Defense abated, as Carlucci, Powell, and Secretary of State George Shultz forged a collegial partnership through the duration of the administration.

The Bush and Clinton Administrations and the Post–Cold War World

Two paradoxes stand out about the George H.W. Bush administration's national security policy and institutions. First, while the Bush administration is known for a substantially different foreign policy approach than the Reagan administration, it largely maintained the same national security institutions that were inherited from the Reagan White House. Second, while the Bush administration presided for four years over some of the most profound shifts in the international order that world history had ever seen, the administration largely eschewed any profound institutional reforms within its own government. Instead, it used status quo institutions to manage revolutionary global change. It later fell to the first exclusively post–Cold War era presidency, the William J. Clinton administration, to adopt more substantial institutional reforms.

Bush's choice of Scowcroft to be Assistant to the President for National Security Affairs largely explains the first paradox. What he had conceived in the Tower Commission report, Scowcroft was able to put into practice as the national security advisor. This structure became the modern NSC system that has continued to this

---

[35] *The Tower Commission Report* (New York: Bantam, 1987), p. 4. For Scowcroft's role in drafting the NSC portions of the report, see George H. W. Bush and Brent Scowcroft, *A World Transformed* (New York: Knopf, 1998), p. 31.

[36] These orders were embodied in National Security Decision Directives 266 and 276, which borrowed language wholesale from the Tower Commission report in restructuring the NSC. Available at http://www.fas.org/irp/offdocs/nsdd/index.html.

day under the three administrations that followed. It is based on a process structure organized around four tiers of escalating rank that extend across the relevant agencies involved in national security. Each tier considers and resolves issues in its domain, and then sends unresolved issues or issues needing higher-level attention up to the next tier. The initial entry point is the Policy Coordinating Committee, consisting of Assistant Secretary-rank officials. The next level is the Deputies Committee, chaired by the deputy national security advisor and comprising officials of the Deputy and Undersecretary rank. The next level, a Scowcroft innovation, is the Principals Committee (PC), chaired by the national security advisor and consisting of cabinet secretaries. The top level is the formal NSC meeting itself chaired by the president.[37] Notably, the PC in a certain manner resembles a return to the earliest days of the NSC under Truman, when the secretary of state or defense would often chair NSC meetings in the president's absence. Rather than indicating a lack of presidential interest or support for the NSC, the PC was designed to make efficient use of the most precious presidential resource—time—by having senior officials first process the relevant issues and then present them in appropriate form for presidential deliberation and decision.[38]

The Scowcroft reform of the NSC system took place just before the strategic shock of the collapse of the Iron Curtain and the end of the Cold War. The Bush administration's national security team by and large performed ably, even expertly, during this seismic turn of events, as well as in its handling of the subsequent Persian Gulf War. In this they were helped by a reasonably well-functioning set of national security institutions. The Bush administration is remarkable for how *little* it did to reform and update institutions. Rather it appears the Bush administration became so immersed in the whirling maelstrom of world events that it had neither the time nor the bandwidth to engage in a sustained institutional reform project.

While in one sense the Bush administration's relative disregard of institutional reforms was very understandable given the overwhelming demands of the turbulent global landscape, the contrast with the Truman administration is still notable. As discussed earlier in this chapter, the Truman administration created new national and international institutions while simultaneously navigating profound global policy challenges. The Bush administration perceived no need to reform institutions amidst unfolding events because the institutions seemed to work, whereas the Truman administration had to create new institutions precisely because it otherwise lacked the tools to deal with the revolutionary new world it encountered.

Yet what in hindsight appears as the smooth and peaceful denouement of the Cold War should not obscure the profound uncertainty, friction, and drama that

---

[37] This structure was established in National Security Directive 1, issued on January 30, 1989. Available on the Bush Presidential Library website at http://bushlibrary.tamu.edu/research/pdfs/nsd/nsd1.pdf. See also Bush and Scowcroft, *A World Transformed,* 31.

[38] For a thoughtful assessment of the Bush and Scowcroft NSC, including the important role of personnel selection, see Bartholomew Sparrow, *The Strategist: Brent Scowcroft and the Call of National Security* (New York: Public Affairs 2015), pp. 265–291. Sparrow asserts that the Scowcroft NSC differed from those under Reagan in one important respect: it elevated the role of the national security advisor to effectively coequal to the secretary of state in policy formulation.

faced President Bush and his team. After all, at the time they did not know how the story would end. And they knew that any misstep could bring serious, even catastrophic consequences.

A memo from Scowcroft to Bush on January 16, 1990 about the American defense budget encapsulated these challenges. In the previous three months alone, the Berlin Wall had crumbled and the Iron Curtain had dissolved. The Soviet Union, however, still loomed as a nuclear-armed superpower adversary, even under the more benign rule of Mikhail Gorbachev. Scowcroft's memo wrestled with "characterizing defense budget reductions," specifically whether and why the administration should reduce the Pentagon budget at this critical juncture. The memo is suffused with the language of uncertainty. The weakening US economy placed additional fiscal pressures on defense spending, especially after its boom during the Reagan years. Even larger loomed the question of the type and size of military needed for what Scowcroft already called "a 'post-containment' world" with "revolutionary changes that are happening all around." Hence Scowcroft recommended that while economic realities dictated some pruning, "we should characterize the defense budget request as the first step in restructuring our defense program and military capabilities in ways that position us for ongoing and prospective changes in the security environment." In an eerily prescient sentiment, considering that Iraq's surprise invasion of Kuwait would take place several months later, Scowcroft cautioned that "our forces must continue to deter the Soviets, but also have increased utility for other, more likely, conflicts." Moreover, "over the longer term we will continue to build a certain degree of reversibility into what we do as a hedge against unforeseen changes." Scowcroft concluded that "such an approach is inherently cautious but ties the defense program to real changes that are occurring in the world . . . it allows the administration to occupy some strategic high ground and use it as a defensible position from which to dampen unrealistic expectations for an immediate and large peace dividend."[39]

As they agonized over the defense budget, Bush and Scowcroft wrestled with an even more basic question: how should they talk about this uncertain global situation? Ideas precede policy, after all, and language helps translate ideas into policy. A revealing moment came on September 11, 1990 (a date now replete with historical irony) as Bush prepared to address a joint session of Congress in the wake of Saddam Hussein's invasion of Kuwait. One early success, thanks largely to Secretary of State James Baker's deft diplomacy, came when the Soviet Union supported a UN Security Council resolution condemning Iraq's aggression. Yet this also sharpened the geopolitical uncertainty facing the Bush administration: was the Soviet Union still a foe, now a friend, or something else altogether? Referencing the decline of East-West antagonisms, Bush's speech draft triumphantly cited the USSR's unprecedented cooperation in opposing Saddam Hussein as evidence that "we could put forty-five years of history behind us. At long last: *The Cold War is over.*"

[39] January 16, 1990 memo from Scowcroft to President Bush on "Characterizing Defense Budget Reductions." From Scowcroft, Brent Collection; Chronological Files; Folder "Other (January–May 1990 (1))"; George H. W. Bush Presidential Library, College Station, Texas.

But Bush never said those words. The day of the speech, Scowcroft deleted those lines in a last-minute set of edits. In sending the revisions forward, NSC Executive Secretary William Sittmann informed White House Deputy Chief of Staff James Cicconi that "General Scowcroft feels very strongly about his changes." Bush evidently agreed with his national security advisor's caution. The more anodyne version of the speech that he actually delivered made no dramatic assertions about a Cold War victory, and noted only that "a new partnership of nations has begun."[40] The speechwriting and editing process provided a poignant illustration not only of the White House's ambivalence about how to describe the world, but also its confusion over the very nature of that world.

The world as it was may have been unclear, but not so the world they wanted to create. The Bush administration's chosen phrase to describe their ambitions became "a new world order." The origins of the term itself remain murky. Scowcroft seems to have come up with the phrase while fishing with Bush on August 23, 1990 in Kennebunkport, Maine, and first used it speaking to the media later that day. Yet even as it became more widely adopted, Scowcroft remained ambivalent about its implied utopianism and admitted it could sound "gimmicky."[41] Bush's first public use of it came a week later during a press conference on August 30, 1990 concerning the Persian Gulf Crisis, when he described the potential significance of the multilateral coalition opposed to Iraq's aggression. "As I look at the countries that are chipping in here now, I think we do have a chance at a new world order." Bush elaborated on this in his September 11, 1990 address to a joint session of Congress in what became known as the "new world order" speech. In it Bush asserted "out of these troubled times . . . a world order can emerge: a new era—freer from the threat of terror, stronger in the pursuit of justice, and more secure in the quest for peace." Bush's frequent invocation of this phrase over the duration of his presidency demonstrated its resonance in his mind. By the count of his own White House staff, he used it in public statements at least forty-two additional times over the next eight months alone.[42]

This phrase may be one of the most emblematic terms of Bush's presidency, yet in another paradox the administration failed to ever define it, let alone translate it into meaningful new institutions. Eventually the administration stopped even using the phrase, and moved away from the idea behind it. According to Sparrow, "Scowcroft accepted responsibility for the idea's demise." The administration let it "drift," he

---

[40] Emphasis original. September 11, 1990 memo from Sittmann to Cicconi with attached speech edits. From Collection: Speechwriting, White House Office of; Chronological Files 1989–1993; Speech File Draft Files; Folder "Address to Joint Session of Congress, 9/11/90"; Bush Presidential Library. The final version of the speech as delivered can be found in the *Public Papers of the Presidents: George H. W. Bush, 1990.* Available at: http://bushlibrary.tamu.edu/research/public_papers.php?id=2217&year=1990&month=9

[41] Sparrow, 479; David F. Schmitz, *Brent Scowcroft: Internationalism and Post-Vietnam War American Foreign Policy* (Lanham, MD: Rowman and Littlefield, 2011), p. 137.

[42] Both references from June 26, 1991 memo from Dan Jahn to Tony Snow on "Presidential References to New World Order," in collection Speechwriting, White House Office of; Folder: Speech File Backup Files "A New World Order 1990–1991"; Bush Presidential Library.

conceded, and 'never invest[ed] in a new program.'"[43] Senior staff such as Richard Haass and Dennis Ross lamented the failure of the Bush administration to develop a coherent strategic vision. Haass later commented that "I wrote memos, suggested presidential speeches, but Bush wasn't comfortable with grand doctrine. His anti-grandness gene kicked in." In the words of Derek Chollet and James Goldgeier's otherwise sympathetic portrayal, "Bush's exhortations about a new kind of global politics implied more forethought and planning than actually existed. He and his advisers were largely making it up as they went along."[44] While this prudence and caution in the face of revolutionary global change is understandable and in hindsight appears vindicated, it also poses a notable contrast to the Truman administration's ambitious development of the containment strategy and construction of new national security institutions during the equally tumultuous early Cold War era.

With the Soviet Union's final dissolution on Christmas Day 1991, the United States emerged in 1992 as the world's hegemonic superpower, possessing a proportion of global power not seen since the end of World War II and perhaps never before. While the Cold War's final dénouement provided its own strategic shock (albeit a positive one), even at this juncture the Bush administration still did not initiate any substantial reforms of America's civilian national security institutions. This was in part because of the administration's judgment that the prevailing institutions worked sufficiently well, and in part because after three exhausting years of management of profound global change, domestic politics returned with a vengeance. Bush found himself facing an economic recession, plummeting approval ratings, and electoral challenges from the right, left, and center in the respective candidacies of Patrick Buchanan, Ross Perot, and Bill Clinton. Any questions of institutional reform in a second term were answered in the negative by Bush's 1992 reelection loss, and inherited by the Clinton administration.

The judgments of history are rarely kind to one-term presidents who lose reelection. This makes the recent favorable reassessments of the George H. W. Bush administration's national security policy all the more remarkable. While this chapter contends that the Bush team did not possess an overarching strategic vision nor advance any significant institutional reforms, this does not render them a failure. In the tasks history handed them—of navigating a peaceful end to one of the most terrifying conflicts the world had ever seen; of helping usher in democracy, prosperity, and peaceful reintegration to a divided Europe; of rolling back tyrannical aggression and restoring a stable balance in the Middle East—the Bush administration was equal to the moment. As Joseph Nye contends, some acute historical challenges demand a "transactional" rather than a "transformational" president, and he lauds Bush as an exemplar of the former. In managing the fraught transactions of international politics that ended the Cold War, Bush and his team performed remarkably well.[45]

When Bill Clinton took the oath of office on January 20, 1993, he embodied another paradox: a president with little preparation or interest in national security

[43] Sparrow, 482.

[44] Derek Chollet and James Goldgeier, *America Between the Wars: From 11/9 to 9/11* (New York: Public Affairs 2008), pp. 8–9. Ross cited on pp. 18–19.

[45] Nye, 55–59.

policy inherited a nation at the zenith of its global power. His relative inattention to foreign policy mirrored that of an American public feeling dispirited by their country's economic recession and more relieved than triumphant about the Cold War's end. As Chollet and Goldgeier describe, "the new president didn't want to make ... any global issue the center of attention when he came into office ... Clinton believed, with reason, that the election had been fought and won on domestic issues and argued privately that international issues had come up on the campaign trail only in questions from journalists who cared about foreign affairs."[46] Partly because national security was not a priority, and partly because he did not want to tamper with what he saw as a successful model, the new National Security Advisor Tony Lake decided to preserve the basic structure of the Scowcroft NSC system. David Rothkopf describes this as an "act of political courage," because "past administrations had seen tinkering with the NSC structure as a way of imposing their identity on the process."[47] Clinton's embrace of the Bush NSC system also mirrored Eisenhower's adoption of the Truman system. Once again, a successor president of the opposing party helped ensure bipartisan support and continuity of institutional reforms.

"It's the economy, stupid" was the memorable mantra invoked by the Clinton team throughout the 1992 campaign. Ironically this focus on domestic policy led directly to what became one of President Clinton's most consequential institutional innovations on international policy. The NSC structure itself may not have been changed, but instead it received an imitator and in some ways even a bureaucratic competitor with Clinton's creation of the National Economic Council (NEC). The new team began to implement the NEC during the presidential transition, designing it as an entity within the Executive Office of the President to coordinate all economic policy, domestic and international. This also reflected Clinton's fascination with the then-new concept of globalization and the growing interdependence of the United States and the world. Clinton shrewdly realized that the efficacy of new institutions depends as much on personnel as on structure. Within weeks of his election, he phoned Goldman Sachs co-chairman Robert Rubin and asked the investment banker to head the new NEC. Rubin eagerly accepted this new role and made it work, enjoying considerable success first in leading the NEC and eventually as Secretary of the Treasury as well. Analyzing why the new NEC survived and even thrived when many other institutional innovations did not, Rothkopf observes

> the most successful reforms of this sort require the absolute commitment of a major source of power, such as the president; an exceptional champion for the reform in its early days, such as Bob Rubin was; and a little bit of luck, skill, or both. The birth of the NEC needed to have all these things going for it, vulnerable as it was of being killed off by those on the NSC or those in individual departments who saw it as diminishing their power or cutting into their turf.[48]

---

[46] Chollet and Goldgeier, 57.
[47] David Rothkopf, *Running the World: The Inside Story of the National Security Council and the Architects of American Power* (New York: Public Affairs 2005), p. 313.
[48] Rothkopf, 307.

The Clinton era also witnessed a recurring theme in postwar institutional reforms: the role of Congress. Just as Congress had played a significant part in past reorganizations such as the 1947 National Security Act and especially the 1986 Goldwater-Nichols Defense Department Reorganization Act, Capitol Hill emerged as an influential actor in a substantial reorganization of multiple Cold War–era agencies. Under the chairmanship of the venerable conservative Jesse Helms, the Senate Foreign Relations Committee developed legislation to abolish the Arms Control and Disarmament Agency (ACDA), the United States Information Agency (USIA), and the United States Agency for International Development (USAID) by merging their functions into a (presumably) strengthened and streamlined State Department.[49] On one level this proposal demonstrated the changed geopolitical landscape with the end of the Cold War. No longer did the United States face an adversary armed with a massive nuclear arsenal and a competing ideological system, the respective domains of the ACDA and USIA. In this case Senator Helms also resurrected an idea that the Clinton administration had once conceived but then dismissed. Secretary of State Warren Christopher had first proposed this merger, only to have Vice-President Al Gore, who was overseeing the administration's government-wide reform efforts, reject it. In convening his first hearing on the issue in 1995, Helms complained to Christopher that "I have had the majority staff look into the way our government executes decisions the President makes in foreign affairs. The way it is now structured, it is a mess." Helms particularly lamented that "No one person is in charge—and I firmly believe that one person must be in charge of all actions that take place outside (the United States), except for military operations, and that one person is the secretary of state."[50] Even though Helms' criticisms were directed in part at the Clinton administration, they likely pleased Christopher in that they reflected his original ideas and sought to strengthen his cabinet position.

Congress passed Helms's first reorganization bill in 1996, but it suffered a Clinton veto, as the president worried it went too far in usurping executive branch management and eliminating agencies that still enjoyed considerable bureaucratic support. Undeterred, Helms secured the Clinton administration's support for a revised version of his State Department reform measure the next year, in exchange for an agreement to allow the Chemical Weapons Convention (CWC) treaty to come to the Senate floor for a ratification vote. Helms had long opposed the CWC, but agreed to a tactical defeat as it passed the Senate in exchange for what he saw as a strategic victory in the dissolution of the ACDA and USIA and subordination of

---

[49] Curiously, as substantial as this interagency reorganization effort was, it receives no mention in two of the standard books on Clinton-era foreign policy by Chollet and Goldgeier and by Rothkopf.

[50] "Helms Blasts Foreign Policy and Vows to Push an Overhaul," *Philadelphia Inquirer*, February 15, 1995, A07. While Helms' concerns about a multiplicity of voices claiming to speak for American foreign policy were directed at the heads of these three agencies, ironically he did not address the position that had emerged as a much more visible challenge to the secretary of state's primacy: the national security advisor.

USAID under the State Department.[51] Although both the Clinton administration and Senator Helms had to compromise on certain points, overall both parties saw the final package of reforms as a necessary measure to bring American diplomacy from the Cold War into the 21st century.

INSTITUTIONAL REFORM IN THE PRESENT ERA: SEPTEMBER 11TH AND BEYOND

The strategic shock of the terrorist attack on September 11, 2001 was accentuated by the searing exposure of the nation's vulnerability during a time when America otherwise still occupied its post–Cold War position as the dominant global power. From this paradoxical position of national strength and vulnerability, under the George W. Bush administration the United States undertook the most extensive set of institutional reforms since the beginning of the Cold War.[52] Yet as extensive as these new reforms were, it should not escape notice that this Bush administration also preserved several of the institutional reforms it had inherited from the Clinton administration, including the National Economic Council and the merger of USIA and ACDA functions into the State Department. Once again, the pattern of a president of an opposing party adopting his predecessor's reforms helped ensure their bipartisan continuity.

As the Bush administration grappled with its response to the September 11th attacks, it self-consciously drew on the historical analogy of the early Cold War years. Just as the Truman administration had constructed a new set of institutions for the global contest with communism, so did the Bush administration regard its own efforts to create a new set of national security institutions for the 21st century global conflict with Islamist terrorism. Bush frequently expressed this theme, such as in a 2006 commencement address at West Point that drew explicit parallels with the Truman administration and the early Cold War:

> President Truman launched a sweeping reorganization of the federal government to prepare it for a new struggle. Working with Congress, he created the Department of Defense, established the Air Force as a separate military service, formed the National Security Council at the White House, and founded the Central Intelligence

---

[51] For more on this process, see William A. Link, *Righteous Warrior: Jesse Helms and the Rise of Modern Conservatism* (New York: St. Martin's, 2008), pp. 456–460, and James M. Lindsay, "The State Department Complex After the Cold War," in Randall Ripley and James M. Lindsay, eds., *U.S. Foreign Policy After the Cold War* (Pittsburgh, PA: University of Pittsburgh Press, 1997), pp. 74–105.

[52] Quality academic literature on the George W. Bush administration remains quite sparse, in part because of limited access to source material until the archival records are processed, declassified, and opened. Some of the extant literature that does exist is marred by partisan bias. At this juncture, some of the more insightful treatments of the Bush administration are journalistic accounts, such as Peter Baker, *Days of Fire: Bush and Cheney in the White House* (New York: Doubleday, 2013), and David Rothkopf, *National Insecurity: American Leadership in an Age of Fear* (New York: PublicAffairs, 2014).

Agency to ensure America had the best intelligence on Soviet threats. . . . Today, at the start of a new century, we are again engaged in a war unlike any our nation has fought before—and like Americans in Truman's day, we are laying the foundations for victory.[53]

Both of the Bush administration's *National Security Strategy (NSS)* documents, issued in 2002 and 2006, respectively, included an entire chapter entitled "Transform America's National Security Institutions to Meet the Challenges and Opportunities of the 21st Century." Each *NSS*, especially the 2006 edition, described the creation of new institutions such as the Department of Homeland Security (DHS), the Director of National Intelligence, the National Counterterrorism Center (NCTC), the Millennium Challenge Corporation (MCC), the President's Emergency Plan for AIDS Relief (PEPFAR), the Director of Foreign Assistance, and the Office of Reconstruction and Stabilization.[54]

The similarities between the George W. Bush administration and the Truman administration on institutional reform may have been even closer than the Bush administration realized. As in Truman's day, the Bush White House faced considerable external pressure for some of the reforms—and like the Truman administration, the Bush administration resisted many of these reforms until compelled to accept them. Thus it was the relentless demands of Congress for the creation of the Department of Homeland Security that caused the Bush administration to drop its opposition and agree to the passage of the Homeland Security Act of 2002. And it was the *National Commission on Terrorist Attacks Upon the United States* (the "9/11 Commission"), created over the Bush administration's objections, that demanded reforms such as the creation of a more integrated intelligence system. The 9/11 Commission Report led directly and rapidly to the passage of the Intelligence Reform and Terrorism Prevention Act of 2004, which among other provisions created the Office of the Director of National Intelligence (ODNI) and the National Counterterrorism Center.[55] Just as in Truman's day, there was a rough consensus on the necessary elements of national power to be brought to bear on the new conflict, but fierce disagreements over how that power should be institutionalized and wielded. In 1947 and

---

[53] President George W. Bush, Commencement Address at the United States Military Academy at West Point, May 27, 2006. Available at http://www.presidentialrhetoric.com/speeches/05.27.06.html.

[54] 2002 *National Security Strategy* available at http://georgewbush-whitehouse.archives.gov/nsc/nss/2002/; 2006 National Security Strategy available at http://georgewbush-whitehouse.archives.gov/nsc/nss/2006/. In full disclosure, the author served as one of the NSC staff responsible for drafting the 2006 *NSS*.

[55] For an authoritative treatment on the passage of the Intelligence Reform and Terrorism Prevention Act of 2004 by a key participant in the legislative process, see Michael Allen, *Blinking Red: Crisis and Compromise in American Intelligence after 9/11* (Washington, DC: Potomac Books, 2013). For the role of the 9/11 Commission in generating this legislation, see Jordan Tama, *Terrorism and National Security Reform: How Commissions Can Drive Change During Crises* (New York: Cambridge University Press, 2011).

in 2003, institutional reforms occurred as contested processes, with competing stakeholders and multiple catalysts, and with a president determined to protect his prerogatives while wielding whatever instruments of power were available to him.

The verdict is still unfolding on these reforms, and the reform processes themselves may not be complete. Thus far the results are mixed, although many of these Bush-era reforms have benefited from the Obama administration's continuation of a notable historical pattern. After campaigning in 2008 on an explicit repudiation of Bush foreign and defense policy, once in office President Obama has largely preserved most of the institutions created under the Bush administration. Some of these are unsurprising, such as Bush's "smart development" initiatives exemplified by PEPFAR and MCC, which Obama has continued, albeit with reduced funding due to budgetary pressures.[56] Much less expected has been the Obama administration's embrace of the Bush administration's intelligence and counterterrorism infrastructure, which if anything has been expanded and used with considerable effect.

The Bush-era intelligence reforms themselves did not have an auspicious beginning, although perhaps initially too much emphasis was placed on new institutional structures rather than personnel and leadership. Commenting on the institutional ambiguities and tensions inherent in the O/DNI and CIA relationship, Paul Pillar has observed that "Even poorly designed institutional structures can be made to work with enough skill and will from the people at the top. Individual working relationships that those people forge are critical, and different people in the same positions might not be as good at forging such ties. Nonetheless, the tone that the people at the top set shapes the work habits of the folks lower down in their organizations. Once formed, the habits can persist even after leaders change."[57] In this vein, current DNI James Clapper, who has held the position since 2010, has taken a cooperative and collegial posture toward the other heads of the intelligence agencies, especially the various CIA directors. Clapper has focused on the development of the coordination and budget responsibilities of his office, and thus cultivated more institutional credibility and respect for the O/DNI, which makes its longer term viability much more promising.[58] Likewise the various NCTC directors have adeptly concentrated on the coordination and analysis responsibilities that the law provides, rather than picking what would have been losing bureaucratic fights with operational entities like the CIA's Counterterrorism Center. Now that a decade has passed since the creation of the ODNI and NCTC under Bush, both entities function as integral parts of Obama's national security system, and will very likely continue under the next presidency.

---

[56] Nicholas van de Walle, "Obama and Africa: Lots of Hope, Not Much Change," *Foreign Affairs*, September/October 2015, 54–61.

[57] Paul Pillar, "Good While It Lasted: Did David Petraeus Leave His Mark at the CIA?" *ForeignPolicy.com*, November 13, 2012. Available at: http://foreignpolicy.com/2012/11/13/good-while- it-lasted.

[58] On the O/DNI's successes and limitations, see Michael Allen and Stephen Slick, "The Office of the DNI's Greatest Hits," *ForeignPolicy.com*, April 21, 2015. Available at http://foreignpolicy.com/2015/04/21/dni-september-11-terrorism-clapper.

The verdict on the Department of Homeland Security (DHS) remains uncertain, but early indications are not promising. The disparate mélange of agencies, offices, and institutions that were forcibly merged under the DHS umbrella have largely resisted true integration of functionality or mission. As one critic recently observed, a "cautionary tale, recently reviewed by the Government Accountability Office, is the eight-year-and-counting attempt to realign the Department of Homeland Security's field office structure. The GAO's review recounted two major reorganization efforts, in 2004 and 2010, both of which were substantially abandoned. It was unable to find enough documentation to even evaluate whether the benefits of these reorganizations would have justified the costs."[59]

For all of its ambitions of transforming institutions, the Bush administration still preserved intact large swaths of the system first created under Truman. From their gruesome nativity in the strategic shock of the Pearl Harbor attack to the vantage point of the 21st century, the reforms of civilian national security institutions during the Truman administration remain the most consequential and enduring in American history. The process lacked a grand design, and its multiple architects competed as much as they cooperated, but in the end that resulted in a system that enabled the Truman administration to establish not just the ideas but also the means for a Cold War grand strategy. The institutions had flaws from the outset, and some of those flaws would bedevil the national security system throughout the Cold War and even up to the present day.[60] However, for all of its weaknesses, the system bequeathed to us then still works, for two fundamental reasons. First, it contained enough flexibility and internal adjustment mechanisms that subsequent administrations could continue to revise and update the national security system to suit the preferences of each president and the changing landscapes of international politics. Second, it succeeded in its most basic purpose, of enabling the president and his lieutenants to wield all instruments of national power on behalf of a broad vision of national security. Put another way, the system may not be good, but for almost seventy-five years it has been good enough.

Yet now, "good enough" may no longer be, in fact, good enough. Further reforms may be necessary as the United States enters an uncertain new era in which our national power may not be as dominant or enduring, and the international security environment encompasses a complex array of possible threats ranging from great power peer competitors to pariah states pursuing weapons of mass destruction to nonstate actors such as terrorist groups. This is where the concept of "sustainable security" becomes most relevant. National security needs to be sustained even when prevailing distributions of power are shifting, and new threats are emerging. However, two cautionary notes are in order. First, while global power distributions are shifting, this does not necessarily mean that American power is substantially

---

[59] Robert M. Simon, "Seven Rules for Wannabe Cabinet Members," *Washington Post*, 16 November 2012. Available at http://www.washingtonpost.com/opinions/seven-rules-for-wannabe-cabinet-members/2012/11/16/76756d06-2d03-11e2-89d4-040c9330702a_story.html?hpid=z3

[60] These flaws, perhaps unavoidable, include persistent service rivalries, tensions and turf wars between the NSC and State, tensions between the NSC's honest broker and advisory roles, insufficient coordination across intelligence agencies, and so on.

declining.[61] Second, the fact that the previous institutional reforms discussed as historical case studies in this chapter generally took place during times of relative power ascendance does not mean that the insights from those reforms do not apply during times of power stagnation or decline.

On the question of American power, this author does not share the premise of some other contributors to this volume that the United States is a declining power. While global power balances are in flux, with the trend appearing to include China's power increasing as that of Japan and the European Union diminishes, overall the United States still retains a position of predominance across several domains such as economic power, military power, and diplomatic power. In economic terms, while America's challenges include anemic growth and a ballooning debt, they pale in comparison with the Eurozone's simmering crisis and economic erosion, or with China's economic slowdown and stalled transition from a low-cost manufacturing and export economy to a domestic consumption economy, or with Russia's continued overreliance on hydrocarbon exports and slow-motion demographic suicide. Setting aside China's slowing growth rates, themselves a crude and imperfect indicator of future trends, Beijing's more enduring economic problem remains the failure to develop a system of widespread innovation. Extrapolating on this, Michael Beckley recently observed that "the United States is now wealthier, more innovative, and more militarily powerful compared to China than it was in 1991."[62] In military terms, the United States remains the dominant global hegemon, even as the declining defense budget of the past few years is now beginning to grow again. Diplomatically, while under the Obama administration the United States has sought to reduce its commitments abroad, no other nation has emerged to replace the United States as the diplomatic convener of first resort, and most other nations in every region still look to America as an essential diplomatic participant in addressing regional and global crises. In international politics, the United States fills the role of what Josef Joffe terms the "default power . . . a nation to which others look when nobody else steps forward."[63]

This is not to assert that the United States will inevitably remain the dominant global power for the next half century, but only that predictions of *inevitable* American decline or even power stagnation are not warranted. Lamentations over national decline have been a perennial feature of American public consciousness since the Puritan new world settlements of the 17th century, a phenomenon that Samuel Huntington labeled "Declinism." Yet they have very often proven unwarranted. As Joffe contends in his 2014 book, *The Myth of America's Decline: Politics, Economics, and a Half Century of False Prophecies*, across a preponderance of metrics that capture not only static capabilities, but more crucially the capacity for

---

[61] For more on the complexities of measuring national power, see William Inboden, "What is Power?" *The American Interest* 5, no. 2 (November/December 2009).

[62] Michael Beckley, "China's Century? Why America's Edge Will Endure," *International Security* 36, no. 3 (Winter 2011/2012): 41–78.

[63] Josef Joffe, *The Myth of America's Decline: Politics, Economics, and a Half Century of False Prophecies* (New York: W.W. Norton 2014), pp. 249–250.

dynamism and renewal, the United States is poised to remain the dominant global power for the foreseeable future.

Yet what if this time the grim, gloomy prophets are correct, and American primacy is coming to an end? Here the second point emerges: shock and flux, not power ascendance, matter most for spurring institutional reform. For purposes of this chapter's historical analysis and current prescriptions, when it comes to reform of civilian national security institutions the lessons still hold. The key determinant of the past phases of institutional reform assessed here—principally the beginning of the Cold War but also the end of the Cold War and the post-9/11 period—was not abundant and increasing national power, but rather strategic shocks and system flux. It was the shock of the Pearl Harbor attack followed by the systemic flux of the emergence of the Soviet threat after World War II that spurred the creation of the NSC, CIA, Defense Department, and related reforms. It was the shock of the Iran-Contra scandal, the Cold War's end, and the systemic flux of globalization that drove the modernization of the NSC and the creation of the NEC. It was the shock of 9/11 that drove the creation of O/DNI, NCTC, DHS, and so on.

And so, if further reform of national security institutions is undertaken, such efforts and those leading them should bear in mind the following principles, borne of history:

- *First do no harm.* If poorly conceived, sometimes the creation of new institutions can be deleterious to national security. The perpetual impulse to build something new should be carefully examined before being acted on. This prudent insight in part shaped Brent Scowcroft's reluctance to replace or completely recreate the NSC in the wake of Iran-Contra and the end of the Cold War.
- *Strengthen what remains.* Just as the Tower Commission and then the Clinton administration found with the NSC, it may be that the current institutions are the best option, and merely need to be updated and strengthened.
- *Define first principles.* Institutions are tools, and before new tools should be designed and used, their purpose needs to be defined. What is the nature of power in the 21st century, and how do we ensure that our national security institutions wield it most effectively? What are the strategic goals that our national security institutions are designed to attain? It was in part these questions that shaped the creation of the NSC and related institutions under Truman. His administration and its Congressional allies determined that the nature of power itself was changing as the Cold War emerged; that economic, diplomatic, and ideological power needed to be integrated with military power; and that the projection of force needed to be better subordinated to political goals determined by the president.
- *Secure bipartisan presidential support.* No reform can succeed without the support, engagement, and commitment of the Oval Office as an institution, beyond individual presidents. The president is not only the chief executive but also the diplomat in chief and the commander in chief, and all of these roles must align in supporting new or reformed institutions. Yet new presidents can often undo the actions of their predecessors, so enduring institutional reforms will be most viable when they are embraced by successive presidents, especially of opposing

parties. The examples of Truman to Eisenhower, Bush 41 to Clinton, Clinton to Bush 43, and Bush 43 to Obama all illustrate this.

- *Enlist multiple stakeholders.* Important actors such as Congress, expert commissions, and existing departments and agencies should be enlisted early in the process, to solicit ideas, generate political will, and ensure sustainability. They will insert themselves anyway, so better to invite them at the outset. From the Eberstadt Commission to the 9/11 Commission, from Forrestal to Kennan to Scowcroft, this characterizes the institutional reforms pursued in every era described in this chapter.

- *Institutionalize adaptation.* In other words, reform and build institutions in a way that allows them to be further revised and adapted by succeeding generations. "Built to last" means "built to be reformed later." Today's NSC little resembles the NSC in its nativity under Truman, yet the 1947 law governing the institution remains the same. It gave the NSC its mandate, yet remained either vague enough or sufficiently silent in other provisions to empower every president since to refashion the NSC according to his preferences.

- *Put people first.* Yes, this is a platitude, but in this case it has the specific purpose of remembering that quality personnel are more important than quality institutions. Good leaders can make bad institutions work; bad leaders cannot make good institutions work. Priority should first be given to recruiting, training, and empowering capable new national security leaders. The real success of the early Cold War era is not just the 1947 law, but the presence of giants such as Marshall, Kennan, Forrestal, Acheson, and Truman himself.

6

TO STARVE AN ARMY
HOW GREAT POWER ARMIES RESPOND
TO AUSTERITY

John W. Hall

How have military institutions in great powers adjusted to severe budget constraints in the past? What can we learn for today?

As the United States slowly crawls its way out of a global recession, extracts itself from the longest war in American history, and attempts to resolve a colossal (and partly derivative) deficit, few responsible observers question the prudence of cuts to the American defense budget. On the magnitude of such cuts or where they should fall, however, there is less agreement. Since 2013, America's armed services have contended with the fiscal bogeyman "sequestration" and jockeyed against one another for their respective slices of a diminishing pie. Grown fat by supplemental funding and a favorable base budget over more than a decade of war, the army has found that the navy and air force have closed ranks against it, offering operational concepts that promise to secure America's future interests with high-tech capabilities that are at once economical and alluring. The army, meanwhile, is relegated to its traditional role of waging conventional or counterinsurgent wars and occupying terrain—competencies for which Americans presently have no enthusiasm, either because of their high cost and meager dividends or (in the case of conventional warfare) their perceived irrelevance to the future operating environment. Compounding the army's problem is its own rhetoric regarding civilian soldiers over the past forty years. Having extolled the virtues of the National Guard and the Army Reserve in order to grow these components, the army must now justify the preservation of a large regular force to do things that part-time soldiers seem capable of doing for a fraction of the price. Thus it appears inevitable that while all of the services will have to surrender their pound of flesh, the army will have to give several.

The army's protestations to the contrary, this is not necessarily a bad thing. To a far greater extent than the other services, the army relies on the most expensive element of American force structure: manpower. Historically, Americans have been loath to pay for big armies in times of relative peace because, despite their positive impact on local economies, they represent torrential drains on public revenues without offering any appreciable return on the nation's investment, save in the exceptional event of war. When it erupts, the republic pours funds into the army for the duration of hostilities—and cuts them off once they have concluded.

Having endured it for nearly two-and-a-half centuries, the US Army is very familiar with this cycle but protests that it hardly provides a model for sustainable national security. In the mid-1980s, the army commissioned an edited volume titled *America's First Battles*, in which respected military historians examined the army's performance in the first engagement in each of America's major wars. With only a handful of exceptions, the army performed very poorly, and the principal inference by the volume's editors was that, by their misguided frugality, the American people and Congress had routinely set their army up for failure. The book found a receptive audience among army officers, making its way onto the Chief of Staff of the Army's reading list and burrowing itself into the curricula at nearly every level of professional military education.[1] Perhaps the most assigned chapter from the volume is Roy Flint's survey of the US Army's abysmal performance at the beginning of the Korean War. The United States threw an understrength, poorly trained battalion in the path of a North Korean juggernaut that brushed aside "Task Force Smith" and the rest of the 24th Division and nearly completed its conquest of the Korean Peninsula.[2] Particularly after the Cold War, army leaders used the expression "no more Task Force Smiths" to warn about the dangers of cutting army spending too drastically or assuming that ground combat power would not be needed again in the future.

But the other "lessons" we might draw from *America's First Battles* are more ambiguous. After all, the United States categorically lost only one of the wars addressed in the volume. Ironically, the American army that deployed *en masse* to Vietnam in 1965 was one of "the best-equipped armies in history."[3] Conversely, the United States' most sweeping and complete victory—that over Mexico in the mid-nineteenth century—was won by a perpetually underfunded and widely maligned army that surprised everyone with its magnificent performance.[4] So whatever

---

[1] In fairness to the volume's editors and contributors, it is solid, scholarly contribution that deserves wide readership. Charles E. Heller and William A. Stofft, eds., *America's First Battles, 1776–1965* (Lawrence: University Press of Kansas, 1986).

[2] Flint is careful to point out, however, that despite its numerous deficiencies, the 24th Division succeeded in delaying the advance of the North Korean forces long enough to allow the US 8th Army to establish a lodgment at Pusan. Roy K. Flint, "Task Force Smith and the 24th Division: Delay and Withdrawal, 5–19 July 1950," in *America's First Battles, 1776–1965*, eds. Charles E. Heller and William A. Stofft (Lawrence: University Press of Kansas, 1986), pp. 266–299.

[3] George C. Herring, "The 1st Cavalry and the Ia Drang Valley, 18 October–24 November 1965," *First Battles*, 303. Unable to blame its eventual defeat on pre-war civilian parsimony, the army eventually developed a "stabbed-in-the-back" narrative that ascribed responsibility to political leaders and the decisions they made during the war.

[4] Although volunteers outnumbered regulars by a margin of two-to-one in this war, their performance was uneven, and the officers of a professional US Army credited their soldiers and (above all) themselves for the victory. Their claims to the lion's share of credit were not without merit, and an American public that had previously viewed the regular army with distrust nominated each of its senior commanders in this war for the presidency. William B. Skelton, *An American*

lesson army leaders and their lobby would *like* for us to draw from history, one point seems clear: robust peacetime spending is no guarantee of future performance or, for that matter, salutary to national interests. Far more important than the gross flow of dollars to the army or other elements of the defense establishment are the ways that those dollars are put to use.

Rather than revisit each of these chapters of American history to evaluate the prudence of interwar defense allocations, this chapter will examine two broad case studies that bear certain similarities to the current fiscal and strategic environment. Broadly speaking, retrenchment in defense spending occurs for one of two reasons, sometimes in combination: economic considerations create an imperative for cost savings; or a nation's assessment of the strategic situation warrants a reduction in military capabilities or capacities and, by extension, expenditure. Arguably, the United States presently finds itself in both situations; the relevant question now is not *whether* the nation should cut defense spending but rather how deeply and at the expense of what capabilities.[5]

To shed some light on these questions, this chapter will examine how effectively the armies of several great powers responded to the austerity of the 1920s and the Great Depression and how the US Army in particular dealt with the Eisenhower administration's discretionary cutbacks under the "New Look" of the 1950s.[6] Collectively, these case studies suggest that responsibility for the prudent commitment of scarce resources is shared by civilian policymakers (and the domestic constituencies to which they answer) and military leaders who develop doctrine and capabilities. Perhaps not surprisingly, nations fare best when they enjoy a reasonably accurate estimate of the strategic situation; a consistent, feasible strategy for safeguarding national interests; and the military capabilities to implement it.

Profession of Arms: The Army Officer Corps, 1784–1861 (Lawrence: University Press of Kansas, 1992), pp. 340–345.

[5] There is little disagreement on the first point. The second is more contentious but reflected in the most recent (2014) Quadrennial Defense Review. Even dissenters such as Andrew Krepinevich, who argues that the United States is "entering a period of heightened security challenges," concede the inevitability of decreased or static defense spending. Andrew F. Krepinevich, "Statement before the Senate Armed Services Committee on Defense Strategy, October 28, 2015," Alternative Approaches to Defense Strategy, Center for Strategic and Budgetary Assessments, 30 October 2015, accessed 31 October 2015 http://csbaonline.org/publications/2015/10/alternative-approaches-to-defense-strategy/.

[6] Primarily as means of containing the scope of this chapter, it focuses exclusively on the interwar cases of Germany, France, Great Britain, and the United States. It omits consideration of the Soviet Union because—although clearly a "great power"—its largely preindustrial, agrarian economy partially insulated the Red Army from the effects of the Great Depression. But more important was the priority afforded to military spending and military-oriented industrialization under the five-year plans. According to Earl F. Ziemke, "the Soviet armed forces had something no other military establishment of the time had, namely . . . an economy entirely devoted to military support." Earl F. Ziemke, "The Soviet Armed Forces in the Interwar Period," in *Military Effectiveness*: Vol. 2, *The Interwar Period*, Allan Reed Millett and Williamson Murray eds. (Cambridge, UK: Cambridge University Press, 2010), pp. 6–7, quotation from 15–16.

No less surprisingly, nations rarely draw such a winning hand. Indeed, its essential components—strategic clarity and doctrinal flexibility—are largely countervailing forces, one achieving its fullest realization only at the expense of the other. Nations facing a single strategic threat are prone to construct military capabilities optimized for that threat alone, while those confronted with an ambiguous strategic environment are likely to hedge their bets, building a range of general (and sometimes competing) capabilities optimal for no single contingency. Each course is fraught with danger. In the former case, any misreading of the strategic situation or misjudgment of the military capabilities required to meet it can result in catastrophic failure (such as France endured in 1940). On the other hand, jacks of all trades are usually masters of none—unless they possess the time, perspicuity, and resources to reorient on threats as they become salient. Complicating matters further, the militaries of democratic nations are rarely able to devise their capabilities in a theoretical vacuum, for they are beholden to public sentiments born of recent conflicts and borne by emotion as much as reason. Similarly, military services are prone to subordinating genuine requirements to parochial interests when they perceive political and fiscal threats to their well-being.

It is therefore not surprising that history is replete with examples of nations and armies that failed to prepare adequately for the future, however astute their reading of the strategic environment. Of the five cases examined here, not one may be judged an unqualified success story, and in no instance were shortcomings attributable solely or even primarily to inadequate peacetime spending. Raw levels of funding proved less important than the projects to which armies applied their limited resources. Ultimately, the nations that fared best possessed armies with learning cultures and enough political security to tolerate—indeed, harness—ambiguity, dissent, and innovation. They also enjoyed enough freedom from operational demands to undertake serious reflection and experimentation. Unfortunately, the US Army today is overextended in the role of a global constabulary even as many Americans question the need for substantial ground forces. Although it tries to look to the future, the army is preoccupied with threats to its immediate front—and to its bottom line. Compounding matters, American partisan politics no longer stop at the water's edge, making it increasingly difficult to craft a consensus strategy and identify the requisite military capabilities. To achieve sustainable security, the United States will have to contend with each of these problems, the most pressing of which is the need to define strategic requirements that realistically serve American interests and ideals.

GERMANY IN THE INTERWAR PERIOD

While sustainable security demands strategic clarity and doctrinal flexibility, these attributes are by themselves insufficient guarantors of national ambition, which may itself be irrational and self-defeating. Such was the case with Germany, which enjoyed exceptional strategic clarity (shared broadly by the national leadership, the military, and society at large) and an almost mythological military culture of innovation. Yet Germany suffered complete defeat by the summer of 1945 because Hitler miscalculated the military and industrial means required to achieve his otherwise clear strategic vision of overturning the Versailles Treaty and establishing Germany as a global hegemon.[7]

From a strictly military point of view, however, the German Army was more successful than any other great power military establishment at anticipating the requirements of the next war and—despite crippling austerity measures imposed at Versailles and exacerbated by the Great Depression—building the requisite military capabilities. The army certainly benefitted (at least in the short run) from the ascension of Adolf Hitler to reich chancellor in 1933 and his aggressive rearmament program, but the money Hitler lavished on the *Wehrmacht* was akin to water spread over seeds planted years earlier. Hitler neither planted these seeds nor, in the case of the army, had any substantive role in their development.[8] The foundations of that force had been laid a decade earlier by a generation of officers determined to both learn from and rewrite the history of the Great War.

Stereotypes notwithstanding, most Germans were not technophiles hoping to manufacture a "revolution in military affairs" that would render obsolete the lessons of the past. To the contrary, the German doctrinal renaissance of the interwar period was a product of intense historical study, opportunity afforded by the Versailles Treaty (which wiped clean the German Army's slate), and an abiding desire on the part of the military to overturn that treaty. Ironically, the austerity imposed by the Treaty of Versailles in some ways, at least, fostered doctrinal innovation in the German Army. Firstly, it deprived that force of the matériel of modern warfare, which allowed the staff to envision ideal technological solutions to future operational problems rather than binding them to stockpiles of legacy equipment. To bend Donald Rumsfeld's infamous phrase, Germany would not have to go to war with the army *it had* because it had no army to speak of. Instead, it could design the army it *wished* it had—and build it once Hitler provided the funding for rearmament. Similarly, the absence of a large body of men under arms relieved the officers of the *Reichswehr* of responsibility for training those men and allowed them more time for theoretical-doctrinal reflection.[9]

---

[7] The historiography of Germany's economic mobilization for World War II is vast and, while relevant to this paper, beyond its scope. Among the more recent and influential works on this point is Adam Tooze, *The Wages of Destruction: The Making and Breaking of the Nazi Economy* (New York: Viking, 2007).

[8] Williamson Murray, *The Change in the European Balance of Power, 1938–1939: The Path to Ruin* (Princeton, NJ: Princeton University Press, 1984), p. 32; Williamson Murray, "German Army Doctrine, 1918–1939, and the Post-1945 Theory of 'Blitzkrieg Strategy,'" in *German Nationalism and the European Response, 1890–1945*, Carole Fink, Isabel V. Hull, and MacGregor Knox eds. (Norman: University of Oklahoma Press, 1985), p. 79; Elizabeth Kier, *Imagining War: French and British Military Doctrine between the Wars* (Princeton, NJ: Princeton University Press, 1997), p. 14.

[9] Citing a persistent culture of doctrinal innovation in the German Army, Williamson Murray argues that historians tend to overemphasize the extent to which Versailles limitations actually facilitated innovation. Nevertheless, he elsewhere obliquely supports this argument. Murray, "German Army Doctrine, 1918-1939," 75–77; Murray, *The Change in the European Balance of Power, 1938–1939*, 31. See also Robert O. Paxton, *Parades and Politics at Vichy: The French Officer Corps under Marshal Pétain* (Princeton, NJ: Princeton University Press, 1966).

The Germans established a deserved reputation for tactical ingenuity and imagination during the Great War.[10] By 1918, the German Army had essentially arrived at its doctrinal solution for restoring mobility and operational maneuver to the battlefield. Yet despite unprecedented success (as measured in depth of penetration) in their 1918 spring offensive, the Germans could not maintain offensive momentum or translate tactical gains into operational success. How to solve this problem became the overriding concern of the German Army's General Staff after the war.[11] Its chief, General Hans von Seeckt, commissioned no less than fifty-seven committees to study the "lessons" of the last war.[12] Out of this ferment arose a commitment to restoring mobility to the battlefield.[13] While their own experience in motorization and mechanization was limited, the Germans were profoundly impressed by the potential of the tank as demonstrated by the British in 1918.[14] Versailles Treaty restrictions reduced the Germans to conducting armored warfare experiments with cars fitted with prosthetics that made them look like tanks, but it did not prevent them from paying close attention to the experiments of other nations, especially the United Kingdom. The Germans devoured the writings of British armor pioneers J.F.C. Fuller and Basil Liddell Hart and keenly observed the British Army's realistic experiments in the late 1920s. In 1935, the commander of Germany's first *Panzer* unit was entirely sincere when he told Sir John Dill "with some pride . . . that the German tank corps had been modelled on the British."[15] Soon afterward, the British lost their enthusiasm for the tank while the Germans assumed the global lead in developing armored formations and doctrine.[16]

[10] Murray, "German Army Doctrine, 1918–1939," 72. For a detailed analysis of Germany tactical innovations during the Great War, see Timothy T. Lupfer, *The Dynamics of Doctrine: The Changes in German Tactical Doctrine During the First World War* (Fort Leavenworth, KS: Combat Studies Institute, 1981).

[11] Technically, the Versailles Treaty outlawed the General Staff, but it nevertheless persevered during the Weimar era under the cover name *Truppenamt* ("troop office").

[12] MacGregor Knox and Williamson Murray, *The Dynamics of Military Revolution, 1300–2050* (Cambridge, UK: Cambridge University Press, 2001), pp. 157–158.

[13] This commitment was originally predicated on the belief that Germany's severe military weakness demanded a mobile defensive doctrine. With Germany's seizure of the Rhineland in 1936 and Hitler's underwriting of a dramatic expansion of the army, the General Staff seized the opportunity to embrace an offensive doctrine not because it facilitated any articulated strategy but for the simple reason that it was good for the army. Murray, *The Change in the European Balance of Power, 1938–1939*, 31–32; Murray, "German Army Doctrine, 1918–1939," 76; Manfred Messerschmidt, "German Military Effectiveness Between 1919 and 1939," in *Military Effectiveness*: Vol. 2, *The Interwar Period*, Allan Reed Millett and Williamson Murray eds. (Cambridge, UK: Cambridge University Press, 2010), pp. 225, 230; Wilhelm Deist, *The Wehrmacht and German Rearmament* (Toronto: University of Toronto Press, 1981), p. 42.

[14] Murray, "German Army Doctrine, 1918–1939," 75, 88.

[15] Murray, *The Change in the European Balance of Power*, 35.

[16] Matthew Cooper, *The German Army, 1933–1945: Its Political and Military Failure* (New York: Scarborough House, 1990), pp. 144–145; Azar Gat, *British Armour Theory and the Rise of the Panzer Arm: Revising the Revisionists* (New York: St. Martin's, 2000), pp. 43–48. The principal "revisionist" alluded to in the title is John Mearsheimer, who argued in 1988 that the then consensus interpretation exaggerated the originality and influence of Basil Liddell

This is not to say, however, that all German commanders were sold on the revolutionary potential of the tank. Whereas General Heinz Guderian and his disciples forwarded an "armored idea" of rapid, strategic penetrations by Panzer units, the senior leadership of the Germany Army remained committed to a more traditional strategy of annihilation carried out by a mass army. Guderian railed especially against the apparent conservatism of Chief of the General Staff Ludwig Beck (1935–1938), whom he accused of retarding the development of Germany's armored potential and rejecting a supposedly superior form of war. So blinded was Guderian by his enthusiasm for the armored idea that he failed to appreciate its risks, limits, and (for Germany in particular) unbearable costs. With a better appreciation of the German Army's logistical limitations and strategic vulnerability, Beck rejected Guderian's radical vision but underwrote continued experimentation and development of mechanized forces, generating the army that enjoyed so much operational success in 1939 and 1940. If he was not a revolutionary himself, he was hardly a reactionary. Nor did he (or for that matter von Seeckt) insist upon a single doctrinal template without room for dissent or innovation. "What separated the German army from the other European armies," writes Williamson Murray, "was the fact that most German army leaders, while remaining skeptical about the armor school's seemingly extravagant claims, acquiesced in the development of the new arm." Once this arm demonstrated its potential in combat, former opponents (among them Erwin Rommel and Gerd von Rundstedt) were quick to change their positions and become champions of the new capability, which they continued to refine through rigorous after-action reviews.[17] This openmindedness and commitment to professional learning extended to all other domains of the German army, and largely explains its astonishing success throughout the first two years of the war.

But tactical acumen obscured fundamental problems that ultimately spelled defeat for the Third Reich. In 1938, Hitler purged the senior leadership of the army (prompting Beck to resign in protest) and began replacing military professionals with fanatics and stooges. Yet this is not to suggest that German Army officers were blameless in the tragedy that befell their nation. According to Manfred Messerschmidt, the Weimar-era army "laid the foundation for a political military order that aimed at ignoring the aims and values of the republic in order to organize a thoroughly militarized society and a modern army ready to wage an industrialized war."[18] Thus, the officers of this army were more than receptive to Hitler's aggressive rearmament programs—but thoroughly disappointed to learn that they had no strategic voice in the Third Reich.[19] From 1936 through the commencement of the Second World War, moreover, rearmament occurred in a void of strategic planning and guidance. There was perfect clarity when it came to the strategic ends desired,

---

Hart, one of Britain's leading prophets of armored warfare. Gatz's counter-revision has restored the consensus interpretation. See John J. Mearsheimer, *Liddell Hart and the Weight of History* (Ithaca, NY: Cornell University Press, 1988).

[17] Cooper, *The German Army, 1933–1945*, 142–158; Murray, "German Army Doctrine, 1918–1939," 77, 80, 85–86 (quotation from p. 85).

[18] Manfred Messerschmidt, "German Military Effectiveness Between 1919 and 1939," 220–221.

[19] Ibid., 218–227.

but none whatsoever when it came to the ways and means required to achieve them. Predictably, the various services of the *Wehrmacht* gobbled up whatever funds Hitler fed them, building forces that served their professional ambitions more than any unified strategy (which Hitler kept to himself). When Hitler at last committed these forces, none of them were deemed operationally ready by their commanders, who had been left to speculate (or fantasize) about their ultimate role.[20] Perhaps the least prepared was the German Navy, prompting its commander, Erich Raeder, to exclaim in 1939, "the navy is not ready for the great fight with England. The only thing the fleet can do is to prove that it can sink honorably."[21]

Nevertheless, the army and *Luftwaffe's* exemplary performance in the first years of the war is a testament to a professional military culture that *had* distinguished Germany from its adversaries. More ably than most, they reexamined the apparent lessons of the Great War and synthesized a new (if not revolutionary) vision of modern warfare. Strapped for resources, they read widely and carefully observed the experiments of other nations. Whether or not the German military actually benefitted from the forced austerity of the Weimar era, the paucity of resources certainly did not hinder its ability to innovate. Unfortunately for the rest of Europe, Germany drew not only tactical and operational lessons from the Great War but also the ill-begotten moral lesson that it had endured an historic injustice. With currency across most of German society, this "lesson" engendered a strategy that was as clear as it was morally bankrupt.

FRANCE IN THE INTERWAR PERIOD

Of course all nations derived their own moral lessons from the Great War; that which predominated among the western Allies was "never again." Victory had come at such an immense human and material cost that it seemed war was no longer a constructive tool of statecraft, let alone the gymnasium of fit nations extolled by fin-de-siècle intellectuals. None of these nations had sacrificed or suffered more than France, yet France alone among the western allies could not simply withdraw from the Continent and make "never again" a functioning component of national strategy.

France provides perhaps the most interesting case study, as it maintained the highest level of defense spending throughout the interwar period and yet had the least to show for it once the smoke cleared. The failure was clearly *not* one of failing to anticipate strategic requirements. Despite the trauma of the Great War, all French political and military leaders recognized the imperative of preparing for another war with Germany. Nor did they underestimate the potential power of a rearmed Germany. Indeed, they assumed that, in the next war, Germany would

---

[20] Ibid., 229–237. See also Deist, *The Wehrmacht and German Rearmament*, 36–85.

[21] Quoted in Messerschmidt, "German Military Effectiveness Between 1919 and 1939," 235. Germany had perhaps the most mature conception of the diverse, complementary roles of airpower of any of the World War II combatants. Nevertheless, Hitler commenced hostilities before German industry could build the balanced air force envisioned by *Luftwaffe* commander General Walther Wever (whose death in 1936 did nothing to improve that force's prospects). Messerschmidt, "German Military Effectiveness," 231–232.

again mobilize the entirety of its society to launch an offensive against France, which prepared itself accordingly.

With only a single contingency to plan for, we might well wonder how the French got it so wrong. We may discount out of hand the popular explanation that France was so traumatized by the experience of the Great War (and, in particular, the bloodletting at Verdun) that it adopted a passive, defensive strategy that was bound to fail when tested by the "revolutionary" blitzkrieg methods of the Germans. After all, the Germans also fought at Verdun and, in fact, suffered more dreadfully. If the psychological scars on France were for some reason more severe, we would expect to see this reflected in their postwar military doctrine—but we do not. Indeed, according to Eugenia Kiesling, "Few armies have emerged from a major war with greater confidence in the future than the French Army felt in 1918."[22] For the next ten years, moreover, French military leaders generally embraced (albeit not without some dissent) an offensive doctrine, and their war plans envisioned the strategic penetration and division of Germany.[23]

Yet where was this confidence and offensive spirit in 1940? Some scholars blame the French Left, which assumed control of the government in 1924 and, they contend, committed a pair of cardinal errors. The first, according to Elizabeth Kier, was to reduce the term of conscription for the French Army to twelve months out of an abiding mistrust for professional (and presumably fascist) forces. Deprived the ability to properly train and indoctrinate their troops, officers of the French High Command scotched their plans for an offensive war against Germany in favor of a static defense—with doleful consequences in May and June 1940.[24] According to Williamson Murray, the Leftist government compounded this error by allocating insufficient resources to rearmament after 1935, setting back the development of French armored and air forces. "Unfortunately, French military leaders *never* confronted political leaders about the serious imbalance between requirements and funding levels."[25]

But these explanations are insufficient by themselves, and they shift too much blame to the usual patsies for military disasters: Leftist politicians. It is quite true that the French High Command preferred that professional soldiers make up a larger component of the French army and that they felt that two years were necessary to transform reservists into effective soldiers. But no one in France (save the iconoclast Charles de Gaulle) envisioned any defense policy that did not rest almost entirely on a massive conscript army.[26] Moreover, the Popular Front government actually gave the French military *more* resources than they requested.[27] According to Robert

---

[22] Eugenia Kiesling, "France Prepares for War, 1918–1939," in *History of the Military Art since 1914*, Steve Waddell ed. (Boston: Pearson, 2005), p. 115.

[23] Kier, *Imagining War*, 41–45.

[24] Ibid.

[25] From 1935–1938, the Italians spent more real dollars on defense than did the French. Williamson Murray, "Armored Warfare: The British, French, and German Experiences," in *Military Innovation in the Interwar Period*, Williamson Murray and Allan R. Millett eds. (New York: Cambridge University Press, 1996), p. 15.

[26] Charles de Gaulle, *Vers l'Armée de Métier [Toward a Professional Army]* (Paris: Presses Pocket, 1934).

[27] Eugenia C. Kiesling, *Arming against Hitler: France and the Limits of Military Planning* (Lawrence: University Press of Kansas, 1996), p. 82.

Doughty, "the dominant characteristics of relations between civil and military leaders between 1919 and 1939 were of accord and accommodation, rather than discord and defiance."[28] Indeed, if there were problems in civil–military relations in the interwar period they were that the French government deferred *too much* to military judgments and that the French Army suspended disbelief regarding manpower policy rather than intrude on the civil domain.[29] Finally, the shift to a predominantly defensive strategy had as much to do with the withdrawal of French forces from the Rhineland and the construction of the Maginot Line as it did changes to the conscription law. Throughout the interwar period, a consistent imperative was to fight the next war somewhere other than France. With the Maginot Line protecting France's Rhine frontier, the French Army no longer had to rush into Germany to save the French people the horror of another war fought on French soil. Instead, it merely had to win a race into Belgium, where it would occupy defensive positions and wait for the inevitable German attack. After letting the Germans wade against torrents of overwhelming firepower for two or three years, the French and their allies would launch a counteroffensive and complete the destruction of a battered and demoralized German force.[30]

Despite Barry Posen's postulation that defensive doctrines are less expensive than offensive ones, this concept required the commitment of substantial resources, and one French general advocated an offensive alternative on the grounds that it was more economical.[31] Channeling the Germans into Belgium and defending the French heartland demanded the construction of the exorbitantly expensive Maginot Line, which (popular memory notwithstanding) performed exactly as intended. Winning the race to the Belgian frontier, moreover, required the development of expensive mobile forces. Accordingly, the French fielded the world's first truck-borne infantry units and armored division.[32] Although the French strategy generally depended on quantity over quality, the French Army sometimes achieved both. When Germany invaded in 1940, the French had more tanks than the Germans, and their SOMUA-35 was the best on the battlefield.[33] Such capabilities did not come cheaply. Indeed, from the conclusion of the Great War until 1935, no World War II combatant spent as much of its GNP on defense as France. The Depression momentarily set French defense spending back to 1927 levels, but by 1938 the French were spending (in real francs) 2.6 times as much on defense as they had on the eve of the Great War.[34] Despite his criticism of laggard French rearmament in the 1930s, even

[28] Robert A. Doughty, "The French Armed Forces, 1918–40," in *Military Effectiveness*: Vol. 2, *The Interwar Period*, Allan Reed Millett and Williamson Murray eds. (Cambridge: Cambridge University Press, 2010), 40–41.

[29] Ibid., 41; Kiesling, *Arming against Hitler*.

[30] Doughty, "The French Armed Forces, 1918–40."

[31] Barry Posen, *The Sources of Military Doctrine: France, Britain, and Germany Between the World Wars* (Ithaca, NY: Cornell University Press, 1984), pp. 18–20; Kier, *Imagining War*, 42.

[32] Kiesling, *Arming against Hitler*, 147.

[33] Doughty, "The French Armed Forces, 1918–40," 45.

[34] Robert A. Doughty, *The Seeds of Disaster: The Development of French Army Doctrine, 1919–1939* (Hamden, CT: Archon, 1985), p. 183; Doughty, "The French Armed Forces, 1918–40," 43; Kier, *Imagining War*, 48.

Williamson Murray acknowledges that "The problem . . . was not so much a lack of funding, but rather how the French prepared."[35]

In their preparation for the next war, the French were no less attentive to the past than were the Germans, but they derived what we might call "negative" lessons from the Great War. Whereas the Germans focused their attention on possibilities that were not quite within their grasp during that conflict, the French instead fixated on the apparent constraints of industrialized warfare. At the level of policy, the French military and government concurred that any future war with Germany would be total in nature, requiring the complete mobilization of French society. In their experience, there was no longer room for partial mobilizations or limited war waged by small professional forces. Thus, when Germany remilitarized the Rhineland in 1936, France had two options: mobilize the entire nation for war or acquiesce. It chose the latter. In the strictly military domain, the French learned one overriding lesson from the Great War: firepower kills. Unlike the Germans, French officers were content to plumb to the past for truisms such as this and did not undertake genuine historical studies of the Great War. Consequently they failed to perceive that technology, which had created the stalemate on the Western Front, also had the potential to restore maneuver to the battlefield.[36] Instead, French officers predicted that advances in technology would only compound the horror of the Western Front many times over.

These lessons—although drawn from a past shared with Germany—took the French Army in a completely different direction. Whereas the Germans assumed that armored and air formations would make operational penetrations and exploitations feasible once more, the French concluded that attackers would wreck themselves on walls of concentrated firepower. In the German conception, the key to success was decentralizing command and control so that subordinate commanders could develop the situation and seize opportunities as they developed. Conversely, the French assumed that they could position their conscript units and mass their fires only by centralized command and control. The result was a doctrine of "methodical battle," which—as the name implies—was very nearly the polar opposite of what the Allies would term "*Blitzkrieg*."[37] Judged by the blinding light of May 1940,

---

[35] Murray, "Armored Warfare: The British, French, and German Experiences," 13–14. This was particularly true in the case of the French Air Force, which falls beyond the scope of this essay but demands some attention. It remained doctrinally tied to the support of traditional ground forces until it gained its independence from the army in 1933 and an air minister who favored strategic bombing in 1936. By then, however, Germany was already surpassing French capabilities in this regard, so the next air minister reprioritized the defense of French air space. As a consequence of shifting priorities and inadequate industrial capacity, French planes were neither numerous nor good on the eve of war. Doughty, "The French Armed Forces, 1918–40," 50–51.

[36] Superficial comparisons of the French and Germany armies during the interwar period suggest just the opposite—that the French remained captives of history while the Germans slipped its suffocating yoke. For an incisive revision of this interpretation, see Kiesling, *Arming against Hitler*, 119–25.

[37] Robert A. Doughty, "The Myth of Blitzkrieg," in *Challenging the United States Symmetrically and Asymmetrically: Can America Be Defeated?*, Lloyd J. Matthews ed. (Carlisle Barracks, PA: US Army War College, 1998), pp. 57–79.

historians have been quick to assert the superiority of the German method. Yet as Douglas Porch reminds us, the German blitzkrieg faltered after two years and some version of the much-maligned "methodical battle" eventually carried the Allies to victory.[38] Nor have historians convincingly suggested that some alternative strategy or doctrine was more appropriate for France in 1940; had the French Army actually been trained in its doctrine, the outcome might have been much different.[39]

Ultimately France fell not because of inappropriate strategy or inadequate funding but because fragile civil–military relations inhibited professional discourse and learning. Whereas the German Army enjoyed a revered station in its society and could subordinate purely parochial concerns to professional inquiry, the French military was much less secure. Although the historical tension between the rightist officer corps and the Left relaxed somewhat during the interwar period, military leaders proved unwilling to challenge French military policy for fear of upsetting the détente they had achieved. Hence, while officers knew that the government's manpower policies (which were, in fact, predicated on a mistrust of the military) precluded the army from adequately training either individual conscripts or the units in which they would serve, they dared not protest. Similarly, a staff college established in 1936 to provide the nation with civil and military experts to superintend the nation's mobilization for total war deliberately avoided the sorts of exercises and war games that might have laid bare the weaknesses of French military policy.[40] Nor would the army tolerate critical reappraisal of the French doctrine of methodical battle or the place of tanks within it. Out of fear of repeating the bloody mistakes of the last war and subjecting itself to renewed attacks from the Left, the high command squashed dissent, requiring officers on active duty to submit virtually any writings on modern warfare to the Ministry of War for approval.[41] Politically insecure, the French Army was unwilling to ask uncomfortable questions and thereby deluded itself (and most foreign observers) that it was ready for the impending showdown with the Wehrmacht.[42]

GREAT BRITAIN AND THE UNITED STATES IN THE INTERWAR PERIOD

Whereas France's shared boundary with Germany provided the war-weary French with an imperative to prepare for the next war, Great Britain and the United States could withdraw beyond the English Channel and the Atlantic and vow "never again" with sincerity. In both nations, isolationist and pacifist sentiments rose while defense budgets fell. With far-flung and largely insular empires to maintain, the navies of each nation retained a clear sense of purpose and at least a modicum of funding. The

---

[38] Douglas Porch, "Military 'Culture' and the Fall of France in 1940: A Review Essay," *International Security* 24, no. 4 (2000): 164–165.

[39] Kiesling, *Arming against Hitler*, 174–175.

[40] Ibid., 43–60.

[41] Ibid., 125–35; Kier, *Imagining War*, 80–83; Murray, *The Change in the European Balance of Power, 1938–1939*, 103–104.

[42] Doughty, "The French Armed Forces, 1918–40," 39; Kiesling, *Arming against Hitler*.

US and British Armies, however, enjoyed neither. A shared Whig political tradition rooted in seventeenth-century England contributed to a historical mistrust of the army in each nation, and neither the disappointments of the Great War nor the Great Depression did anything to improve the soldiers' standing in either society. Not that the soldiers knew exactly where they stood or were supposed to stand in the event of another war. The strategies of the two nations were remarkably similar, each affording priority to the defense of the homeland and the preservation of their overseas empires but generally forswearing another continental great-power war.[43] As a consequence, both nations maintained capable (albeit insufficient) naval forces during the interwar period but left their ground forces starved for resources and otherwise to their own devices. In the latter regard the two armies provide a study in contrasts, as the Americans navigated austerity more successfully than their British cousins thanks to a marginally better organizational culture and the blessings of geography.

The British Army

After the Great War, Britons resolved to never again relive its horrors and substituted the sentiment "never again" for a viable strategy. Such a strategy asked very little from the British military, which in turn could expect very little from Parliament. All of the services were neglected, but none more so than the army. The "Mistress of Seas" enjoyed both a robust lobby and a special place in Britain's conception of itself as an empire, and the Royal Air Force captured the imagination— and with it the solicitude—of the British people.[44] But while the Royal Navy and Air Force represented the ghosts of British military greatness past and future, the British Army remained nothing more than a necessary evil. Exactly *why* it was necessary remained open to question—even within the army. According to one defense planner, "the salient difference between us and Germany ... [is that] they know what army they will use and, broadly, how they will use it and can thus prepare ... in peace for such an event. In contrast, we here do not even know what size of army we are to contemplate for purposes of supply preparations between now and April 1939."[45]

When Britain began rearming in 1935, it hoped to deter Japan and Germany with seapower and airpower, respectively. Having withered on the vine for nearly twenty years, the British Army was unfit for actual deployment by design. It therefore was unconvincing as a deterrent and received minimal funding even as Europe rearmed.[46] Neville Chamberlain did nothing to improve the situation upon becoming prime minister in the spring of 1937. Instead, he decisively committed Britain to a strategy of "limited liability," reaffirming the following priorities: (1) defending

[43] Brian Bond and Williamson Murray, "The British Armed Forces, 1918–39," in *Military Effectiveness: Vol. 2, The Interwar Period*, Allan Reed Millett and Williamson Murray eds. (Cambridge, UK: Cambridge University Press, 2010), 99; Ronald H. Spector, "The Military Effectiveness of the US Armed Forces, 1919–39," ibid., 78.

[44] Brian Bond and Williamson Murray, "The British Armed Forces, 1918–39," ibid., 101–104.

[45] Quoted in Murray, "Armored Warfare: The British, French, and German Experiences," 12.

[46] Bond and Murray, "The British Armed Forces, 1918–39," 100.

the British Isles, (2) protecting trade routes, (3) maintaining the Empire, and (4) upholding obligations to allies. In no case could Chamberlain envision a situation that required the commitment of a large British ground force to the Continent, so he slashed £70 million from the army's budget even as Germany was building a juggernaut in plain view.[47] Although British Army officers themselves had extolled the virtues of a strategy of limited liability, *de-armament* was, under the circumstances, too much to bear quietly. After all, Chamberlain's top priority—protecting the home isles—demanded the capability to keep Channel ports in the Low Countries out of German hands. Their French allies shared this objective but depended on the contributions of Belgium, which declared neutrality in 1936, and Great Britain, which foreswore continental intervention in 1937. In short, Chamberlain had widened a cavernous capability gap and left the army without the means of closing it. Its leaders duly protested, albeit meekly considering the gravity of the situation. The fact of the matter was that most British officers shared their countrymen's aversion to preparing for another continental war. "In fact," conclude leading scholars of the interwar British Army, "the whole sorry story of the interwar period suggests that British military institutions, like British society in general, made every effort to escape the realities of the last war and to forget the hard lessons of that conflict."[48]

Thus, while the British government (particularly under the leadership of Neville Chamberlain) may be faulted for providing the British Army with inadequate funding, the army itself was culpable for a complacent, unprofessional service culture that retarded strategic thought and doctrinal innovation. The British Army did not undertake serious study of the Great War until 1932. When the new chief of the Imperial General Staff, Field Marshal Archibald Montgomery-Massingberd, found the results unflattering to the British profession of arms, he suppressed the report.[49] This is not to say that the British Army was devoid of intellectual talent during the interwar period, but it lacked both the means and motivation to harness it. As already addressed, the Germans built their armored formations and doctrine largely by reading the seminal works of Britons J.F.C. Fuller and Basil Liddell Hart. Their ideas were too radical for the conservative hierarchy of the British Army, however, and few senior commanders paid them much heed in matters of tactics.[50] One exception was Field Marshall Sir George Milne who, during his 1926–1933 tenure as CIGC, underwrote some of the most demanding and realistic armored experiments ever conducted. Unfortunately, the armored warfare pioneers were displeased by Milne's measured approach and the (far more numerous) skeptics were unimpressed by the demonstrated potential of the tank. Once Milne left office, the British Army largely abandoned the development of armored doctrine and forces.[51] In 1938, the British Army allocated less than £8 million for the acquisition

---

[47] Murray, "Armored Warfare: The British, French, and German Experiences," 10.

[48] Bond and Murray, "The British Armed Forces, 1918–39," 117.

[49] Murray, "Armored Warfare: The British, French, and German Experiences," 20; Knox and Murray, *The Dynamics of Military Revolution, 1300–2050*, 157–158.

[50] Michael Howard, "The Liddell Hart Memoirs," *Journal of the Royal United Services Institution* 111(1966): 59.

[51] Murray, *The Change in the European Balance of Power, 1938–1939*, 84–91.

of tracked vehicles—and over half as much for horse fodder! The following year, the British Army cashiered one of its most innovative armored commanders, General Percy Hobart, who had been in Egypt training the 7th Armoured Division. Although Heinz Guderian recognized Hobart's genius and had his writings translated to German, the British cavalry establishment (and their allies in Parliament) considered Hobart a heretical nuisance. "The Army must stand together and show a solid front to the politicians," admonished one CIGS.[52] Hobart did not relent, and by 1940 he found himself a corporal in the Home Guard. The force he had trained went on to win glory and distinction as the "Desert Rats."[53]

For the most part, however, British feats of arms during the Second World War resulted from (in Lord Tedder's words) "an excess of bravery and a shortage of brains."[54] The venerable British military historian Michael Howard has acknowledged that the interwar British Army "contained a high proportion of men of deep and far-ranging intelligence," but he questions how much influence these men wielded in an establishment that was "as firmly geared to the pace and perspective of regimental soldiering as it had been before 1914." "Too many of its members," Howard concludes, "looked on soldiering as an agreeable and honourable occupation rather than as a serious profession demanding no less intellectual dedication than that of the doctor, the lawyer, or the engineer."[55] Part of the problem was the British regimental system, which promoted esprit but did little or nothing to advance modern notions of professionalism.[56] "They are such nice chaps, socially," Hobart wrote of his subordinate officers before his relief. But they were "so conservative of their spurs and swords and regimental tradition" that it was hard to get any real work out of them.[57] For this leisurely lifestyle, the soldiers of the British Army paid a steep price during the Second World War.

Yet it is perhaps too easy to caricaturize the "gentleman-officers" of the British Army and to hold them exclusively accountable for its lackluster performance in 1940 and afterward.[58] Fundamentally, Britain's disappointments during the Second World War were a product of leaders—political and military—willfully misreading the nation's strategic requirements and failing to generate even a modicum of the military capabilities needed to fulfill them. Whether a more professional officer corps might have more carefully studied the past and developed appropriate, skeletal capabilities during the lean years is largely beside the point. The entire nation was in the thrall of a powerful moral lesson that precluded a rational assessment of the nation's strategic situation until the last moment. Then,

[52] Quoted in Howard, "The Liddell Hart Memoirs," 61.

[53] Murray, "Armored Warfare: The British, French, and German Experiences," 25–27; Bond and Murray, "The British Armed Forces, 1918–39," 115–16, 22–23.

[54] Quoted in Williamson Murray, "British Military Effectiveness in the Second World War," in *Military Effectiveness: Volume 3, The Second World War*, Allan Reed Millett and Williamson Murray eds. (Cambridge: Cambridge University Press, 2010), p. 111.

[55] Howard, "The Liddell Hart Memoirs," 61.

[56] Bond and Murray, "The British Armed Forces, 1918–39."

[57] Quoted in Murray, "British Military Effectiveness in the Second World War," 111

[58] Porch, "Military 'Culture' and the Fall of France in 1940: A Review Essay," *International Security* 24, no. 4 (2000): 163–164, 174–178.

the British adopted the most rational strategy available: they turned to the United States for deliverance.

The US Army

Like their allies, most Americans were thoroughly disillusioned with the dividends of the Great War. While their sacrifices paled in comparison to the other combatant nations, none of the domestic constituencies Woodrow Wilson cobbled together to support the war got what they wanted out of it.[59] Disillusionment with the outcome collided with fiscal retrenchment to create a climate of austerity that, according to Army Chief of Staff Peyton March, punished the US Army more severely than the Versailles Treaty had the Germans.[60] After their 1924 convention, Republican Party leaders crowed that "our standing Army is now below 125,000 men, the smallest regular military force maintained by any great power."[61] The consequences for the readiness of that force were perhaps predictable. According to Russell Weigley, "the Army during the 1920's and early 1930's may have been less ready to function as a fighting force than at any time in its history."[62] The situation had not materially improved by the beginning of World War II. According to the relevant chapter of *America's First Battles*, the US Army "was still seriously undermanned and underrequipped, practiced obsolete procedures with outmoded weapons, and from 1933 ranked seventeenth in size among the armies of the world."[63]

[59] David M. Kennedy, *Over Here: The First World War and American Society* (Oxford: Oxford University Press, 1980); Edward M. Coffman, "The Meuse-Argonne Offensive: The Final Battle of World War I," in *Between War and Peace: How America Ends its Wars*, Matthew Moten ed. (New York: Free Press, 2011), pp. 179–196.

[60] Russell F. Weigley, *History of the United States Army* (New York: Macmillan, 1967), p. 403.

[61] Quoted in Spector, "The Military Effectiveness of the US Armed Forces, 1919–39," 71.

[62] He continued, "It lacked even the combat capacity that the Indian campaigns had forced on it during the nineteenth century and the pacification of the Philippines had required early in the twentieth century." Weigley, *History of the United States Army*, 402–403.

[63] Martin Blumenson, "Kasserine Pass, 30 January–22 February 1943," in *America's First Battles, 1776–1965*, Charles E. Heller and William A. Stofft eds. (Lawrence: University Press of Kansas, 1986), p. 227. By comparison, the US Navy fared relatively well. The Washington and London Naval Conferences of 1922 and 1930, respectively, amounted to voluntary submissions to Versailles-style restrictions on force structure. This allowed the US Navy (like the German Army) to concentrate its efforts on modernizing and training the best force allowable under the restrictions. Naval officers chafed under these restrictions, especially the Five Power Washington Treaty, which demilitarized much of the Pacific and thus compromised the United States' ability to wage a successful war against Japan. (The US Marine Corps eagerly stepped into the resulting capability gap, however, by developing and marketing the capability to seize the advance bases denied by this treaty. This was a relatively rare instance in which strategic necessity and service parochialism converged.) The navy received a boon with the 1932 election of Franklin D. Roosevelt to the presidency. A former assistant secretary of the navy who had always looked fondly on America's sea service, he provided the navy an advocate in the highest of places. Naval expansion became part of FDR's New Deal program of public works, and naval expenditures increased yearly after 1933. See Allan R. Millett and Peter Maslowski, *For the Common Defense: A Military History of the United States of America*, Revised and expanded edition

Yet within three years, this army would prove itself capable of conducting large-scale combat operations against veteran German forces and demonstrate a capacity for operational learning that eluded most other forces. How did this come to pass? Did the Americans, like the Germans, commit themselves to the rigorous study of the Great War and devise concepts that required only the addition of dollars to blossom into an effective fighting doctrine? Not quite. Instead the US Army squandered much of the interwar period by maintaining the hulks of understrength divisions and clinging to doctrine that would have little place in the Second World War. The US Army provided an intellectual climate that was somewhat (and sometimes) more receptive to new ideas than that of the British Army, but it performed better in the Second World War largely due to factors beyond its institutional control. Alone among the interwar cases examined here, the US Army did not *need* to be ready for a European war in 1939. Ultimately, it performed better than the British Army because it had more time and space to prepare.

Like the Germans, the Americans studied the "last war," but they did so without the introspective curiosity born of defeat. Studies abounded, but different officers embraced whichever lessons resonated with them most. Officers who had endured frontline combat frequently emphasized the importance of firepower to modern warfare while traditionalists and many senior commanders asserted that the war had validated the Americans' prewar doctrine of infantry-centered "open warfare."[64] These divergent interpretations were reflected in two of the army's most important doctrinal publications of the interwar era, the 1923 edition of *Field Service Regulations* and the 1930 *The Manual for Commanders of Large Units*.[65] Citing "the glaring inconsistencies in doctrine" reflected in those two publications, one chief of infantry complained that they were "based upon two distinct military philosophies

(New York: Free Press, 1994), 383–384; ibid., 383; Spector, "The Military Effectiveness of the US Armed Forces, 1919–39," 72–74; Jeter Allen Isely and Philip A. Crowl, *The US Marines and Amphibious War: Its Theory, and Its Practice in the Pacific* (Princeton, NJ: Princeton University Press, 1951).

[64] In 1919, the army's plenary "Superior Board" attempted to reconcile these positions, genuflecting to American military tradition while arguing (as the French would) that advances in firepower were likely to exacerbate the stalemated conditions of the Western Front and recommending that the army enhance its capabilities for trench warfare. Having commanded the American Expeditionary Force in France but having seen little actual combat, General John J. Pershing represented the traditionalist point of view and dissented. Nothing in *his* experience challenged his faith in fighting élan of the individual infantryman or the superiority of open warfare over European methods, and he considered it unlikely that the army would again operate on a large scale overseas. Brian M. Linn, *The Echo of Battle: The Army's Way of War* (Cambridge, MA: Harvard University Press, 2007), p. 120; Russell F. Weigley, "The Interwar Army, 1919–1941," in *Against all Enemies: Interpretations of American Military History from Colonial Times to the Present*, Kenneth J. Hagan and William R. Roberts eds. (Westport, CT: Greenwood, 1986), p. 257.

[65] William O. Odom, *After the Trenches: The Transformation of US Army Doctrine, 1918–1939* (College Station: Texas A & M University Press, 1999), pp. 118–123; Mark E. Grotelueschen, *The AEF Way of War: The American Army and Combat in World War I* (New York: Cambridge University Press, 2007), pp. 362–364.

as opposite as night and day."[66] The army's belated effort to resolve these discrepancies, *FM 100-5, Tentative Field Service Regulations, Operations* (1939), amounted to little more than an expanded version of the 1923 manual. It failed to account for any significant military advancements since World War I and had no bearing on the army's matériel acquisition strategy.[67] As a consequence, the US Army would deploy to North Africa with outdated, contradictory doctrine and equipment reflecting the traditional American preference for highly mobile operations. The consequences for American tankers and tank destroyer crews were dreadful.[68]

They were not, however, strategically significant. Indeed, General Dwight D. Eisenhower was unaware his tanks were inferior until late 1944.[69] Ultimately, the Americans improvised a combined arms doctrine that mitigated the army's failure to develop the army (and better armored vehicles) before the war. Yet why, with so much time to observe developments in other countries and to prepare for an explicit strategic threat, did the US Army fail to do so? According to one historian, the blame falls largely on the US Congress, which assigned the army immense responsibilities in the 1920 National Defense Act yet subsequently cut defense spending to the bone.[70] Nevertheless, army leaders were responsible for the decision to prioritize force structure and end strength over all other concerns. A principal reason for this decision was the US Army's traditional fixation on manpower policy. Since the 1790s, army leaders had lobbied for more control of militia regulation and training, but they made little headway against the popular view that unindoctrinated citizen soldiers were paragons of republican virtue. These popular prejudices slowly eroded over the course of the nineteenth century and were, by 1920, at last subordinated to reason. The National Defense Act of that year provided for a three-tiered mobilization scheme comprising the active duty US Army, the National Guard, and a skeletal Organized Reserve. The army was to maintain nine full-strength divisions and was responsible for the training of the Guard and Reserve units assigned to its nine corps commands. Unfortunately, Congress began whittling away the end strength of the army as early as 1921. By 1927, less than 120,000 men filled formations designed for 280,000. Rather than reduce the number of formations, the army clung to its nine divisions, compromising not only their deployability but also their ability to conduct realistic training.[71] Indeed, "[b]y 1939, the Army had virtually forgotten how to conduct training on a broad scale."[72]

---

[66] Quoted in Spector, "The Military Effectiveness of the US Armed Forces, 1919–39," 90. That chief of infantry was Major General George A. Lynch, who had been primary author of the 1923 *Field Service Regulations*; Odom, *After the Trenches*, 121.

[67] Blumenson, "Kasserine Pass, 30 January–22 February 1943," 229; Odom, *After the Trenches*; Linn, *The Echo of Battle*, 130–131.

[68] Russell F. Weigley, *Eisenhower's Lieutenants: The Campaign of France and Germany, 1944–1945* (Bloomington: Indiana University Press, 1981), pp. 5–12; David E. Johnson, *Fast Tanks and Heavy Bombers: Innovation In The US Army, 1917–1945* (Ithaca, NY: Cornell University Press, 1998), pp. 189–201; Blumenson, "Kasserine Pass, 30 January–22 February 1943," 226–265.

[69] Johnson, *Fast Tanks and Heavy Bombers*, 197–201.

[70] Odom, *After the Trenches*, 199–220.

[71] Weigley, *History of the United States Army*, 406–407; Millett and Maslowski, *For the Common Defense*, 385–386, 396–397; Spector, "The Military Effectiveness of the US Armed Forces, 1919–39," 72.

[72] Blumenson, "Kasserine Pass, 30 January–22 February 1943," 229.

As army chief of staff from 1930 to 1935, Gen. Douglas MacArthur had tried to address this problem by focusing resources on select units that would form an "Instant Readiness Force." He also instituted a research, development, and reequipment program designed to improve the army's material readiness, but MacArthur could stretch sparse funds—and his imagination—only so far.[73] He foresaw the potential of motorized warfare but opposed spending army money on research and development or "expensive toys" (such as tanks) because, in the event of war, America's automotive industry would provide the requisite hardware. When, according to Brian Linn, "congressional reformers tried to cut personnel and obsolescent organizations in order to fund tanks and airplanes, MacArthur fought them with a crusader's zeal."[74] MacArthur retarded the development of armored doctrine by disbanding an experimental mechanized force in 1931 and relegating its future development to the Cavalry and Infantry Schools. In 1928, the General Staff had entrusted the direction of this force to its brilliant operations officer, Major Adna R. Chaffee, Jr. His command consisted of little more than the decrepit relics of the last war, yet he was able to recognize the potential to create a wholly new combat arm characterized by speed and shock power. By letting the Infantry and Cavalry schools generate their own concepts, MacArthur essentially placed Chaffee's vision at the mercy of branch parochialism. Nevertheless, Chaffee was retained first as the executive officer and later as the commander of the Cavalry School's test outfit, the 7th Cavalry Brigade (Mechanized). In this capacity, he was able to further his own ideas against organizational conservatism. When General George Marshall reversed MacArthur's decision and constituted a new Armored Force in 1940, Chaffee commanded it.[75]

To the credit of the US Army, it empowered Chaffee to develop an American vision for independent mechanized warfare even when the chiefs of cavalry and infantry viewed tanks merely as tools for the traditional branches. To Chaffee's credit, he continued to toil within the system and make a difference rather than making himself a pariah (as in the cases of de Gaulle and Fuller).[76] It is worth

---

[73] Weigley, *History of the United States Army*, 406–407. From 1925 to 1940, War Department expenditures totaled $6.2 billion. Only $344 million of this was allocated to procurement for ground forces. According to Ronald Spector, "The entire research and development program [of the US armed forces during the interwar period] amounted to about one-twentieth of the cost of a contemporary battleship and less than one four-hundredth of what it cost to develop the atomic bomb." Millett and Maslowski, *For the Common Defense*, 399; Spector, "The Military Effectiveness of the US Armed Forces, 1919–39," 74.

[74] Linn, *The Echo of Battle*, 134.

[75] Weigley, *History of the United States Army*, 410–411; Johnson, *Fast Tanks and Heavy Bombers*, 116–117, 127–128, 139–148. One of the most egregious examples of this conservatism was the army's insistence that medium tanks weigh no more than fifteen tons so as to not exceed the load capacity of the bridging equipment then in the army's inventory. This led to disproportionate attention to the development of light tanks that would prove nearly useless in World War II and to the rejection of the superior designs of American tank designer J. Walter Christie. He sold them to the Soviets, who used them to produce the T-34, widely regarded as the best heavy tank of the war. Weigley, *History of the United States Army*, 411; Johnson, *Fast Tanks and Heavy Bombers*, 74.

[76] David E. Johnson depicts Chaffee as an essentially conservative force who innovated only within the cavalry paradigm familiar to him. Yet Chaffee compares quite favorably to genuinely

considering the extent to which the United State's relatively "free security" provided the space for competing ideas to coexist and compete. Outside those forces
assigned to the Pacific theater, the army did not design their capabilities against
a single most likely threat.[77] Undeniably, American forces paid a heavy price for
mismatched doctrine and equipment, but the consequences might have been
much worse had army leaders (like the French) actually achieved a unitary vision
of future warfare. Whether by design or accident, ambiguity allowed the development of competing models that, once tested in combat, could be modified to suit
the actual conditions.

Of course, it is questionable whether France had the luxury of pursuing such
an option. The United States' relative geographic isolation and awesome industrial
capacity allowed it to overcome the "lost years" of the 1920s and 1930s, during
which the army officer corps at least envisioned the force it would eventually command. This was in many respects an intellectual exercise that demanded little in
the way of resources, which had always been sparse in peacetime. The "board system" by which branch chiefs established requirements and the army chief of staff
set priorities worked reasonably well and provided the mold into which Congress
eventually poured dollars to cast a warfighting army. The officers who would command it, meanwhile, received a rigorous education at the army's service schools,
where the army sent its top officers both as students and faculty. As in the French
case, students learned a "school solution"—but without the political imperative of
conformity as war approached.[78] At the Command and General Staff School at Fort
Leavenworth, Kansas, the future commanders of regiments and divisions learned
the rudiments of combined arms operations that, while incomplete and conflicted,
would eventually defeat Nazi Germany.[79]

reactionary influences such as cavalry chief Major General John K. Herr and infantry chief Major
General Stephen O. Fuqua. If he did not grasp the apparent potential of "blitzkrieg," it is worth
remembering that neither did most Germans. See Johnson, *Fast Tanks and Heavy Bombers*,
127–128, 139–145. For more sympathetic portrayals of Chaffee, see Mildred Hanson Gillie,
Forging the Thunderbolt: A History of the Development of the Armored Force (Harrisburg,
PA: Military Service Pub. Co., 1947); George F. Hofmann, *Through Mobility We Conquer: The
Mechanization of US Cavalry* (Lexington: The University Press of Kentucky, 2006).

[77] Brian Linn describes the US Army in the Pacific as almost a separate service with unique strategic requirements and even culture. Brian McAllister Linn, *Guardians of Empire: The US Army
and the Pacific, 1902–1940* (Chapel Hill: University of North Carolina Press, 1997).

[78] The situation was different under the fiscally conservative Republican administrations of
Warren Harding and Calvin Coolidge, which censured officers for public comments regarding
defense spending, chilling professional discourse within the army. See Johnson, *Fast Tanks and
Heavy Bombers*, 66–71.

[79] US Army Heritage and Education Center, "*Maintaining and Modernizing the Force in Periods of
Reduced Resources*," (Carlisle, PA: United States Army War College and Carlisle Barracks, 2012),
p. 2; Peter J Schifferle, *America's School for War: Fort Leavenworth, Officer Education, and Victory
in World War II* (Lawrence: University Press of Kansas, 2010). For a more critical appraisal of the
Leavenworth curriculum, see Jörg Muth, *Command Culture: Officer Education in the US Army and
the German Armed Forces, 1901–1940, and the Consequences for World War II* (Denton: University
of North Texas Press, 2011).

In the twenty-seven months between the German invasion of Poland and the US-British invasion of North Africa, the Americans dramatically expanded their armed forces, fielded equipment that existed only in prototype just a few years before, and conducted realistic combined arms training on an unprecedented scale. Culminating in the Louisiana and Carolina maneuvers of 1941, these exercises not only trained legions of newly inducted soldiers but provided an opportunity to test and revise theoretical doctrine against the then manifest capabilities of the German Army.[80] The army that landed in North Africa in 1942 was undertrained and inadequately equipped to employ a doctrine that remained fraught with problems, but it proved equal to the task at hand. In this regard, it was fairly typical of all American armies up to that time.

THE PENTOMIC ARMY

Soon after World War II, the proliferation of long-range strategic bombers and nuclear weapons deprived the United States of the luxury of preparing for the next war *after* it had begun. Disillusioned with the United States' lackluster performance in the Korean War yet demanding a curtailment in defense spending, the American people in 1952 elected Dwight David Eisenhower to the presidency with a mandate to at once enhance the nation's security and rein in runaway defense spending. Despite the paradoxical nature of such sentiments, they were entirely in line with Eisenhower's thinking on the subject. In accordance with traditional Republican fiscal conservatism, he regarded a strong economy as the foremost guarantor of national security.[81] In accordance with American political thought dating back to the eighteenth century, any drain on the national treasury that did not at least pay for itself in the long run was prejudicial to the public weal. And nothing fit this description more squarely than a standing professional defense establishment, which was considered both fiscally *and* ideologically odious to the republic. Now and again, navalists and shipbuilders would make a compelling case that overseas trade depended on a strong navy—but the army could muster no such arguments. For most of its existence, the US Army had coped with acute fiscal austerity during peacetime, but its leaders were nevertheless surprised when one of their own threatened to reduce the force to something approaching irrelevancy.

But here also Eisenhower's views accorded with those of the population at large. The Korean War suggested to most Americans the limited utility of ground combat in the nuclear age. Years of desperate fighting had produced only stalemate and—in Truman's relief of MacArthur—a national scandal. When contrasted with the dazzling, high-tech capabilities of the newly independent US Air Force, the army

---

[80] Blumenson, "Kasserine Pass, 30 January–22 February 1943," 233–238.

[81] NSC 162/2, approved in October 1953, outlined the Eisenhower administration's thinking on defense policy. The paper was issued by the National Security Council Planning Board, which Eisenhower created "to regularize and make more reliable the activities of the NSC." Russell F. Weigley, *The American Way of War: A History of United States Military Strategy and Policy* (Bloomington: Indiana University Press, 1977), p. 401; John Lewis Gaddis, *Strategies of Containment* (New York: Oxford University Press, 2004), pp. 131–133.

appeared at once unglamorous and incompetent. The overriding moral lesson from Korea was not "never again" but rather "not *that way* again." As Eisenhower saw it, his principal duty as commander in chief was to prepare the nation and the military for a single contingency: an unrestrained nuclear war against the Soviet Union. Eisenhower hoped very much to avoid this, so he and his secretary of state threatened the Soviet Union with "massive retaliation" as a means of deterring such an event. Naturally, this strategy relied on a strong US Air Force to make the deterrent threat credible, and it relied on the army only as a theoretical afterthought. Eisenhower could envision calling on the army to establish military rule over a land devastated by a nuclear attack (whether the homeland or a foreign country), but the prospects of participating in another maneuver-based land war were exceedingly slim.[82]

Thus under Eisenhower's watch the army entered what one chief of staff termed its "Babylonian Captivity."[83] Along with funding, the morale and prestige of the force plummeted. Quality recruits flocked to the air force and navy but left the army well enough alone, and junior officers resigned their commissions in droves.[84] One major who stayed in the service and went on to become a general officer lamented, "I do not know what the Army's mission is or how it plans to fulfill its mission. And this, I find, is true of my fellow soldiers. At a time when new weapons and new machines herald a revolution in warfare, we soldiers do not know where the Army is going and how it is going to get there."[85]

Led by Chief of Staff Matthew B. Ridgeway, the army confronted this existential crisis by attacking the concept of massive retaliation on the grounds of morality and practicality, in the latter regard asserting that it would be nearly impossible to forward any genuine national interests in a postapocalyptic world. Indeed, the army recommended forswearing the use of atomic weapons or, at the very least, restricting their use to tactical targets. To Eisenhower these protestations were as ridiculous as they were insubordinate. He shared Ridgway's doubts about the dividends of a postnuclear "victory" but considered it fantasy to assume that any war with the Soviet Union would not involve nuclear weapons.[86] In any event, the concept of massive retaliation was intended primarily to serve a strategy of deterrence. Eisenhower could envision no war with the Soviets but a nuclear one—and his goal was to avoid it altogether.

Frustrated by their commander in chief, army leaders next argued that, once the Soviets achieved parity in nuclear forces, deterrence would fall apart. Stalemated at the highest end of the spectrum of conflict, the initiative would fall to the antagonist with asymmetric capabilities elsewhere. With a manifest superiority in conventional forces, the Soviets would be able to pursue a campaign of subversion and revolution with relative impunity.[87] The most logical course available, argued army

[82] Andrew J. Bacevich, *The Pentomic Era: The US Army Between Korea and Vietnam* (Washington, DC: National Defense University Press, 1986), 16.

[83] Ibid., 9; Maxwell D. Taylor, *The Uncertain Trumpet* (New York: Harper, 1960), p. 108.

[84] Bacevich, *The Pentomic Era*, 20.

[85] Quoted in ibid., 21.

[86] Gaddis, *Strategies of Containment*, 133.

[87] Bacevich, *The Pentomic Era*, 25–33.

leaders, was for the United States to grow "balanced" forces capable of countering the Soviets and seizing opportunities across the spectrum of potential conflict. Eisenhower disagreed, but on December 3, 1954, he allowed Ridgway to make his final case to the National Security Council. He impressed the president as sincere but unrealistic. To the economically minded Kansan, "the United States could not afford to prepare to fight all kinds of wars and still preserve its free economy and its basic institutions."[88] Treasury Secretary George Humphrey emphatically agreed: maintaining "all kinds of forces designed to fight all kinds of war at all times . . . was absolutely impossible."[89]

Ridgeway saw it differently and continued to be a thorn in Eisenhower's side beyond his June 1955 retirement as chief of staff of the army.[90] His successor, Maxwell Taylor, shared most of Ridgeway's misgivings about the "New Look" but proved receptive to candid advice offered by the president and his secretary of defense. If the army wanted money, it was going to have to sell itself as something other than the force that had recently bogged down in Korea. Eisenhower was not entirely unsympathetic to the plight of his old service, and he urged Taylor to "sex up" the army's public image as a means of winning congressional support.[91] Defense Secretary Charles Wilson issued similar guidance after reviewing an army budget request that appeared too conventional. According to Taylor, the secretary directed him "to substitute requests for 'newfangled' items with public appeal instead of the prosaic accoutrements of the foot soldier."[92]

Unable to convince the administration that the United States needed the capabilities the army offered, the army changed its tack under the leadership of Taylor. For the duration of the Eisenhower administration, at least, the army would develop the capabilities Congress appeared willing to buy and worry afterward about how they would fulfill strategic requirements. The result was the "Pentomic" division, a neologism coined by Taylor as a means of staking the army's claim to the nuclear pie. Armed with "Honest John" nuclear rockets and the ludicrous "Davey Crockett" nuclear recoilless rifle, soldiers of the Pentomic division were to fight from dispersed positions on an atomic battlefield out of the recognition that most of them would die in the initial attack. Those who survived would form islands of resistance against attacking Soviet forces; relief would

[88] Memorandum of Discussion at the 227th Meeting of the National Security Council, Friday, December 3, 1954, in *Foreign Relations of the United States, 1952–1954.* Vol. 2, John P. Glennon ed. (Washington, DC: G.P.O., 1986), 804.

[89] Memorandum of Discussion at the 227th Meeting of the National Security Council, Friday, December 3, 1954, ibid., 805.

[90] For the rest of Eisenhower's administration, Ridgway and his compatriots worked to undermine the president's defense policy by whatever means available: published doctrine, congressional testimony, leaked correspondence, and critical memoirs. Collectively, these efforts did not shake Eisenhower's commitment to massive retaliation, but they swayed public opinion to the point that a Democratic presidential candidate would, in 1960, make Taylor's vision for a balanced defense policy his own.

[91] Quoted in Ingo Trauschweizer, *The Cold War US Army: Building Deterrence for Limited War* (Lawrence: University Press of Kansas, 2008), 270n26.

[92] Quoted in ibid., 56.

come in the form a tactical nuclear counterattack that would likely expose the defenders to as much radiation as the enemy. Were the Pentomic soldiers to live long enough to assume the offensive, they would wait for nuclear missiles to blast holes in the Soviet defenses before plunging forward in a frontal attack reminiscent of World War I.[93]

The absurdity of such a concept was not lost on most army leaders, who railed against it in later years. When the army undertook earnest studies of tactical nuclear warfare, it concluded that tactical nuclear weapons would not be able to offset the Soviet manpower advantage and that forces built around such capabilities would have to be larger rather than smaller.[94] This did not accord with the political imperative of reducing end strength, however, so the army shrank most of its divisions. Most officers doubted the prudence of these reductions, but Maxwell Taylor's principal concern in 1956 was not generating a combat-ready force but rather to combat the growing popular opinion that "sizable Army forces may no longer be required."[95] According to Ingo Trauschweizer, the Pentomic division was a political ploy designed "to enhance the army's position with respect to the other armed services, to help redefine the role of the institution in the Cold War, and to contribute to a change in national military strategy."[96] Indeed, even while committing exorbitant resources to the development of a force that he and his colleagues knew to be deeply flawed, Taylor began to articulate the alternative strategy of "flexible response," which was essentially the same strategy for which Ridgway had argued in 1954. With the election of John F. Kennedy, Taylor got his way—but only after squandering millions of dollars rather than letting them go to another service or some other purpose.

OBSERVATIONS

Collectively, these case studies do little to inspire confidence in professional militaries' ability to prepare for the next war—an endeavor that nearly always occurs under conditions of peace and, by extension, austerity. In reflections on a study of military effectiveness during the Second World War, retired Lt. Gen. John H. Cushman noted that the evaluated officer corps demonstrated "for the most part less than general professional military competence and sometime abysmal incompetence."[97]

---

[93] Bacevich, *The Pentomic Era*, 103–127.

[94] Weigley, *The American Way of War: A History of United States Military Strategy and Policy*, 419, 422. Collecting usable data, however, was not always the topic priority of these experiments. The after action report of Operation DESERT ROCK VI matter-of-factly acknowledged that "planning proceeded from the basic decision that first priority be given to demonstrating the Army at its best." Quoted in Bacevich, *The Pentomic Era*, 113.

[95] Quoted in Trauschweizer, *The Cold War US Army: Building Deterrence for Limited War*, 56.

[96] Ibid., 58.

[97] Cushman was also that major who worried about the purpose and direction of the army under the Eisenhower administration. John H. Cushman, "Challenge and Response at the Operational and Tactical Level," in *Military Effectiveness: Vol. 3, The Second World War*, Allan Reed Millett and Williamson Murray eds. (Cambridge, UK: Cambridge University Press, 2010), p. 322.

It is doubtful that the US Army's ministrations during the Eisenhower years would rate any more favorably. Indeed, it is apparent from these case studies that there are no exemplars worthy of emulation. For this we may be thankful, however, as the formulas derived from these unique cases would undoubtedly be found wanting once applied to contemporary problems. Nevertheless, we may venture some observations.

The principal of these is that robust peacetime defense spending is not necessarily an indicator of performance in a future war. The real issue, unsurprisingly, is how the resources allocated are actually spent. Two considerations prevail: the accuracy of a nation's perception of strategic requirements and the adequacy of the military capabilities generated to fulfill them. During times of peace (and thus relative austerity) these capabilities are never fully developed; some remain theoretical abstractions, and the rest lack the capacity (i.e., numbers of platforms, men, etc.) demanded of a major war. Typically, the allocation of funds to realize or expand these capabilities is belated and insufficient—but this is true for all nations and rarely spells the difference between victory and defeat. Far more important is the organizational culture of the forces that design and employ military capabilities, specifically their tolerance for innovation.

Of the nations analyzed, only the British drew a losing hand on both the counts of recognizing strategic requirements and generating the relevant military capabilities. Arguably, only the British were guilty of the fundamental error of miscalculating the strategic situation.[98] This shortsightedness, when combined with a hidebound army culture, resulted in "the scandalously bad performance" of the British Army in World War II.[99] Fortunately, the British were delivered by something old, something new, something borrowed, and something blue: respectively, the Royal Navy, the Royal Air Force, American largess in the form of Lend-Lease assistance, and the English Channel.

As the other cases make clear, however, strategic clarity is, by itself, insufficient to guarantee the creation of appropriate military capabilities. Indeed, the distinction between strategic clarity and myopia is very fine. If a nation and its military have a clear, common conception of their interests and the military means of safeguarding them, the production of relevant military capabilities may be reduced to an engineering problem. One error in calculation or implementation (to say nothing of the emergence of new strategic problems), however, and the solution will not work. The error in this case is not of recognizing strategic requirements but in designing and building the appropriate military capabilities to fulfill them. There are perhaps no clearer examples than the French Army of 1940 and the Pentomic army of the late 1950s. Closing their eyes to all contingencies but (respectively) a German invasion of France and total nuclear war with the Soviet Union, these armies developed forces that were presumed optimal for these purposes and adequate for all "lesser included" missions. In

---

[98] The others, to one degree or another, designed the wrong capabilities to fulfill those requirements (France, the Pentomic army) or developed insufficient capacity (Germany, the United States—especially in the Pacific).

[99] Murray, "Armored Warfare: The British, French, and German Experiences," 29n85.

hindsight, we can appreciate that they were instead (to borrow Washington's phrase) *incompetent to every exigency*.[100]

Indeed, these cases suggest that *too much* strategic clarity removes the impetus for innovation as well as toleration for competing ideas. None of the nations addressed here tolerated dissent that threatened to subvert civil control of the military, as the American aviator Billy Mitchell and the French armor pioneer Charles de Gaulle could well attest.[101] But strategic myopia had a tendency to squelch productive debate *within* the services as well. This was especially so when the affected services felt cornered or neglected by their civilian masters. The imperative of "closing ranks" against presumably hostile administrations produced in the French and Pentomic armies almost fatalistic resignation to defense policies that were not of their own design. The result was, in each case, a carefully engineered yet inflexible doctrine and a force ill prepared for the challenges of modern warfare.

Conversely, the most effective armies were those afforded sufficient leeway to grow their own competing conceptions of future warfare. As the contrasting cases of the interwar German and American armies suggest, it did not really matter whether this professional space was a product of social deference or neglect; nor did it require robust funding. (Indeed, Samuel Huntington has argued that the isolation and austerity of the late-nineteenth-century Western frontier provided the US Army with an ideal crucible for professionalization.)[102] Nor did competing ideas demand resolution before the next war. Far more important were professional minds conditioned to tolerate ambiguity and dissent and to capitalize on the ideas of others once their merit became apparent. It is worth remembering that as late as 1939, the *infantryman* Erwin Rommel was highly skeptical about the potential of tanks. Within every service, proponents for new capabilities developed their own consensus about how to optimally employ those capabilities—and they never got it entirely right. Naval commanders considered aircraft carriers and submarines as auxiliaries to battleships, most armies thought of tanks primarily as reconnaissance and infantry support vehicles, and aviators were steadfast in their commitment to strategic bombing at the expense of all other missions. In war, each of these communities proved stubborn in their convictions, but visionaries among them were allowed to assert themselves— provided they had been able to develop their alternative visions in the years before the war.

---

[100] Washington to John Hancock, December 16, 1776, *The Papers of George Washington*. Vol. 7, *Revolutionary War Series*. Philander D. Chase ed. (Charlottesville: University Press of Virginia, 1997), p. 352.

[101] Furthermore, Eisenhower essentially relieved Ridgeway by not renewing him for a second term as chief of staff.

[102] Samuel P. Huntington, *The Soldier and the State: The Theory and Politics of Civil–Military Relations* (Cambridge: Belknap Press of Harvard University Press, 1957), p. 229. John M. Gates has since dismantled the notion that the army officer corps of this era was truly isolated from the sources of political influence and society at large, but the austerity under which it labored is beyond dispute. John M. Gates, "The Alleged Isolation of US Army Officers in the Late-19th Century," *Parameters* 10, no. 3 (1980).

Significantly, the most accurate of these visions were historically based yet *aspirational*. Their authors studied the last war carefully—not with an eye to refighting its battles but to identify needs and opportunities for innovation. Fixated on the disastrous Nivelle Offensive of 1917, the French "learned" the putative limits of maneuver in an age of overwhelming firepower. The Germans likewise studied their failed offensives but drew completely different conclusions. Instead of looking for "lessons," they identified tactical and operational problems as a means of designing their solutions. Popular misconceptions notwithstanding, the resulting "blitzkrieg" formations and doctrine were anything but revolutionary. They were historically derived and evolutionary.

Problems arose for armed forces, however, when they assumed that new technology would render old methods (and their historical study) obsolete. This is a perennial vice of aviators who, from the earliest days of military aviation, have espoused millenarian views about the promise of airpower.[103] Especially in Britain and the United States, they captured the imagination of the broader public and assured themselves at least a modicum of funding in an era of austerity. Popular enthusiasm also granted them, to one degree or another, independence from the armies that spawned them.[104] Untethered, the acolytes of Hugh Trenchard and Billy Mitchell advocated strategic bombing as the one true use of air power, and they generally ignored the development of doctrine or aircraft for close air support or air defense. Moreover, they dogmatically clung to the theory of strategic bombing well after experiments and experience demonstrated its shortcomings.[105] If most of the cases examined here suggest that overly conservative organizations have a tendency to suppress or marginalize their visionaries, the cases of the Royal Air Force and US Army Air Forces reveal the danger of giving the visionaries too much leash. By the time the Second World War erupted, their once original and provocative ideas had hardened into dogma. Indeed, the most innovative officers in each of these air services represented Thermidorian reactions to organizational revolutions gone too far. In their respective development of Britain's air defense system and America's pursuit tactics, Hugh Dowding and Claire Chennault

---

[103] Michael S. Sherry, *The Rise of American Air Power: The Creation of Armageddon* (New Haven: Yale University Press, 1987).

[104] The Royal Air Force became an independent service in 1918. American aviators had to wait longer, but an "American love affair with military aviation flowered in 1925–26." The latter year Congress authorized a new US Army Air Corps, which was still technically part of the army but answered directly to the chief of staff. Henceforth, the visionaries did not need to fight the establishment to forward their views; they were the establishment. See Millett and Maslowski, *For the Common Defense*, 390.

[105] Richard Overy, *Why the Allies Won* (New York: W.W. Norton, 1995), pp. 105–113; Johnson, *Fast Tanks and Heavy Bombers*, 153–75, 202–211. "That there was a disastrous first raid on Schweinfurt by the Eighth Air Force in August 1943 is neither surprising nor necessarily avoidable," write Allen Millett and Williamson Murray. "But what should have been avoidable was the follow-on raid in October 1943, which proved even more costly and repeated the errors of the first raid in nearly every way." Allan Reed Millett and Williamson Murray, *Military Effectiveness*: Vol. 2, *The Interwar Period*, new edition (Cambridge: Cambridge University Press, 2010), xv.

labored against the grain of the airpower community and in so doing attempted to compensate for its failings.[106]

Perhaps the most alarming observation from these studies is the extent to which perceived *moral* lessons from past wars can influence military policy—rarely for the better. Indeed, these cases suggest that we should perhaps revisit and revise the old saw about generals preparing to fight the last war. As already suggested, the more careful the generals' attention to the last war, the better their performance in the next tended to be. Societies, on the other hand, are not configured like general staffs and have a harder time extracting meaningful lessons from the past. To the contrary, they are prone to draw sweeping moral lessons from the last war that tend to distort the past and complicate the formulation of strategies that actually serve the national interest.

CONCLUSION/RECOMMENDATIONS

As the United States enters another era of uneasy peace and uncertainty, it should strive for as much strategic clarity as possible without ever looking for certitude. Certain Cold Warriors wax nostalgically about the days when the United States had a clear-cut enemy and a well-defined strategy for confronting it. They neglect to consider the enormous cost, fiscal and social, incurred in that contest or how America's myopic attention to a single strategic problem helped created the multitude of challenges the United States confronts today.[107] We should be thankful that the strategic environment is less clear than it once seemed, if only so we can avoid building forces such as the French Army of 1940 or the US Army of 1955.

Yet as the world's lone superpower in an age in which two oceans no longer provide a strategic buffer, the United States is unlikely to revert to the pre–World War II practice of building combat-ready forces and developing a strategy for their employment only in the event of a national emergency. Prudently, the United States seeks not merely to monitor but to shape the strategic environment, and it quadrennially reviews the priorities and programs of the Defense Department as a means of ensuring that its limited (if considerable) resources are being well-spent on capabilities that fulfill strategic requirements. Unfortunately, such measures are prone to producing modern equivalents of the Pentomic army. By subjecting the services to what is essentially a competition for slices of a fixed pie, the government incentivizes them to promote concepts and weapons that appear most relevant to the existing strategy or congruent with popular sentiment. Neither is necessarily constructive, particularly when strategy reflects an aversion to ground combat, counterinsurgency, or any other mission that the American people ostensibly will not tolerate—until they must. In those instances in which the services win funding for future-looking programs of questionable relevance to the contemporary environment, they prove tenacious in their defense regardless of cost or merit.[108]

---

[106] Spector, "The Military Effectiveness of the US Armed Forces, 1919–39," 84.

[107] Odd Arne Westad, *The Global Cold War: Third World Interventions and the Making of Our Times* (New York: Cambridge University Press, 2005).

[108] The US Army's most recent example of this was the ill-fated (and by some accounts misbegotten) Future Combat System.

As with military forces that feel politically insecure, it is beyond the ken of organizations engaged in such budgetary contests to be genuine learning organizations. Wargames and experiments intended to generate new ideas and challenge existing paradigms are likely to become charades designed instead to "validate" favored concepts. Moreover, the necessity of fielding combat-ready forces places a premium on training that, while entirely warranted, acts as a brake on meaningful innovation and intellectual reflection. Rather than staffing their schoolhouses with the "best and brightest," the services expect their "best" to stay in command of troops. When they do go to school, they are encouraged to "recharge their batteries" (recuperate) and reconnect with the families they have neglected—perfectly understandable priorities, but not those associated with a learning organization.

The greatest challenge currently confronting the armed forces of the United States is neither uncertainty nor austerity. Rather, it is the preoccupation with what amount to global constabulary obligations and the constraint of being perpetually ready for a major war against every identifiable threat. As the service chiefs brace for further "sequestration," they have made clear their priority of providing the president with the broadest range of strategic options *now*. Doing so requires the recapitalization of aging equipment vice modernization and prioritizes the training of fighting units over the education of their leaders. In other words, they are mortgaging the future viability of the force in the name of operational readiness for the moment. Far from happy about this state of affairs, the chiefs have been very vocal about the strategic risks it imposes.[109] They are chary of admitting, however, that the cuts imposed by sequestration have thus far been less severe than the drawdowns following each of America's twentieth-century wars.[110] As a matter of fact, the US military is not entering an era of austerity at all. Rather, it is resuming its nineteenth-century role as a constabulary force (albeit on a much larger scale) with the late-twentieth-century conviction that it must be prepared for conventional warfare at all times. Not surprisingly, it is discovering that even the defense budgets of a decade ago cannot accommodate both traditions.

Reconciling them and achieving sustainable security will demand a strategic consensus that the United States presently appears incapable of achieving. Partisan politics have, for the past generation, exerted an increasingly powerful and dysfunctional force on the formulation of national foreign and military policy. Since the 1980s, the Republican Party has all but abandoned its traditional fiscal conservatism regarding defense spending (which contributed to each of the eras of austerity addressed in this chapter). It has replaced it with a narrative that American military might has made the world safe for democracy and that only American "leadership" can keep it so. A competing narrative—more popular on the left—maintains

---

[109] John T. Bennett, "Military Chiefs Warn Anew About Sequester Cuts," *DefenseNews*, February 2, 2015, accessed April 26, 2016 http://www.defensenews.com/story/defense/policy-budget/congress/2015/01/28/sequestration-military-isis-budget/22462259; Cheryl Pellerin, "Service Chiefs Detail 2014 Sequestration Effects," *American Forces Press Service*, September 19, 2013, accessed October 12, 2013 http://www.defense.gov/news/newsarticle.aspx?id=120825.

[110] Todd Harrison, "Defense Cuts Conundrum: Weighing the Hard Choices Ahead," *Foreign Affairs*, September 29, 2013, accessed October 12, 2013 http://www.foreignaffairs.com/articles/139965/todd-harrison/defense-cuts-conundrum.

that American military misadventures since 1945 have engendered instability and that the American people will not tolerate another Korea ... or Vietnam ... or Beirut ... or Somalia ... or Iraq. Between these problematic moral lessons there is little common ground upon which to achieve a rational appreciation of the United States' strategic requirements.

Yet beneath disagreements about ways and means, there exists greater consensus about the United States' strategic aims than is readily apparent. Ultimately, the United States seeks to maintain the global order it has constructed over the past seventy years, mitigate threats to it, and maintain a position of preeminence. The problem, therefore, is not fundamentally the absence of strategic clarity; it is the lack of strategic realism. These interests are—practically speaking, if not morally—indefensible in the long term. If, as many argue, the threats to American interests are greater today that at any time since World War II, it is principally because the United States has defined its interests more broadly than ever before. While most Americans deny that the United States exercises imperial power, they are loath to surrender the privileges it conveys. Hence, the United States today implicitly defines its interest as the preservation of a favorable status quo that will be—inevitably and perpetually—challenged by "revisionist" powers. Countering them at every turn and in every domain is infeasible, so the Defense Department has proposed that it instead devise "offset" strategies that play American strengths off of competitor weaknesses.[111] But such strategies are most effective when wielded by the revisionists—not the guardians of the status quo—and they are unlikely to close the gap between America's strategic aims and the means it is willing or able to commit. Solving this dilemma will require nothing less than a reassessment of the United States' truly vital interests and place in the world. Until then, the US Army will dutifully perform the constabulary mission it has been assigned while preparing for its next major contest: the next quadrennial defense review.

---

[111] US Department of Defense, "The Third U.S. Offset Strategy and its Implications for Partners and Allies: As Delivered by Deputy Secretary of Defense Bob Work, Willard Hotel, Washington, D.C., January 28, 2015," accessed 31 October 2015, http://www.defense.gov/News/Speeches/Speech-View/Article/606641/the-third-us-offset-strategy-and-its-implications-for-partners-and-allies.

7

CLIMATE CHANGE AND US NATIONAL SECURITY
SUSTAINING SECURITY AMIDST
UNSUSTAINABILITY

Joshua William Busby

As global negotiations over addressing climate change lumber on, the problem itself has increasingly moved from a long-run threat to a more urgent problem.[1] Scientists put this starkly when they say that current concentrations of carbon dioxide, the main greenhouse gas, are higher than they have been for 800,000 years.[2] The effects of climate change are already manifesting in higher temperatures as well as extreme weather events that scientists can increasingly attribute to climate change.[3] Since the 2007 release of a series of think tank reports on climate change and national security, the US national security apparatus has moved to incorporate climate change into its strategic planning, both in terms of preparing for direct threats to the homeland and indirect threats to the country's overseas interests.

How should the United States properly align means and ends at a time of constrained resources? In a world of pressing security problems, how can those concerned about climate change make a compelling case for dedicating scarce resources to this problem? This volume has an expressed aim of encouraging triage and goal-setting: that some problems are more important than others and "all of the above" is not a national security strategy.[4] Climate change is a problem that asks the United States to do more at a time when public opinion, military exhaustion, and domestic economic imperatives counsel doing less.

---

[1] Savannah Kumar assisted in the research for this chapter.

[2] CBS NewsMay CBS News, "First Time in 800,000 Years: April's CO2 Levels above 400 Ppm," May 6, 2014, http://www.cbsnews.com/news/first-time-in-800000-years-aprils-co2-levels-above-400-ppm.

[3] The field of attribution, whereby scientists seek to connect individual weather events to climate change, is a young and somewhat controversial field, but increasingly scientists are able to tease out whether climate change enhanced the likelihood and severity of individual weather events. BMAS, "Explaining Extreme Events of 2013 from a Climate Perspective," *Bulletin of the American Meteorological Society* 75, no. 9 (September 2014), http://www2.ametsoc.org/ams/index.cfm/publications/bulletin-of-the-american-meteorological-society-bams/explaining-extreme-events-of-2013-from-a-climate-perspective; Climate Central, "2014 Extreme Weather: Looking for Climate Ties," *Climate Central*, October 8, 2014, http://www.climatecentral.org/news/2014-extreme-weather-attribution-18150.

[4] See introduction to this volume.

This chapter seeks to reconcile that tension, beginning with the general case for incorporating climate change into the broader strategic calculus of the United States, given concerns about imperial overstretch and the need for more selective engagement on the world stage. My general argument is that self-interest and preservation demands US leadership on climate alongside China, which has now superseded the United States as the world largest emitter of greenhouse gases. Changes in relative economic power between the United States and China create a danger of the equivalent of the interwar period between World War I and World War II, with both countries unable and unwilling to provide sufficient leadership to generate the global public good of climate protection. While the breakdown in cooperation on climate change is a possibility, US–China policy coordination in the lead up to the 2015 Paris climate negotiations suggest this is not destiny.

At the same time, even as climate change demands more attention, US policymakers have to be mindful of the risks of threat inflation by "securitizing" climate change. Labeling climate change a security threat has a certain attraction, as it may increase attention, resources, and support for action, particularly among conservatives. However, advocates of this strategy may have to be careful what they wish for. While it might deliver new efforts to mitigate climate change (that is to reduce greenhouse gases), the climate security agenda will likely lead to attention to homeland security and the consequences for the American military at home and abroad. A climate security agenda might also lead to a narrow agenda. Most academic studies focus on whether climate change will lead to conflicts such as civil wars, for which the evidence is mixed and the causal chains complex and poorly understood. Climate change already poses a present security danger through extreme weather events and their direct effects on populations and critical infrastructure. While a wide variety of climate security concerns have been incorporated into national security planning documents, major investments in climate proofing infrastructure and investments domestically and internationally have only just begun. More attention needs to be paid to understanding the full set of risks, including potentially catastrophic impacts of low or unknown probability such as ocean acidification and permafrost melt.

In this chapter, I first discuss the origins of climate security both among practitioners and academics before synthesizing the state of knowledge on climate change and US national security, drawing from both US government assessments and the wider academic literature on climate and security. I focus on three dimensions of the problem: the direct effects on the US homeland; the indirect effects on US national security through overseas impacts; and the geostrategic implications of the policy environment as climate change becomes an increasingly top tier issue in international relations. For each, I review the claims about the security connections and the state of knowledge. I close with some thoughts on US policy, risk assessment, and the meaning of sustainability and security.

THE ORIGINS OF CLIMATE AND SECURITY

To know what level of self-protection against climate change is warranted, it is helpful to understand the origins of the interest in environmental and, in turn, climate

security. This section walks through the turn to climate security both among practitioners and scholars that began in the mid-2000s.

Environmental security has an established pedigree dating back to the 1990s
and 2000s in policy and academic circles, led by the likes of the scholar Thomas
Homer-Dixon, who sought to demonstrate that environmental stresses had a major
role in triggering conflicts.[5] The Woodrow Wilson Center's Environmental Change
and Security Program was founded in 1994 as a transmission mechanism for connecting this kind of academic work to policy audiences.[6] Environmental scarcity
was explicitly explored as a cause of conflict and state collapse in the work by the
State Failure Task Force in 1999 (later renamed the Political Instability Task
Force), a US government-sponsored research project.[7] Given data availability, much
of the environmental security literature was based on qualitative case studies, and
ultimately, the efforts were somewhat inconclusive, with the association between
environmental factors and security outcomes, notably conflict, contingent on other
political phenomena such as the degree of government inclusiveness and the extent
of societal cleavages.[8]

The connections between climate change and security did not emerge until
later in the mid-2000s. In the face of political opposition to addressing the
climate problem, climate advocates, particularly in the United States, began
casting about for new ways to frame climate change as a way to broaden their
coalition.[9] One way was to frame climate change as a security threat. In the
aftermath of the 9/11 terror attacks, Tom Friedman and others began this framing, linking fossil fuel dependence to unsavory regimes and also highlighting
the connections between climate change and security outcomes at home and
abroad.[10]

One of the early efforts to connect climate and security was a piece I coauthored
with Nigel Purvis in 2004—commissioned by the Woodrow Wilson Center for the

---

[5] Thomas F. Homer-Dixon, "On the Threshold: Environmental Changes as Causes of Acute
Conflict," *International Security* 16, no. 2 (1991): 76–116; Thomas F. Homer-Dixon, "Environmental
Scarcities and Violent Conflict: Evidence from Cases," *International Security* 19, no. 1 (1994):
5–40; Thomas F. Homer-Dixon, *Environment, Scarcity, and Violence* (Princeton, NJ: Princeton
University Press, 1999).

[6] That program was still operative in 2015. See http://www.wilsoncenter.org/program/
environmental-change-and-security-program.

[7] Daniel C. Esty et al., "State Failure Task Force Report: Phase II Findings," Environmental
Change and Security Project Report (Woodrow Wilson Center, 1999), https://www.wilsoncenter.
org/sites/default/files/Phase2.pdf.

[8] Colin H. Kahl, *States, Scarcity, and Civil Strife in the Developing World* (Princeton, NJ: Princeton
University Press, 2006).

[9] For a discussion, see Josh Busby and Alexander Ochs, "From Mars and Venus Down to
Earth: Understanding the Transatlantic Climate Divide," in *Climate Policy for the 21st Century:
Meeting the Long-Term Challenge of Global Warming*, David Michel ed. (Washington: Center for
Transatlantic Relations, Johns Hopkins University, 2004), pp. 35–76.

[10] Thomas L. Friedman, *Hot, Flat, and Crowded: Why We Need a Green Revolution—and How It
Can Renew America* (New York: Farrar, Straus and Giroux, 2008).

UN Secretary General's project on Threats, Challenges, and Change—where we emphasized that the most important emergent threat was increasing humanitarian crises that might require military support.[11] The climate security drumbeat began to accrue a constituency in policy circles in Washington beginning with some think tank studies in 2007 and 2008 by the CNA Corporation,[12] my paper for the Council on Foreign Relations,[13] and an edited volume from the Center for a New American Security and the Center for Strategic and International Studies.[14] All of these studies tentatively approached the causal role of climate change in security outcomes, notably conflict, by referring to climate change as a "threat multiplier" and as an additional "stressor."

Governments began commissioning studies on the effects of climate change and security such as the 2008 National Intelligence Assessment on climate and security by the National Intelligence Council,[15] its subsequent report on water security,[16] as well as reports and meetings by the Defense Science Board[17] and the National Academy of Sciences.[18]

While this interest in climate and security may not endure across presidential administrations if a Republican is elected in 2016, the Obama administration's incorporation of climate change in national security planning documents sprawls across multiple executive branch agencies. Prompted by an Executive Order from the president in 2009 (followed by others in 2013 and 2014) and the work of the Interagency Climate Adaptation Task Force, the Obama administration

---

[11] Nigel Purvis and Josh Busby, "The Security Implications of Climate Change for the UN System," Policy Brief, The United Nations and Environmental Security, *Environmental Change and Security Project*, 2004, http://www.wilsoncenter.org/topics/pubs/ecspr10_unf-purbus.pdf.

[12] CNA Corporation, "National Security and the Threat of Climate Change," 2007, https://www.cna.org/cna_files/pdf/national%20security%20and%20the%20threat%20of%20climate%20change.pdf.

[13] Joshua Busby, "Climate Change and National Security: An Agenda for Action" (Council on Foreign Relations, 2007), p. 2, www.cfr.org/publication/14862.

[14] Kurt M. Campbell et al., "The Age of Consequences," Center for Strategic and International Studies, 2007, http://www.csis.org/media/csis/pubs/071105_ageofconsequences.pdf; John Podesta and Peter Ogden, "The Security Implications of Climate Change," *The Washington Quarterly* 31, no. 1 (2007): 115–138.

[15] Thomas Fingar, "Testimony to the House Permanent Select Committee on Intelligence House Select Committee on Energy Independence and Global Warming", June 25, 2008, http://www.dni.gov/testimonies/20080625_testimony.pdf. I was an external reviewer of this report.

[16] Office of the Director of National Intelligence, "Global Water Security: Intelligence Community Assessment," US Department of State, February 2, 2012, http://www.state.gov/e/oes/water/ica.

[17] Defense Science Board, "Report of the Defense Science Board Task Force on Trends and Implications of Climate Change for National and International Security" (Office of the Secretary of Defense, Defense Science Board, October 2011), http://www.acq.osd.mil/dsb/reports/ADA552760.pdf.

[18] John Steinbruner, Paul Stern, and Jo Husbands, eds., *Climate and Social Stress: Implications for Security Analysis* (Washington, DC: National Academies, 2013).

directed executive agencies to take climate change adaptation concerns into their operations.[19]

Climate change has thus subsequently been incorporated into US Pentagon planning documents like the Quadrennial Defense Review (2010, 2014)[20] and the 2014 Department of Defense Adaptation Roadmap[21] as well as planning documents by other agencies, including the 2012 Department of Homeland Security Climate Change Adaptation Roadmap,[22] and the 2010 and 2014 Quadrennial Homeland Security Review.[23] The United States also issued strategic documents on the implications of climate change as part of the 2010 and 2015 national security strategy documents[24] as well as more focused investigations for the Navy and

---

[19] The 2009 Executive Order directed agencies to cooperate with the Task Force as it examined "the domestic and international dimensions of a US strategy for adaptation to climate change." White House, Office of the Press Secretary, "Executive Order: Federal Leadership in Environmental, Energy, and Economic Performance," October 5, 2009, https://www.whitehouse.gov/assets/documents/2009fedleader_eo_rel.pdf.

The Task Force's 2010 report recommended that adaptation planning be mainstreamed across all federal agencies, with a government-wide strategy to bring adaptation into foreign assistance programs and enhanced coordination between national security, international development, and technical programs. White House Council on Environmental Quality, "Progress Report of the Interagency Climate Change Adaptation Task Force: Recommended Actions in Support of a National Climate Change Adaptation Strategy," October 5, 2010, https://www.whitehouse.gov/sites/default/files/microsites/ceq/Interagency-Climate-Change-Adaptation-Progress-Report.pdf. The 2013 executive order focused on the homeland, creating a Council on Climate Preparedness and Resilience which assumed the functions of the adaptation task force. White House, "Executive Order 13653—Preparing the United States for the Impacts of Climate Change," Federal Register, Vol. 78, no. 215, November 6, 2013, http://www.gpo.gov/fdsys/pkg/FR-2013-11-06/pdf/2013-26785.pdf. The 2014 order directed that all international development work include climate-resilience considerations into its operations. White House, "Executive Order Climate-Resilient International Development," September 23, 2014, https://www.whitehouse.gov/the-press-office/2014/09/23/executive-order-climate-resilient-international-development.

[20] Department of Defense, "Quadrennial Defense Review Report 2010," February 2010, http://www.defense.gov/Portals/1/features/defenseReviews/QDR/QDR_as_of_29JAN10_1600.pdf; Department of Defense, "Quadrennial Defense Review 2014," 2014, http://www.defense.gov/pubs/2014_Quadrennial_Defense_Review.pdf.

[21] Department of Defense, "2014 Climate Change Adaptation Roadmap," October 2014.

[22] Department of Homeland Security, "Department of Homeland Security Climate Change Adaptation Roadmap," June 2012, https://www.dhs.gov/sites/default/files/publications/Appendix%20A%20DHS%20FY2012%20Climate%20Change%20Adaptation%20Plan_0.pdf.

[23] Department of Homeland Security, "2010 Quadrennial Homeland Security Review," 2010, http://www.dhs.gov/publication/2010-quadrennial-homeland-security-review-qhsr; Department of Homeland Security, "2014 Quadrennial Homeland Security Review," June 2014, http://www.dhs.gov/publication/2014-quadrennial-homeland-security-review-qhsr.

[24] White House, "National Security Strategy 2010," National Security Strategy Archive, May 2010, http://nssarchive.us/?page_id=8; White House, "2015 National Security Strategy," February 2015, https://www.whitehouse.gov/sites/default/files/docs/2015_national_security_strategy.pdf.

the Arctic.[25] USAID has also carried out research projects to assess the significance of climate change for state fragility,[26] and climate security concerns were incorporated in to the 2015 Quadrennial Diplomacy and Development Review (QDDR), a State Department planning document.[27] In May 2015, President Obama pulled these threads together in a 2015 commencement speech at the US Coast Guard academy.[28] Subsequent speeches by National Security Advisor Susan Rice and Secretary of State John Kerry reinforced these themes.[29] As of fall 2015, most of these appear to be planning documents with multibillion-dollar investments in protecting critical infrastructure and spending patterns for combatant commands and foreign assistance yet to materialize.

Outside of government, in addition to the longtime work of the Woodrow Wilson Center, there is a newer policy community in Washington that works on climate change and security nearly full time, including at the CNA Corporation, the Center for Climate and Security,[30] the American Security Project,[31] and various universities. These professionals meet regularly to mainstream climate considerations into policy, mostly in terms of an adaptation and response agenda for the traditional US national security establishment. There are similar constituencies in other countries, notably the United Kingdom. Internationally, the UN Security Council held its first ever debate on the topic

[25] White House, "National Strategy for the Arctic Region," May 2013, http://www.white-house.gov/sites/default/files/docs/nat_arctic_strategy.pdf; Task Force Climate Change/Oceanographer of the Navy, "Climate Change Roadmap" (US Navy, April 2009); US Navy, "US Navy Arctic Roadmap 2014–2030," February 2014, http://www.navy.mil/docs/USN_arctic_roadmap.pdf.

[26] Jeffrey Stark, "What Climate Conflict Looks Like: Recent Findings and Possible Responses," *New Security Beat*, December 16, 2014, http://www.newsecuritybeat.org/2014/12/climate-change-conflict-findings-responses/; USAID, "Climate Change and Conflict: Findings and Lessons Learned from Five Case Studies in Seven Countries," African and Latin American Resilience to Climate Change Project, July 2014, http://community.eldis.org/.5b9bfce3/CCC%2004%20FESS%20Synthesis%20Paper_CLEARED.pdf.

[27] State Department, "Enduring Leadership in a Dynamic World: Quadrennial Diplomacy and Development Review 2015," William and Mary: Government Information, 2015.

[28] White House, "Findings from Select Federal Reports: The National Security Implications of a Changing Climate," Washington, DC: The White House, May 2015, https://www.whitehouse.gov/sites/default/files/docs/national_security_implications_of_changing_climate_final_051915_embargo.pdf; White House, "Remarks by the President at the United States Coast Guard Academy Commencement," Whitehouse.gov, May 20, 2015, https://www.whitehouse.gov/the-press-office/2015/05/20/remarks-president-united-states-coast-guard-academy-commencement.

[29] John Kerry, "Remarks on Climate Change and National Security," US Department of State, November 10, 2015, http://www.state.gov/secretary/remarks/2015/11/249393.htm; Susan Rice, "Remarks by National Security Advisor Susan E. Rice on Climate Change and National Security at Stanford University—As Prepared for Delivery," Whitehouse.gov, October 12, 2015, https://www.whitehouse.gov/the-press-office/2015/10/12/remarks-national-security-advisor-susan-e-rice-climate-change-and.

[30] See http://climateandsecurity.org.

[31] See http://www.americansecurityproject.org/issues/climate-security.

in 2007.[32] The European Union,[33] the G-7,[34] and various other governments also began engaging the security dimensions of the problem.[35]

Alongside this policy preoccupation with climate and security, academics have also engaged the topic with a large literature proliferating since the late 2000s, much of it quantitative in nature and narrowly focused on whether or not climate change causes internal conflict within countries.[36] A broader more qualitative literature has focused on the "human security" implications of climate change and wider harms to human welfare. From this perspective, in addition to food security and climate-induced migration, the cultural integrity of communities and the effects of climate change on livelihoods are threats to human security.[37] The surge in academic research on the topic was sufficient to elicit a full chapter on human security in the 2014 IPCC Fifth Assessment Report.[38]

This background is important because the diverse motivations for framing climate change as a security problem and the various ways climate security is understood have major implications for how the problem is currently dealt with. Importantly, in order to justify action in this space, either to address the security implications themselves or to trigger a broader commitment to mitigation, climate security professionals have strong incentives to dramatize the problem and make sweeping claims about the contribution of climate change to global conflict trends[39] or the contribution of climate change to

[32] United Nations: Meeting Coverages and Press Releases, "Security Council Holds First-Ever Debate On Impact Of Climate Change On Peace, Security, Hearing Over 50 Speakers," April 17, 2007, http://www.un.org/News/Press/docs/2007/sc9000.doc.htm.

[33] Javier Solana, "Climate Change and International Security: Paper from the High Representative and the European Commission to the European Council," March 14, 2008, http://www.consilium.europa.eu/ueDocs/cms_Data/docs/pressData/en/reports/99387.pdf.

[34] Lukas Rüttinger et al., "A New Climate for Peace," Adelphi, Wilson Center, International Alert, and The European Institute for Security Studies, 2015, http://www.newclimateforpeace.org.

[35] See for example the work in Germany and the UK. WBGU, German Advisory Council on Global Change, "Climate Change as a Security Risk: Summary for Policymakers," Flagship Report 2007, http://www.wbgu.de/wbgu_jg2007_kurz_engl.html.

[36] See for example the review Nils Petter Gleditsch, "Whither the Weather? Climate Change and Conflict," *Journal of Peace Research* 49, no. 1 (January 1, 2012): 3–9, doi:10.1177/0022343311431288.

[37] Jon Barnett and W. Neil Adger, "Climate Change, Human Security and Violent Conflict," *Political Geography* 26, no. 6 (2007): 639–655.

[38] See chapter 12 in Neil Adger et al., "Climate Change 2014: Impacts, Adaptation, and Vulnerability. Part A: Global and Sectoral Aspects." Contribution of Working Group II to the Fifth Assessment Report of the Intergovernmental Panel on Climate Change Cambridge, UK: Intergovernmental Panel on Climate Change, 2014.

[39] Solomon Hsiang, Marshall Burke, and Edward Miguel, "Quantifying the Influence of Climate on Human Conflict," *Science* 341, no. 6151 (September 13, 2013); Marshall B Burke et al., "Warming Increases the Risk of Civil War in Africa," *Proceedings of the National Academy of Sciences* 106, no. 49 (November 23, 2009): 20670–20674, doi:10.1073/pnas.0907998106.

particularly salient geopolitical events such as the Arab Spring[40] and the conflict in Darfur.[41]

This effort to "securitize" climate change is a familiar project that groups seeking policymakers' attention have engaged in to jump their particular issues up the queue. As Daniel Deudney noted in a 1990 *Millennium* article, evoking security allows normal politics and the standard policy process to be swept aside in favor of extraordinary measures. These may be expensive and focus on parochial national interests at the expense of wider global public goods concerns.[42]

Aside from these risks, securitizing a problem potentially leads to threat inflation as groups hype their preferred cause *du jour* because they think the instrumental use of security language will generate more interest and resources for their problem. The downside is that if those security consequences do not materialize, the issue might not have staying power on the international agenda. Though HIV/AIDS remained a high priority in the 2000s for other reasons, the security dimensions of HIV/AIDS largely dissipated as an active area of research and policy despite earlier claims that AIDS orphans were being recruited to become child soldiers and other ills.[43] The other negative consequence of successful securitization is that it identifies the military as primarily responsible for addressing the security consequences of climate change, even if other agencies and instruments are more appropriate for dealing with the issue.

This is not a negation of the connections between climate change and security but a recognition of incentives and motivations that have impelled the security cast of the problem to prominence.

THE SECURITY CONSEQUENCES OF CLIMATE IMPACTS

From the previous discussion, the strategic imperative that emerges is to review and evaluate the specific consequences of climate change that pose a real threat to

---

[40] Caitlin E. Werrell and Francesco Femia, eds., *The Arab Spring and Climate Change* (Washington, DC: Center for American Progress 2013), http://www.americanprogress.org/issues/security/report/2013/02/28/54579/the-arab-spring-and-climate-change.

[41] Alex de Waal, "Is Climate Change the Culprit for Darfur?" 2007, http://africanarguments.org/2007/06/25/is-climate-change-the-culprit-for-darfur/; Thomas Homer-Dixon, "Cause and Effect," Aug. 7, 2007, https://web.archive.org/web/20110429011738/http://blogs.ssrc.org/sudan/2007/08/02/cause-and-effect; Ban Ki-Moon, "A Climate Culprit in Darfur," *Washington Post*, June 16, 2007, http://www.washingtonpost.com/wp-dyn/content/article/2007/06/15/AR2007061501857_pf.html.

[42] Daniel Deudney, "The Case Against Linking Environmental Degradation and National Security," *Millennium* 19, no. 3 (1990): 461–476. On the wider topic of securitization, see Ole Waever, "Securitization and Desecuritization," in *On Security*, Ronnie D. Lipschutz ed. (New York: Columbia University Press, 1995), pp. 46–86.

[43] Tony Barnett and Indranil Dutta, "HIV and State Failure: Is HIV a Security Risk?" New York, USA: Aids, Security and Conflict Initiative (ASCI), September 2007, https://www.escholar.manchester.ac.uk/api/datastream?publicationPid=uk-ac-man-scw:67900&datastreamId=SUPPLEMENTARY-1.PDF.

US national security. This requires a tractable definition of national security that is both consistent with practice in policy circles and logically defensible. This section begins with a review of definitions of national security and provides a conceptual framework for thinking about climate security threats, as well as for distinguishing between direct threats to the homeland, indirect threats to a country's interests overseas, and the geostrategic implications of responses to climate change.[44]

Definitions of national security

Historically, national security threats were narrowly construed as armed external attacks by state actors against other states. Post 9/11, when nonstate actors carried out attacks against the United States, that definition appeared anachronistic. However, even expanding the definition to include terrorists and other nonstate actors as security threats still implies human agents actively seeking to harm another state. Some threats, such as diseases like Ebola, might not be directed by human agents but still constitute security threats to the United States. The consequences of a disease outbreak could kill large numbers of Americans and disrupt national confidence and stability enough to constitute security threats.[45]

By the same token, climate change might also give rise to consequences of similar severity to disease outbreaks. Put more generally, a threat that potentially causes massive challenges or disruptions to a country's way of life and poses a danger to the survival of large numbers of people is a national security threat. Another way of imagining security threats is to ask if those consequences were wrought intentionally, what would the state's response be? If a state, in other circumstances, would be prepared to use military force to prevent such an outcome, then that would also signal that the problem is severe enough to constitute a threat to national security, even if the tools required to address that challenge are not necessarily military ones. Indeed, if the military is required to deal with these threats, then that in and of itself is an indicator of failure of civilian early warning systems and humanitarian action to prevent hazard exposure from escalating into disasters that require emergency military mobilization.

There are two main ways that climate change could constitute a national security threat: as a *direct* threat to a country's homeland and as an *indirect* threat to its overseas or international interests.[46] This distinction between direct threats to the homeland and indirect threats overseas is largely consistent with how the wider policy community conceptualizes the nature of the threat. For example, the report that accompanied the 2015 commencement speech by President Obama emphasized this perspective. "The implications of climate change on national security are not all beyond US borders—they pose risks here at home."[47]

[44] This mirrors a similar distinction made by Marc A. Levy, "Is the Environment a National Security Issue?" *International Security* 20, no. 2 (1995): 35–62.

[45] Joshua Busby, "Who Cares About the Weather? Climate Change and US National Security," *Security Studies* 17, no. 3 (2008): 468–504.

[46] Ibid., 470.

[47] White House, "Findings from Select Federal Reports: The National Security Implications of a Changing Climate."

For both direct and indirect threats, I consider the causal connections between climate change and security outcomes, focusing on the claims and the state of knowledge for a select few processes along with some policy recommendations.

Direct threats to the homeland

For both direct and indirect security threats of climate change, we can identify the main potential pathways and evaluate the available evidence connecting each threat to security consequences that policymakers might care about given their relatively short-term time horizons. Climate change could conceivably constitute a security threat to a homeland if it threatened (1) the existence of the country, (2) its seat of government, (3) the state's monopoly on the use of force, (4) disruption or destruction of critical infrastructure, (5) catastrophic short-run losses in human life or well-being calling into question the legitimacy of the government (6) causation of sudden large-scale internal or cross-border refugee movements, or (7) alteration of a country's territorial borders or waters.[48]

For the United States, four physical forces might bring about some (though certainly not all) of these consequences, including: (1) abrupt climate change, (2) sea-level rise, (3) extreme weather events, and (4) Arctic ice melt.[49] Of these, extreme weather and Arctic ice melt are two physical phenomena for which scientific evidence suggests a high probability of occurrence in the following one or two decades (though the pace of sea-level rise is accelerating quickly).[50] Focusing on the more probable consequences of climate change creates space for climate change as a security problem using conservative assumptions.[51]

Extreme weather events

The claims: Physical phenomena of extreme weather can be connected to possible security consequences for the United States. These include the effects of swift onset hazards like cyclones and floods on major urban populations, military bases, and critical infrastructure. Such events can lead to domestic humanitarian emergencies and compromise law enforcement and public safety in affected communities subject to looting, vandalism, and other damage to property. Moreover,

---

[48] Busby, "Who Cares About the Weather?" 477.

[49] Ibid., 481.

[50] The scientific community had yet to resolve the extent to which climate change will enhance both severity and frequency of extreme weather events. For heat waves and heavy precipitation events, the scientific evidence was clear, whereas for other hazards like cyclones the evidence was not conclusive. See IPCC, "Managing the Risks of Extreme Events and Disasters to Advance Climate Change Adaptation (SREX)," Working Groups I and II, December 2011, http://ipcc-wg2.gov/SREX.

[51] In a paper for the Pentagon, prominent futurists assessed the implications of a highly improbable ice age scenario of abrupt climate change (akin to the disaster movie *The Day After Tomorrow*). Peter Schwartz and Doug Randall, "An Abrupt Climate Change Scenario and Its Implications for United States National Security," San Francisco: Global Business Network, Department of Defense, 2004, http://www.climate.org/PDF/clim_change_scenario.pdf.

failure by government to respond effectively can lead to protest and loss of public confidence.

The state of knowledge: Hurricane Katrina, for example, killed more than 1,800 people and dislocated another 270,000, caused eighty billion dollars in damages, and took off line critical energy infrastructure. Moreover, the mobilization of thousands of members of the National Guard diverted resources and attention that otherwise could have been dedicated to important national security priorities such as the ongoing conflict in Iraq. Indeed, the government's hamhanded response to that episode was a stain on the George W. Bush presidency and created ongoing challenges for the federal government's relationship with the New Orleans populace.

This take on the threats posed by extreme weather events is mirrored in official documents from the US government. Drawing on evidence from the third national assessment of climate change impacts on the United States,[52] the Obama administration warned of the risks by mid-century of flooding and sea-level rise in coastal areas:

> Critical infrastructure, major military installations, and hurricane evacuation routes are increasingly vulnerable to impacts, such as higher sea levels, storm surges, and flooding exacerbated by climate change. Sea-level rise, coupled with storm surge, will continue to increase the risk of major coastal impacts on transportation infrastructure, including both temporary and permanent flooding of airports, ports and harbors, roads, rail lines, tunnels, and bridges.[53]

The White House referenced the response to Superstorm Sandy that affected the eastern seaboard in 2012, leaving 8.5 million without power and causing tens of billions of dollars in damage. Like Hurricane Katrina, the storm required mobilization of the National Guard, the Coast Guard, and other elements of the defense establishment to lead domestic humanitarian response, including delivery of emergency supplies and efforts to restore infrastructure.[54]

The Obama administration noted that these effects potentially go beyond humanitarian emergencies and storms. The Department of Homeland Security flagged the effects of heat: "In Western States, higher temperatures and more frequent or severe heat waves could buckle railways, damage roads, and strain power systems."[55] Together, the effects of storms, floods, sea-level rise, and irregular rainfall pose problems for energy production and electricity grids, and threaten to "overwhelm the capacities of critical infrastructure, causing widespread disruption

[52] US Global Change Research Program "National Climate Assessment: Climate Change Impacts in the United States," *National Climate Assessment*, 2014, http://nca2014.globalchange.gov/downloads.

[53] White House, "Findings from Select Federal Reports: The National Security Implications of a Changing Climate."

[54] Ibid.

[55] Department of Homeland Security, "Department of Homeland Security Climate Change Adaptation Roadmap," 10.

of essential services across the country."[56] Particular military installations such as the naval base in Norfolk, Virginia are often identified as at risk from frequent flooding.[57]

Although climate-induced migration is frequently identified as an international problem likely to affect countries overseas, the United States itself might experience some cross-border migration of this nature.[58] The Department of Homeland Security for its part also recognized domestic threats from regional migration, noting that extreme weather events ultimately could spur migration to the United States: "More severe droughts and tropical storms, especially in Mexico, Central America, and the Caribbean, could also increase population movements, both legal and illegal, across the US border."[59]

Slow onset hazards such as droughts arguably may also constitute security concerns of a different nature. In the late 2000s and early 2010s, the Southwest, from Texas to California, experienced devastating droughts. There are fears among scientists that these drought conditions across parts of the Southwest may endure for extended periods, perhaps for several decades.[60] While on some level this is a domestic economic problem, an issue of water resources and agriculture, a multi-decadal megadrought could have wider ramifications for power generation, water access, and agriculture. Some cities and states could face existential questions for human habitability, requiring concerted efforts that go well beyond reforming decades old water withdrawal rights for farmers.

Policymakers would have to consider providing emergency water provision in the short run and expensive investment in desalinization in the long run. While some residents might vote with their feet in a reversal of the historic Dust Bowl migration, the US government might have to engage in more proactive efforts to facilitate population movements out of affected areas. With numerous military bases and training facilities dotting Western states, the confluence of persistent droughts, inadequate power generation from hydropower, declining agricultural yields, and insufficient drinking water might elevate aridity in the Southwest to a chronic national emergency.

---

[56] White House, "Findings from Select Federal Reports: The National Security Implications of a Changing Climate."

[57] Department of Defense, "2014 Climate Change Adaptation Roadmap."

[58] Busby, "Who Cares About the Weather?" 489.

[59] Department of Homeland Security, "2014 Quadrennial Homeland Security Review," 22; Alexander Bollfrass and Andrew Shaver, "The Effects of Temperature on Political Violence: Global Evidence at the Subnational Level," *PLoS ONE* 10, no. 5 (May 20, 2015): e0123505, doi:10.1371/journal.pone.0123505; Shuaizhang Feng, Alan B. Krueger, and Michael Oppenheimer, "Linkages among Climate Change, Crop Yields and Mexico–US Cross-Border Migration," *Proceedings of the National Academy of Sciences* 107, no. 32 (2010): 14257–14262.

[60] B. I. Cook, T. R. Ault, and J. E. Smerdon, "Unprecedented 21st Century Drought Risk in the American Southwest and Central Plains," *Science Advances* 1, no. 1 (February 1, 2015): e1400082–e1400082, doi:10.1126/sciadv.1400082; Eric Holthaus, "The United States of Megadrought," *Slate*, February 12, 2015, http://www.slate.com/articles/technology/future_tense/2015/02/study_climate_change_may_bring_about_megadroughts_this_century.html.

Some scholars, such as Roger Pielke, Jr., downplay the significance of climate change as a driver of more storms and damages, instead attributing these changes to increasing numbers of people living along coasts and more valuable infrastructure to lose. Indeed, he notes, improved humanitarian response capacity and early warning systems have resulted in declines in mortalities caused by natural hazards.[61] While that perspective itself has been disputed by those who see a clearer signal in the empirical record for climate change's role in increasing the number and intensity of cyclones,[62] the reality is that America's coastal cities, infrastructure, and bases are vulnerable to extreme weather, and the Boy Scout motto "Be Prepared" is apropos regardless. Ongoing reviews of national vulnerabilities to climate hazards should create additional impetus for billions of dollars to climate-proof infrastructure investments such as New York initiated in the wake of hurricane Sandy.

Arctic ice melt

The claims: In terms of Arctic ice melt, the risks are distinct from extreme weather, as the opening of possible sea lanes and territory is leading to jockeying by various countries with claims to the Arctic, including Canada, Russia, Norway, and Denmark. Climate change is contributing to more ice-free days in the Arctic, making it possible to navigate, at least for more days in the summer, the two Arctic sea routes, the northern sea route and the Northwest Passage. The northern route could potentially cut by two weeks the travel time from China to Europe in lieu of the longer route through the Suez Canal.[63] With Russia investing in ice fleet capabilities and exercising control over the route, there is concern that Russia could impede or impose costs on the movement of goods as this route becomes increasingly viable in coming decades.

The state of knowledge: While an increasing number of ships have been able in recent years to make it through the northern route that connects the Atlantic to the Pacific above Siberia, they often require icebreakers to accompany them. Analysts have raised concerns about whether the United States (with one, possibly two icebreakers) and regional ally Canada (with six) possess an adequate number and quality of icebreakers to defend their claims to the Arctic or respond to accidents, especially compared to Russia's more robust fleet of eighteen to twenty-seven icebreakers and China which has commissioned a second icebreaker.[64] While the

---

[61] Roger Pielke, Jr., "Disasters Cost More Than Ever -- But Not Because of Climate Change," *FiveThirtyEight*, March 19, 2014, http://fivethirtyeight.com/features/disasters-cost-more-than-ever-but-not-because-of-climate-change; Roger Pielke Jr., "Signals of Anthropogenic Climate Change in Disaster Data," January 4, 2011, http://rogerpielkejr.blogspot.com/2011/01/signals-of-anthropogenic-climate-change.html.

[62] Kerry Emanuel, "MIT Climate Scientist Responds on Disaster Costs And Climate Change," *FiveThirtyEight*, March 19, 2014, http://fivethirtyeight.com/features/mit-climate-scientist-responds-on-disaster-costs-and-climate-change.

[63] Chester Dawson, "Arctic Shipping Volume Rises as Ice Melts," *Wall Street Journal*, October 29, 2014, http://www.wsj.com/articles/arctic-cargo-shipping-volume-is-rising-as-ice-melts-1414612143.

[64] Scott Borgerson, "Arctic Meltdown," *Foreign Affairs*, March/April 2008, https://www.foreignaffairs.com/articles/arctic-antarctic/2008-03-02/arctic-meltdown.

Department of Homeland Security in December 2013 suggested that three heavy and three medium icebreakers might be required, the expense of a single heavy icebreaker could be nearly equivalent to the Coast Guard's entire annual budget of $1.1 billion.[65]

With the Arctic a source of valuable hydrocarbons, the risk of disputes over territory and sea lanes harkens back to the kinds of disputes that resulted in armed conflict in previous centuries. The Arctic has seen a spate of action by states anticipating more regular access as sea ice melts, including plans approved by the Obama Administration in May 2015 to allow Shell to drill for oil.[66]

Though institutions like the Arctic Council likely will help facilitate transnational cooperation to minimize the risks of conflict, increasing ease of transit, albeit seasonal, is creating new sources of friction between states.[67] The Obama administration downplayed the risk of conflict over the Arctic but noted that melting ice will open the region and that will require more international cooperation:

> While the Region is expected to remain a low-threat security environment where nations resolve differences peacefully, the Navy will be prepared to prevent conflict and ensure national interests are protected. In the coming decades, the Arctic Ocean will be increasingly accessible and more broadly used by Arctic and non-Arctic nations seeking the Region's abundant resources and trade routes.[68]

The administration concluded that increased traffic will potentially lead to disruptions in marine food systems as well as more accidents:

> As ice coverage in the Arctic continues to recede and shorter shipping routes become more accessible and more profitable, increased ship traffic and human activity in the region will require that the United States be more prepared to respond to emergencies in this remote region.[69]

Beyond investments in icebreaking technology that could help shore up the US ability to defend its interests in the Arctic, another policy that the US should move

---

[65] Brad Plumer, "The US Only Has Two Polar Icebreakers. That's a Problem If the Arctic Keeps Melting," *Vox*, March 30, 2015, http://www.vox.com/2015/3/30/8312473/arctic-icebreakers; Richard O'Rourke, "Coast Guard Polar Icebreaker Modernization: Background and Issues for Congress," Congressional Research Service 7-5700, Marxh 21, 2016, https://fas.org/sgp/crs/weapons/RL34391.pdf.

[66] Coral Davenport, "US Will Allow Drilling for Oil in Arctic Ocean," *The New York Times*, May 11, 2015, http://www.nytimes.com/2015/05/12/us/white-house-gives-conditional-approval-for-shell-to-drill-in-arctic.html.

[67] Busby, "Who Cares About the Weather?" 489–490. I explored these issues in the brief for the Council on Foreign Relations as well. Busby, "Climate Change and National Security: An Agenda for Action."

[68] US Navy, "US Navy Arctic Roadmap 2014–2039," 3.

[69] White House, "Findings from Select Federal Reports: The National Security Implications of a Changing Climate," 7.

forward on is ratification of the Law of the Sea Treaty. Russia pushed forward its territorial claims to the Arctic by submitting claims to the UN Commission on the Limits of the Continental Shelf. Other countries like Denmark are poised to do the same. By not being party to the Law of the Sea Treaty, the United States cannot put forward its own claims for jurisdiction of an extended continental shelf.[70] The potential loss of influence over the fate of the Arctic ought to be the final impetus for the long-delayed US ratification of the Law of the Sea Treaty. In asserting its own territorial claims, the US also needs to work with other countries on measures to discourage oil exploration in the Arctic, which would only make the climate problem worse. After having earlier authorized drilling in the Arctic, the Obama administration in October 2015 cancelled planned future lease sales.[71]

Official government statements asserting future security risks do not necessarily make them true. Some of these potential effects such as migration are arguably more speculative than others or depend on longer causal chains and perhaps less predictable human behavior. While the fingerprint of climate change on the magnitude and number of extreme weather events remains a source of debate, we already have vivid examples in Hurricane Katrina and Superstorm Sandy that underscore the risks of inaction. The potential effects of climate change on US national security extend beyond direct effects on the US homeland to the country's interests abroad. Again, it is important to examine the validity of potential threats that analysts have raised, reviewing the claims and the available evidence.

Indirect threats to the United States

Much emphasis in the climate security literature has been placed on the potential effects on US security interests overseas as a consequence of climate effects abroad. Climate change poses at least four sets of potential problems for US interests including: (1) US overseas assets including embassies and military bases, (2) violent conflict, (3) state failure, and (4) humanitarian disasters.[72] Migration, whether or not it leads to conflict, is often evoked as an independent climate security concern. Others include changes in the operating environment for the military and disruptions to strategically important raw materials and global supply chains. Of these, the connections between climate change and conflict have received the most attention, particularly by scholars.

[70] Asaf Shalev, "Russia Just Claimed a Broad Swath of the Arctic Shelf; Why Isn't the US Doing the Same?" *Arctic Newswire*, August 8, 2015, http://www.adn.com/article/20150808/russia-just-claimed-broad-swath-arctic-shelf-why-isnt-us-doing-same; Editorial Board, "Russian Arctic? A New Reason for the US to Ratify Law of the Sea," *Pittsburgh Post-Gazette*, August 6, 2015, http://www.post-gazette.com/opinion/editorials/2015/08/06/Russian-Arctic-A-new-reason-for-the-U-S-to-ratify-Law-of-the-Sea/stories/201508060025.
[71] Those sales already faced limited private sector demand in the face of low oil prices and Shell's disappointing and highly controversial drilling in summer 2015. Timothy Cama, "Obama Cancels Arctic Drilling Lease Sales," Text, *TheHill*, (October 16, 2015), http://thehill.com/policy/energy-environment/257191-obama-cancels-arctic-drilling-lease-sales.
[72] Busby, "Who Cares About the Weather?" 496.

Overseas assets and operations

The claims: In terms of US assets vulnerable to climate change, low-lying military installations such as Diego Garcia and Guam are exposed to extreme weather events.[73] This mirrors the emphasis in discussions of homeland security on vulnerable physical infrastructure and bases.

The state of knowledge: The 2014 Department of Defense Adaptation Roadmap discussed an ongoing assessment of seven thousand military installations and flagged the need to assess how "the changes in storm patterns and sea levels will impact the Department's Pacific Island installations, including their water supplies."[74] In addition, embassies located in countries vulnerable to climate change such as Bangladesh might face high physical exposure themselves, or, at the very least, be called upon to coordinate or assist humanitarian responses.[75]

The Obama administration has identified additional challenges—the effects on military operations, training and testing equipment, and provisioning and supporting military missions coming from increasing temperatures, changes in precipitation patterns, increases in the frequency or intensity of extreme weather, and rising sea levels and storm surge. The Adaptation Roadmap argued: "sea level rise may impact the execution of amphibious landings; changing temperatures and lengthened seasons could impact operation timing windows; and increased frequency of extreme weather could impact overflight possibility as well as intelligence, surveillance, and reconnaissance capability."[76] In terms of supply chains, the Obama administration highlighted the risk of "reduced or changed availability and access to food and water sources to support personnel."[77] Pending the outcome of the various infrastructure vulnerability assessments, the likely outcome is the need for investments that would enhance the resilience of facilities to climate damages through relocation, refurbishment, enhanced building codes, physical barriers, and improved emergency response measures.

Conflict and state failure

The claims: The contribution of climate change to the increased likelihood of conflict has been the central analytical focus of much academic and think tank work in the climate security space and to a lesser extent government studies. This research has focused largely on internal conflict—namely civil wars; communal conflict;

---

[73] Others have also identified these risks. CNA Corporation, "National Security and the Threat of Climate Change," https://www.cna.org/cna_files/pdf/national%20security%20and%20the%20threat%20of%20climate%20change.pdf; CNA Military Advisory Board, "National Security and the Accelerating Risks of Climate Change," Alexandria, VA: CNA Military Advisory Board, May 2014; Catherine Foley, "Military Basing and Climate Change," Washington, DC: American Security Project, November 2012.

[74] Department of Defense, "2014 Climate Change Adaptation Roadmap," 8.

[75] Busby, "Who Cares About the Weather?"

[76] Department of Defense, "2014 Climate Change Adaptation Roadmap," 4.

[77] Ibid., 7.

and protests, strikes, and riots. While there has been some limited discussion of disputes over shared aquifers and upstream-downstream tensions as a consequence of dam construction along the Nile, the Mekong, and other rivers, most work in this space is rather dismissive of the prospects for interstate conflict. This is likely a function of the decline in interstate wars[78] as well as the history of interstate cooperation over river basins and aquifers, even in highly adversarial political situations such as between Israel and Palestine.[79]

While interstate war is frequently discounted, tensions and conflict emanating from the cross-border movement of people is often evoked as a specific risk, but these risks are seen less as transnational or international conflicts and more as internal ones between migrants and their new host states and populations. Migration, particularly from low-lying island countries in the Pacific as well as Bangladesh, is often identified as a likely consequence of climate change independent of whether or not it escalates to conflict. There is extensive debate about the likely magnitude of climate-induced migration and its consequences, as in many cases the climate signal driving migration is only one of many factors.[80]

The state of knowledge: As I noted earlier, based on the challenges of teasing out the specific contribution of environmental factors to conflict, the think tank community initially used the language of "threat multiplier," "stressor," "exacerbate," and "conflict accelerant" to describe the risks posed by climate change to the increased likelihood of conflict. That language and approach to the problem has permeated policy documents. For example, in the public Congressional testimony that accompanied the classified 2008 National Intelligence Assessment, the National Intelligence Council's Tom Fingar argued:

> We assess that climate change alone is unlikely to trigger state failure in any state out to 2030, but the impacts will worsen existing problems—such as poverty, social tensions, environmental degradation, ineffectual leadership, and weak political institutions. Climate change could threaten domestic stability in some states, potentially contributing

---

[78] Steven Pinker, *The Better Angels of Our Nature: Why Violence Has Declined* (Penguin, 2012); Joshua S. Goldstein, *Winning the War on War: The Decline of Armed Conflict Worldwide* (New York: Plume, 2012).

[79] Lucia De Stefano et al., "Climate Change and the Institutional Resilience of International River Basins," *Journal of Peace Research* 49, no. 1 (January 1, 2012): 193–209, doi:10.1177/0022343311427416; Jaroslav Tir and Douglas M. Stinnett, "Weathering Climate Change: Can Institutions Mitigate International Water Conflict?" *Journal of Peace Research* 49, no. 1 (January 1, 2012): 211–225, doi:10.1177/0022343311427066; Aaron T. Wolf, "Conflict and Cooperation along International Waterways," *Water Policy* 1, no. 2 (1998): 251–265.

[80] Clionadh Raleigh, Lisa Jordan, and Idean Salehyan, "Assessing the Impact of Climate Change on Migration and Conflict," *The Social Dimensions of Climate Change*, 2008, World Bank Group, http://siteresources.worldbank.org/EXTSOCIALDEVELOPMENT/Resources/SDCCWorkingPaper_MigrationandConflict.pdf; Nils Petter Gleditsch, Ragnhild Nordås, and Idean Salehyan, "Climate Change and Conflict: The Migration Link," *Coping with Crisis: Working Paper Series*, 2007, https://www.ipinst.org/2007/05/climate-change-and-conflict-the-migration-link; Idean Salehyan and Kristian Skrede Gleditsch, "Refugees and the Spread of Civil War," *International Organization* 60, no. 2 (2006): 335–366.

to intra- or, less likely, interstate conflict, particularly over access to increasingly scarce water resources.[81]

In its 2012 successor report on water, the NIC and the Office of the Director of National Intelligence emphasized the near-term risks from too much and too little water and how this would translate into problems of food and energy production for particular places of interest to the United States in North Africa, the Middle East, and South Asia:

> During the next ten years, many countries important to the United States will experience water problems—shortages, poor water quality, or floods—that will risk instability and state failure, increase regional tensions, and distract them from working with the United States on important US policy objectives.[82]

The Navy's 2009 climate roadmap made a similar case: "Economically unstable regions will be more vulnerable to the effects of climate change, and climate change will be one of several factors that may increase instability."[83] Policy documents like the 2010 QDR evade the challenge of establishing causality by saying that climate change on its own is not likely to cause conflict, but in concert with other factors will increase, magnify, or accelerate the risk.[84]

In its 2011 report, the Defense Science Board also exercised caution in its statements attributing causality to climate effects, focusing on the "indirect effects" on conflict in countries with low state capacity, where climate stresses are likely to be an "an exacerbating factor for failure to meet basic human ends and for social conflict, rather than the root cause."[85] The 2014 QDR adopted the language of "threat multiplier" and sought to identify the potential pathways between physical effects of climate hazards and conflict emergence from the effects on water and food to local scarcities and competition for resources.[86]

While the policy community is largely content with this formulation of the problem, the academic community has plowed ahead to assess whether the likely

---

[81] Fingar, "Testimony to the House Permanent Select Committee on Intelligence House Select Committee on Energy Independence and Global Warming," 4–5.

[82] Office of the Director of National Intelligence, "Global Water Security: Intelligence Community Assessment," ii.

[83] Task Force Climate Change/Oceanographer of the Navy, "Climate Change Roadmap," 5.

[84] Department of Defense, "Quadrennial Defense Review Report 2010," 85. The 2010 QDR argued: "Climate change will contribute to food and water scarcity, will increase the spread of disease, and may spur or exacerbate mass migration. While climate change alone does not cause conflict, it may act as an accelerant of instability or conflict, placing a burden to respond on civilian institutions and militaries around the world." For its part, the 2010 National Security Strategy was more strident in tone than the other documents, linking climate change to "conflicts over refugees and resources." White House, "National Security Strategy 2010," 47.

[85] Defense Science Board, "Report of the Defense Science Board Task Force on Trends and Implications of Climate Change for National and International Security," United States Defense Science Board, 2011.

[86] Department of Defense, "Quadrennial Defense Review 2014," 8.

future consequences of climate change (extreme temperatures, rainfall volatility, droughts, extreme weather events, etc.) historically have been correlated with the increased likelihood of different forms of conflict. That peer-reviewed literature has somewhat ambiguous and conflicting findings. In their review of the scholarly literature on the connections between climate and conflict, a 2013 National Academy of Sciences study stressed the nuanced nature of the connections, emphasizing that climate change together with other "socioeconomic and political conditions" can lead to social and political stresses and concomitant security risks.[87] The 2014 IPCC Fifth Assessment echoed this conclusion, focusing on "a need for theories and data that explain the processes that lead from changes in climate to violence, including on the institutions that help avoid violent outcomes."[88]

Most of the new work on climate and conflict is quantitative statistical research that seeks to test the direct relationship between a climate variable of interest (such as rainfall scarcity) and conflict onset (such as civil wars). Many take Africa as their specific region of focus. Initially, studies focused on national level analyses and found promising results that suggested rainfall volatility in particular might be an important trigger for conflict.[89] Improvements in data made disaggregated subnational analysis increasingly possible. Studies found different effects for different kinds of climate-related phenomena. Some studies found no association between drought and civil wars in Africa.[90] Others found evidence that undermined the nascent theory that scarcity was driving conflict. Rather, it appeared that abundance might be a more potent mechanism triggering certain forms of conflict as groups had more reason to clash in time of plenty. Indeed, better rains might give groups, particularly raiding parties engaged in communal conflict, more forage cover to conceal attacks.[91]

---

[87] Steinbruner, Stern, and Husbands, *Climate and Social Stress: Implications for Security Analysis*, 134.

[88] Adger et al., "Climate Change 2014: Impacts, Adaptation, and Vulnerability. Part A: Global and Sectoral Aspects. Contribution of Working Group II to the Fifth Assessment Report of the Intergovernmental Panel on Climate Change." For similar and even more strident declarations about the state of the field, see Gleditsch, "Whither the Weather?"; Idean Salehyan, "Climate Change and Conflict: Making Sense of Disparate Findings," *Political Geography, Special Issue: Climate Change and Conflict*, 43 (November 2014): 1–5, doi:10.1016/j.polgeo.2014.10.004; Idean Salehyan, "From Climate Change to Conflict? No Consensus Yet," *Journal of Peace Research* 45, no. 3 (2008): 315–332.

[89] Marc A. Levy et al., "Freshwater Availability Anomalies and Outbreak of Internal War: Results from a Global Spatial Time Series Analysis," June 2005, http://www.ciesin.org/pdf/waterconflict.pdf; Cullen S. Hendrix and Sarah M. Glaser, "Trends and Triggers: Climate Change and Civil Conflict in Sub-Saharan Africa," *Political Geography* 26, no. 6 (2007): 695–715.

[90] Ole Magnus Theisen, Helge Holtermann, and Halvard Buhaug, "Climate Wars? Assessing the Claim That Drought Breeds Conflict," *International Security* 36, no. 3 (January 2012): 79–106.

[91] Cullen S. Hendrix and Idean Salehyan, "Climate Change, Rainfall, and Social Conflict in Africa," *Journal of Peace Research* 49, no. 1 (January 2012): 35–50; Patrick Meier, Doug Bond, and Joe Bond, "Environmental Influences on Pastoral Conflict in the Horn of Africa," *Political Geography* 26, no. 6 (August 2007): 716–35; Clionadh Raleigh and Dominic Kniveton, "Come Rain or Shine: An Analysis of Conflict and Climate Variability in East Africa," *Journal of Peace Research* 49, no. 1 (January 1, 2012): 51–64.

Despite these findings, some scholars made broad claims of a causal connection between climate impacts and violence. For example, a 2009 Miguel paper found a strong correlation between temperature and civil war onset and concluded that for every one-degree increase in Celsius, there was a 4.5 percent increase in the incidence of violent conflict. Using climate projections, Miguel estimated that Africa would experience a fifty-four percent increase in civil conflict by 2030 and nearly 400,000 additional battle deaths based on average conflict deaths.[92] Those claims were rejected by Halvard Buhaug, who suggested the results did not hold up when one included additional data or used alternative model specifications.[93]

A follow-on meta-analysis by Solomon Hsiang and coauthors bundled a variety of climate effects (temperature increases, positive deviations in rainfall, negative deviations in rainfall) and sought to examine the average effect on violence across sixty different studies. They examined both "personal violence" (which included studies of baseball pitchers beaning more batters on hot days) as well as "intergroup" violence (which included studies of state collapse, civil wars, and other measures). Their provocative claim in *Science* was that: "For each one standard deviation change in climate toward warmer temperatures or more extreme rainfall, median estimates indicate that the frequency of interpersonal violence rises four percent and the frequency of intergroup conflict rises fourteen percent."[94]

This particular study came under criticism again from Halvard Buhaug and others on methodological grounds that resulted in a series of point-counterpoint arguments about model specification and other arcana.[95] The Hsiang et al. piece included studies of ancient Egypt and fifteenth-century China, whose relevance to the contemporary period is questionable. In addition, in the meta-analysis, the authors combined a number of different climate phenomena together to try to establish some average effects across studies at a time when the field was increasingly moving to try to establish differentiated causal pathways between specific climate phenomena (such as too much rain) and specific categories of conflict outcomes (such as increases in communal violence). On some level, this meta-analysis resembles early debates of the "democratic peace," the empirical finding that democracies almost never go to war with each other, which was likened to a finding in need of a theory.

---

[92] Burke et al., "Warming Increases the Risk of Civil War in Africa."

[93] Halvard Buhaug, "Climate Not to Blame for Africa's Civil Wars," *Proceedings of the National Academy of Sciences* 107, no. 38 (2010): 16477–16482. I joined Buhaug on the initial methodological critique of the *Science* article.

[94] Hsiang, Burke, and Miguel, "Quantifying the Influence of Climate on Human Conflict." An earlier study looked at the effects of El Niño and La Niña events on conflict onset. Solomon M. Hsiang, Kyle C. Meng, and Mark A. Cane, "Civil Conflicts Are Associated with the Global Climate," *Nature* 476, no. 7361 (print 2011): 438–441, doi:10.1038/nature10311.

[95] H. Buhaug et al., "One Effect to Rule Them All? A Comment on Climate and Conflict," *Climatic Change* 127, no. 3 (October 27, 2014): 391–397, doi:10.1007/s10584-014-1266-1; Solomon M. Hsiang and K. C. Meng, "Reconciling Disagreement over Climate-Conflict Results in Africa," *Proceedings of the National Academy of Sciences* 111, no. 6 (February 11, 2014): 2100–2103, doi:10.1073/pnas.1316006111; Halvard Buhaug, "Concealing Agreements over Climate–Conflict Results," *Proceedings of the National Academy of Sciences* 111, no. 6 (February 11, 2014): E636–E636, doi:10.1073/pnas.1323773111.

The emergent findings in the climate security literature, to the extent they are robust, still lack clear causal arguments that link climate hazards and security outcomes.[96] As I mentioned earlier, most of the academic studies have tested direct relationships between a physical hazard and conflict, rather than indirect pathways through plausible mechanisms such as economic growth or food prices.[97] As the IPCC chapter on human security noted, climate hazards are correlated with effects that are known correlates of conflict: "Though there is little agreement about causality, there is robust evidence that shows that low per capita incomes, economic contraction, and inconsistent state institutions are associated with the incidence of civil wars. These factors are sensitive to climate change."[98]

Some policymakers are ready to accept that climate change will be a conflict accelerant in the absence of scientific guidance on the specific connections. However, without clarity of the conditions under which climate hazards might lead to conflict, it is impossible to identify nodes of leverage by which one might intervene to make conflict less likely.

A number of questions still beg answers: Under what climatic or weather conditions do people fight? When it is hot? If so, why? Do they become more aggressive in the heat? How hot is too hot? Do people fight when it is wet? Does wetness increase forage and pasture, leading to more abundant valuable resources that trigger competition? Does rainfall scarcity lead to conflict by lowering the opportunity costs of fighting? Does rainfall scarcity affect conflict patterns through agricultural production or economic growth? Do extreme weather events trigger conflict resolution or escalation? Are certain kinds of states more subject to these kinds of problems than others? Without better understanding of the configurations of factors that together yield violence, policymakers could invest in efforts to reduce imaginary or misplaced vulnerabilities for the wrong threats and places.

This challenge is made all the more difficult by the fact that the historic data testing correlations between climate phenomena and conflict may be a poor guide to future patterns. The geographic distribution and intensity of weather events (of rainfall, temperature, etc.) may not resemble past patterns, making causal inference from history a problematic basis for planning for the future.[99] In terms of policy, this is an area where greater research on the causal pathways linking climate hazards to

[96] Joshua Busby, "Why Do Climate Changes Lead to Conflict? Provocative New Study Leaves Questions," *New Security Beat*, September 12, 2013, http://www.newsecuritybeat.org/2013/09/climate-lead-conflict-provocative-study-leaves-questions.

[97] Exceptions include: Vally Koubi et al., "Climate Variability, Economic Growth, and Civil Conflict," *Journal of Peace Research* 49, no. 1 (January 1, 2012): 113–127, doi:10.1177/0022343311427173; Todd Graham Smith, "Feeding Unrest Disentangling the Causal Relationship between Food Price Shocks and Sociopolitical Conflict in Urban Africa," *Journal of Peace Research* 51, no. 6 (November 1, 2014): 679–695, doi:10.1177/0022343314543722.

[98] Adger et al., "Climate Change 2014: Impacts, Adaptation, and Vulnerability. Part A: Global and Sectoral Aspects." Contribution of Working Group II to the Fifth Assessment Report of the Intergovernmental Panel on Climate Change. IPCC, 2014.

[99] Joshua W. Busby et al., "Of Climate Change and Crystal Balls: The Future Consequences of Climate Change in Africa," *Air & Space Power Journal Africa and Francophonie*, no. 3 (2012): 4–44, http://www.airpower.maxwell.af.mil/apjinternational/apj-af/2012/2012-3/eng/2012_3_05_Busby.pdf.

conflict outcomes could help identify the various factors that conjoin to make conflict onset more likely. With more robust understanding, it may be possible to identify indicators of early warning as well as investments that might mitigate conflict potential. Absent this improved comprehension of the conditions under which climate hazards trigger different forms of conflict, policymakers may be hard-pressed to identify appropriate interventions.

Humanitarian emergencies and natural disasters

The claims: With the causal connection between climate outcomes and conflict difficult to disentangle, perhaps more proximate security threats of climate change for US national security are the effects of climate change yielding more humanitarian emergencies from natural disasters, leading to more demands for US military mobilization for humanitarian assistance.[100]

The state of knowledge: While scientists continue to dispute whether or not climate change will yield more numerous or intense cyclones and other extreme weather events,[101] the world has ample evidence of climate-related hazards causing massive dislocations requiring emergency response from the international community, from Typhoon Haiyan in the Philippines in 2013; to the famine that afflicted Somalia in 2011; to the floods that displaced millions in Pakistan in 2010; to Cyclone Nargis that killed thousands in Myanmar in 2005.

In these cases, the United States government was frequently called upon (or offered) to provide lift support, relief, and logistics. For example, after Haiyan, 9500 military personnel helped respond to the crisis, with delivery of 750,000 pounds of relief supplies and the airlift of almost 6,000 survivors from the affected city of Tacloban.[102] In response to the 2010 floods that affected some twenty million people in Pakistan, the United States delivered approximately $390 million in aid and twenty million pounds of relief supplies.[103] After both the Somalia and

---

[100] Busby, "Climate Change and National Security: An Agenda for Action"; Busby, "Who Cares About the Weather?"; Purvis and Busby, "The Security Implications of Climate Change for the UN System"; Joshua W. Busby et al., "Locating Climate Insecurity: Where Are the Most Vulnerable Places in Africa?," in *Climate Change, Human Security and Violent Conflict*, Jurgen Scheffran et al. eds., Hexagon Series on Human and Environmental Security and Peace 8 (New York: Springer: 2012), pp. 463–512; Joshua W. Busby et al., "Climate Change and Insecurity: Mapping Vulnerability in Africa," *International Security* 37, no. 4 (2013): 132–172; Joshua W. Busby, Todd G. Smith, and Nisha Krishnan, "Climate Security Vulnerability in Africa Mapping 3.0," in "Special Issue: Climate Change and Conflict," ed. Idean Salehyan, special issue, *Political Geography* 43 (November 2014): 51–67, doi:10.1016/j.polgeo.2014.10.005.

[101] IPCC, "Managing the Risks of Extreme Events and Disasters to Advance Climate Change Adaptation (SREX)."

[102] White House, "FACT SHEET: US Response to Typhoon Haiyan," Whitehouse.gov, November 19, 2013, https://www.whitehouse.gov/the-press-office/2013/11/19/fact-sheet-us-response-typhoon-haiyan.

[103] American Forces Press Service, "Military Reaches Pakistan Flood Relief Milestone," Defense Media Activity, October 28, 2010, https://www.dvidshub.net/news/59006/military-reaches-pakistan-flood-relief-milestone#.Vvfw5-IrIQ8.

Myanmar disasters, the international community had difficulty delivering aid supplies. In the case of the 2011 Somalia famine, the Islamist al Shabaab militia impeded relief supplies, resulting in the excess deaths of some 250,000 people.[104] Similarly, in Myanmar, offers by the United States to provide relief, including landing 4,000 US Marines to deliver aid,[105] were partially rebuffed. Ultimately, 140,000 people were estimated to have died.[106]

More broadly, between FY 2000 and FY 2009, the US government spent some $25.3 billion on disaster response globally (in 2009 inflation-adjusted dollars). That includes funding for complex emergencies, particularly for the conflict in Darfur (which some attribute to resource conflicts between herders and grazers as a result of drought conditions), although aid for explicitly climate-related disasters was about one out of ten of the overall total.[107]

Although the contribution of anthropogenic climate change to those particular events is debatable, they remind us of the terrible power of nature. Some of the places affected are locations of strategic interest to the United States. And, while the literature on whether disasters contribute to conflict remains contested,[108] the US government and the military in particular is increasingly called upon to play a supporting role in major humanitarian emergencies.

While academics have been slow to recognize this dynamic, the US government has integrated this concern centrally into its planning documents with the 2010

[104] Francesco Checchi and W. Courtland Robinson, "Mortality among Populations of Southern and Central Somalia Affected by Severe Food Insecurity and Famine during 2010-2012" (FAO and FEWS NET, 2013), http://reliefweb.int/sites/reliefweb.int/files/resources/Somalia_Mortality_Estimates_Final_Report_1May2013.pdf.

[105] Amy Kazmin and Colum Lynch, "American Admiral Takes Plea To Burma," *The Washington Post*, May 13, 2008, http://www.washingtonpost.com/wp-dyn/content/article/2008/05/12/AR2008051200158.html.

[106] Ian MacKinnon, "Burmese Regime Deliberately Blocked International Aid to Cyclone Victims, Report Says," *The Guardian*, February 27, 2009, accessed June 12, 2015, http://www.theguardian.com/world/2009/feb/27/regime-blocked-aid-to-burma-cyclone-victims.

[107] USAID-OFDA, "USAID-OFDA and USG Disaster Response FY 2000-2009", Washington, DC: USAID, 2010; Busby et al., "Climate Change and Insecurity: Mapping Vulnerability in Africa." Exclusively climate-related disasters accounted for about twelve percent of the Office of Foreign Disaster Assistance's total (excluding complex emergencies but including floods, droughts, fires, winter emergencies, typhoons, and food security).

[108] Philip Nel and Marjolein Righarts, "Natural Disasters and the Risk of Violent Civil Conflict," *International Studies Quarterly* 52, no. 1 (2008): 159–185; Dawn Brancati, "Political Aftershocks: The Impact of Earthquakes on Intrastate Conflict," *The Journal of Conflict Resolution* 51, no. 5 (2007): 715–743; Rune T Slettebak, "Don't Blame the Weather! Climate-Related Natural Disasters and Civil Conflict," *Journal of Peace Research* 49, no. 1 (January 2012): 163–176, doi:10.1177/0022343311425693; Drago Bergholt and Päivi Lujala, "Climate-Related Natural Disasters, Economic Growth, and Armed Civil Conflict," *Journal of Peace Research* 49, no. 1 (January 2012): 147–162, doi:10.1177/0022343311426167; Alastair Smith and Alejandro Quiroz Flores, "Disaster Politics," *Foreign Affairs*, July 15, 2010, http://www.foreignaffairs.com/articles/66494/alastair-smith-and-alejandro-quiroz-flores/disaster-politics; Alejandro Quiroz Flores and Alastair Smith, "Leader Survival and Natural Disasters," *British Journal of Political Science* 43, no. 4 (October 2013): 821–843.

QDR and the 2014 Pentagon Adaptation, both recognizing that extreme weather events at home and abroad will lead to increased demands for humanitarian assistance.[109] For its part, the 2013 National Academy of Sciences report concluded that these complex emergencies are likely to become more frequent and "produce consequences that exceed the capacity of the affected societies or global systems to manage and that have global security implications serious enough to compel international response."[110] As the 2008 NIC report noted, the implications of increased demands of disaster response could be potential strains on US capacity, readiness, and strategic depth for combat operations.[111]

Beyond these concerns, leaders have periodically invoked the wider strategic implications of disaster relief for public diplomacy. After the 2004 Asian tsunami, the 2006 earthquake in Pakistan, and the 2010 Pakistani floods, the United States saw opportunities for improving its image in the region. However, a 2012 Pew study found that Indonesian attitudes toward the United States improved slightly after the 2004 tsunami but deteriorated thereafter and only returned to pre-Iraq War levels when Barack Obama was elected president. Pakistani public opinion deteriorated further despite America's flood relief.[112]

The United States could reject or scale back such global responsibilities if it were to find its military too stretched in a world of many severe humanitarian emergences. The experience in South Asia suggests that there is no automatic or durable public favorability boost from relief efforts, but it is not clear if failure to respond to a humanitarian emergency would have *no* effect on the country's international reputation. States may not get a lot of credit or permanent boosts in international goodwill from a single act of altruism or enlightened self-interest, but they potentially face international opprobrium for failure to act (or act with sufficient vigor, as China experienced in response to its lackluster support for efforts to suppress the Ebola virus in West Africa).[113] The United States, as the architect of the liberal international order, would potentially face greater international condemnation than other countries if it decided that it had to scale back its disaster response. As a matter of policy, the United States should minimally identify the places most likely to be severely affected by such climate-related humanitarian disasters through vulnerability assessments. Beyond this, the United States should use such assessments to pre-position humanitarian supplies for likely hot spots of vulnerability and support civilian efforts by local actors to shore up resilience.

[109] Department of Defense, "Quadrennial Defense Review Report 2010"; Department of Defense, "2014 Climate Change Adaptation Roadmap."

[110] Steinbruner, Stern, and Husbands, *Climate and Social Stress*, 136.

[111] Fingar, "Testimony to the House Permanent Select Committee on Intelligence House Select Committee on Energy Independence and Global Warming," 16.

[112] Richard Wike, "Does Humanitarian Aid Improve America's Image?" *Pew Research Center's Global Attitudes Project*, March 6, 2015, accessed June 12, 2015, http://www.pewglobal.org/2012/03/06/does-humanitarian-aid-improve-americas-image.

[113] Chris Liens, "China's Evolving Ebola Response: Recognizing the Cost of Inaction," *Atlantic Council*, November 10, 2014, http://www.atlanticcouncil.org/blogs/new-atlanticist/china-s-evolving-ebola-response-recognizing-the-cost-of-inaction.

Geostrategic implications

The previous observation raises a third dimension where actions or inactions on climate change could have wider strategic significance for the United States. I address the reputational consequences of climate diplomacy before turning to the potential strategic considerations of policies that countries might pursue to either mitigate climate change or adapt to its consequences such as geoengineering, territorial claims, land concessions in other countries, border tax adjustments, divestment campaigns and bans on international finance for carbon-intensive energy sources, and possibly even more coercive measures to keep fossil fuels in the ground.

Climate diplomacy and reputation

The claims: The elevation of climate change to the sphere of higher if not high politics potentially affects US standing in the world and pursuit of its national interests. While the Bush administration was able to endure nearly a decade of international opprobrium for its hostility to action on climate change, failure in the future could engender negative reputational consequences for the United States.

The state of knowledge: What significance does negative international standing have on the US power position in the world, if at all? States that are powerful, determined, and view acquiescence to international opinion as costly can endure international disdain and even sanctions (witness Vladimir Putin in Russia). Normative pressure and shame on their own are weak signals. Even when accompanied by material punishment, the costs may ultimately be modest since punishment is costly.[114] However, states with bad reputations face higher transactions costs of achieving cooperative outcomes on issues they care about.[115]

George W. Bush was able to pursue the Iraq War despite the hostility of traditional European allies. A future US administration that takes a hard line on climate policy, as the Bush administration did, may raise the costs of securing cooperative agreements with others on defense, trade, etc. It is an interesting counterfactual to ask if the Bush administration been less obstructionist on climate and other multilateral initiatives, might it have had an easier time leveraging the support of its European allies for the war effort in Iraq, or at least the rebuilding phase?

We will never know, but as concerns about climate change increase and expectations of progress rise, international processes like the climate negotiations in Copenhagen in 2009 and in Paris in 2015 create opportunities for politicians to either burnish or damage their international standing with repercussions for their room for maneuver at home.

---

[114] Joshua Busby, "The Hardest Problem in the World: Leadership in the Climate Regime," in *The Dispensable Hegemon: Explaining Contemporary International Leadership and Cooperation*, Stefan Brem and Kendall Stiles eds. (London: Routledge, 2008), pp. 73–104; Joshua W. Busby and Kelly M. Greenhill, "Ain't That a Shame: Hypocrisy, Punishment, and Weak Actor Influence in International Politics," in *The Politics of Leverage in International Relations: Name, Shame, and Sanction*, Richard Friman ed. (New York: Palgrave Macmillan, 2015), pp. 105–122.

[115] Michael Tomz, *Reputation and International Cooperation: Sovereign Debt across Three Centuries* (Princeton, NJ: Princeton University Press, 2007).

Thus when it appeared that the Copenhagen climate negotiations would fail to reach an agreement or an agreement that met advocates' expectations, the Obama Administration sought to deflect blame for the outcome on China. The US delegation suggested that the United States was prepared to leverage $100 billion in public and private money to assist developing countries, but China was blocking a final agreement, thus pitting the rest of the developing world against China.[116] As China's carbon dioxide emissions now dwarf those of the United States (some twenty-eight percent of the global total for China in 2013 compared to fourteen percent for the United States), that strategy of blame defection may increasingly work, but will not solve the problem.

At the same time, it is not as if the United States can avoid blame. It is still the second largest emitter, and the country's cumulative emissions between 1870 and 2013 lead the world at twenty-six percent. Countries will still be prepared to label the United States a climate scofflaw, all the more so because its per capita emissions exceed much of the rest of the world by orders of magnitude. Moreover, the United States contribution to current emissions rises still further if one includes the carbon content of imported products from countries such as China.[117]

From a strategic perspective, countries, the United States included, will not do things that are very costly for them even if highly desirable by other states, unless other states possess tremendous coercive power. That said, countries facing high climate exposure will increasingly look for venues to remind the world of their plight, as the Philippines did after Typhoon Haiyan at the 2013 climate negotiations. Even if the science of event attribution is not settled, vulnerable countries will blame climate change for disasters and in turn implicate countries responsible for the problem.

The United States and China are going to be the primary recipients of that finger-pointing. Climate change presents a curious problem for the two countries, especially given the power transition process that is currently underway with the United States experiencing relative decline and China a rapid ascent. We know from history that such moments are especially dangerous times, as fading hegemons face revisionist challengers seeking to remake the world in their image. Yet that logic of relative gains and preoccupation with narrow national self-interest runs against the wider liberal logic of mutual gains from trade.[118]

[116] Josh Busby, "China and Climate Change: A Strategy for US Engagement," *Resources for the Future*, 2010, http://www.rff.org/research/publications/china-and-climate-change-strategy-us-engagement; Joshua Busby, "After Copenhagen: Climate Governance and the Road Ahead," *Council on Foreign Relations Press*, August 2010, http://www.cfr.org/publication/22726/after_copenhagen.html.

[117] Global Carbon Project, "Global Carbon Budget 2014," *Global Carbon Project*, 2014, http://www.globalcarbonproject.org/carbonbudget/archive/2014/GCP_budget_2014_lowres_v1.02.pdf.

[118] Jacek Kugler, "The Asian Ascent: Opportunity for Peace or Precondition for War?" *International Studies Perspectives* 7, no. 1 (February 1, 2006): 36–42, doi:10.1111/j.1528-3577.2006.00228.x; Ronald L. Tammen et al., *Power Transitions: Strategies For the 21st Century* (New York: Seven Bridges Press, 2000).

Moreover, climate protection is a global public good; neither the United States nor China, despite being the largest emitters, can resolve the problem on their own. From the standpoint of self-protection against global climate change, states have strong incentives to band with coalitions of the relevant (i.e., the major emitters) to stave off suboptimal outcomes for everyone. Despite its relative decline, the United States is, as Bruce Jones notes, "the largest minority shareholder" in the international order, and, as such, still possesses sufficient capability to lead by example and shepherd consolidation of a liberal international order in which China is embedded.[119]

As a consequence, even as there is inevitable friction over China's ambitions in the South China Sea, the United States and China possess shared goals and vulnerabilities because of economic interdependence and exposure to climate hazards. In this context, the countries need to rise above their sources of discord and enter into a mature relationship of quasi-rivalry on some dimensions of policy and cooperation on others. Even in the climate space, the United States may have to engage in technical cooperation on emissions monitoring, but at the same time prepare for different ambitions regarding climate change by exploring coercive instruments such as border tax adjustments to induce greater Chinese engagement.[120]

There are positive signs that the United States and China are heeding this advice. In November 2014, China and the United States reached a potentially historic agreement on greenhouse gas emissions. China for the first time pledged to peak its greenhouse gas emissions by around 2030 and to increase the share of non-fossil energy (nuclear and renewables) to twenty percent by that same year. The United States, for its part, extended its target to reduce greenhouse gas emissions by twenty-six to twenty-eight percent below 2005 levels. This agreement put pressure on other fast-developing countries such as India to play a constructive role going into the 2015 Paris climate talks where a new kind of climate agreement based on country pledges of action was set to be negotiated.[121]

That dynamic of somewhat competitive and virtuous promise-making over climate change with China, what Levy called tote-board diplomacy, may be a useful

[119] Bruce Jones, "The Changing Balance of Global Influence and US Strategy," Brookings Institution, Foreign Policy Series 25, March 2011, http://www.brookings.edu/research/papers/2011/03/global-order-jones.

[120] Joshua Busby and Sarang Shidore, "How The United States Can Reinforce Chinese Action on Climate Change" (Chicago: Paulson Institute, 2015), paulsoninstitute.org/think-tank/2015/07/20/how-the-united-states-can-reinforce-chinese-action-on-climate-change; Joshua Busby, "A Green Giant? Inconsistency and American Environmental Diplomacy," in America, China, and the Struggle for World Order, G. John Ikenberry, Wang Jisi, and Zhu Feng eds. (New York: Palgrave Macmillan, 2015), 245–274.

[121] David Nakamura and Steven Mufson, "China, US Agree to Limit Greenhouse Gases," Washington Post, November 12, 2014, http://www.washingtonpost.com/business/economy/china-us-agree-to-limit-greenhouse-gases/2014/11/11/9c768504-69e6-11e4-9fb4-a622dae742a2_story.html; Joshua Busby, "Historic Bilateral Climate Agreement Between the US and China," Duck Of Minerva, November 11, 2014, http://duckofminerva.com/2014/11/historic-bilateral-climate-agreement-between-the-us-and-china.html.

one if ultimately followed up by action.[122] This approach might need to extend beyond the mitigation (emissions reduction) agenda to support for adaptation (preparing for climate change), particularly in East Asia. For example, outside of Guam, small island countries in the Pacific may not be all that consequential for US national security or the world. That said, the United States will have stronger incentives to react to claims from larger, more populated countries in the region like Indonesia and the Philippines. Those countries have historical and ongoing value to the United States, in terms of concerns about Islamist radicalization, bases, and Chinese territorial claims in the South China Sea. Densely populated countries in South and Southeast Asia may be valuable partners on other issues of importance to the United States, and if they come to believe that their future security depends on climate adaptation and mitigation efforts, then the United States may have compelling reasons to do more.

Beyond its own actions to mitigate its own greenhouse gas emissions, the United States should also put a high priority on overcoming its own domestic impasse over providing climate finance. In 2014, the Obama administration committed three billion dollars to the Green Climate Fund over four years, but found its contributions snared in partisan politicization over the budget.[123] Moreover, at the 2009 Copenhagen meeting, the Obama Administration created political space for a new bottoms-up process of country commitments on climate change based on the promise to leverage by 2020 $100 billion annually in public and private money to address climate change in the developing world. Failure to make good on that commitment would undermine the credibility of the US response but also limit the international community's ability to invest in climate and conflict management.

Unilateral climate mitigation and adaptation

The claims: From the perspective of system and order maintenance, the United States also risks damaging the legitimacy of international, rule-based processes if the climate arena, like other domains, increasingly is seen as irrelevant and ineffectual. If that outcome of "ossified" zombie politics returns to the climate arena,[124] individual countries or groups of countries may take matters in to their hands, by seeking to shore up their own position through resource and territorial claims, acquisition of access rights to land in other countries, and through dam-building to the detriment of downstream users.

The state of knowledge: Though somewhat far-fetched, people are beginning to worry about how legal regimes could regulate how countries engage in

---

[122] Marc A. Levy, "European Acid Rain: The Power of Tote-Board Diplomacy," in *Institutions for the Earth: Sources of Effective International Environmental Protection*, Peter M. Haas, Robert O. Keohane, and Marc A. Levy eds. (Cambridge, MA: MIT Press, 1993), pp. 75–132.

[123] Sophie Yeo, "Obama Pledges $500m for Green Climate Fund in 2016 Budget," *Climate Home News*, March 2, 2015, http://www.climatechangenews.com/2015/02/02/obama-pledges-500m-for-green-climate-fund-in-2016-budget.

[124] Joanna Depledge, "The Opposite of Learning: Ossification in the Climate Change Regime," *Global Environmental Politics* 6, no. 1 (2006): 1–22.

geoengineering, such as efforts to alter the atmosphere to insulate countries from the effects of climate change. If left as an ungoverned free-for-all, such schemes might be highly risky and lead to unanticipated and catastrophic global consequences, including countermeasures by states trying to stop others' geoengineering projects.[125] Other policy responses to climate change, such as foreign land acquisitions to shore up domestic food security, may become contested as "land grabs."[126] In this context, the United States has an interest in steering these unilateral or small-group impulses in a constructive direction as it has on hydrofluorocarbons (HFCs)—potent contributors to the greenhouse effect—through the Climate and Clean Air Coalition.[127] While some of these various unilateral initiatives remain on the horizon, the United States has an interest in establishing multilateral codes of conduct and dialogue to ensure that states do not seek to shore up their own protection with disastrous consequences for others.

CONCLUSION: US POLICIES, RISK ASSESSMENT, AND SUSTAINABLE SECURITY

The starting premise of this volume when we began our collective deliberations was based on a sense of US overextension and diminished national capacity. Since then, the country's economic recovery from the 2008 financial crisis and newfound domestic energy supplies may have eased some of the exigency and urgency of a retrenchment agenda. At the same time, the rise and specter of ISIS in Syria and Iraq has frightened the American public, providing them with renewed appetite to engage internationally. Moreover, as the introduction to this volume noted, even if one acknowledges the need for selective engagement, that is distinct from counseling isolation and withdrawal from the international scene. What that means, however, is that climate change, arguably a more long-run threat than many contemporary emergencies, has to compete for attention with other pressing concerns. In this crowded landscape with increased competition for resources, the justification for acting now to combat climate change is to minimize later costs that would be considerably more expensive, highly undesirable, and/or irreversible.[128]

The previous sections included a range of policies that the United States should pursue to address specific threats to the homeland, its overseas interests, and wider

---

[125] David Victor et al., "The Truth About Geoengineering," *Foreign Affairs*, March 27, 2013, https://www.foreignaffairs.com/articles/global-commons/2013-03-27/truth-about-geoengineering.

[126] David Smith, "The Food Rush: Rising Demand in China and West Spark African Land Grab," *The Guardian*, July 3, 2009, http://www.theguardian.com/environment/2009/jul/03/africa-land-grab; Michael Kugelman, "The Global Farmland Rush," *The New York Times*, February 5, 2013, http://www.nytimes.com/2013/02/06/opinion/the-global-farmland-rush.html.

[127] The US does not always steer policy in a constructive direction. From a climate perspective, the Obama administration's imposition of a tax on Chinese solar cells in late 2014, which was ruled illegal by the WTO, may not have been all that productive. John Upton, "US Tariffs on Chinese Solar Panels Break Trade Rules, WTO Says," *Grist*, July 14, 2014, http://grist.org/news/u-s-tariffs-on-chinese-solar-panels-break-trade-rules-wto-says.

[128] Trevor Houser et al., *Economic Risks of Climate Change: An American Prospectus* (New York: Columbia University Press, 2015).

geostrategic position. Beyond this, there is a wider philosophy of governance, namely risk management, which ought to infuse US approaches to climate, much as it already does for defense establishment and the corporate sector.

Those concerned about climate change increasingly have justified action by evoking the language of managing risk. While many climate impacts are known and highly likely, some of the most severe potential impacts of climate change such as melting permafrost, changes to the Gulf Stream, or more catastrophic sea-level rise are likened to the threat of nuclear war during the Cold War, presenting so-called "tail risks" of low probability but very high impact.[129] A challenge is that some of these most extreme consequences are highly uncertain, but may become more likely at higher temperatures and concentrations of greenhouse gases. Some kinds of climate events have an irregularly high likelihood of catastrophic consequences, referred to as "fat tails" of the probability distribution. Others reference similar kinds of high impact but are hard-to-predict "black swan" events.[130] Under such circumstances, a risk management perspective would invest in contingency plans to ensure that the worst consequences do not come to pass.[131]

Preparing for contingencies and investing in risk management are familiar practices for national security officials. During the Cold War, the United States invested vast amounts of money and intellectual energy to ensure that the (generally) low probability but high consequence risk of a nuclear exchange with the Soviet Union did not come to pass. Similarly, in the contemporary era, the US military has to prepare for possible contingencies of war-fighting in multiple theaters and the remote possibility of military conflict with a rising China over flashpoints such as the South China Sea. In addition to regional deployment of troops through the Pacific Fleet, the US military also engages in regular military exercises with allies.[132]

One of the challenges of this "fat tail" problem is that it becomes difficult to anticipate how much preparation is enough. Traditional cost-benefit analysis based on expected outcomes may lead us to be insufficiently prepared for the Hurricane

[129] Risky Business Project, "Risky Business: The Economic Risks of Climate Change in the United States," 2014, 9, http://riskybusiness.org/site/assets/uploads/2015/09/RiskyBusiness_ Report_WEB_09_08_14.pdf; Nick Mabey et al., "Degrees of Risk: Defining a Risk Management Framework for Climate Security," E3G, 2011, http://www.e3g.org/images/uploads/Degrees_ of_Risk_Defining_a_Risk_Management_Framework_for_Climate_Security_Executive_ Summary.pdf.

[130] Nassim Nicholas Taleb, *The Black Swan: Second Edition: The Impact of the Highly Improbable* (New York: Random House Trade Paperbacks, 2010).

[131] Gernot Wagner and Martin L. Weitzman, *Climate Shock: The Economic Consequences of a Hotter Planet* (Princeton, NJ: Princeton University Press, 2015); Martin L. Weitzman, "Fat-Tailed Uncertainty in the Economics of Catastrophic Climate Change," *Review of Environmental Economics and Policy* 5, no. 2 (July 1, 2011): 275–292, doi:10.1093/reep/rer006; IPCC Working Group III, "Climate Change 2014: Mitigation of Climate Change," IPCC, 2014, 246, http://mitigation2014.org; Ian Bremmer and Preston Keat, *The Fat Tail: The Power of Political Knowledge in an Uncertain World* (Oxford; New York: Oxford University Press, 2010).

[132] Jim Gomez, "Admiral Assures Asian Allies US Forces Ready for Contingency," *The Big Story*, July 17, 2015, http://bigstory.ap.org/article/813b11a6edec403185ab6a4785868cab/admiral-assures-asian-allies-us-forces-ready-contingency.

Sandy- and Katrina-type events. On the other hand, we cannot spend an infinite amount of money to prepare for possible climate catastrophe. The strategic dilemma is ultimately calibrating the appropriate level of insurance given other competing priorities.

With such considerations, how should we conceive of "sustainable security" amidst a world that manifestly appears to be on an unsustainable path with respect to nature? In this book, sustainability refers to the material resources that sustain US national security and the reservoir of public support to use those resources for their intended purposes. However, in environmental circles, the word "sustainability" has a historically contingent meaning referencing the work of the 1987 World Commission on Environment and Development. The commission's report, *Our Common Future*, introduced the concept of "sustainable development" into the lexicon, defining it as "development that meets the needs of the present without compromising the ability of future generations to meet their own needs."[133] Since its introduction, sustainable development has become an elastic concept with little operational value, simultaneously used by people to support environmental protection and by those who favor human development at the expense of the environment.

There is an effort to reclaim the environmental roots of "sustainability." Indeed, *In Pursuit of Prosperity*, a 2014 book from the environmental advocacy group WWF, sought to put environmental sustainability at the heart of US foreign policy. That project is an explicit framing attempt to convince national security elites to care about conservation and the environment.[134] While that project may be successful, connecting environmental issues to security consequences potentially has unintended effects. On climate change, the security discussion has, alongside an expanded set of actors interested in the issue, brought attention and resources to an array of other concerns, from climate and conflict to defending US sovereignty over the Arctic. For advocates of using climate and security as a means to boost support for climate mitigation, that may not be what they had in mind.

While sustainable development has little analytical leverage, it would be ironic if a book on sustainable security lacked that environmental connotation. What then does sustainable security look like with an environmental sensibility? Sustainable security must mean calibrating ends and means in the current period with the need to sustain the planet's core life-sustaining ecological functions in the future. This dynamic view of security has to anticipate future risks to humanity and the natural world arising from demographic change and increasing consumptive possibilities, particularly in Asia where demand for resources has led to unprecedented air and water pollution and pressures on global stocks of fish, wildlife, timber, and other resources. Without dramatic decoupling of economic growth from carbon-based fuels, adoption of modern pollution control, improvement in the productivity of agriculture and aquaculture, and change in the consumptive patterns of individuals, the 21st century may yield a dystopian polluted and degraded future.

---

[133] World Commission on Environment and Development, *Our Common Future* (Oxford: Oxford University Press, 1987).

[134] David Reed, ed., *In Pursuit of Prosperity: U.S Foreign Policy in an Era of Natural Resource Scarcity* (New York: Routledge, 2014).

For the United States, the challenge narrowly is how much insurance is necessary to protect the country from catastrophic damages from global public adverse consequences like climate change. Economists will counsel some cost-benefit calculus such that the discounted future benefits of avoided climate damage exactly equal the costs of action. However, this quickly devolves into a somewhat unproductive discussion about the appropriate discount rate by which we value future benefits.[135] It also requires burden sharing with other major emitters and confidence that our actions are being matched by others.

In this context, political leaders have established a somewhat artificial goal of preventing global greenhouse gas emissions from reaching concentrations that would cause global average temperatures to rise two degrees Celsius above preindustrial levels. This goal was somewhat informed by scientists who described it as a threshold above which the world might experience dangerous climate change. The reality is that so little has been done that this goal is unlikely to be achieved, and it is unclear if it in fact represents a singularly critical threshold.[136]

In general, on the mitigation front, there is consensus that the world needs to move dramatically toward decarbonization of the energy supply by the mid-21st century. What that means for policy is ultimately a price on carbon and other incentives to keep hydrocarbons in the ground and technological innovation to either sequester carbon dioxide underground or to have some biological or chemical process for taking it out of the air. Putting a price on carbon through a tax or establishing some sort of quantity limit on emissions (and allowing for actors to trade emissions permits depending on their costs of mitigation) are thought of as cost-efficient strategies, relative to other efforts that have been tried. A comprehensive survey of the various actions major emitting economies are pursuing on this front is beyond the scope of this chapter, but the hardest part of the mitigation challenge has simply been getting started and being able to send clear, consistent signals to the private sector that greenhouse gases are pollution and need to be eliminated.

In terms of adaptation and preparation for the security consequences of climate change, which is really the heart of this chapter, we do not know how likely certain outcomes will be, either in terms of direct impacts on the homeland or US overseas interests (though some are known better than others). In terms of domestic infrastructure, we will ultimately have to make some rules about what flood, storm, and other extreme weather risks the country's infrastructure specifications should be built around. New York, after Hurricane Sandy, adopted new building codes to ensure resilience of new construction, such as wind-resistant windows

---

[135] This was at the heart of critiques of the Stern report by Nicholas Stern, an advisor to the UK government who used a very low discount rate to heavily weigh future benefits of climate protection. HM Treasury, "The Stern Review on the Economics of Climate Change," 2006, http://webarchive.nationalarchives.gov.uk/20080910140413/http://www.hm-treasury.gov.uk/independent_reviews/stern_review_economics_climate_change/sternreview_index.cfm; Richard S.J. Tol and Gary Yohe, "A Critique of the Stern Review," *World Economics* 7, no. 4 (2006): 233–250, http://www.fnu.zmaw.de/fileadmin/fnu-files/publication/tol/RM551.pdf.

[136] David G. Victor and Charles F. Kennel, "Climate Policy: Ditch the 2 °C Warming Goal," *Nature* 514, no. 7520 (October 1, 2014): 30–31.

and elevation of base-level construction to account for flood risks.[137] New York is better positioned to adopt such changes given its relative wealth, but poor countries in the developing world facing high exposure to climate risks lack the capacity to afford or implement such measures.

While the United States and other rich countries pledged to mobilize up to $100 billion in public and private finance annually for climate mitigation and adaptation by 2020, it is difficult to see those amounts fully materializing. Indeed, the US three-billion-dollar pledge to the Green Climate Fund housed in Korea is in doubt, given President Obama's difficulty in securing appropriations in the US Congress.[138] Beyond these challenges, the international community underinvests in disaster risk reduction (DRR) because the political rewards for emergency response, despite being more expensive, are greater than preventive activities. Voters do not necessarily reward decision makers for averted disasters.

There is a robust international framework in place to encourage more front-end investments in DRR, which began with the ten-year Hyogo Framework for Action in 2005.[139] In March 2015, a new commitment was developed in Sendai, Japan.[140] The challenge going forward is both analytical and financial. To start with, the United States can and is supporting analytical work to identify the places where large numbers of people could die from exposure to climate hazards. Second, the United States should use leverage resources from the World Bank and other multilateral bodies to help communities plan for those situations. Finally, the United States should work with other donors and financial institutions, including the Asian Infrastructure Bank, to find additional support to fund early warning systems, infrastructure investments, and capacity-building so communities and countries can protect themselves in times of need.

The United States, as the most influential country in the international system, can at least rally the resources to begin the process of better understanding the vulnerabilities and helping countries jump-start the planning process.[141] In June

[137] Jillian Jorgensen, "Bloomberg Talks 'Nitty Gritty' Building-Code Changes to Make NYC Safer after Hurricane Sandy," SILive.com, June 14, 2013, http://www.silive.com/news/index.ssf/2013/06/bloomberg_talks_nitty_gritty_p.html.

[138] Jason Plautz, "House Republicans Dismiss Obama's $3 Billion Climate Pledge," National Journal, June 2, 2015, http://www.nationaljournal.com/energy/climate-fund-republicans-obama-appropriations-20150602.

[139] World Conference on Disaster Reduction, "Hyogo Framework for Action 2005–2015: Building the resilience of nations and communities to disasters," UNISDR: Kobe, Hyogo, Japan, January 2005, http://www.unisdr.org/we/coordinate/hfa.

[140] Third UN World Conference on Disaster Risk Reduction, "Sendai Framework for Disaster Risk Reduction 2015–2030," United Nations Office for Disaster Risk Reduction: Sendai, Japan, 2015, http://www.wcdrr.org.

[141] It has already funded a number of efforts, including water anomaly data project from the company ISciences. See isciences, Water Security Indicator Model, http://www.isciences.com/water-security-indicator-model. I have been involved in two such efforts, one a five-year $7.6 million project to study Climate Change and African Political Stability (CCAPS, https://www.strausscenter.org/ccaps/about.html) and another three-year $1.9 million project to study Complex Emergencies and Political Stability in Asia (CEPSA, https://www.strausscenter.org/cepsa/about.html).

2015, the Obama administration announced a new thirty-four million dollar initiative with partner organizations that included in-kind contributions from the Red Cross, Google, and ESRI to support climate contingency measures in three vulnerable developing countries, Bangladesh, Colombia, and Ethiopia.[142] Such investments in the millions can minimize if not eliminate the number of multimillion and/or billion dollar emergency disaster responses later, conserving US strategic assets and financial resources for other purposes. All of this is happening at a potentially dangerous moment in the international system as the relative economic advantage of the United States declines as China rises. As the United States becomes more selective in its choice of areas of strategic investment, climate change has to be one of those areas.

---

[142] Chris Mooney, "White House Launches $ 34 Million Plan to Help Developing Countries Prepare for Climate Change," *The Washington Post*, June 9, 2015, http://www.washingtonpost. com/news/energy-environment/wp/2015/06/09/the-obama-administration-wants-to-help-developing-countries-map-their-climate-risks.

Regional Security Commitments

Benjamin Valentino

The foundation of American foreign policy is America's network of overseas alliances and defense commitments. As of 2014, the United States maintained defense pacts with over sixty-eight countries, totaling twenty-five percent of the world's population. The United States has over 160,000 troops deployed abroad in more than 150 countries, not including those deployed on operations. These foreign commitments are where the rubber of any sustainable security strategy hits the road of the world beyond our shores. Strategic principles that look good on paper must be matched with the reality of constrained resources and regional politics. Critical choices about diplomatic initiatives, military budgets, and force structure proceed from the requirements of protecting specific commitments against specific threats. The forces, assets, and diplomatic agreements needed to assist Japan in a naval conflict with China are not the same as those needed to help defend South Korea in a war against the North or disrupt terrorist groups in Pakistan.

In recent years, scholars have begun to focus increased attention on the long-neglected debate about America's grand strategy. Virtually all parties to the current debate concur that a careful reevaluation of America's strategy is long overdue in light of the dramatically changed international environment. For some, like Steven Brooks, John Ikenberry, and William C. Wohlforth, such a reevaluation leads to the conclusion that the United States must remain deeply engaged militarily around the world, preserving most of its current allies and overseas bases. This position is supported by policymakers on both sides of the political spectrum, with only a few exceptions. As the Obama administration declared in its 2010 Quadrennial Defense Review, "America's interests and role in the world require Armed Forces with unmatched capabilities and a willingness on the part of the nation to employ them in defense of our national interests and the common good." Others, like Barry Posen, have argued that such a revaluation makes clear that many of America's current commitments are unnecessary to American security in the post-Cold War era and that some may be fundamentally unsustainable in the long term. Although few policymakers support retrenchment of the kind Posen advocates, many have expressed the fear that the public may soon demand it. Speaking to a gathering of NATO ministers in 2011 on the eve of his retirement as Secretary of Defense, Robert Gates warned "The blunt reality is that there will be dwindling appetite and patience in the U.S. Congress—and in the American body politic writ large—to expend increasingly precious funds on behalf of nations that are apparently unwilling to devote the necessary resources or make the necessary changes to be serious and capable partners in their own defense."

Despite this renewed attention on the grand strategic debate, few scholars have focused their attention on a careful reevaluation of the specific commitments that alternate grand strategies might entail. For the most part, the argument has been conducted in general terms, with scholars debating whether America's allies in general tend to "free ride" or entrap the United States, and whether the overall benefits of an engaged foreign policy outweigh its costs. But all of America's commitments are not created equal. Proponents of deep engagement may agree to scale back commitments to some allies and proponents of restraint may wish to retain some.

What is needed now, therefore, is a careful reexamination of American commitments to specific countries and regions. This section begins to fill that important void in the debate. The section begins with an analysis of public opinion on American foreign commitments, to help assess whether the fears of policymakers' fears of rising isolationism are well founded. In subsequent chapters, regional experts examine America's commitments to Europe, the Middle East, East Asia, and South Asia. The authors forward a diverse set of recommendations for reforming or maintaining alliances in different parts of the world, but this exercise serves to emphasize the insights that can be gained by approaching each region on its own terms.

8

AT HOME ABROAD
PUBLIC ATTITUDES TOWARD AMERICA'S
OVERSEAS COMMITMENTS

Benjamin Valentino

On November 23, 2010, North Korean troops fired over 150 artillery shells at Yeonpyeong Island in South Korea, killing two South Korean soldiers and two civilians. Within hours, President Obama condemned the attack, reminding the DPRK and the rest of the world that "South Korea is our ally. It has been since the Korean War and we strongly affirm our commitment to defend South Korea as part of that alliance . . . Along with our alliance with Japan, this is the cornerstone of US security in the Pacific region."[1] The following day, Obama ordered the aircraft carrier USS George Washington to the region to emphasize US resolve.

Fortunately, there were no further hostilities in November 2010. But we will never know how close the United States came to war, potentially a nuclear war, with North Korea during that confrontation. What may be most remarkable about the incident, however, were the events that did not occur. Despite the fact that the United States was already embroiled in two major wars in the Middle East, neither the President nor his top advisors felt pressured to explain in any detail to the American people exactly why South Korea was a "cornerstone" of American security or how American interests would be harmed if American leaders decided not to help defend it. No Oval Office speech or major press conference with the President was called. Indeed, the incident passed with little reaction from the press or the public and is now mostly forgotten. After fifty years, the alliance with South Korea did not seem to require further justification. No one suggested that the fact that the alliance was formed so long ago might actually have been reason to question whether the arrangement still made strategic sense today.

Indeed, the domestic reaction (or non-reaction) to the North Korean attack seems to reflect a broader pattern of American attitudes toward its overseas commitments. Although political leaders, scholars, pundits, and America's foreign allies have been warning that the public might embrace a "new isolationism" since the end of the Cold War, no significant argument for retrenchment has entered the public discourse on American foreign policy. In the past years only a handful of

---

[1] ABC News Transcript, "A Thanksgiving Visit with President and Mrs. Obama," November 26, 2010, http://abcnews.go.com/Politics/transcript-barbara-walters-interviews-president-barack-obama-lady/story?id=12250047.

political leaders—including Patrick Buchanan, Dennis Kucinich, Ron and Rand Paul—have advocated a meaningful reduction of America's foreign commitments. None of them have attracted a significant national following. Commenting on Rand Paul's 2016 Presidential prospects, William Kristol, an influential neoconservative commentator told *The Washington Post* that "Rand Paul is a lonely gadfly ... Rand Paul speaks for a genuine sentiment that's always been in the Republican Party, but maybe it's ten percent? Fifteen percent? Twenty percent? I don't think he's going to be a serious competitor for guiding Republican foreign policy."[2] More recently, Donald Trump, who has advocated reducing American expenditures on foreign alliances, including NATO, has garnered much higher support among Republican voters. Nevertheless, an April 2016 survey showed that only 19% of Americans agree that there is no longer any need for the United States to belong to NATO and only 26% agreed that the United States should remove its troops from Western Europe.[3] The percent of the public supporting each of these policies was actually lower in the 2016 survey than in polls conducted before Trump's candidacy. Some observers have pointed to the declining support for America's wars in Iraq and Afghanistan as evidence of growing isolationism, but ending these costly wars cannot be said to constitute a fundamental shift in American grand strategy.[4] In fact, there remains a significant possibility that the United States will establish new defense commitments to the governments we promoted in Iraq and Afghanistan, binding America to the defense of these countries for many years to come. Still others have suggested that the lingering effects of the 2008 financial crisis or America's continuing fiscal problems may yet tempt the public to retreat into isolationism. To date, however, few political leaders have proposed the kinds of defense budget cuts that would necessitate a fundamental shift in American foreign policy.[5]

Understanding the nature of public attitudes about American foreign policy is critical if the United States wishes to craft a more sustainable national security strategy. Whether America seeks to achieve sustainability by reining in American commitments or by significantly reorienting them, in the long run, new policies must be accepted by the American public. Although it is sometimes asserted that the public plays little role in the realm of foreign policy, the consensus among recent scholarship is that public opinion has a significant influence over America's foreign policy decisions. Contrary to conventional wisdom, attitudes about foreign policy can sometimes be an important determinant of voting behavior, which means that

[2] Philip Rucker, "In Paul-Rubio Feud over Cuba, A Preview of 2016," *Washington Post*, December 20, 2014, p. A1. A September 2015 survey of Republican voters, for example, found that only five percent of respondents selected Rand Paul as the Republican primary candidate they believed could "best handle foreign policy." Cable News Network. CNN/ORC International Poll, September 2015 [survey question]. USORC.092015.R11C. ORC International. Storrs, CT: Roper Center for Public Opinion Research. Accessed October 29, 2015.

[3] Rasmussen Reports, April 6, 2016, accessed April 22, 2016, http://www.rasmussenreports.com/public_content/politics/general_politics/march_2016/should_the_u_s_leave_nato.

[4] Ross K. Baker, "Bipartisanship We Don't Want: Isolationism," *USA Today*, June 28, 2011, p. 19A.

[5] Niall Ferguson, "America's Dumbest Budget Cut," *Newsweek* 158, no. 2, July 4, 2011.

decision makers who seek to maintain their positions ignore it at their peril.[6] For this reason, every American President since Franklin Roosevelt has closely tracked public opinion on important foreign policy decisions.[7] Because the public is generally not well informed about foreign affairs, elites probably do have a greater opportunity to shape public opinion on foreign policy than they do in the domestic arena. Over the longer term, however, if elites cannot convince the public to support their policies or if the public becomes convinced the policies have failed, they will be punished at the polls.[8] Indeed numerous studies have found that public opinion can affect important foreign policy choices, including the timing, duration, and conduct of war.[9]

This chapter, therefore, investigates American attitudes toward US foreign commitments, drawing on recent public opinion polls including the results of an original foreign policy survey conducted on a representative sample of Americans in the spring of 2012.[10] We know surprisingly little about US public opinion on these issues. Although pollsters frequently survey American attitudes regarding ongoing military conflicts, the American public is only rarely asked its opinions on longstanding security commitments to places like Japan, Korea, Taiwan, Europe, or Kuwait—and even then, often only during times of crisis. Surveys that do explore foreign policy attitudes tend to address these issues only at the highest level of generality, such as gauging overall levels of public support for a particular military intervention, public fears about terrorism, presidential approval in the conduct of foreign policy, American favorability toward specific foreign countries, and attitudes about the defense budget. To understand how the public is likely to react to

---

[6] John H. Aldrich, John L. Sullivan, and Eugene Borgida, "Foreign Affairs and Issue Voting: Do Presidential Candidates 'Waltz Before a Blind Audience?'" *American Political Science Review* 83, no. 1 (1989): 123–141; Sowmya S. Anand and Jon A. Krosnick, "The Impact of Attitudes Toward Foreign Policy Goals on Public Preferences Among Presidential Candidates," *Presidential Studies Quarterly* 33, no. 1 (2003): 31–71; Christopher Gelpi, Peter D. Feaver, and Jason Reifler. *Paying The Human Costs of War: American Public Opinion and Casualties In Military Conflicts* (Princeton, NJ: Princeton University Press, 2009).

[7] Adam Berinsky, *In Time of War: Understanding American Public Opinion from World War II to Iraq* (Chicago: University of Chicago Press, 2009).

[8] John E. Mueller, *Policy and Opinion in the Gulf War* (Chicago: University of Chicago Press, 1994); John Zaller, "Elite Leadership of Mass Opinion," in *Taken by Storm: The Media, Public Opinion, and US Foreign Policy in the Gulf War*, W. Lance Bennett and David L. Paletz eds. (Chicago: University of Chicago Press, 1994), pp. 186–209; Carrie Lee Lindsay, "Politics at War: Military Operations and Electoral Politics in Iraq and Afghanistan," 2014 *American Political Science Association Meeting Paper*, accessed October 29, 2015, http://papers.ssrn.com/sol3/papers.cfm?abstract_id=2453599; Matthew A Baumand and Philip B. K. Potter, *War and Democratic Constraint: How the Public Influences Foreign Policy* (Princeton, NJ: Princeton University Press, 2015).

[9] John E. Mueller, *Policy and Opinion in the Gulf War* (Chicago: University of Chicago Press, 1994).

[10] Thus survey was conducted with the support of the Tobin Project. Numerous scholars submitted questions for the survey. The full results of the poll are available at http://www.dartmouth.edu/~benv/data.html. The survey interviewed 1056 respondents and has a margin of error of +/− 3.16 percent.

proposals for significant changes in American grand strategy, however, we need to know not simply what the public thinks, but why.

The results of the 2012 survey and other related polls provide clear evidence that the American public is not ready to support a major foreign policy retrenchment. On the contrary, although Americans seem to recognize that our foreign commitments are expensive and worry about free riding by our allies, sizable majorities continue to support all of America's major commitments from Asia to Europe to the Middle East. Americans see the current world as even more dangerous than it was during the Cold War and believe that our allies and alignments help to guard against these dangers. They do not favor significantly reducing our alliance commitments in the effort to help balance the federal budget. Although Republicans generally favor a significantly more expansive, forceful interventionist foreign policy than do Democrats, attitudes are not as polarized as in domestic politics. Large numbers of Democrats support preserving our long-term alliance commitments as well.

On the other hand, the survey also reveals that Americans have a relatively poor understanding of the nature and extent of Americas' commitments. Many Americans could not identify which countries the United States has formally pledged to defend and which it has not. On most questions in the survey, a significant percentage of respondents answered "don't know" or indicated they did not have an opinion about the foreign policy issue mentioned in the question. These results suggest that public opinion remains at least somewhat malleable on these issues and strong political leadership or dramatic external events could still undermine the internationalist consensus in the years ahead. The current internationalist consensus, after all, emerged in America in the early years of the Cold War not due to pressure from the public, but only after a coordinated effort on the part of elites to convince the American people of the need for international engagement.

THE INTERNATIONALIST CONSENSUS

One of the most well-known and consistently asked survey questions on American attitudes toward foreign policy asks respondents whether they agree or disagree with the statement that "the United States should mind its own business internationally and let other countries get along the best they can on their own." By this measure, support for isolationism seems to be at an all-time high, with fifty-two percent of Americans agreeing that the United States should "mind its own business" in 2013 (see Figure 8.1).[11]

On closer examination, however, it seems likely that this trend primarily reflects growing dissatisfaction following America's wars in Iraq and Afghanistan rather than a significant decline in support for America's international leadership role. Indeed, as shown in Figure 8.2, responses to another even longer-running survey

---

[11] Pew Research Center, "Public Sees US Power Declining as Support for Global Engagement Slips," Washington DC, December 3, 2013, http://www.people-press.org/2013/12/03/public-sees-u-s-power-declining-as-support-for-global-engagement-slips.

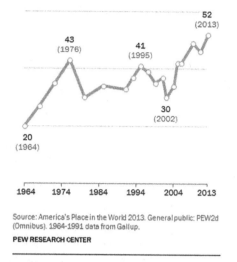

Figure 8.1 Majority Says United States Should "Mind Its Own Business Internationally"
Source: Pew Research Center.

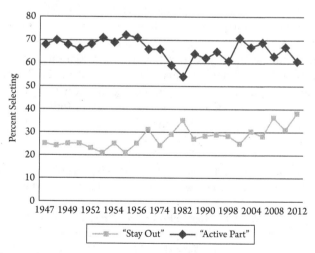

Figure 8.2 Support for an Active Part in World Affairs

question—"Do you think it will be best for the future of the country if we take an active part in world affairs or if we stay out of world affairs?"—suggest only a small decline in internationalism, while a sizable majority of Americans continues to support a substantial international role for the United States.[12]

---

[12] "Global Views 2012: U.S. Public Topline Report," Data from The Chicago Council on Global Affairs, July 27, 2012, http://www.thechicagocouncil.org/sites/default/files/2012Topline(1).pdf.

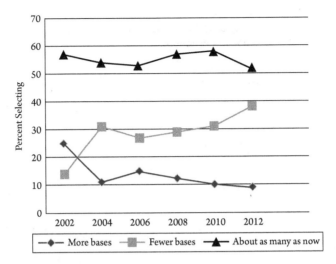

Figure 8.3 Support for Overseas Military Bases

In 2012, seventy-four percent of the public agreed that it is very or somewhat important "for United States to remain the world's number one military power."[13] More to the point, when the public was asked specifically about support for "long-term military bases the United States has overseas," large majorities approve of maintaining or expanding the number of US bases (see Figure 8.3).[14]

Polls show strong support for a variety of specific military commitments as well. Fifty-six percent of Americans agree that NATO is "still essential to our country's security" compared to only thirty-five percent who say it is no longer essential.[15] A May 2012 Gallup poll found that nearly ninety percent of the public believes the Japan-US Security Treaty, which commits the United States to the defense of Japan, "should be maintained."[16] In April 2013, sixty-one percent of Americans said they would support using "military troops to help defend South Korea" in the event of an invasion by the North (only thirty-six percent would not support using troops).[17] Thirty-one percent of Americans reported

---

[13] Eleven percent said it was "a little important," and only five percent said it was "not important at all." Eleven percent chose "don't know." Valentino poll (http://www.dartmouth.edu/~benv/data.html).

[14] "Global Views 2012: U.S. Public Topline Report," data from The Chicago Council on Global Affairs, July 27, 2012, http://www.thechicagocouncil.org/sites/default/files/2012Topline(1).pdf.

[15] Transatlantic Trends 2012 Survey, June 2012. Accessed November 21, 2012 from the iPoll Databank, The Roper Center for Public Opinion Research, University of Connecticut. http://ropercenter.cornell.edu/ipoll-database.

[16] Kirk Spitzer, "Americans Choose Up Sides—Japan Over China," *Time Magazine*, May 22, 2012, http://nation.time.com/2012/05/22/americans-choose-up-sides-japan-over-china/#ixzz2Csxq7gHF.

[17] CNN/ORC International Poll, April 2013. Accessed May 31, 2013 from the iPOLL Databank, The Roper Center for Public Opinion Research, University of Connecticut. http://ropercenter.cornell.edu/ipoll-database.

that they would be less likely to vote for a candidate who "proposed to end the current US military alliance with South Korea," while only twelve percent said it would make them more likely to vote for the candidate.[18] Forty-one percent even favored establishing "new military alliances to help defend emerging democratic states like Brazil and India," with only nineteen percent opposing such alliances. Americans appear less enthusiastic about Taiwan than our formal Asian alliance partners, but a plurality in 2012 (forty-eight percent in favor to forty-three percent against) still favored using military force to defend Taiwan in the event of an attack by China.[19]

In the Middle East, support for America's close ties with Israel also remains strong. In March 2015, only eighteen percent of Americans indicated that they felt the United States has been "too supportive" in its relationship with Israel, while twenty-nine percent felt America had not been supportive enough and forty-eight percent said the level of support was "about right."[20] In 2012, a *CBS News/New York Times* Poll asked Americans "If Israel were to attack Iran to prevent Iran from developing nuclear weapons, then what should the United States do?" Fifty-five percent said the United States should "support Israel's military action" and only thirty-eight percent said the United States "should not get involved."[21]

COMMITMENT COSTS

Despite the public's endorsement of internationalism, most Americans acknowledge that America's overseas commitments come at a high price. Sixty-one percent of Americans agree that "The United States can no longer afford to maintain its commitments to defend all of its current allies around the world" compared to only thirteen percent who disagree.[22] In addition, Americans remain concerned that our allies are not bearing a fair share of the burden of our alliances. Seventy-seven percent of respondents, for example, believe that "most of America's allies get more help from the United States than the United States gets from them."[23] Americans overwhelmingly agree (fifty-three percent to nine percent) that "Japan spends less on its own defense than it should because of the security provided by Japan's military alliance with the United States."[24] Similarly, fifty-nine percent agree and only seven

[18] Valentino poll (http://www.dartmouth.edu/~benv/data.html). Fifty-seven percent, however, reported that it would make them neither more nor less likely to vote for the candidate.

[19] Pew Global Attitudes Project Poll, Apr, 2012. Accessed November 21, 2012 from the iPOLL Databank, The Roper Center for Public Opinion Research, University of Connecticut. http://ropercenter.cornell.edu/ipoll-database.

[20] Pew Research Center Poll, February 26, 2015. Accessed October 30, 2015 from http://www.people-press.org/2015/02/27/more-view-netanyahu-favorably-than-unfavorably-many-unaware-of-israeli-leader/2-27-2015_03.

[21] CBS News/New York Times Poll, November, 2012. USCBSNYT.201211A.Q47. Accessed October 30, 2015 from the iPoll Databank, The Roper Center for Public Opinion Research, University of Connecticut. http://ropercenter.cornell.edu/ipoll-database.

[22] Valentino poll (http://www.dartmouth.edu/~benv/data.html).

[23] Ibid.

[24] Ibid.

percent disagree that "America's European allies spend less on their own defense than they should because of the security provided by the NATO military alliance with the United States."[25]

In addition to these financial costs, the public also concedes that some of America's commitments have political/strategic costs. Sixty-one percent, for example, agree that "current US military, economic, and political support for Israel angers many Muslims and makes terrorist attacks against the United States and our interests more likely," while only seven percent disagree.

Despite the recognition of these costs, the public mostly opposes specific measures to reduce the costs of America's foreign commitments. Only thirty-five percent say they would support "major cuts in military spending" and only thirty percent would support any level of tax increase "to help keep the United States military the strongest in the world."[26] Just twenty-five percent support the establishment of a "war surtax" to "pay for [future] war[s] and avoid adding to our nation's debt," while fifty-three percent oppose it.[27] Although some scholars have suggested that the United States should not oppose or might even encourage allies like Germany and Japan to build nuclear weapons, only twenty-one percent agreed (and forty-two percent disagreed) that "it would be a good thing if countries like Germany and Japan had their own nuclear weapons since then they would not have to rely as much on the United States for their defense."[28]

A DANGEROUS WORLD

Why does the American public continue to support our overseas commitments in spite of these serious costs? There is no single answer to this question, but the results of the original survey described in this paper suggest that most Americans perceive the world as an exceptionally dangerous place and believe that our foreign alliances continue to play a vital role in protecting the United States and its vital interests. Perhaps most strikingly, more than sixty-three percent of Americans agreed that "The United States faces greater threats to its security today than it did during the Cold War," while only fourteen percent disagree.[29]

Much of this concern probably stems from Americans' persistent fears of terrorist attacks. Seventy-four percent of Americans agree that it is very or somewhat likely that a "terrorist attack causing large numbers of American lives to be lost will happen in the near future."[30] Fifty-five percent believe that it is very or somewhat

---

[25] Ibid.

[26] Ibid.

[27] Ibid.

[28] Ibid.

[29] Ibid.

[30] Only 15 percent said it was not very likely or not likely at all. Quinnipiac University Poll, December 2015, USQUINN.122315.R58, Quinnipiac University Polling Institute. Accessed April 22, 2016 from the iPoll Databank, The Roper Center for Public Opinion Research, http://ropercenter.cornell.edu/ipoll-database. This high level of concern does not appear to be the result of recent ISIS attacks. These survey results are essentially unchanged since 2011. Fox News Poll, August, 2011. Accessed November 21, 2012 from the iPOLL Databank,

likely that "the United States will be attacked by terrorists using nuclear weapons in the next decade."[31] The fear of terrorism may be intensified by Americans' views of the causes of terrorist attacks directed against the United States. Forty-nine percent of Americans (including seventy-one percent of Republican respondents) agreed that "terrorists attack the United States mostly because they hate America's values," while just thirty-seven percent said that "terrorists attack the United States mostly because they hate America's foreign policies."[32] The view that terrorism is primarily motivated by a hatred of American values suggests that terrorists will continue to target the United States until we either change our values or defeat them. Perhaps this is also why ninety percent of Americans polled in April 2013 agreed that "Americans will always have to live with the risk of terrorism."[33]

Another possible explanation for Americans' sense of insecurity could be that Americans lack faith in the power of deterrence to keep America safe. For example, sixty-nine percent of the public agreed that if Iran succeeded in developing a nuclear weapon it would be very or somewhat likely to use it against Israel. Only seventeen percent said it was not too likely or not at all likely. A separate poll found that only thirty-two percent of Americans believed that if Iran developed nuclear weapons it "would be deterred from striking Israel for fear of being destroyed in a nuclear retaliatory strike" by Israel.[34] Indeed, arguments about the futility of deterrence figured prominently in the Bush administration's case for war against Iraq in 2003 and in the administration's wider policy of preempting military threats, which came to be known as the "Bush Doctrine." Subsequent polls have continued to show that a majority of Americans agree that the use of military force can at least be sometimes justified "against countries that may seriously threaten the United States, but have not attacked," although support for preemption has declined from sixty-six percent in 2003 to fifty-two percent in 2009, the last time this question was polled.[35]

Americans see our foreign alliances as important to protecting the United States from these threats and minimizing the chances that the United States will be directly attacked. For example, fifty percent of Americans agreed and just twenty-five percent

The Roper Center for Public Opinion Research, University of Connecticut. http://roper-center.cornell.edu/ipoll-database.

[31] Thirty percent said such an attack was "not too likely" and fifteen percent said it was "not likely at all." CNN/Opinion Research Corporation Poll. April 9–11, 2010, http://www.pollingreport.com/defense.htm.

[32] Valentino poll (http://www.dartmouth.edu/~benv/data.html).

[33] CBS News/New York Times Poll, April, 2013. Accessed May 31, 2013, from the iPOLL Databank, The Roper Center for Public Opinion Research, University of Connecticut. http://ropercenter.cornell.edu/ipoll-database.

[34] PIPA/Knowledge Networks Poll, March, 2012. Accessed May 31, 2013 from the iPOLL Databank, The Roper Center for Public Opinion Research, University of Connecticut. http://ropercenter.cornell.edu/ipoll-database.

[35] Pew Global Attitudes Project Poll, April, 2003. Accessed June 14, 2013 from the iPOLL Databank, The Roper Center for Public Opinion Research, University of Connecticut. http://ropercenter.cornell.edu/ipoll-database; Pew Research Center for the People, Oct, 2009. Accessed June 4, 2013 from the iPOLL Databank, The Roper Center for Public Opinion Research, University of Connecticut. http://ropercenter.cornell.edu/ipoll-database.

disagreed that "the United States must keep a strong military presence in the Middle East to prevent terrorist attacks against the United States homeland."[36] Fifty-two percent also agreed that "the United States depends on the support of Israel to protect vital US interests in the Middle East," with only eighteen percent disagreeing.[37]

In Asia, on the other hand, Americans see our commitments as vital to protecting important economic interests. Americans agreed by a margin of sixty-four percent to nine percent that "The United States must maintain its current naval forces in Asia and the Pacific to protect the cargo ships that carry most of trade between the United States and Asia."[38]

Americans also registered concern that *failing* to support our formal or informal commitments would deal a serious blow to US credibility. Americans agreed by a margin of fifty-eight to twelve percent that "if the United States decided to end its commitment to help defend South Korea, our enemies would doubt America's resolve to defend other American allies and interests in the future."[39] Thirty-nine percent agreed and only seventeen percent disagreed that "if China attacked Taiwan and the United States decided not to help defend Taiwan, our enemies would doubt America's resolve to defend our key interests in the future."[40] Americans were also skeptical that our allies would stand up for themselves in the absence of American support. Thirty-six percent agreed (compared to twenty-two percent who disagreed) that "most of America's allies, even the wealthy and powerful ones, fear war so much that if they are threatened by a determined enemy, they will give in, unless they are defended by the United States."[41]

CONCLUSION

The survey results reviewed in this paper strongly indicate that the American public has not embraced a "new isolationism," the rise of which has been forecast repeatedly since the end of the Cold War. Although there is some evidence that the public has begun to move away from the most expansive and interventionist varieties of US foreign policy in recent years, these shifts have been relatively subtle and seem just as likely to reflect a reaction to the increasingly unpopular wars in Iraq and Afghanistan as the early signs of a larger shift toward isolationism. Americans do not appear to have chosen these views uncritically. They recognize that our commitments come with substantial economic, political, and military costs, but Americans seem to believe these costs are worth paying to defend the United States from what they see as a highly threatening world.

These findings have important implications for the effort to produce a more sustainable security strategy for the United States. For supporters of America's current forward-leaning foreign policy, a group that includes the leaders of both Republican and Democratic parties, these findings suggest that they can largely put aside concerns that the public will soon demand a fundamental reevaluation of our foreign policy.

[36] Valentino poll (http://www.dartmouth.edu/~benv/data.html).

[37] Ibid.

[38] Ibid.

[39] Ibid.

[40] Ibid.

[41] Ibid.

Although the public may question the wisdom of particular policies or military interventions, the belief that America must retain its overseas commitments and its leadership role in global affairs remains largely unshaken more than two decades after the
Cold War. For those who believe that substantial retrenchment is necessary for sustainability, on the other hand, these results suggest that if a fundamental change in US
foreign policy is to occur, the impetus for change is not likely to come from the public.

Although the surveys reported in this paper show that public support for a forward-leaning foreign policy is wide, it is not as clear how deep this support runs.
Many of the questions elicited a very high rate of "don't knows" or "neither agree
nor disagree" responses—often more than twenty percent.[42] This pattern is consistent with the often-observed lack of American public interest in and knowledge of
foreign affairs. Indeed, the survey revealed that most Americans have a very poor
understanding of our foreign commitments. As shown in Table 8.1 below, when
asked to choose from a list of countries which ones the United States has pledged
via a formal treaty to defend, only 4.8 percent of Americans correctly identified that
America is committed to defend Latvia as part of the NATO alliance. More than
fifty-five percent incorrectly assume that the United States has a treaty to defend

Table 8.1 Percent of Respondents Who Believe "the
United States Currently Has a Formal Treaty That
Pledges the United States to Help Defend" (Italicized
Countries are Correct)

Israel	55.30%
South Korea	*46.70%*
Japan	*42.40%*
Germany	*36.60%*
Kuwait	27.70%
Taiwan*	23.40%
Saudi Arabia	21.30%
Mexico	20.70%
Turkey	*17.30%*
India	11.80%
Egypt	10.40%
Romania	*7.50%*
Latvia	*4.80%*

* The Taiwan Relations Act is not considered a formal defense
treaty. As part of the agreement, the United States pledges to "make
available to Taiwan such defense articles and defense services in
such quantity as may be necessary to enable Taiwan to maintain
a sufficient self-defense capability" but whether or not to do so
remains at the sole discretion of the President of the United States.

---

[42] This may reflect in part the structure of the YouGov survey which, unlike many other surveys,
explicitly invited subjects to answer "don't know" rather than only recording that response if the
subject spontaneously offered it.

Israel—significantly more than correctly identified America's treaty commitments to Germany or Japan.

The fact that public opinion on America's foreign commitments does not rest on particularly well-informed foundations reminds us that we should not conclude that our current, forward-leaning foreign policy is the best one for America simply because a majority of the public supports it. In this case, as with many complex foreign policy issues, public opinion may be more likely to represent a reflection of the elite consensus rather than an independent affirmation of it.[43]

This is, after all, how America's current international consensus was fashioned. In the years immediately following the Second World War, most Americans longed for a return to isolationism and were not prepared for the idea of large peacetime armies and their associated budgetary expenses. America's postwar foreign policy, first articulated in NSC-68, represented a major departure from the public consensus. Secretary of State Dean Acheson, one of the key authors of NSC-68, worried that "the American people have a false sense of security and ... must be made to realize the gravity of our situation and must become reconciled to the fact that we must make certain sacrifices in order to meet the problem of Soviet aggression."[44] Senator Arthur Vandenberg famously urged Truman to "scare the hell out of the American people" if that is what it took to get them to accept the new internationalist strategy.

The challenge for proponents of major change in American foreign policy, then, is either to fracture the current elite consensus about American grand strategy, or to convince the public that our current strategy has failed, thereby putting pressure on elites from below. Both strategies are likely to prove difficult. Change from above is improbable because powerful political, organizational, and psychological pressures in favor of the status quo make major shifts in elite opinion exceedingly rare. Change from below also seems unlikely. Since the end of the Cold War, the American public has been shielded from the direct costs of the current policy, since the country's current wars have been waged by a small, all-volunteer military and paid for through borrowing rather than tax increases. The most painful costs of an unsustainable grand strategy, therefore, will be borne in the future when American debts come due or when American alliance commitments compel the United States to fight a war it would have rather stayed out of. It is possible that only a major crisis, such as an even more serious economic calamity or failed military adventure abroad, will prompt elites and the public to consider a change of course.

---

[43] See for example, Eric V. Larson, *Casualties and Consensus: The Historical Role of Casualties in Domestic Support for U.S. Military Operations* (Santa Monica: RAND, 1996).

[44] Steven Casey, *Selling the Korean War: Propaganda, Politics, and Public Opinion in the United States 1950–1953* (Oxford: Oxford University Press, 2007), p. 68.

9

THE RIGHT CHOICE FOR NATO

William C. Wohlforth

The case for an agonizing reappraisal of the US security commitment to Europe has never seemed stronger. In the early 1990s, the costs and risks of preserving NATO after the disappearance of its Soviet *raison d'être* were still matters of speculation. Now critics can point to concrete evidence. The huge and growing gap between US and allied military capabilities shows that the free-rider problem that has dogged the alliance from its earliest days is not going away. NATO's 2011 intervention in Libya exposed Europe's critical dependence on US capabilities even against a militarily weak opponent close to Europe's shores in an operation the United States was trying not to lead. In Georgia in 2008 and more dramatically in Ukraine in 2014, the impulse to expand the alliance played a role in exacerbating tensions with Russia. With the expected costs of sustaining US security commitments in East Asia rising along with intense pressure on the Pentagon's budget, the United States confronts newly salient incentives to scrutinize the value-added of its legacy commitment to Europe.

Russia's new assertiveness has transformed the debate on European security, but, for the purposes of this volume, the essential question remains: would a reduced US role increase, or at least not unduly harm, US security interests? This chapter makes the case—heretical in many corners of academe and increasingly outside it as well—that America's core NATO commitment continues to serve its national interests. Radical policy departures, moreover, are unlikely to be necessary in order for the alliance to continue to work. The United States should not attempt to shock its allies into radically increased military spending or intra-European defense cooperation by threatening to radically restructure or abrogate its security commitment. Nor certainly should it seek to solve NATO's problems by promulgating new, expansive roles and missions for the alliance, as was its habit until recently. Instead, it should refocus on the essential NATO purposes of deterring Russia while not foreclosing cooperation with Moscow, providing a hedge against other threats to European security, and serving as a useful if somewhat inefficient institution for inter-allied security cooperation. Not only is this what the United States *should* do about NATO, it is what it *is* doing. For the path I find optimal is simply muddling through. It is the "strategy" that emerges willy-nilly from budget pressures, domestic distractions, ad hoc responses to the new challenges from the East, embedded institutional and bureaucratic interests, and the whole ghastly array of democratic politics and myopic satisficing that grand-strategic scolds love to excoriate. In this case, muddling through is not just expedient, and it's not just what will happen. It is in fact optimal.

I make this case in four steps. First, I establish the necessary background concerning the nature of the commitment. Second, I provide a preliminary assessment of the commitment's costs and risks. I find that the costs and risks are low but vary with the alliance's objectives. The more policymakers insist that the alliance must expand its objectives or die, the more costs and risk they assume. The contretemps with Russia over Ukraine may have the salutary effect of driving this point home. In addition, if the free-riding problem is considered a cost, it must be acknowledged that it is endemic to the alliance and no feasible solution is available. Third, I outline the array of policy options that currently preoccupy the expert debate. Here I show that the real choice is muddling through versus "shock therapy": making a substantial policy departure from the status quo intended to reduce US costs and risks while simultaneously creating incentives for the Europeans to up their defense game. In the concluding section, I compare the likely gains and losses the two main policy options would generate. I argue that shock therapy would marginally reduce US costs, but the probability of its working optimally by producing a militarily capable, independent Europe is low, yielding a different and not necessary better set of risks than the current policy. Muddling through, therefore, preserves a useful array of benefits—deterrence of and leverage on Russia; a hedge against future threats; a vehicle for inter-allied security cooperation; a potential legitimacy enhancer; a major logistical hub for operations around Eurasia, etc.—at an acceptable level of costs and risk.

THE US COMMITMENT TO NATO

The United States' security commitments to Europe fall into three categories: Article 5 commitments, expanded Article 5 commitments, and non-Article 5 commitments. Under Articles 5 and 6 of the North Atlantic Treaty, the United States is explicitly committed to assist in the defense any of its twenty-seven NATO allies should they come under "armed attack." The treaty's text limits the commitment in three key ways: only classical cross-border armed assault is covered, as opposed to more ambiguous threats; only attacks in the North Atlantic area are covered; and the United States, like all members, is obligated only to take those actions in response to an attack on an ally "that it deems necessary." The point is so often missed that it bears repeating: actual treaty text does not commit the United States to war should any ally be attacked. The obligation is to consider doing something in response.

The United States also promoted and endorsed successive NATO "strategic concepts," issued in 1991, 1999, and 2010, which set forth a hugely expanded set of less explicit commitments.[1] Each document endorses commitments of increased geographical and functional scope. Some of these commitments count as expansions

---

[1] Available at NATO, "Strategic Concepts," November 11, 2014, http://www.nato.int/cps/en/natolive/topics_56626.htm.

of the notion of territorial defense beyond conventional armed attack, encompassing the security challenges posed by civil wars or humanitarian crises in Europe (Bosnia, Kosovo) and such modern threats as ballistic missile attacks; terrorism; cyberattacks; nuclear proliferation; and transnational activities such as human, narcotics, and weapons trafficking. The 1999 and 2010 strategic concepts enshrined additional commitments to crisis prevention, response to humanitarian emergencies, post-conflict stabilization, and a raft of other global objectives that go well beyond even a most expansive interpretation of Article 5.

While the obligations undertaken in Article 5 seem clear, the nature of the expanded commitments is ambiguous, reflecting NATO's ad hoc evolution from a collective defense alliance into a cooperative security institution. A reading of the 2010 concept, and official commentary surrounding it, suggests that the United States' Article 5 commitments would come into play if the "fundamental security" of a member state were threatened by conventional threats or "emerging security challenges."[2] President Barack Obama reiterated this commitment when addressing the Baltic allies after Russia's intervention in Ukraine, promising in a speech in Tallinn in September 2014 that "We'll be here for Estonia. We'll be here for Latvia. We'll be here for Lithuania. You lost your independence once before. With NATO, you'll never lose it again."[3] That followed NATO's summit in Wales, where the allies stressed that "the greatest responsibility of the Alliance is to protect and defend our territories and our populations against attack."[4] But the stress on independence and protection of populations from attack provides some wiggle room. NATO's muted response to the cyberattack on Estonia in 2007 further suggests the limits of Article 5, which has thus far been invoked only once, after the 9/11 attacks. Collectively over the years, the Alliance's actions appear to have erected a something of a firewall around Article 5, reserving it for the most serious threats.

Most of the real NATO action over the last two decades is the product of its "cooperative security institution" side as opposed to its "collective defensive alliance" side. The major NATO missions of this period include: military and peace support operations in the Balkans: SFOR, KFOR (1996–ongoing); counterterror operations in the Mediterranean: Operation Active Endeavor (2003–ongoing); International Security and Assistance Force (ISAF): Afghanistan (2001–ongoing); training support for the international force in Iraq: NMTI (2003–2011); counterpiracy

---

[2] Paragraph 4 (a) of the Concept, concerning collective defense, states that "NATO members will always assist each other against attack, in accordance with Article 5 of the Washington Treaty. That commitment remains firm and binding. NATO will deter and defend against any threat of aggression, and against emerging security challenges where they threaten the fundamental security of individual Allies or the Alliance as a whole." In a speech on the Concept, Secretary of State Clinton argued that cyber- and energy-security threats should fall under Article V. See Atlantic Council, "Hillary Clinton on NATO's Future," http://www.atlanticcouncil.org/component/content/article?id=2722:transcript-hillary-clinton-on-nato-s-future.

[3] Colleen McCain Nelson, "Obama Pledges NATO Backing for Baltic Allies," *Wall Street Journal*, Sept. 3, 2014.

[4] NATO, Wales Summit Declaration, September 5, 2014, http://www.nato.int/cps/en/natohq/official_texts_112964.htm.

operations in the Gulf of Aden: SNMG (2008–ongoing); No-fly zone/civilian protection in Libya: Operation Unified Protector (February–October 2011).

The obligations the United States undertakes as a part of its commitment to NATO as a cooperative security institution are much harder to establish than in the case of NATO as a defensive alliance. In some of the operations noted above (Iraq, Afghanistan), NATO is clearly operating as an appendage of US strategy. In others (Mediterranean, Somalia) it is a coordinating mechanism for deploying forces in a common objective. The US commitments to the Balkan and Libyan operations were, however, partly the result of its alliance obligation. While US officials had other reasons to intervene in these cases, the incentive to maintain alliance cohesion and credibility played a role.

These commitments reflect an evolving constellation of interests. The original Article 5 goal, thought to be a necessary condition of US territorial security, was to prevent Soviet hegemony in the region. Because neither Russia nor any other power has the potential capability to physically conquer Europe today or a plausible interest in doing so, this goal is no longer relevant. To achieve classic threat balancing goals, however, Washington found itself managing incipient security tensions among European states. American leaders came to see that German rearmament and especially nuclear proliferation—both necessary conditions of balancing Soviet power without an American military presence—would make war more rather than less likely.[5] Dwight Eisenhower's preference for eliminating US deployments in Europe would therefore not work, not just because of the difficulty of countering formidable Soviet military capabilities, but more immediately because incipient political and security contradictions *within* the region forbade it. The relevance of US security provisions in dampening intra-European security tensions is debated. Most analysts discount it, but some prominent experts hold that at least low-level varieties of geopolitical competition would reemerge were the United States to come home.[6]

But US grand strategy in the Cold War saw global preeminence as a necessary condition of US security and prosperity. From early on, the US commitment to Europe was intertwined with America's perceived interest in global engagement and activism. Even in the middle and later years of the Cold War, the probability of a Soviet attempt to conquer Europe was seen as extremely low. The operative issues concerned bolstering US allies against Soviet political influence, buying allied deference to US preferences, providing a political and military platform for US engagement in Eurasia's geopolitics, and enhancing the legitimacy of US global leadership. These did circle back to security interests because the political influence and other goods the United States purchased via its NATO commitments were seen as assets in shaping global politics in ways that would reduce long-term security challenges. And institutionalized security cooperation in NATO also served as a hedge against the possibility that the Soviets might suddenly become highly risk-tolerant and seek military aggrandizement in Europe.

---

[5] Marc Trachtenberg, *A Constructed Peace* (Princeton, NJ: Princeton University Press, 1999).

[6] See, for example, Sten Rynning, "Germany is More Than Europe Can Handle: NATO as Europe's Pacifier," Research Paper No. 96 (Sept. 2013) NATO Defense College, Rome.

In short the transformation of NATO from a straightforward military alliance into a key foundation stone supporting the edifice of US global leadership had begun long before the collapse of the Soviet Union. After 1991, the mix between classical security and global leadership goals shifted, but the basic strategic calculation that US core interests are best served by a forward-leaning activist global posture remained the same.

Thus in Europe as in US grand strategy writ large, US security and global leadership goals are mixed, and it is not easy to determine where one ends and the other begins. Post–Cold War goals included:

- Keeping the United States engaged as a hedge against a renewed threat from Russia;
- Preserving US access to permanent bases, logistical assets, overflight rights, etc;
- Preserving US influence and leverage over allies;
- Institutionalizing security and intelligence cooperation among like-minded allies;
- Reducing the risk of conflict and competitive rivalries among European states;
- Legitimizing US leadership of western nations;
- Fostering a belt of democratic, peaceful, and secure states on Europe's eastern flank via "socializing" postcommunist societies into the liberal west.

Article 5 guarantees remained relevant at first because extending them to former Soviet satellites and republics could promote stability and democracy in Europe. Although expanding NATO is widely believed to have served that objective, it is decreasingly seen as necessary to sustain it. But the Article 5 guarantees still remain relevant, many argue, as an essential part of the institutional bargain that sustains the alliance and allows the United States to obtain the other goods the alliance provides. And while Russia is generally not seen as either capable of or seriously interested in large-scale territorial conquest, fears that it might seek to use subtler coercive techniques against alliance members—especially Latvia and Estonia, with their large Russian populations—heighten the salience of Article 5 in assuring allied security.

COSTS AND RISKS

The cost of the commitment to NATO is the cost of things the United States does because of its alliance commitment that it would not otherwise do. This is hard to estimate in any precise way because we cannot answer with certainty the counterfactual question concerning what America would do if it were not bound by treaty obligations to its allies. Because military forces are relatively fungible, the fact that they may be located in Europe does not mean that they are there because of the commitment to Europe. Forces stationed in Europe can be used elsewhere, as the United States demonstrated when it shifted forces to Vietnam in the Cold War and to Iraq and Afghanistan more recently. Capabilities that might defeat a hypothetical Russian invasion of Estonia might also be used to counter other more immediate threats. Similarly, the fact that a military operation is designated a NATO mission does not mean that the United States would not have undertaken it had it been freed from alliance obligations. The missions in both Afghanistan and Iraq, for example, began as non-NATO missions, and so obviously they would have happened with or without NATO.

The implication of most studies relevant to this question is that marginal cost of defending Europe is small—that is, that the United States is not doing much to prepare for fighting in for Europe that it would not otherwise do.

Russia's capabilities and intentions are central to these assessments. Until 2014, NATO treated Russia officially as a friendly state, welcoming its participation in alliance affairs via the NATO–Russia Council. Consistent with this approach to Moscow, no alliance forces were permanently stationed east of the Elbe River. Even after Russia's invasion of Georgia in 2008, classified NATO assessments remained dismissive of Russian military capabilities.[7] But Russia began energetically reforming its military in 2007, seeking to create a leaner, more professional, better-equipped force. Although progress was uneven, analysts generally rated this as the most serious, most effective, and certainly the most expensive Russian military reform effort since the Soviet collapse.[8]

Moscow's intervention in Crimea revealed a highly competent elite force within the larger conscript army.[9] In turn, the Syria operation in 2015 showcased expeditionary capacity that is modest only in comparison to the United States. Russia has reorganized its conventional forces into nimbler brigades and instituted a vigorous weapons modernization program. Strategic forces, naval forces, and air defense have improved; Russia's military-industrial complex retains the capacity to develop and deploy highly capable systems in some areas; and Russian military thinkers have worked hard on strategies and plans for effective coercion.[10]

Nevertheless, the consensus remains that Russia's military challenge is of a different order than China's in East Asia.[11] Vladimir Putin's Russia is assertive, but it is not a rising power. Its economy is unbalanced and is poised for a prolonged period of low to negative growth that will increase the gap with NATO countries. Its military

[7] According to one 2009 cable released by Wikileaks: "Russia has limited capability for joint operations with air forces, continues to rely on aging and obsolete equipment, lacks all-weather capability and strategic transportation means . . . has an officer corps lacking flexibility, and has a manpower shortage." Wikileaks, accessed May 2, 2016, https://wikileaks.org/plusd/cables/09USNATO546_a.html.

[8] See Jim Nichol, "Russian Military Reform and Defense Policy," Congressional Research Service Report for Congress 7-5700 (August 27, 2011), https://www.fas.org/sgp/crs/row/R42006.pdf.

[9] Timothy Thomas, "Russia's Military Strategy and Ukraine: Indirect, Asymmetric—and Putin-Led," *Journal of Slavic Military Studies* 28 (2015): 445–461.

[10] See Paul Bernstein et al., "Putin's Russia and US Defense Strategy," Workshop Report, CGSR and Lawrence Livermore National Laboratory, August 19–20, 2015 (LLNL-PROC-678215), Washington DC, https://cgsr.llnl.gov/content/assets/docs/RussiaWorkshopReport.pdf.

[11] See, for example, "CSIS—An Assessment of Russian Defense Capabilities and Security Strategy," July 30, 2014, http://csis.org/event/assessment-russian-defense-capabilities-and-security-strategy; and "2016 Index of US Military Strength—Threats to the Homeland: Europe," Heritage Foundation, http://index.heritage.org/military/2015/chapter/threats/europe.

modernization confronts demographic, political, social, and especially economic challenges in the years ahead. NATO can deploy some two million troops (compared to Russia's 800,000), and its dramatically larger and more advanced economy allows it to mobilize and rearm far more effectively and quickly than Russia.[12] In this perspective, Russia's "nonnuclear military power is woefully insufficient for the conquest of the major states of Eurasia."[13] The International Institute of Strategic Studies assessment stresses that the purpose of the reforms is to move away from "the mass-mobilization model intended for large-scale conflict" and instead is "more aligned with the combat requirements of low- and medium-intensity local and regional warfare."[14]

The bottom line is an overall imbalance in favor of the West but a credible Russian capability to quickly seize territory near its borders—including that of Baltic NATO members—which it could then defend via highly capable A2/AD capabilities. The circumstances under which Moscow might risk such a move are hard to define. But a fair summary of the many assessments conducted in the wake of the Ukraine crisis is that NATO can "develop the capability to deter this type of Russian operation, not necessarily to comprehensively defeat it . . . at a reasonable cost."[15] Predeployed equipment and dedicated forces not necessarily stationed in the Baltics, as well as command and control and infrastructure improvements, would make such a move extremely risky and costly for Moscow and yet keep both overall costs and potential escalation risks low.

NATO's deployments continued to reflect the assessment that substantial strategic warning would long precede any change in this state of affairs, and that vulnerable states like Estonia and Latvia can be secured via general deterrence rather than fully credible forward defensive postures. The chief constraint on forward deployments in Central Europe and the Baltics has been concern over alienating Russia. At Poland's insistence, NATO began planning for the defense of Central European allies from Russian attack, and after 2008 contingency planning was extended to encompass the Baltic states. Whether these plans were credible, especially if Russia were to attempt unconventional destabilizing operations, remained open to question.[16] As of this writing (November 2015), NATO was discussing potential

---

[12] Jim Nichol, "Russian Political, Economic, and Security Issues and US Interests." See also International Institute for Strategic Studies, *Military Balance 2014*, (London: IISS 2014), pp. 161–162; Michael Kofman and Matthew Rojansky, "A Closer Look at Russia's 'Hybrid War,'" April 2015, Washington, DC: Wilson Center, https://www.wilsoncenter.org/sites/default/files/7-KENNAN%20CABLE-ROJANSKY%20KOFMAN.pdf; Keir Giles and Andrew Monaghan, "Russian Military Transformation—Goal in Sight?" May 2014, Carlisle, PA: US Army War College, Strategic Studies Institute, http://www.strategicstudiesinstitute.army.mil/pdffiles/PUB1196.pdf.

[13] Barry Posen, "Ukraine: Part of America's 'Vital Interests'?" *National Interest*, May 12, 2014, http://nationalinterest.org/feature/ukraine-part-americas-vital-interests-10443.

[14] "Military Balance 2014," pp. 161–162, http://www.iiss.org/en/publications/military-s-balance.

[15] Bernstein, et al, *Putin's Russia*, 8.

[16] "US Embassy Cables: US Plans to Defend Eastern Europe against Russia," *The Guardian*, Monday December 6, 2010, http://www.theguardian.com/world/us-embassy-cables-documents/

brigade-size rotational deployments and more vigorous exercises that appear to entail very modest cost increases over the pre-1914 status quo.[17] But the core assessment that the overall NATO–Russia balance would remain favorable without major new infusions of expensive US forces remained in place.

The scale of direct and indirect US budgetary outlays reflects this governing assessment. Direct outlays seem most clearly connected to the NATO commitment (and thus most likely to constitute savings if the United States withdrew), but they are modest. Even though America's economy accounts for over fifty percent of NATO's GDP, the United States pays less than twenty-five percent of NATO's budget: roughly $70 million for the civilian budget, $440 for the military budget, and $250 million for the Security Investment Program (mainly operational infrastructure) for a total of about $760 million.[18] Given that much of what NATO does has little directly to do with European security, at least some of that money would still be spent even if the United States revoked its security commitment to Europe.

But that sum factors in only direct payments, not deployments of personnel. Estimating those costs depends on what proportion of US forces deployed in Europe one assumes exists only because of the US commitment to Europe. As of late 2013, roughly 80,000 troops were stationed in Europe, with that number set to decline to the mid-60,000 range.[19] If these forces would be needed in any case, then the cost is simply the cost of stationing them in Europe as opposed to the United States. Because host counties cover many infrastructure costs, the marginal cost of keeping forces in Europe is surprisingly low. Studies suggest that simple redeployment of existing army troops home would entail short-term increases in outlays and only some modest savings in over the long term. For example, the General Accounting Office estimates that bringing two brigades home from Europe would save some $1.6 billion over a twenty-year period, but in the first two years it would add $900 million in new outlays.[20] But such a redeployment implies more expensive

A somewhat dated RAND study estimates that NATO's contingency plans for defending the Baltics were in fact credible with existing capabilities, under the (to my mind unrealistic) assumption that Russia would refrain from covert destabilizing operations. See Eric V. Larson et al., "Assuring Access in Key Strategic Regions," RAND Arroyo Center, www.rand.org/pubs/monographs/2004/RAND_MG112.pdf.

[17] Julian E. Barnes and Gordon Lubold, "US Military Officials Aim to Bolster Troop Presence in Europe," *Wall Street Journal*, Nov. 8, 2015.

[18] Figures are averages for 2010–2013. See Carl Ek, "NATO Common Fund Burdensharing: Background and Current Issues," Congressional Research Service 7-5700, February 2012.

[19] "Total Military Personnel and Dependent End Strength By Service, Regional Area, and Country." United States Department of Defense, December 31, 2012, accessed December 12, 2013, http://www.defense.gov/faq/pis/mil_strength.html; Donna Miles, "Force Changes in Europe to Preserve Strategic Edge," American Forces Press Service, May 7, 2012, http://www.eur.army.mil/news/2012/05072012-Force-changes-in-Europe-to-preserve-strategic-edge.htm.

[20] See GAO-10-745R, "Defense Planning: DOD Needs to Review the Costs and Benefits of Basing Alternatives for Army Forces in Europe" at http://www.gao.gov/new.items/d10745r.pdf; and CBO, "Options for Changing the Army's Overseas Basing," May 2004 at http://www.cbo.gov/doc.cfm?index=5415&type=0&sequence=1. The 1.6 billion estimate is thus net of the initial cost increase. My thanks to Cindy Williams for pointers on this issue.

logistics should those forces be needed in western and central Eurasia, the Middle East, or Africa. US defense officials argue that the operational hub in Europe is key even for offshore, "light footprint" style military presence in CENTCOM and AFRICOM, which is headquartered in Stuttgart. Even if the United States continues to move away from major expeditionary operations, if it wants to continue special-operations and other light footprint activity around Eurasia, it will want some infrastructure in Europe—a place where permanent US military installations are much less toxic politically than almost anywhere else in the world.

The upshot is that even if the United States follows the counsel of many NATO critics and chooses a grand strategy of restraint or offshore balancing, it is still going to want to retain some presence and infrastructure in Europe.[21] If, however, reducing the US commitment to Europe were part of a much more radical retrenchment that would truly cause America to "come home" and decommission a substantial portion of troops deployed there, then the savings are more serious, perhaps in the multiple billions per year.[22] Establishing exactly how much infrastructure needs to be kept in Europe to sustain US light footprint military operations around Eurasia and in Africa would take a very elaborate analysis. But it is likely to require some significant portion of current outlays. And if the United States were no longer committed to NATO, host country financial and logistical support might not be available as widely and cheaply as it is today. The real budgetary savings, therefore, are unlikely to be realized by cutting the commitment to Europe. It is only by rethinking the need for global military reach that the big dollars would be freed up.

As Cindy Williams demonstrates in this volume, pressure to reduce the defense outlays can be expected to remain a permanent feature of US domestic politics for the foreseeable future.[23] Yet the analysis here suggests that the scale of US grand strategic retrenchment would have to reach very radical proportions, and the marginal value of defense dollars saved would have to escalate dramatically, for pulling back from Europe to look like a promising option to American leaders. As long as US policymakers retain a strong interest in global leadership and the ability to conduct military operations around Eurasia, and as long as they value the NATO "coalition in waiting" that they can draw upon as the situation warrants, they are unlikely to see the net savings of reducing the security commitment to Europe as compellingly large.[24]

[21] These grand strategic options are parsed in Robert J. Art, *A Grand Strategy for America* (Ithaca, NY: Cornell University Press, 2003).

[22] The Task Force on a Sustainable Defense Budget estimated that decommissioning one-third of the US troops stationed in Europe and Asia would save $80 billion over a ten-year period. But that was in 2010, and the commitment has already been downsized in the years since. See Sustainable Defense Task Force, "Debt, Deficits, and Defense: A Way Forward," June 2010 at http://www.comw.org/pda/fulltext/1006SDTFreport.pdf. On the strategic option of truly "coming home" see Eugene Gholz, Daryl G. Press, and Harvey M. Sapolsky, "Come Home, America: The Strategy of Restraint in the Face of Temptation," *International Security* 21, no. 4 (Spring 1997): 5–48;

[23] See this volume, Cindy Williams, "Preserving National Strength in a Period of Fiscal Restraint."

[24] "Coalition in waiting" is the phrase used by NATO Deputy Director Gen. Alexander Vershbow. See Paul D. Shinkman, "The NATO Problem: Ukraine Edition," *US News & World Report*,

Hence the importance of security risks: the chance that the commitment will drag America into fighting wars that are not in the country's national interest. While such risk is inherent in any alliance, NATO raises it in particularly acute form for two reasons. First is the unusually large asymmetry in military capabilities that is a feature of all US alliances. This raises a moral hazard problem. In any asymmetric alliance between a strong state and weaker allies, smaller allies may be emboldened by the security offered by the powerful partner to run risks they would not otherwise have done, provoking an attack that triggers the alliance commitment. Most alliances are carefully written to protect the stronger power from this risk.[25] Other than leaving the nature of promised assistance in case of attack to the discretion of each alliance member, the North Atlantic Treaty contains no such provisions. As discussed below, this problem is acute in NATO because the United States has a near monopoly on certain kinds of military capacity, running the risk that wars sought by other alliance members will perforce demand US support.

The second worrisome feature of NATO is mission creep. At least until the Ukraine crisis, the relatively low salience of the classic defensive rationale generated incentives to create new missions merely to sustain the institution and calls to use the institution simply because it was there. NATO's highly bureaucratized nature means that there are hundreds of officials, analysts, think tanks, and other stakeholders whose livelihoods depend on NATO's relevance. They can be counted on to generate ideas for new roles and missions. For critics, the enlargement of NATO to include former Soviet allies and, especially, former Soviet republics (Latvia, Lithuania, and Estonia) represents the prime example of such mission creep. New allies with potentially toxic relations with Moscow add little capability to the alliance and impose the cost of potentially souring relations with a great power. Careful studies show that NATO expansion did, in fact, help "socialize" newly democratic former communist states into the liberal west, but, critics wonder, how did this become a key national interest for the United States?[26] Expansion, in turn, has led to a highly complex decision-making apparatus ripe for logrolls and other bargaining that might generate otherwise unsought alliance commitments. Precisely this kind of logroll may make it harder for the alliance to unambiguously forswear further expansion, a stance which imposes the costs of helping to stymie a possible bargained solution to the Ukraine crisis.

This yields two kinds of risks: (1) the small probability of a very costly US involvement in a war with Russia whose origins lie in some moral hazard behavior that would not have occurred without the alliance; and (2) the larger probability of lower cost interventions that may not be in the US national interest. Analyses of Russia's interests and capabilities discount the former risk for the near to medium term. In addition, there is very little evidence of this dynamic at work in the quarter

---

May 20, 2014, http://www.usnews.com/news/articles/2014/05/20/natos-very-existence-to-blame-for-ukraine-violence-ukrainian-pol-says.

[25] See TongFi Kim, "Why Alliances Entangle but Seldom Entrap States," *Security Studies* 20, no. 3 (2011): 350–377.

[26] On socialization, see, especially, Alexandra Gheciu, *NATO in the "New Europe": The Politics of International Socialization After the Cold War* (Palo Alto: Stanford University Press, 2005).

century since the Cold War's end. The potentially riskiest move, extending Article 5 to the Baltic states, thus far has not prevented those governments from taking apparently sufficient palliative measures to prevent the alienation of their Russian minorities.[27] States neighboring Russia would likely be more solicitous of Moscow's interests were they unallied, but it is hard to find examples of provocative, war-risking behavior enabled by the alliance.[28] Indeed, substantial pressure on the Estonian and Latvian governments to ease citizenship rules and integrate their minority Russian populations comes from NATO and the EU.

The latter problem—of mission creep to encompass lower cost operations—is where most of the action has been. While NATO cannot make the United States do anything, concern for the alliance's credibility may conspire to commit Washington to interventions that emerge from a suboptimal NATO process. Bosnia, Kosovo, and Libya are all examples of this dynamic, though none offers strong evidence of "wag-the-dog" dynamics. In each, the alliance credibility argument played a role, but actors within the US government argued for the intrinsic merits of intervention. In the Libya case, France and Britain were the strongest supporters of intervention. But extant accounts of President Obama's decision to intervene do not feature alliance credibility as part of the story.[29]

But by far the main story of the last two decades has been the dog emphatically wagging the tail. The costliest operations were those pushed by Washington, with allies dragged in because of *their* felt need to sustain the alliance. Sixty-seven percent of all the casualties and sixty-four percent of all the budget costs of all the wars the United States has fought since 1990 were caused by Iraq. Twenty-seven percent of the causalities and twenty-six percent of the costs were related to Operation Enduring Freedom in Afghanistan. All the other interventions—the 1990–1991 Persian Gulf War, the subsequent airstrike campaigns in Iraq, Somalia, Bosnia, Haiti, Kosovo, Libya, and so on—account for three percent of the casualties and ten percent of the costs.[30] As Michael Beckley has shown, moreover, in all interventions

---

[27] I write this as someone who opposed NATO expansion and expected it to generate much higher costs than it ultimately did. For a retrospective analysis, see W. C. Wohlforth, "Policy Evaluation After Paradigm-Shattering Events: How Well Do the Experts Do?" in Melvyn Leffler and Jeffrey Legro eds., *In Uncertain Times: American Foreign Policy after the Berlin Wall and 9/11* (Ithaca, NY: Cornell University Press, 2011)

[28] A circumstantial case can be made that close relations with the United States and talk of NATO membership may have emboldened Georgia in the run up to its five-day war with Russia in 2008. Needless to say, the fact that NATO was under no obligation to defend Georgia is likely to have figured in Moscow's response. See Ronald Asmus, *A Little War that Shook the World: Georgia, Russia, and the Future of the West* (New York, NY: Palgrave MacMillan, 2010).

[29] The main issue that comes up in journalistic accounts is humanitarianism. See, for example, Michael Lewis, "Obama's Way," *Vanity Fair*, September 2012.

[30] Casualties as of 2010 calculated from: Hannah Fischer, "A Guide to U.S. Military Casualty Statistics: Operation Freedom's Sentinel, Operation Inherent Resolve, Operation New Dawn, Operation Iraqi Freedom, and Operation Enduring Freedom", CRS 7-5700, (Washington, DC.: Congressional Research Service, 2010). Costs are actual budget outlays (not estimated total cost) as of 2011, calculated from: Stephen Daggett, "Costs of Major US Wars," CRS 7-5700, (Washington, DC: CRS, June 2010); Jeremiah Gertler, "Operation Odyssey Dawn

except Iraq, allies either spent more than the United States, suffered greater relative casualties, or both. In the 1990–1991 Persian Gulf War, for example, the United States ranked fourth in overall casualties (measured relative to population size) and fourth in total expenditures (relative to GDP). In Bosnia, European Union budget outlays and personnel deployments ultimately swamped the United States' as the Europeans took over post-conflict peace-building operations. In Kosovo, the United States suffered one combat fatality, the sole loss in the whole operation, and it ranked sixth in relative monetary contribution. In Afghanistan, the United States was the number one financial contributor (it achieved that status only after the 2010 surge), but its relative combat losses ranked fifth.[31] In Libya, Britain, France, Norway, and Denmark all dramatically outspent the United States as a proportion of their economies. And if talk of NATO expansion to Georgia and Ukraine is partly to blame for the deterioration in relations with Moscow, it is important to note that most of that talk came from Washington itself and was resisted by most of the most powerful NATO allies.

In sum, the evidence strongly suggests that the countries running the real risk of getting dragged into conflicts of others' making are America's allies. 45,000 allied NATO troops have served in Afghanistan. Were they as effective as US troops? Mostly no. Were they a net plus? Unquestionably. That the American dog ends up wagging the NATO tail is hardly surprising, given that the United States dominates the alliance. And that is arguably the biggest problem with the "wag-the-dog" argument: all the post-1991 intervention cases occurred in a context in which the United States itself was pushing NATO toward a larger global role. This was the era of "out of area, or out of business" logic. As James Goldgeier put it: "If NATO isn't outward looking, it's got nothing to do."[32] Because this was the message emanating from Washington, it is hard to portray these episodes as an outgrowth of the alliance dragging the United States into conflicts it did not seek. Washington sets the agenda. If it doesn't like what NATO is doing, it should change that agenda.

TODAY'S NATO "CRISIS": POLICY OPTIONS

If the foregoing analysis is right, why does everyone think NATO is in a crisis that requires a dramatic policy departure? Why did Secretary of Defense Gates read NATO leaders the riot act in Munich in 2011, warning of the alliance's potential demise? The answer is that analysts, commentators, and political leaders frequently elide the distinction between the NATO commitment's costs to the United States and the gap between US and allied defense efforts. US defense spending accounted for seventy-five percent of total NATO outlays in 2010, up from sixty percent in 1991. And even though US spending is heading down steeply, so is Europe's, with

(Libya): Background and Issues for Congress," CRS 7-5700, (Washington, DC.: CRS, March 2011); and Nina Serafino, "Military Contingency Funding for Bosnia, Southwest Asia, and Other Operations: Questions and Answers" (Washington, DC: CRS, 1999).

[31] Data from Michael Beckley, "The Unipolar Era" (PhD diss., Columbia University, 2012).

[32] Steven Erlanger, "Shrinking Europe Military Spending Stirs Concern," *New York Times*, April 22, 2013.

only four NATO allies currently willing and able to sustain defense commitments at or above the alliance's official target of two percent of GDP. The EU's austerity policies will long constrain allied defense efforts, weakening even such relatively capable states as France and Britain more than major cuts in the United States will reduce American capabilities. As unimpressive as some allies' efforts in Libya were, currently projected defense cuts will render them incapable of even that level of military activity in short order.[33]

The gap in military power between the United States and its NATO allies is enormous and likely to grow.[34] And it clearly matters. Stronger allies are better than weaker ones. But it matters in assessing the cost of NATO only if the United States maintains high relative defense spending *because* of its commitment to Europe, and, as I've shown above, that is demonstrably not the case. US military spending increased by over eighty percent in the years after 2001, virtually none of which was generated by NATO commitments. On the contrary, the United States continued to draw down forces in Europe, concentrating first on Afghanistan and Iraq and then on East Asia. Far from being a driver of US military efforts, NATO was a reserve on which Washington drew to pursue various global objectives.

If there is a crisis in NATO, then, it is not a matter of costs and risks. Rather it has to do with the fact that the allies' military deficiencies lower their value, and thus lower the net benefits of the alliance to the United States. Even though costs to the United States are small and risks are manageable, the allies' military weakness risks making the alliance a losing proposition for Washington. This was the gist of Secretary of Defense Robert Gates' oft-quoted swansong speech in Brussels.[35] Concern about this issue has fed into a vigorous expert debate over what to do about NATO.

Four options emerge. Option 1 is *full-scale retrenchment.* As Barry Posen puts it, transform NATO into a political alliance.[36] Perhaps with some window for adjustment, the United States would renounce Article 5 of the North Atlantic Treaty, abrogating any military commitment to European security. In this view, US security provision to Europe is "welfare for the rich." Allies can easily provide for their

[33] F. Stephen Larrabee, et al., *NATO and the Challenges of Austerity* (Santa Monica, CA: RAND National Defense Research Institute, 2012).

[34] There are multiple caveats that weaken the case for free-riding—US and European commitments to NATO are near their historical averages; some trends point to a decreasing gap; many European contributions fall outside of defense budgets, etc.—but my main point here is that the alliance's value is not strictly dependent on the burden sharing debate. See Jordan Becker and Edmund Malesky, "Pillar or Pole? The Effect of Strategic Culture on Burden Sharing and NATO's Future," (October 1, 2013). Available at SSRN, http://papers.ssrn.com/sol3/papers.cfm?abstract_id=2333290.

[35] "The Security and Defense Agenda (Future of NATO)" Secretary of Defense Robert M. Gates, Brussels, Belgium, Friday, June 10, 2011, http://archive.defense.gov/speeches/speech.aspx?speechid=1581.

[36] Barry M. Posen "Pull Back," *Foreign Affairs* 92, no. 1 (January–February 2013): 116–148. For similar analyses, see Andrew Bacevich, "Let Europe Be Europe," *Foreign Policy* 178 (March/April 2010): 70–71; and David C. Ellis, "US Grand Strategy Following the G.W. Bush Presidency," *International Studies Perspectives* 10, no. 4 (November, 2009): 361–377.

own security through increased spending, reorganization of inefficient military institutions, and pooling of capabilities via the European Union's Common Foreign and Security Policy (CFSP). Revoking Article 5 is just the shock needed to prod complacent allies to get their act together. And if they fail, the downsides would be manageable, given low background threats to European security.

A second option is *NATO-friendly retrenchment*. Announce a limited window during which America would assist the Europeans in developing intrinsic capacity for neighborhood (e.g., Libya, Balkans) operations; restrict the US role to Article 5 contingencies, a commitment that can be sustained mainly from offshore; and hand over ultimate allied command (SACEUR) to Europe at the end of the window.[37] Ending the organizational basis for US "leadership" would truly incentivize allies to increase defense cooperation and pooling and spending and finally ramp CFSP into a real capability.

Option 3 is to *muddle through,* accepting that NATO's capacity for large-scale expeditionary operations will progressively decline. Continue reductions in permanent presence as currently planned without either renouncing Article 5 or instigating any reform in the alliance's organization. Allow the alliance to function as an institutionalized cooperation shop that reduces transactions costs for ad hoc coalitions of the willing—in which allies have to reckon with probability that the United States will be unwilling in some cases. Realities on the ground in terms of real US deployments and commitments might incentivize some increased allied defense efficiencies *a la* the France–Britain defense cooperation treaty.[38]

Doubling down is the fourth option: the United States and its allies minimize defense cuts, the United States sustains at least current level of military presence in Europe, and NATO continues to be thought of as global or at least wider-neighborhood interventionist alliance. [39]

CONCLUSION: THE OPTIMALITY
OF MUDDLING THROUGH

We will, of course, muddle through. This was already the Obama administration's policy before Russia's newfound assertiveness, and arguably is compatible with the

[37] See, Sarwar Kashmeri, *NATO 2.0: Reboot or Delete?* (Washington, DC: Potomac Books, 2011); Sean Kay, "A New Kind of NATO," http://walt.foreignpolicy.com/posts/2012/01/11/a_new_kind_of_nato.

[38] The analysis most closely reflecting this view (though its author would reject the name I've given it) is Sten Rynning, *NATO In Afghanistan: The Liberal Disconnect* (Stanford, CA: Stanford University Press, 2012).

[39] See, for example, Luke Coffey, "2014 NATO Summit: Laying the Groundwork Now," Heritage Foundation Issue Brief #4603 on NATO, http://www.heritage.org/research/reports/2013/10/2014-nato-summit-laying-the-groundwork-now. Earlier analyses in this vein include James Goldgeier, "The Future of NATO," New York: Council on Foreign Relations, Special Report No. 51, 2010; and Ivo Daalder and James Goldgeier, "Global NATO," *Foreign Affairs,* Council on Foreign Relations, September/October 2006.

modal allied response to NATO's recent experiences in Afghanistan and Libya as well as Ukraine. But if advocates of Option 1 (full-scale retrenchment) are right about the benign strategic environment and advocates of a deep engagement grand strategy are right about that strategy's core requirements, then Option 3 is not just expedient, it is in fact optimal.

Strategic Environment : NATO is only in crisis if the North Atlantic area faces critical threats that require robust high-end military intervention capabilities from the European allies. But it is hard to argue with the basic claim of advocates of grand strategic retrenchment: security threats to the wealthy, powerful, and institutionally robust states of the North Atlantic area are extremely low by any historical comparative standard. Vladimir Putin's Russia now boasts a more coherent and functional state that wields a much more effective military tool than it had for most of the post–Cold War period. Russia's actions in Georgia and Ukraine show that, where the balance of interests favor it, Moscow can exploit its proximity to call the west's bluff about further eastward expansion. But using military power to coerce NATO is a different kettle of fish. There, Russia faces the same tight local balancing constraint the Soviet Union confronted in the Cold War. More bellicosity generates painful pushback in the form of sanctions, lost cooperation, and enhanced allied military efforts. By the autumn of 2015, Russian assertiveness had pushed Finland and Sweden more seriously than ever to consider joining NATO.

It follows that the "crisis" created by the growing gap in US and allied military capacity is really no crisis at all. Or, perhaps more accurately, it is a crisis only for a particular, liberal-global vision for NATO rather than a down-to-earth vision focused on the North Atlantic.[40] Declining allied defense commitments portend a reduced capacity to intervene *early* (e.g., long before any real security threat is manifest) and at extremely *low human cost* to allied military personnel in *optional* operations like Libya, justified mainly on human rights grounds, or exceedingly conjectural threats emerging from various sorts of instability. Because the threats are low, wealthy North Atlantic countries do not want to risk serious casualties to address them, hence they substitute expensive technology. This creates the impression of dire deficits in defense provision. Europe's effort to mimic the United States in this regard is what creates the false impression that capable states like the United Kingdom or France risk becoming military pygmies when they pare defense outlays to under two percent of their economies. They only seem such when the United States is the reference point. Having stronger allies is better than the alternative, but that fact that European allies' defense cuts may reduce the attractiveness of military responses to humanitarian operations or conjectural security threats is hardly a real crisis for American national security.

A further, critical implication of this assessment of the strategic environment is rarely noted: it is entirely inconsistent with shock therapy's assumption about the lack of serious threats to European security to say that calling the United States' Article 5 commitment into question will cause European governments step up and create more military capacity via increased spending or cooperation. On the contrary, a relatively benign security setting is arguably more conducive to allowing

---

[40] See Rynning, *NATO In Afghanistan.*

narrow national perspectives to trump EU-wide initiatives and to foster the continuation of minimalist defense efforts than the status quo of US leadership. America's NATO allies make up nearly a fifth of global military spending. Britain is the fourth biggest military spender in the world, with France close behind (after another US ally, Japan) as sixth. Germany, Italy, Turkey, and Canada all rank among the world's fifteen biggest spenders.[41] Very secure states like Norway and Canada purchase sophisticated weaponry from the US military-industrial complex and order their soldiers into battle in America's wars in far off lands. Why? A major reason is the alliance with the United States—it is the existence of the overseas hegemon and the perceived need to retain access to it and standing with it that drive much of this behavior.[42]

Options 1 and 2 are based on the assumption that the international system generates strong pressures for European states to do one or all of three very costly things: ramp up spending on defense; reform entrenched domestic defense practices and institutions; and set aside national prerogatives to generate genuine supranational military defense and decision making at the EU level. Take away Uncle Sam's "welfare for the rich" and the logic of anarchy will somehow force this outcome. It cannot be ruled out that there is something special about Europe that would cause it to act in this collectively martial way without the US umbrella. But that expectation is inconsistent with most of what we know about international politics and with the lived experience of the EU's European Security and Defense Policy and Common Foreign and Security Policy. Governments just don't do extremely expensive and politically costly things without a major prod of some sort. The problem is that there is neither a compelling external security incentive nor a European hegemon to help solve the collective action problem. Germany may play this role in economics, but it is not going to do so in security.[43] The likelihood that a US revocation of Article 5 would spur France and Britain to set aside national feeling and unite defense efforts—and that middle powers from Poland to Turkey would acquiesce— is exceedingly low. Indeed, the downward trend in European defense spending has continued despite the continuing decline in American military forces in Europe and despite increasingly loud calls for retrenchment.

Three consequences follow from this analysis. First, doubling down is unlikely—because Americans won't pay for it—and neither form of retrenchment will work—because Europeans won't pay the political or economic costs even if the United States steps aside. Second, major changes to the current benign macro-security environment are likely to occur only after substantial strategic warning, and therefore projected low costs and risks for US security provision will likely remain adequate. And third, there is no net security benefit to the United States

---

[41] See SIPRI military expenditures database, http://www.sipri.org/research/armaments/milex/milex_database.

[42] On the Norway case, see Nina Græger, "From 'Forces for Good' to 'Forces for Status'? Status-Seeking For Small States: The Case of Norway," in Iver B. Neumann and Benjamin de Carvalho eds., *Small States and Status Seeking* (New York: Routledge, 2015).

[43] See Sten Rynning, "Germany is More than Europe can Handle: NATO as Europe's Pacifier," Research Paper No. 96 (Sept. 2013) NATO Defense College, Rome.

of administering a shock to NATO via even more dramatic reductions in presence or commitment. Indeed, there are serious expected costs in terms of lost security cooperation and even less capable and interoperable allies. With militarily capable allies like NATO and the Republic of Korea, a major benefit of presence is security cooperation (joint training, planning, etc.) that is difficult or impossible to replicate with rotational deployments. According to a recent comprehensive RAND study, the US presence in NATO is getting near the floor of deployed personnel needed to sustain security cooperation at current level.[44]

Now let's consider how this vision of NATO aligns with American grand strategy. The US grand strategy of deep engagement is essentially about three objectives: managing the external environment to reduce near- and long-term threats to US national security; promoting a liberal economic order to expand the global economy and maximize domestic prosperity; and creating, sustaining, and revising the global institutional order to secure necessary interstate cooperation on terms favorable to US interests.[45]

NATO's declining capability for large-scale optional expeditionary operations to address conjectural security threats or humanitarian ideals does little to impede this grand strategy. The Obama administration's policy pronouncements and military deployments do not in any way represent a change away from deep engagement. They reflect a refocus on the strategy's core. For that core, NATO retains value as an institutional framework for:

- Coordinating transatlantic security cooperation;
- Maintaining key infrastructure and lines of communications to sustain a US-led containment strategy in the greater Middle East;
- Reducing inefficient duplication of defense efforts among allies, preventing full renationalization of security;
- Hedging against the emergence of a more threatening Russia or the appearance of a new, serious security threat.

The retrenchment options (One and Two) put these benefits at risk. Full retrenchment does so because it is obviously inconsistent with deep engagement. "NATO-friendly" retrenchment does so because it confuses secondary aims with the grand strategy's core aims. It is willing to trade US leadership of the alliance for ephemeral and likely unattainable gains in indigenous European capability. Doubling down on NATO makes the same mistake of viewing optional capacities as essential, and magnifies it by ultimately imposing its costs on the US taxpayer, as it has no answer to the "free rider" problem aside from exhortation.

If the United States engineers a dramatic shift in its grand strategy to a strong version of restraint that devalues the capacity to mount light footprint military operations around Eurasia as well as the incipient "coalition in waiting" represented

---

[44] Michael J. Lostumbo et al., "Overseas Basing of US Military Forces: An Assessment of Relative Costs and Strategic Benefits," Santa Monica, CA: RAND, 2013.

[45] For more, see S.G. Brooks, G.J. Ikenberry, and W.C. Wohlforth "Don't Come Home, America: The Case Against Retrenchment," *International Security* 37, no. 3 (Winter 2012–2013): 7–51

by NATO, then the alliance would cease to make sense. But if, as is likely, it pares the deep engagement strategy to its core objectives, then muddling though, with no new grand bargains, no grand "rebooting" of the alliance, no sudden new infusion of defense dollars and euros, and no "post-American" NATO emerges as the optimal choice. In other words, the transatlantic bargain should contain three parts: NATO should continue to guarantee territorial defense; external operations in Europe's neighborhood where the United States has no interest should fall under the EU or individual European allies (e.g., France in Mali, Central African Republic); and NATO should only engage beyond Europe's borders when the United States wishes to be involved.

10

THE UNITED STATES AND THE MIDDLE EAST
INTERESTS, RISKS, AND COSTS

Daniel Byman and Sara Bjerg Moller

The United States has long been involved in the Middle East, and its role has only grown since the end of the Cold War. Yet in contrast to Europe, another region of long-standing interest, or Asia, where the United States plans to "pivot" in the years to come, trade relations and cultural ties remain weak, and the region's military power marginal. During the Cold War, the Middle East's energy supplies and several communist-leaning regimes rendered it part of the US-Soviet chessboard. In the 1990s the United States expanded its security presence in the region to contain Saddam Hussein's Iraq and the clerical regime in Iran. At the same time, Washington engaged in an energetic and sustained, but ultimately unsuccessful, effort to bring about peace between Israel and its Arab neighbors.

Following the 9/11 attacks, US involvement grew even greater. The United States deepened counterterrorism cooperation with long-standing allies like Egypt and Jordan and pushed to establish more extensive ties with hitherto neglected or adversarial regimes, like Yemen and Libya. Most dramatically, of course, in 2003, the United States invaded Iraq and, in so doing, triggered an insurgency that led to a sustained US presence in the country until the end of 2011. And then, just as US forces departed Iraq, the so-called "Arab Spring" shook the region, toppling long-standing US allies in Egypt, Tunisia, and Yemen, and creating civil wars in several countries, most notably Syria. Although the Obama administration resisted a large-scale US military commitment in the region, after the 2014 Islamic State advances in Iraq, it began air strikes against Islamic State forces and stepped up its efforts to work with regional allies and local partners against the group.

Today's posited US interests in the Middle East can be broken down into five areas: ensuring the free flow of oil; preventing nuclear proliferation; fighting terrorism; maintaining the security of Israel; and promoting democratization. Iran, the Islamic State, and al-Qaeda at times pose real threats to these interests, but we argue that the threat they represent is often overstated and that many US interests in the region stand little risk of disruption. In fact, it is our allies' own problems that present a bigger concern, and the Arab Spring and subsequent civil wars brought many of these into the forefront. The US approach to managing these problems has generated many benefits, including deterring and disrupting foes and successfully reassuring allies. However, it has at times exacerbated internal problems and contributed to anti-Americanism. To protect its interests, the United States should try to contain the violence in Iraq and Syria, weaken the Islamic State, and reenergize its efforts to promote peace between Israel and the Palestinians. Washington must also recognize the limits of its power as it tries to protect its interests in this turbulent region.

The remainder of this essay is divided into four parts. Section one describes the array of US security commitments to states in the Middle East, ranging from formal military agreements to more rhetorical declarations of interest. Section two assesses the posited US interests in the region, presenting the arguments to their importance and raising questions about the validity of many of the justifications on which they are based. It also reviews the threats to these interests and evaluates which represent the most worrisome cases. Section three attempts to prioritize US interests and discusses those over which the United States can exert meaningful influence. The essay concludes in section four by presenting the implications of this dissection and the recommendations for policy.

US SECURITY RELATIONSHIPS IN THE MIDDLE EAST: A REVIEW

The United States maintains a range of security relationships in the Middle East. These include defense cooperation agreements, basing and access rights, the prepositioning of equipment, and other "hard" forms of cooperation. In addition, the United States has made rhetorical commitments to several of its allies (and explicit and implicit threats to its enemies) and fulfills the role of major arms supplier to the region. These relations are particularly extensive with states of the Arabian Peninsula, Egypt, and Israel.

The US basing network in the Middle East is quite extensive. Even taking the US presence in Afghanistan out of the picture, the United States positions numerous bases, Forward Operation Sites (FOS), and Cooperative Security Locations (CSL) and forces along the Gulf littoral, as well as in the eastern Mediterranean and along the Horn of Africa. Although accurate numbers are hard to come by due to the political sensitivities of the host nations and regular changes in the specifics of basing as operational needs vary, US military sites in the region number in the dozens. Among the major US Army military installations located in the CENTCOM theater are Kuwait's Camps Arifjanin and Buehring along with Camp As Saliyah in Qatar.[1] The US Air Force also maintains installations in Kuwait, UAE, and Qatar. In 2015, the US Air Force also began deploying air assets from Incirlik Air Force Base in Turkey.[2] Additionally, at any given time, as many as two of the navy's three forward-deployed aircraft carriers are also deployed in the region.[3] The conversion

[1] Michael Lostumbo et al. 2013, "Overseas Basing of US Military Forces: An Assessment of Relative Costs and Strategic Benefits," (Santa Monica, CA: RAND Corporation), p. 24.

[2] Jeff Schogul, "F-15Cs Deploy to Incirlik to Protect Turkish Airspace," *Air Force Times*, November 6, 2015, http://www.airforcetimes.com/story/military/2015/11/06/f-15cs-deploy-incirlik-protect-turkish-airspace/75288330/>.

[3] In mid-2013 the number of aircraft carriers deployed in the Fifth Fleet dropped from two to one due to budget cuts.

Associated Press, "US to Cut Carrier Fleet in Persian Gulf to 1," *Seattle Times*, February 7, 2013. http://www.seattletimes.com/seattle-news/politics/us-to-cut-carrier-fleet-in-persian-gulf-to-1/

of one of the navy's oldest transport ships in 2012 into a floating forward base marks the introduction of yet another basing platform in the region.[4] Taken together, this arrangement provides the United States the ability to deploy forces at or near a wide range of potential crisis points.

This basing network is reinforced by several thousand troops deployed in various states throughout the Persian Gulf. The United States also retains several dozen personnel in Oman and an advisory presence in Saudi Arabia. To strike the Islamic State, the United States and its allies have stepped up cooperation with Turkey and bombed from bases there and in Jordan and other states in the region. In addition, the United States maintains several hundred troops afloat in the region at any given time.[5] The United States still retains an unmatched ability to quickly ramp up additional assets in the region should events there warrant it, as evidenced by the late summer 2013 US Navy positioning of an additional ten ships, including the aircraft carrier the USS Nimitz, into the Red Sea in preparation for a possible limited strike against Syria.[6] As such, the United States will continue to maintain a strong military presence in the region for the foreseeable future.

Washington also holds numerous long-standing security agreements with the smaller states of the Arabian Peninsula that give the United States access to facilities and bases in the region and the right to pre-position equipment. Kuwait is a "Major Non-NATO ally" and the country served as a base for over 20,000 US troops during the Iraq War. Despite withdrawal of US forces from Iraq, Kuwait (along with Qatar) has remained an important regional hub, with the US bases there coordinating logistical and training support. The United States also deploys missile defense systems to the country and helps train the Kuwaiti military.[7] Further south, Bahrain is home to the American Fifth Fleet and, like Kuwait, is a "Major Non-NATO Ally," enabling it to buy advanced American weapons systems. The United States has supplied Bahrain with surplus military equipment and helped Bahrain expand its air

---

[4] Thom Shanker, "Floating Base Gives US New Footing in the Persian Gulf," *New York Times*, July 11, 2012.

[5] These figures are from a June 2012 Senate Foreign Relations Committee report, except for the figures for Oman, Saudi Arabia, and afloat which come from a Department of Defense report and *The New York Times*. See "The Gulf Security Architecture: Partnership With the Gulf Cooperation Council," Majority Staff Report, Committee on Foreign Relations, United States Senate, June 19, 2012; "Active Duty Military Personnel Strengths by Regional Area and by Country," Department of Defense, December 31, 2011; Thom Shanker, Eric Schmitt, and David E. Sanger, "US Adds Forces to the Persian Gulf, a Signal to Iran," *The New York Times*, July 3, 2012. (The United States in July 2012 deployed another aircraft carrier to the Gulf, further increasing the troop numbers.) Adam Entous and Julian E. Barnes, "Pentagon Bulks Up Defenses in the Gulf," *Wall Street Journal*, July 17, 2012.

[6] Andrea Shalal-Esa, "More Than 10 Ships Near Syria As USS Nimitz Carrier Group Movies Into the Red Sea," Reuters, September 2, 2013.

[7] Anthony Cordesman et al, "Iran and the Gulf Military Balance – I," 4th Working Draft *CSIS*, June 28, 2012, p. 30, http://csis.org/files/publication/120612_Burke_IRan_Gulf_Military_Balance.pdf; Kenneth Katzman, "Kuwait: Security, Reform, and US Policy," CRS Report for Congress, *Congressional Research Service*, June 20, 2012.

and coastal defenses.[8] Bahrain also provided basing and other support for US operations in Iraq and Afghanistan.

Qatar's importance as a US base dates to the 1990s when Washington sought alternatives to Saudi Arabia. Qatar is the forward-deployed base of CENTCOM and houses the Combined Air and Space Operations Center. In 2011, Doha signed a bilateral security agreement with Washington regarding information sharing, aviation, cybersecurity, and other homeland defense-related issues. Qatar also hosts a missile defense radar station.[9]

The UAE's Jebel Ali is the most visited foreign port in the world for the American Navy. In addition, the United States positions several air defense systems in the country, which also functions as the base for the Integrated Missile Defense Center. The United States trains large numbers of Emiratis and other Gulf students in the UAE, and there is a considerable effort to develop and support the country's air forces.[10] Oman is home to several US Air Force bases and prepositioned American equipment. US forces maintain access to bases in Oman for contingencies and engage in a range of training programs and joint exercises with the Omani armed forces.[11]

The United States has long cooperated militarily with Saudi Arabia and has worked extensively—though without much success—to train the Saudi military. The United States is widely perceived as firmly committed to Saudi Arabia's security, but no formal defense agreement exists between the two countries. In the 1990s, the United States deployed tens of thousands of troops to Saudi Arabia, primarily to defend the region against Iraq, but withdrew in 2003 after the fall of Saddam Hussein. Several hundred troops remain in the country to administer training programs. Washington has also undertaken a range of counterterrorism cooperation efforts with the Saudi regime, including measures to work together to combat terrorism financing.[12]

In addition to formal defense cooperation agreements with traditional allies on the Arabian peninsula, and the implicit guarantee of Saudi security, the United

[8] Kenneth Katzman, "Bahrain: Reform, Security, and US Policy," *Congressional Research Service*, August 13, 2012; "US Relations with Bahrain," Fact Sheet, *Bureau of Near Eastern Affairs*, July 31, 2015.

[9] "Qatar, US Sign Security Pact on terrorism, airport security," *AFP*, January 3, 2011, http://www.dailystar.com.lb/News/Middle-East/2011/Jan-03/90496-qatar-us-sign-security-pact-on-terrorism-airport-security.ashx; Christopher M. Blanchard, "Qatar: Background and US Relations," *Congressional Research Service*, June 6, 2012, http://www.au.af.mil/au/awc/awcgate/crs/rl31718.pdf; Adam Entous and Julian E. Barnes, "Pentagon Bulks Up Defenses in the Gulf," *Wall Street Journal*, July 17, 2012.

[10] Kenneth Katzman, "The United Arab Emirates: Issues for US Policy," *Congressional Research Service*, July 17, 2012; Anthony Cordesman and Alexander Wilner "Iran and the Gulf Military Balance – I," *CSIS*, June 28, 2012.

[11] Kenneth Katzman, "Oman: Reform, Security and US Policy," *Congressional Research Service*, August 30, 2012; Anthony Cordesman and Alexander Wilner, "Iran and the Gulf Military Balance," *CSIS*, June 28, 2012, p. 31.

[12] Christopher M. Blanchard, "Saudi Arabia: Background and US Relations." *Congressional Research Service*, June 14, 2010; Cordesman and Wilner, "Iran and the Gulf Military Balance."

States signed a "Strategic Framework Agreement" with Iraq in 2011. Although this promises cooperation in various areas, it comes after unsuccessful attempts to conclude a more formal defense arrangement, which foundered on Iraq's unwillingness to grant US forces a separate legal status. A Memorandum of Understanding on Security Cooperation concluded between the two countries in December 2012 provides additional mechanisms for increased defense cooperation.[13] Given the ongoing war against the Islamic State in much of Iraq, the Obama administration has deployed additional forces to train and advise the Iraqi Army as well as work with Iraqi tribes and Kurdish forces. It has also deployed special operations forces.[14]

To back up these various formal agreements, the United States engages in repeated public declarations of support for the security of its allies in the region. President Obama, former Secretary of State Hillary Clinton, Secretary of Defense Leon Panetta, and their successors have repeatedly declared their commitment to individual states' and to the security of the region as a whole.[15] As further evidence of these strong ties, senior US administration officials undertake frequent trips to the region.

States in the Middle East also serve as major purchasers of US military equipment. In 2011 Saudi Arabia agreed to purchase over eighty F-15SA fighter aircraft and upgrade its existing fleet of seventy F-15s, along with air-to-air and air-to-ground packages. The $29.4 billion sale was the largest of its kind to a single recipient. In recent years the UAE, though far smaller than Saudi Arabia, agreed to purchase over ten billion dollars of US equipment, including up to 80 F-16s.[16] Other sales to these and other regional states have included not only high-end aircraft, tanks, and other military systems, but also packages for system support, logistics, and upgrades. As part of these sales, the US has also agreed to deploy standoff weapons to Saudi Arabia and UAE. And, as in the past, US military personnel will jointly train with the Emirati and the Saudi pilots.[17]

---

[13] "U.S.-Iraqi Strategic Framework Agreement: Update on Implementation," Office of the Spokesperson, U.S. Department of State, August 15, 2013, http://www.state.gov/r/pa/prs/ps/2013/08/213170.htm.

[14] Euan McKirdy, Jim Sciutto and Jamie Crawford, "US sending more troops, Apaches to Iraq," *CNN*, April 18, 2016, http://www.cnn.com/2016/04/18/politics/defense-secretary-carter-iraq/.

[15] Among many, see for example Associated Press, "Obama: Kuwait Has Been 'Outstanding' Host," *CBS News*, August 3, 2009, http://www.cbsnews.com/news/obama-kuwait-has-been-outstanding-host/; Habib Toumi, "Clinton Reiterates US Commitment to Security in the Gulf," *Gulfnews.com*, December 4, 2010; Leon E. Panetta, "Remarks at the US Forces-Iraq End of Mission Ceremony," (speech, Baghdad, Iraq, December 15, 2011); Arshad Mohammed, "Kerry gently presses Bahrain on rights, praises security ties," *Reuters*, April 7, 2016, http://www.reuters.com/article/us-mideast-crisis-gulf-bahrain-idUSKCN0X40XM.

[16] Kenneth Katzman, "The United Arab Emirates: Issues for US Policy," *Congressional Research Service*, July 17, 2012; "Kingdom of Saudi Arabia – Intelligence, Surveillance, and Reconnaissance (ISR) Suites and Support," News Release, Defense Security Cooperation Agency, August 15, 2012.

[17] US Department of Defense, "Background Briefing on Secretary Hagel's Trip to Israel, Jordan, Saudi Arabia, Egypt, and the United Arab Emirates from the Pentagon Briefing Room," April 19, 2013.

The United States does not hold a defense treaty with Egypt, but it is a major recipient of US assistance, particularly military aid. From 1987 through the present, Egypt received $1.3 billion a year in military aid and has long stood as the second largest recipient, after Israel, of US foreign assistance. Much of this aid goes towards military acquisitions, upgrades of existing equipment, and maintenance. Some analysts believe that US aid covers perhaps eighty percent of Egypt's weapons procurement costs.[18] Egyptian arms acquired from the US include M1A1 Abrams tanks, F-16s, and other advanced equipment.[19] Congressional pressure following the Egyptian military's violent ouster of President Mohammed Morsi prompted the Obama administration to undertake a case-by-case formal review of aid programs and suspend much of this aid in October 2013. The importance of the United States–Egypt relationship however ultimately led the administration to lift the suspension after 17 months in May 2015. In addition to imposing new restrictions requiring that all aid be channeled to either counterterrorism, maritime, border, or Sinai security, the Administration cancelled the financing system that had allowed Egypt to buy American arms on credit from future foreign aid.[20]

The United States maintains a wide range of security cooperation efforts with Israel. Washington helps Israel preserve its "Qualitative Military Edge," with legislation ensuring Israel's superiority over "any conventional military threat from any individual state or possible coalition of states or from nonstate actors."[21] In 2007, the Bush administration agreed to a ten-year, $30 billion military aid package. Israel is the top recipient of US Foreign Military Financing, through which it has received F-35s/Joint Strike Fighters, bunker-busting bombs, and much of its most advanced equipment. Israel also has access to many of the top US weapon systems. Pentagon officials described the military sales as part of an ongoing US effort to ensure Israel maintains unprecedented air superiority into the next generation.[22]

US and Israeli defense companies often work together on projects, including on missile defense programs such as the Arrow and Arrow II antimissile systems. The United States also maintains a large emergency stockpile of material on Israeli soil for US contingencies, with the possibility of its use by Israel in a crisis

[18] Jeremy M. Sharp, "Egypt: Background and US Relations," *Congressional Research Service*, September 13, 2012.

[19] "News Release: Egypt–Service Life Extension Program for F-110-GE-100 Engines," Defense Security Cooperation Agency, December 18, 2009, http://www.dsca.mil/major-arms-sales/egypt-service-life-extension-program-f-110-ge-100-engines; "News Release: Egypt–Co-production of M1A1 Abrams Tank," Defense Security Cooperation Agency, July 5, 2011, http://www.dsca.mil/major-arms-sales/egypt-co-production-m1a1-abrams-tank.

[20] Gabriel Kohan, "On the Restoration of Aid to Egypt," *Lawfare* (blog), May 15, 2015, https://www.lawfareblog.com/restoration-aid-egypt.

[21] Barbara Opall-Rome, "Hagel: US Arms to Augment Israeli Military Edge," *Defense News*, April 22, 2013, http://rpdefense.over-blog.com/hagel-u.s.-arms-to-augment-israeli-military-edge.

[22] "Background Briefing on Secretary Hagel's Trip to Israel, Jordan, Saudi Arabia, Egypt and the United Arab Emirates from the Pentagon Briefing Room," April 19, 2013.

situation.[23] The "Iron Dome" antimissile system, which helps protect Israel from Hamas and Hizballah rockets, was a joint United States–Israel effort. US officials repeatedly emphasize America's commitment to Israel's security in public rhetoric as well.

The United States also enjoys substantial trade relationships with several Middle Eastern states, though these are usually dwarfed by the US trade relationship with more advanced industrialized economies in Europe and Asia. In 2012 (the latest year for which data is available), the United States exported almost twenty-five billion dollars' worth of goods to the UAE and an equal amount to Saudi Arabia. The United States imported almost fifty-six billion dollars in goods, primarily petroleum, from Saudi Arabia and billions more from other Gulf States (the figure varies dramatically depending on the price of oil). Israel exported over twenty-seven billion dollars to the United States.[24] (Japan, in contrast, in 2012 exported over $173 billion in goods to the United States and imported $116 billion.[25])

POSITED US INTERESTS TO THE REGION— AND THREATS TO THESE INTERESTS

US leaders have declared a range of vital (and not-so-vital) American interests in the Middle East. These have varied by administration and historical era, but they have long included ensuring the free flow of oil and maintaining Israel's security. The United States has also expressed a strong desire to prevent further nuclear proliferation in the Middle East, and since 9/11 has placed particular emphasis on counterterrorism. In addition, Washington has demonstrated an episodic commitment to the spread of democracy in the region. This section describes these interests, examines questions concerning their validity, and surveys potential threats posed to them.

Oil

Ensuring the free flow of oil represents perhaps the most constant, and many would say the most important, US interest in the Middle East. Since at least the 1970s, America's key strategic interests in the region have involved not only securing easy

---

[23] Jeremy M. Sharp, "US Foreign Aid to Israel," *Congressional Research Service*, March 12, 2012, http://emetnews.org/documents/us-foreign-aid-to-israel-2012.pdf.

[24] "US-Saudi Arabia Trade Facts," Office of the United States Trade Representative, http://www.ustr.gov/countries-regions/europe-middle-east/middle-east/north-africa/saudi-arabia; "US – United Arab Emirates Trade Facts," Office of the United States Trade Representative http://www.ustr.gov/countries-regions/europe-middle-east/middle-east/north-africa/united-arab-emirates; "US-Israel Trade Facts," Office of the United States Trade Representative, https://ustr.gov/countries-regions/europe-middle-east/middle-east/north-africa/israel.

[25] "Japan, Korea, & APEC," Office of the United States Trade Representative, https://ustr.gov/countries-regions/japan-korea-apec/japan.

access for itself but also guaranteeing an open and secure market for Japan and Europe. Middle East countries, especially the states of the Persian Gulf, are key oil producers, exporting far more than they consume. In 2015, Persian Gulf states produced almost thirty percent of total world oil production, with the United States receiving roughly twenty-one percent of its imports from the region in the first six months of 2015.[26] Europe, China, and Japan all also depend on oil imports for their energy needs.

One common myth is that the country of origin of the oil is what matters most. Iran has often been referred to as a major supplier of particular European or Asian countries. In 2011, for example, Italy and Spain together imported over ten percent of their oil from Iran.[27] In reality, however, oil is a global market—who supplies whom at any given moment matters far less than the overall supply and demand, which is what sets the overall price. Thus Iran's value to a particular economy depends largely on how much oil it contributes to the global market. The stability or instability in a particular country consequently matters equally for the whole world based on how much oil they use for their overall economy.

It is possible that the Gulf may, in the near future, play a lesser role not only for US energy interests but also in world oil supplies. Both Republican and Democratic administrations have voiced their commitment to American energy independence and the Obama administration has introduced several policy measures aimed at reducing American reliance on Middle East oil. Technological improvements have enabled production from so-called "tight" oil, increasing overall world supply as well as the relative US share, and that of stable allies like Canada, of production.[28] Due in part to rapid growth in new petroleum sources in the Western hemisphere like shale energy or the use of fracking to exploit fields once thought exhausted, analysts now anticipate a fifty percent drop in US oil imports from the region by 2035.[29] Most analysts project that US domestic oil output will rise significantly over the next decade.[30] However, increases in global demand are likely to match supply increases, particularly if China and India continue high growth rates. On the supply side, most of the growth in OPEC petroleum production is expected to come mainly from the Persian Gulf countries, with current US government

---

[26] "Monthly Energy Review October 2015," US Energy Information Administration, www.eia. gov/totalenergy/data/monthly/pdf/sec11_5.pdf; "2015 Crude Oil Imports from Persian Gulf Highlights," US Energy Information Administration, February 29, 2016, www.eia.gov/petroleum/imports/companylevel/summary.cfm.

[27] "Iran Oil Exports: Where Do They Go," *The Guardian*, February 6, 2012, http://www.guardian.co.uk/news/datablog/2012/feb/06/iran-oil-exports-destination.

[28] Frank A. Verrastro, "The Role of Unconventional Oil and Gas: A New Paradigm for Energy," *CSIS*, April 17, 2012; Daniel Yergin, "America's New Energy Reality," *The New York Times*, June 9, 2012 (for a more skeptical view).

[29] Angel Gonzalez, "Expanded Oil Drilling Helps US Wean Itself From Mideast," *Wall Street Journal*, June 27, 2012.

[30] Mahmoud A. El-Gamal and Amy M. Jaffe, "Oil Demand, Supply, and Medium-Term Price Prospects: A Wavelets-Based Analysis" (working paper, Baker Institute for Public Policy, Rice University, June 2013): 19.

projections putting their market share within OPEC at roughly seventy percent by 2040.[31] Although both the total likely additional demand and supply remain speculative at this point, recent projections in both supply and demand suggest the Persian Gulf will continue to a major player in the global oil market for years to come.[32]

In many ways, a stable price is as important as a low price. The United States and other advanced economies have proven that, over time, they can adjust to both high and low energy prices and maintain economic growth. In addition, oil exporters often use any surge in their wealth from exports to increase their own imports from Western countries and increase investment there as well, thus balancing some of the economic losses that would otherwise accrue to the West.[33]

The greater danger comes from sudden price shocks: oil is notoriously inelastic, as it is difficult to quickly change consumption should the price of oil rise. Yet even here there may be good news. During the postwar period through the 1970s, oil price elasticity was as high as -0.29: when the price of oil increased ten percent, real GNP figures declined a staggering 2.9 percent. However, this fell sharply from the 1980s on, as the market became more accustomed to volatility: elasticity fell to an average of -0.02 in the first year after a sudden price increase and -0.05 in the second, leading to a GDP decline of 0.2 percent and 0.5 percent in the first and second year: high figures (particularly if, say, the price of oil increased thirty percent in a year) but not catastrophic.[34]

Eugene Gholz and Daryl Press point out "potential supply disruptions are less worrisome than scholars, politicians, and pundits presume."[35] They go on to argue that spare consumption, changes in transport routes, and consumer adaptation can reduce the cost of oil shocks. In addition, oil companies often diversify their portfolios, accounting for political risk and, in so doing, anticipating the likelihood of unexpected decreases in global supply. Moreover, oil shocks lead to increases in exploration and production elsewhere, leading to an increase in supply over time.[36] However, as these authors also note, the Strait of Hormuz is perhaps "the world's only true chokepoint," and they contend that preventing the conquest, and thus the

---

[31] "Annual Energy Outlook 2013 with Projections to 2040," US Energy Information Administration, April 2013, DOE/EIA-0383, 194, www.eia.gov/forecasts/AEO/pdf/0383(2013).pdf.

[32] For an argument that "tight" oil will add dramatically to global oil supply, see Leonardo Maugeri, "Oil: The Next Revolution," Discussion Paper 2012-10, Belfer Center for Science and International Affairs, Harvard Kennedy School, June 2012; for a more skeptical view, see Claudia Cattaneo, "Will Tight Oil Change the World?" *Financial Post*, July 21, 2012.

[33] "Oil, Scarcity, Growth, and Global Imbalances," in "World Economic Outlook: Tensions from the Two-Speed Recovery," International Monetary Fund, April 2011.

[34] Robert Hoffman, "Estimates of Oil Price Elasticity," International Association for Energy Economics, 19–23.

[35] Eugene Gholz and Daryl G. Press, "Protecting 'The Prize': Oil and the US National Interest," *Security Studies* 19, no. 3 (2010): 453. See also Gholz and Press, "Energy Alarmism: The Myths that Make Americans Worry about Oil," CATO Institute Policy Analysis no. 589, April 5, 2007.

[36] Gholz and Press, "Energy Alarmism," 9–11.

consolidation, of major Persian Gulf suppliers represents an important US interest, albeit one that they do not see as facing serious threat today.[37]

Notionally, the threat to oil arises in two forms. First, a hostile state could invade and occupy an oil producer or cut off a key chokepoint such as the Strait of Hormuz. The hostile producer, of course, would almost certainly want to sell the oil—thus in the long term, supply would likely remain constant. However, the short-term disruption caused by invasion (and perhaps an insurgency in response) could prove highly disruptive. In addition, it is possible that the invading power, if it gained control of a significant percentage of the world's reserves, would acquire the ability to manipulate the market, deliberately creating price spikes.

Here the variation in current and spare production in the region must be taken into account. As the world's reaction to the crisis in Libya and, before that, the disruption in Iraqi oil supplies showed, world oil markets can adjust to losing the production of one of the region's suppliers. Because of the concentration of the world's oil supplies in the Gulf region—and much larger portion of spare production there—the possibility of disruption of the region in general (i.e., the production of more than one state), or of Saudi Arabia in particular, deserves additional scrutiny.[38]

Historically, only Iran and Iraq posed a threat to oil from the Gulf region—Iraq from conquest, as it attempted in Kuwait in 1990, and Iran through subversion. With Saddam Hussein gone and Iraq in turmoil, in the near- to medium-term, Iran represents the country of greatest concern with regard to invasion. However, even a cursory look at Iran's capabilities suggests how difficult this would be. Tehran's military lacks the ability to project power outside its borders in a sustained way. Iraq's military is weak and unable to "balance" Iran, but Iran's seizure of oil-rich parts of Iraq would be difficult to achieve and would probably lead to a protracted insurgency on the part of local Iraqis. Striking across the Gulf at Kuwait and Saudi Arabia would be exponentially harder, requiring sea and air capabilities the Islamic Republic lacks and exposing attacking forces to strikes from the forces of the Gulf States, which are prepared for this eventuality. Politically, Tehran does not claim the territory of any of its neighbors (a few disputed minor islands aside), and the Islamic Republic still bears the scars from the country's long struggle with Iraq. Tehran has no appetite for another large-scale war.

In recent years, one much-touted concern is that Iran might try to block the Strait of Hormuz, perhaps the world's most important chokepoint for oil supplies: thirty-three percent of all oil shipped by sea and nearly twenty percent of all oil traded worldwide passed through the two-mile-wide shipping lane in 2009.[39] Stopping traffic through the Strait would cut off over eighty percent of the Gulf states' oil exports, driving up shipping costs, and otherwise lead to a major spike in the price of oil—and one that could not be quickly made up from other sources.[40] Caitlin

---

[37] Gholz and Press, "Protecting 'The Prize'," 463 and 474.

[38] Gholz and Press, "Energy Alarmism," 15.

[39] Rick Gladstone, "Noise Level Rises Over Iran Threat to Close Strait of Hormuz," *New York Times*, December 28, 2011.

[40] Daniel Yergin, "Ensuring Energy Security," *Foreign Affairs* 85, no. 2 (March/April 2006): 78.

Talmadge finds that Iran has significant capabilities to close the Strait for perhaps a month, using a combination of mines, anti-ship cruise missiles, and land-based air defense.[41] Even so, the potential disruption to the global oil market stemming from a crisis over the Strait could be significant, especially in the short term. In December 2011, after Iranian Vice-President Mohammad Reza-Rahimi threatened to close the Strait if new sanctions were levied, oil prices jumped over two percent in one day. However, the ensuing week—which witnessed both Iranian and American naval exercises—saw oil prices quickly return to pre-incident levels.[42] Still, some energy analysts predict the price of oil could rise by as much as fifty percent within days of the Strait's closure.[43]

One reassuring counterargument is that it would be self-defeating for Iran to close the Strait as Iran itself is dependent on the Strait to export its oil. However, it is plausible (though not likely) that Iran might still try to close the Strait: scenarios might include a full boycott of Iranian oil should Iran renew its nuclear program, which means Iran has no significant exports to lose, or a more ideological or desperate regime in Tehran. Such an action, however, would create a counterbalancing coalition, including Europe and China, that would lead to economic and diplomatic isolation as well as support for aggressive US military action.

Moreover, Washington's existing regional assets provide it with options should Iran choose to disrupt traffic in the vital shipping channel. In 2012, President Obama reportedly sent a private letter to Tehran declaring Iranian closure of the Strait of Hormuz a "red line" for the United States.[44] When the Iranian Coast Guard seized a Marshall Islands-flagged Maersk cargo ship in April 2015 the administration demonstrated its commitment to protecting the passageway by sending the guided missile destroyer USS Farragut to patrol the channel. In addition to sending American warships to shadow US-flagged merchant ships CENTCOM announced it was considering offering its assistance to non-US flagged merchant ships, an effort to bring the Strait under US extended deterrence.[45] The ongoing US naval presence in the region should afford Washington continued deterrence opportunities.

[41] Caitlin Talmadge, "Closing Time: Assessing the Iranian Threat to the Strait of Hormuz," *International Security* 33, no. 1 (2008): 82–117.

[42] The price of a barrel of crude oil on December 27, 2011, the first day of the crisis, was $101.12 compared with $99.77 the day prior. Although oil prices reached a high of $102.92 in early January 2012, prices were back down around the $98 mark by the next month. Daily oil prices taken from xroilprice.com; Steve Hargreaves. "Oil Jumps over 2% as Iran Threatens Supplies," CNN.com, December 27, 2011. http://money.cnn.com/2011/12/27/markets/oil_iran.

[43] Clifford Krauss. "Oil Price Would Skyrocket if Iran Closed the Strait of Hormuz," *New York Times,* January 4, 2012.

[44] Michael Crowley, "Iran's Dire Strait,' Politico, May 2, 2015 http://www.politico.com/story/2015/05/irans-dire-strait-117566.

[45] Agence France-Presse, "US Navy Bolsters Presence in Gulf," May 3, 2015, http://www.defensenews.com/story/defense/international/mideast-africa/2015/05/03/us-navy-bolsters-presence-gulf-iran-seizure/26835345/; Asa Fitch, "Iranian Authorities Release Maersk Tigris," *Wall Street Journal,* May 7, 2015, http://www.wsj.com/articles/iranian-authorities-release-maersk-tigris-1430991500.

Another risk comes from Iranian-supported subversion and perhaps even limited military strikes on Gulf oil facilities. Tehran in the past sponsored a coup in Bahrain and various terrorist attacks in Kuwait and Saudi Arabia. The circumstances for this are far from impossible given the growing polarization of Sunni and Shi'a in the Muslim world, the proxy wars between Iran and Saudi Arabia in Syria and Yemen, and other issues. Here the direct threat to supply would be less, but the increased risk premium would lead to price increases and perhaps even a short-term spike until the situation stabilized one way or another.

The potential for non-state actors to disrupt the region's oil supply, while in the realm of possibility, remains low. Although the Islamic State's control of several Iraqi and Syrian oil refineries and distribution assets since 2014 garnered significant news coverage, the oil fields controlled by the organization are responsible for only a fraction of regional output capacity. Rather than destroy many of these sites, the group has kept several oilfields operational as part of an elaborate oil smuggling operation in order to fund its activities. While troublesome from a counterterrorism perspective—illicit oil sales reportedly netted the organization several million dollars a month in 2014—terrorist groups like the Islamic State do not as yet pose a serious and consistent challenge to the region's oil supply.[46]

Regional allies are also at risk of internal strife unrelated to foreign subversion. In Iraq during the height of the civil war in 2006, in Libya during the revolt against Qaddafi, and in Iran during the early days of the revolution, internal unrest led to significant decreases in oil production.[47] The Arab Spring embodies the latest reminder that many regimes in the Middle East rest on fragile foundations. While oil-rich Gulf States have largely escaped massive unrest, they have witnessed some demonstrations though these have tapered off. Because of its large share of global production and world spare capacity, Saudi Arabia represents a particular concern in terms of internal instability. Yet even here there may be less cause for concern than some suggest. Domestic instability may not be as destabilizing to oil production as previously thought. Mahmoud El-Gamal and Amy Jaffe find that regime change by itself historically has "not resulted in significant medium term (32–64 month) disruptions in output." The authors conclude that while regime change may hamper investment and production in the immediate short term, only outright wars that destroy production and transportation infrastructure would produce significant medium-term output disruption.[48]

[46] Fazel Hawramy, Shalwa Mohammed, and Luke Harding, "Inside Islamic State's Oil Empire: How Captured Oilfields Fuel ISIS Insurgency," *The Guardian*, November 19, 2014; Jay Solomon, "ISIS's Oil Revenue is Falling, Administration Says," *Wall Street Journal*, December 15, 2014; Michael R. Gordon, "Iraqi Forces and Shiite Militias Retake Oil Refinery From ISIS," *New York Times*, October 16, 2015.

[47] Jim Krane, "Iraq Oil Output Lowest Since Invasion," *Associated Press*, April 18, 2006, http://www.washingtonpost.com/wp-dyn/content/article/2006/04/28/AR2006042801082.html; Clifford Krause, "After the Revolution, Hurdles in Reviving the Oil Sector," *New York Times*, August 23, 2011, http://www.nytimes.com/2011/08/24/business/global/libya-faces-hurdles-in-reviving-its-oil-sector.html.

[48] Gamal and Jaffe, "Oil Demand," 23–24.

Nuclear proliferation

Preventing the spread of nuclear weapons represents a central and oft-cited by leaders US interest in the Middle East. In part this policy intends to prevent any hostile state from gaining enough power to threaten US interests regarding oil security. But this issue also involves concerns relating to the security of Israel and a more general viewpoint that proliferation is dangerous, particularly with regard to "rogue" or hostile regimes.

The arguments against proliferation (or, more rarely, in favor of it) are well known and thus only briefly summarized here. While some contend that nuclear weapons make leaders more cautious, others argue that their spread risks the use of nuclear weapons in war or by accident, either way a catastrophic event. A particular fear is the so-called "stability-instability paradox": Even if states become more cautious in their willingness to go to war, they will be more willing to engage in limited aggression (including supporting terrorists and insurgents) in the belief that their nuclear capability insulates them from conventional attack.[49] As Robert Jervis has argued, "To the extent that the military balance is stable at the level of all-out nuclear war, it will become less stable at lower levels of violence."[50] This more pessimistic view is the common wisdom in policy circles.

The United States does not view the Israeli nuclear program, which dates back to the 1960s, as a threat because Israel is an ally. US officials are further reassured by the fact that Israel did not use nuclear weapons even when its security was threatened in the 1973 war. Successive US administrations have deemed Israel a stable and rational actor with a professional military that will be careful to prevent a nuclear accident and will ensure proper command and control.

Today the biggest risk of proliferation comes from Iran. Tehran developed an extensive nuclear program and has enriched uranium to twenty percent, but comprehensive sanctions helped convince Iran to go to the negotiating table. In 2015, the United States and Iran signed the Joint Comprehensive Plan of Action (JCPOA) designed to disband Iran's nuclear weapons program in exchange for sanctions relief.[51]

Tehran is hostile to the United States and Israel, and its command and control and accident-prevention procedures are uncertain. Many critics of the deal argue that Iran cannot be trusted to uphold its end of the bargain, that inspection procedures are too lenient, and that the eventual expiration of the agreement enables Iran to eventually get a nuclear weapon. However, should Tehran acquire a nuclear weapon, it is highly unlikely to use it as a "bolt from the blue"

---

[49] Kenneth Waltz, "The Spread of Nuclear Weapons: More May Be Better," *Adelphi Papers* 21, no. 171 (1981); Scott Sagan, *The Limits of Safety: Organizations, Accidents, and Nuclear Weapons* (Princeton, NJ: Princeton University Press, 1993); Peter Lavoy, "The Strategic Consequences of Nuclear Proliferation," *Security Studies* 4, no. 4 (1995): 695–753.

[50] Robert Jervis, *The Illogic of American Nuclear Strategy* (Ithaca, NY: Cornell University Press, 1984), p. 31.

[51] See US Department of State, "Joint Comprehensive Plan of Action," at http://www.state.gov/e/eb/tfs/spi/iran/jcpoa/.

or pass it to terrorist groups, though the possibility of an accident remains quite real.[52]

Even assuming that Iran eventually gets a bomb, much comes down to the "stability-instability paradox."[53] Tehran sponsors a range of terrorist and insurgent groups, and analysts fear it would become more aggressive as its nuclear capability would act as a deterrent to conventional military attacks. So a nuclear Iran could mean a risk of greater terrorism, subversion, and support for insurgency. However, although the Iranian regime aspires to greater influence in the near-abroad, sectarian issues have prevented Tehran from achieving its goal of becoming a leader of the Muslim world. Save for in Syria and Iraq, where Iranian influence has grown in recent years, the Arab street's perception of Iran and its proxy Hizballah has markedly declined.

Another concern is so-called "reactive" or "tit-for-tat" proliferation: when the acquisition of a nuclear weapon by one country triggers a response by that country's neighbors, thus greatly increasing the number of nuclear powers, and thus the risk of accident and war. Saudi Arabia, Turkey, Egypt, and other regional countries are all cited as potential reactive proliferators should Iran's program lead to a nuclear weapon. However, Philipp Bleek's research indicates that reactive proliferation is far from automatic but is more likely when a state exhibits an intense rivalry with another, possesses its own indigenous research and industrial base to build a bomb, and lacks a security guarantee from a nuclear-armed ally.[54] Iran's rivalry with its neighbors is significant but not necessarily intense by the standards of, say, India versus Pakistan. Even more reassuringly, Saudi Arabia lacks the necessary industrial and technological resource base, though in contrast to most potential proliferators, it might have the ability to purchase a weapon outright from an ally like Pakistan. Turkey, however, possesses the necessary resource base, but it too does not have an intense rivalry that would drive the development of a weapon. Most important, many of the potential proliferators are US allies and thus can "balance" against the greater Iranian threat. At one time a cause for concern in Washington, Syrian efforts to build a nuclear program of their own have effectively been stopped by the 2007 Israeli air strike and the ongoing civil war, suggesting that the main threat to nuclear proliferation in the coming years in the region will continue to be Iran alone.

Regarding the proliferation (and use) of chemical and biological weapons, the picture is mixed. The Bush administration succeeded in getting Libya to abandon its programs for the development of biological, chemical, as well as nuclear weapons in 2003. The Obama administration was also able to compel the Syrian regime to dismantle its chemical weapons programs. Rather than state proliferation, the more immediate concern is that the Islamic State or its associates may acquire access to

---

[52] Daniel Byman, "Iran, Terrorism, and Weapons of Mass Destruction," *Studies in Conflict and Terrorism* 31, no. 3 (2008): 169–181.

[53] For an exposition with a Cold War framework, see Glenn Snyder, *Deterrence and Defense* (Princeton, NJ: Princeton University Press, 1961).

[54] Philipp Bleek, "The Nuclear Domino Myth: Why Proliferation Rarely Begets Proliferation" (PhD diss., Georgetown University, 2010).

these dangerous materials.[55] Going forward, deterring CBRN proliferation in the region will continue to remain a major goal of all American administrations.

Security of Israel

Since the 1960s, the United States has had an increasingly close relationship with the state of Israel.[56] Administrations of all stripes have repeatedly declared that the security of Israel represents a significant US national interest. This alliance is based on three pillars: security interests, shared values, and domestic support.

The United States and Israel have long opposed common foes in the Middle East. This ranged from pro-Soviet (or at least not pro-American) regimes like Nasser's Egypt and Saddam's Iraq, to the clerical regime in Tehran and, more recently, a range of terrorist groups. Israel played an important role in helping the United States set back Iran's nuclear program in the years before the JCPOA. Champions of the US-Israel alliance also stress that Israel represents an island of democracy in the authoritarian sea of the Middle East. In helping defend Israel, the United States is thus defending its own values. In addition, Israeli public opinion of the United States—in contrast to Arab state public opinion—is favorable, and the alliance is based on people-to-people as well as government-to-government relations.

Americans strongly support close ties to Israel. A 2015 poll found that over seventy percent of Americans view Israeli favorably—far higher than support for other countries in the Middle East.[57] Support is particularly high among the American Jewish community and the white evangelical Protestant communities.[58] In recent years support has become especially strong within the Republican party, with Democratic party supporters being more ambivalent about Israel's policies. This strong domestic support makes it likely that any president will strongly support Israel. However, in some cases—notably Obama's championing of the Iran deal— US leaders will pursue regional goals even against Israel's objections.

There are several arguments made against the designation of the security of Israel as a critical US interest. First, as John Mearsheimer and Stephen Walt have

---

[55] Ahmed Rasheed, Aref Mohammed and Stephen Kalin, "Exclusive: Radioactive material stolen in Iraq raises security concerns," *Reuters*, February 17, 2016, http://www.reuters.com/article/us-mideast-crisis-iraq-radiation-idUSKCN0VQ22F; Ian Johnston, "Brussels attacks: Belgium fears ISIS seeking to make 'dirty' nuclear bomb," *The Independent* March 24, 2016, http://www.independent.co.uk/news/world/europe/brussels-attacks-belgium-fears-isis-seeking-to-make-dirty-nuclear-bomb-a6951661.html.

[56] Warren Bass, *Support Any Friend: Kennedy's Middle East and the Making of the US-Israel Alliance* (Oxford: Oxford University Press, 2004).

[57] Lydia Saad, "Seven in Ten Americans Continue to View Israel Favorably," Gallup, February 23, 2015, http://www.gallup.com/poll/181652/seven-americans-continue-view-israel-favorably.aspx.

[58] "AJC Survey of American Jewish Opinion Highlights," *American Jewish Committee*, April 30, 2012, http://www.jewishdatabank.org/studies/downloadFile.cfm?FileID=2841; "Evangelical Support for Israel," *Pew Research Center*, April 6, 2011, http://www.pewresearch.org/daily-number/evangelical-support-for-israel.

contended, among their other criticisms of the US-Israel partnership, Israel is widely reviled in the Arab and Muslim worlds. Thus close US ties to Israel and support for its unpopular policies drag down favorable opinion of the United States. Many of the reasons the United States has enemies in the region, they contend, are due to its ties to Israel.

This argument is both true and overstated. US support for Israel remains a grievance held by friends and enemies alike in the Arab and Muslim world and does increase anti-US sentiment. In many cases, however, this grievance figures as simply one among many. So Iran is hostile to the United States because of Washington's support for Israel, but also because of past US meddling in Iran, US support for Iraq in the Iran-Iraq War, US opposition to Iran's attempt to expand its influence, rejection of US secular values, and other concerns. Al-Qaeda of course strongly rejects Israel and repeatedly identifies US support for Israel as a reason to the attack the United States. Al-Qaeda propaganda, however, also cites a range of other supposed US crimes. Some of these are factual such as the US military presence in the Middle East and historical support for authoritarian regimes. Others are tied to US values, such as support for women's rights, religious minorities and, increasingly, the rights of homosexuals. Still others tend toward the delusional, such as a supposed US campaign aimed at subordinating Muslims and undermining Islam throughout the world. As the Syrian civil war has heated up and other concerns have risen to the fore, the importance of Israel as a grievance has declined.

A second argument leveled against the partnership is that Israel represents simply one power among many in the region, and the hostility regional governments hold towards the Jewish state creates difficulties in US diplomacy and hinders US alliances. But often this hostility is more public than private: a number of US allies in private have shown little concern about Israeli activities and even expressed indirect support for an Israeli attack on Iran's nuclear facilities. And one of the ironies of the US-Iran deal is that Israel joined Saudi Arabia and other foes of Iran in opposing the deal.

The actual US role in helping secure Israel is unclear. Israel does not face a threat from conventional military attack. Even before Syria collapsed into civil war, Israel's forces were far more capable than those of its neighbors combined, and while US support increases the capabilities gap, without Washington's backing Israel's forces would still enjoy a considerable advantage. The last decade has witnessed a steady increase in Israeli capabilities, with little comparable growth in that of its neighbors. The United States and civil war shattered Iraq's military power. Egypt, in theory, could again become hostile, but the conventional gap in military capabilities remains considerable and the Sisi government there has furthermore reaffirmed its support for the peace treaty.

The security threat to Israel today comes primarily from terrorism or from rocket attacks from Hamas, Hizballah, and other substate or quasi-state foes. Israel has gone to war with Hamas several times since the terrorist group seized power in Gaza, often over the threat of rockets. Working with the United States, Israel has developed the "Iron Dome" and "Arrow" systems, improving its defenses against missiles and rockets.[59] Such systems, however, are unlikely to

---

[59] Jeremy M. Sharp, "U.S. Foreign Aid to Israel," *Congressional Research Service*, March 12, 2012, http://thehill.com/images/stories/blogs/flooraction/jan2012/crsisrael.pdf.

present a cure-all to a weapon that, in the end, is primarily psychological. Rockets have killed relatively few Israelis, but the risk of rocket attack remains disruptive to Israeli society. Israel, using its own intelligence and military capabilities, has dramatically reduced the scale and scope of terrorism in the last ten years. The United States has at best a limited role to play by helping Israeli diplomacy and assisting Israeli research.

Israel faces political and diplomatic jeopardy in that it risks becoming a world pariah. Israel's increasing isolation is a threat to its security, and the United States can help lessen its pariah status. Already it does not have diplomatic relations with many states, and constant pressure for sanctions and other punishments against Israel persists due to its continued occupation of the West Bank. Indeed, some of this hostility would continue regardless of the status of peace talks, but the lack of progress on peace with the Palestinians means this pressure is likely to continue, and perhaps grow. US efforts to move the peace process forward require encouraging both Israelis and Palestinians to make difficult and politically unpopular concessions in the name of peace.

Democratization

The United States also professes an interest in the spread of democracy throughout the world. For many years various US administrations embraced a "Middle East exceptionalism," wherein the United States acted as if democracy in the region represented both an unlikely and undesirable development. This policy changed significantly in the George W. Bush administration, but the disastrous occupation of Iraq and the success of Hizballah and Hamas in elections in Lebanon and Gaza respectively made the embrace of democratization appear naïve and counterproductive.[60] The unexpected occurrence of the Arab Spring, however, returned democracy promotion to center stage, though democratization ardor cooled as the Arab Spring devolved into civil wars and led to a coup in Egypt.

Several arguments emerged for democracy promotion. Mubarak's Egypt, Qaddafi's Libya, Salih's Yemen, and other authoritarian regimes produced terrorists who often targeted the United States as well as local authorities: dictatorship, it seemed, provided al-Qaeda both a grievance to exploit and a large pool of recruits. In addition, US support for dictatorship tarnished the image of the United States in the eyes of many Arabs. Thus, democracy promoters anticipated that a change in policy would lead to a change in hearts, as democracy is genuinely popular in the region.[61] Supporting democracy also aligns with US values, while, strategically, the most enduring and close US alliances are with strong democracies. Consequently, if democracy was successfully fostered, Israel would not be the only regional country with shared political values.

---

[60] For a review of this debate, see Tamara Wittes, *Freedom's Unsteady March: America's Role in Building Arab Democracy* (Washington, DC: Brookings, 2008).
[61] "Most Muslims Want Democracy, Personal Freedoms, and Islam in Political Life," *Pew Research Center*, July 10, 2012.

Critics, however, point to several weaknesses in these arguments. First, US endorsement of democracy under President George W. Bush, and then belatedly under Obama, has won little support for the United States in the Arab world. In Jordan, approval of the United States is at just fourteen percent. In Egypt, among Palestinians, and in other countries of the region, rates remain similarly low, largely unchanged since before the Arab Spring.[62]

Second, many of the dictators were staunch US allies, and two of them, Jordan and Egypt, maintained peace with Israel—something far harder for popularly elected governments to accomplish given widespread public hostility toward Israel. So in supporting democratic movements, the United States was in essence abandoning friends, while their replacements were still unknown. Indeed democratic regimes are not likely to be more pro-American than their authoritarian predecessors and, indeed, have good reason to adopt a more hostile position. Broad anti-American sentiment in the Arab world suggests that regimes responsive to the mood of their people are likely to oppose close relations with the United States. In addition, Islamists emerged as one strong alternative, and they hold views on personal freedoms and the role of religious minorities, among other issues, that diverge sharply from those held by the United States, rendering the "shared values" objective a much less likely outcome.

Third, fighting terrorism requires strong governments, and, for the short term in particular, democratization actually weakens governments, while the risk of civil strife creates opportunities for al-Qaeda and like-minded groups.[63] So while the grievances that foster support for terrorists may decline, governments' abilities to fight them will too. The collapse of weak governments in Yemen and Libya despite hopes for democratization—and the growth of jihadist terrorism in Egypt since the Arab Spring—are in part because of the collapse of government authority. In addition, if governments are more hostile, their intelligence services are less likely to cooperate with the United States.

Finally, skeptics point out that the most important dynamics are domestic. Active US backing of democracy, if anything, backfired under President George W. Bush, and the Arab Spring had little to do with US policy. The United States, they would contend, should simply pursue its interests unconcerned with the type of government in the Arab world, as it cannot effect this type of change through its own efforts.

The primary threats to democratization are internal. Regimes are entrenched and resist reform. New actors that come to power after the collapse of dictators may not accept the premise of democracy or may implement it fitfully. Most regional economies are in poor shape, and the rule of law is often weak. On the margins Washington might influence these dynamics, but US intervention, even in small ways, could easily backfire, discrediting those we seek to help.

---

[62] "Global Indicators Database," *Pew Research Center,* June 23, 2015, http://www.pewglobal.org/database/indicator/1/; "Arab Spring Fails to Improve US Image," *Pew Research Center,* May 17, 2011, http://www.pewglobal.org/2011/05/17/arab-Spring-fails-to-improve-us-image/.

[63] F. Gregory Gause, "Can Democracy Stop Terrorism?" *Foreign Affairs* 84, no. 5 (September-October 2005): 62–76.

Yet the threat posed to democracy is not completely internal. In Syria, Iran has backed the Assad regime in its efforts to resist a popular revolution. In Egypt, organizations in Saudi Arabia showered money on Salafi groups that are opposed to liberal interpretations of democracy, and Saudi Arabia and the United Arab Emirates backed the Sisi coup with billions of dollars. Most dramatically, the Kingdom of Saudi Arabia backed the Bahraini government's 2011 crackdown on dissent, deploying its troops to shore up government control. Bruce Riedel argues that Saudi Arabia is implementing a version of the Brezhnev doctrine, using force and money to ensure that revolutions do not occur in its backyard.[64]

Nowhere have the intricacies of America's position toward democratization in the Middle East been more apparent than in Egypt. The White House's reluctance to publically condemn the Egyptian military's July 2013 overthrow of the democratically elected Morsi government as well as its initial dismissal of congressional calls for the suspension of foreign aid demonstrated once more the fine line Washington walks when its own interests clash with democratic tenets. Although numerous foreign policy commentators and members of Congress argue that Washington's annual foreign aid package to Cairo provides the United States with leverage in influencing Egyptian politics, the truth is more complicated. In exchange for the $1.3 billion in military aid given to Egypt each year the United States receives overflight rights, preferential access to the Suez Canal, prepositioning at Cairo West Air Base, and intelligence on al-Qaeda. Were Washington to further restrict or re-suspend aid to Cairo, the United States could be on the "losing end" of the relationship as well.[65]

In Egypt, the Obama administration's position was further complicated by the Egyptian public's support for the military's ouster of Morsi and subsequent crackdown against the Muslim Brotherhood. Faced with supporting a democratically elected but anti-American regime or the widely popular Egyptian military, many of whose leaders had long established ties to US officials and close relations with Israel, the Obama administration came down on the side of stability and order over democracy. However, lingering concerns over democracy and the harsh crackdown in Egypt strained relations with the Sisi government. With the aftershocks of the Arab Spring likely to continue to ripple through the region in the coming years, Washington may resort to taking a long view on democracy in the Middle East.

Terrorism and counterterrorism

Since the 9/11 attacks in particular, the United States has prioritized counterterrorism in its policy towards the Middle East. Egypt, Jordan, Saudi Arabia, and Yemen became especially valued for their counterterrorism cooperation, and Washington has expanded ties to previously neglected countries like Algeria. In Saudi Arabia

---

[64] Bruce Riedel, "Brezhnev in the Hijaz," *The National Interest* 115 (Sept.–Oct. 2011).

[65] Tom Curry, "White House Rebuffs Calls To Cut US Aid to Egypt, Ducks Coup Label," *NBC News*, July 8, 2013, http://nbcpolitics.nbcnews.com/_news/2013/07/08/19356446-white-house-rebuffs-calls-to-cut-us-aid-to-egypt-ducks-coup-label?lite.

and other wealthy Gulf states, both the George W. Bush and Obama administrations pushed hard for a crackdown on terrorist financing and on support for jihadist movements in general. The intelligence services of Egypt, Jordan, Morocco, and Syria have all reportedly penetrated al-Qaeda with human assets.[66]

Al-Qaeda, the Islamic State, and associated movements can be seen as posing three categories of threats. First, they might directly plot attacks on US and allied targets, both in the Middle East and in the West. The al-Qaeda core itself has attempted several attacks in Europe and the United States since 9/11, and al-Qaeda of the Arabian Peninsula came close to success—nearly downing a US passenger plane in 2009 and a US cargo aircraft in 2010. The al-Qaeda core has not successfully attacked the West for some time.

However, the emergence of the Islamic State has raised a range of terrorism fears. Western officials have long worried that young European Muslims who have gone off to fight in Syria as anti-Assad idealists will return to Europe as anti-Western terrorists directed by the Islamic State. As FBI director James Comey warned, "All of us with a memory of the '80s and '90s saw the line drawn from Afghanistan in the '80s and '90s to Sept. 11." He then warned, "We see Syria as that, but an order of magnitude worse in a couple of respects."[67]

Those warnings came true on November 13, 2015 when a series of ISIS-orchestrated terror attacks struck Paris killing 130 people in the deadliest attack in Europe since the Madrid train bombings in 2004.[68] In March 2016, members belonging to the same network struck Brussels airport and metro. In both cases some of the perpetrators were French and Belgian nationals who had trained with the Islamic State in Syria.[69]

Despite these attacks and the real danger that motivates them, the Islamic State-linked Syrian foreign fighter threat can easily be exaggerated.[70] Fears about foreign fighters were raised concerning many conflicts, including after the US invasion of

---

[66] Martin Rudner, "Hunters and Gatherers: The Intelligence Coalition against Islamic Terrorism," *International Journal of Intelligence and CounterIntelligence* 17, no. 2 (2004): 217.

[67] Sari Horowitz and Adam Goldman, "FBI Director: Number of Americans Traveling to Fight in Syria Increasing," *Washington Post*, May 7, 2014, https://www.washingtonpost.com/world/national-security/fbi-director-number-of-americans-traveling-to-fight-in-syria-increasing/2014/05/02/6fa3d84e-d222-11e3-937f-d3026234b51c_story.html.

[68] Mariano Castillo, Margot Haddad, Michael Martinex and Steve Almasy, "Paris suicide bomber identified; ISIS claims responsibility for 129 dead," *CNN*, November 2016, 2015, http://www.cnn.com/2015/11/14/world/paris-attacks.

[69] Rukmini Callimachi, "How ISIS Built the Machinery of Terror Under Europe's Gaze," *New York Times*, March 29, 2016, http://www.nytimes.com/2016/03/29/world/europe/isis-attacks-paris-brussels.html; Gabriele Steinhauser, Natalia Drozdiak and Julian E. Barnes, "Brussels attacks linked to Paris cell," *Wall Street Journal*, March 23, 2016, http://www.wsj.com/articles/manhunt-for-brussels-terror-suspect-continues-1458722020.

[70] For additional thoughts on this subject see Daniel Byman, "The Homecomings: What Happens when Arab Foreign Fighters in Iraq and Syria Return?" *Studies in Conflict & Terrorism* 38, no. 8 (May 1, 2015); and Daniel Byman and Jeremy Shapiro, "Homeward Bound? Don't Hype the Threat of Returning Jihadis," *Foreign Affairs* 93, no. 6 (November/December 2014): 37–46.

Iraq, but this did not lead to massive anti-Western terrorism. Previous cases and the information already emerging from Syria suggest several mitigating effects that reduce—but do not eliminate—the potential terrorist threat from foreign fighters who have gone to Syria. Many of the most radical die, blowing themselves up in suicide attacks or perishing quickly in firefights with opposing forces. Many of the most radical never return home, but continue fighting in the conflict zone or at the next battle for jihad. Some of those who go quickly become disillusioned, and even those who return often are not violent. Others are arrested or disrupted by European intelligence services. Indeed, becoming a foreign fighter—particularly with today's heavy use of social media—makes a terrorist far more likely to come to the attention of security services.[71]

This is not to say that the danger is not real—it is, as the 2015 attack in Paris and the 2016 strike in Brussels so painfully suggest. The Islamic State has increased its focus on Europe and the West in general. Indeed, as it has lost territory in the Middle East it has incentives to go more global both for revenge and to show its constituents that it is "winning."

Less directly, but more significantly for the region, al-Qaeda actively backs insurgencies. Algeria, Iraq, and Yemen are all threatened by sizeable insurgencies linked to al-Qaeda. Zawahiri's organization also backs insurgents outside the Arab world such as in Somalia and Chechnya, and is closely tied to a number of Pakistani groups.[72] These insurgencies have claimed tens of thousands of lives and risk fundamentally destabilizing the countries in question. Mali, Nigeria, Syria, and the Sinai Peninsula all represent areas that offer potential opportunity for an al-Qaeda-like movement to expand its presence. The Islamic State also tries to create "provinces"—and has gained the loyalty of groups in Nigeria, North Africa, Sinai, and Afghanistan, among others. So far it has used these relationships primarily for prestige, and—with the exception of Libya and Sinai—has not devoted significant resources to supporting them.

Counterterrorism cooperation helps all concerned. Through cooperative efforts, the United States gains access to vital intelligence, local services use their agents and capabilities to target and disrupt terrorists at home, and in some cases, such as Yemen, the United States secures physical access in order to launch drone strikes. In 2010, the Saudis played a critical role in foiling an AQAP plot to bomb a US airliner, and joint United States–Saudi efforts against the group disrupted similar plots.[73]

---

[71] Rukmini Callimachi, "How ISIS Built the Machinery of Terror Under Europe's Gaze," *New York Times*, March 29, 2016, http://www.nytimes.com/2016/03/29/world/europe/isis-attacks-paris-brussels.html.

[72] Daniel Byman, "Breaking the Bonds between Al-Qaeda and Its Affiliate Organizations," *Saban Analysis Paper* 27, Brookings Institute, August 2012, http://www.brookings.edu/research/papers/2012/07/alqaida-terrorism-byman.

[73] Yochi J. Dreazen, "Foiled Bomb Plot Highlights Growing CIA-Saudi Arabian Ties," *The National Journal*, May 9, 2012; "News Report: Would-Be Bomber was a Double-Agent," *CNN*, May 8, 2012.

For alliance purposes, counterterrorism importance and terrorism have a symbiotic relationship. Today, Pakistan and Yemen host dangerous anti-United States terrorist groups, and these governments' policies at times augment the strength of the jihadists. Wealthy individuals in Saudi Arabia have long been the primary financiers for jihadist groups. Similarly, much of the reason for the growth of the Islamic State is the Assad regime's deliberate fostering of sectarianism and the Iraqi government's discriminatory policies against the country's Sunnis. In many of these cases, flawed government policies and government weakness have amplified the problem of terrorism. Because the problem is grave, however, the importance of these allies increases. Thus, the gravity of the threat and the importance of the alliance vary together.

In counterterrorism, much depends on where the line is drawn. Hamas and Hizballah are two powerful terrorist organizations that also function as important political players. In contrast to al-Qaeda, both are hostile to the United States, but neither is actively planning operations against Americans. However, both have regularly attacked Israel, and Hizballah is often cited as likely to attack the United States should there be a military confrontation with Iran.

Counterterrorism often goes against democracy promotion. By working with allies to fight terrorism, in reality the United States is working to bolster their intelligence services—often the least democratic part of an undemocratic regime. Counterterrorism also risks creating a self-fulfilling prophecy. By aiding allies and acting unilaterally, the argument goes, the United States puts itself in the terrorists' crosshairs. Moreover, the manner in which the United States responded to the threat only reinforced the jihadist narrative.

Perhaps the most common argument against prioritizing counterterrorism is that the threat today is low.[74] Since 9/11, the US homeland has suffered almost no terrorist attacks emanating from abroad, despite several near misses. Moreover, the United States has suffered over 6,000 deaths in Iraq and Afghanistan so far, more than twice as many as died on 9/11—suggesting the risks of supposedly decisive interventions in the Middle East. Several reports suggest the al-Qaeda core has been hit hard and is far weaker than it was ten years ago. The death of Bin Laden, setbacks in Iraq, the Arab Spring, and an ideological critique within the Salafist community are all cited as sources of the organization's decline.[75] The paucity of recent al-Qaeda core attacks also suggest the movement's weakness. This argument, however, depends on whether al-Qaeda's weakness is due in part to a constant US counterterrorism campaign or whether it is largely independent of US actions. It also depends on whether al-Qaeda affiliate groups are considered part of the core movement and a threat to the United States or simply local groups that pose at best an indirect threat to US interests.[76]

---

[74] John Mueller and Mark Stewart, "The Terrorism Delusion: America's Overwrought Response to September 11," *International Security* 37, no. 1 (Summer 2012).

[75] Peter Bergen and Paul Cruickshank, "The Unraveling," *The New Republic,* June 11, 2008; Daniel Byman, "Al Qaeda's Terrible Spring," *Foreign Affairs,* May 24, 2011, https://www.foreignaffairs.com/articles/2011-05-24/al-qaeda-s-terrible-spring.

[76] See Byman, "Breaking the Bonds," for a discussion.

Regional threats and challenges to US interests

In meeting these key interests, the United States faces a number of challenges. Iran could present obstacles to several core US interests in the region, including securing access to oil, counterterrorism, nuclear proliferation, and protecting Israel's security. With regards to securing both regional and global access to oil, the good news is that the United States can prevent Iran from using its conventional military power to dominate oil reserves. The poor condition of Iran's conventional forces and the weakness of most other potentially hostile states' forces indicate that allies can do reasonably well on their own, particularly if they have access to US backing in a crisis. To ensure this, the United States would want rapid-deployment forces and the basing and access structure to enable rapid deployment to the region—both to tip the military balance further in allies' favor and to signal resolve. However, it already possesses this capability, and a further reduction of US forces in the region would not significantly reduce this. Given the unlikelihood of a sudden Iranian attack, the United States does not need a large on-the-ground presence but can rely more on an over-the-horizon one.

While the 2015 JCPOA did not eliminate the Iranian nuclear proliferation threat in its entirety, the agreement did reduce the danger of a near-term military confrontation between the US and Iran. The agreement also made possible the addition of several safeguards: monitoring and verification procedures will be conducted by the International Atomic Energy Agency (IAEA) on a regular—and in some cases, continual—basis.[77] Additionally, the involvement of the EU+3 in the drafting and implementation of the agreement suggests that should the Iranian regime renege on its commitments the United States will be in a stronger position to secure widespread international support should it choose to respond with punitive measures.

Iranian regional subversion is harder to stop, but the threat it presents remains more limited. Iran's primary capacity to meddle involves the Shi'a populations of neighboring states, and it has undertaken such efforts with varying degrees of success in Afghanistan, Bahrain, Iraq, Lebanon, and Saudi Arabia. However, the Arab/Persian divide and local nationalism often lead to resentment of, rather than loyalty to, Tehran among the Arab Shi'a. In addition, regime security forces have long focused on this threat, since the 1979 revolution, and have successfully cowed and penetrated Shi'a communities. Furthermore, in Sunni-majority societies, little danger exists of Shi'a radicals gaining broader popular support. At most they could launch a limited terrorism campaign that would raise the price of oil somewhat, but not catapult it into the stratosphere.

A second internal challenge comes from the festering Arab–Israeli conflict. Without a lasting solution agreed upon by the two main parties, violent clashes between Israelis and Palestinians will continue to erupt with regularity every couple of years, negatively impacting other US interests in the region. The United States should work to prevent Israel from becoming a complete pariah state: vetoing UN

---

[77] Under the agreement, the centrifuges and enrichment infrastructure at Natanz will be under continuing IAEA monitoring. See Joint Comprehensive Plan of Action, State Department, July 14, 2015, http://www.state.gov/documents/organization/245317.pdf.

resolutions, pushing for trade to stay open, and otherwise defending Israel in international fora, while also trading with the Jewish state. Peace with the Palestinians would greatly reduce Israel's pariah status and somewhat improve the US image in the Middle East, though only marginally. Here, ironically, the United States would be pushing on behalf of its ally against the wishes of the ally's own government. The Netanyahu government's support for peace initiatives is tepid, at best, and for the United States to drive Israel to the negotiating table would require a sustained and public quarrel with a close and politically powerful ally.

In contrast to the challenges posed by Iran and the Arab–Israeli conflict, the challenge of combating the Islamic State requires the investment of additional resources in the region; specifically, a significant US air presence to augment the forces of local allies. To date, the United States has tried—with little success—to arm and train large numbers of capable local forces (Iraqi and Syrian Kurds, moderate Syrian opposition forces, and Iraqi tribes) to fight the Islamic State. The United States should continue these efforts but also work to contain the fires burning in Syria.[78] Part of this involves reducing the conventional and insurgent military threat the Islamic State poses. It also requires working with refugees and shoring up the border defenses and counterterrorism capabilities of neighboring states like Lebanon and Jordan.

Other threats and potential challenges to US interests

In addition to the internal regional challenges to US interests mentioned above, the United States faces a number of challenges originating from outside of the region. The Middle East has long been a source of contention for great powers. Driven by their own national interests, many of which often do not align with those of Washington, outside actors have the potential to serve as spoilers for the United States. Chief among the list of states able to influence dynamics within the region and, in the process, potentially undermine US interests there, is China, and to a lesser extent, Russia. While the United States has faced great power competition in the region before (from Great Britain during its initial foray into the Middle East and later from Moscow), competition from an ascending China is unlikely to resemble past challenges. In contrast to the United States-Soviet clash during the Cold War, China's main strategic interests in the Middle East are economic. Even so, the potential for Chinese interests to interfere with US objectives in the region is real.

Nowhere is China's growing presence in the Middle East more visible than in the oil and gas industry. The largest energy consumer in the world, China became the second largest net oil importer in the world behind the United States in 2009. As the largest source of China's crude oil imports, more oil flows from the Middle East to China than to any other destination in the world. Saudi Arabia alone accounts for nearly one-quarter of all Chinese oil imports. In 2014, the region as a whole made up fifty-two percent (3.2 mil bbl/d) of total crude oil imports to China.[79] In an effort

---

[78] For a more detailed overview, see Daniel Byman, "Containing Syria's Chaos," *The National Interest*, October 20, 2015, http://nationalinterest.org/feature/containing-syrias-chaos-14102.

[79] "US Energy Information Agency: China," Last updated: May 14, 2015, https://www.eia.gov/beta/international/analysis_includes/countries_long/China/china.pdf.

to secure continued access, major Chinese oil and gas companies like the Sinopec Group have invested heavily across the region, with the largest investments occurring in Iran, Iraq, and Saudi Arabia. Moreover, unlike its American counterpart, Chinese investment comes with "no strings attached."

In the billions of dollars, these investments not only buy access but also influence. Regional governments and their publics are keenly aware that after more than two decades of unmatched influence, an alternative to US authority now exists. Beijing has increasingly become the destination of choice for new leaders upon assuming office: not counting regional trips both Saudi Arabia's King Abdullah and Egypt's President Morsi undertook their first official foreign trips to China.[80] The change is also reflected on the streets. China's favorability ratings surpass those of the United States by double digits throughout much of the region. In Jordan, a long-time US ally, forty-seven percent of the population views China favorably compared with just twelve percent for the United States. The outlook is equally bleak in Egypt where support for China outshines that for the United States by more than thirty percent.[81]

Although access to energy is at the crux of China's interests in the Middle East, Beijing remains a key player with respect to other US strategic interests in the region. China is a leading source of arms in the region. Currently the third-largest supplier behind the United States and Russia, Chinese military sales are on the rise. Although the main destinations for Chinese arms in the past have been Iraq and Iran, Beijing recently signed several major arms deals with Algeria and Morocco.[82] With a proven track record of doing business with everyone, regardless of international pariah status or regime type, Chinese interests may also clash down the road with US efforts to promote democratization in the region. One area in which the two countries do see eye to eye on in the region, however, is guaranteeing a stable and secure oil flow. Another shared common interest is counterterrorism. Still, as China's power continues to grow, it is unclear whether the United States will be able to get Beijing to support Washington's broader goals for the Middle East. However, China still lacks strong security ties to any state in the region, and its ability to project military power to the Middle East is limited.

Moscow too has the potential to serve as a spoiler to US interests in the region. In 2015, Russia intervened in Syria on behalf of the Assad regime, using its air force to bomb opposition forces. By focusing on the more moderate Syrian opposition

---

[80] King Abdullah visited China in 2006. The visit was not only his first outside the Middle East since being crowned a year earlier but also marked the first time a Saudi head of state traveled to the country. In 2012, Morsi's first visit outside of the Middle East was to China. See Brian Spegele and Matt Bradley, "Egypt's Morsi Firms China Ties," *Wall Street Journal*, August 29, 2012; Anand Giridharadas, "Oil Needs in Asia Spur Saudi Attentions," *International Herald Tribune*, January 27, 2006.

[81] Pew Research Center Global Attitudes Project, "Global Opinion of Obama Slips, International Policies Faulted," June 13, 2012, 37, http://www.pewglobal.org/2012/06/13/global-opinion-of-obama-slips-international-policies-faulted.

[82] Paul Holtom, et al. "Trends in International Arms Transfers, 2012," SIPRI Fact Sheet, March 2013.

rather than the Islamic State, Russia's actions not only directly challenged US counterterrorism and democracy promotion objectives in the region but also increased the likelihood of unintended military "friendly fire" incidents or other accidents between the two former Cold War superpowers.

While the United States is hardly the only foreign power interested (or currently engaged) in the region, it remains the most powerful external actor in the Middle East today. China's interests are largely economic and unlikely to directly challenge US security interests, while Russia's increasing involvement in the region represents more of an irritant than a viable challenge to American influence there. Additionally, Moscow's military and political support for the Assad regime in the Syrian conflict places Russia firmly in the Iranian camp in the wider Shi'a-Sunni regional struggle, a development which is likely to draw the ire of the Gulf monarchies and limit Russia's regional gains.

A final challenge to US strategic interests in the Middle East comes from within the United States itself. Following a decade of war, the American public is wary of becoming embroiled in overseas missions be they military or diplomatic. Americans are also increasingly skeptical of democratization. A September 2012 poll found a marked shift in American perceptions about the Arab Spring: where nearly half of the respondents thought the uprisings in the Arab world were about ordinary people seeking freedom in 2011, the figure had dropped to just fifteen percent by the end of 2012. By contrast, the number of Americans believing the uprisings were the result of Islamist groups seeking power more than doubled to 38 percent over the same period.[83] However, Americans are highly concerned about the Islamic State. Although polls show continued skepticism about US involvement in the Middle East, because of fears of Islamic State terrorism and anger at its brutality, the vast majority favor military action against the group.[84]

WHICH ALLIES MATTER MOST, AND WHERE DOES THE UNITED STATES HAVE INFLUENCE?

The US ability to secure many of its interests and influence events is both relatively easy and extremely limited. Counterterrorism cooperation is one area where US influence is considerable. Washington both augments local capabilities, particularly with its superior signals intelligence and analytic resources, and serves as a regional and global orchestra conductor, bringing together information and assets from different countries that would otherwise function in isolation. Allies' information represents an even more vital resource to Washington as they are well-positioned to disrupt activities and gather intelligence.

In securing a range of interests, Washington also gains some ability to influence allies' policies toward one another and toward other regional actors through its

[83] Shibley Telhami, "Americans on the Middle East: A Study of American Public Opinion," Brookings, October 8, 2012.

[84] Dan Balz and Peggy Craighill, "Poll: Public Supports Strikes in Iraq, Syria; Obama's Ratings Hover Near His All-Time Lows," *Washington Post*, September 9, 2014, https://www.washington-post.com/politics/poll-public-supports-strikes-in-iraq-syria-obamas-ratings-hover-near-his-all-time-lows/2014/09/08/69c164d8-3789-11e4-8601-97ba88884ffd_story.html.

military assistance efforts. The Middle East in general is weak on regional institutions—there is no OSCE or even an ASEAN equivalent, let alone something like the European Union. As an outside actor, the United States can use its good offices to work behind the scenes and ease regional disputes and personal rivalries. In addition, the US role in logistics and support gives the United States a near-veto on independent military operations. For example, after the 1995 attempted assassination of Egyptian President Mubarak in Addis Ababa, Egypt sought to conduct military strikes on Khartoum, which it blamed for the attack. The United States, however, refused to cooperate, and Egypt lacked the ability to strike on its own.

Table 10.1 Posited US Interests and Possible Threats

Country	Free Flow of Oil*	Nuclear Proliferation Concern	Terrorism Problem?	Counterterrorism Assistance	Security of Israel	Democratization
Algeria	+		--	++		
Bahrain						
Egypt			-	++	++	-
Iran	++/--†	---	--	--	--	
Iraq	++		---	++		
Israel				+	+++	
Jordan			-	++	+	
Kuwait	++			+		
Libya	++		--	+		--
Morocco				++		
Oman						
Palestinian Territories (WB)			-	+	++	
Palestinian Territories (Gaza)			--	-	--	
Qatar	++			+		
Saudi Arabia	+++	+	-	+++		-
Syria			--	+/---‡	--	--
Tunisia			--			+
UAE	++			+		
Yemen			---	+++		--

Note: Plus signs mean regime is of interest in a positive way from a US point of view. Minus signs mean country is a threat to that interest.

* Although Oman, Yemen, and other regional states also export oil, they are not among the top suppliers to the global market.

† Iranian reserves and exports are beneficial to US energy interests in the Middle East. Iran's military posture and actions are seen as a potential threat to this interest.

‡ Syria was a US counterterrorism partner until the Arab Spring. Now violence there is generating terrorism and the regime is not working with the United States.

The alliance posture the United States pursues in the region should depend on which, if any, of the above interests the United States should emphasize and which can be discarded. Table 10.1 gives a review of the various countries in the region and the posited US interests. For energy, key states include of course Saudi Arabia, but also (and to a lesser degree) Algeria, Iran, Iraq, Kuwait, Libya, Qatar, and the United Arab Emirates. Nuclear proliferation represents a far more bounded problem, with Iran of greatest concern, and only Saudi Arabia deserving scrutiny among other states. The security of Israel prioritizes not only the Jewish state, but also its neighbors, especially Egypt, and the Palestinian territories. Counterterrorism positions countries with an Islamic State or al-Qaeda presence near the top of the list, along with regimes that are effective in fighting them. So Algeria, Egypt, Iraq, Jordan, Libya, Saudi Arabia, and Yemen figure prominently. Democratization prioritizes countries that have a chance of making a successful transition: a list that, at the time of writing, includes just one country, Tunisia.

The above classification scheme suggests that several countries should continue to be alliance priorities, while others could be downgraded. For example, a cursory view of Table 10.1 reveals that Saudi Arabia offers the potential for cooperation on the most (3) number of US interests. An alternative metric would be to prioritize or rank interests, with oil, counterterrorism, nonproliferation, and Israel's security scoring high and democratization lower.

Egypt

With neither enough oil to support an export industry nor a viable nuclear program, Egypt's significance stems largely from its ability to affect—either adversely or positively—US efforts at counterterrorism and democracy promotion as well as Israel's security. Historically, a leader in the Arab world, Egypt is still very much in transition as it continues to adjust to developments following the Arab Spring.

The Sinai region however continues to be a source of instability for both Egypt and Israel; though the Sisi government—following a spate of kidnappings and violence—has recently begun to crack down on terrorism and lawlessness there.[85] Both Washington and Cairo share a common desire to seal the vast security vacuum in the Sinai, the source of many of the terrorist incidents in the country. Clamping down on extremists in the Sinai is also having a stabilizing effect on the Israeli–Egyptian relationship, which has faltered since Mubarak's fall. Egypt also has the potential to affect Libya and other Maghreb states from becoming terrorist footholds. Ongoing political and economic instability though threaten counterterrorism efforts. The Sisi government's crackdown on the Muslim Brotherhood, however, risks driving peaceful members of that group into the arms of radical terrorists and in general of perpetuating Egypt's political crisis.

Geography and history dictate that Egypt is a key player in the Israeli–Palestinian conflict, and going forward it will continue to be so. Cairo not only controls the

---

[85] Ben Hubbard, "Egypt Sends Show of Force to Sinai After Kidnappings," *New York Times*, May 20, 2013.

Rafah border crossing into Gaza, the location of the smuggling tunnels the Israelis frequently complain about, but has successfully brokered a number of ceasefires between Hamas and Israel in the past.

In Egypt, as elsewhere in the region, the US ability to promote democratization and economic reform is extremely limited. America's recent record should give us pause: the George W. Bush administration's energetic efforts failed and perhaps backfired, discrediting regional reformers, while the Obama administration's initial inaction did not halt the Arab Spring nor the emergence of several more democratic movements. Nor was the United States able to prevent a military coup. Even relatively low-level US efforts, like funding civil society organizations, lead to charges of US meddling and, given the unpopularity of the United States in general, can discredit the very organizations it aims to help.

Iraq

Iraq plays a pivotal role in three of America's interests in the region: democratization, counterterrorism, and oil. However, after the 2003 war and a decade-long occupation the reality is such that America will be linked with Iraq whether it chooses to be or not.

Never great to begin with, America's influence in Iraq (and correspondingly Washington's ability to affect its interests there,) declined considerably in the wake of the withdrawal of US combat troops. After years of failed reforms, mounting corruption, and poor services, the Iraqi population has largely given up on Baghdad. Ongoing Sunni exclusion from the political process, repression of Sunni leaders, the exclusion of former Sunni fighters from the security services, and the failure to broker a lasting power-sharing agreement has led to an upsurge in sectarian violence. In 2014 the Islamic State capitalized on these sectarian tensions, gaining considerable Sunni support when it stepped up operations in Iraq in 2014, eventually taking Mosul and large swathes of the country. Iraqi security forces have recovered from this nadir and in 2015 and 2016 made limited progress against the Islamic State, retaking important cities and parts of Iraq.

One positive note is that Iraqi oil production has been increasing strongly. With 3.1 million barrels per day, Iraq now accounts for one-tenth of all OPEC production.[86] Political instability and poor infrastructure however has led to disenchantment with Iraq's oil sector among the international community. Many foreign oil companies prefer to operate in Iraqi Kurdistan rather than the more volatile and dangerous south. Although the Iraqi government reached an agreement with the Kurdish Regional Government (KRG) over the management of the country's oil and natural gas resources in December 2014 implementation of the arrangement has proved sporadic with Baghdad calling for a new deal.[87] Growing Turkish

[86] Stanely Reed, "OPEC Holds Steady on Output Targets," *International Herald Tribune,* June 1, 2013.

[87] Matt Bradley, Sarah Kent and Ghassan Adnan, "Iraq and Kurdistan Agree on Oil Deal," *Wall Street Journal,* December 2, 2014, http://www.wsj.com/articles/iraq-agrees-kurdistan-oil-deal-1417513949; Matt Bradley, "Iraq, Kurdistan Oil Deal Close to Collapse, *Wall Street Journal,* July 3, 2015, http://www.wsj.com/articles/iraq-kurdistan-oil-deal-close-to-collapse-1435922324;

influence in Kurdistan along with plans to build a new pipeline with a western outlet have officials in Baghdad concerned while, for its part, Washington is monitoring growing Chinese influence in the Iraqi oil industry from afar.[88] According to the International Energy Agency, one quarter of all Iraqi oil will be destined for China by 2035.[89]

Saudi Arabia

Saudi Arabia remains critical in terms of oil and counterterrorism, but its hostility regarding the Arab Spring and the Iran deal has placed it at odds with Washington. Riyadh's role varies considerably depending on US priorities.

Saudi Arabia possesses much of the world's spare oil capacity, roughly 3.5 million barrels a day, enabling it to play a critical role in support of US policies. Although the United States is becoming less dependent on Saudi oil with time, Saudi Arabia's role as swing producer makes this largely irrelevant for most economic circumstances, as this role places the Kingdom at the top of the list in maintaining an open and secure global market. The Kingdom's spare capacity allows it to mitigate disruption of the market should there be a price shock, such as the collapse of Libya's supplies during the Libyan revolution, or an unexpected surge in demand.[90]

Riyadh's oil wealth also affords it unmatched influence among its neighbors. In an effort to counter what they perceive to be growing Iranian influence in the region, the Saudis have embarked on an active campaign of backing local politicians and political parties abroad. Riyadh's ability to sway events was on full display in 2011 when Saudi forces intervened in Bahrain in order to quell a growing uprising there. Though most demonstrations of Saudi influence are tacit, their ability to shape regional events is nonetheless significant.

After an initial slow start, United States-Saudi counterterrorism cooperation has greatly improved following the 2003 Riyadh bombing. The Saudi government maintains a "robust" counterterrorism relationship with the United States and has

---

"Baghdad calls for striking new oil deal with Iraq's Kurdistan Regional Government," *Daily Sabah*, March 22, 2016, http://www.dailysabah.com/energy/2016/03/22/baghdad-calls-for-striking-new-oil-deal-with-iraqs-kurdistan-regional-government.

[88] Massimo Morelli and Costantino Pischedda, "Oil, Federalism, and Third-Party Intervention: An Assessment of Conflict Risk in Iraqi Kurdistan" (working paper, Columbia University, May 15, 2013).

[89] Chazan, "Iraq's Appeal Wanes for Oil Majors."

[90] "World Total Liquids Production By Region and Country, Reference Case," in "The International Energy Outlook 2011," US Energy Information Administration, September 19, 2011, http://www.eia.gov/oiaf/aeo/tablebrowser/#release=IEO2011&subject=0-IEO2011&table=38-IEO2011&region=0-0&cases=Reference-0504a_1630; "Crude Oil Imports From the Persian Gulf," US Energy Information Administration, August 30, 2012, http://www.eia.gov/petroleum/imports/companylevel/summary.cfm; Marianne Lavelle, "Iran's Undisputed Weapon: Power to Block the Strait of Hormuz," *National Geographic News*, February 7, 2012.

welcomed enhanced bilateral cooperation with Washington.[91] The Saudis have made significant headway in their counterradicalization and rehabilitation programs in an effort to check the flow of new recruits and stem the extremist tide. Much progress has been made on intelligence sharing and combatting terrorist financing as well. The United States and Saudis have also cooperated extensively in protecting critical infrastructure targets in the Kingdom, such as oil installations.[92] Riyadh's support will also be necessary for dealing with the terrorist threat emanating from Yemen, though here, as on other issues, Washington's efforts are likely to complicated by Saudi Arabia's (sometimes) opposing interests.

The potential US military role

Given the interests and threats identified above, what level of capabilities can and should the United States invest in the region? To protect against Iran or another hostile power, the United States requires military access to a range of countries— to protect states from conventional attack and to deter Iran should it go nuclear. To react immediately, the United States would need a presence in the Persian Gulf comparable to what it has today. To be able to react relatively quickly, the United States would need basing and access privileges and prepositioning, enabling a rapid deployment in the event of a crisis.

Given internal instability and the vagaries of local politics, Washington also values diverse basing, allowing it to pick and choose as necessary ensure backups should a regime turn against the United States. This basing and access is also important for contingencies outside the region. For example, bases in the Middle East provide partial support to the campaign in Afghanistan.

Similarly, America's ability to strike at the Islamic State depends on ongoing access to regional bases and a continued naval presence in the region. Defeating or downgrading ISIS does not require a heavy US combat presence, however. Rather, the United States should encourage, empower, and equip regional partners to confront and destroy the organization and restore the territorial integrity of Iraq and Syria. This may require limited numbers of trainers and special operations forces, but not large numbers of conventional combat troops.

Alliances between the United States and countries in the region also enhance deterrence. Many US allies, particularly the smaller states of the Persian Gulf, but also Jordan and even Saudi Arabia, have weak conventional military forces.[93] An

---

[91] "Chapter 2, Country Reports: Middle East and North Africa Overview," Country Reports on Terrorism 2012, US State Department, May 30, 2013.

[92] "Combating Terrorism: US Agencies Report Progress Countering Terrorism and Its Financing in Saudi Arabia but Continued Focus on Counter Terrorism Financing Efforts Needed," GAO Report, September 2009, available at http://www.gao.gov/new.items/d09883.pdf.

[93] The problem for many of these states is not just their small size but the overall skill levels of their militaries. In many cases they possess state-of-the-art arsenals, and regional predators' forces are weak, but US allies are unable to leverage the systems they own. See Kenneth Pollack, *Arabs at War: Military Effectiveness, 1948–1991* (Lincoln: University of Nebraska Press, 2002).

alliance with the United States enables them to resist pressure from hostile neighbors while simultaneously providing protection from outright invasion. So should Iran threaten the Gulf states with military force or increased subversion, the presence of American troops is a visible symbol that the United States will aid its allies in resisting Tehran.

The United States pays a price for its willingness to use its military to deter and repel regional aggressors in the Middle East. Even putting aside the 2003 war in Iraq as a policy approach unlikely to be repeated, the human cost can be considerable. Limited US uses of force and deterrence attempts may involve casualties comparable to the deterrence and coercion campaign of 1990 and 1991, after Iraq invaded Kuwait. Over one hundred Americans died in combat in the 1991 Gulf war, and almost five hundred were wounded—small figures compared to previous and subsequent wars, but nevertheless considerable given the limited long-term strategic results.[94]

The financial costs are difficult to determine precisely, but are large by any measure. Much of the size of the US military is determined by multiple contingencies as well as domestic concerns, so part of the air, naval, and ground presence in the region would have been developed and maintained for other reasons.

Furthermore, the US role in the region increases the risk of local "free riding" off the American security guarantee. The wealth of the Gulf states, and even their purchase of massive stocks of the most advanced aircraft, has not directly translated into military power. This weakness is due in part to the assumption that they can rely on the United States as a security guarantor and thus do not need to take the politically painful steps to dismiss incompetent generals, implement conscription, or otherwise expand their militaries and reduce coup-proofing measures to increase effectiveness.[95]

Deep anti-Americanism can weaken the stability of US allies in the region. The peacetime US military presence remains unpopular, and was a source of controversy in Saudi religious circles in the 1990s. The regional US military role is still a concern, though it represents a far less emotive issue today as concerns like the Syrian civil war have risen to the fore. Even so, however, radical groups, including those linked to al-Qaeda but also those with Iranian support, are quick to deride any form of cooperation with the United States as a sign of the regime's fundamental illegitimacy. In their eyes, US troops often represent the highest form of betrayal. And, indeed, the US presence is a visible sign that US allies are not able to ensure their own security, a potential humiliation.

The most important current US military role is in fighting the Islamic State. This involves a mix of forces to help arm and train local allies combined with regular airstrikes against Islamic State forces and leaders. The United States also helps manage the broader air campaign of its many allies, including both Arab and European states.

---

[94] This figure excludes casualties from accidents. Dennis Cauchon, "Why US Casualties Were Low," *USA Today*, April 20, 2003, http://www.usatoday.com/news/world/iraq/2003-04-20-cover-usat_x.htm.

[95] James Quinlivan, "Coup-Proofing: Its Practice and Consequences in the Middle East," *International Security* 24, no. 2 (Fall 1999): 131–165.

POLICY IMPLICATIONS AND RECOMMENDATIONS

Although recognizing that US influence in the Middle East is often at best limited, the above analysis suggests several policy changes for the United States.

First, there is little need for a larger deployment of US forces given the conventional weaknesses of potential adversaries, but the United States will want a significant air component and some special operations and ground forces in the region to oppose the Islamic State. At the same time, maintaining a network of bases, prepositioned equipment, and access agreements assist in US deterrence and thus make Iran less likely to cheat on any deal and enable the United States to deploy quickly should deterrence fail or should an unexpected contingency occur requiring the use of military assets from the region. In addition, Washington should continue to emphasize maintenance and logistics as well as arms sales, as these functions provide it considerable influence over allied uses of force.

The good news is that for the first time in many years there appears to be strong regional support for a US security presence. If anything, many Gulf countries would like to see the US *expand* its military assurances to the region.[96] Washington should resist the temptation to do a massive expansion, however, and focus on the more limited capabilities necessary to fight the Islamic State and other immediate threats. Instead, the US should leverage its existing contributions to ensure our allies are pulling their own weight.

Second, a behind-the-scenes approach represents the most valuable method for securing the majority of US interests. Basing and access agreements, in contrast to troop deployments, can be low-profile. Counterterrorism cooperation is both clandestine and does not involve a large US footprint. Given the unpopularity of the United States, democracy promotion is also best done behind the scenes. A low profile on democratization is advantageous as it reduces the risk of a US–Saudi rupture on this issue. Furthermore, a higher profile has not proven to significantly help pro-democratic forces in the region. Inevitably, the United States will be damned for not aggressively supporting democracy, but given that doing so would probably have little impact and might be counterproductive both for the alliance in general and for democratization itself, it is best to err on the side of caution.

Third, reenergizing the Middle East peace process represents a vital step both for Israel's security and for US interests. Overall cooperation with the United States is affected negatively by the continued regional and worldwide hostility toward Israel. This hostility would not vanish with a Palestinian state, but it would be diminished. For Israel's sake, pressure that could lead it to become a pariah would diminish, as would the costs and risks inherent in its ongoing occupation of the Palestinian territories.

Fourth, to further reduce the danger from foreign fighters going to Syria, several steps are necessary beyond fighting the Islamic State. These include increasing

---

[96] Karen DeYoung and Juliet Eilperin, "Persian Gulf leaders to Press Obama to Strengthen Us Security Relationship," *Washington Post*, May 11, 2015, https://www.washingtonpost.com/ world/national-security/persian-gulf-leaders-to-press-obama-to-strengthen-us-security-relationship/2015/05/11/60d16ece-f811-11e4-a13c-193b1241d51a_story.html.

community engagement efforts to dissuade potential fighters from going to Syria; working more with Turkey to disrupt transit routes; improving deradicalization programs to "turn" returning fighters into intelligence sources or make them less likely to engage in violence; and avoiding blanket prosecution efforts. Most important, security services must be properly resourced and organized to handle the potential danger. Given Europe's many problems, US technical assistance there is also vital.

Additionally, the United States must recognize that its overall ability to influence some threats to its interests remains limited. Many of the dangers to the region are not amenable to the greatest tool of US influence—overwhelming conventional force—and some involve complex political dynamics that will often defy pressure from Washington. In particular, several states in the region are now or at risk of being failed states. Given strong anti-United States sentiment and often limited interests, Washington can do little to alter this situation, but it can prepare for the aftermath. Washington should prepare for a period of prolonged instability, along with the possibility that the eventual victors may prove hostile to US interests.

Such a strategy is not only prudent and wise, it is sustainable. In an era of constrained resources, the task for America's leaders is to craft a national security strategy that will protect US interests in the Middle East while being affordable in the long term. Given the complexities of the region, the potential for the Middle East to suck in further American military forces and resources will always be there. A sustainable national security will be one that guards against this ever-present danger while still protecting US interests. Part of having a sustainable national security means not only curtailing ineffective or less vital obligations but also getting our allies to do more. Heightened insecurity among the Gulf states stemming from Iran's growing influence and the rise of the Islamic State means the United States may, at least in the short term, find itself in the unusual position of having to turn down invitations from regional allies to increase its security footprint in the region.

11

KEEP, TOSS, OR FIX? ASSESSING US ALLIANCES IN EAST ASIA

Jennifer Lind

Changing strategic and economic conditions have prompted a debate about the future of US national security strategy and American alliances. Since the George W. Bush administration, the United States has run budget deficits that ballooned in the wake of the financial crisis, recession, and wars in Afghanistan and Iraq. As a result of these deficits, the United States accumulated a national debt that today exceeds $18 trillion. At the same time, as Cindy Williams has argued in this volume, the United States is entering a period (for demographic reasons) in which government expenditures for entitlements will soar (Social Security, Medicare, and Medicaid). Combined with interest on the debt, these expenditures will vastly outpace revenues. To deal with this problem, the 2011 Budget Control Act, or sequestration, capped discretionary spending and imposed cuts on defense spending. Unless other legislation is passed, the US defense budget will be cut by about $500 billion over the 2012–2021 period, relative to where it would have been had it kept pace with inflation. Defense spending in the United States, then, will fall.[1]

Meanwhile, scholars warn that in East Asia, the United States faces a gathering storm. Since the collapse of the Soviet Union, the United States enjoyed uncontested regional dominance in East Asia, but this has changed with the growth of Chinese power in the region.[2] China's economy has grown rapidly for three decades, unseating Japan to rank second only to the United States in terms of aggregate GDP. China has also engaged in significant military modernization, pursuing an asymmetric strategy that is challenging US access to the Western Pacific.[3] To be sure,

---

[1] On US national security policy in an age of austerity see Michael Mandelbaum, *The Frugal Superpower: America's Global Leadership in a Cash-Strapped Era* (New York: PublicAffairs, 2010); Daniel W. Drezner, "Military Primacy Doesn't Pay (Nearly As Much as You Think)," *International Security* 38, No. 1 (2013): 52–79.

[2] John Mearsheimer, *The Tragedy of Great Power Politics*, 2nd Ed. (New York: W.W. Norton, 2014); John Mearsheimer, "The Gathering Storm: China's Challenge to U.S. Power in Asia," *Chinese Journal of International Politics* 3, no. 4 (2010): 381–396; Hugh White, *The China Choice: Why America Should Share Power* (New York: Oxford University Press, 2013); Aaron Friedberg, *A Contest for Supremacy: China, America, and the Struggle for Mastery in Asia* (New York: W.W. Norton, 2012).

[3] Jennifer Lind and Daryl G. Press, "The Sources of the Sino-American Spiral," *National Interest*, September 18, 2013; Joshua Rovner, "Three Paths to Escalation with China," *National Interest*,

China's economy may falter, or political turmoil may derail Chinese growth, thus allowing the United States to retain its dominant position.[4] But Asia's transformation from a region of uncontested US dominance to a region in which two great powers compete for space warrants a debate about the future of American national security policy there.

Given the profound transformation in the US budgetary and strategic environment, is it possible, as Jeremi Suri and Benjamin Valentino query in the introduction to this volume, that "the same basic policies, allies, and budgets that protected us from the Soviet Union in 1988" are "the optimal ones for defending American interests" in East Asia? Or do changed budgetary and strategic conditions warrant changes in US national security policy as well?

This chapter joins an ongoing debate about US grand strategy about maintaining, or retrenching from, the current American grand strategy. Many scholars have argued that global peace and prosperity depend on the United States maintaining dominant military capabilities, deploying American military personnel overseas, and continuing to offer security guarantees to US allies.[5] Critics, however, argue that the expansive US grand strategy—known variously as "deep engagement," "primacy," or "hegemony"—encourages "free riding" among US allies; it threatens to undermine US economic prosperity, provoke counterbalancing, and drag the United States into unnecessary wars.[6] Such critics argue for adopting a strategy

July 19, 2012; Michael McDevitt, "The PLA Navy's Antiaccess Role in a Taiwan Contingency," in Phillip C. Saunders, Christopher D. Yung, Michael Swaine and Andrew en-Dzu Yang, eds., *The Chinese Navy: Expanding Capabilities, Evolving Roles* (Washington, DC: National Defense University, 2011).

[4] David Shambaugh, *China's Future* (London: Polity Press, 2016); Michael Pettis, *The Great Rebalancing: Trade, Conflict, and the Perilous Road Ahead for the World Economy* (Princeton, NJ: Princeton University Press, 2013); Nicholas Lardy, *Sustaining China's Economic Growth After the Global Financial Crisis* (Washington, DC: Peterson Institute for International Economics, 2012); Minxin Pei, *China's Trapped Transition: The Limits of Developmental Autocracy* (Cambridge, MA: Harvard University Press, 2006).

[5] Robert Kagan, *The World America Made* (New York: Knopf, 2012); Stephen Brooks, G. John Ikenberry, and William C. Wohlforth, "Don't Come Home, America: The Case against Retrenchment," *International Security* 37, no. 3 (Winter 2012–2013): 7–51; Stephen G. Brooks, G. John Ikenberry, and William C. Wohlforth, "Lean Forward: In Defense of American Engagement," *Foreign Affairs* 92, no. 1 (January/February 2013); Robert J. Lieber, *Power and Willpower in the American Future: Why the United States Is Not Destined to Decline* (New York: Cambridge University Press, 2012); Michele Flournoy and Janine Davidson, "Obama's New Global Posture," *Foreign Affairs* (July–August 2012); G. John Ikenberry, *Liberal Leviathan: The Origins, Crisis, and Transformation of the American World Order* (Princeton, NJ: Princeton University Press, 2011); Carla Norrlof, *America's Global Advantage: U.S. Hegemony and International Cooperation* (New York: Cambridge University Press, 2010); Robert J. Art, *A Grand Strategy for America* (Ithaca, NY: Cornell University Press, 2003); Joseph S. Nye, Jr., *Bound to Lead: The Changing Nature of American Power* (New York: Basic Books, 1990).

[6] Christopher Preble, *The Power Problem: How American Military Dominance Makes Us Less Safe, Less Prosperous, and Less Free* (Ithaca, NY: Cornell University Press, 2009); Barry R. Posen, *Restraint: A New Foundation for US National Security Policy* (Ithaca, NY: Cornell University Press, 2014); Barry R. Posen, "Pull Back: the Case for a Less Activist Foreign Policy," *Foreign Affairs*

("offshore balancing" or "restraint") that ends security guarantees and brings many or all US military forces home.

This article contributes to this debate in two ways. First, it focuses attention on US alliances in East Asia. This region is the world's most consequential for US national security policy: it is home to a rising great power that could end unipolarity and upend the liberal order that the United States and its partners created after the Second World War.[7] In this region, do American alliances continue to advance the US national security interest? Are they in need of reform—or outright termination—because they are outdated, dangerous, or too costly? If so, what kind of reform? Second, as I examine these questions, I draw upon international relations theory to establish counterfactuals for what the region would look like in the absence of US security guarantees, and how it might look in the future.

In this chapter, I argue that, assuming the United States plans to abandon its grand strategy of deep engagement (which indeed it shows no signs of doing), it makes little sense to "toss" American alliances in East Asia. The alliances advance several key national security goals: most compellingly, they enhance regional deterrence, reduce the spread of nuclear weapons, and dampen regional spirals of insecurity. Without US alliances, the costs to China of pursuing military action or applying pressure on its neighbors would be far lower, so Beijing might feel emboldened to increase its assertiveness in its regional disputes over Taiwan or contested islands. Without US security guarantees, South Korea would almost certainly, and Japan would possibly, acquire nuclear weapons. Furthermore, a US withdrawal from its alliance commitments increases the danger of regional arms racing among in particular China, Japan, and South Korea.

Second, though keeping American alliances makes sense under the current grand strategy, Washington should "fix" them in a few key ways, to maximize the utility of those alliances, and to reduce their costs and risks. Toward this end, US military bases in allied countries should, to the greatest extent possible, be maintained or reformed into "hubs," which are useful in both the regional and global US military network. Furthermore, Washington should adapt its diplomacy so as to reduce growing entanglement risks and to reduce strategic mistrust with China.

In the rest of this chapter, I first describe current US alliance commitments in East Asia. In sections three and four, I describe American foreign policy goals there and assess how these alliances do (and do not) serve these goals. Section five

(January/February 2013); Christopher Layne, "China's Challenge to U.S. Hegemony," *Current History* (January 2008); Eugene Gholz, Benjamin H. Friedman, Daryl G. Press, and Harvey M. Sapolsky, "Restraining Order for Strategic Modesty," *World Affairs* (Fall 2009); Eugene Gholz, Daryl G. Press, and Harvey Sapolsky, "Come Home, America: The Case for Restraint in the Face of Temptation," *International Security* 21, no. 4 (Spring 1997): 5–48. On entanglement risks see Michael Beckley, "The Myth of Entangling Alliances: Reasssessing the Risks of US Defense Pacts," *International Security* 39 no. 4 (Spring 2015): 7–48.

[7] On polarity see Stephen G. Brooks and William C. Wohlforth, *World Out of Balance: International Relations and the Challenge of American Primacy* (Princeton, NJ: Princeton University Press, 2008); William C. Wohlforth, "The Stability of a Unipolar World," *International Security* 24, no. 1 (Summer 1999): 5–41. On the American-led order see Ikenberry, *Liberal Leviathan*.

describes the costs and risks that America's Asian alliances bring. I conclude by describing how the United States might change its alliance policies in order to minimize these costs and risks.

US ALLIANCES AND MILITARY PRESENCE IN EAST ASIA

After World War II, the United States established formal alliances with several East Asian countries. To support the US-Japan Security Treaty, signed in 1951, the United States currently stations 35,000 forces in Japan, the vast majority of which are air force, Marines, and navy.[8] Though there are a few US military installations on the main islands, the majority of the US forces in Japan are stationed on the small island of Okinawa to the far south. Okinawa is proximate to the East Asian sea lanes in the South China Sea, and to Taiwan. It hosts several US military facilities, notably US Marine Corps bases (among them Camp Schwab and Camp Hansen) and the large Kadena Air Base.

The presence of US military forces in Okinawa is a sore spot for many residents, who live with the noise, accidents, and crime associated with the bases.[9] In response to such complaints, and in an effort to create a more sustainable US–Japan alliance, Washington plans to relocate 8,000 US Marines off of the island to Guam, has negotiated with Tokyo to relocate Futenma Air Station elsewhere on the island, and is consolidating other forces. The Futenma relocation has stalled in the face of significant local resistance; the problem—and more generally the future of the US Marines on Okinawa—remains unresolved.[10]

The Mutual Defense Treaty with the Republic of Korea (ROK) obligates the United States to come to the defense of South Korea in the event that it is attacked. The original purpose of the alliance was to deter an attack from hostile North Korea, which in 1950 invaded South Korea to attempt to unify the divided peninsula. To deter an attack, the United States has stationed ground and air force personnel in the ROK. For many years, substantial numbers of American troops were stationed near the DMZ as a "tripwire" force, and the United States also had a large military footprint within Seoul.

US forces in Korea have shrunk in recent years.[11] Particularly since the 1990s, North Korea's economic and military power has waned, and the threat of invasion

---

[8] For a useful accounting of US overseas forces see Michael J. Lostumbo, et al., "Overseas Basing of U.S. Military Forces: An Assessment of Relative Costs and Benefits," RAND Corporation, Santa Monica, CA, 2012.

[9] On the politics of the Okinawa base issue see Kent E. Calder, *Embattled Garrisons: Comparative Base Politics and American Globalism* (Princeton, NJ: Princeton University Press, 2007), pp. 166–175. The issue of American violence against the people of Okinawa has a long and fraught history: most notoriously, in 1995, three US soldiers gang-raped an Okinawan schoolgirl, fueling the island's anti-base movement. See Martin Fackler, "Arrests of 2 U.S. Sailors in Rape Case Threaten to Fan Okinawa's Anger," *New York Times*, October 16, 2012.

[10] On the Futenma debate see Shannon Tiezzi, "Beyond Futenma: Okinawa and the US Base Conundrum," *The Diplomat*, November 4, 2015.

[11] For an overview, see Lostumbo, et al., "Overseas Basing of U.S. Military Forces."

has fallen. Fighting two wars in the Persian Gulf since 1991, the United States withdrew (and sent to Iraq) forces from the Korean peninsula. 28,500 troops remain, consisting of two brigades of the army's Second Infantry Division (2ID), and several air force tactical squadrons. Washington and Seoul have negotiated a phased reduction and reorganization of American forces that will move and consolidate troops and facilities southward.[12] The United States also agreed to transfer wartime operational control ("OPCON") to the South Korean military, although Seoul has delayed this move multiple times.[13]

In Southeast Asia, the United States guarantees the security of the Philippines, Australia, and New Zealand. With the latter two, the United States in 1951 concluded the ANZUS security pact. Australia previously hosted only a handful of US military personnel, but after 2012, as part of the Obama administration's "pivot" or "rebalancing" effort, agreed to host 2,500 US Marines. The US–Philippine alliance was signed in 1952, and US bases there (Clark Air Force Base and US Naval Base Subic Bay) served as important Cold War hubs. Physical damage to the bases caused by the eruption of Mt. Pinatubo, and Philippine domestic political dissatisfaction with the US presence, led Manila to eject the US military from these bases in 1991–1992. The United States, however, has continued to guarantee the security of the Philippines; military cooperation since the end of the Cold War has primarily continued in the realm of counterterrorism. But more recently, the increasing salience of territorial disputes in the South China Sea (in which Manila is a claimant) has led to a reinvigorated US–Philippine alliance.[14]

As for Taiwan, in 1952 the United States and the Republic of China (ROC) signed a Mutual Defense Treaty. They cooperated within the framework of this alliance in military crises in the Taiwan Strait in the 1950s. Under the leadership of the Nixon administration, Washington normalized diplomatic relations with the People's Republic of China (PRC) in 1979—agreeing that there was one China, ending its security treaty with the ROC, and withdrawing diplomatic recognition from Taipei. The United States currently has no formal security alliance (nor diplomatic relations) with Taiwan, but in 1979 the US Congress passed the "Taiwan Relations Act," declaring its support for maintaining a military balance in the strait, and saying it would view any use of force to resolve the Taiwan dispute with "grave concern." Despite the lack of formal defense commitment, many American foreign policy elites argue that the relationship constitutes a "functional equivalent of a defense pact."[15]

---

[12] The United States has agreed to return Yongsan garrison and other bases in Seoul. US forces in Korea will be consolidated south of Seoul in US Army Garrison Humphreys in Pyeongtaek, and in Osan Air Base. Also, tours in Korea will now be accompanied tours. See "U.S. Changing Its Mission in Korea," *Washington Times*, March 5, 2009.

[13] On "opcon" see "Ash Carter Assures South Korea On US Support," *Wall Street Journal*, November 1, 2015; "S. Korea, U.S. to Decide Timing of Opcon Transfer Next Year," *Korea Herald*, October 14, 2013.

[14] Javier C. Hernández, "Warily Eyeing China, Philippines May Invite U.S. Back to Subic Bay," *New York Times*, September 19, 2015; Prashanth Parameswaran, "Philippines to Revive Former US Naval Base Near South China Sea in 2016," *The Diplomat*, July 17, 2015.

[15] Robert J. Art, *A Grand Strategy for America*, 138.

Finally, American territories in East Asia also provide forward military presence. Long-range aircraft access the region from Alaska, and the United States has significant naval and Marine forces in Hawaii. Even more proximately, the United States maintains a naval base and Anderson Air Force Base on Guam, which is home to attack submarines and B-2 bombers. Over the next several years, the United States plans to redeploy to Guam 8,000 US Marines and their 9,000 dependents from Okinawa, as well as Trident submarines, a ballistic missile task force, and F-22 fighter jets.[16] Preparations are also being made in Guam to accommodate aircraft carriers.

GOALS OF AMERICA'S ASIAN ALLIANCES

US alliances in East Asia aim to serve several broad goals. The first is to deter attacks on allied nations. South Korea has the most heightened threat: the alliance seeks to protect South Korea from attack by North Korea. Additionally, in recent years the region has seen an intensification of island disputes between China and its neighbors in the South China Sea, and between China and Japan in the East China Sea.[17] Proponents of US engagement in the region cite the deterrent role played by American alliances, and by the US military presence that they facilitate.[18]

Second, US alliances in East Asia further the goal of maintaining regional stability in a region of great economic and political significance. The notion of regional stability encompasses several different ideas:

- *Prevention of nuclear spread.* The United States government takes the position that the spread of nuclear weapons is detrimental to international stability. It pledged under the 1968 Nuclear Non-Proliferation treaty to cooperate to reduce the spread of nuclear weapons, and to reduce the size of its own arsenal over time. In East Asia, US alliance commitments are partly aimed at reducing the likelihood of nuclear spread throughout the region through the provision of a nuclear umbrella to Japan and South Korea.

[16] Gina Harkins, "Marines Identify Units That Will Move from Japan to Guam," *Marine Corps Times*, October 1, 2015.

[17] Bonnie S. Glaser, "Armed Clash in the South China Sea," Council on Foreign Relations, Contingency Planning Memorandum No. 14, April 2012; Stephanie Kleine-Ahlbrandt, "Dangerous Waters," *Foreign Policy*, September 17, 2012, http://foreignpolicy.com/2012/09/17/dangerous-waters/; James Manicom, *Bridging Troubled Waters: China, Japan, and Maritime Order in the East China Sea* (Washington, DC: Georgetown University Press, 2014); Sheila A. Smith, "A Sino-Japanese Clash in the East China Sea," Contingency Planning Memorandum No. 18, Council on Foreign Relations, April 2013; Su-Won Park, "The East China Sea Dispute: Short-Term Victory and Long-Term Loss for China?" Brookings Institution, November 1, 2010.

[18] Brooks, Ikenberry and Wohlforth, "Don't Come Home, America"; Robert Kagan, "Superpowers Don't Get to Retire," *New Republic*, May 26, 2014; Nancy Tucker and Bonnie Glaser, "Should the United States Abandon Taiwan?" *The Washington Quarterly* 34, no. 4 (Fall 2011): 23–37; Art, *A Grand Strategy for America*.

- *Prevention of conventional arms races.* Due to historical animosities, territorial disputes, and the growth of Chinese power, East Asian countries may feel mistrust and uncertainty that would lead them to build up their conventional military power. Through the logic of the security dilemma (in which one country's effort to increase its own security reduces the security of another), this has the potential to fuel arms racing.[19] Such arms racing would hinder beneficial economic relations in the region, would be inefficient for the global economy, could sour broader political relations, and could raise the risk of conventional conflict. The United States aims to reduce arms races in East Asia by guaranteeing the security of several states in the region, and by maintaining a powerful military presence there.

- *Free and uninterrupted access to sea lanes.* The United States (specifically the US Seventh Fleet, based on Yokosuka, Japan) is the dominant naval power in a region home to some of the busiest trade routes in the world. The prosperity of the United States (as well as China, South Korea, Japan, and so on) relies upon the uninterrupted flow of shipping through regional sea lanes. Analysts argue that the interruption of those trade flows due to war or terrorist attacks would create supply chain problems and other costly economic disruptions. The smooth flow of sea traffic, military as well as commercial, depends on managing threats such as piracy, and on the region's respect for the law of the sea. The UN Convention of the Law of the Sea (UNCLOS) governs the sovereignty, rights of transit, and economic rights to the millions of miles of coastline and thousands of islands throughout the region.[20]

- *Generally cooperative relations among US allies and partners.* The United States benefits from friendly relations among like-minded countries in East Asia. Close ties among these countries reduce the likelihood of regional disputes and crises, and facilitate diplomacy in a variety of realms. Good state-level relations among the United States and these countries improve the lives of their very intermingled people, who intermarry, work, and travel in these countries.

Third, the United States seeks to keep these countries "on its team"—namely, within the US political orbit (and, by definition, out of a rival political orbit).[21] A country can be said to be in the US political orbit if it has friendly relations and

---

[19] On the security dilemma see John Herz, "Idealist Internationalism and the Security Dilemma," *World Politics* 2, no. 2 (1950): 171–201; Robert Jervis, "Cooperation under the Security Dilemma," *World Politics* 30, no. 2 (January 1978): 167–214; and Jervis, *Perception and Misperception in International Politics* (Princeton, NJ: Princeton University Press, 1976), pp. 58–113.

[20] The United States signed, but has not ratified, UNCLOS. However, US policy follows UNCLOS as standard international law. On the controversy surrounding ratification of UNCLOS see Scott G. Borgeson, "The National Interest and the Law of the Sea," Council on Foreign Relations, May 2009.

[21] On the US orbit in East Asia see Yuen Foong Khong, "The American Tributary System," *Chinese Journal of International Politics* 6, no. 1 (Spring 2013): 1–47; Ikenberry, *Liberal Leviathan*; Kagan, *The World America Made.*

broadly overlapping national interests with the United States, and if it frequently cooperates with Washington. Many analysts argue that countries in the US orbit are more likely to be receptive to concluding trade and other economic agreements.[22] They are more likely to cooperate with US diplomatic goals, and to cooperate militarily (such as training with the US military, providing overflight routes, and even contributing forces for US-led military operations). Countries in the US orbit are more likely to ally with the United States if trouble arises and less likely to succumb to external pressure.

While military alliances (i.e., security guarantees or mutual defense agreements) send a clear sign that a country lies within the US orbit, "orbit" and "alliance" are not synonymous. Israel, for example, is within the US orbit; it cooperates broadly with the United States in many different realms (including national security) without a formal defense agreement. Many other countries occupy this category: Bahrain, Kuwait, Saudi Arabia, Singapore, Taiwan, Thailand, and (previously) Egypt.

In some analysts' eyes, the United States has a fourth critical goal, as important of any of the above: namely, the goal of maintaining US military power and presence in the region. They argue that the United States has an interest in having substantial power in Asia due to its importance: the region's economic dynamism and the emergence of China. Such analysts see power projection capabilities and military presence as an end in and of itself.

By contrast, I treat US military presence and power projection in East Asia as a means to an end: to deter, to contain, to assure, to stabilize. The questions, examined in this chapter, are whether US military presence and commitments actually promote these goals, and whether the gains are worth the costs and risks they bring.

A final word about liberalism. After all, a plank of US foreign policy writ large is to encourage the spread of democracy and to promote US values abroad. In Asia, the United States promoted the development of democracy in Japan, and explains continued support for Taiwan in part by noting shared democratic values. Washington today encourages nascent political reform in Myanmar.[23] However, democracy promotion has not been a first-order goal in Asia: for decades, Washington supported anticommunist dictators in the region (notably in South Korea, Taiwan, and South Vietnam). The United States, including the Obama administration, has also pursued a pragmatic approach toward China that prioritizes stable Sino-American relations over concerns about the Chinese Communist Party's political repression and human rights violations.[24] Although the spread of liberalism remains a broad American goal, it is not a first-order national security goal in East Asia.

---

[22] Brooks, et al., "Don't Come Home America"; for a competing view see Drezner, "Military Primacy Doesn't Pay."

[23] Tucker and Glaser, "Should the United States Abandon Taiwan?" On Myanmar see Agence France-Presse, "US Hails Myanmar Vote as 'Important Step Forward,'" November 9, 2015.

[24] "Clinton: Chinese Human Rights Can't Interfere with Other Crises," CNN.com, February 22, 2009.

DO AMERICA'S ASIAN ALLIANCES ADVANCE ITS NATIONAL SECURITY GOALS?

Deterrence

Deterring war in East Asia is a key goal of American alliances, and the alliance with South Korea aims to deter a second war on the Korean peninsula. North Korea invaded the South in 1950; after the 1953 armistice that ended the Korean War, Pyongyang continued to claim that it was the sole legitimate government of the Korean people, and continued to advocate unification under North Korean rule. For the past half-century, however, North Korea has been deterred from once again attempting to conquer the South.

At the same time, Pyongyang *not* been deterred from initiating lower-level acts of violence. Over the past six decades, North Korea has repeatedly launched egregious attacks on the ROK (e.g., terrorist bombings and assassination attempts of South Korean presidents) albeit below the level of full-scale conventional war.[25] The most recent attacks were North Korea's sinking of the South Korean warship *Cheonan* (which killed forty-six sailors) and its shelling of Yongpyeong Island, in March and November 2010.

A debate over whether deterrence should be characterized as "working" or "failing" is merely semantic: major attacks are being deterred; lesser acts of violence are not. The crucial question for US national security policy is: what is deterring major war on the Korean peninsula? Is the US-ROK alliance causing peace, or are South Korean military capabilities independently sufficient to prevent major war?

The dramatic power asymmetry in the South's favor suggests that North Korea would be deterred from attacking South Korea even without a US-ROK alliance. South Korea is an advanced OECD country (the fourteenth largest economy in the world), whose GDP dwarfs North Korea's ($1.8 trillion compared to $40 billion).[26] South Korea also has a large and well-trained military, with advanced technology that outclasses its antiquated North Korean counterpart. For example, North Korea's most modern tank was built in 1962; North Korea's army would be beset by problems related to lack of fuel, ammunition, and spare parts. Military analysts thus long ago concluded that South Korea would dominate in any conventional war with North Korea.[27] North Korean soldiers are also likely to be hamstrung by hunger,

---

[25] Such events include the 1968 commando raid on the South Korean Blue House; the 1983 attempted assassination of President Chun Doo Hwan during a visit to Burma (which killed sixteen South Korean officials in the delegation and wounded fifteen others); and the 1987 terrorist bombing of a KAL airliner, which killed 115 people. For a description and context of these attacks see Don Oberdorfer and Robert Carlin, *The Two Koreas: A Contemporary History* (New York: Basic Books, 2013).

[26] CIA World Factbook, 2015.

[27] Michael O'Hanlon, "Stopping a North Korean Invasion: Why Defending South Korea is Easier than the Pentagon Thinks," *International Security* 22, no. 4 (1998): 135–170; Nicholas Beldecos and Eric Heginbotham, "The Conventional Military Balance in Korea," *Breakthroughs* 4, no. 1 (Spring 1995): 1–9.

low morale, and leadership ineptitude, because the Kim regime's policies of "coup-proofing" reduce military effectiveness.[28] In sum, borrowing from John Mueller, if North Korea were to attack South Korea absent a US alliance, it would be like jumping off the 5th floor of a building. If North Korea attacked South Korea *and* the United States, it would be like jumping off the 50th floor. If Pyongyang is rational enough to fear for its own existence, it is unclear how much practical difference those additional stories make.[29]

Taiwan. Despite the absence of a formal alliance with Taiwan, US policy deters conflict in the Taiwan Strait. Since the founding of the People's Republic of China, the Chinese Communist Party (CCP) has consistently stated that Taiwan is part of China, that "national unification" is a core interest of the CCP, and that a Taiwanese declaration of independence would lead Beijing to use military force. Although the United States ended its 1954 security treaty with Taiwan more than three decades ago, the Taiwan Relations Act passed by Congress in 1979 has been interpreted as an expression of American interest and potential involvement in a crisis in the strait. Many American officials and foreign policy analysts still express frequent support for Taiwan, and argue that Washington would experience a serious loss of credibility if it did not respond to a Chinese use of force against Taipei.[30] The fact that the United States *might* come to Taiwan's aid helps deter China from using force; the fact that it *might not* come to Taiwan's aid helps deter Taiwan from declaring independence.[31]

Japan and the Philippines. Second, US alliances with Japan and the Philippines likely deter the use of force in regional territorial disputes. In recent years Beijing has changed the territorial status quo and has adopted more assertive military and diplomatic policies. China has pursued extensive island reclamation in the South China Sea, creating nearly 3,000 acres of land, what PACOM Commander Admiral Harry Harris has dubbed a "Great Wall of Sand."[32] Analysts argue that through island reclamation and the construction of military runways and other facilities,

---

[28] Daniel L. Byman and Jennifer Lind, "Pyongyang's Survival Strategy: Tools of Authoritarian Control in North Korea," *International Security* 35, no. 1 (Summer 2010): 44–76; James T. Quinlivan, "Coup-Proofing: Its Practice and Consequences in the Middle East," *International Security* 24, no. 2 (Fall 1999): 131–165.

[29] ". . . anyone who finds life even minimally satisfying is extremely unlikely to do either." John Mueller, *Retreat from Doomsday: The Obsolescence of Major War* (New York: Basic Books, 1989), p. 116.

[30] Tucker and Glaser, "Should the United States Abandon Taiwan?"; Denny Roy, "The Impossible Price of a U.S.-China Grand Bargain: Dumping Taiwan," *National Interest*, June 24, 2015. For a competing view see Charles L. Glaser, "A U.S.-China Grand Bargain? The Hard Choice between Military Competition and Accommodation," *International Security* 39, no. 4 (Spring 2015): 49–90.

[31] For a discussion of US policy see Nancy Bernkopf Tucker, "Strategic Ambiguity or Strategic Clarity?" in Nancy Tucker, ed., *Dangerous Strait: The U.S.-Taiwan-China Crisis* (New York: Columbia University Press, 2005), chapter 8.

[32] Derek Watkins, "What China Has Been Building in the South China Sea," *New York Times*, October 27, 2015; "US Admiral: China 'Creating a Great Wall of Sand' in Sea," Associated Press, March 31, 2015.

China is expanding its ability to project power across the area, and to intimidate neighbors who dispute Chinese territorial claims.[33]

Beijing's policies have also grown increasingly assertive in disputed areas. Chinese ships and submarines more frequently enter disputed territorial waters around the Spratly and Paracel islands in the South China Sea, and have harassed other countries' fishing ships, coast guards, and naval vessels.[34] In 2012, China negotiated an agreement with the Philippines to demilitarize the disputed Scarborough Shoal—but after the Philippines withdrew its military forces, China left its own forces there and has since cut off Philippine access. James Kraska writes, "China's control of access to the feature is dependent upon coercive law enforcement and militia fishing vessel operations, including ramming and shouldering Philippine ships, and harassment of Philippine fishermen."[35] In 2014 in the Paracel Islands (disputed with Vietnam), the Chinese national oil company CNOOC installed an oil rig in disputed waters and drilled for oil, sparking diplomatic protests and anti-Chinese rallies in Hanoi. Vietnam has also protested China's construction of a two-kilometer runway on one of the disputed islands, which enhances its local power projection capabilities.[36] In the East China Sea, a growing number of Chinese ships and jets enter waters around the Senkaku/Diaoyu islands disputed with Japan. In 2013, Beijing declared an Air Defense Identification Zone or ADIZ over the islands.[37] Observers attribute China's assertive policies to a long, patient strategy of "salami tactics" in which China increasingly seeks to dominate the region by changing the "facts on the ground" one step at a time.[38]

US alliances with the Philippines and Japan, by linking these countries to the region's military superpower, help deter Chinese aggression in these regional territorial disputes. In the absence of the US commitments, Philippine military weakness, and the anticipation of a weak response from Japan,[39] might convince the

[33] John Chen and Bonnie Glaser, "What China's 'Militarization' of the South China Sea Would Actually Look Like," *The Diplomat*, November 5, 2015; Andrew Erickson, "Lengthening Chinese Airstrips May Pave Way for South China Sea ADIZ," *National Interest*, April 27, 2015; Alexander Vuving, "Think Again: Myths and Myopia about the South China Sea," *National Interest*, October 16, 2015.

[34] Jane Perlez and Keith Bradsher, "In High Seas, China Moves Unilaterally," *New York Times*, May 9, 2014; Glaser, "Armed Clash in the South China Sea"; Mark Valencia, "High-Stakes Drama: The South China Sea Disputes," *Global Asia* 7, no. 3 (Fall 2012); Park, "The East China Sea Dispute."

[35] James Kraska, "A Legal Analysis of the Philippine-China Arbitration Ruling," *The Diplomat*, November 2, 2015.

[36] Jane Perlez "Beijing Exhibiting New Assertiveness in South China Sea," *New York Times*, May 31, 2012; John Boudreau, "China's Airstrip in Paracel Islands Heightens Vietnam Tensions," Bloomberg, October 10, 2014.

[37] On China's declaration of an Air Defense Identification Zone in November 2013, see Chris Buckley, "China Claims Air Rights over Disputed Islands," *New York Times*, November 23, 2013; Thom Shanker, "U.S. Sends Two B-52 Bombers into Air Zone Claimed by China," *New York Times*, November 26, 2013.

[38] Robert Haddick, "Salami Slicing in the South China Sea," *Foreign Policy*, August 3, 2012.

[39] On the strong strain of antimilitarism in Japanese defense policy see Thomas U. Berger, *Cultures of Antimilitarism: National Security in Germany and Japan* (Baltimore: Johns Hopkins

Chinese government that it might successfully advance its interests through *faits accompli*. The Chinese Communist Party, facing challenges to its domestic legitimacy and an increasingly nationalistic and noisy populace, has political incentives for diversionary efforts.[40] Such pressures may grow increasingly intense at a time of declining Chinese economic growth.[41] In a climate of increasing Chinese assertiveness in its territorial claims (an assertiveness that is only likely to grow),[42] America's Asian alliances help deter Beijing from using force.

Nuclear nonproliferation

US alliances unquestionably reduce the spread of nuclear weapons in East Asia. Japan and South Korea's acquisition of nuclear weapons is still possible even within the context of their relationship with the United States, but nuclear and conventional US security guarantees make this outcome much less likely.

Out of the various factors that affect countries' decisions to acquire nuclear weapons, the security motivation is among the most powerful.[43] According to this explanation, countries will acquire nuclear weapons if they are facing a potentially hostile actor that acquires nuclear weapons, or that outmatches them conventionally. Scholars have also found, however, that proliferation can be reduced through security guarantees—that sometimes threatened actors will not acquire nuclear weapons if they can rely on an ally's protection.[44] According to this logic, the loss of a security guarantee would encourage the abandoned and threatened ally to decide to acquire nuclear weapons.

American security guarantees have kept, and may yet keep, South Korea from acquiring nuclear weapons of its own. When Seoul signed the Nuclear

---

University Press, 2003); Jennifer Lind, "Evolution in Japan's Security Policy," Cato Institute, Washington, DC, forthcoming 2016.

[40] On Chinese nationalism see Jessica Chen Weiss, *Powerful Patriots: Nationalist Protest in China's Foreign Relations* (Oxford: Oxford University Press, 2014); Peter Hays Gries, *China's New Nationalism: Pride, Politics, and Diplomacy* (Berkeley: University of California Press, 2005); Susan L. Shirk, *China: Fragile Superpower* (New York: Oxford University Press, 2007).

[41] On Chinese economic decline see Shambaugh, *China's Future*; Pettis, *The Great Rebalancing*; Pei, *China's Trapped Transition*.

[42] Alastair Iain Johnston, "How New and Assertive Is China's New Assertiveness?" *International Security* 37, no. 4 (Spring 2013): 7–48.

[43] See, for example Scott D. Sagan, "Why Do States Build Nuclear Weapons? Three Models in Search of a Bomb," *International Security* 21, no. 3 (Winter 1996–1997): 54–86. On NATO's use of nuclear weapons to deter the conventionally superior Soviet Union see Keir A. Lieber and Daryl G. Press, "The Rise of U.S. Nuclear Primacy," *Foreign Affairs* 85, no. 2 (March–April 2006). For a review of the proliferation literature see Nuno P. Monteiro and Alexandre Debs, "The Strategic Logic of Nuclear Proliferation," *International Security* 39, no. 2 (Fall 2014): 7–51.

[44] Monteiro and Debs, "The Strategic Logic of Nuclear Proliferation"; Philipp C. Bleek and Eric B. Lorber, "Security Guarantees and Allied Nuclear Proliferation," *Journal of Conflict Resolution* 58, no. 3 (2014): 429–454; Alexander Lanoszka, "The Alliance Politics of Nuclear Statecraft," (Ph.D. diss., Princeton University, 2014).

Nonproliferation Treaty (NPT) in 1968, it stated that its membership "would only be contingent on robust US security commitments."[45] Indeed in the past when the United States contemplated significant changes in its policy or force posture in Korea, Seoul began a nuclear program (as seen in 1969 under the Guam Doctrine, or in 1977 when the Carter administration planned a troop withdrawal).[46] And that was *before* North Korea acquired nuclear weapons. Today, because South Korea faces a nuclear-armed North Korea, the security model would predict that, if Washington ended its security guarantee, South Korea would acquire nuclear weapons.

In fact, even a robust US alliance may no longer be sufficient to prevent Seoul from acquiring an independent nuclear capability. (During the Cold War, after all, American allies France and the United Kingdom both acquired nuclear weapons despite US and NATO protection.) In the past several years, Pyongyang has conducted nuclear and missile tests, and has engaged in acts of violence toward the South such as the 2010 sinking of the naval vessel *Cheonan* and the shelling of Yongpyeong Island. After North Korea's 2013 nuclear test, poll data showed that over two-thirds of South Koreans favored going nuclear.[47] Short of that, Seoul might negotiate for the reintroduction of US tactical nuclear weapons to the peninsula (removed in 1991), or might seek a nuclear sharing agreement such as the one in effect among the United States and several NATO countries (Germany, Belgium, and Italy: all states, like South Korea, that are nonnuclear states and NPT signatories).

As for Japan, the end of the US–Japan alliance could indeed lead Tokyo to acquire nuclear weapons. Given that during the Cold War the Soviets were bristling with nuclear weapons, and that the Chinese and North Koreans also acquired them, Japan probably would have acquired nuclear weapons by now absent the US nuclear umbrella. As Prime Minister Sato Eisaku told the US ambassador in 1964, "it is common sense that we should possess nuclear weapons if everyone else does."[48] Japanese leaders for decades have declared that acquiring nuclear weapons would not violate Japan's constitution.[49] Today, Japan lives next to an avowedly hostile North Korea—which not only has nuclear weapons, but threatens to turn Japanese cities into a "sea of fire." Japan lives among nuclear-armed

---

[45] Mitchell Reiss, *Without the Bomb: The Politics of Nuclear Nonproliferation* (New York: Columbia University Press, 1988), pp. 92–108; Etel Solingen, *Nuclear Logics: Contrasting Paths in East Asia and the Middle East* (Princeton, NJ: Princeton University Press, 2007).

[46] Joseph Cirincione, *Bomb Scare: The History and Future of Nuclear Weapons* (New York: Columbia University Press, 2008), chapter 4.

[47] Martin Fackler and Choe Sang-hun, "South Korea Flirts With Nuclear Ideas As North Blusters," *New York Times*, March 10, 2013; Byong-chul Lee, "South Korea on the Fence: Nukes or No Nukes?" 38North.org, September 30, 2011, at http://38north.org/2011/09/bclee093011/.

[48] Quoted in George Packard, *Edwin O. Reischauer and the American Discovery of Japan* (New York: Columbia University Press, 2010), p. 197.

[49] Jennifer M. Lind, "Pacifism or Passing the Buck? Theories of Japanese Security Policy," *International Security* 29, no. 1 (2004); on Japan's nuclear hedge see Ariel Levite, "Never Say Never Again: Nuclear Reversal Revisited," *International Security* 27, no. 3 (Winter 2002–2003): 59–88.

Russia and a nuclear-armed China that is modernizing its maritime forces, and increasingly sending them into what Tokyo believes to be Japanese territorial waters. Given this strategic environment, it is very possible that absent the US security guarantee, Japan would feel compelled to acquire an independent nuclear weapons capability.

But Japan's nuclear acquisition in this situation should not be seen as a foregone conclusion.[50] Japan's people are highly antinuclear since suffering two nuclear strikes by the United States in World War II, as well as a 1954 domestic crisis over the "Lucky Dragon" fishing boat, whose crew and catch was irradiated by US nuclear testing. Antinuclear sentiment was reinvigorated after the 2011 tsunami and nuclear disaster at Fukushima. A decision to acquire nuclear weapons would thus be politically fraught and costly.[51] Externally, Japan's acquisition of nuclear weapons could have undesirable effects because Japan's neighbors are sensitive to increases in Japan's military power. Finally, Japan is an NPT member and (as the sole country to have suffered nuclear attacks) has taken a leadership role in the global nonproliferation effort. A turnabout of this magnitude would be a dramatic move decried by many Japanese, and by many other countries.

Given domestic, regional, and global sensitivities; given Japan's more secure status as an island nation; and given its strong maritime military capabilities, Tokyo might therefore decide against acquiring nuclear weapons, at least in the short or medium term. It might quietly take steps that moved Japan closer to a nuclear weapons capability—an approach designed to shorten the time it would take to deploy a full nuclear deterrent while avoiding the costs associated with nuclear acquisition. Japan's large stockpile of plutonium would greatly facilitate development of such a "virtual" nuclear deterrent.[52]

In sum, absent US security guarantees, nuclear weapons would likely spread to South Korea and possibly to Japan. Some scholars would not be troubled by this prospect: some view the spread of nuclear weapons as stabilizing in world politics, arguing that (because nuclear weapons raise the costs of war) nuclear weapons deter wars among states that possess them. Furthermore, such scholars would view the countries in question (Japan and the ROK) as responsible stewards of nuclear technology—being democratic, technologically advanced, wealthy, and politically stable.[53] But the bottom line is that the end of US security guarantees in East Asia would almost certainly lead to the spread of nuclear weapons to Korea and might lead to nuclear spread to Japan.

---

[50] For a detailed analysis see Llewelyn Hughes, "Why Japan Will Not Go Nuclear (Yet): International and Domestic Constraints on the Nuclearization of Japan," *International Security* 31, no. 4 (Spring 2007): 67–96.

[51] On domestic political considerations in decisions to acquire nuclear weapons see Solingen, *Nuclear Logics*; Hughes, "Why Japan."

[52] On Japanese plutonium stocks see Hughes, "Why Japan."

[53] On the stability-inducing effects of nuclear weapons, see Kenneth N. Waltz, "More May Be Better," in Kenneth Waltz and Scott Sagan, eds., *The Spread of Nuclear Weapons: A Debate Revised*, 2nd ed. (New York: W.W. Norton, 2002).

Arms races

The withdrawal of US security guarantees in East Asia could lead to elevated threat perception and arms race dynamics.[54] US security guarantees reduce the amount of military capabilities that these countries need to build in order to protect themselves, and thus reduce how threatening they appear to their neighbors. An end to the security guarantees means that countries would perceive the need to acquire the capabilities to conduct the missions that the United States has largely performed, which could have the effect of increasing a sense of insecurity and fueling arms races. The effects of arms races are uncertain; international relations scholarship has had trouble demonstrating that arms races lead to war.[55] Arms races do, however, significantly sour political relations. As countries begin to observe each other's improvements in military capabilities, and as they increasingly see them as aimed at undermining their own security, competition in the military realm spills over into the political and societal realms, poisoning formerly amicable relations.

For example, under the US–ROK alliance, the South Koreans have focused on ground forces, with the United States carrying the heaviest burden of air and naval forces for Korea contingencies. The result is that Seoul has not built as much capability that could reach and worry Japan. As for Japan, alliance with the United States has enabled it to acquire less military capability than it otherwise would, particularly in the area of air and naval forces.[56] In the absence of a US security guarantee, Japan would likely increase its military spending, the pace of its training, and (given the North Korean missile threat) its offensive and preemptive strike capabilities. It would also likely pursue legal reforms, such as revision of Article 9 of Japan's "Peace Constitution," that would provide the institutional framework for a more assertive foreign policy.[57] Thus in the absence of US security guarantees, both Japan and the ROK would likely increase their conventional military spending, and would do so in ways that might alarm the other. This would be taking place in a climate of chilly relations between Seoul and Tokyo, in a region in which the Chinese have been engaged in a vigorous program of military modernization.[58]

[54] Brooks and Wohlforth, "Don't Come Home, America"; Adam P. Liff and G. John Ikenberry, "Racing Toward Tragedy: China's Rise, Military Competition in the Asia Pacific, and the Security Dilemma," *International Security* 39, No. 2 (Fall 2014): 52–91; Thomas J. Christensen, "China, the U.S.-Japan Alliance, and the Security Dilemma in East Asia," *International Security* 23, no. 4 (Spring 1999): 49–80.

[55] Toby J. Rider, Michael J. Findlay and Paul Diehl, "Just Part of the Game? Arms Races, Rivalry, and War," *Journal of Peace Research* 48, no. 1 (January 2011): 85–100.

[56] Lind, "Pacifism or Passing the Buck?"

[57] On the reform of Japan's national security laws see Adam P. Liff, "Japan's Security Policy: Abe the Evolutionary," *Washington Quarterly* 38, no. 15 (2015); Jennifer Lind, "China's Growing Assertiveness is Transforming Japan's Security Policy," *Al Jazeera America*, July 9, 2014.

[58] On Japan-ROK relations see Brad Glosserman and Scott A. Snyder, *The Japan-South Korea Identity Clash: East Asian Security and the United States* (New York: Columbia University Press, 2015); on Chinese military modernization see Friedberg, *A Contest for Supremacy*; James Steinberg and Michael E. O'Hanlon, *Strategic Reassurance and Resolve: U.S.-China Relations in the Twenty-First Century* (Princeton, NJ: Princeton University Press, 2014).

International relations scholarship highlights several factors that affect the severity of the security dilemma, and the likelihood of arms races, in East Asia. Scholars have pointed out that maritime geography has a palliative effect on threat perception: "the stopping power of water" (in John Mearsheimer's words) complicates offensive military operations, deterring would-be aggressors, and reassuring would-be targets.[59] Arms race dynamics in maritime East Asia should thus be less severe relative to continental regions.[60]

Other factors beyond geography raise concerns about East Asian arms races. Asia's maritime geography does dampen the security dilemma by reducing fears of homeland invasion. But countries worry about more than the threat of homeland invasion; among the most relevant threats in East Asia are territorial disputes. In these disputes, aspects of maritime warfare—including first-mover advantage—exert a destabilizing influence.[61] Furthermore, identity politics in East Asia—rooted in resentment over historical issues, and animated through nationalistic politics in the region—increase threat perception and make the security dilemma more severe. In other words, in China and South Korea, Japanese moves to increase its power projection capability would be viewed through the lens of Japan's failure to acknowledge or repudiate past aggression.[62] All of these factors elevate the risk of regional arms racing in the absence of American security guarantees.

Freedom in the sea lanes

US alliances in East Asia support the US maritime presence in the region, which is said to provide a public good of ensuring freedom of passage through the vital East Asian sea lanes. Writes Barry Posen, "US military power underwrites world trade, travel, global telecommunications, and commercial remote sensing, which all depend on peace and order in the commons."[63] Would the absence of the US

---

[59] On the palliative effect of defense-dominance on the security dilemma, see Charles Glaser, "Will China's Rise Lead To War?" *Foreign Affairs* 90, no. 2 (March–April 2011); Stephen Van Evera, *Causes of War* (Ithaca, NY: Cornell University Press, 1999), chapter 6; Robert Jervis, "Cooperation Under the Security Dilemma," *World Politics* 30, no. 2 (January 1976): 167–214; Sean M. Lynn-Jones, "Offense-Defense Theory and Its Critics," *Security Studies* 4, no. 4 (1995): 660–691.

[60] Jennifer Lind, "The Geography of the Security Dilemma," in Saadia M. Pekkanen, John Ravenhill, and Rosemary Foot, eds., *The Oxford Handbook of the International Relations of Asia* (Oxford: Oxford University Press, 2014).

[61] Jennifer Lind and Daryl G. Press, "Geography, Maritime Power, and the Pacific Rivalry," Paper presented to the Annual Meeting of the International Studies Association, New Orleans, Louisiana, February 2015.

[62] On the role of historical memory see Christensen, "China, the U.S.-Japan Alliance, and the Security Dilemma"; Jennifer Lind, *Sorry States: Apologies in International Politics* (Ithaca, NY: Cornell University Press, 2008); Thomas U. Berger, *War, Guilt, and World Politics after World War II* (Cambridge, UK: Cambridge University Press, 2012).

[63] Barry R. Posen, "Command of the Commons: The Military Foundation of U.S. Hegemony," *International Security* 28, no. 1 (Summer 2003): 46; Michael D. Swaine, *America's Challenge: Engaging a Rising China in the Twenty-First Century* (Washington, DC: Carnegie

military presence in East Asia threaten this peace and order in the commons? And would an end to US military dominance in the sea lanes undermine US national security goals in other ways?

When answering these questions, it's important to distinguish between peacetime and wartime conditions. In peacetime, the US Seventh Fleet patrols the sea lanes, provides maritime assistance, and engages in counterpiracy activity in cooperation with other East Asian countries. It trains and learns regional waters. The US Navy is on location in the event that disaster strikes and so can provide rapid humanitarian assistance, as it did following the Indian Ocean tsunami (2004), Japanese tsunami (2011), and the Haiyan typhoon in the Philippines (2013). The US peacetime naval presence promotes the flow of commerce in the sea lanes and helps save lives after natural disasters. It also overlaps with and enhances other US national security goals—as many commentators have argued, US leadership in providing humanitarian relief enhances American soft power, and patrol and presence reinforces the deterrence/assurance missions.[64]

In peacetime, countries with tense relations routinely use their navies to interfere with one another's trade. Countries obstruct trade by demanding inspections, or playing chicken with another country's vessels, forcing them to change course. Such behavior has been increasing in East Asia. Washington and Tokyo on the one hand, and Beijing on the other, all point to each other as culpable of such harassment, as in incidents involving the *USS Cowpens* in 2013, and the *USS Impeccable* in 2009.[65] Although such incidents have occurred in a region with a strong US military presence, the end of US dominance in the sea lanes would likely make such low-intensity harassment more common among regional navies.

US naval dominance in East Asia would also confer advantages on the United States during wartime. Its powerful regional base network and naval presence enhances the US ability to destroy the naval forces of rivals, or to create or break a blockade. Relative to performing such missions from Hawaii or other distant locations, the United States could do the same missions with a smaller force due to the efficiencies gained from a local base structure. Furthermore, as Michele Flournoy and Janine Davidson argue, not only do regional bases cut response times, "moving troops from the United States to a conflict zone just as tensions begin to rise can exacerbate or escalate a crisis."[66]

One might challenge these arguments for several reasons. First, one might doubt that a major war will erupt in East Asian waters, and might discount the peacetime benefits of US sea lane dominance. After all, US alliances in East Asia are

---

Endowment, 2011), p. 164; David Schenker, "China's Middle East Footprint," *Los Angeles Times*, April 26, 2013.

[64] Robert Farley, "'Smart Power' and Humanitarian Assistance," *The Diplomat*, December 28, 2013; Larissa Forster, "The Soft Power Currencies of US Navy Hospital Ship Missions," *International Studies Perspectives* 16, no. 4 (2015): 367–387.

[65] Carl Thayer, "*USS Cowpens* Incident Reveals Strategic Mistrust Between U.S. and China," *The Diplomat*, December 17, 2013; "Pentagon Says Chinese Vessels Harassed U.S. Ship," CNN.com, March 9, 2009.

[66] Flournoy and Davidson, "The Logic of U.S. Foreign Deployments."

not necessary for the US Navy to engage in such activities; it would be possible to deliver humanitarian relief, train with regional navies, and participate in counter-piracy missions in the absence of security pacts with regional nations. While this is true, a regional base presence provides efficiency due to shorter distances. Transit from Hawaii to Manila requires eleven days steaming time; the United States can respond much more quickly to East Asian crises from bases at (for example) Yokosuka, Japan.

Secondly, one might argue that, as export-dependent, globalized countries, East Asia's naval powers have no interest in disrupting regional sea lanes. Japan and China—needing to bring home oil and other essential inputs, and needing to export their goods abroad–have every incentive to keep the sea lanes open.[67] Chinese economic growth (and the legitimacy of the CCP) depends on the free transit of a vast and growing amount of natural resources to its shores, and of exports from its shores to global markets. Therefore the United States need not worry about regional navies challenging freedom of commerce or navigation: no one has an incentive to do so.

While countries have a general interest in keeping the sea lanes open, even highly economically interdependent countries use naval forces to disrupt other countries' trade for coercive purposes. The United States, a leading globalized country, has long engaged in coercive diplomacy, such as its embargo of Iranian oil.[68] Such activities are the modern manifestations of "gunboat diplomacy" and "demonstrations" by the Royal Navy during Pax Britannica—another country that benefited from the global trading system, and indeed generally used its navy to keep the sea lanes open.[69]

In sum, US naval predominance in East Asia is not necessary but is useful for the US to engage in the kinds of activities (both supportive and coercive) that Washington might want to engage in. Allies provide the United States with a regional base network that increases efficiencies and reduces force requirements. The US naval presence enhances the missions of assurance and deterrence, and contributes to US soft power.

Good Relations Among Partners

Although some American partners in East Asia have warm relations, American alliances do not necessarily translate to good relations among partners (and in some cases may do the opposite). The remarkable turnaround in relations between

---

[67] Swaine, *America's Challenge*, 178. On economic interdependence and peace see Edward D. Mansfield and Brian Pollins, "The Study of Interdependence and Conflict: Recent Advances, Open Questions, and Directions for Future Research," *Journal of Conflict Resolution* 45, no. 6 (2001): 834–859; Jennifer Lind, "Democratization and Stability in East Asia," *International Studies Quarterly* 55, no. 2 (2011): 409–436.

[68] On US sanctions against Iran see Josh Rogin, "Inside the Iran Sanctions Debate," *Foreign Policy*, December 15, 2009.

[69] Kevin Rowlands, "'Decided Preponderance at Sea': Naval Diplomacy and Strategic Thought," *Naval War College Review* 65, no. 4 (Autumn 2012).

the United States and Japan after World War II was echoed in relations between Australia and Japan; today their relations are excellent, as are relations between Japan and the Philippines (another country Japan victimized in World War II).[70] But relations between Japan and South Korea show that alliances with the United States do not necessarily forge bonds among allies. In over sixty years of sharing an ally, Japan and South Korea have cultivated strong economic ties, but their political and military relations have ranged from civil to frosty. Many analysts argue that, given China's growing power and assertiveness, and given that Japan and South Korea are both liberal democracies, the two countries should increase their security cooperation. However Seoul has resisted greater cooperation with Tokyo.[71] Within the ROK, Japan remains a useful target that politicians can attack for domestic political gain—on the issues of history textbook coverage, demands for apologies for wartime misdeeds, and the Tokdo/Takeshima islands disputed by the two countries.[72] In Japan, conservative leaders, catering to influential constituencies, assert sovereignty over disputed islands and favor history-telling that omits Japan's historic aggression.[73] All of this ill will has festered despite sixty-plus years of longstanding American alliances with both countries.

Some evidence suggests that, rather than encourage amity among allies, US commitments may actually do the reverse—allowing allies to nurse grievances. James Schoff and Dunyeon Kim note that US alliance commitments can "foster Seoul-Tokyo estrangement, ironically, if such relations lead Japanese and South Korean policymakers to believe that they have a sturdy bulwark against any truly damaging implications of their row."[74] Victor Cha, in his study of the trilateral relationship, writes that when the United States reduced its level of military presence and involvement in East Asia, Japan and South Korea made efforts to reconcile their historical and other disputes, in order to pursue the closer diplomatic and military relations necessitated by the more dangerous security environment.[75] By contrast, as Robert Kelly notes, US alliances "encourage maximalists and zealots on both sides not to compromise."[76] According to this logic, the end of US alliances with

[70] Kevin Placek, "Australia and Japan's Special Relationship," *The Diplomat*, July 9, 2014; Mina Pollman, "Amid South China Sea Tensions, Japan Strengthens Ties With Philippines, Vietnam," *The Diplomat*, December 2, 2015.

[71] Glosserman and Snyder, *The Japan-South Korea Identity Clash*; Robert E. Kelly, "Three Hypotheses on Korea's Intense Resentment of Japan," *The Diplomat*, March 13, 2014.

[72] On history education see Choe Sang-hun, "South Korea to Issue State History Textbooks, Rejecting Private Publishers," *New York Times*, October 12, 2015. On history issues in Japan-ROK relations see Lind, *Sorry States*, chapter 2.

[73] Berger, *War, Guilt, and World Politics*, 186–187.

[74] James L. Schoff and Dunyeon Kim, "Getting Japan-South Korea Relations Back on Track," Carnegie Endowment for International Peace, November 9, 2015.

[75] Victor D. Cha, *Alignment Despite Antagonism: The United States-Korea-Japan Security Triangle* (Stanford, CA: Stanford University Press, 2000). Also see Jennifer Lind, "Making Up Isn't Hard to Do," *Foreign Affairs*, March 5, 2015.

[76] Robert E. Kelly, "Unintended Consequences of U.S. Alliances in Asia," *The Diplomat*, April 7, 2014; also see Ralph Cossa, "Japan-South Korea Relations: Time to Open Both Eyes," Council on Foreign Relations, July 2012.

Japan and South Korea would incentivize Seoul and Tokyo to improve their relations. That said, the two countries have different interests and diverging perceptions of the threat posed by China, making it unclear whether an end to their alliances would push the two countries closer together.[77] One thing is very clear, however: US alliances have not produced that outcome.

Political orbit

Do US security guarantees in East Asia keep Japan, the ROK, and other countries within the "US orbit," and would a withdrawal from those alliances push those countries into Beijing's arms? Although a Chinese economic orbit is already emerging, uncertainties exist about a) the extent to which this will translate to regional political leadership, and b) even if it does, whether countries in the region would tilt toward Beijing.

China's stunning economic rise has already transformed regional (and global) trade and financial flows, giving rise to a Chinese economic orbit.[78] China has become the number-one trading partner for Australia, Japan, Malaysia, the Philippines, Singapore, South Korea, and Vietnam, among others. China's currency has joined the ranks of the world's most influential currencies, as represented by the International Monetary Fund's decision to include the renminbi (along with the dollar, euro, pound, and yen) in the basket of "special drawing rights."[79] Beijing is increasing its influence through policies of economic integration and international lending such as the "New Silk Road" and the Asian Infrastructure Investment Bank.[80]

Beijing's orbit would have a different character than the current liberal order. Rebecca Liao notes, "Western aid and development efforts are geared toward spreading liberal democracy and their own institutional frameworks. China, on the other hand, has stuck to its policy of distancing itself from the domestic affairs of other nations."[81] Chinese institutions, in other words, will eschew the Bretton Woods agenda of spreading liberalism; they will direct business toward Chinese state-owned enterprises that enrich and sustain the CCP. China's orbit is not a liberal one.

[77] Lind, "Making Up Isn't Hard to Do."

[78] John Wong, "A China-centric Economic Order in East Asia," *Asia Pacific Business Review* 19, no. 2 (2013): 286–296; "The World's Shifting Centre of Gravity," *The Economist*, June 28, 2012.

[79] Ian Talley, "China Joins World's Elite Currency Club," *Wall Street Journal*, November 30, 2015; "Maiden Voyage," *The Economist*, December 5, 2015.

[80] Min Ye, "China's Silk Road Strategy," *Foreign Policy*, November 10, 2014; Jane Perlez, "China Creates a World Bank of Its Own, and the U.S. Balks," *New York Times*, December 4, 2015; Daniel Bob, Tobias Harris, Masahiro Kawai, and Yun Sun, "Asian Infrastructure Investment Bank: China As Responsible Stakeholder?" Sasakawa Peace Foundation, Washington, DC, August 7, 2015.

[81] Rebecca Liao, "Out of the Bretton Woods: Why the AIIB is Different," *Foreign Affairs*, July 27, 2015.

The extent to which China's economic influence will translate to the creation of a powerful Chinese political orbit—to which countries in a "post-American Asia" would be attracted and deferential—is uncertain. First, China has risen in the context of a half-century old political and economic system created by the United States and its liberal partners after World War II. China's ability to displace this system is very much in question. As John Ikenberry writes, "The capitalist democratic world is a powerful constituency for the preservation—and, indeed, extension—of the existing international order. If China intends to rise up and challenge the existing order, it has a much more daunting task than simply confronting the United States."[82]

Not only does China confront a regional and international system that, in Ikenberry's words, is "hard to overturn," Beijing arguably has a strong interest in not overturning it. China has profited immensely from the current order, and its future prosperity (and thus the resilience of the CCP) depends on its access to trading partners within this nondiscriminatory trading system. More likely, rather than seek to create a different system that challenges the current regional order, Beijing will seek greater influence *within* it. Such behavior is already evident in China's efforts to reform existing institutions (such as the greater influence it has sought and received at the IMF and World Bank), and to create new institutions (such as the AIIB) that allow Beijing to exercise greater influence.[83]

Observers are divided on how receptive Asian countries would be to the pull of a Chinese orbit. In the early years of China's rise, neighbors responded positively to its growing power; at that time, Chinese diplomacy emphasized multinational coordination within regional institutions and compromise in territorial disputes.[84] Some scholars argue that China's neighbors will not resist and will defer to growing Chinese power—in part due to regional norms of hierarchy (the regional dominance of the "Middle Kingdom" during the seventeenth and early eighteenth centuries).[85] According to this view, countries in a "post-American Asia" would embrace Beijing's orbit.

By contrast, another view holds that even in the absence of American alliances, countries (though they may be economically close to China) would not necessarily defer to Chinese political leadership. This position is supported by evidence of regional dismay at China's growing assertiveness in its territorial disputes, and by broader unease about Chinese intentions.[86] Beijing's diplomacy aside, scholars

[82] G. John Ikenberry, "The Rise of China and the Future of the West," *Foreign Affairs* (January–February 2008).

[83] Benjamin Cohen, "The China Question: Can its Rise Be Accommodated," in Eric Helleiner and Jonathan Kirshner, eds., *The Great Wall of Money: Power and Politics in China's Monetary Relations* (Ithaca, NY: Cornell University Press, 2014), chapter 1.

[84] M. Taylor Fravel and Evan Medeiros, "China's New Diplomacy," *Foreign Affairs* (November–December 2003); this was the period discussed in Kang, "Getting Asia Wrong."

[85] David C. Kang, *China Rising: Peace, Power, and Order in East Asia* (New York: Columbia University Press, 2007).

[86] Liff and Ikenberry, "Racing toward Tragedy?"; Mearsheimer, *Tragedy of Great Power Politics*, 2nd ed., chapter 10.

who believe in a powerful balancing tendency in international politics would argue that power and geography alone would make it likely that Australia, Japan, the Philippines, and the ROK would balance against a rising China.[87]

The extent to which countries in a "post-American Asia" would fall into China's orbit would vary by country. Southeast Asian countries—even diplomatically unified (which they are not)—are too weak (economically and militarily) and too economically dependent on China to offer a counterweight to Chinese power. In the absence of its alliance with the United States, the Philippines (despite its disputes with Beijing) would have no choice but to accept Chinese regional leadership.

South Korea has already moved toward Beijing. Seoul is hedging between the two great powers: it maintains its alliance with the United States but diplomatically has moved close to China, its most important economic partner, and the country that holds the greatest sway over North Korea.[88] Hugh White argues, "China simply has too many cards to play on issues that matter to Seoul for it to be willing to break with China in any but the most extreme circumstances."[89] Indeed, South Korea has demonstrated acceptance of Chinese regional leadership and has distanced itself from anything that might resemble an anti-China coalition.[90] It has done so chiefly by distancing itself from Tokyo: rejecting closer security cooperation,[91] stoking domestic rancor over history disputes,[92] and crafting with China a shared anti-Japanese identity.[93] Seoul's drift toward Beijing should not be exaggerated: Korea has a longstanding strategic tradition ("shrimp among whales") of navigating among great powers.[94] This tradition suggests that South Korea's approach in a China-led Asia would resemble its current approach in US-led Asia: Seoul would seek to cultivate friendly ties with both great powers, but would create distance when doing so advanced its interests.

[87] On balancing see Kenneth Waltz, *Theory of Great Power Politics*; Mearsheimer, *Tragedy of Great Power Politics*, 2nd ed., chapter 10. On geography and its influence on threat perception see Stephen Walt, *The Origins of Alliance* (Ithaca, NY: Cornell University Press, 1987).

[88] Jennifer Lind, "Between Giants: South Korea and the US-China Rivalry," *The Atlantic*, July 19, 2012.

[89] White, *The China Choice*, 92.

[90] Shannon Tiezzi, "South Korea's President and China's Military Parade," *The Diplomat*, September 3, 2015; Hiroyuki Akita, "US Jittery over South Korea's Tilt Toward China," *Nikkei Asian Review*, April 24, 2014.

[91] On Seoul's rejection of the THAAD ballistic missile defense system (out of concerns about China's reaction) see Kang Seung-woo, "Seoul Cornered in THAAD Talks," *Korea Times*, November 26, 2011.

[92] South Koreans have legitimate disputes with Tokyo, which itself could do more to promote reconciliation with Seoul. However other countries that experienced trauma have adopted conciliatory policies on historical issues in the interest of increasing cooperation. Historical rancor is the result, not the cause, of strategic distance between Seoul and Tokyo. See Lind, "Making Up Isn't Hard to Do"; also see Tiezzi, "South Korea's President and China's Military Parade."

[93] Jennifer Lind, "Burying the Dead in East Asia," *Journal of Northeast Asian History* 11, no. 2 (Winter 2014).

[94] Lind, *Sorry States*, 83.

Japan would be (and already is) most resistant to a Chinese orbit in East Asia. With its large economy and capable military (and its water buffer between itself and China), Japan enjoys the greatest freedom of action. Japan has a territorial dispute and tense political relations with China, making it more inclined to resist attempts at Chinese encroachment. Japan—quite unlike its neighbors—has already resisted China's attempt to enlarge its regional orbit through the creation of the AIIB; Tokyo and Washington conspicuously refused to sign on.[95] The extent to which Japan would be willing to balance against China is debatable; Japan faces a serious demographic crisis that will reduce future economic growth,[96] and the Japanese people evince strong opposition to raising defense spending or increasing the country's military activism.[97] But in the absence of the US-Japan alliance, relative to any other country in the region, Japan is the least likely to fall into a Chinese orbit.

COSTS AND RISKS OF US ALLIANCES IN EAST ASIA

The above assessment of US alliances suggests that they advance many, though not all, US security goals. Most importantly, the alliances strengthen deterrence, prevent the spread of nuclear weapons, and prevent regional arms races. The next important issue to consider is whether these alliances promote these US national security goals at an acceptable level of cost and risk.

Financial cost

The United States spends more on defense than any country in the world: more, indeed, than the next seven countries combined. The American defense budget for 2014 was $610 billion.[98] This large sum supports a vast infrastructure of alliances and overseas bases. To what extent would ending America's Asian alliances create budgetary savings?

Supporters of America's Asian alliances frequently downplay their financial costs because the United States receives host nation support from allies. For example, in 2011 the United States and Japan signed an agreement for $2.02 billion per year for the next five years.[99] South Korea pays about $700 million per year toward the expense of stationing US military forces there.[100] Were the United States to

[95] "To Join or Not To Join," *The Economist*, May 30, 2015.

[96] "The Incredible Shrinking Country," *The Economist*, March 25, 2014; Milton Ezrati, "The Demographic Timebomb Crippling Japan's Economy," *The National Interest*, March 25, 2015.

[97] Sheila A. Smith, "All He is Saying is Give War a Chance," *Foreign Policy*, September 18, 2015; Sheila A. Smith, "Japan's Diet Uproar," Asia Unbound blog, Council on Foreign Relations, July 15, 2015; Jake Adelstein, "In Japan, Protests Intensify as Vote Nears on 'War Bills,'" *Los Angeles Times*, September 15, 2015.

[98] Stockholm International Peace Research Institute, SIPRI Military Expenditure Database, April 2015.

[99] Hana Kusumoto, "U.S., Japan Sign New Five-Year 'Host Nation Support' Agreement," *Stars and Stripes*, January 21, 2011.

[100] Lee Chi-dong, "S. Korea, U.S. Start Talks on 'Host Nation Support' for American Troops," *Yonhap News*, July 3, 2013.

end its alliance relationships with those countries and simply reassign those forces elsewhere (to the United States or to another foreign base), this move would yield no savings (and may indeed cost *more* unless sent to another country paying host nation support). Thus the relevant comparison is to compare the cost of those troops stationed in East Asia against the prospect of both bringing those troops home and decommissioning them. If the troops were both brought home and decommissioned, this would result in savings for the United States.

Calculating the exact expense of stationing US troops in allied countries is difficult. Rather than calculate the cost of stationing forces in a particular country, analysts have tried to estimate the savings of shifting to a more restrained grand strategy, which would end US security guarantees not only to Asian allies but also to NATO—thus enabling the United States to save in the force structure required to uphold those security guarantees. An estimate by the Cato Institute calculated in this fashion reported cost savings of $1.2 trillion over the next decade.[101] According to their analysis, the end-strength of the army and Marine Corps would be cut by one-third; the United States would field eight rather than twelve carrier battle groups and would cut a commensurate number of ships from the navy; it would cut six fighter wing equivalents from the air force. These cuts would permit further administrative savings.

In sum, budgetary savings could be substantial, but to realize those savings the United States would need to change its policy of providing peacetime presence and preparing for wartime contingencies; it would need to bring its forces home and decommission them. Assuming that the United States intends to keep a strong regional forward presence, basing US forces in Japan or South Korea may even save money because those countries pay host nation support. Force structure can be reduced, and cost savings realized, if and only if the United States reduces its regional forward military presence—which would mean a change in its broader grand strategy.

A US-China arms race

While (as described earlier) America's Asian alliances likely reduce the incidence of arms races among regional countries, US alliances are fueling an arms race between the United States and China.[102] America's alliance commitments obligate it to maintain the ability to project massive force into the region in order to come to the defense of its allies. But, as argued earlier, with its increased military power, and its pursuit of an "anti-access, area denial" (A2/AD) strategy, China is eroding the

[101] Benjamin H. Friedman and Christopher A. Preble, "Budgetary Savings from Military Restraint," Policy Analysis no. 667, Cato Institute, September 21, 2010.

[102] On a US-China spiral see Lind and Press, "The Sources of the Sino-American Spiral," *The National Interest*, September 18, 2013; Robert S. Ross, "The Problem with the Pivot," *Foreign Affairs*, November–December 2012; White, *The China Choice*. On escalation risks in US–China relations see Lind and Press, "Geography, Maritime Power, and the Pacific Rivalry"; Avery Goldstein, "First Things First: The Pressing Danger of Crisis Instability in U.S.-China Relations," *International Security*, 37, no. 4 (Spring 2013): 49–89.

ability of the US military to introduce force into the region.[103] This starts to call into question the credibility of US alliances: alliances will be credible only if an ally has the military capabilities to fulfill its obligations.[104]

A United States-China arms race is already underway. In order to counter China's A2/AD efforts, the US military has countered with changes in both weaponry and doctrine—notably, the doctrine of Air Sea Battle, later known as Joint Concept for Access and Maneuver in the Global Commons, or "JAM-GC." Under this doctrine, the US military seeks to identify and target the critical nodes of China's A2/AD strategy. In addition to missile launchers, these nodes include sensing platforms: the sensors, radar sites, satellite control facilities, and the command and control facilities that integrate information from the various sensing platforms and would orchestrate attacks against US vessels. Not surprisingly, given their strategic importance, the Chinese have installed these sites deep within the Chinese hinterlands. JAM-GC thus requires the United States to develop weapons and doctrines for attacking these critical military targets. The doctrine also includes targeting launch facilities, and shooting down or decoying away Chinese missiles that would attack US targets.

The action-reaction pattern that has formed in US-China relations—A2/AD producing a change in US doctrine; Chinese advances in weaponry prompting US responses—is highly destabilizing. According to US doctrine, if China and the United States find themselves in the middle of a military crisis, Washington would be considering military strikes against target sets that are located deep within the Chinese interior. Analysts have noted that this carries with it chilling escalatory risks to the nuclear level. Heinrichs warns, "Such an attack, even if it relied solely on conventional systems, could easily be misconstrued in Beijing as an attempt at preemptively destroying China's retaliatory nuclear options."[105]

In classic spiral dynamics, the status quo United States cites the need for JAM-GC, while the Chinese view it as a highly alarming doctrine aimed at containing Chinese power. A *Global Times* editorial argues, "China's anti-access strategy does not challenge the US hegemony. So the US should not seek to achieve its global strategy by pursuing absolute military superiority in Chinese coastal waters and threatening the country's security."[106] In sum, in an era of growing Chinese military

---

[103] Lind and Press, "The Sources of the Sino-American Spiral"; Michael McDevitt, "The PLA Navy's Antiaccess Role in a Taiwan Contingency," in Phillip C. Saunders, Christopher D. Yung, Michael Swaine and Andrew en-Dzu Yang, eds., *The Chinese Navy: Expanding Capabilities, Evolving Roles* (Washington, DC: National Defense University, 2011); Andrew Krepinevich, "Why Air-Sea Battle?" Center for Strategic and Budgetary Assessments, February 19, 2010; White, *The China Choice*.

[104] Daryl G. Press, *Calculating Credibility* (Ithaca, NY: Cornell University Press, 2004).

[105] Keir A. Lieber and Daryl G. Press, "Superiority Complex: Why America's Growing Nuclear Supremacy May Make War with China More Likely," *The Atlantic* (July–August 2007); Raoul Heinrichs, "America's Dangerous Battle Plan," *The Diplomat*, August 17, 2011; Rovner, "Three Paths to Escalation with China"; McDevitt, "The PLA Navy's Antiaccess Role in a Taiwan Contingency."

[106] "AirSea Battle Plan Renews Old Hostility," *Global Times*, November 14, 2011.

power, US alliance commitments in East Asia are leading the United States to take steps that Beijing will view as highly inflammatory—which, in the event of crisis over one of their multiple flashpoints, create serious escalation risks.

Some critics would counter that this vision of East Asia might never become reality. China, like other countries previously expected to unseat the United States, may see its growth falter, making it unable to challenge the United States in the Pacific. Many "China bears" make compelling arguments that predict a Chinese slowdown, and indeed one has already begun.[107] Other critics might argue that China will eschew a grand strategy of driving the United States out of the region.[108] Some analysts persuasively argue that a "revisionist" grand strategy would be costly and detrimental to China's interests.[109] Perhaps, then, China will not challenge continued US military dominance in the Pacific.

To be sure, China's growth has already slowed, and China will likely reject a highly confrontational, revisionist grand strategy. But the United States should nonetheless be worried about the future. First, China has already acquired a great deal of wealth; the relative size of its economy is already larger than was that of the Soviet Union, which for a half-century presented a formidable geopolitical challenge to the United States. As Joshua Itzkowitz Shifrinson points out, Imperial Japan pursued regional domination when its per capita GDP was barely a third of the United States.[110] And China need not pursue a revisionist grand strategy to pose serious security challenges to the United States—threatening US access to the region, jeopardizing the credibility of US alliance commitments, and creating friction with Washington.[111] Concerns about arms races are not speculation about the future, but about the current state of US–China relations.

Entanglement

US alliances in Asia create risks of entanglement in wars that the United States otherwise need not fight. Scholars note that although alliances can help a country balance against a security threat, they confer entanglement risks. "Entanglement" is when a state "is compelled to aid an ally in a costly and unprofitable enterprise because of the alliance" ("entrapment" is a subset of entanglement caused by an

[107] Shambaugh, *China's Future*; Pettis, *The Great Rebalancing*; Nicholas Lardy, *Sustaining China's Economic Growth*; Pei, *China's Trapped Transition*.

[108] Outlining different Chinese strategic options are Lind and Press, "The Sources of the Sino-American Spiral." On different visions of grand strategy see Zhang Wenmu, "Back to Yalta: A Roadmap for Sino-U.S. Relations," *China Security* 19 (2011); Wang Jisi, "China's Search for a Grand Strategy," *Foreign Affairs* (March–April 2011).

[109] Jisi, "China's Search for a Grand Strategy"; Jia Qingguo and Richard Rosecrance, "Delicately Poised: Are China and the U.S. Headed for Conflict?" *Global Asia* 4, no. 4 (Winter 2010).

[110] Joshua R. Itzkowitz Shifrinson and Michael Beckley, "Debating China's Rise and U.S. Decline," *International Security* 37, no. 3 (Winter 2012): 172–181.

[111] Lind and Press, "Sources"; White, *The China Choice*; Mearsheimer, "The Gathering Storm"; Thomas J. Christensen, "Posing Problems Without Catching Up: China's Rise and Challenges for U.S. Security Policy," *International Security* 25, no. 4 (Spring 2001): 5–40.

ally's risky or aggressive actions).[112] Kim argues that because of these risks, countries craft alliance agreements carefully to reduce the likelihood of being dragged into war by an aggressive ally over an issue of little strategic import.[113]

America's Asian alliances bring serious entanglement risks. First, the US-ROK Mutual Defense Treaty (MDT) could drag the United States into a serious military conflict or full-blown war. The United States could be involved in conflict on the peninsula if North Korea attacks South Korea. While no one expects North Korea to win this war, it could be very costly to the victors nonetheless. US war fighting plans, by targeting the North Korean government, create major risks of nuclear escalation.[114] The US government believes that North Korea has, and would use, large amounts of chemical and biological weapons on the battlefield as an asymmetric instrument. In the wake of Afghanistan and Iraq, the United States does not need another major theater war, yet its alliance with South Korea could draw the United States into war at any time.

Furthermore, in the event of North Korean collapse, the MDT would likely involve the United States in dangerous stabilization missions on the peninsula. North Korea's government might collapse under its own weight, or it could collapse following a war. South Korean forces might intervene in a post-collapse, anarchic North Korea to provide humanitarian relief or to locate North Korea's nuclear weapons.[115] The Chinese may also decide to intervene for similar reasons. This could create a perilous situation in which US/ROK and Chinese military forces are inserted in North Korea in an uncoordinated fashion, raising the risk of misperception and escalation.

Risks of US entanglement in a Korea crisis are high given periodic bursts of North Korean violence. In 2010 North Korea shelled South Korean territory (Yongpyeong Island) and sank a South Korean naval vessel, killing forty-eight sailors. Since then, Seoul has vowed it would retaliate if North Korea uses force again: "If there is any provocation against South Korea and its people," declared South Korea's president Park Geun-hye, "there should be a strong response in initial combat, regardless of the political considerations."[116] What both sides hope would be a symbolic or limited use of force thus has the potential, through misperception, to escalate to full-blown war on the peninsula, and to draw in the United States by virtue of the MDT.

---

[112] Tongfi Kim, "Why Alliances Entangle but Seldom Entrap States," *Security Studies*, 20, no. 3, (July 2011): 355–356; Glenn H. Snyder, "The Security Dilemma in Alliance Politics," *World Politics* 36, no. 4, (July 1984): Glenn H. Snyder, *Alliance Politics* (Ithaca, NY: Cornell University Press, 1997).

[113] Kim, "Why Alliances Entangle." An empirical study of American alliances argues that historically the risk of entanglement has been low. See Beckley, "The Myth of Entangling Alliances;" for a critique see Jennifer Lind, H-Diplo/ISSF Article Review 52 on "The Myth of Entangling Alliances," *International Security* 39, no. 4 (Spring 2015).

[114] Keir A. Lieber and Daryl G. Press, "The Next Korean War," *Foreign Affairs*, April 1, 2013.

[115] Bruce W. Bennett and Jennifer Lind, "The Collapse of North Korea: Military Missions and Requirements," *International Security* 2, no. 36 (2011): 84–119.

[116] Justin McCurry, "South Korea Warns It Will Retaliate If North Attacks," *The Guardian*, April 1, 2013.

Japan and the Philippines. Until recently, the US–Japan alliance was long characterized by *Japan's* fears of entanglement; for seventy years the Japanese resisted being dragged into one of America's adventures (in Korea, Vietnam, or the Persian Gulf), and feared finding itself in the middle of a US–Soviet nuclear exchange.[117] Today, however, things are different: the growth of Chinese power and China's increased threat to the Senkaku/Diaoyu islands now mean that Japan risks entangling the United States in a war with a nuclear-armed adversary. US officials (including President Obama) have announced that although Washington does not take a position on the sovereignty of the islands, they do indeed fall under the US–Japan security treaty because they are "administered" by Japan. Thus, the entanglement risk in the US–Japan alliance—for a half-century predominantly borne by Tokyo—today has shifted toward the United States.[118]

Alliance with the Philippines also brings a growing risk of entanglement. Security ties between the United States and the Philippines waned after the 1990s (when Manila ejected American troops from its bases at Clark and Subic Bay), but the US security commitment remained in place. Today the alliance presents a growing risk of entanglement because of the sovereignty dispute over the Spratly islets in the South China Sea.

The entanglement risks posed by US alliances with the Philippines and Japan are a relatively recent development. Although for years these territorial disputes sat relatively dormant, they have grown more salient in these countries' foreign relations with China. Sino-Japanese relations have nosedived in recent years, in large part due to their territorial dispute. The growth of Chinese maritime power, and increased Chinese incursions into these disputed areas in recent years, have elevated the risk of crises.[119] Thus although for decades alliances with Japan and the Philippines did not pose a significant entanglement risk for the United States, today this risk is growing—over islets in which the United States has no clear strategic interest.

Buck-passing

Critics of the current US grand strategy identify "buck-passing" as one of its costs. Indeed, current US national security policy has encouraged buck-passing among friendly and potentially militarily powerful countries. As Barry Posen writes, America's Cold War alliances "have provided US partners in Europe and Asia with

---

[117] Kim, "Why Alliances Entangle," 364–368; Jennifer Lind, "Japan's Security Evolution," Policy Analysis 78 (Washington DC: CATO Institute, 2016); Yasuhiro Izumikawa, "Explaining Japanese Antimilitarism: Normative and Realist Constraints on Japan's Security Policy," *International Security* 35, no. 2 (Fall 2010): 123–160; Evelyn Goh, "How Japan Matters in the Evolving East Asian Security Order," *International Affairs* 87, no. 4 (July 2011): 887–902.

[118] See discussion in Jennifer Lind, "Pivot Problems: What Washington Should Concede in East Asia," *Foreign Affairs*, June 25, 2014.

[119] Lind and Press, "Geography, Maritime Power, and the Pacific Rivalry"; Goldstein, "First Things First"; Taylor Fravel, "China's Strategy in the South China Sea," *Contemporary Southeast Asia* 33, no. 3 (2012): 292–319.

such a high level of insurance that they have been able to steadily shrink their militaries and outsource their defense to Washington." Since the end of the Cold War, European countries that previously contributed to balancing against the Soviet Union now collectively spend only 1.6 percent of the GDP on defense—lower than either the United States or the global average in defense spending.[120]

Similarly, Tokyo (during and since the Cold War) has pursued a low level of defense spending for a great power—less than one percent of its GDP. Japan's high GDP means that this is a nontrivial sum, so even with this low level of effort, Japan developed a capable maritime military force.[121] However Japan's level of defense effort, and its regional and global leadership, could be far greater. Critics of US grand strategy argue that an important negative effect of the US commitment to Japan is that it has led one of the most potentially powerful countries in the world, a wealthy liberal democracy friendly to the United States, to act as a secondary diplomatic and military power.

Importantly, Japanese buck-passing is not an unfortunate *cost* of the current grand strategy: it is a *goal* of the current grand strategy. Allied buck-passing means that countries are not balancing against the preponderance of American power. Furthermore, allied buck-passing means that countries in key regions are not building up independent capabilities that could trigger security dilemma dynamics. As discussed earlier, the prevention of arms races is an explicit US national security goal. Therefore, far from being a cost of the current grand strategy, allied buck-passing is the manifestation of its goals being achieved.

Confusion may stem from the fact that proponents of the current US grand strategy sometimes call for greater allied burden sharing. Indeed, American officials have over the years negotiated with Tokyo to increase to increase its host nation support, level of military capability, and activism in different alliance roles. In particular, Congress and US officials in the Nixon and Carter administrations sought greater Japanese burden sharing, and Japan's inaction (despite its large financial donation) to the first Persian Gulf War triggered criticism in the United States.[122]

Although Washington would prefer that Japan contribute more to the alliance, this should not be misconstrued as a desire for a change in the East Asian distribution of power. Under deep engagement, an underperforming Japan, rather than an unfortunate side effect of the current US grand strategy, is a desired outcome. The fact that American blood and American treasure substitute for what could be Japanese balancing—lamented by Posen as "welfare for the rich"[123]—is a necessary requirement of this grand strategy.

---

[120] Posen, "Pull Back." Also on allied buck-passing see Gholz and Press, "Come Home America"; Christopher Layne "From Preponderance to Offshore Balancing: America's Future Grand Strategy," *International Security* 22, no. 1 (Summer 1997): 118.

[121] Richard C. Bush, *The Perils of Proximity: China-Japan Security Relations* (Washington, DC: Brookings Institution, 2010); Lind, "Pacifism or Passing the Buck."

[122] Susumu Awanohara, "The Burden-sharing Issues in US-Japan Security Relations: A Perspective from Japan," East-West Center, Honolulu, Hawaii, Occasional Paper #2, March 1990; on the Gulf War see Steven R. Weisman, "Japan Counts the Costs Of Gulf Action–Or Inaction," *New York Times,* January 27, 1991.

[123] Posen, "Pull Back."

FUTURE DIRECTIONS FOR AMERICA'S ASIAN ALLIANCES

As described earlier, US alliances in East Asia advance some national security goals but not others; they also come with important costs and risks. Given US budgetary realities, and given changes in East Asia's strategic environment, how should Washington change its national security policies vis-à-vis these alliances to advance US national security goals, while minimizing their costs and risks?

When one considers alternative national security postures in East Asia, an important point should be kept in mind: a US regional military presence does not depend upon the existence of formal alliances. The United States could end one or more of its alliances there in favor of new basing arrangements in the Western Pacific that do not include mutual defense treaties. This would mirror the model the United States currently uses with Bahrain and Singapore. Alternatively, the United States could project military power into the region from Alaska, Guam, and Hawaii (currently major hubs for US Pacific forces). The point is that "alliance" and "military presence" should not be conflated, and the arguments for both must be assessed independently.

Withdrawal from alliances

With this in mind, one possible course is for the United States to withdraw from some or all of its East Asian alliances.[124] Advocates of "offshore balancing" or "restraint" argue that if China did emerge as threatening to its neighbors, the rich and capable countries in East Asia could themselves balance against it. If the United States were to itself buck-pass to the countries most proximate and most affected by China's rise, this would confer significant savings in US defense if the current US force structure for the ROK and Japanese alliances was decommissioned. American buck-passing would also encourage greater national security efforts by Japan, thus giving the United States a like-minded, militarily capable foreign-policy actor with which Washington could cooperate in the region. Most importantly, an end to these security guarantees would reduce serious dangers that they bring: the growing spiral of distrust in US–China relations (only exacerbated by the recent "pivot"), and the risks of entanglement in regional military crises or war.

Withdrawal from these alliances would of course undermine other American national security goals. The end of US alliances with South Korea and Japan would likely lead to nuclear spread to the former, and possibly to the latter. In the absence of the US alliances, as Japan adopted a more assertive regional role, and as South Korea developed more maritime capabilities, this could lead to elevated regional tensions and arms races among Australia, China, Japan, and South Korea. China would likely develop stronger political influence over ASEAN countries, over South Korea (and to a lesser extent possibly Australia). Others argue that these alliances—and more generally the US grand strategy of global leadership—confer significant economic gains on the United States, and that discarding these

---

[124] Posen, "Pull Back"; Layne, "China's Challenge"; Gholz, et al., "Come Home America."

alliances would thus disadvantage the United States in international institutions and trade.[125]

US withdrawal from its Asian alliances would represent a dramatic departure from current US policy and is therefore unlikely. As Benjamin Valentino shows in chapter 8 of this volume, American public opinion broadly supports the continuation of these longstanding alliances. And in Washington, America's post–World War II grand strategy enjoys a broad bipartisan consensus. This is truly striking in an era when every *domestic* public policy issue produces bitter partisan vitriol. To be sure, while liberals and conservatives advocate somewhat different flavors of deep engagement, overall the US foreign policy establishment supports keeping the postwar US alliance system, maintaining overwhelming US military dominance, intervening across the globe, and frequently using force to advance US foreign policy interests.[126] As Aaron O'Connell argues, "Today, there are just a select few in public life who are willing to question the military or its spending, and those who do—from the libertarian Ron Paul to the leftist Dennis Kucinich—are dismissed as unrealistic."[127]

Reforming US alliances

Given that the United States is likely to retain its grand strategy of deep engagement, Washington should reform its East Asian alliances so to make them less dangerous, more useful, and more sustainable.

Terminals to Hubs. America's global alliances can be thought of as having two types: hubs and terminals. "Hubs" provide bases and a flexible legal and regulatory infrastructure that make them useful to the United States across a range of missions across the region, and in conflicts in other regions. Vital American hubs include Ramstein and Aviano Air Force Bases in Europe, and US bases in Okinawa. "Terminals," on the other hand, provide bases that serve only the purpose of defending a particular ally. The bases and American troops deployed there are not used in regional or global missions, and, in the event of a conflict elsewhere in the region or globe, the United States would be unable to draw upon them. Obviously from the US standpoint, a hub is far more useful than a terminal; for the United States to accept a "terminal" arrangement, that ally should be incapable of independent

---

[125] On this issue see Brooks et al., "Lean Forward"; Beckley, "China's Century?" Other analysts take the opposite position, such as Drezner, "Why Military Primacy Doesn't Pay"; Gholz et al., "Come Home America."

[126] Interventionists on the right are dismissive of allies and international institutions; they believe in preventive wars but have less interest in humanitarian ones. Liberal interventionists, on the other hand, pay greater attention to international public opinion; they often advocate fighting wars of humanitarian intervention; and are more skeptical of preventive wars (though they authorized the war against Iraq). On the bipartisan American grand strategy see Posen, "Pull Back"; Michael A. Cohen, "Can't We All Just Not Get Along?" *Foreign Policy*, June 22, 2012; Robert Kagan, "Bipartisan Spring," *Foreign Policy*, March 4, 2010.

[127] Aaron O'Connell, "The Permanent Militarization of America," *New York Times*, November 4, 2012.

defense against the threat it faces; its defense should have vital strategic import to the United States; and ideally the alliance should also confer a low risk of entanglement. The MDT between South Korea and the United States was initially designed as a "terminal," but because of changing strategic circumstances, it should be reformed into a "hub." The alliance was created at a time when South Korea was militarily weak, and was outmanned and outgunned by an economically dynamic North Korea. The Korean peninsula was seen as a key "domino" in America's Cold War strategy of containment of Soviet communism. Given all of this, the United States agreed to defend South Korea under an arrangement in which South Korea refused to allow base usage for other regional operations, and refused to allow military personnel or assets on the peninsula to be used "off-pen."

All of these strategic circumstances have changed; the US-ROK alliance thus cries out for reform. South Korea no longer meets the criteria to be a "terminal"— it is more than capable of defending itself against a weak adversary, and the alliance brings a high entanglement risk to the United States. If Washington decides to keep this alliance, it should be reformed into serving a broader strategic purpose— namely, by making it into a regional and global hub. The current posture is expensive because the United States has to buy adequate force structure to support its deployment on the peninsula, which then serves no other regional or global role. In keeping with this theme of creating a more flexible hub, the United States should also transition its forces in ROK away from ground forces toward a naval forward presence.

These trends have already begun, and should be continued. In recent years the United States has adopted a posture of "strategic flexibility" in which US forces in Korea will evolve into a high-mobility, expeditionary force.[128] And as part of this, the United States has negotiated with Seoul to relax its regulations against using US assets (personnel and materiel) on the peninsula elsewhere in the region. Some such assets were thus dispatched to a US-Japan joint exercise in 2012; US forces in Korea were sent to participate in Operation Tomodachi, the disaster relief operation in Japan; and in 2004 the United States dispatched the 2nd Brigade of the 2nd Infantry Division to Iraq. Washington should continue in this direction, transforming this outdated alliance into one that gives the United States a true regional and global hub.[129]

Moving the US presence in the ROK toward a naval mission would confer several advantages. First, instead of being tied to the peninsula, such naval forces would be of broader use to the region and to the Persian Gulf region if the need arose. Second, the United States could shift to the peninsula naval assets that are currently stationed in Hawaii or San Diego. This would bring budgetary savings because the United States currently has to buy additional force structure to account for long transit times to the region. Finally, (anticipating Korean unification) the

---

[128] "USFK Role Expands as U.S. Seeks Flexibility," *Korea Herald*, February 6, 2012; "USFK's New Strategic Flexibility," *The Hankyoreh*, March 21, 2011.

[129] Given Seoul's strategic drift toward Beijing, described earlier in this chapter, Washington would have to discuss in advance with Seoul the conditions under which the US military could project force from bases in the ROK.

change would make the US forward presence in Korea less inflammatory to China than American ground troops on its border. Although in the case of Korean unification Beijing might indeed object to *any* US military forces left on the Korean peninsula, ground troops would be far more inflammatory (since they would appear to be aimed at China) than would naval forces envisioned to serve a broader regional purpose.

Second, assuming that the United States remains obligated to guarantee Japanese security, Washington should maintain its "hubs" in Japan against local pressure to downgrade the utility of its bases. As noted earlier, Okinawans have in recent years used the debate about the future of the Futenma air base to express their frustration with the large US military footprint in their prefecture, and have argued for moving the US Marines not within Okinawa, but out of it all together.[130] Washington should resist this pressure. To be sure, it may be that the US Marines stationed at Futenma are not necessary or are not the right types of forces for likely missions; the specific configuration of which US forces belong in Japan is beyond the scope of this article.

In general, however, Washington should resist a trend in which a more threatened Japan is expecting US military protection while being less willing to host US forces. Of course, the US military must conduct its operations in Okinawa so that its people are safe; it must deal respectfully with Okinawans; and it must understand Tokyo's dilemmas as it negotiates with the prefecture that bears such a high share of the US defense burden. But ultimately, the seventy-year old deal between the United States and Japan—that the United States will protect Japan, and Japan will provide the bases—would no longer be much of a deal if (at a time when Japan is more threatened and more of an entanglement risk) Japan wants the United States to protect it offshore and at higher expense. If Washington intends to maintain the alliance, it should thus maintain a "hub" in Okinawa. Similarly, as the evolution of the US–Philippine alliance continues, and as the United States negotiates for renewed access to Philippine bases, these same ideas should also be applied.[131]

Dual Deterrence. Changing strategic conditions in East Asia also suggest changes in US alliance diplomacy. China's growing maritime power, and its increased assertiveness over its island claims, have raised the salience of island disputes in the South China and East China Seas. Inflammatory Japanese policies—such as Tokyo's 2012 purchase of the Senkaku/Diaoyu islands from its private owner, an action that Washington urged against,[132] risk creating crises and wars into which the United States could be dragged. Washington should thus adopt, in its alliances with Japan and the Philippines, policies that reduce the risk of entanglement. As

---

[130] Tokyo and Washington have made progress toward resolving this dispute (and toward keeping the US Marines in Okinawa). However, Okinawans remain opposed to moving the Futenma facility, and have continued to stall it. See Tiezzi, "Beyond Futenma; Stacie Pettyjohn, "The Battle of Futenma Isn't Over Yet," *National Interest,* January 3, 2014.

[131] Paolo Romero, "Military Base-Sharing Scheme with U.S. Proposed." *The Nation,* February 23, 2012.

[132] "U.S. Warned Government Against Buying Senkaku Islands: Campbell," *Japan Times,* April 10, 2013.

Michael Beckley describes, such policies include "dual deterrence" and "loopholes" that reduce the chance of the US military having to fight a war with China over islets in the South or East China Seas.[133] For example, though Washington describes its security commitment to defend the Philippines as "ironclad,"[134] it has reduced its entanglement risk through a loophole. Washington maintains that because sovereignty over the Spratly Islands is disputed, the United States does not have an obligation to defend territory that is not clearly part of the Philippines.

Given increased entanglement risks, Washington should adopt a strategy of "dual" or "pivotal" deterrence in its alliances with Manila and Tokyo.[135] It has already pursued such a strategy in the Taiwan Strait; this was particularly necessary during the tenure of Taiwanese President Chen Shui-bian, who routinely engaged in actions that provoked diplomatic crises with China. According to the logic of dual deterrence, Washington should express its intention to uphold its security obligations, and should warn China of the consequences of using force to resolve its territorial disputes. On the other hand, Washington should warn its allies of the consequences of them engaging in provocative actions. In the case of Taiwan, Logan Wright argued that if Chen Shui-bian "refuses to moderate his rhetoric and shelve his referenda, the United States should make gradual, measured reductions in US–Taiwan military-to-military cooperation, while clearly telling the Taiwanese leadership privately of the reasons for this downgrade." Wright argued that if private warnings are ignored, "public statements condemning his moves should follow, preferably in advance of the policy initiatives."[136] To be sure, Taiwan is not a military ally of the United States, whereas Japan and the Philippines both are. Keeping in mind the need to maintain the credibility of the US commitment, Washington will thus have to carefully weigh what it considers provocative behavior on the part of its ally, and what the consequences to such behavior would be. But the broader point is that because of a greater risk of US entanglement by these allies, the United States needs to move toward a posture of dual deterrence.

Strategic Reassurance. As argued earlier, a serious risk of the US alliance system in East Asia is that the US regional force posture necessary to uphold the credibility of US security guarantees is deeply threatening to China. Because of the cost, instability, and souring of bilateral relations that its East Asian forward presence is causing in US–China relations, Washington should look for ways to reassure Beijing. To be sure, perhaps it is ultimately not possible to square the circle of maintaining a force posture in East Asia that would both reassure American allies and not threaten Beijing. But Washington should only arrive at this conclusion after careful study. US officials and military analysts should discuss: are there aspects of American force structure or operations that could be reformed so to not overly antagonize China? Scholars have already begun a productive discussion

[133] Beckley, "The Myth of Entangling Alliances," 17–21.

[134] Mark Felsenthal and Matt Spetalnick, "Obama Says U.S. Commitment To Defend Philippines 'Ironclad,'" Reuters, April 29, 2014.

[135] Timothy Crawford, *Pivotal Deterrence: Third-Party Statecraft and the Pursuit of Peace* (Ithaca, NY: Cornell University Press, 2003); Richard C. Bush, *Untying the Knot: Making Peace in the Taiwan Strait* (Washington, DC: Brookings Institution Press, 2005), pp. 263–264.

[136] Logan Wright, "Dual Deterrence: A New Taiwan Strategy," *National Interest*, March 31, 2004.

about strategic reassurance; James Steinberg and Michael O'Hanlon identify four tools (restraint, reciprocity, transparency, and resilience), arguing "it is crucial to find ways of transcending or minimizing such a classic security dilemma."[137] Washington should work with Beijing in nonmilitary areas to build cooperation and trust. Lyle Goldstein advocates a "spiral of cooperation," noting that, "Since the Sunnylands summit, a string of positive, albeit small-scale joint activities has been undertaken by the US and Chinese armed forces." Goldstein points to encouraging progress in the areas of "carbon emissions, trade, easing visa requirements, and military confidence-building."[138] Although Washington is unlikely to be so fearful of a US–China spiral as to end American alliances in the region, American military leaders and foreign policy officials should be looking for ways in which they can adapt US policy so as to avoid creating undue fear in Beijing. In sum, in this era of strategic and budgetary change, in which Americans continue to support the country's Asian alliances, foreign policy leaders should fix these alliances in ways that minimize their costs and risks, and better serve the US strategic interest.

ACKNOWLEDGMENTS

The author wishes to thank several colleagues for their thoughtful and generous comments on earlier drafts of this chapter: Michael Beckley, Stephen G. Brooks, Daniel L. Byman, Jeffrey Friedman, Lindsey O'Rourke, Daryl G. Press, Sebastian Rosato, Benjamin Valentino, Siddharth Shah, Joshua Ifkowitz Shifrinson, Stephen Van Evera, and William C. Wohlforth.

---

[137] James B. Steinberg and Michael O'Hanlon, "Keep Hope Alive: How to Prevent US–China Relations from Blowing Up," *Foreign Affairs* (July–August 2014); also see Steinberg and O'Hanlon, *Strategic Reassurance*.

[138] Lyle J. Goldstein, *Meeting China Halfway: How to Defuse the Emerging US-China Rivalry* (Washington, DC: Georgetown University Press, 2015); also see White, *The China Choice*.

12

TERMINATING THE INTERMINABLE?

Sumit Ganguly

INTRODUCTION

How might the India-Pakistani rivalry terminate? The question is far from trivial for a number of compelling reasons. Of the post-war rivalries it remains one of the most intractable.[1] It has led to four wars (1947–1948, 1965, 1971, and 1999) and multiple crises since the two states emerged from the collapse of the British Indian Empire in 1947.

Additionally, what role has the United States played in either exacerbating the rivalry or contributing to peace and stability in the region? More to the point, why should the United States devote any effort to the termination of this rivalry? Some have argued that the US role, especially in the early Cold War years, was quite pernicious. Their arguments mostly focused on the forging of the US-Pakistan strategic nexus as early as 1954, subsequent American support for military regimes in Pakistan, and the Nixon administration's tilt toward Pakistan during the 1971 East Pakistan crisis.[2] Others have suggested that the US role in the subcontinent has been decidedly more mixed.[3]

This analysis has three key foci. First, it will spell out why efforts to terminate the India-Pakistani rivalry are in the interest of the United States. Second, the chapter will focus on three competing models of rivalry termination and show their relevance (or the lack thereof) to the triangular relationship among the United States, India, and Pakistan. The chapter unfolds in the following fashion: It will briefly summarize the origins of the rivalry, discuss the significance of the India-Pakistani rivalry to the United States, focus on US efforts at various junctures to broker an end to the rivalry, and deal with what leverage the United States has over both states. Third, and finally, it will discuss the implications for the United States in managing this rivalry. The United States, it will argue, has long sought to bring

---

[1] For a number of perspectives on the rivalry see T.V. Paul, ed., *The India-Pakistan Conflict: An Enduring Rivalry* (New York: Cambridge University Press, 2005).

[2] See Baldev Raj Nayar, "Treat India Seriously," *Foreign Policy* 18, Spring 1975, pp. 133–154; also see M.S. Venkatramani, *The American Role in Pakistan, 1947–1958* (Hyderabad: Radiant Publishers, 1982).

[3] Stephen P. Cohen, "U.S. Weapons and South Asia: A Policy Analysis," *Pacific Affairs* 49, no. 1 (Spring 1976): 49–69; also see Lawrence Wright, "The Double Game," *The New Yorker*, May 16, 2011.

about an alignment of its interests with those of Pakistan. It has attempted to pursue these goals through the use of military and economic assistance, periodic pressures on India, and occasional threats to curb Pakistani adventurism. American goals have ranged from anticommunism during the Cold War years; to the ousting of the Soviets from Afghanistan during their occupation; to preventing Pakistan from pursuing nuclear weapons; and finally, since 9/11, to removing Afghanistan as a sanctuary for al-Qaeda.

THE ORIGINS OF THE RIVALRY

The origins of the rivalry can be traced to a territorial dispute involving the state of Jammu and Kashmir. The dispute, in turn, underpins the competing ideological visions of the two states: Pakistan, based upon a conception of primordial nationalism, and India, a state created on the basis of civic, secular nationalism.[4] Multilateral, bilateral, and even unilateral attempts to resolve this conflict have accomplished little. It is possible that the overt, mutual acquisition of nuclear weapons in 1998 has effectively ruled out the prospects of full-scale war in the region.[5] However, bilateral tensions have yet to significantly diminish and the dispute over the state of Jammu and Kashmir, the original source of discord, remains unresolved. Even though the ethnoreligious insurgency that erupted in the Indian-controlled portion of the state in 1989 has ebbed, thanks to an amalgam of both concessions and coercion, tensions within much of the Muslim populace of the state continue to simmer, as they nurse a range of grievances against India. Were they to flare up once again, there is little question that Pakistan would attempt to fan the flames and thereby contribute to renewed bilateral tensions.

US INTERESTS IN THE RIVALRY

What, if any, interest does the United States have in an amelioration and possible termination of the rivalry? The rivalry is of considerable significance to the United States for a number of compelling reasons. Even as it draws down from Afghanistan, it cannot remain oblivious to the India-Pakistani rivalry, as it constitutes the principal strategic fault line in the region.

First, since the Cold War's end, the United States has come to see India as a potential strategic partner. Even though Indian elites remain ambivalent about the scope and the dimensions of partnership with the United States, they share a common concern about the dramatic rise of the People's Republic of China (PRC). Such

[4] On the India-Pakistani conflicts see Sumit Ganguly, *Conflict Unending: India-Pakistan Tensions Since 1947* (New York: Columbia University Press, 2001); on the crises see P.R. Chari, Pervaiz Iqbal Cheema, and Stephen P. Cohen, *Four Crises and a Peace Process: American Engagement in South Asia* (Washington, DC: The Brookings Institution, 2007).

[5] Sumit Ganguly and Devin T. Hagerty, *Fearful Symmetry: India-Pakistan Crises in the Shadow of Nuclear Weapons* (New Delhi: Oxford University Press, 2005); also see Sumit Ganguly, "Nuclear Stability in South Asia," *International Security* 33, no. 2 (Fall 2008): 45–70.

misgivings have been exacerbated because of the growing assertiveness of the PRC both in the South China Sea and along the disputed Himalayan border with India. Consequently, despite India's *idée fixe* about maintaining its "strategic autonomy," it will pursue a level of quiet strategic cooperation with the United States. Such cooperation, however, could be undermined if the United States finds itself forced to choose between India and Pakistan in the event of yet another bilateral conflict. Consequently, a dampening of the India-Pakistani rivalry is clearly in the United States' interest.

Second, and in a related vein, the United States quite correctly remains concerned about the presence of a range of terrorist organizations within Pakistan and their willingness and ability to carry out strikes in Indian-controlled Kashmir. These groups, whether within the control of the Pakistani security establishment or not, can wreak havoc between the two warring nations.

Third, because both India and Pakistan are nuclear-armed rivals, continued tensions in the subcontinent remain a source of concern to the United States. The region has seen its share of crises since the overt India-Pakistani acquisition of nuclear weapons. None of these have spiraled into full-scale war. However, the fear of such escalation and the subsequent usage of nuclear weapons have long been on the minds of American policymakers. Not surprisingly, ensuring that the nuclear taboo is not broken in South Asia remains an enduring policy interest of the United States, and a reduction in India-Pakistani tensions is critical to that end.

US LEVERAGE OVER INDIA AND PAKISTAN

What leverage does the United States have over India and Pakistan? American leverage over India is probably at its peak today. During the Cold War, when the two states were mostly at odds, even in times of dire distress India demonstrated that it could afford to fend off US pressures to change its policies. In considerable part this was possible because it could almost always turn to the Soviet Union to balance American power. Today, however, the principal successor state to the Soviet Union, Russia, is neither able nor willing to play such a role. Consequently, India's room for maneuver is more limited. More to the point, India is far more enmeshed with the United States along a number of important dimensions, such as military-to-military contacts, weapons sales, trade, investment, and diplomatic cooperation in multilateral fora. That said, given the country's political culture, Indian policymakers still remain fiercely committed to the pursuit of an autonomous foreign policy. However, the current level of Indian involvement with the United States makes it more difficult for Indian policymakers to remain oblivious to American concerns. There is some evidence to suggest that US prodding in the wake of a major India-Pakistani crisis in 2001–2002 contributed to the commencement of the "composite dialogue" with Pakistan.[6]

What about US leverage over Pakistan? Since the US involvement in Afghanistan in the wake of 2001 terrorist attacks on the United States, it has poured well over

[6] See Chari et al., 2007.

$20 billion in economic and military assistance into the country. However, given the US dependence on the land access to Afghanistan for the prosecution of the war against the Taliban and the remnants of al-Qaeda, American policymakers were always hesitant to exert any real pressure on Pakistan to alter any aspect of its foreign or security policies. With the US drawdown from Afghanistan, is this relationship likely to change? Obviously, the US dependence on Pakistan to maintain the logistical chain to Afghanistan will soon draw to a close. Consequently, American policymakers should no longer feel as beholden to the demands of the Pakistani military establishment.

The question of American leverage, however, depends on whether or not US policymakers remain wedded to untenable assumptions of another era. If, for example, they continue to harbor the belief that any pressure on Pakistan is likely to drive it further into the arms of the PRC and thereby lead to a loss of any residual US leverage, they will become victims of a self-fulfilling prophecy. On the other hand, if they recognize that both the elected leadership as well as the military establishment remain dependent on the United States for economic and military assistance and that the PRC (and Saudi Arabia) do not constitute easy substitutes, they can exert more pressure on Pakistan to abandon some of its past policies that have either piqued or exacerbated relations with India. Given that the United States does have a substantial interest in limiting the possibility and scope of conflict between these two nuclear-armed rivals in South Asia, it may be useful to turn to an examination of some literature on rivalry termination that deals with the role of external actors in fostering an improved climate of relations in an enduring rivalry.

COMPETING MODELS

Three recent works on rivalry termination provide some useful clues and suggestions about how external actors may facilitate the process of a reduction in tensions and the promotion of amity. In this section we turn to the key elements of these analyses.

Kristina Mani, in a recent work, underscores the significance of democratization in promoting rivalry termination. Even though her analysis draws on Latin American cases, there is no reason to believe that it cannot be usefully applied to the study of rivalries in other regional contexts with suitable and appropriate modifications.[7]

At bottom, her theory holds that as a new democratizing regime assumes office it will seek to adopt policies of compromise and conciliation in the domestic arena and avoid political polarization. In turn it will also try to avoid arbitrariness in the use of political power that had characterized the previous regime. These habits of compromise, negotiation, and reasonableness, she argues, are also likely to spill over into the international arena. Such strategies, she argues, especially if they meet with some reciprocity from rivals, then enable the democratizers to shift critical

---

[7] Kristina Mani, *Democratization and Military Transformation in Argentina and Chile: Rethinking Rivalry* (Boulder, CO: First Forum, 2011).

resources away from national security; to weaken other domestic actors who are opposed to reform; and to also to secure access to international markets, capital, and technology.

Mani is also attentive to the presence of potential "veto players" within the political order who could undermine or hobble the efforts of democratizers. These "veto players," in turn, are defined as *partisan* and *institutional*. *Partisan veto players* are individuals or groups who stem from alignments within the political system while *institutional veto players* are those who enjoy such status on the basis of constitutional arrangements.

The task of democratizing agents then is to find ways to either neutralize or win over the potential veto players as they seek to consolidate democracy at home and reduce tensions abroad. To do so, Mani argues that the likely veto players have to be engaged for extended periods of time and thereby have their preferences altered. Obviously, if external tensions can be reduced, the ability of veto players, most notably military establishments, to forestall or hobble reforms can be diminished. This model has considerable logical as well as intuitive appeal. However, it will be shown that it is nevertheless of rather limited utility in the India-Pakistani case, especially because her model grants no explicit role to external actors. The absence of a role for external actors greatly reduces the relevance of her model for this particular project.

Charles Kupchan, whose work deals with a different set of cases from other regions, offers a second model of rivalry termination. The key elements of his model can be summarized as follows. Kupchan's argument is located in the larger body of literature dealing with "the democratic peace."[8] His analysis is composed of four distinct segments or stages toward rivalry termination. In the first phase, one which involves *unilateral accommodation*, one party makes a unilateral gesture with the hope of eliciting a reciprocal reaction. Such accommodation will be facilitated if both parties see a common threat. The second phase moves toward *mutual accommodation* when the hopes of tension reduction give way to *mutual confidence*. The third phase leads to *societal integration* when confidence expands, contributing to a milieu of mutual *trust*. The fourth and final phase culminates in the generation of new political narratives, with the two polities coming to share a common *identity*.[9]

It is really the first two phases of Kupchan's model that are of significance to this analysis, as they deal specifically with the process of rivalry termination. The subsequent phases are invaluable in explaining how a rivalry may eventually culminate in the creation of a security community. While the model is elegantly laid out, however, the relevant components of the model which account for its success elsewhere have not been present in South Asia and are unlikely to obtain anytime in the

---

[8] The literature on "the democratic peace" is vast and was pioneered by Michael Doyle. See Michael Doyle, *Liberal Peace: Selected Essays* (London: Routledge, 2011); also see Bruce Russett, *Grasping the Democratic Peace* (Princeton, NJ: Princeton University Press, 1994); John Owen, *Liberal Peace, Liberal War: American Politics and International Security* (Ithaca, NY: Cornell University Press, 2000).

[9] Charles A Kupchan, *How Enemies Become Friends: The Sources of Stable Peace* (Princeton, NJ: Princeton University Press, 2010).

foreseeable future. More to the point, his model, like that of Mani, has no particular role assigned to external actors.

Our third and final model is derived from the work of William Thompson. His model has the following components. They involve *expectations, shocks, policy entrepreneurs, reciprocity,* and *reinforcement.* Each of these components requires some discussion and explication. *Expectations* are based upon what rivals have done in the past and what they are presently engaged in. *Shocks* are defined as transitional situations that can provoke a significant change in adversarial relations by changing key *expectations.* (Shocks, in turn, can be either endogenous or exogenous and third parties can play a vital role in generating exogenous shocks). Next, *policy entrepreneurs* are decision makers who prove to be critical in seeking de-escalation. Their role, in turn, can be bolstered through a process of *third-party interventions.* Additionally, for this process to culminate in the de-escalation of the rivalry, there must be *reciprocity* and *reinforcement.* In the absence thereof, a de-escalatory process will not ensue.[10] Finally, if all six variables are present, the likelihood of the model's expectations being realized is that much greater. That said, *policy entrepreneurs* and *third parties*, though desirable, are not critical to the working of the model.

The presence of the role of *third parties* renders his model most useful for our purposes. Specifically, using his model, we will highlight the role of the United States at key junctures and turning points in this relationship when the possibility of a breakthrough toward amity loomed large. As this analysis will demonstrate, the United States has not always played a particularly positive role on all occasions.

CLOSE CALLS AND MISSED OPPORTUNITIES

The following section will examine three important moments when the rivalry may have deescalated but did not and what role, if any, the United States played in the process. The first will focus on the period after the 1971 India-Pakistani conflict, the second on the era after the death of General Zia-ul-Haq and the restoration of democracy in Pakistan, and the third during the last years of General Pervez Musharraf following a major crisis in India-Pakistani relations between 2001 and 2002. Of the three episodes, it is believed in some quarters that the most recent attempt came closest toward generating a rapprochement.

Several moments in the India-Pakistani relationship should have provided suitable opportunities for a reduction in tensions as Pakistan made a transition from military rule to democracy. The first such episode came about in the wake of the country's disastrous defeat in the India-Pakistani conflict of 1971.[11] The origins of this particular crisis and its culmination in the third India-Pakistani war have been

[10] William R. Thompson, "Expectancy Theory, Strategic Rivalry De-escalation, and the Evolution of the Sino-Soviet Case," in William R. Thompson, ed., *Evolutionary Interpretations of World Politics* (New York: Routledge, 2001), pp. 218–240; also see Karen Rasler, William R. Thompson, and Sumit Ganguly, *How Rivalries End* (Philadelphia: University of Pennsylvania Press, 2013).

[11] Leo E. Rose and Richard Sisson, *War and Secession: Pakistan, India, and the Creation of Bangladesh* (Berkeley: University of California Press, 1990).

explored elsewhere. Suffice it to say that it stemmed from the unwillingness of the West Pakistani civilian elite as well as the military establishment to share power with their East Pakistani counterparts in the aftermath of Pakistan's first free and fair election in December 1970. As the negotiations collapsed, the Pakistani military embarked upon a brutal crackdown in East Pakistan, leading to the flight of nearly ten million refugees into India. After exhausting diplomatic options, Indian policymakers, unwilling to absorb such a large influx of refugees into its already turgid population, chose to provoke Pakistan into a war.[12]

The US role during this crisis was, without question, malign.[13] The military dictatorship of General Yahya Khan in Pakistan had facilitated Henry Kissinger's visit to Beijing in July 1971.[14] Consequently, the Nixon administration was unwilling to exert any pressure on Pakistan despite evidence of the military's brutal and egregious conduct against hapless East Pakistani civilians in March 1971. Instead, it adopted an overtly hostile stance toward India on the mistaken belief that the country was acting at the behest of the Soviet Union.[15] American support for Pakistan during this crisis not only alienated Indian elites but helped drive India into a strategic alignment with the Soviet Union.

Furthermore, despite US support for Pakistan, India prevailed militarily in the conflict. Pakistan's defeat was decisive in that it led to the breakup of the country. Furthermore, it also contributed to the discrediting of the Pakistani military because of its unprofessional conduct in suppressing the civil unrest in East Pakistan and its subsequent incompetence in the conduct of the war with India.[16]

In the aftermath of the war, however, President Zulfiquar Ali Bhutto, through very deft negotiations with his Indian counterpart, Prime Minister Indira Gandhi, in 1972, managed to reach a very favorable postwar settlement. Specifically, he arranged for the release of 90,000 Pakistani prisoners of war; reiterated a commitment to abjure from the use of force in resolving the Kashmir dispute; and accepted a change of nomenclature, which altered the Cease Fire Line (CFL) in Kashmir to the Line of Actual Control (LOAC).[17] The disastrous performance of the Pakistani

[12] Robert Jackson, *South Asian Crisis: India, Pakistan, and Bangladesh* (New York: Praeger, 1975).

[13] On this issue see Gary J. Bass, *The Blood Telegram: Nixon, Kissinger, and a Forgotten Genocide* (New York: Knopf, 2013).

[14] On this subject see also William Burr, ed., "The Beijing-Washington Back-Channel and Henry Kissinger's Secret Trip to China: September 1970–July 1971," Washington, DC: National Security Archive Electronic Briefing Book, Number 66, February 27, 2002. Available at: http://www.gwu.edu/~nsarchiv/NSAEBB/NSAEBB66/.

[15] The best statement on this issue remains, Christopher van Hollen, "The Tilt Policy Revisited: Nixon-Kissinger Geopolitics and South Asia," *Asian Survey* 20, no. 4, (April 1980): 339–361.

[16] On the discrediting of the Pakistani military see Hasan Zaheer, *The Separation of East Pakistan: The Rise and Realization of Bengali Muslim Nationalism* (New York: Oxford University Press, 1998).

[17] The Line of Actual Control reflected the disposition of troops at the conclusion of the 1971 war. It is important to note that the Indian military played little or no role in the postwar settlement. The entire negotiation with Pakistan was the preserve of civilians. Mrs. Gandhi and a close coterie of advisers participated in the negotiations and were solely responsible for determining

armed forces in the 1971 war, coupled with Bhutto's adroit diplomacy in the wake of military defeat, gave him an opportunity to reduce the salience of the military in Pakistan's politics and to move toward a rapprochement with India while consolidating democracy at home.

Unfortunately, neither he nor his party did much to utilize this opportunity to alter the internal political arrangements within the country and promote a culture of negotiation, compromise, and reasonableness when dealing with political opponents. Consequently, no democratic consolidation took place either in normative or institutional terms. Instead, he chose to promote populist ventures, nationalized several industries, alienated the civil service, and failed to win the trust of the military. Furthermore, he undermined the independence of the Pakistan Civil Service, arbitrarily retired several hundred civil servants, and abolished service guarantees. He also created the Federal Security Force (FSF), an organization designed for his personal protection and one that he used to victimize his political opponents. In an effort to emplace his party in the province of Baluchistan, he summarily dismissed the National Awami Party in the province. In the wake of this dismissal, an armed rebellion erupted in the state. Bhutto banned the party, arrested its principal leaders, and charged them with conspiracy and high treason. He also used the military to suppress the uprising and granted them considerable leeway in the use of force. When his popularity started to sag, far from resorting to a strategy of political conciliation, he chose instead to wrap himself in the mantle of Islam and thereby even alienated segments of his own supporters. His final error, of course, was the attempt to rig the national elections in 1977. This decision led to widespread discontent across the country and his eventual overthrow in a military coup.[18]

Not surprisingly, given the domestic turmoil that his policies had engendered and his preoccupation with the suppression of the uprising in Baluchistan, his regime could make no meaningful gestures toward India. To compound matters, in an effort to compensate for Pakistan's conventional inferiority he also embarked upon a clandestine nuclear weapons program.[19] To the extent that there was any reorientation in Pakistan's foreign policy, it involved a significant turn toward the Middle East. [20]

A long period of peace did ensue between the two adversaries in the wake of the 1971 war. However, this period of peace cannot be attributed to the beginnings of a rapprochement. It was little more than a reflection of the conventional military asymmetry between the two states. Pakistan, the revisionist power, was simply

---

the scope of the discussions that ensued. For details pertaining to the bilateral negotiations at Simla in 1972 see P.R. Chari and Pervaiz Iqbal Cheema, *The Simla Agreement 1972: Its Wasted Promise* (New Delhi: Manohar, 2001); also see the discussion in S.M. Burke and Lawrence Ziring, *Pakistan's Foreign Policy: An Historical Analysis*, 2nd ed. (Karachi, Pakistan: Oxford University Press, 1990), p. 420.

[18] Roedad Khan, *Pakistan—A Dream Gone Sour* (Oxford: Oxford University Press, 1997), pp. 64–65.

[19] Samina Ahmed, "Pakistan's Nuclear Weapons Program: Turning Points and Nuclear Choices," *International Security* 23, no. 4 (Spring 1999): 178–204.

[20] Marvin Weinbaum and Gautam Sen, "Pakistan Enters the Middle East," *Orbis*.

in no position to militarily provoke India, given the latter's considerable military superiority.

Indeed the next crisis did not take place until 1987. An ethnoreligious insurgency had broken out in the Indian border state of Punjab. In the mid-1980s, this crisis peaked, and Pakistan sought to exploit India's difficulties in suppressing the rebellion through the provision of sanctuaries, training, and weaponry for the insurgents.[21] This crisis stemmed from India's decision to resort to a strategy of coercive diplomacy to dissuade Pakistan from continued meddling.

It is important to note that certain permissive conditions within India were conducive to the adoption of this strategy of forceful persuasion. A largely untested prime minister, Rajiv Gandhi, who was also a political neophyte, was in office; the Minister of State for Defense, Arun Singh, enjoyed a close rapport with the Chief of Staff (COAS) of the Indian Army, General Krishnaswami Sundarji; and the COAS was known for his flamboyance as well as a propensity for risk-taking. Taken together, these factors created an ideal conjuncture for the events that transpired.

The United States, along with the Soviet Union, played a mostly helpful role in defusing this crisis.[22] During or shortly after this crisis, it is widely believed that Pakistan crossed a threshold in its quest to acquire a nuclear weapons option.[23] Though its security establishment had long utilized an asymmetric war strategy against India, the growth in its nuclear weapons capability certainly emboldened them to adopt a more aggressive stance toward India.[24] Though US and Soviet intercession played critical roles in containing this crisis, neither power did much to follow up with the two warring parties to further the cause of conflict resolution.

A second opportunity for deescalating the rivalry with India arose in the wake of the abrupt death of General Zia-ul-Haq in a plane crash in the summer of 1988. After a decade of military rule, popular disaffection with the military in Pakistan was at its apogee. Consequently, his successors made no attempt to try and sustain military rule. Furthermore, the United States, which had granted General Zia-ul-Haq considerable leeway and had indeed, by default, bolstered military rule, encouraged the Pakistani military not to interfere in the political process. Almost immediately, Benazir Bhutto, Zulfiquar Ali Bhutto's daughter who had returned to Pakistan from exile, entered the political fray. When national elections were held in November 1988, the Pakistan People's Party (PPP), which she now headed, swept the polls.

In the meanwhile, Prime Minister Indira Gandhi had been assassinated in India in 1984. Her son and successor, Rajiv Gandhi, had won a significant mandate

---

[21] Mark Tully and Satish Jacob, *Amritsar: Mrs. Gandhi's Last Battle* (London: Jonathan Cape Ltd, 1985).

[22] For details see Kanti Bajpai, Sumit Ganguly, et al., *Brasstacks and Beyond: Perception and the Management of Crisis in South Asia* (New Delhi: Manohar, 1997).

[23] Devin T. Hagerty, *The Consequences of Nuclear Proliferation: Lessons from South Asia* (Cambridge: MIT Press, 1998).

[24] In this context it is important to underscore that this analysis firmly challenges those that seek to link Pakistan's feckless use of asymmetric forces to its acquisition of nuclear weapons. For a statement of that argument see S. Paul Kapur, *Dangerous Deterrent* (Stanford: Stanford University Press, 2007).

when elections had been held later that year. With both leaders enjoying substantial domestic popularity, it proved possible for Rajiv Gandhi to make an overture toward Pakistan to try and reduce tensions. These hopes for improved relations were also enhanced because of the relative age of both national leaders, neither of whom had searing memories of the horrors that had accompanied the partition of the subcontinent in 1947. Indeed, the initial efforts to improve relations proved quite promising.

While visiting Pakistan for the South Asian Association for Regional Cooperation (SAARC) summit in December 1988, Gandhi signed three important agreements with his Pakistani counterpart. The first and easily the most significant of these was a pact whereby both sides agreed that they would not attack each other's nuclear facilities.[25] The other agreements outlined plans to work toward ending the confrontation on the Siachen Glacier and the delimitation of a boundary along Sir Creek near the Indian state of Gujarat and the Pakistani province of Sindh. In this context, it is important to note that even though the Indian military had distinct views about the demilitarization of the Siachen Glacier, they were in no position to exercise a unit veto on the subject.[26]

Throughout the year thereafter, a series of high-level meetings ensued, which were designed to improve bilateral relations. Many of these meetings dealt with contentious issues including the Siachen Glacier question. Furthermore, in July 1988, Rajiv Gandhi became the first Indian prime minister to visit Pakistan in thirty years. Benazir Bhutto had expected Rajiv Gandhi to make some concession on the Kashmir question to enable her to deal with pressures from radical Islamists and the military at home. Rajiv Gandhi, however, was unwilling to make any such gesture.[27] Accordingly, despite the goodwill that had been generated as a consequence of the prior agreements, the visit did not prove to be especially fruitful, barring the formal agreement not to attack each other's nuclear installations. Nevertheless, other high-level meetings between key officials that had been in the cards continued throughout most of the year.[28]

The sudden eruption of an ethnoreligious insurgency in the Indian-controlled portion of the disputed state of Jammu and Kashmir brought these negotiations to a halt. The origins of this insurgency were indigenous and could be traced to the exigencies of Indian politics.[29] However, almost immediately after its outbreak, the Pakistani military, despite the presence of a civilian and democratically elected government, jumped into the fray.[30] Recognizing that she could ill-afford to continue the discussions with India given her domestic milieu as well as the antagonism of the military, Bhutto promptly did an about-face and ratcheted up her hostile rhetoric.

[25] J.N. Dixit, *India-Pakistan in War and Peace* (New Delhi: Books Today, 2002).

[26] V.R. Raghavan, *Siachen: Conflict Without End* (New Delhi: Viking, 2003).

[27] Dixit, *India-Pakistan in War and Peace*, p. 270.

[28] J.N. Dixit, *Across Borders: Fifty Years of India's Foreign Policy* (New Delhi: Picus Books, 1998), pp. 198–201.

[29] Sumit Ganguly, *The Crisis in Kashmir: Portents of War, Hopes of Peace* (New York: Cambridge University Press, 1997).

[30] For evidence of Pakistan's involvement in the insurgency see Peter Chalk, "Pakistan's Role in the Kashmir Insurgency," *Jane's Intelligence Review* 13, no. 9 (September 1, 2001): 26–27.

Any prospect of some accommodation with India that had arisen was now irretrievably lost for well over a decade, especially as Rajiv Gandhi had lost the national election in 1989, with a coalition government coming to power.[31]

The coalition government was at a loss when confronted with the Kashmir insurgency. To compound matters, the Indian security forces, which had no dearth of experience in coping with domestic insurgencies, initially adopted a mailed fist strategy in their efforts to crush the insurgents. This approach almost immediately backfired and actually widened the scope and intensity of the uprising.[32] Of course, Pakistan's quick involvement in supporting elements of the rebels led to a dramatic escalation of violence.[33]

Faced with the abrupt eruption of this insurgency, the United States could do little to address its underlying causes. However, as the crisis threatened to spiral out of control in 1990, and rumors of an Indian strike across the Line of Control became rife, the United States did engage in some crisis diplomacy. To that end, it dispatched Robert Gates, the US deputy national security adviser, to both India and Pakistan in May 1990. In Islamabad, Gates made clear that the United States had simulated every plausible India-Pakistani war game scenario and in every case Pakistan lost. Accordingly, he urged Islamabad to end its support for the insurgency in Kashmir, while he told his Indian interlocutors in New Delhi that they should exercise military restraint and also not seek to suppress the insurgency with mailed fist tactics.[34] Subsequent American efforts to reduce India-Pakistani tensions during the first Clinton administration, however, were seen to be blatantly partisan and set back the cause of peacemaking in the region.[35]

The third and final case that will be discussed started under a military regime in Pakistan and in the aftermath of a major India-Pakistani crisis. The origins of this attempt at rapprochement remain somewhat murky. However, it is widely believed that an external actor, the United States, played a critical role in prodding the two sides to embark upon a peace process.[36] US pressures, no doubt, were taken seriously in both Islamabad and New Delhi because much international pressure had been brought to bear on the two countries in the wake of the 1998 nuclear tests.[37]

---

[31] Her domestic constraints are clearly summarized in Husain Haqqani, *Pakistan: Between Mosque and Military* (Washington, DC: Carnegie Endowment for International Peace, 2005).

[32] On India's experiences with counterinsurgency as well as a discussion of the Kashmir case see Sumit Ganguly and David P. Fidler, eds., *India and Counterinsurgency: Lessons Learned* (London: Routledge, 2009).

[33] On Pakistan's involvement see Praveen Swami, *India, Pakistan, and the Secret Jihad* (London: Routledge, 2007).

[34] Much of this is discussed in Devin Hagerty, "Nuclear Deterrence in South Asia: The 1990 Indo-Pakistani Crisis," *International Security* 20, no. 3 (Winter 1995–1996): 79–114.

[35] John F. Burns, "US Remarks Over Kashmir Anger Indians," *The New York Times*, March 10, 1994.

[36] Howard B. Schaffer, *The Limits of Influence: America's Role in Kashmir* (Washington, DC: The Brookings Institution, 2009).

[37] On the role of external pressures, especially from the United States, see Strobe Talbott, *Engaging India: Diplomacy, Democracy, and the Bomb* (Washington, DC: The Brookings Institution, 2006).

The backdrop to the initiation of this process was hardly propitious. The Pakistani state had been implicated in a terrorist attack launched on the Indian parliament on December 13, 2001.[38] In the aftermath of this attack India had embarked on a massive military mobilization designed to forcefully persuade Pakistan to not only desist from allowing any more terrorist attacks but to also end its involvement with the use of terror.[39] This crisis stretched out for most of the spring and summer of 2002 and concluded in the early fall of the year. In its wake, it is believed that the George W. Bush administration, which was keenly interested in eliciting Pakistan's cooperation in the "war on terror" and in eviscerating al-Qaeda in Afghanistan, urged the two parties to move toward a reduction of tensions. A more cordial India-Pakistani relationship, the administration believed, might enable Pakistan to direct its military resources to its border with Afghanistan.

In any event, Indian Prime Minister Atal Behari Vajpayee offered a resumption of talks with Pakistan in mid-April 2003. Significantly, this offer was made in Srinagar, the capital of the Indian-controlled portion of the disputed state of Jammu and Kashmir.[40] Later that year, General Musharraf reciprocated with two important gestures. In November, he banned three terrorist organizations, the Hezb-ul Tehrir, the Jamiat-ul Furqan, and the Jamait-ul Ansar, and agreed to a cease-fire along the Line of Control in Kashmir.[41] Also in November, the Pakistani prime minister, Zafarullah Khan Jamali, proposed an unconditional cease-fire.[42] Subsequently, in December 2004, a few weeks prior to the 12th SAARC Summit in Islamabad, Musharraf demonstrated some apparent flexibility on the Kashmir question. Most importantly, he suggested that the contentious issues of the UN plebiscite, a long-standing Pakistani demand harking back to the late 1940s, could be set aside.[43] However, faced with intense domestic criticism, the Pakistani Foreign Office sought to reduce the significance of his statement while insisting that they remained open to meaningful discussions with India to resolve the Kashmir question.[44]

As in the past, on the sidelines of the SAARC Summit, Vajpayee and Musharraf reached an understanding that met the basic expectations of both sides for a viable dialogue. Significantly, India conceded that Kashmir did indeed constitute an international dispute and Pakistan agreed to prevent terror emanating from its soil. In the wake of these developments, a full-scale "composite dialogue" ensued.

---

[38] On Pakistan's involvement in the 2001–2002 crisis see Sumit Ganguly and R. Harrison Wagner, "India and Pakistan: Bargaining in the Shadow of Nuclear War," *The Journal of Strategic Studies* 27, no. 3 (2004): 479–507.

[39] Sumit Ganguly and Michael R. Kraig, "The 2001–2002 Indo-Pakistani Crisis: Exposing the Limits of Coercive Diplomacy," *Security Studies* 14, no. 2 (April–June 2005): 290–324.

[40] *Press Trust of India*, "Talk, Not Guns, Will Solve Issues: Vajpayee," April 18, 2003.

[41] Thomas Wagner, "Musharraf Bans Three Islamic Militant Groups," *The Boston Globe*, November 21, 2003.

[42] Praful Bidwai, "Time to Seize the Initiative," *Frontline* 20, no. 25, December 6–19, 2003, http://www.frontline.in/static/html/fl2025/stories/20031219008712300.htm.

[43] Ahmed Rashid, "Musharraf Offers 'Flexibility' on Kashmir Dispute," *The Telegraph*, December 19, 2003; also see Stephen P. Cohen, "The Pakistan Time Bomb," *The Washington Post*, July 3, 2007.

[44] TNN, "Who Said We'd Forget Plebiscite Demand?" *The Economic Times*, December 20, 2003.

The dialogue encompassed a range of issues, from nuclear confidence-building measures to the possible demilitarization of the Siachen Glacier. It is believed that considerable progress toward the resolution of a number of nettlesome issues was being made. Most importantly, it is also argued that a preliminary roadmap was also drawn up for the eventual settlement of the Kashmir dispute.[45] This possible pathway to rapprochement had five significant features. First, the two sides had agreed that there would be no significant changes in the Line of Control but that some minor adjustments were possible. Second, they agreed that the two governments would devolve considerable autonomy to their respective parts of Kashmir; the specifics would have to be dealt with in due course. Third, they also agreed on various steps to bring about a process of reciprocal demilitarization. Fourth, India did not agree to a proposed "joint management" of the affairs of the whole state but did express willingness to consider such an approach for the management of watersheds, forests, and glaciers. Fifth and finally, they agreed to open the border to the free movement of people and goods.[46]

Others, however, claim that despite the fashioning of a possible roadmap, it was far from clear that Musharraf was in a position to make a credible commitment. This analysis cannot adjudicate between those two competing positions. What is known, however, is that two different regimes in India, with markedly divergent political orientations, sustained the peace process.

Even after Vajpayee remitted office following the electoral defeat of his National Democratic Alliance (NDA) coalition government, his successor, Prime Minister Manmohan Singh, continued the nascent peace process, and with much vigor. Musharraf's ability to sustain the peace process, however, was undermined because of the exigencies of Pakistan's domestic politics. Specifically, the removal of the Chief Justice of the Pakistan Supreme Court, Iftikhar Muhammad Chaudhury, in November 2007, triggered a significant backlash and undermined Musharraf's position.

Faced with the possibility of impeachment, President Musharraf resigned from office in 2008. Soon thereafter, elections were held and a civilian regime under the aegis of the Asif Ali Zardari, the husband of the assassinated Benazir Bhutto, assumed office. It is possible that this regime may have continued the process that had been initiated under Musharraf's watch. However, a major terrorist attack on Bombay (Mumbai) in late November 2008, which was traced back to Pakistan, effectively brought the dialogue to a close.[47] No prime minister in India could possibly sustain the talks in the immediate aftermath of the terrorist attacks, which made clear that that the Indian state was acutely vulnerable to a determined terrorist onslaught stemming from Pakistan.

[45] Steve Coll, "The Back Channel," *The New Yorker*, March 2, 2009.

[46] Praveen Swami, "An Explosion on the Road to Peace," *The Hindu*, February 27, 2008.

[47] The Lashkar-e-Taiba, a terrorist organization based in the town of Muridke in Pakistan's Punjab, was implicated in the attacks. The full scope and extent of the complicity of the Pakistani military and intelligence establishments in aiding and abetting the LeT remains a matter of debate. For the LeT's role see Stephen Tankel, *Storming the World Stage: The Story of Lashkar-e-Taiba* (New York: Columbia University Press, 2011).

The US role in prodding the two parties in the wake of the 2001–2002 crisis was, in many ways, an important catalyst in promoting the "composite dialogue." Consequently, in this particular case the role of the United States as a *third party* was a critical factor in boosting the prospects of conflict resolution and eventual reconciliation.

CONCLUSIONS

Based on the analysis of these three cases, it is possible to conclude that the Thompson model offers the best explanation for the prospects of rivalry de-escalation or its failure. The variables of the model provide a number of useful apertures through which to examine the conditions under which a rivalry can stagnate, escalate, or dissipate. The model is distinctive in that it pays heed to structural, national, and decision-making-level factors. The focus on *shocks* provides opportunities to examine the impact of various disjunctures; the issue of *expectations* helps clarify the views of each side of the other; the emphasis on *change-seeking entrepreneurs* as well as *third-party pressures* directs attention to the role of human agency; and, finally, the questions of *reciprocity* and *reinforcement* highlight the importance of the critical need for positive interactions. These variables enable the model to have sufficient flexibility to ensure broad application—unlike Mani's model, for example, which requires *democratization* as a precedent for a process of rapprochement to ensue.

Relying on Thompson's model, what might be the key elements of a possible scenario for the de-escalation of the rivalry? It may stem from a situation where the domestic crises in Pakistan become so acute that they constitute an *endogenous shock*. Unable to cope with widespread domestic disorder and maintain vigilance on its eastern border, and fearful of the safety and security of their nuclear arsenal, Pakistan's civilian and military elites may revise their *expectations* of their ability to compete with India and offer to end their unremitting hostility. Quite fortuitously, a *change-seeking entrepreneur* is on hand in India and responds favorably to the Pakistani gesture. Simultaneously, key external actors (*third parties*), including the United States and the PRC, exert suitable diplomatic pressures, thereby sustaining the momentum for a dialogue. US pressure, of course, happens to be crucial because it signals to India that, unlike in the past, the United States is no longer willing to countenance Pakistan's continued intransigence, nor is it willing to perpetuate its continued reliance on the Pakistani military. India then decides to make suitable and viable concessions on the Kashmir question and thereby sets in motion a process of *reciprocity*. Pakistani decision makers, recognizing that India's concessions are significant, respond favorably and thereby start a virtuous spiral of *reinforcement* which steadily contributes to the eventual de-escalation of the rivalry.

How might the United States then fashion a sustainable national security strategy toward this enduring rivalry? Such a discussion necessitates a focus on risks, enablers, and pitfalls. At the outset, three risks in particular should concern US policymakers. First, the India-Pakistani rivalry in Afghanistan is likely to intensify as the US drawdown in 2016 approaches. Second, Pakistani policymakers have growing misgivings about the growth in and transformation of India-United States ties.[48] Third, the vortex of Pakistan's domestic politics also raises questions about the long-term stability of the state, especially given that it possesses a significant nuclear arsenal.

What might be the enablers of such a strategy? One step, though bold, could have a dramatic impact on tamping down the conflict. This would require the United States to declare that it recognizes the LoC as the international border. This would deliver a significant *shock* and could well change Pakistani *expectations*. Also, it would enable India to place its own house in order within the segment of Kashmir that it controls, free of the fear of Pakistani interference.[49]

In the more immediate term, however, as the United States seeks to reduce its presence in Afghanistan, it could benefit from India's cooperation. To that end, it can quietly work to reduce India-Pakistani hostility through the pursuit of some concrete, tangible projects. Specifically, the United States has expressed an interest in promoting economic ties between Central and South Asia. Accordingly, it could gently prod India-Pakistani collaboration on the construction of gas pipelines linking India with various states in Central Asia. Pakistan may well perceive a "relative gains" problem at the outset.[50] However, given its own dire energy needs, it may be amenable to suitable US side payments to overcome these misgivings.

Though US engagement in the region has been intermittent, apart from rare exceptions, its support for the Pakistani military establishment has been consistent. Such backing has helped foster a self-fulfilling prophecy: the military, for all practical purposes, has long emerged as the only functioning institution in the country. In turn, whenever faced with a foreign or security policy exigency in the region, American policymakers have turned to the military to pursue their interests. The military order, in turn, has exacted a price: it has ensured that the bulk of US assistance has helped to strengthen its own position within the Pakistani polity.

Any discussion, of course, would fall short without an examination of possible pitfalls. Accordingly, it will behoove US policymakers to remain alert to these. Three likely and significant dangers need to be highlighted. The first would be yet another Pakistan-backed terrorist attack on India. Unlike in the past, when the Indian state has shown both restraint and forbearance, its patience may not hold on this occasion. Calls for a more vigorous response are likely to ensue from right-wing political parties, hawkish strategic commentators, and even segments of the afflicted citizenry. Under these circumstances any US effort to promote the de-escalation of India-Pakistani tensions would reach a swift standstill.

In a related vein, any American effort designed to reduce India-Pakistani tensions must remain alert to the vagaries of India's domestic politics. An attempt that is overt and heavy-handed is bound to provoke a backlash among India's attentive

[48] Sumit Ganguly and S. Paul Kapur, "The Transformation of U.S.-India Relations," *Asian Survey* 47, no. 4 (July–August 2007): 642–656.

[49] This argument is developed some length in C. Christine Fair and Sumit Ganguly, "A New Approach for Kashmir," *The National Interest*, November 12, 2012; available at: http://nationalinterest.org/commentary/new-approach-kashmir-7754.

[50] On this subject see Robert Powell, "Absolute and Relative Gains in International Relations Theory," *American Political Science Review* 85, no. 4 (December 1991): 1303–1320.

public. Such a concern is hardly chimerical. Despite the dramatic improvement in India-United States relations over the past decade or so, much distrust of American intentions continues to pervade the views of segments of Indian elite opinion. To reverse Robert Axelrod's famous dictum, the "shadow of the past" continues to haunt India-United States relations.[51]

Furthermore, a US strategy must also be sensitive to the growing fragmentation of Indian politics. Despite the unitary constitutional dispensation of the Indian state, politics in India increasingly resemble those of a highly federal polity. Owing to the presence (and likely persistence) of coalition governments, state-level regimes are today exercising a disproportionate influence on a range of foreign policy issues. Any strategy that is oblivious to this feature of the Indian political terrain is bound to encounter resistance.

Additionally, the PRC, which has long enjoyed a strategic partnership with Pakistan, and has used the latter as a strategic surrogate in South Asia, may be disinclined to see the emergence of an Indian-Pakistani rapprochement. The reasons for their unwillingness to see a more cordial relationship develop are straightforward. Such reconciliation could enable India to direct the bulk of its strategic resources to the Sino-Indian frontier and thereby attenuate India's security concerns. All of these possible pitfalls are compelling. Any American strategy that hopes to deescalate the India-Pakistani rivalry can ill afford to ignore these potential limits.

Finally, the United States needs to eventually confront a "moral hazard" problem that it has long overlooked in its attempts to influence and alter Pakistan's behavior.[52] During the Cold War, Pakistan was at best a partial partner. It did provide the United States bases in the country which enabled surveillance flights over the Soviet Union and also provided opportunities for intelligence collection on the USSR. However, weaponry that the United States had provided to steel Pakistan's resolve against Communist expansion was used to start a war against India in 1965.[53] In 1970, the United States chose to resurrect the relationship after having imposed an arms embargo on Pakistan (and India) in the wake of the war. This renewal of the partnership again came at a cost. The Nixon administration, beholden to Pakistan for enabling a diplomatic opening to the PRC, chose to ignore its client's resort to a genocidal strategy to quell domestic discontent in East Pakistan.[54] This episode, thanks to the feckless actions of the military dictatorship in Pakistan, tainted the United States through its association with the regime.

Later, during the Soviet invasion and occupation of Afghanistan, Pakistan once again proved to be a limited partner. It did allow the United States to use its territory to train, organize, and arm the Afghan insurgents. However, this relationship came at a price; for all practical purposes the United States willfully ignored Pakistan's

---

[51] Robert Axelrod, *The Evolution of Cooperation* (New York: Basic Books, 2006).

[52] For a discussion of "moral hazards" in the context of US alliance commitments see Daniel Byman, "Friends Like These: Counterinsurgency and the War on Terrorism," *International Security* 31, no. 2 (Fall 2006): 79–115.

[53] Robert McMahon, *The Cold War on the Periphery: The United States, India and Pakistan* (New York: Columbia University Press, 1994).

[54] Gary J. Bass, *The Blood Telegram*, 2014.

headlong pursuit of nuclear weapons, thereby undermining US nonproliferation efforts in South Asia and beyond.[55] In the wake of the terrorist attacks of September 11, 2001, the United States once again forged a strategic relationship with Pakistan with the goals of toppling the Taliban regime and eviscerating al-Qaeda. Yet again Pakistan has proven to be, at best, a reluctant partner. It has acted against al-Qaeda but has consistently failed to rein in key terrorist organizations ranging from the Lashkar-e-Taiba to the Afghan Taliban. In the meanwhile, it has continued to make demands on the United States for both financial and military assistance. US policymakers, in the hope of changing Pakistan's behavior, have continued to provide such assistance. But American policy, though designed to alter Pakistan's preferences, yet again is failing. A more appropriate strategy might involve one that shifts support away from the Pakistani military and focuses American assistance toward building up civilian institutions that would discourage Pakistan's continued dalliance with agents of terror. In the absence of these policy shifts it is hard to envisage how the United States might actually further its strategic interests in the region.[56]

[55] Adrian Levy and Catherine Scott-Clark, *Deception: Pakistan, the United States and the Secret Trade in Nuclear Weapons* (New York: Walker, 2007).

[56] C. Christine Fair and Sumit Ganguly, "The Unworthy Ally: Time for Washington to Cut Pakistan Loose," *Foreign Affairs* 94, no. 5 (September–October 2015): 160–171.

13

A SUSTAINABLE APPROACH TO
AFGHANISTAN: NEUTRALIZATION

Audrey Kurth Cronin

Developing a sustainable security policy for future US policy toward Afghanistan requires dispassionately weighing American interests within the context of competing global and domestic challenges. Since al-Qaeda's attacks in 2001, the top American priority has been to prevent future threats against the United States and its allies emanating from Afghan territory. Relatedly, a viable and legitimate Afghan government serves American interests. After a vast investment of American lives and treasure, US credibility would be damaged if Afghanistan again reverted to being a failed state. Establishment of a second Afghan Taliban regime could reverse all the post-2001 development gains and provide a further breeding ground for anti-West Islamist violence. Finally, at the heart of the famous Silk Road that once ran from the Eastern Roman Empire to China (300 BCE to 200 AD), Afghanistan plays a key role in Eurasia's changing current geopolitical picture. Chinese President Xi Jinping's Silk Road Initiative, announced in 2013, seeks to cut China-Europe transport from four to six weeks by sea to fourteen days by road or rail. This may or may not accord with US interests, depending upon whether it benefits Afghanistan economically and increases China's incentives to pressure Pakistan not to export Islamist radicalism. Above all else, then, American interests are served by an Afghanistan that is stable, autonomous, economically developing, unthreatening to others, and constructively committed to by its neighbors.

Afghanistan's neutralization is the best way to ensure a stable state that cannot threaten itself, the region, or the United States. It also accords with Afghan tradition by echoing the most peaceful, prosperous periods of Afghan history. While Afghanistan is by no means a developed country, it has been at the crossroads of civilizations for centuries, with archaeological roots rivaling those of Egypt and a trading culture that dates back to at least 2,000 BCE. The great conquerors of history, including Genghis Khan and Alexander the Great, passed through the area, helping to establish a warrior tradition. Afghan statesmen have built a legacy of balancing off the interests of rival empires, achieving stability only when they have kept themselves politically separate and independent of them all. In the last two hundred years, Afghanistan has been at the crossroads of Tsarist Russia, British India, the Soviet Union, the United States, Pakistan, Saudi Arabia, Al-Qaeda, and now NATO and the United States again—with Pakistan, Iran, and China waiting in the wings. As US troops draw down, the Afghan government is resuming its role as geopolitical pivot; the United States should shape that process by helping to build a sturdy regional framework that discourages meddling neighbors and reduces the threat to both Afghanistan and the United States.

Afghanistan has been most dangerous to itself and others when it has drawn too close to any one power or group, and most stable when it has acted as a political buffer and economic crossroads between two or more. The key to the most peaceful period in recent history—what the Afghans call the "Era of Tranquility" between 1929 and 1978—was a strict policy of neutrality and nonalignment. That is also the most promising approach today, but with a regional accord to back it up.

Neutralization is a reciprocal agreement, usually between a weak state and two or more external powers, in which the state agrees to be perpetually neutral and the external powers guarantee that neutrality. Neutralization agreements are designed to guard a state's territorial integrity and independence while keeping external actors at bay. Like any other tool of statecraft, these agreements do not always work; but when they do, they can change regional dynamics in ways that serve inhabitants and stabilize the entire global system. There are many examples of disadvantaged, strategically important states gaining leverage against stronger powers by crafting a regional solution; the conditions under which they have succeeded or failed are readily apparent. Intelligently crafted, a neutralization agreement could provide an overarching diplomatic and legal framework for Afghanistan that counterbalances competitive regional powers externally, and shores up the national interests of the Afghans internally, to lay the groundwork for the stability and independence of the state into the twenty-first century and beyond.

Many argue that the key question for Afghanistan is not whether or not it allies with external powers, but whether the Afghans will dissolve into further internal conflict and reestablish safe havens for terrorists committed to attacking the United States. That perspective is backwards: the country has best avoided internal strife when acting as a buffer state, evading all alliances and external interference. The civil wars of the late twentieth century grew out of Russian, Saudi, US, Iranian, and Pakistani interventions, picking winners and losers and carrying out their proxy battles via Afghan warlords and government leaders on Afghan soil. Moving forward, the goal must be to break this pattern by establishing a political framework where the major powers collectively agree to stay out and give Afghan nationalism and institutions the space in which to work. Instead, the current trajectory is to increase Pakistan's intervention in Afghanistan as the United States draws down, a risky scenario for the United States because the groups that threaten US and allied territory come mainly from Pakistan, not Afghanistan (e.g., Lashkar-e-Taiba, Tehrik-i-Taliban Pakistan). To prevent a future safe haven for terrorists, the critical objective must be to keep *all* of the external powers out of Afghanistan. That is exactly what a neutralization agreement does.

Neutralization is complicated, and only a fool would argue that a 21st century neutralization of Afghanistan would be easy. The most successful instances of neutralization have involved states, cities, and principalities in Europe. But looking at the history of the practice, successfully neutralized states have had consistent strategic, structural, economic, and political conditions that may be relevant to Afghanistan. Strategically, the neutralized states or territories have been of limited intrinsic importance to any one other state, thus important enough to deny to a neighbor but not worth the sacrifice of a risky occupation. Structurally, they have had challenging geographical characteristics, such as mountainous terrain or landlocked borders, making them difficult to conquer and occupy. Economically, they have been important to broader regions as hubs of trade, with multilateral access to resources or markets, offering neighbors a pay-off for respecting the arrangement. And politically, they have had external affirmation of their neutralized status—by the Church, an international body, or through covenant by more than one major military power—adding legitimacy and potential force to the arrangement.

Afghanistan's current situation does not perfectly fit *all* conditions of successful neutralization, but there are enough promising factors to make the approach worth trying. States have been successfully neutralized even when they lacked perfectly clear borders, suffered occasional violations of their neutrality, or even experienced domestic conflicts. The method is chosen after other options have failed. The Afghans have been at war for more than thirty years. They are looking for a new approach that avoids the tired pattern of instability, civil war, and invasion of the recent past. And from the American perspective, neutralization is a solution whose costs are low and potential benefits—of even a short-term success—high.

This chapter proceeds in four sections. First it explains and defines neutralization, distinguishing it from other related concepts. Second, it carries out a structured comparison of all historical cases of neutralization over the past five hundred years. Third, it explains the conditions under which neutralization succeeds or fails. Fourth, it tests those conditions against this case, while also considering alternative pathways for post-ISAF Afghanistan. Close study of the historical record indicates that Afghanistan can be neutralized if classic pitfalls are avoided. Neutralization represents the best available option for the future of Afghanistan and the broader region.

"NEUTRALIZATION": DEFINING THE CONCEPT

Neutralization is a multilateral arrangement designed to advance regional and domestic stability where the goals of competing military powers intersect. It discourages enemies from clashing over a territory whose strategic significance affects them all. The purpose of a neutralization accord is to discourage military intervention by one power that might be met by counterintervention by another power, ultimately catalyzing a war where everyone would lose. The small state commits to remain perpetually neutral and to prevent force projection from its territory, and the external powers guarantee the political independence and territorial integrity of that state. In a sense, then, the actors being "neutralized" are not just the state but also the major powers vying to invade, intimidate, or control it.

Neutralization is often confused with related, similar-sounding concepts.[1] "Neutrality," the oldest of these, was first used by the Swiss in 1536 to refer to a

---

[1] International law with respect to neutrality will not be comprehensively covered here (e.g., this study does not cover the governing of waterways or short-term demilitarization of a contested territory during a war). See J. H. W. Verzijl, *International Law in Historical Perspective*. Part IX-B: *The Law of Neutrality* (The Netherlands: Sijthoff & Noordhoff, 1979).

state's deliberate policy to stay out of a particular war.[2] The term has often been used incorrectly in political discourse (especially during the Cold War) but its meaning is clear: there is no formal legal neutrality *except* in time of war.[3] Neutralization is a more long-lasting status that exists in war or peace and cannot be declared unilaterally. Unlike neutrality, neutralization requires both a state declaration and an external guarantee on the part of neighboring powers.

"Nonalignment" and "neutralism" are political (not legal) terms made popular following the Second World War.[4] In the postwar wave of decolonization, both concepts maximized a new state's maneuverability and independence by keeping it out of the bipolar contest between the Soviet Union and the United States. In 1961, the nonaligned states paradoxically aligned themselves in the Non-Aligned Movement (NAM), led initially by Yugoslavia, India, Indonesia, Egypt, and Ghana. The movement was dedicated to peace, territorial integrity, independence, anticolonialism, and other activist policies. NAM members made no promise to be nonbelligerents in wartime: there were scores of conflicts among members, notably India/Pakistan, Iran/Iraq, Ecuador/Peru, and Libya/Chad. After the Cold War ended, the movement struggled to redefine itself. Its present *raison d'être* is to support the rights of developing states; reform the structure of the United Nations (especially the Security Council); and criticize the policies of the traditional powers (especially the United States). Afghanistan is a member of the Non-Aligned Movement, whose August 2012 meeting was held in Tehran, Iran.

Unlike any of these other arrangements—neutrality, nonalignment, neutralism, and so forth—there is both an internal and an external dimension to a neutralization agreement. "Permanent neutrality" is the internal dimension, declared by the state, involving a promise not to participate in or prejudice the outcome of any current or future war.[5] While "permanent neutrality" or "enduring neutrality" may be self-declared, neutralization must involve an external recognition or guarantee of that status. The external angle is crucial. It is difficult for a state to be neutralized by only one major power: while major powers have collected buffer states (or "satellites") around them for centuries, those arrangements amount to protectorates, placing the weaker

---

[2] Edgar Bonjour, *Swiss Neutrality: Its History and Meaning*, trans. Mary Hottinger, 2nd ed (London: Allen & Unwin, 1948), p. 12; A.W. Stargardt, *Problems of Neutrality in Southeast Asia: The Relevance of the European Experience*, Occasional Paper 12 (Singapore: The Institute of Southeast Asian Studies, 1972), p. 1; and Cyril E. Black et al., *Neutralization in World Politics* (Princeton, NJ: Princeton University Press, 1968), p. 21.

[3] This is also called "customary neutrality." See "Conception officielle Suisse de la neutralite," Schweizerisches Jahrbush fur internationals Recht, XIV (1957), pp. 195–199, cited by Black et al., *World Politics*, 22n; and Nils Andren, "Sweden: Neutrality, Defense, and Disarmament," in *The European Neutrals in International Affairs*, edited by Hanspeter Neuhold and Hans Thalberg, The Laxenburg Papers 7 (Laxenburg, Austria: Austrian Institute for International Affairs, 1984), p. 40.

[4] Paul F. Power, *Neutralism and Disengagement* (New York: Scribner, 1964), p. 2; and Marvin C. Ott, *The Neutralization of Southeast Asia: An Analysis of the Malaysian/ASEAN Proposal*, Papers in International Studies, Southeast Asia Series 33 (Athens, OH: Ohio University Center for International Studies, 1974), 2–3.

[5] The terms "self-neutralization" and "autonomous neutralization" were also used. See, for example, Stewart MacMaster Robinson, "Autonomous Neutralization," *The American Journal of International Law* 11, no. 3 (July 1917): 607–616.

state at risk vis-à-vis its stronger neighbor.[6] The key is to neutralize not only the weak state (the internal dimension), but also the stronger powers whose interests clash over it (the external dimension). Without at least two outside powers agreeing to the arrangement, there can be no "neutralizing" the interests of competing major powers.

In a neutralization accord, the external guarantee may vary from an explicit enforcement agreement with control machinery to a more ambiguous multilateral recognition of the state's permanent neutrality. Historically, the formal mechanisms have been diverse, from that of Belgium, whose nineteenth-century neutralization by the European powers came closest to a classic model, to that of Austria, first neutralized under a 1955 bilateral agreement with the Soviet Union then recognized by France, Britain, and the United States.[7] (More on these cases later.) The way to establish whether a state has been neutralized is to determine whether outside powers would be militarily involved if its territory were violated. A "neutralized" state must defend its territorial integrity if it is to avoid triggering competitive intervention. In short, neutralization carries risks for both the state and neighboring powers. So why consider it?

Under certain conditions, neutralization serves the interests of the weak state, major powers, and the broader international system. From the viewpoint of the inhabitants of a neutralized state, the costs of alliance exceed the benefits.[8] Neutralization can increase a country's security and independence without enlarging the risk and burden of defense expenditures. Indeed some neutralization agreements have called for the elimination of military assets that could be used for external aggression so that a government may focus its army on internal order and territorial defense. Neutralization can also aid in unifying a country divided between two or more major powers (permanent neutrality is better than partition) or two or more domestic factions associated with different outside sponsors (neutral unity beats civil war). The reduction of the threat of military intervention by bigger states can increase the political maneuverability of the neutralized state, giving it a larger role in international politics than it otherwise would have. Indeed it is often in the interests of neutralized states to demonstrate independence of their guarantors so as to reinforce the image of impartiality. States that choose neutralization prefer strong affordable defense, intact survival, maneuverability, and independence over external military alliances.

Major powers also have specific reasons to consider neutralization. In the simplest terms, major powers have three options with respect to contested weaker powers: (1) to acquire a weaker state as a client or ally; (2) to allow the state to be neutral; or (3) to yield the weaker state as a client or ally of a rival. Situations that are ripe for neutralization often follow in the wake of unsuccessful attempts to invade or acquire a weaker power (option one), where major powers settle for option two so as to avoid option three.[9] Through diplomatic means, neutralization agreements

---

[6] Although some write of the neutralization of Finland by a single state (the Soviet Union), that is inaccurate. Finland's 1948 Treaty of Friendship, Cooperation and Mutual Assistance was an agreement for limited and conditional military cooperation, aimed against Germany. Neutrality was not a condition for Soviet troop withdrawals from Finnish territory; military cooperation was.

[7] Black et al., *World Politics*, 20.

[8] Neutralization aligns with the qualifications for small and weak countries described by Mancur Olson and Richard Zeckhauser, "An Economic Theory of Alliances," *The Review of Economics and Statistics* 48, no. 3 (August 1966): 271–272.

[9] I am indebted to Peter Krause for this formulation.

remove small states from the threat of attack or annexation by rival stronger powers, by denying the state to any one of them. Unable to control the state unilaterally, competing powers hedge their bets.

Neutralization accords also play a broader role in the stability of the collective international system. Both guaranteed and guarantor states enter into this kind of diplomatic agreement to diffuse international tensions in a region that is vulnerable to war and potentially destabilizing to the international system. The framework deters conflict and enhances predictability. A weak state can act as a power vacuum, inviting the meddling of stronger states that prolong civil wars and might precipitate an international crisis. Neutralization decreases the chance of a conflict that could escalate to major war. Whatever its design, neutralization cannot *remove* the possibility of external intervention, but it raises the cost to the intervener by heightening the risk that another major power will counteract it. It also weakens the intervener's legitimacy by forcing it to violate an international agreement, making it more likely that other states will counterattack. At its heart, then, neutralization strengthens the deterrent capability of a militarily weak state that is an object of strategic interest by major powers.

Neutralization protects a contested state's self-determination by ensuring its autonomy. In return it places obligations upon it. By the terms of most agreements, the country may not go to war except in self defense, may not influence the course of any international hostilities that do occur, and may not take any actions that could lead to involvement in those hostilities.[10] The state's principal duty is to protect its impartiality and territorial integrity, and the guarantors threaten to intervene if it aligns with one of them. These obligations and restrictions are weighed against alternative pathways for contested states, including partition, satellite status, occupation by one or more external powers, or civil war aggravated by meddling powers. For contested states, neutralization is the least unattractive of the available options.

NEUTRALIZATION IN PRACTICE:
THE UNIVERSE OF CASES

The following considers the thirteen historical cases of neutralization and is confined to neutralization cases: myriad other historical cases of protectorates,[11] satellites,[12] buffer states,[13] nonalignment,[14] or customary neutrality[15] are not included here. In each neutralization case study, there are seven key variables examined: geographic features, clarity of borders, level of economic value to neighbors, nature of the external guarantee, level of defenses within the state, and the degree of indigenous support for the agreement, as summarized in Table 13.1.

[10] Some experts argued that neutralization was an intolerable infringement upon state sovereignty. See F.W. Baumgartner, "Neutralization of States," *Bulletin on the Department of History and Political and Economic Science* 25 (October 1917), (Kingston, ON: The Jackson Press, 1917), 25.

[11] For example, Uganda and The Solomon Islands, under the British.

[12] For example, most of the states of Eastern Europe under the Soviet Union during the Cold War.

[13] For example, Paraguay between Argentina and Brazil, or Afghanistan between Russia and British India.

[14] For example, members of the nonaligned movement during the Cold War, such as India, Yugoslavia.

[15] For example, Sweden during the Cold War.

Table 13.1 Neutralization Cases

Territory or State Neutral Period	Negotiating Parties	Key Geographic Features	Contested Borders?	History of Domestic Conflict?	Economic Value to the Region	Binding Guarantee? Guarantor	Demilitarized?	Broad Indigenous Support?	Outcome*
Channel Islands 1483–1689	English and French kings	Islands in key waterway	No Islands (under English sovereignty)	No	High	Yes The Pope	Yes	No, imposed	Success
Liege 1492–1518	Liege inhabitants, France, the Netherlands	Flat lowland, valley of the Meuse River	No City-state	Yes Civil war with outside intervention	High	No	No (defensive forces only)	Yes Initiated by the inhabitants	Success
Malta 1802–1814 (*de facto* much earlier)	Mainly Britain and France Divided Maltese participants (incomplete)	Island with excellent fortresses, dramatic natural cliffs	No Island	No Passed between external powers	High Maritime way-station to the colonies	No	No (defensive forces only)	No, imposed	Failure
Upper Savoy 1815–1919	Austria, Great Britain, Portugal, Prussia, Russia France, Sweden, and Spain	Controlling access to a key mountain pass	Yes Small territory on the border of Switzerland; in 1919 it became part of France.	No	Low	Yes All the signatory powers	No	No, imposed	Success
Cracow 1815–1846	Austria, Great Britain, Portugal, Prussia, Russia France, Sweden, and Spain	On the Vistula River, in a key mountain pass	No City	No	High Economic hub; coal reserves, later steel center	Yes Austria, Russia, Prussia	Yes, completely	No, imposed	Failure

(continued)

Table 13.1 Continued

Territory or State Neutral Period	Negotiating Parties	Key Geographic Features	Contested Borders?	History of Domestic Conflict?	Economic Value to the Region	Binding Guarantee? Guarantor	Demilitarized?	Broad Indigenous Support?	Outcome*
Switzerland 1815–present (*de facto* much earlier)	Austria, Great Britain, Portugal, Prussia, Russia, France, Sweden, and Spain	Landlocked, formidable mountains, control over key Alpine passes	Yes Settled during negotiations	Yes Centuries of conflict between Cantons; external border disputes	High Long tradition of open access to commerce.	Yes All the signatory powers	No. Strong territorial defenses	Yes. Initiated by the Swiss	Success
Moresnet 1815–1914	Netherlands, Prussia (and to a lesser extent, all Congress of Vienna signatories)	Forested, mines, near borders of Germany and Belgium	Yes Settled during negotiations	No	High One of two zinc mines in Europe at the time.	Yes Netherlands, Prussia	Yes.	No. Product of a tense compromise between the Dutch and Prussians for the mine	Failure. Germany invades at the start of World War I
Belgium 1831–1914	1831: Great Britain, Austria, France, Prussia, and Russia; 1839: Holland.	Flat, lowlands, no natural barriers.	Yes Settled during negots.	Yes Revolution to secede from Holland	High Steel and coal, key transportation hub (roads, ports, canals, rail)	Yes Great Britain, Austria, France, Prussia, and Russia (individual guarantees)	Yes. Ancient forts destroyed; v. ltd defensive forces retained	No, imposed	Mixed; ultimately Failure

	Guarantors	Geography			Strategic Value	Guarantee	Guarantors	Demilitarized	Imposed/Initiated	Outcome
Luxembourg 1867–1914	Great Britain, Austria, Belgium France, Italy, Netherlands, Prussia, and Russia	Landlocked citadel, transformed into an "open city"	No	No But lost territory in the Belgian Revolution	High Iron and steel; banking	Yes Great Britain, Austria, France, Italy, the Netherlands, Prussia, and Russia (collective guarantee)	Yes, completely	No, imposed	Failure
Congo 1885–1914	US, UK, Austria, France, Germany, Italy, Russia, Belgium, Denmark, Holland, Portugal, Sweden, Norway, and Turkey	Coastal plain, large arable river basin	No Corporate state/ colony, under Belgian control	No	High Rubber, copper, other minerals	No A *"garantie restreinte"*: individual commitment to respect the neutrality of the Congo Basin.	No, but weak defenses	No, imposed	Failure
Austria 1955–present	Great Britain, United States, France, and USSR, along with Austria	Landlocked; plain and mountains; border disputes w. Italy	Yes Post–WWII southern border disputes; resolved during negots.	Yes Two attempted coups; riots; unrest, border skirmishes	High Long tradition of trade through Vienna	Yes United Kingdom, USSR, United States, France	No. Strong territorial defenses	Yes; initiated by the Austrians	Success

(continued)

Table 13.1 Continued

Territory or State Neutral Period	Negotiating Parties	Key Geographic Features	Contested Borders?	History of Domestic Conflict?	Economic Value to the Region	Binding Guarantee? Guarantor	Demilitarized?	Broad Indigenous Support?	Outcome*
Laos 1962 (almost immediately violated)	Burma, Cambodia, Canada, PRC, both Vietnams, France, India, Poland, Thailand, USSR, United States, United Kingdom, and Laos	Landlocked; mountainous, elongated, with historically fluid borders	Yes	Yes Civil war, Pathet Lao vs. Royal Lao Army	Low Not a major trading center	No Just an agreement by the parties to "consult" if there is a violation	No, but weak defenses	Yes. (Laotian government participated but did not initiate)	Failure
Turkmenistan 1995-present	None. Unilaterally declared; codified in the Constitution	Mainly flat; desert; borders Caspian sea.	No Borders were settled in 1924, but under Soviet control.	No But highly repressive regime; human and drug trafficking	High Extensive oil and natural gas reserves; on historic Silk Road trade route	No Recognized by UN General Assembly.	No. Conscript-based armed forces.	No. Unilateral, with UN recognition	?

Afghanistan ?	Min.: Pakistan, China, Iran, India, Saudi Arabia, United States. **Max.**: also NATO, Central Asian republics	Landlocked; mainly mountainous; plains in north and southwest; fluid eastern border	Yes	Durand Line with Pakistan (to be addressed during negotiations?)	Repeated civil wars	High Mineral wealth, key trade routes	Yes	Multilateral; China, Iran, Pakistan India, Saudi Arabia, Russia, United States	No. Strong national army required, probably with technical assistance re the border and monitoring air space	Must be initiated by the Afghan government, strongly supported by the US	? To be determined

*Note:

Cases of neutralization are labeled a **"Success"** if they held for more than twenty years, preserved the entity's independence OR played a stabilizing role in the region during a crisis or conflict. Cases are labeled a **"Failure"** if they lasted fewer than twenty years, failed to preserve the independence of the entity, or helped to catalyze a broader regional war or crisis.

(This chart does not reflect more nuanced results, such as the achievement of short- or medium-term success in the face of long-term failure, as in the case of Laos.)

Origins of the concept (fifteenth to eighteenth centuries)

Beginning in the fifteenth century, major European powers tried to isolate territories because they were important to commerce or might be a catalyst for war. The earliest recorded example is the neutralization of the Channel Islands during the late fifteenth century. The English and French kings drew up the arrangement and then asked for the protection of the Pope, who in 1483 issued a Bull stating that anyone who violated it would be excommunicated.[16] The inhabitants sought the 1492 neutralization of Liege, then a loosely federated state commanding French access to the Rhine. France and the Netherlands kept it out of their bloody conflicts until 1518, when Liege entered into a mutual defense treaty with the Netherlands.[17]

During the seventeenth and eighteenth centuries there were numerous examples of *imposed* neutrality, but none with reciprocal agreements that characterize neutralization. Most were part of the barrier system against France.[18] Under the first barrier treaty of October 29, 1709, for example, the Dutch were allowed to maintain a line of forts along the French border in the Austrian Netherlands (now Belgium), as a "dyke, rampart and barrier against France," in the common interests of Austria, Holland, and England.[19] This boundary line in the middle of Europe foreshadowed the neutralizations of Belgium and Luxembourg a century later. In 1802, under the Treaty of Amiens, France (with her allies) and England provided for the neutralization of Malta, an island with a prior tradition of self-declared neutrality, but it soon fell to Great Britain in the war of the Third Coalition.[20]

The Congress of Vienna, 1815

The end of the Napoleonic Wars and the attempt to establish a new European order resulted in the first far-reaching neutralization accords at the Congress of Vienna. Switzerland was the greatest success of the Congress and will be treated in detail below. But the 1815 settlement also neutralized upper Savoy (on the Swiss border),

---

[16] E. Toulmin Nicolle, "Neutrality of the Channel Islands during the Fifteenth, Sixteenth, and Seventeenth Centuries," *Journal of Comparative Legislation and International Law*, 3rd Series 2, no. 3 (1920): 238–239.

[17] W.S.M. Knight, "Neutrality and Neutralization in the Sixteenth Century – Liege," *Journal of Comparative Legislation and International Law*, 3rd Series 2 (1920), 98–104.

[18] Malbone W. Graham, Jr., "Neutralization as a Movement in International Law," *The American Journal of International Law* 21, no. 1 (January 1927): 82.

[19] James Marshall-Cornwall, *Geographic Disarmament* (London: Oxford University Press, 1935), 18–19.

[20] Clair Francis Littell, *The Neutralization of States: A Study in Diplomatic History and International Law* (New York: Columbia University, 1921), 16–19; Cyrus French Wicker, *Neutralization* (London: Oxford University Press, 1911), pp. 11–12; See also Graham, "Neutralization as a Movement," 82 and Baumgartner, "Neutralization of States," 20. Malta remained part of the British Empire until its independence in 1964 and declared its own permanent neutrality in 1980. Costa Rica has been neutral since 1983, Sweden since 1812, and Ireland since the 1930s. None of these was an externally guaranteed neutralization.

Moresnet (between Prussia and the Netherlands), and the city of Cracow (Poland), three small territories whose fates yield insights into how the concept was applied both well and badly.

Upper Savoy

The neutralization of Upper Savoy was an attempt to build a buffer around the borders of Switzerland. It was neutralized under the Final Act of the Congress of Vienna, as well as Article 3 of the Treaty of Paris (November 1815). Upper Savoy provided a territorial cushion for the Swiss cantons of Valais and Geneva by cutting off access to a key mountain pass (Simplon) that might be used by the French to invade Switzerland. Switzerland was even permitted to place troops there to defend her neutrality.[21] The Versailles Treaty abrogated the neutralized status in June 1919, and Upper Savoy became a normal part of France (Haute-Savoie).[22]

Moresnet

The neutrality of Moresnet lasted for almost a century and kept the European powers from dragging the continent into a war over resources. Moresnet was a tiny territory now within the city of Kelmis, Belgium that in 1815 was caught between the Prussians and the Dutch. The Congress of Vienna had settled the main outline of the border between the Kingdoms of Prussia and the Netherlands, but Moresnet held a valuable zinc spar mine that both sides wanted. So the European powers neutralized and demilitarized the territory, barring both Kingdoms from occupying it and putting it under the jurisdiction of a combined royal commission. This was the situation until the Germans invaded in 1914. Under the Versailles treaty Belgium formally annexed it in 1920.

Cracow

The 1815 attempt to neutralize the city of Cracow is a classic example of what *not* to do. The Congress of Vienna made it an independent republic, with Austria, Russia, and Prussia guaranteeing perpetual neutrality. All three powers wanted control of the city, which had become vulnerable after the Grand Duchy of Warsaw dissolved.

---

[21] "Letter from the Swiss Federal Council to Dr. Kern," *Correspondence Relating to the Affairs of Italy, Savoy & Switzerland*. Presented to both Houses of Parliament by Command of Her Majesty (London: Harrison and Sons, 1860), pp. 46–51; and Adda Bruemmer Bozeman, *Regional Conflicts Around Geneva: An Inquiry into the Origin, Nature, and Implications of the Neutralized Zone of Savoy and of the Customs-free Zones of Gex and Upper Savoy* (Stanford, CA: Stanford University Press, 1949).

[22] See Permanent Court of International Justice, "Case of the Free Zones of Upper Savoy and the District of Gex," (France V. Switzerland), 1929 P.C.I.J. (ser. A) No. 22 (Order of Aug. 19); accessible at http://www.worldcourts.com/pcij/eng/decisions/1929.08.19_savoy_gex.htm.

The treaty of June 9, 1815 made Cracow a free, independent and neutral city, then denuded it of self-defense or restrictions on external intervention. All three then freely violated its borders, giving it all the drawbacks and none of the advantages of neutralization. In 1846, the city was incorporated into the Austrian Empire, with Prussia and Russia trading it for compensation elsewhere and the British and the French protesting in vain.

Switzerland

Switzerland would not have survived as an independent, unified state without building a tradition of neutrality. Characterized from the outset by internal fractiousness, a strong warrior culture, and repeated conquest of (and by) its neighbors, Switzerland found permanent neutrality essential to its welfare—not least because every other policy had proven disastrous.

The Swiss confederation emerged during the disintegration of the Carolingian Empire between the tenth and thirteenth centuries, when strong central power devolved to feudal lords, local authorities, monasteries, and cities. During a complicated process of confederation, including a civil war (1436–1450), the Swiss developed a reputation for military prowess. They conquered new territories in the north and east, enlarging their borders at the expense of Austria, and defeated the Emperor and South German princes in the Swabian War (1499). Especially after the Swiss defeated Charles the Bold of Burgundy (1477), European leaders vigorously sought Swiss mercenary soldiers. By the start of the sixteenth century, the Swiss had unparalleled military prestige and were at the forefront of political power on the continent.[23]

Defeat at the battle of Marignano, September 13–14, 1515, marked the reversal of Swiss military fortunes. The goal had been to drive the French from northern Italy, but the Swiss lost and sued for peace. Under the peace agreement that followed, they retained crucial Alpine passes and received a subsidy in return for the French government's right to enlist Swiss mercenaries, marking the last time the Swiss launched a military conquest in their own name. On May 5, 1521, shortly after the peace accord, the Swiss entered an offensive and defensive alliance with France that was renewed in 1663, 1715, and 1777.[24]

The Swiss first officially used the term "neutrality" in 1536, but it did not characterize their foreign policy until the Thirty Years War (1618–1648). Divided between Catholic and Protestant cantons, the Swiss confederation remained neutral to avoid being torn apart. Switzerland's governing body, the Diet, issued a 1638 order forbidding the passage of foreign troops through Swiss territory. By 1647, the Diet organized a federal army of 36,000 men to protect the common frontier, establishing the principle of territorial defense.[25] In the 1648 treaties of Westphalia, the European

[23] Ibid., 10.

[24] Gordon E. Sherman, "The Neutrality of Switzerland," *The American Journal of International Law* 12, no. 2 (April 1918): 241; and Baumgartner, "Neutralization of States," 12.

[25] Baumgartner, "Neutralization of States," 14–15; Cornwall, *Disarmament*, 20.

powers recognized the thirteen cantons as an independent state, acknowledging the collective stance they had adopted during the war.[26]

Although now recognized as one state, the cantons were bitterly divided over religious issues and maintained the loosest possible unity. Although they were no longer launching their own military campaigns, the Swiss continued to send tens of thousands of mercenary soldiers to fight under foreign flags, especially the French tricolor. By the end of the seventeenth century, yearly pensions paid to Swiss soldiers abroad amounted to some 1.5 million francs.[27] The religious ties on the one hand between the Protestant cantons and the Dutch and the English, and on the other hand between the Catholic cantons and the French and the Spanish, led to a supply of Swiss mercenaries for each of these powers. Tragically, in the War of the Spanish Succession (1701–1714), thousands of Swiss soldiers confronted each other on the battlefield as a result. Irrespective of the activities of Swiss soldiers and the weaknesses of the federal structure—indeed, partly *because* of the latter—the state continued to maintain a policy of neutrality in all European conflicts.

In addition to its warrior tradition, geography and economics have been crucial to Swiss neutrality. Switzerland is both a vital strategic gateway and a fortified enclave from attack. Largely through its jurisdiction over key mountain passes, the state has been central to the interests of each of the major European powers during wartime. Otherwise, isolated from the rest of Europe by mountain barriers, lacking in raw materials, and with limited amounts of arable land, Switzerland has been a peripheral concern. This odd combination of qualities ultimately benefited the Swiss, as no power wanted to see Switzerland's routes controlled by rivals, yet few sought to control Swiss territory itself. Switzerland's economic vitality was likewise crucial. Swiss free trade policies and the abundance of their markets gave seventeenth and eighteenth century belligerents strong motives to respect Swiss neutrality.

The French Revolution catalyzed the emergence of modern Switzerland. Revolutionary ideology found eager adherents in Switzerland, making the state vulnerable to Napoleon's armies. In 1798, Napoleon and his armies invaded, annexing Geneva to France and proclaiming the establishment of the "Helvetic Republic," modeled after republican France. It had a strong central government consisting of an elected chamber of deputies, a senate, and a directory of five men at the top. Under Napoleon's oversight, the Helvetic constitution eliminated the original cantons, reallocating territory to twenty-three smaller units. The two republics entered into an offensive and defensive alliance, whereby France guaranteed the independence and unity of the Helvetic Republic and Switzerland supplied 12,000 men for the French armies. Being now essentially a vassal state of Napoleon's France, Switzerland forfeited any claim to neutrality, and most of the wars of the Second Coalition (1798–1802) were fought on Swiss soil.[28]

---

[26] Wicker, *Neutralization*, 14; Baumgartner, "Neutralization of States," 16; Sherman, "The Neutrality of Switzerland," 242; Cornwall, *Disarmament*, 20; and Bonjour, *Swiss Neutrality*, 24–25.

[27] Baumgartner, "Neutralization of States," 17.

[28] Baumgartner, "Neutralization of States," 18–19; Sherman, "The Neutrality of Switzerland, 244–245; and Bonjour, *Swiss Neutrality*, 45–46.

With the treaty of Amiens (March 27, 1802), French troops withdrew and the state seemed to regain its autonomy. But the Swiss so resisted Napoleon's centralized constitution that by the end of the year he was forced to send 30,000 French troops back again.[29] Summoning Swiss leaders to Paris, Napoleon forced the writing of a "mediation constitution," completed on February 19, 1803. Dividing the state into nineteen cantons, it better reflected Swiss political traditions but remained a product of French domination. Soon they were supplying 20,000 men for Napoleon's armies.[30]

Napoleon's defeat in the battle of Leipzig (October 16–19 1813) had powerful implications for Switzerland. With allied armies approaching the Swiss frontier, the central government declared its neutrality; but the allies barreled through in pursuit of the French. A small defensive contingent of about 12,000 Swiss soldiers fell to overwhelming force.[31] The outcome was removal of French dominance and the establishment of a multipower allied protectorate over Switzerland.[32]

Switzerland's future was a major agenda item at the Congress of Vienna, 1814–1815. Subject to the approval of the Swiss government, on March 20, 1815, the powers announced their intention to neutralize Switzerland. For its part, Switzerland wanted clarification of its territorial dimensions, as France had annexed Geneva, Neuchatel, and several other territories during the war. Deliberations were abruptly interrupted by the return of Napoleon to Paris. Having solemnly promised to respect the perpetual neutrality of Switzerland, the allied powers asked the Swiss to allow allied armies to pass across Swiss soil again. Under the circumstances the Swiss could hardly refuse. Meanwhile, the Swiss Diet acceded to the March declaration of the powers, signifying satisfaction with the territorial adjustments and political arrangements. Delayed by Napoleon's campaign of a hundred days, final signature was part of the second Peace of Paris, November 20, 1815. In the treaty Austria, Great Britain, Portugal, Prussia, Russia, and France acknowledged Switzerland's permanent neutrality and provided a formal guarantee of the "integrity and inviolability" of Swiss territory. Shortly thereafter, Sweden and Spain also acceded to the declaration.[33]

Since 1815, the military readiness of the Swiss to defend their borders and to prevent foreign use of their territory has been crucial to the success of neutralization. In 1870, Switzerland was almost drawn into war when the French army, fleeing the Prussians, passed into Swiss territory; the Swiss disarmed and interned the French soldiers for the remainder of the war. Before the First World War, the German general staff considered sweeping through Switzerland to outflank the French defensive line at the southern end but decided that an invasion would be too costly.[34] The

[29] Geoffrey Bruun, *Europe and the French Imperium, 1799–1814* (New York: Harper, 1938), 58.

[30] Ibid., 137.

[31] Baumgartner, "Neutralization of States," 20; and Bonjour, *Swiss Neutrality*, 51.

[32] Gordon E. Sherman, "The Permanent Neutrality Treaties," *Yale Law Journal* 24, no. 3 (January 1915): 223.

[33] See Wicker, *Neutralization*, 14; Black et al., *World Politics*, 21; and Baumgartner, "Neutralization of States," 26–28.

[34] See William McElwee, *The Art of War: Waterloo to Mons* (Bloomington: Indiana University Press, 1974), pp. 103–105.

Swiss mobilized their entire army on July 31, 1914 and were poised to make life difficult for any invading force. The Swiss also successfully deterred invasion of their territory during the Second World War, mobilizing some 430,000 men for defense of the frontiers. The Swiss define and enforce their own permanent neutrality, and since 1815 have never called upon the guarantors to intervene on their behalf.

Following Switzerland's neutralization, the European powers tried to duplicate the formula just north, in Belgium and Luxembourg.

Belgium, 1831

Following the Napoleonic wars, the Congress of Vienna agreed to unite the Austrian Netherlands (Belgium) and Holland to form the Kingdom of the Netherlands; but the Belgians opposed the arrangement and grew steadily unhappy over the next fifteen years. On October 4, 1830, Belgium declared its independence, and the European powers hastily called a conference in London. On January 20, 1831, the European powers agreed in principle that the state of Belgium would be independent and, so as to preserve the "balance of Europe," neutralized. The neutralization of Belgium fully satisfied no one (including the Belgians); however, it seemed the best solution to a destabilizing threat.

Several months passed before the European representatives could agree on the terms of a peace accord; the outlines of the final settlement had been sketched in London. On June 24, 1831, they prepared a preliminary treaty of eighteen articles, designed formally to separate Belgium from Holland and to recognize the independence, territorial integrity, and permanent guaranteed neutrality of the new state. The Belgians had not even been consulted, and opposition was initially strong.[35] Eventually, they accepted it. But Dutch King William angrily disagreed. On August 2, 1831, he broke off the armistice and sent the Dutch army into Belgium. In response, the Belgian Congress, taking just the action that the major powers had hoped to avert, asked the French for assistance; an army of 50,000 Frenchmen was soon advancing toward Brussels. In a short time, the French forced the Dutch to withdraw from all occupied areas except the port of Antwerp, where Dutch troops barricaded themselves against attack.

To avert disaster, including another major war in Europe, the powers framed a second treaty more favorable to Holland that defined Belgian frontiers virtually as they are today. The treaty of independence and neutralization of Belgium was signed in London on November 15, 1831 by the five major European powers, accepted by the Belgian congress, but rejected, as before, by Holland. On December 14, the Dutch government formally protested it to the major powers. The protest received unexpected support from Austria, Prussia, and Russia, who began to fear that they had gone too far in appeasing revolutionaries; but the remaining powers moved immediately to protect the treaty.[36] Britain and France made arrangements to blockade the coast of Holland, to seize Dutch ships in British and French ports,

---

[35] Fred Greene, "Neutralization and the Balance of Power," *The American Political Science Review* 47, no. 4 (December 1953): 1048.

[36] Wicker, *Neutralization*, 25.

and to send French forces into Antwerp, where Dutch troops remained in occupation.[37] On May 21, 1833, the Dutch yielded and agreed to an armistice on the basis of the status quo; but they still refused to become a party to the treaty separating Belgium from Holland.

Eight years after the initial treaty's signing, the Dutch finally gave in, acceding to the neutralization of an independent Belgium. On April 19, 1839 a further Treaty of London was signed, incorporating the terms of the 1831 treaty. Supplementary treaties were concluded on the same day between the European powers and Holland, and between Belgium and Holland. The five principal signatory powers each separately guaranteed all terms of the 1839 treaty, including Belgium's independence and neutralization. Holland undertook only an obligation to recognize and respect Belgium's permanent neutrality, not guarantee it. Thus, with the reluctant approval of the Dutch, Belgium was formally neutralized and guaranteed by the major European powers. Under the terms of the agreement, they stripped Belgium of her permanent defenses (including a vast line of fortresses built to contain the French), while still permitting Belgium to maintain defensive armed forces.[38] Later with the outbreak of the Franco-Prussian War in 1870, the Gladstone government signed an additional treaty between Britain and Prussia, on the one hand, and then Britain and France, on the other, designed to shore up the 1839 agreement on Belgian neutrality and defuse the crisis on the Continent.

Luxembourg, 1867

Like its Belgian neighbor, Luxembourg was pinched between the dominance of France and emerging Germany. After Louis XIV captured Luxembourg in 1684, the great strategist of sieges, Marquis de Vauban, strengthened Luxembourg's capital into a formidable fortress. Like Belgium, Luxembourg was part of a barrier treaty against France, a failed effort as Napoleon's France overran and annexed it completely in 1795.[39] At the Congress of Vienna the European powers, trying again to restrain France, decided to place Luxembourg under the sovereignty of the Dutch king; but it was also to be permanently garrisoned against the French by Prussian troops. The elaborate arrangement called for three-quarters of the troops in Luxembourg to be Prussian and the remainder Dutch.

In 1866, at the start of the Austro-Prussian War, the Grand Duchy of Luxembourg demanded the withdrawal of the Prussian garrison of about four thousand men. The Prussian government, led by Prime Minister Otto von Bismarck, flatly refused. Jealous of Prussia's territorial gains in the war, Napoleon III then insisted that France be compensated for Prussia's growing strength by the acquisition of Belgium and Luxembourg. Again, Bismarck refused. Convinced that it would cost him nothing, however, Bismarck whetted the French appetite: England would never tolerate the annexation of Belgium, he observed. But as for Luxembourg, why didn't the emperor of France approach Dutch king William III himself? Bismarck was sure, he

---

[37] Sherman, "The Permanent Neutrality Treaties," 236.

[38] Wicker, *Neutralization*, 27–28; and Cornwall, *Disarmament*, 25.

[39] Cornwall, *Disarmament*, 25–26.

said, that the King would be only too pleased to sell the Luxembourgers and their territory for an appropriate sum.[40]

Following Bismarck's advice, during the winter of 1866–1867 Napoleon III pressured the King of the Netherlands to sell Luxembourg to France. To ensure French forbearance as he united the German confederation, Bismarck encouraged him. Writing to his representative in Paris, Bismarck said that the French "must be induced to go on hoping and, above all, to retain their faith in our good will without being given any definite commitment."[41]

This subterfuge lasted until March 1867, when Bismarck abruptly double-crossed and humiliated Napoleon III. As Bismarck had predicted, the Dutch King agreed to sell Luxembourg to France for five million guilders, but only on the condition that the King of Prussia explicitly approve the sale. When Napoleon approached him to seek it, Bismarck now sharply protested that Prussia could not sanction the giving away of any German soil and that the views of all the major European powers must be sought. The Dutch king hastily withdrew his consent; but the affair leaked to the press, exposing Napoleon's scheme and provoking nationalist hysteria among the Germans. The result was an acute European crisis.[42] To deter the outbreak of war, the major European powers hastily gathered in London on May 7 and decided that Luxembourg should be neutralized.

Although modeled after Belgium, Luxembourg's neutralization differed in three key respects. First, while Belgium was allowed to maintain armed forces for her own defense, Luxembourg was not. The European powers disarmed Luxembourg, mandating the destruction of all fortresses and permitting only the minimum number of troops necessary to maintain order. In one stroke, they transformed the city of Luxembourg from one of the greatest fortresses in Europe to an "open city."[43] Second, under the 1867 agreement Luxembourg remained within the customs union of the German federation, as the major powers thought it was not economically viable on its own.[44] Finally, Luxembourg's guarantee contrasted with Belgium's. Belgium's permanent neutrality and territorial independence had been guaranteed severally by the signatory states, meaning that each of the major European powers individually committed to uphold the arrangement.[45] For Luxembourg, the major powers provided only a *collective* guarantee, a weaker formulation that meant the Luxembourg guarantee was ambiguous from the start.

Effectiveness of the neutralizations of Belgium and Luxembourg?

Determining whether the neutralizations of Belgium and Luxembourg were effective is not straightforward. While Belgian neutrality played a role in stabilizing the

---

[40] Edward Crankshaw, *Bismarck* (London: Macmillan, 1982), pp. 247–248.

[41] *Les origins diplomatique de la guerre de 1870-71 XII*, 29 vols. (Paris, 1910–1932), pp. 200 and 226, and Herman Oncken, *Die Rheinpolitik*, Vol. 2, 201; cited by Crankshaw, *Bismarck*, 248.

[42] Crankshaw, *Bismarck*, 249–253.

[43] Black et al., *World Politics*, 26; Cornwall, *Disarmament*, 28; and Harold J. Tobin, "Is Belgium Still Neutralized?" *The American Journal of International Law* 26 (July 1932), 518.

[44] Wicker, *Neutralization*, 32.

[45] Sherman, "The Permanent Neutrality Treaties," 239.

continent for decades, especially during the crisis of the 1870 Franco-Prussian war, in 1914 it helped precipitate the bloody catastrophe of the First World War.

Executing their notorious Schlieffen Plan in August 1914, the Germans invaded both Luxembourg and Belgium as their opening gambit in the West. Luxembourg complained but, having been demilitarized, provided no resistance. The Belgians were not so cooperative. On August 3, 1914, the Germans sent Brussels an ultimatum promising a guarantee of Belgium's territorial integrity if the Belgians would allow German troops to pass through their territory on the way to France. The Belgians refused, and on August 4 the German army invaded Belgium. On the same day, Great Britain declared war on Germany and the entire continent was at war.

Five years and nine million soldiers' deaths later, both neutralizations were abrogated in the 1919 Versailles treaty. The Belgians welcomed the move.[46] Luxembourg's status was more complicated. The German occupation, being primarily about free passage of troops and supplies across Luxembourg territory, had been less oppressive than Belgium's. The Germans controlled the rail lines but did not interfere in the activities of the civilian government. So Luxembourg did not declare war on Germany, was not a belligerent, and did not participate in the peace conference. So Luxembourg did not accept the termination of its neutralized status and considered the 1867 treaty to remain in force—until the second German invasion at the start of the Second World War.

The Belgian Congo, 1885

Although called a "neutralization" at the time, this agreement had nothing to do with protecting the independence, stability, and territorial integrity of the Congo Basin. Belgium's King Leopold II wanted to exploit Congo's resources—a problem since a neutralized state presumably should not have colonies. To accommodate him, the European powers declared its neutrality at the 1885 Congress of Berlin. They also gave King Leopold personal financial control over the territory and named it the Congo Free State. There were fifteen signatories, and for the first time even the Americans endorsed it. Each pledged to respect the neutral status of the "free state," but there was neither a binding guarantee nor any right for the Congolese to protect themselves. Like Cracow, it had all of the drawbacks and none of the benefits of neutralization. In any case, Congo's legal status proved virtually meaningless, as the British, Germans, and Belgians ignored it in the brutal East African campaign of the First World War.[47]

Austria, 1955

Without neutralization, Austria would have been partitioned between East and West throughout the Cold War. The agreement under the Austrian State Treaty was

---

[46] Black et al., *World Politics*, 25. See Article 31 of the treaty. Green H. Hackworth, *Digest of International Law*, 8 vols. (Washington, DC: US Govt. Printing Office, 1940), Vol. 1, 69.

[47] Jonathan E. Helmreich, "The End of Congo Neutrality, 1914," *The Historian* 28, no. 4 (August 1966): 610–624.; William Roger Lewis, *Ends of British Imperialism: The Scramble for Empire,*

the outcome of years of fractious negotiations between France, Britain, the United States, and the Soviet Union—the four occupying powers after the Second World War. Looking at this prosperous country today it is difficult to envision ten years of allied occupation with bitter disputes over Austria's borders, dangerous riots, internal unrest, and two attempted coups (1947 and 1950). Yet, in 1955, the four powers suddenly came to an understanding and agreed to withdraw their armies. Austria's neutral, unified status stood as an intriguing exception to Europe's partition, and the state remains permanently neutral today.

Like the Swiss, the Austrians played a crucial role in pursuing their own interests and in their country's eventual neutralization.[48] Only three months after the Allied occupation began, the Austrians held their first postwar election and established a provisional national government. This government doggedly rebuilt Austria's institutions and sense of national identity during the occupation. With the death of Stalin in March 1953 and evidence of a Kremlin leadership struggle, the Austrians took the initiative to approach the Soviet government and propose military neutrality. Molotov told the Austrians that a declaration of neutrality was mere words.[49] The Western powers were not much more enthusiastic, especially at first. The Chairman of the Joint Chiefs of Staff, Arthur Radford, privately expressed concern about the strategic implications of signing any treaty that would make Austria a neutral state—especially if neutrality precluded the use of Austrian territory by the newly established North Atlantic Treaty Organization.[50] Meanwhile, to the dismay of Pentagon analysts, the British and the French confided that they could no longer bear the economic burden of the occupation and would have to withdraw two-thirds of their troops even without a treaty.[51]

Meanwhile Soviet policy was moving in the opposite direction, toward long-term occupation. At the Berlin Conference of Foreign Ministers, January–February 1954, Soviet Foreign Minister Molotov insisted that allied troops remain in Austria until a German peace treaty was signed. In other words, with or without an Austrian

---

Suez, and Decolonization (London: I.B. Taurus, 2006), especially chapter 3, "The Berlin Congo Conference and the (non-) Partition of Africa, 1884–85," 112–114; Littell, *Neutralization of States*, 144–151; and Wicker, *Neutralization*, 33–36.

[48] Gunter Bischof, *Austria in the First Cold War, 1945–55: The Leverage of the Weak* (New York: Palgrave Macmillan, 1999).

[49] US Department of State, Office of Intelligence Research, Report no. 6403, "Austria Attempts Independent Foreign Policy," August 31, 1953, and State Department Memorandum (from R. B. Knight to Mr. Merchant and Mr. MacArthur), July 9, 1953, R.G. 59, 763.00/6-953; both read in the Diplomatic Documents Division, US National Archives, Washington, D.C.

[50] Memorandum from Arthur Radford, chairman of the US Joint Chiefs of Staff, to the Secretary of Defense, October 9, 1953, R.G. 330, Records of the Office of the Secretary of Defense, Modern Military Records Division, NA.

[51] Memorandum from Vice Admiral A.C. Davis, deputy US representative to the Standing Group of the North Atlantic Military Committee, to the Chairman of the Joint Chiefs of Staff, September 9, 1953, and memorandum from the JCS to the Secretary of Defense, September 11, 1953; both in Records of the Office of the Secretary of Defense, Modern Military Records Division, NA.

treaty, the Red Army would stay in Austria until the fate of Germany was settled to Soviet satisfaction. The proposal was unacceptable to the Western powers as well as to the Austrians, so the four-power talks collapsed again. For the remainder of 1954, Austria's fate was eclipsed by an international fixation on West German rearmament. The Soviet Union warned repeatedly that the fates of Germany and Austria were intertwined; plans to rearm Germany would result in "new impediments for the final settlement of the Austrian question." The implication was that Moscow would partition Austria if West Germany were rearmed.[52] As the debate over West German rearmament continued into the early days of 1955, Austria's future looked bleak.

Yet in February 1955 Soviet policy suddenly changed, paving the way for the final agreement. In a February 8 speech before the Supreme Soviet, Molotov announced that the USSR might countenance an Austrian state treaty independent of a German peace treaty. Two months later, invited by Molotov, the Austrians sent another delegation to Moscow for bilateral discussions. There the Austrian government agreed to declare Austria a permanently neutral state, adhering to "neutrality after the Swiss model," following the signing of a treaty among the major powers and the withdrawal of foreign troops. In a few days the Austrians and the Russians settled all the outstanding disagreements.[53] The final treaty was much more favorable to the Austrians than the draft treaty had been. The Russians agreed, for instance, to drop limitations on the size of the Austrian army, and they accepted economic terms more liberal to Austria than any they had previously considered. Khrushchev, in a state of buoyant good humor, advised Austrian Chancellor Raab: "Follow my example and turn Communist . . . But if I really can't convince you then for God's sake stay as you are!"[54]

The decision to sign the Austrian State Treaty directly resulted from the failure of the Soviet government's efforts to use Austria as a bargaining chip against the rearmament of West Germany, and Soviet desire to see a neutral corridor on its western frontier from Finland and Sweden through Germany, Austria, and Switzerland down to Italy and Yugoslavia.[55] A vigorous Soviet attempt to improve relations with neutral or "uncommitted" states in Europe followed the signing of the accord, including a Soviet delegation's trip to Yugoslavia, the return of the Porkkala naval base to Finland, and an invitation to West German Chancellor Konrad Adenauer to visit Moscow. More importantly, Khrushchev anticipated that the new Soviet

---

[52] US Department of State, *The Austrian State Treaty: An Account of the Postwar Negotiations Together with the Text of the Treaty and Related Documents*, European and British Commonwealth Series 49 (Washington, DC: US Govt. Printing Office, 1957); and Sven Alard, *Russia and the Austrian State Treaty: A Case Study of Soviet Policy in Europe* (University Park: Pennsylvania State University Press, 1970), pp. 134–135.

[53] Interview with former Chancellor Bruno Kreisky, Vienna, December 2, 1983.

[54] Kurt Waldheim, *The Austrian Example*, trans. Ewald Osers (London: Weidenfeld & Nicolson, 1973), pp. 66–67.

[55] William B. Bader, *Austria between East and West, 1945–1955* (Stanford, CA: Stanford University Press, 1966), pp. 206–207; and Gerald Stourzh, "The Austrian State Treaty and the Origins of Austrian Neutrality," Part 1 of *Austria and Its Permanent Neutrality* (Vienna: Austrian Federal Ministry for Foreign Affairs, n.d.).

attitude toward neutrality would be favorably received in the developing world. By the end of 1955, Khrushchev and his followers had affected a dramatic demarche, including state visits to India, Burma and Afghanistan; flamboyant denunciations of Western "colonialism"; and offers of assistance to any underdeveloped Arab or Asian country.

After giving varying degrees of support over the years to the diplomatic effort, France, Britain, and the United States also reached consensus on terms both proposed and desired by the Austrian government. The Americans had worried that Austria's neutrality would tempt the West Germans, but Chancellor Konrad Adenauer gave US Secretary of State Dulles assurances to the contrary.[56] In short, there were no losers in the signing of the Austrian State Treaty. Permanent neutrality became a part of the Austrian Constitution on October 26, 1955, and that status continues today.

Of course, the Austrian case differs from the current situation in Afghanistan. Although the European state was under four-power occupation in the wake of the Second World War, it elected a strong central government three months after hostilities ended. The Austrian government played a key role in breaking the deadlock between the major powers, with leaders traveling to Moscow to negotiate with the Soviet government. They sought a permanently neutral status and by 1955 had developed a territorial army to defend their frontiers. On the other hand, there were serious disputes over Austria's southern border and considerable domestic unrest, including two attempted Communist coups. Without clever diplomacy and dogged persistence, Austria would have been partitioned rather than neutralized.

Laos, 1962

Like Austria, the neutralization of Laos had an impressive lineage of high-powered negotiations by smart diplomats; yet it was a failure before it even began. It is a cautionary tale about the pitfalls of neutralizing a peninsular territory, geographically unsuitable and ensnared in a neighbor's civil war.

In the wake of the defeat of French colonial forces at the battle of Dien Bien Phu, the 1954 Geneva Conference sought to end the war in Vietnam and establish peace in the Indochina peninsula. Being a French protectorate, Laos's future was already entangled with Vietnam's. The 1954 Geneva Conference participants (UK, US, USSR, France, PRC, North and South Vietnam, Cambodia, and Laos) divided Vietnam along the 17th parallel, affirmed the independence of Laos, mandated the withdrawal of Vietnamese troops, and called for democratic elections. Immediately upon his election, the Laotian Prime Minister declared the state's policy of "peace and neutrality," but at this point there was no external guarantee. By 1959, Laos was already infiltrated by the North Vietnamese (aligned with the Communist Pathet Lao) and aided by the United States (aligned with the Royal Lao Government). A Laotian civil war prevailed along the Eastern border, a dividing line that ran the entire length of the country.

---

[56] M.S. Handler, "Bonn Disavows Aim to be Neutral State," *New York Times*, 30 April 1955, 1.

In May 1961 the Second Geneva Conference began, including the participants of the first conference along with Canada, Poland, India, Burma, and Thailand. By now there were three warring factions within Laos: the Communist Pathet Lao, the centrist Laotian government, and the right-wing military anticommunists. The Second Geneva Conference produced an agreement formally neutralizing Laos, with thirteen states pledging to guarantee the status, and a tripartite Laotian government also officially committed to its own neutrality. According to the Geneva Accord (July 23 1962), the government of Laos agreed to not to participate in any alliances or allow "the establishment of any foreign military bases on Laotian territory, nor allow any country to use Laotian territory for military purposes or for the purposes of interference in the internal affairs of other countries . . . ," while the thirteen other signatories agreed to respect the neutrality and territorial integrity of Laos. The agreement contained no provision for consequences (other than consultation) in the event of violation. But it did establish an International Control Commission comprising Canada, India, and Poland, who were to supervise the observance of the ceasefire and Laotian neutrality.

In the long term, the neutralization of Laos had little chance to succeed. Although on paper it had the essential internal and external dimensions of a good neutralization accord, the Laotians were too weak to protect their own territorial integrity and the external actors never meant to do so. The Canadians, Poles and Indians could not enforce a status that was secretly being violated by their own allies and co-signatories. The North Vietnamese had already established the Ho Chi Minh trail, a robust supply line that was merely masked by the 1962 neutralization three years later. The United States then provided robust aid to the Hmong, an indigenous tribe living in the mountains along the long border with Vietnam, and from 1965–1973 dropped some two million tons of bombs on neutral Laotian territory. Even without the Vietnam War drawing it in, however, Laos's geographical position on the northwest portion of the Indo-Chinese peninsula would have doomed any neutralization effort. Although there have been various proposals through the years, including in Southeast Asia (Malaysian Proposal, 1970) and on the Korean Peninsula, there has never been a case of successful neutralization along a peninsula.

Although it did not end the fighting or result in long term protection for the state, the neutralization of Laos did accomplish key short- and medium-term aims for US policy. The agreement detached the country from the larger bipolar contest between the United States and the Soviet Union, sidestepping another proxy war there between the superpowers. Following the agreement, the Laotian Prime Minister, Souvanna Phouma, took a far more conciliatory approach toward the West. It also eliminated the possibility of US troop commitments in Laos, a policy option supported by some of President John F. Kennedy's advisors. And there were important domestic political benefits for President Kennedy, demonstrating his earnest desire to end the conflict and act as a peacemaker in the region. While the neutralization accord was a clear failure in the long term, it did yield valuable results and a measure of stability for a time. [57]

[57] I am indebted to Fredrik Logevall for these observations. See his *Choosing War: The Lost Chance for Peace and the Escalation of War in Vietnam* (Berkeley: University of California Press, 2001), p. 41.

This case has both similarities and differences with the situation in Afghanistan. Similarities include the presence of an internal civil war fed by the ideology of its neighboring state, a weak central government, and the powerful interests of combatants in a neighboring conflict that easily overwhelmed any legal or moral commitment to respect Laotian neutrality. Neutralization accords cannot create a confluence of interests that does not exist. On the other hand, there are key differences between the Laotian and Afghan cases. The geography of Laos is narrow, landlocked, mountainous, accessible, and difficult to defend, and the inhabitants lacked a tradition of territorial defense in any case. Neutral Laotian territory provided a key protected logistical pathway for supplying the insurgency in Vietnam. Afghanistan, although it provides important strategic depth vis-à-vis Pakistan and India, is not the direct access point for the conflict between its regional neighbors. And the Afghans have a strong tradition of successfully repelling foreigners; indeed, it is one of the few things that have united them in the past.

Turkmenistan, 1995

Turkmenistan, a highly autocratic republic of the Soviet Union, declared its independence in 1991 and continued single-party rule into the post-Soviet era. It is one of the world's most repressive countries.[58] The state, which is mainly flat desert, borders the Caspian Sea and has important oil and natural gas reserves. Its national army acts as a territorial defense force and is forbidden to operate outside the borders of the country. In 1995, the government asked the UN General Assembly to pass a resolution recognizing Turkmenistan's permanently neutral status, and the government then enshrined that status in the national constitution. The resolution was cosponsored by major powers including the United States, Russia, Iran, Pakistan, and Turkey, but there was no enforceable guarantee. With a vague collective external endorsement, the neutralization accord parallels Luxembourg's 1867 neutralization and has yet to be seriously tested.

BUILDING A THEORY OF NEUTRALIZATION

The foregoing provides an overview of neutralization attempts (summarized in Table 13.1). Comparative analysis highlights the following:

1. **Key Geographic Features:** There has never been a successful neutralization along a peninsula, and flat areas such as coastal plains or open lowlands are also unpromising. Landlocked countries with mountainous features are well suited for neutralization, a concept heavily dependent upon traditional geopolitical factors.

---

[58] Jim Nichol, "Central Asia: Regional Developments and Implications for US Interests," CRS Report for Congress #RL33458, January 9, 2013, p. 31.

2. **Contested Borders:** The existence of a border dispute in the territory of the state does not reduce the likelihood of successful neutralization, especially because the negotiations often provide a forum for their resolution. Neutralized countries or territories with contested borders include Switzerland, Moresnet, Belgium, Upper Savoy, Austria, and Laos. The neutralization of Switzerland included ambiguity about the sovereign status of neighboring provinces such as Upper Savoy (also neutralized), where the Swiss could send troops to protect their own neutrality. Belgium's borders were disputed for years after the neutralization. Although the great powers agreed that the main outlines of Austria would be the pre-*Anschluss* territory, Yugoslav partisans engaged in violent incursions in the south; those claims were not resolved until 1949. The Soviet delegation refused to sign an Austrian treaty until the port of Trieste was finally divided between Italy and Yugoslavia in 1954. The only case in which there was no attempt to clarify the status of disputed borders was Laos—also the only case to quickly fail.

3. **History of Domestic Conflict:** There is no apparent relationship between domestic conflict and whether or not neutralization succeeded. This counterintuitive finding is clearly born out by comparative examination of the thirteen cases presented here. Switzerland's history of civil war is virtually unparalleled in the history of modern Europe. Indeed, the Swiss decision to become a neutral state was elemental to its emergence and survival as a political entity. With the revolution to secede from Holland, Belgium's unrest was a key reason for neutralizing it, in order to contain the revolutionary contagion. Austria's domestic unrest in the aftermath of the Second World War was in part a result of foreign occupation and the desperate economic circumstances of the domestic population; however, it included two attempted coups and serious border skirmishes in the south. States or territories without domestic conflict included Moresnet, Luxembourg, Cracow, Malta, and Congo—all failures.

4. **Economic Value to the Region:** High economic value to the surrounding region is a necessary but not sufficient condition for successful neutralization. There is no case of successful neutralization in the absence of economic assets of interest to the neighbors, especially control of key trade routes. The only example of a successfully neutralized territory in the *absence* of commercial value was Upper Savoy, which had proximity to key mountain passes.

5. **Enforceable Guarantee:** Neutralization accords formally recognize stalemates between major powers and all those with the ability to intervene must acquiesce. Acquiescence to the status quo often follows costly and unsuccessful attempts to alter it unilaterally. Napoleon's France tried fruitlessly to conquer Switzerland. The Soviet Union tried and failed to execute two communist overthrows in eastern Austria. If any party holds out hopes of unilateral victory, the agreement will fail. The neutralizations of Belgium and Luxembourg yielded decades of stability but failed when Germany invaded. Related to this, the major powers must commit to an enforceable guarantee, meaning that they police each other if there is a violation of the state's neutrality. Agreeing to "respect" the neutrality of the state is not sufficient: the individual commitment to respect the neutrality of the Congo basin failed, as did the agreement to "consult" if Laos's neutrality was violated. It remains to be seen whether the 1995 UN recognition of Turkmenistan's neutrality will suffice.

6. **Strong Defenses:** There must be international agreement about the defensive military posture of the state, and the neutralized state must be able to fulfill its commitments. Foreign actors must not be able to use the neutralized state's territory for their own military purposes. Will the state be armed or unarmed? Will there be limits on armaments? This aspect has evolved in the past two centuries away from the emphasis upon external military guarantors toward stronger emphasis on internal territorial defenses. A key reason for the eventual failures in Belgium and Luxembourg was the demilitarization of both territories. As in the case of Laos, belligerent foreign powers can drag the neutralized state unwillingly into a conflict even if intervention occurs without permission. All parties wanted both Switzerland and Austria armed. Switzerland had a storied and unparalleled tradition of territorial defense, which was a deterrent to potential meddlers for centuries. Austria stayed out of military alliances (most notably NATO) and developed a territorial army to deter the actions of any stronger power.

7. **Indigenous Support:** The state and its people must be dedicated to their own permanent neutrality. The concept of neutralization has evolved along with modern international law and the nation-state itself. It has shifted emphasis over the centuries, especially the relative importance of the external versus the internal dimensions. The degree to which the neutralized state's inhabitants accept and, better yet, initiate the accord is more important than the strength, nature, and form of the external guarantee. The neutralization must be initiated by the state in question, as was the case in Austria and Switzerland, rather than imposed by external powers, as in the Belgian Congo and Cracow. Austria had a provisional national government from the earliest months of the postwar occupation, and that leadership steadily gained strength, helped by the Western powers (especially the United States). But a centralized form of government is not critical: Switzerland's loose federation of cantons fought for control over the mountainous territory for centuries, organically developing a tradition of neutrality as a way to keep the state from breaking apart. National identity is more important than type of government. With the exception of the 1962 neutralization of Laos, every example of failure has been a case of imposed or reluctantly accepted neutrality, without the support of the government and its people. The role of the state has gradually overshadowed that of its guarantors.

AFGHANISTAN AS A CASE STUDY

Historical background

Seeing the Afghans merely as victims of neighborly aggression is ahistorical and counterproductive. Had Afghan leaders not been wily diplomats and warriors, independent Afghanistan would have disappeared long ago.

In the nineteenth century, the state was caught in the expansion of European empires, with the Russians pushing their boundaries southward into Central Asia and the British reaching northward from India. The British, anxious to protect against tsarist encroachment into British India, twice invaded Afghanistan (1839–1842 and 1878–1879) and twice found themselves forced by fierce local resistance to withdraw. Although they were repulsed, after the second Anglo-Afghan war the British gained the right to occupy the Khyber Pass and to control Afghan foreign policy. To counter British influence, the Afghans approached the Russians and, through complicated diplomatic maneuvers, successfully played one power against the other while protecting the autonomy of the state. Eventually the imperial powers colluded; in 1907, they entered into an entente, which among other things formally established Afghanistan as a buffer state between the two empires and again ceded Afghanistan's foreign policy to the British. The Afghans had no say in the accord, but gradually accepted it and found satisfaction in the preservation of their independence.

Independence from outside control was more important in Afghanistan's emergence as a state than was internal unity. The martial tradition of the Afghan tribes was directed against not only outside invaders but also those attempting to impose centralized rule. Apart from the campaigns against the British, much of nineteenth-century Afghanistan was characterized by civil struggle between rival tribal leaders, vying for local control with varying sources of power and authority. The only focus of legitimate national authority was the monarchy, and that was weak: the title of amir passed from ruler to ruler, as leaders were overthrown, murdered, or militarily defeated.

Afghanistan's policy of neutrality and nonalignment between rival international powers was a rallying point for nationhood. Despite strong pressure from the Germans and domestic agitation in favor of alliance with the Turks, Afghanistan remained neutral in both world wars. Between the wars, the Afghans took advantage of the war-weariness of the British and tried to incite the Muslims of India to revolt. In 1919, looking for both a diversion from internal strife and potential political gains, the Afghan Amir, Amanullah, proclaimed a religious war, called upon the tribes, and began to invade British India (now Pakistan). But Afghan forces were repulsed by a larger and more technologically advanced British force, relying upon Royal Air Force raids against Kabul. The two sides signed a peace treaty in August 1919 that included reaffirmation of the Durand Line. But the British also stopped paying the Afghan government an annual subsidy, and the Afghans regained control of their own foreign policy. This is arguably when Afghanistan emerged as a truly independent state. Again to offset the British, the Afghans turned to the Russians, concluding treaties of friendship and nonaggression with the Bolshevik regime. This pattern of playing one power against the other is ingrained in Afghan statecraft, which, although not always successful in fending off invasions, has been neither passive nor naive.

After the 1947 partition of India and British withdrawal, the Afghan government's rivalry was transferred to Pakistan. Two years later, in 1949, Kabul and Karachi began a border dispute that continues today. The crux of the dispute is the status of the peoples of the Pashtun tribes who were divided from Afghanistan by the British-drawn Durand Line. For more than fifty years, Afghanistan pursued a policy of trying to reclaim the Pashtun areas first from the British and then from the Pakistanis.

Meanwhile, the Afghan elite sought aid and loans for the economic development of the country. With the British no longer a major factor in the region (and no longer providing a lucrative subsidy), the government approached the United States for aid, receiving some $524 million between 1949 and 1979.[59] Following their foreign policy tradition, the Afghans openly tried to gain leverage by playing the United States off the Soviet Union, just as they had for decades balanced the Russians off against the British. But this time the policy failed; unlike the British, American policymakers considered Afghanistan distant and unimportant.

By the mid-1950s, the United States had decided to arm Afghanistan's rival, Pakistan, and to encourage participation in anticommunist alliances. The Eisenhower administration aligned itself with the position that the Durand Line was a fixed border, thus opposing Afghan claims and alienating the leadership. The Afghan government turned increasingly to the Soviet Union. Between 1954 and 1978, Afghanistan slowly came under Soviet influence, receiving more than twice the aid received from the United States (c. $1.3m), and approximately the same amount again in Soviet military aid. Numerous other Soviet-Afghan agreements, such as those providing for the training of Afghan military personnel in the Soviet Union, followed.[60]

By walking a fine line between rival powers in the region for centuries, Afghanistan succeeded in its primary aim: independence. This pattern abruptly ended in 1973 with the overthrow of the monarchy, which increased still further the country's vulnerability to external influences. President Mohammed Daoud's rise to power signaled the end of a short-lived flirtation with constitutional monarchy and resulted in the exile of the king. Military power had been directly responsible for bringing Daoud to power, but the disaffected social and economic forces that had facilitated the coup began to undermine his government almost as soon as it was established.

Again the answer was to try to balance the interests of neighboring powers off each other. In foreign affairs, Daoud began to move the country away from its Russian oriented policy and search for new sources of foreign support, accepting aid from the Shah of Iran, seeking more aid from the United States, travelling to India, Yugoslavia, Egypt, Saudi Arabia, and even improving relations with Pakistan. None of this was viewed favorably in Moscow. Daoud was attempting to reduce Afghanistan's dependence upon the Soviet Union at a time when the superpower to the north was growing stronger than ever before, the United States and Britain had withdrawn, and there was no equivalent power in the region to offset that strength.[61]

Meanwhile, in the mid-1970s, the Soviet Union began a serious effort to provide support to the Afghan communists, who were split between rival Khalq and Parcham factions. When a communist coup occurred in April 1978, Nur Mohammed Taraki became president and prime minister, and Hafizullah Amin became foreign minister. Both were in the Khalq faction of the Afghan communist party, the more ideologically pure and less pro-Soviet faction. Amin, a military

---

[59] Henry S. Bradsher, *Afghanistan and the Soviet Union*, 2nd edition (Durham, NC: Duke University Press, 1985), p. 24.

[60] Bradsher, *Afghanistan*, 24–25.

[61] US Department of Defense, "The Declassified Documents 1979 Collection" (Washington, DC: US Government Printing Office, 1979), no. 33A; quoted and cited by Bradsher, 60–67.

strongman, had been largely responsible for organizing the coup. His control of the military and the secret police gave him a formidable base for consolidating his internal power. Seven months after the coup, Taraki had become little more than a figurehead, with Amin wielding most of the power within Afghanistan. In Soviet eyes, Taraki was a benign, malleable Marxist, but Amin clashed repeatedly with Moscow. In September 1979, a Soviet plot to kill Amin failed: Taraki was killed instead and Amin rose to the Presidency.

Amin was a nationalistic, strong-willed leader, determined to resist Soviet control even as he pressured the Russians to provide more aid to the faltering communist regime. Domestically, he attempted widespread modernization, including land reform and a literacy campaign that defied Islamic traditions. He was ruthless and cruel, ordering the execution of thousands of his political opponents. These actions alienated much of the population and eliminated whatever chance there might have been to gain broad support for the Kabul regime. With the fall of the shah and the radicalization of neighboring Iran, Soviet leaders were doubly determined to remove Amin so as to stabilize the fledgling communist state and prevent the spread of Islamist extremism on their border. In December 1979, Soviet troops invaded. Soviet leaders installed Babrak Karmal, a leader from the Parcham faction of the Afghan Communist Party who was much more amenable to their interests, and began an occupation and war against the Mujahideen resistance force that ended in the deaths of some 13,833 Soviet troops (469,685 sick or wounded), the defeat of the communist government, the withdrawal of Soviet forces in 1989, and the end of the Soviet Union itself a few years after that.[62]

The story of the rise of the mujahideen during the 1990s, the 9/11 attacks on the United States, and the 2001 invasion is well known. Parallels with the Soviet military experience are thin: the initial cause of the invasion, the multinational nature of the ISAF force, and the much greater amount of US aid are all sharp contrasts. But the tradition of playing major powers against one another persists, with US troops targeted by insurgents supported by Pakistan and Iran. The violent interplay between major powers, and Kabul's active role in the geopolitical drama, are nothing new.

Neutralization for Afghanistan?

While it is obviously not Switzerland or Austria, Afghanistan does meet most of the seven criteria for successful neutralization. The first three are straightforward. Geographically Afghanistan is mountainous and landlocked. While the state is not inclined toward centralized government, neither was Switzerland. ISAF's well-meaning efforts to encourage Afghan centralization are reminiscent of Napoleon's folly two centuries earlier: it is possible that the optimal government for twenty-first

---

[62] Casualty figures from Lester R. Grau, *The Bear Went over the Mountain: Soviet Combat Tactics in Afghanistan*, translated from the original Russian version, (Moscow: Frunze Academy, 1991) (London: Frank Cass, 1998), xix, citing the manuscript of Aledsandr Lyakhovskiy, *Tragediya I doblest' Afghan* [The Tragedy and Valor of the Afghan Veterans], (Moscow: Iskona, 1995).

century Afghanistan is a loosely aligned confederation. Second, the borders of Afghanistan are clear, with the important exception of the Durand Line. But the cases of Switzerland, Belgium, and Austria demonstrate that this is not an insurmountable obstacle. Establishing a process for finalizing the borders during the framework negotiations would be crucial. Third, the notorious record of domestic conflict in Afghanistan, following the Soviet invasion of 1979 and now with the resurgence of the Taliban, is not a disqualifier. Neutralization could help the inhabitants coalesce around the common aim of protecting Afghan territory against foreign interveners instead of killing fellow Afghans.

Afghanistan has important economic value to the region—the fourth criterion. Drug trafficking and illicit trade are serious concerns; however, strengthening border controls and developing the Afghan security forces could enhance state control at the expense of nonstate actors and warlords. The Chinese are especially motivated to protect the investments they have made in Afghan minerals and resources, and the Iranians, whose population suffers from the highest levels of drug addiction in the world,[63] would support Afghan efforts to reduce the flow of heroin. Responsibly developing the resources and mineral wealth of Afghanistan would serve the entire region and contribute to the long-term stability and development of the country, as well as its neighbors.

Fifth, the exact nature of the guarantee would be important. Regional actors share the need for Afghan stability but have conflicting national agendas. Those with an interest in the future of the state include Pakistan, India, China, Iran, Saudi Arabia, and Russia, along with the United States and possibly NATO. Neighbors such as Uzbekistan, Turkmenistan, and Tajikistan might play a role, although Austria's neutralization demonstrates that contiguous states need not be guarantors. China's role could be crucial, given its ties to Pakistan, its concerns about Uighur radicalization, its interest in avoiding a destabilizing India-Pakistan nuclear conflict, and its desire to avoid a permanent American military presence on its border. Although such ambitious regional diplomacy would present challenges, the neighbors share a strong common interest in a stable Afghan government and preventing the return of a radical Sunni government.

Pakistan's own internal problems have reduced enthusiasm for another Taliban-ruled neighboring state, as well. Preventing radical spillover and further unrest among Pakistani Pashtuns are key objectives in Islamabad. Relatedly, the Pakistan military fears the possibility of Indian influence in Afghanistan, stoking up Pashtun nationalism on the Pakistani side of the border and Baluch nationalism in Baluchistan. A stable, neutralized Afghanistan, removed from Indian involvement (or that of any other state), would serve Pakistan's interests, especially if the accord resulted, at least eventually, in recognition of the Durand line. This is likewise the case with respect to Iran. Judging by Iran's behavior in the immediate aftermath of 9/11, it could theoretically play a constructive role. Iran does not want a radicalized Sunni regime on its border, and it has a strong interest

---

[63] Karl Vick, "Opiates of the Iranian People; Despair Drives World's Highest Addiction Rate," *The Washington Post*, September 23, 2005.

in protecting trade routes through Afghanistan. Neutralization could return the loosely aligned Afghan provinces to their traditional focus upon controlling local trade routes and ensuring local security. Afghanistan might return to a potpourri of types of governance in the country loosely aligned with Kabul but empowered to provide local security against outsiders. Iranian efforts to encourage Shia identity in Afghanistan would be less threatening if the state were stable and neutralized.

Sixth, the level and quality of defenses would be very important, as only a well-armed Afghanistan could defend itself against both outside intervention and internal unrest. The intense US effort to develop the Afghan national army and police is well targeted to meet this need. During the height of its occupation, the United States built Afghanistan a counterinsurgency army; however, the Afghan Ministry of Defense, arguing that insurgents mainly target western forces, preferred to transition to a conventional army focusing particularly on the threats from Pakistan and Iran. The Afghans would like to be able to control their own air space, with radar and artillery capabilities that could respond to threats across the border. Under a multilateral framework agreement, the United States and NATO could beef up Afghanistan's defensive forces, including increased capabilities to monitor incursions using reconnaissance drones and night-vision capabilities. That kind of territorial army would perfectly suit a neutralized state.

Neutralization accords require the withdrawal of foreign forces, at least eventually, and the state's eventual assumption of responsibility for military control of its own territory. Such an outcome could be approached in phases, with the United States engaging in training Afghan security forces for their role as a territorial army and helping to monitor Afghan territory in the short or medium term. The process of withdrawal need not be precipitous. The 5,500 American troops projected to be deployed to Afghanistan for some time could play the role of garrison force protecting Kabul in the near term. Also the United States will want to retain its counterterrorism mission in Afghanistan, as well as the capability to spy on Pakistan, Iran, and China. Intelligence cooperation with a neutral government is nothing new: Austria played a vital role in this regard during the Cold War.

An Afghanistan government determined to hew to its own permanent neutrality, defensively armed and supported by a multilateral accord among the neighboring powers, would be stronger and more aligned with American interests than a government that quickly fell under Pakistan's control or influence—an outcome that would only magnify the influence of the Taliban. In this respect, moves by the recently-elected Ashraf Ghani government to draw closer to the Pakistan government are worrisome steps in the wrong direction.

Which leads to the final requirement: indigenous support. The state must be dedicated to its own permanent neutrality. Successful neutralization of Afghanistan would require both the initiative and active involvement of the Afghan people, either through their government in Kabul or through a federated association of more local provincial leaders (parallel to the Swiss cantons). The Afghans themselves would have to pursue a declaration of permanent neutrality, a move that would serve Afghanistan's broader long-term national interests but could be hard to achieve, given domestic disunity. (Here parallels with Laos come to mind.) Admittedly Afghan elites may prefer to continue to enrich themselves by cutting deals with external powers. Monitoring and enforcing such an agreement would be a challenge. It would require a means of verifying noninterference from outside powers, and spoilers—both external and internal to Afghan territory—could compromise success and spur further intervention. But the key to success would be to make this concept an Afghan initiative.

Alternative pathways for Afghanistan

There is no denying that neutralization is challenging and could fail. So, what are the alternatives? Apart from neutralization, there are four: partition, satellite status, military occupation, or civil war.

Partition

Senior US officials such as Ambassador Robert Blackwill have argued that partition is the only feasible solution for post-ISAF Afghanistan, ceding the south and east to the Taliban and concentrating on protecting the non-Pashtun areas in the north and west.[64] But partition is an unpromising means to end the conflict in Afghanistan, not least because the Afghans do not want it. The country has experienced partition twice before, with poor results. The British first brought about *de jure* partition during the late nineteenth century, when they drew the Durand line between Afghanistan and British India. This did not reduce conflict in subsequent decades.[65] Almost a century later, following the Soviet retreat, Afghanistan entered a period of civil war that led to a division between vast Taliban-controlled Pashtun-dominated areas in the south, center, and west and smaller United Front areas in the north and east. That de facto partition enabled Al–Qaeda to use Afghan territory as a launching pad for the September 2001 attacks against the United States. In short, Afghanistan is a textbook case of a country that did not experience greater stability and reduced civil conflict following its past partition, and there is no reason to believe that it will do so in the future.[66]

Satellite status

Afghanistan can be an economic and military satellite of the United States or another major power. Some point to the large amounts of foreign aid provided by one major power—first the British, then the Soviets, and finally the United

---

[64] Robert D. Blackwill, "Plan B in Afghanistan: Why De Facto Partition Is the Least Bad Option," *Foreign Affairs* 90, no. 1 (2011): 42–50.

[65] Running directly through Pashtun-dominated territory, the partition did not include separation of ethnic groups.

[66] On whether partition ends civil wars, see Carter Johnson, "Partitioning to Peace: Sovereignty, Demography, and Ethnic Civil Wars," *International Security* 32, no. 4 (Spring 2008): 140–180;

States—as stabilizing factors throughout the twentieth century. But clientelism has been a key source of weakness in the past. After losing British subsidies in the 1920s, Afghan elites followed a conscious policy of seeking funds from powerful patrons, becoming so dependent on foreign aid that by 1973, two-thirds of Afghanistan's annual revenue came from foreign loans and grants.[67] This dependency contributed to weak governance and endemic corruption, as successive regimes relied upon external patronage and their own control of the aid. The ability to tax its citizens declined: direct taxation brought in the bulk of government revenue in the 1920s, thirty percent in the 1950s, and less than one percent in the 1970s.[68] Foreign aid was effective in securing and enriching government elites, less so building the indigenous institutions required to strengthen state governance.[69] Economic dependency upon a single major power would serve neither Afghan interests nor those of the United States.

Military occupation

Afghanistan has been occupied by the Russians, the British, and now (mainly) the Americans. Potential candidates for future military occupation include Pakistan, Iran, and China. Pakistan's paranoia about potential Indian military activities at their back door could prompt it to send troops across the border. Likewise, in the absence of effective Afghan security, China and Iran will be tempted to control the areas nearest to them—as is already happening to some degree. But this is a counterproductive strategy for the entire region, not to mention the United States. Historically military occupation has neither reduced the level of conflict in the country nor facilitated the building of a strong, stable, and prosperous state within a vibrant region.

Civil war

Civil war is the most likely outcome of continuing on the current path. Recent attempts to transport Afghanistan from its deeply embedded tribal and cultural roots to a modern centralized democratic government ignored the five-hundred-year consolidation needed by other ethnically complex nation-states. Endemic

Michael C. Horowitz, Alex Weisiger, and Carter Johnson, "Correspondence: The Limits to Partition," *International Security* 33, No. 4 (Spring 2009): 203–210; and Nicholas Sambanis and Jonah Schulhofer-Wohl, "What's in a Line?: Is Partition a Solution to Civil War?" *International Security* 34, no. 2 (2009): 82–118.

[67] Thomas Barfield, *Afghanistan: A Cultural and Political History* (Princeton, NJ: Princeton University Press, 2010), pp. 204–205; and Maxwell J. Fry, *The Afghan Economy: Money, Finance, and the Critical Constraints to Economic Development* (Leiden, The Netherlands: Brill, 1974), pp. 158–160.

[68] Fry, *The Afghan Economy*, 155 and 183–186, cited by Barfield, *Afghanistan: A Cultural and Political History*, 205.

[69] Barnett Rubin, *The Fragmentation of Afghanistan: State Formation and Collapse in the International System* (New Haven, CT: Yale University Press, 1995).

factionalism, sectarianism, corruption, and weak institutions will continue in the short or medium term. ISAF made important strides, especially with the Afghan National Army; but outside powers cannot impose long-term order and unity any more than Napoleon could crush the independent-minded Swiss into a centralized nation-state. Afghanistan is a semifeudal, developing state that must be built indigenously, with economic support but without further political and military meddling. Yet the current trajectory is for neighboring powers to align themselves with internal factions within Afghanistan, potentially tearing the country apart. In this regard, the Taliban's September 2015 capture of northern Afghan city of Kunduz, after five months of fighting Afghan security forces, was the first time the Taliban had taken control of a major city since 2001. If the current trajectory continues, the Taliban will grow in strength, forcing Afghanistan to again become a potential sanctuary for violent, anti-American nonstate actors such as the Islamic State and Al-Qaeda.

Of these various possibilities, Afghanistan's neutralization is the best available long-term option for American interests. It is the only one that would enable Afghanistan to maintain its independence and sovereignty for any period of time, and the most likely to lead to a stable state that is not a threat to itself or others.

CONCLUSION

Neutralization is not a panacea, but it is the only promising way forward for protecting both American interests and Afghan stability. Neutralization poses few costs and has high potential payoff for the United States and all the other actors should it succeed. It would commit major powers such as China, Russia, and Iran to the stability and viability of the state, offsetting Pakistan's growing influence; another radical Sunni Islamist regime would threaten them all. The current trajectory toward renewed internal conflict in Afghanistan is clear: the emergence of a small ISIS-aligned force in Afghanistan and its August 2015 declaration of war against the Afghan Taliban provides insight into the ongoing struggle between local and international radical forces. Oddly, it is more in American interests to support the Afghan government's negotiations with the Afghan Taliban than to increase the incentives for the latter to align with external groups. The current pathway could drive nationalists and global Islamists together, repeating the tired pattern of instability in a region that now includes two nuclear powers, a dangerous radical ideology, and unprecedented potential for power projection.

After fourteen years of war, the American people are no longer willing to spend the lives and treasure needed to stabilize Afghanistan with large numbers of US troops. Neutralization could change the strategic matrix in the region, buying time and staving off the regional and domestic instability that currently looms. Like Belgium, Afghanistan's neutralization need not succeed over the long term to be beneficial: even a short- or medium-term respite could bring important gains.[70]

---

[70] On how to implement a neutralization agreement, see Audrey Kurth Cronin, "Thinking Long on Afghanistan: Could It Be Neutralized?" *The Washington Quarterly* 36, no. 1 (Winter 2012–2013): 55–72.

Neutralization does not necessarily guarantee peace within a state. Instead, it quarantines the state from outside interference so that internal conflicts are not exacerbated and made contagious to the region. It contains the problem. Some will argue that the presence of nonstate actors and powerful Taliban, Haqqani network, and other warring factions within Afghanistan make neutralization impossible. In fact, the opposite is true: only a pact of noninterference and verification can remove Afghanistan from an endless cycle of civil war at home and potential projection of violence abroad. In other words, both Afghanistan and the United States will be much better off with a neutralization agreement than without it.

CONCLUSION

Jeremi Suri and Benjamin Valentino

The contributors to this volume have advanced different perspectives on the challenges facing the United States in crafting a sustainable national security policy. They have offered diverse recommendations about how the United States can most effectively respond to those challenges. Nevertheless, our contributors are unanimous in one conclusion: The United States has reached a strategic crossroads. The extraordinary domestic and international transformations that have occurred in the last decade now demand a similarly profound transformation in our thinking, our policies, and our institutions. The need for such a reevaluation should have been evident years ago, but the scholarship presented in the volume strongly suggests that change can no longer wait.

Our contributors also agree that the prognosis for the future is neither irreversible decline nor a return to America's previous ascendancy, but something in between. To master the more uncertain, fragmented, and challenging international environment, however, American policymakers will have to make some hard choices. First, American leaders will have to reexamine the resources and institutions that underpin the United States' diplomacy, strategy, and military affairs. Building on lessons from previous eras of upheaval in American national security, the contributors to this volume have proposed a variety of ways to recalibrate America's resources and institutions to serve contemporary policy needs better. Second, American leaders must critically reexamine the United States' foreign commitments and assess whether America's complex web of military alliances and partnerships, many of which were formed seventy years ago, still serve the nation's interests today, or whether some of these commitments should be reformed or even discontinued. Many of these commitments cost little on a daily basis, and their costs are largely hidden from public view. Those characteristics have made it easy to carry them forward year after year, even as the costs—financial and strategic—accumulate. Like the "off-balance-sheet" risks that ultimately bankrupted several of America's largest banking institutions during the financial crisis of 2007–2008, the real price of these commitments may only be recognized in times of emergency. Drawing on a close examination of various legacy commitments, the contributors offer a number of suggestions for refocusing American resources.

Underpinning the need to reevaluate American resources, institutions, and commitments is the need to reassess our understanding of American power. Traditional American definitions of power are too narrow and are often premised on a time horizon that is too short. The authors of this book offer numerous insights on how

American leaders should rethink national power and its implementation for greater long-term sustainability. Effective power, in historical and contemporary terms, is affordable, effective, and even efficient. The chapters speak to these qualities and the need to enhance them in current American policy.

KEY FINDINGS AND THEMES

Six key findings and themes emerge from the contributions to this volume. First, nearly all of the authors emphasize the need to recognize explicitly the difficult tradeoffs the United States now faces in crafting a sustainable national security policy. Even at the height of its power, the United States lacked the resources, capabilities, and attention to respond to every potential threat in its environment. The need for prioritization is even more salient today in an era of constrained resources and globalized interests. Focusing our efforts on one threat or region, therefore, will inevitably come at the expense of others. Cindy Williams's contribution reveals most directly, for example, the more dollars the United States devotes to pay and benefits for military and civilian personnel and military retirees, the less it will have for force modernization and training. Jennifer Lind observes that the more military and political resources the United States dedicates to Asian alliances or to counter the threat of a rising China, the less it can use in Europe to contain a resurgent Russia or in the Middle East to confront the threat of terrorist groups like ISIS. As Joshua Busby argues, efforts to contain China militarily and politically run counter to America's strong interests in working with China to address climate change. Making these choices will be difficult, and our contributors do not all agree on which choices will be best for American security. One of the central functions of a national security strategy is to weigh these kinds of competing priorities and prune the burgeoning list of claims on America's resources that have rendered the nation's current strategy unsustainable. Effective strategy turns on the discipline to observe limits.

Second, the contributors agree that even those aspects of American national security that should remain relatively unchanged require new justification in light of the dramatically changed strategic environment facing the United States. William Wohlforth, for example, concludes that the United States should "muddle through" with its current commitments to NATO, but he argues that the alliance has transitioned from its original role as a defensive organization to an institutional and military vehicle for US global leadership. Recognizing this new role for the alliance is critical, however, because doing so should influence America's position on contemporary policy questions such as the further enlargement of NATO and the increasing demands for "out of area" interventions—neither of which Wohlforth believes make sense for the United States today.

Third, although our contributors agree that a clearly articulated strategy is necessary for the United States to achieve sustainable security, they also agree that we must move beyond the "one-size-fits-all" approach to foreign policy that has sometimes characterized previous grand strategic debates. America's strategic environment is simply too complex to make either global retrenchment or global engagement the optimal choice. As Daniel Byman and Sara Bjerg Moller demonstrate in their analysis of the Middle East, America's diverse interests in the region argue for increasing ties with some partner states, and curtailing them with others.

The need to avoid a one-size-fits-all approach also applies to the way the United States structures its interactions with other states. American leaders should think more creatively about the ways they exercise power and influence—using the full spectrum of capabilities and institutional arrangements. As Jennifer Lind writes, in Asia the United States need not face the stark choice between scrapping its existing alliances, which some argue have outlived their usefulness, or maintaining them in their current form. Instead, she argues, the United States should consider transforming these alliances from "terminals," which served the main function of protecting America's allies, into "hubs," which are designed to enhance America's ability to project power throughout East Asia.

Similarly, Audrey Kurth Cronin argues that the debate regarding American strategy toward Afghanistan must evolve beyond the unattractive options of immediate withdrawal or indefinite war. Rather she suggests the United States should work with other nations to "neutralize" Afghanistan. Under this arrangement, the government of Afghanistan would agree to remain neutral in the political and military disputes in South Asia, and external actors like India, Pakistan, Iran, Russia, and the United States would agree not to intervene in Afghanistan's internal affairs. Creative and carefully customized solutions such as these will allow the United States to maximize its influence, even in an era of decreasing resources.

Fourth, American foreign policy leaders must pay close attention to the essential domestic sources of power. Jonathan Kirshner and Jeremi Suri both elucidate the importance of managing financial and monetary markets by providing incentives for productive capital investments that ultimately serve consumer and security needs. Kirshner emphasizes intelligent financial regulations that protect a strong currency. Suri focuses on the institutional capacity for taxing citizens and attracting foreign capital at low cost. Managing currency, taxation, and capital markets needs more attention and calibration with foreign commitments, according to these authors. If the United States regulates and taxes intelligently, it will have more resources for its global aims.

Fifth, institutions matter more than policymakers often realize. The organizations that govern American representatives abroad must become more flexible, focused, and efficient to better match constrained resources with ambitious policy aims. John Hall argues that creating a culture of innovation within the armed services is crucial, particularly among military officers rising through the ranks. This requires more emphasis on free thinking, and even dissent, within military education and promotion boards. William Inboden observes that the national security decision-making process, frequently reformed, requires continual readjustment to ensure that presidents get the kinds of advice they need for the challenges of their time. The National Security Council (and its associated bodies) has often lacked creativity because it expends too much energy on turf battles and gives too little attention to integrating different perspectives into a coherent policy discussion among principals. The military, the NSC, and other US security organizations must learn to embrace change and controlled risk taking, rather than the slow-moving accumulation of claims on resources that have characterized past bureaucratic battles. Leaner institutions can be more effective and sustainable.

Sixth, and perhaps most fundamental, all of the chapters in this volume recognize that sustainability is a moving target. Yesterday's wise and efficient decisions can quickly become misguided and exorbitant in tomorrow's security environment. The geopolitics of the international system change faster than ever before, and the nation's security strategy must adjust faster to keep up. The deliberations and disciplined thinking that the chapters call for must occur continuously within the US government, and policymakers must be willing to rethink inherited positions and commitments with greater frequency. America must have institutional structures in place that provide incentives for the individuals entrusted with formulating and implementing American national security strategy to engage in this kind of continual reevaluation. Strategy is a process, and the chosen policy outcomes are neither foreordained nor permanent.

An ever-adjusting strategy is more likely to bring success than a traditional strategy, like containment, that becomes totemic, freezing American commitments. In recent decades, the United States has often chosen to adjust strategy by adding more—more foreign commitments, more weapons, and more spending. That approach multiplies the problems and the costs. A sustainable strategy will have to give up some old things to do new things; it will have to reduce its emphasis in some places as it increases its actions in others. Strategic wisdom requires tough choices, frankly addressed and implemented. This is where political will must accompany disciplined thought. Strategy, like war, is the extension of politics by other means.

FUTURE RESEARCH

The contributors to this volume have offered original perspectives on the future of American foreign policy and marshaled new evidence on the costs and benefits of America's most important foreign policy choices. Although this scholarship represents the beginning of a much longer debate, it also highlights key areas in need of further research. Several critical questions deserve more sustained attention from scholars in the years ahead.

Americans tend to assume that their democratic system and values naturally translate into international power. That is not necessarily the case. Often, as the chapters show, domestic American behaviors misdirect attention and resources from their most important needs abroad. Foreign actors understand the American system, and they frequently seek to exploit it for their own purposes. Therefore, scholars should give more attention to how democratic policymakers can better leverage the American economy, political system, and military to maximize national security. What are the best ways to conduct a democratic and strategic foreign policy? How should leaders redesign democratic institutions for a sustainable foreign policy? How should leaders acquire the necessary resources, and how should they educate the public about their policies?

Contributors to this volume have examined examples of American commitments to NATO, South Asia, East Asia, and the Middle East, but these analyses have only scratched the surface. Since the United States must evaluate its foreign commitments on a case-by-case basis, a systematic country-by-country inventory of all foreign commitments remains urgently necessary. Such an enterprise will require the work of historians and political scientists with deep regional expertise; it is not a task that any single scholar can undertake alone. It is, in fact, well suited to the kind of collaborative effort that produced this volume.

While the chapter authors have explored the direct costs and benefits of alliances to American security, further research is required to understand the indirect and non-security consequences of America's foreign commitments. The debate surrounding the value of these commitments involves more than just the important question about how efficiently our alliances provide security for the United States and its friends. Alliances offer other potential costs and benefits as well. Do America's alliances allow us to secure important economic concessions from our partners? Do they allow the United States to constrain allies from risky behaviors that could lead to conflict? Or, do American security guarantees generate a "moral hazard" that emboldens allies to initiate conflicts with more powerful neighbors, assuming US protection if risk taking provokes disaster? Do America's alliances generate anger or apprehension in regional powers like Russia, China, and Iran, making cooperation with them more difficult? Or do they dampen regions security dilemmas, reducing the risk of war? Does America's presence abroad deter or provoke nonstate challengers, especially terrorist groups like the Islamic State in Iraq and Syria (ISIS)?

The proposals in this volume to change the process and substance of American policymaking hinge on the ability of leaders to imagine a different world—one where the United States curtails some long-standing foreign commitments and establishes new ones; one where American resources are concentrated on fewer priorities, with greater attention to the balance between costs and benefits. Redesigning security policy in these terms requires a broader exploration of options and a more rigorous analysis of unintended outcomes than is standard in current policy deliberations, as the chapters in this volume show. Above all, policy planners will need to undertake a more systematic counterfactual analysis of likely results from changes in US policy—analysis more open to different judgments than the worst-case assumptions that accompany most assessments of commitment reform and military de-escalation, especially around lingering regional and terrorist crises.

Drawing on history and theory, several of the contributors suggest how more rigorous and open counterfactual analysis can be conducted. They point to the importance of interrogating assumptions, looking to alternative historical precedents, and applying strict cost accountings. Developing these and other methodologies further is a continuing task for scholars. It is indeed our job to expand the imagining of overworked policy-makers.

POLICY RECOMMENDATIONS

The scholars represented in this volume strongly agree that American foreign policy should result from deliberate choices about what is best for America and the world, rather than inertia or fear of the unknown. Unfortunately, the contributors also recognize that the American political system provides few incentives to conduct the thorough policy reevaluation that the United States sorely needs. If anything, current politics encourage tough talk and multiplying commitments to avoid the appearance of weakness or to cater to domestic and international interest groups, often with inadequate funding and limited preparations for negative consequences. We suggest three mechanisms that might help to generate the pressures necessary for fundamental policy change.

First, political leaders, scholars, and other advocates of reforming America's national security strategy must work harder to get the public actively involved in foreign policy debates. As Benjamin Valentino's chapter on public opinion shows, the American public places little pressure on elites to make the kinds of hard choices in foreign policy that all the contributors to this volume believe are necessary. Although the public recognizes the heavy costs of America's foreign commitments, they have been offered no other option for maintaining American security in what they perceive to be an increasingly dangerous world. More important, much of the public remains apathetic and detached from foreign policy issues. Even widespread public fears of terrorism are strangely separated from any serious public engagement with US policy in the Middle East.

The majority of American citizens do not follow foreign affairs in any region closely. The main costs of American foreign policy are borne by the increasingly small and unrepresentative segment of society that serves in the nation's all-volunteer military. The public is largely shielded from the enormous financial costs of American military interventions because recent wars have been financed primarily through borrowing, not taxing. One way to bring about change in American national security strategy is to educate the public better about the ways in which American foreign policy affects their lives. Citizens need to understand the real trade-offs in allocating resources, and they need to be presented with alternative strategies for maintaining America's security. We hope that this volume represents a contribution to that effort.

Second, the United States government should work to streamline American foreign policy budgeting—including the "black" intelligence budget and various "off-budget" costs—to make it easier for citizens to understand where and how their dollars are being spent. At present, the complexity of the US government and its budgeting procedures makes it nearly impossible for even the best-informed citizens to assess where our money is going and what it is buying. Many citizens, for example, vastly overestimate how much the United States spends on foreign aid. They also underestimate the true size of the American military budget, including intelligence and other related agencies.

More transparency about the true costs of our national security would have many beneficial effects. It would allow citizens and leaders to recognize where the nation's deepest ambitions do not match allocated resources—either because the government is short-changing its priorities or overspending on nonpriority commitments. Transparency would also have the general effect of educating citizens about what national security costs in the contemporary world, and how those burdens are distributed—often unfairly—across the population. Most important, clearer reporting about government policies would encourage more substantive debate about policy choices, their costs, and their consequences. If sustainable choices require more knowledge about policy and strategy, then revitalized democratic accountability around international affairs should prove transformative.

Finally, our contributors believe that a thorough reassessment of American national security strategy will be more likely, and more fruitful, if America's leaders are compelled to articulate a grand strategy—to be specific about America's interests in the world, what the key threats to those interests are, and how best to respond to them. A vague and ambiguous strategy is a key enabler of strategic inertia and bloat. Platitudes like "strengthening an unrivaled alliance system," or "sustaining American leadership" or building a military that will "remain dominant in every domain"—all drawn from the 2015 National Security Strategy—promise everything and nothing at once.[1]

Without the discipline provided by a clearly articulated strategy, America becomes the country that can't say no. In these undisciplined circumstances, each branch of government and military service is incentivized to make its own assumptions about where America's interests lie and how best to defend them. Every domestic interest group or foreign lobby is free to make its own claims on US foreign policy. A sustainable national security strategy, therefore, must specify not only what America will do, but also what it will not do. Advocates of change must demand specifics and hold policymakers to account when they fail to provide them.[2]

Together, these policy recommendations point to the potential for a more sustainable and successful American foreign policy, despite resource constraints and multiplying challenges. The United States continues to benefit from favorable geopolitical circumstances, a stable government, and rich resource endowments. There is no country the United States would trade places with. The greatest threat to the long-term security of the United States comes not from a foreign enemy, but from the misuse of American capabilities.

This volume offers the foundation for a renaissance of American strategy that will study, promote, and ultimately implement a more sustainable approach to securing the nation. More than anything, the future of the United States will turn on the strategic wisdom of the next generation. Cooperation between scholars and policymakers, exemplified in the making of this volume, will be crucial for that necessary work. Current difficulties open a promising opportunity.

---

[1] See "National Security Strategy," February 2015, Washington, DC: The White House, https://www.whitehouse.gov/sites/default/files/docs/2015_national_security_strategy.pdf.

[2] For more on these points, see James Goldgeier and Jeremi Suri, "Revitalizing the U.S. National Security Strategy," *Washington Quarterly* 38, no. 4 (Winter 2016), 35–55.

INDEX